Alfred Plummer

The Gospel according to S. John

Edited for the syndics of the University Press

Alfred Plummer

The Gospel according to S. John
Edited for the syndics of the University Press

ISBN/EAN: 9783337281502

Printed in Europe, USA, Canada, Australia, Japan

Cover: Foto ©Thomas Meinert / pixelio.de

More available books at **www.hansebooks.com**

The Cambridge Bible for Schools and Colleges.

General Editor:—J. J. S. PEROWNE, D.D.,
Bishop of Worcester.

THE GOSPEL ACCORDING TO

S. JOHN.

WITH MAPS, NOTES AND INTRODUCTION

BY

THE REV. A. PLUMMER, M.A., D.D.

MASTER OF UNIVERSITY COLLEGE, DURHAM,
FORMERLY FELLOW AND TUTOR OF TRINITY COLLEGE, OXFORD.

EDITED FOR THE SYNDICS OF THE UNIVERSITY PRESS

Cambridge:
AT THE UNIVERSITY PRESS.
1891

PREFACE
BY THE GENERAL EDITOR.

THE General Editor of *The Cambridge Bible for Schools* thinks it right to say that he does not hold himself responsible either for the interpretation of particular passages which the Editors of the several Books have adopted, or for any opinion on points of doctrine that they may have expressed. In the New Testament more especially questions arise of the deepest theological import, on which the ablest and most conscientious interpreters have differed and always will differ. His aim has been in all such cases to leave each Contributor to the unfettered exercise of his own judgment, only taking care that mere controversy should as far as possible be avoided. He has contented himself chiefly with a careful revision of the notes, with pointing out omissions, with suggesting occasionally a reconsideration of some question, or a fuller treatment of difficult passages, and the like.

Beyond this he has not attempted to interfere, feeling it better that each Commentary should have its own individual character, and being convinced that freshness and variety of treatment are more than a compensation for any lack of uniformity in the Series.

CONTENTS.

		PAGES
I. INTRODUCTION.		
	Chapter I. The Life of S. John............................	9—18
	Chapter II. The Authenticity of the Gospel	18—32
	Chapter III. The Place and Date	32—34
	Chapter IV. The Object and Plan	34—38
	Chapter V. The Characteristics of the Gospel ...	38—46
	Chapter VI. Its Relation to the Synoptic Gospels	46—50
	Chapter VII. Its Relation to the First Epistle ...	50—51
	Chapter VIII. The Text of the Gospel	51—52
	Chapter IX. The Literature of the Gospel.........	53—54
	Analysis of the Gospel in Detail......	55—58
II. TEXT AND NOTES		59—378
III. APPENDICES		379—382
IV. INDICES		383—388
MAP OF GALILEE ....*facing title*		
„ „ SEA OF GALILEE .... *at end of volume*		
„ „ PALESTINE IN THE TIME OF OUR SAVIOUR		do.
PLAN OF JERUSALEM		do.

⁂ The Text adopted in this Edition is that of Dr Scrivener's *Cambridge Paragraph Bible*. A few variations from the ordinary Text, chiefly in the spelling of certain words, and in the use of italics, will be noticed. For the principles adopted by Dr Scrivener as regards the printing of the Text see his Introduction to the *Paragraph Bible*, published by the Cambridge University Press.

INTRODUCTION.

CHAPTER I.

THE LIFE OF S. JOHN.

THE life of S. John falls naturally into two divisions, the limits of which correspond to the two main sources of information respecting him. (1) From his birth to the departure from Jerusalem after the Ascension; the sources for which are contained in N. T. (2) From the departure from Jerusalem to his death; the sources for which are the traditions of the primitive Church. In both cases the notices of S. John are fragmentary, and cannot be woven together into anything like a complete whole without a good deal of conjecture. But the fragments are in the main very harmonious, and contain definite traits and characteristics, enabling us to form a portrait, which though imperfect is unique.

(i) *Before the Departure from Jerusalem.*

The date of S. John's birth cannot be determined. He was probably younger than his Master and than the other Apostles. He was the son of Zebedee and Salome, and brother of James, who was probably the older of the two. Zebedee was a fisherman of the lake of Galilee, who seems to have lived in or near Bethsaida (i. 44), and was well enough off to have hired servants (Mark i. 20). He appears only once in the Gospel-narrative (Matt. iv. 21, 22; Mark i. 19, 20), but is mentioned frequently as the father of S. James and S. John. Salome (see on xix. 25) was probably the sister of the Virgin, and in that case S. John was our Lord's first cousin. This relationship harmonizes well with the special intimacy granted to the beloved disciple by his Lord, with the fact of S. James also being among the chosen three, and with the final committal of the Virgin to St John's care. Salome was one of those women who followed Christ and 'ministered to Him of their substance' (Mark xv. 40 ; comp. Matt. xxvii. 55 ; Luke viii. 3). This was probably after Zebedee's death. S. John's parents, therefore, would seem to have been people of means; and it is likely from xix. 27 that the Apostle himself was fairly well off, a conclusion to which his acquaintance with the high-priest (xviii. 15) also points.

S. John, therefore, like all the Apostles, excepting the traitor, was a Galilean ; and this fact may be taken as in some degree accounting for that fieriness of temper which earned for him and his brother the name of 'sons of thunder' (Mark iii. 17). The inhabitants of Galilee, while they had remained to a large extent untouched by the culture of the rest of the nation, remained also untouched by the enervation both in belief and habits which culture commonly brings. Ignorant of the glosses of tradition, they kept the old simple faith in the letter of the Law. Uninterested alike in politics and philosophy, they preferred the sword to intrigue, and industry to speculation. Thus, while the hierarchy jealously scrutinise all the circumstances of Jesus' position, the Galileans on the strength of a single miracle would 'take Him by force' (vi. 14, 15) and make Him king. Population was dense and mixed, and between the Syrians and Jews there were often fierce disputes. To this industrious, hardy, and warlike race S. John belonged by birth and residence, sharing its characteristic energy and its impatience of indecision and intrigue. Hence, when the Baptist proclaimed the kingdom of the Messiah, the young fisherman at once became a follower, and pressed steadily onwards until the goal was reached.

Christian art has so familiarised us with a form of almost feminine sweetness as representing the beloved disciple, that the strong energy and even vehemence of his character is almost lost sight of. In his writings as well as in what is recorded of him both in N. T. and elsewhere we find both sides of his character appearing. And indeed though apparently opposed they are not really so; the one may beget the other, and did so in him.

In yet another way his Galilean origin might influence S. John. The population of the country, as has been said, was mixed. From a boy he would have the opportunity of coming in contact with Greek life and language. Hence that union of Jewish and Greek characteristics which are found in him, and which have led some to the conclusion that the author of the Fourth Gospel was a Greek. We shall find as we go along that the enormous preponderance of Jewish modes of thought and expression, and of Jewish points of view, renders this conclusion absolutely untenable.

The young son of Zebedee was perhaps never at one of the rabbinical schools, which after the fall of Jerusalem made Tiberias a great centre of education, and probably existed in some shape before that. Hence he can be contemptuously spoken of by the hierarchy as an 'illiterate and common' person (Acts iv. 13). No doubt he paid the usual visits to Jerusalem at the proper seasons, and became acquainted with the grand liturgy of the Temple; a worship which while it kindled his deep spiritual emotions and gave him material for reverent meditation, would insensibly prepare the way for that intense hatred of the hierarchy, who had made the worship there worse than a mockery, which breathes through all the pages of his Gospel.

While he was still a lad, and perhaps already learning to admire and love the impetuosity of his older friend S. Peter, the rising of 'Judas of Galilee in the days of the taxing' (see on Acts v. 37) took place. Judas, like our own Wat Tyler, raised a revolt against a tax which he held to be tyrannical, and proclaimed that the people had 'no lord or master but God.' Whether the boy and his future friend sympathized with the movement we have no means of knowing. But the honest though ill-advised cry of the leaders of this revolt may easily have been remembered by S. John when he heard the false and renegade priests declare to Pilate, 'We have no king but Caesar' (xix. 15).

There was another movement of a very different kind, with which we know that he did sympathize heartily. After centuries of dreary silence, in which it seemed as if Jehovah had deserted His chosen people, a thrill went through the land that God had again visited them, and that a Prophet had once more appeared. His was a call, not to resist foreign taxation or to throw off the yoke of Rome, but to withstand their own temptations and to break the heavy bondage of their own crying sins: 'Repent ye, for the Kingdom of Heaven is at hand!' S. John heard and followed, and from the Baptist learnt to know and at once to follow 'the Lamb of God' that was to do (what the lambs provided by man in the Temple could never do)—'take away the sin of the world.' Assuming that the unnamed disciple (i. 40) is S. John, we infer (i. 41) that he proceeded to bring his brother S. James to Jesus as S. Andrew had brought S. Peter. But from 'that day' (i. 39), that never to be forgotten day, the whole tenour of the young man's life was changed. The disciple of the Baptist had become the disciple of Christ.

After remaining with Jesus for a time he seems to have gone back to his old employment; from which he was again called, and possibly more than once (Matt. iv. 18; Luke v. 1—11), to become an Apostle and fisher of men. Then the group of the chosen three is formed. At the raising of Jairus' daughter, at the Transfiguration, and in the Garden of Gethsemane, 'Peter, James, and John' are admitted to nearer relationship with their Lord than the rest; and on one other solemn occasion, when He foretold the destruction of Jerusalem (Mark xiii. 3), S. Andrew also is with them. In this group, although S. Peter takes the lead, it is S. John who is nearest and dearest to the Lord, 'the disciple whom Jesus loved.'

On three different occasions the burning temper of the 'sons of thunder' displayed itself. (1) 'And John answered Him, saying, Master, we saw one casting out devils in Thy name, and he followeth not us: and we forbad him, because he followeth not us' (Mark ix. 38; Luke ix. 49); a touch of zealous intolerance which reminds us of Joshua's zeal against Eldad and Medad (Numb. xi. 28), as Christ's reply recalls the reply of Moses. Probably his brother S. James is included in the '*we* forbad him.' (2) When the Samaritan villagers refused to receive Him, 'because His face was as though He would go to Jerusalem,' His disciples James and John said, 'Lord, wilt Thou that we command fire to come down from heaven and consume them?' (Luke ix. 54). Once again their zeal for their Master makes them forget the spirit of their Master. (3) On the last journey to Jerusalem Salome, as the mouthpiece of her two sons (Matt. xx. 20; Mark x. 35), begs that they may sit, the one on the Messiah's right hand, and the other on His left, in His kingdom. This is their bold ambition, shewing that in spite of their close intimacy with Him, they are still grossly ignorant of the nature of His kingdom. And in their reply to His challenge the same bold temper and burning zeal is manifest. They are willing to go through the furnace in order to be near the Son of God. When S. John and his mother stood beside the Cross, and when S. James won the crown of martyrdom, Christ's challenge was taken up and their aspiration fulfilled.

It will not be necessary to recount at length the history of the last Passover, in which S. John is a prominent figure. As he gives us so much more than the Synoptists about the family at Bethany, we may infer that he was a more intimate friend of Lazarus and his sisters. He and S. Peter prepare the Last Supper (Luke xxii. 8), at which S. Peter gets him to ask who is the traitor; and after the betrayal S. John gets his friend introduced into the high-priest's palace. He followed his Master to judgment and death, and received His Mother as a farewell charge (xviii. 15, xix. 26, 27). His friend's fall does not break their friendship, and they visit the sepulchre together on Easter morning. (On the characteristics of the two as shewn in this incident see notes on xx. 4—6.) We find them still together in Galilee, seeking refreshment in their suspense by resuming their old calling (xxi. 2); and here again their different characters shew themselves (see notes on xxi. 7). And the Gospel closes with Christ's gentle rebuke to S. Peter's natural curiosity about his friend.

In the Acts S. John appears but seldom, always in connexion with, and always playing a second part to his friend (Acts iii., iv., viii. 14—25). We lose sight of him at Jerusalem (viii. 25) after the return from Samaria; but he was not there at the time of S. Paul's first visit (Gal. i. 18, 19). Some twelve or fifteen years later (c. A.D. 50) he seems to have been at Jerusalem again (Acts xv. 6), but for how long we cannot tell. Nor do we know why he left. Excepting his own notice of himself, as being 'in the island called Patmos for the word and testimony of Jesus' (Rev. i. 9), the N. T. tells us nothing further respecting him.

(ii) *From the Departure from Jerusalem to his death.*

For this period, with the exception of the notice in the Apocalypse just quoted, we are entirely dependent upon traditions of very different value. The conjecture that S. John lived at Jerusalem until the death of the Virgin, and that this set him free, is unsupported by evidence. Some think that she accompanied him to Ephesus. It would be during this prolonged residence at Jerusalem that he acquired that minute knowledge of the topography of the city which marks the Fourth Gospel.

It is quite uncertain whether the Apostle went direct from Jerusalem to Ephesus; but of two things we may be confident: (1) that wherever he was he was not idle, (2) that he was not at Ephesus when S. Paul bade farewell to that Church (Acts xx.), nor when he wrote the Epistle to the Ephesians, nor when he wrote the Pastoral Epistles. That S. John did work at Ephesus during the latter part of his life may be accepted as certain, unless the whole history of the subapostolic age is to be pronounced doubtful; but neither the date of his arrival nor of his death can be fixed. He is described (Polycrates in Eus.

H. E. III. xxxi. 3, V. xxiv. 3) as a priest wearing the sacerdotal plate or mitre (*petalon*) which was a special badge of the high-priest (Exod. xxxix. 30); and we learn from the Apocalypse that from Ephesus as a centre he directed the churches of Asia Minor. What persecution drove him to Patmos or caused him to be banished thither is uncertain, as also is the date of his death, which may be placed somewhere near A.D. 100.

Of the traditions which cluster round this latter part of his life three deserve more than a passing mention. (1) John, the disciple of the Lord, going to bathe at Ephesus, and perceiving Cerinthus within, rushed out of the bath-house without bathing, crying out, 'Let us fly, lest even the bath-house fall on us, because Cerinthus, the enemy of the truth, is within' (Iren. III. iii. 4). Epiphanius (*Haer.* XXX. 24) substitutes Ebion for Cerinthus. Both Cerinthus and the Ebionites denied the reality of the Incarnation. This tradition, like the incidents recorded, Luke ix. 49, 54, shews that in later life also the spirit of the 'son of thunder' was still alive within him.

(2) After his return from Patmos he made a tour to appoint bishops or presbyters in the cities. In one place a lad of noble bearing attracted his attention, and he specially commended him to the bishop, who instructed and at last baptized him. Then he took less care of him, and the young man went from bad to worse, and at last became chief of a set of bandits. The Apostle revisiting the place remembered him and said, 'Come, bishop, restore to me my deposit,' which confounded the bishop, who knew that he had received no money from S. John. 'I demand the young man, the soul of a brother;' and then the sad story had to be told. The Apostle called for a horse, and rode at once to the place infested by the bandits and was soon taken by them. When the chief recognised him he turned to fly. But the aged Apostle went after him and entreated him to stay, and by his loving tears and exhortations induced him to return with him to the church, to which in due time he restored him (Eus. *H. E.* III. xxiii. from Clement of Alexandria).

(3) Towards the very end of his life, when he was so infirm that he had to be carried to church and was too weak to preach,

he used often to say no more than this, 'Little children, love one another.' His hearers at last wearied of this, and said, 'Master, why dost thou always say this?' 'It is the Lord's command,' he replied, 'and if this alone is done, it is enough' (Jerome, *Comm. in Ep. ad Gal.* VI. 10).

Other traditions may be dismissed more briefly; that in his old age he amused himself with a partridge, and pleaded that a bow could not always be bent, but needed relaxation; that he was thrown into a cauldron of boiling oil at Rome and was none the worse; that he drank hemlock without being harmed by it; that after he was buried the earth above him heaved with his breathing, shewing that he was only asleep, tarrying till Christ came. This last strange story S. Augustine is disposed to believe: those who know the place must know whether the soil does move or not; and he has heard it from no untrustworthy people.

These fragments form a picture, which (as was said at the outset) although very incomplete is harmonious, and so far as it goes distinct. The two sides of his character, tender love and stern intolerance, are the one the complement of the other; and both form part of the intensity of his nature. Intensity of action, intensity of thought and word, intensity of love and hate—these are the characteristics of the beloved disciple. In the best sense of the phrase S. John was 'a good hater,' for his hatred was part of his love. It was because he so loved the truth, that he so hated all lukewarmness, unreality, insincerity, and falsehood, and was so stern towards 'whosoever loveth and maketh a lie.' It is because he so loved his Lord, that he shews such uncompromising abhorrence of the national blindness that rejected Him and the sacerdotal bigotry that hounded Him to death. Intolerance of evil and of opposition to the truth was sometimes expressed in a way that called for rebuke; but this would become less and less so, as his own knowledge of the Lord and of the spirit of the Gospel deepened. With his eagle gaze more and more fixed on the Sun of Righteousness, he became more and more keenly alive to the awful case of those who 'loved the darkness rather than the light, because their works were evil' (iii. 19). Eternity for him was a thing not of the future but of the present (iii. 36, v. 24, vi. 47, 54); and whereas the world tries to make time the measure of eternity, he knows that eternity is the measure of time. Only from the point of view of eternal life, only from its divine side, can this life, both in its nothingness and in its infinite consequences, be rightly estimated: for 'the world passeth away and the lust thereof, but he that doeth the will of God abideth for ever' (1 John ii. 17).

We thus see how at the end of a long life he was specially fitted to write what has been well called 'the Gospel of Eternity' and 'the Gospel of Love.' It is at the end of life, and when the other side of the grave is in sight, that men can best form an estimate both of this world and of the world to come. If that is true of all men of ordinary seriousness, much more true must it have been of him, who from his youth upwards had been an Apostle, whose head had rested on the Lord's breast, who had stood beside the Cross, had witnessed the Ascension, had cherished till her death the Mother of the Lord, had seen the Jewish dispensation closed and the Holy City overthrown, and to whom the beatific visions of the Apocalypse had been granted. No wonder therefore if his Gospel seems to be raised above this world and to belong to eternity rather than to time. And hence its other aspect of being also 'the Gospel of Love:' for Love is eternal. Faith and Hope are for this world, but can have no place when 'we shall see Him as He is' and 'know even as we are known.' Love is both for time and for eternity.

> "They sin who tell us Love can die,
> With life all other passions fly,
> All others are but vanity.
> In heaven ambition cannot dwell,
> Nor avarice in the vaults of hell;
> Earthly, these passions of the earth
> They perish where they had their birth,
> But Love is indestructible.

> Its holy flame for ever burneth,
> From heaven it came, to heaven returneth.
> Too oft on earth a troubled guest,
> At times deceived, at times oppressed,
> It here is tried, and purified,
> Then hath in heaven its perfect rest:
> It soweth here with toil and care,
> But the harvest-time of Love is there."
>
> Southey.

CHAPTER II.

THE AUTHENTICITY OF THE GOSPEL.

The Fourth Gospel is the battle field of the New Testament, as the Book of Daniel is of the Old: the genuineness of both will probably always remain a matter of controversy. With regard to the Gospel, suspicion respecting it was aroused in some quarters at the outset, but very quickly died out; to rise again, however, with immensely increased force in the eighteenth century, since which time to the present day the question has scarcely ever been allowed to rest. The scope of the present work admits of no more than an outline of the argument being presented.

i. *The External Evidence.*

In this section of the argument two objections are made to the Fourth Gospel: (1) the *silence* of the Apostolic Fathers; (2) its *rejection* by Marcion, the Alogi, and perhaps another sect.

(1) *The silence of the Apostolic Fathers*, if it were a fact, would not be an insuperable difficulty. It is admitted on all sides that the Fourth Gospel was published long after the others, and when they were in possession of the field. There was nothing to lead men to suppose that yet another Gospel would be forthcoming; this alone would make people jealous

of its claims. And when, as we shall see, it was found that certain portions of it might be made to assume a Gnostic appearance, jealousy in some quarters became suspicion. The silence, therefore, of the first circle of Christian writers is no more than we might reasonably expect; and when taken in connexion with the universal recognition of the Gospel by the next circle of writers (A.D. 170 onwards), who had far more evidence than has reached us, may be considered as telling for, rather than against the authenticity.

But the silence of the Apostolic Fathers is by no means certain. The EPISTLE OF BARNABAS (c. A.D. 120—130) probably refers to it: Keim is convinced of the fact, although he denies that S. John wrote the Gospel. The shorter Greek form of the IGNATIAN EPISTLES (c. A.D. 150) contains allusions to it, and adaptations of it, which cannot seriously be considered doubtful. Bishop Lightfoot[1] says of the expression 'living water' (Rom. vii.) "Doubtless a reference to John iv. 10, 11, as indeed the whole passage is inspired by the Fourth Gospel," and of the words 'knows whence it cometh and whither it goeth' (*Philad.* vii.), "The coincidence (with John iii. 8) is quite too strong to be accidental;" and "the Gospel is prior to the passage in Ignatius;" for "the application in the Gospel is natural: the application in Ignatius is strained and secondary." Again, on the words 'being Himself the Door of the Father' (*Philad.* ix.) he says, "Doubtless an allusion to John x. 9." The EPISTLE OF POLYCARP (c. A.D. 150) contains almost certain references to the First Epistle of S. John: and as it is admitted that the First Epistle and the Fourth Gospel are by the same hand, evidence in favour of the one may be used as evidence in favour of the other.

Besides these, PAPIAS (martyred about the same time as Polycarp) certainly knew the First Epistle (Eus. *H. E.* III. xxxix.). BASILIDES (c. A.D. 125) seems to have made use of the Fourth Gospel. JUSTIN MARTYR (c. A.D. 150) knew the

---

[1] I am enabled to make these quotations from the great work of his life through the great kindness of the Bishop of Durham.

Fourth Gospel. This may now be considered as beyond reasonable doubt. Not only does he exhibit types of language and doctrine closely akin to S. John's, but in the *Dialogue with Trypho*, LXXXVIII. (c. A.D. 146) he quotes the Baptist's reply, 'I am not the Christ, but the voice of one crying' (comp. John i. 20, 23) and in the *First Apology*, LXI., he paraphrases Christ's words on the new birth (John iii. 3—5). Moreover Justin teaches the great doctrine of S. John's Prologue, that Jesus Christ is the Word. Keim regards it as certain that Justin knew the Fourth Gospel.

When we pass beyond A.D. 170 the evidence becomes full and clear: TATIAN, the EPISTLE TO THE CHURCHES OF VIENNE AND LYONS, CELSUS, the MURATORIAN FRAGMENT, the CLEMENTINE HOMILIES, THEOPHILUS OF ANTIOCH (the earliest writer who mentions S. John by name as the author of the Gospel—c. A.D. 175), ATHENAGORAS, IRENAEUS, CLEMENT OF ALEXANDRIA, AND TERTULLIAN. Of these none perhaps is more important than IRENAEUS, the pupil of Polycarp, who was the friend of S. John. It never occurs to him to maintain that the Fourth Gospel is the work of S. John; he treats it as a universally acknowledged fact. He not only knows of no time when there were not four Gospels, but with the help of certain quaint arguments he persuades himself that there *must* be four Gospels, neither more nor less (*Haer*. III. i. 1, XI. 8: comp. V. xxxvi. 2). So firmly established had the Fourth Gospel become considerably before the end of the second century.

(2) The *rejection* of the Fourth Gospel by Marcion and some obscure sects is of no serious importance. There is no evidence to shew that the Gospel was rejected on critical grounds; rather because the doctrines which it contained were disliked. This is almost certain in the case of Marcion, and probable enough in the other cases.

Whether the obscure sect mentioned by Irenaeus (*Haer*. III. xi. 9) as rejecting the Fourth Gospel and the promises of the Paraclete which it contains are the same as those whom Epiphanius with a contemptuous *double entendre* calls *Alogi*

INTRODUCTION.   21

('devoid of [the doctrine of] the Logos' or 'devoid of reason'), is uncertain. But we can easily understand how a party might arise, who in perfectly good faith and with the best motives might reject the Fourth Gospel both for the doctrine of the Logos and for other peculiarities which seemed to favour the Gnosticism of Cerinthus. None of the Synoptists, none of the Apostles, had thus far used the term 'Logos'; and the fact that Cerinthus made use of it must have made its prominence in the Prologue to the Fourth Gospel doubly suspicious. Cerinthus maintained that Jesus was a mere man on whom the Logos or Christ descended in the form of a dove at his baptism: and the Fourth Gospel says nothing about the miraculous conception of Christ, or about the wonders that attended and attested His birth, but begins with the Baptism and the descent of the Spirit. The Evangelist pointedly remarks that the miracle at Cana was the first miracle: perhaps this was to insinuate that previous to the Baptism Jesus (being a mere man) *could* do no miracle. This Gospel omits the Transfiguration, an incident from which a participation of His human Body in the glory of the Godhead might be inferred. The 'prince' or 'ruler of this world,' an expression not used previously by any Evangelist or Apostle, might possibly be understood to mean the *Demiurgus* of the Cerinthian system, the Creator of the world, and the God of the Jews, but inferior to and ignorant of the Supreme God. Again, the Fourth Gospel is silent about the wonders which attended Christ's death; and this also harmonizes with the system of Cerinthus, who taught that the Logos or Christ departed when Jesus was arrested, and that a mere man suffered on the Cross; for what meaning would there be in the sympathy of nature with the death of a mere man[1]? All this tends to shew that if the Fourth Gospel was rejected in certain quarters for a time, this tells little or nothing against its genuineness. Indeed it may fairly be said to tell the other way; for it shews that the universal recognition of the Gospel, which we find existing from A.D. 170 onwards, was no mere blind enthusiasm, but a victory

---

[1] See Döllinger's *Hippolytus and Callistus*, Chap. v.

of truth over baseless though not unnatural suspicion. Moreover, the fact that these over-wary Christians assigned the Gospel to Cerinthus is evidence that the Gospel was in their opinion written by a contemporary of S. John. To concede this is to concede the whole question.

ii. *The Internal Evidence.*

We have seen already that there are some features of this Gospel which would seem to harmonize with a Gnostic system, and that it need not surprise us if some persons in the second century hastily concluded that it savoured of Cerinthus. It is more surprising that modern critics, after a minute study of the Gospel, should think it possible to assign it to a Greek Gnostic of the second century. To say nothing of the general tone of the Gospel, there are two texts which may almost be said to sum up the theology of the Evangelist and which no Gnostic would even have tolerated, much less have written: 'The Word became flesh' (i. 14); 'Salvation is of the Jews' (iv. 22). That the Infinite should limit itself and become finite, that the ineffable purity of the Godhead should be united with impure matter, was to a Gnostic a monstrous supposition; and this was what was implied in the Word becoming flesh. Again, that the longed-for salvation of mankind should come from the Jews was a flat contradiction of one of the main principles of Gnosticism, viz. that man's perfection is to be looked for in the attainment of a higher knowledge of God and the universe, to which the Jew as such had no special claim; on the contrary (as some Gnostics held), the Jews had all along mistaken an inferior being for the Supreme God. Other passages in the Gospel which are strongly adverse to the theory of a Gnostic authorship will be pointed out in the notes. And here the Gnostics themselves are our witnesses, and that in the second century. Although the Fourth Gospel was frequently used against them, they never denied its genuineness. They tried to explain away what told against them, but they never attempted to question the Apostolic authority of the Gospel.

But the Gospel not only contains both direct and indirect evidence which contradicts this particular hypothesis; it also supplies both direct and indirect evidence of the true hypothesis.

(1) There is *direct evidence* that the author was an *eye-witness* of what he relates. In two places (according to far the most reasonable, if not the only reasonable interpretation of the words) the Evangelist claims for himself the authority of an eyewitness: in a third he either claims it for himself or others claim it for him. 'We beheld His glory' (i. 14), especially when taken in conjunction with 'which we beheld and our hands handled' (1 John i 1), cannot well mean anything else. Scarcely less doubtful is 'He that hath seen hath borne witness, and his witness is true, &c.' (xix. 35). 'This is the disciple who witnesseth concerning these things, and who wrote these things; and we know that his witness is true' (xxi. 24), even if it be the addition of another hand, is direct testimony to the fact that the Evangelist gives us not second-hand information, but what he himself has heard and seen. (See notes in all three places.)

Of course it would be easy for a forger to make such a claim; and accomplices or dupes might support him. But it would also be easy in so wide a field of narrative to test the validity of the claim, and this we will proceed to do by examining the *indirect* evidence. But first it will be well to state the enormous difficulties which would confront a writer who proposed in the second century to forge a Gospel.

The condition of Palestine during the life of Jesus Christ was unique. The three great civilisations of the world were intermingled there; Rome, the representative of law and conquest; Greece, the representative of philosophical speculation and commerce; Judaism, the representative of religion. The relations of these three elements to one another were both intricate and varied. In some particulars there was a combination between two or more of them; as in the mode of conducting the census (Luke ii. 3) and of celebrating the Passover (see on xiii. 23); in others there was the sharpest opposition, as in very many ceremonial observances. Moreover, of these three factors it was exceedingly difficult for the two that were Gentile to comprehend the third.

The Jew always remained an enigma to his neighbours, especially to those from the West. This was owing partly to proud reserve on his part and contempt on theirs, partly to the inability of each side to express itself in terms that would be intelligible to the other, so utterly different were and still are Eastern and Western modes of thought. Again, if a Greek or Roman of the first century had taken the pains to study Jewish literature with a view to becoming thoroughly acquainted with this strange people, his knowledge of them would still have remained both defective and misleading, so much had been added or changed by tradition and custom. To a Gentile of the *second* century this difficulty would be very greatly increased; for Jerusalem had been destroyed and the Jewish nation had been once more scattered abroad on the face of the earth. With the destruction of the Temple the keeping of the Mosaic Law had become a physical impossibility; and the Jews who had lost their language in the Captivity had now to a large extent lost the ceremonial law. Even a Jew of the second century might easily be mistaken as to the usages of his nation in the early part of the first. How much more, then, would a Gentile be likely to go astray! We may say, therefore, that the intricate combination of Jewish and Gentile elements in Palestine between A.D. 1 and A.D. 50 was such that no one but a Jew living in the country at the time would be able to master them; and that the almost total destruction of the Jewish element in the latter part of the century would render a proper appreciation of the circumstances a matter of the utmost difficulty even to a careful antiquarian. Finally, we must remember that antiquarian research in those days was almost unknown; and that to undertake it in order to give an accurate setting to a historical fiction was an idea that was not born until long after the second century. We may safely say that no Greek of that age would ever have dreamed of going through the course of archæological study necessary for attempting the Fourth Gospel; and even if he had, the attempt would still have been a manifest failure. He would have fallen into far more numerous and far more serious errors than those which critics (with what success

INTRODUCTION. 25

we shall see hereafter) have tried to bring home to the Fourth Evangelist (see on xi. 49).

(2) There is abundant *indirect evidence* to shew that the writer of the Fourth Gospel was a Jew, and a Jew of Palestine, who was an eyewitness of most of the events which he relates. If this can be made out with something like certainty, the circle of possible authors will be very much reduced. But in this circle of possible authors we are not left to conjecture. There is further evidence to shew that he was an Apostle, and the Apostle S. John. (See Sanday, *Authorship of the Fourth Gospel*, Chap. xix.)

The Evangelist was a Jew.

He is perfectly at home in **Jewish opinions and points of view.** Conspicuous among these are *the ideas respecting the Messiah* current at the time (i. 19—28, 45—49, 51; iv. 25; vi. 14, 15; vii. 26, 27, 31, 40—42, 52; xii. 13, 34; xix. 15, 21). Besides these we have the *hostility between Jews and Samaritans* (iv. 9, 20, 22; viii. 48); estimate of *women* (iv. 27), of the *national schools* (vii. 15), of the '*Dispersion*' (vii. 35), of *Abraham and the Prophets* (viii. 52, 53), &c. &c.

He is quite familiar also with **Jewish usages and observances.** Among these we may notice *baptism* (i. 25; iii. 22, 23; iv. 2), *purification* (ii. 6, iii. 25, xi. 55, xviii. 28, xix. 31), the Jewish *Feasts* (ii. 13, 23, v. 1, vi. 4, vii. 2, 37, x. 22, xiii. 1, xviii. 28, xix. 31, 42), *circumcision* and the *Sabbath* (vii. 22, 23), law of *evidence* (viii. 17, 18).

The **form of the Gospel**, especially the style of the narrative, is **essentially Jewish.** The language is Greek, but the arrangement of the thoughts, the structure of the sentences, and a great deal of the vocabulary are Hebrew. And the source of this Hebrew form is the O. T. This is shewn not only by frequent quotations but by the imagery employed;—the lamb, the living water, the manna, the shepherd, the vine, &c. And not only so, but the Christian theology of the Evangelist is based upon the theology of the O. T. 'Salvation is of the Jews' (iv. 22); Moses wrote of Christ (v. 46; i. 45); Abraham saw His day (viii. 56); He was typified in the brazen serpent (iii. 14), the manna (vi. 32), the paschal lamb (xix. 36); perhaps also in the water from the rock (vii. 37) and the pillar of fire (viii. 12). Much that He did was done 'that the Scripture might be fulfilled' (xiii. 18, xvii. 12, xix. 24, 28, 36, 37; comp. ii. 22, xx. 9): and these fulfilments of Scripture are noticed not as interesting coincidences, but 'that ye may believe' (xix. 35). Judaism is the foundation of the Christian faith. No one but a Jew could have handled the O.T. Scriptures in this way.

THE EVANGELIST WAS A JEW OF PALESTINE.

This is shewn chiefly by his **great topographical knowledge**, which he uses both with ease and precision. In mentioning a fresh place he commonly throws in some fact respecting it, adding clearness or interest to the narrative. A forger would avoid such gratuitous statements, as being unnecessary and likely by being wrong to lead to detection. Thus, one *Bethany* is 'nigh unto Jerusalem, about fifteen furlongs off' (xi. 18), the other is 'beyond Jordan' (i. 28); *Bethsaida* is 'the city of Andrew and Peter' (i. 44); 'Can any good thing come out of *Nazareth*' (i. 46); *Cana* is 'of Galilee' (ii. 1, xxi. 2); *Aenon* is 'near to Salim,' and there are 'many waters' there (iii. 23); *Sychar* is 'a city of Samaria, near to the parcel of ground that Jacob gave to his son Joseph. Now Jacob's well was there' (iv. 5); *Ephraim* is a city 'near to the wilderness' (xi. 54). Comp. the minute local knowledge implied in vi. 22—24, iv. 11, ii. 12.

This familiarity with topography is the more remarkable in the case of Jerusalem, which (as all are agreed) was destroyed before the Fourth Gospel was written. *Bethesda* is 'a pool by the sheep-gate, having five porches' (v. 2); *Siloam* is 'a pool, which is by interpretation Sent' (ix. 7); *Solomon's porch* is 'in the Temple' (x. 23). Comp. the minute knowledge of the city and suburbs implied in xviii. 1, 28, xix. 13, 17—20, 41, 42.

The way in which the author quotes the O. T. points to the same conclusion. He is not dependent on the LXX.

for his knowledge of the Scriptures, as a Greek-speaking Jew born out of Palestine would very likely have been: he appears to know the original Hebrew, which had become a dead language, and was not much studied outside Palestine. Out of fourteen quotations three agree with the Hebrew against the LXX. (vi. 45, xiii. 18, xix. 37); not one agrees with the LXX. against the Hebrew. The majority are neutral, either agreeing with both, or differing from both, or being free adaptations rather than citations. (See also on xii. 13, 15.)

The Evangelist's **doctrine of the Logos** or Word confirms us in the belief that he is a Jew of Palestine. The form which this doctrine assumes in the Prologue is Palestinian rather than Alexandrian. (See note on 'the Word,' i. 1.)

THE EVANGELIST WAS AN EYEWITNESS OF MOST OF THE EVENTS WHICH HE RELATES.

The narrative is crowded with figures, which are no mere nonentities to fill up space, but which live and move. Where they appear on the scene more than once their action throughout is harmonious, and their characteristics are indicated with a simplicity and distinctness which would be the most consummate art if it were not taken from real life. And where in the literature of the second century can we find such skilful delineation of fictitious characters as is shewn in the portraits given to us of the Baptist, the beloved disciple, Peter, Andrew, Philip, Thomas, Judas Iscariot, Pilate, Nicodemus, Martha and Mary, the Samaritan woman, the man born blind? Even the less prominent persons are thoroughly lifelike and real; Nathanael, Judas not Iscariot, Caiaphas, Annas, Mary Magdalene, Joseph.

Exact notes of time are frequent; not only *seasons*, as the Jewish Feasts noticed above, but *days* (i. 29, 35, 43, ii. 1, iv. 40, 43, vi. 22, vii. 14, 37, xi. 6, 17, 39, xii. 1, 12, xix. 31, xx. 1, 26) and *hours* (i. 39, iv. 6, 52, xix. 14; comp. iii. 2, vi. 16, xiii. 30, xviii. 28, xx. 1, 19, xxi. 4).

The Evangelist sometimes knows the exact or approximate number of persons (i. 35, iv. 18, vi. 10, xix. 23) and objects (ii. 6, vi. 9, 19, xix. 39, xxi. 8, 11) mentioned in his narrative.

Throughout the Gospel we have examples of graphic and vivid description, which would be astounding if they were not the result of personal observation. Strong instances of this would be the accounts of the cleansing of the Temple (ii. 14—16), the feeding of the 5000 (vi. 5—14), the healing of the man born blind (ix. 6, 7), the feet-washing (xiii. 4, 5, 12), the betrayal (xviii. 1—13), almost all the details of the Passion (xviii., xix.), the visit to the sepulchre (xx. 3—8).

To this it must be added that the state of the text of the Gospel, as we find it quoted by early writers, shews that before the end of the second century there were already a great many variations of readings in existence. Such things take time to arise and multiply. This consideration compels us to believe that the original document must have been made at a time when eyewitnesses of the Gospel history were still living. See notes on i. 13, 18 and ix. 35.

THE EVANGELIST WAS AN APOSTLE.

He knows the thoughts of the disciples on certain occasions, thoughts which sometimes surprise us, and which no writer of fiction would have attributed to them (ii. 11, 17, 22, iv. 27, vi. 19, 60, xii. 16, xiii. 22, 28, xx. 9, xxi. 12). He knows also words that were spoken by the disciples in private to Christ or among themselves (iv. 31, 33, ix. 2, xi. 8, 12, 16, xvi. 17, 29). He is familiar with the haunts of the disciples (xi. 54, xviii. 2, xx. 19). Above all, he is one who was very intimate with the Lord; for he knows His motives (ii. 24, 25, iv. 1—3, v. 6, vi. 6, 15, vii. 1, xiii. 1, 3, 11, xvi. 19, xviii. 4, xix. 28) and can bear witness to His feelings (xi. 33, 38, xiii. 21).

THE EVANGELIST WAS THE APOSTLE S. JOHN.

The contents of the two previous sections are almost sufficient to prove this last point. We know from the Synoptists that three disciples were specially intimate with Jesus, Peter, James, and his brother John. S. Peter cannot be our Evangelist: he was put to death long before the very earliest date to which the Fourth Gospel can be assigned. Moreover the style of the Gospel is quite unlike the undoubted First Epistle of S. Peter. Still less can S. James be the author, for he was martyred long before S. Peter. Only S. John remains, and he not only entirely fits in with the details already noticed, but also having long outlived the rest of the Apostles he is the one person who could have written a Gospel considerably later in date than the other three.

But we have not yet exhausted the evidence. The concluding note (xxi. 24) declares that the Gospel was written by 'the disciple whom Jesus loved' (*êgapa*, xxi. 20). This disciple is mentioned in three other places under the same title (xiii. 23, xix. 26, xxi. 7;—xx. 2 is different). He is some one who is intimate with S. Peter (xiii. 24, xxi. 7; comp. xviii. 15, xx. 2), and this we already know from the Synoptists that S. John was, and we learn from the Acts that he remained so (iii. 1, 3, 11, iv. 13, 19, viii. 14). He is one of those enumerated in xxi. 1, and unless he is one of the two unnamed disciples he must be S. John.

One more point, a small one, but of very great significance, remains. The Fourth Evangelist carefully distinguishes places and persons. He distinguishes Cana 'of Galilee' (ii. 1, xxi. 2) from Cana of Asher; Bethany 'beyond Jordan' (i. 28) from Bethany 'nigh unto Jerusalem' (xi. 18); Bethsaida, 'the city of Andrew and Peter' (i. 44), from Bethsaida Julias. He distinguishes also Simon Peter after his call from others named Simon by invariably adding the new name Peter, whereas the Synoptists often call him simply Simon. The traitor Judas is distinguished as the 'son of Simon' (vi. 71, xii. 4, xiii. 2, 26) from the other Judas, who is expressly said to be 'not Iscariot' (xiv. 22), while the Synoptists take no notice of the traitor's parentage. S. Thomas is thrice for the sake of additional clearness pointed out as the same who was called Didymus (xi. 16, xx. 24, xxi. 2), a name not given by the Synoptists. Comp. the careful identification of Nicodemus (xix. 39) and of Caiaphas (xi. 49, xviii. 13). And yet the Fourth Evangelist altogether neglects to make a distinction which the Synoptists do make. They distinguish John the son of Zebedee from his namesake by frequently calling the latter 'the Baptist' (more than a dozen times in all). The Fourth Evangelist never does so; to him the Baptist is simply 'John.' He himself being the other John, there is for him no chance of confusion, and it does not occur to him to mark the distinction.

iii. *Answers to objections.*

We are now on too firm ground to be shaken by isolated difficulties. It would take a great many difficulties of detail to counterbalance the difficulty of believing that the Fourth Gospel was written by some one who was neither an Apostle nor even a contemporary. But there are certain difficulties supposed to be involved in the theory that the Evangelist is S. John the Apostle, some of which are important and deserve a separate answer. They are mainly these;—

(1) The marked dissimilarity between the Fourth Gospel and the three others.

(2) The marked dissimilarity between the Fourth Gospel and the Revelation.

(3) The difficulty of believing that S. John (*a*) would have "studiously elevated himself in every way above the Apostle Peter;" (*b*) would have magnified himself above all as 'the disciple whom Jesus loved.'

(4) The use made by S. Polycarp of S. John's authority in the Paschal controversy.

(1) The answer to the first of these objections will be found below in Chapter VI. of the *Introduction*, and in the introductory note to Chapter iii. of the Gospel.

(2) The answer to the second belongs rather to the Introduction to the Apocalypse. The answer to it is to a large extent a further answer to the first objection; for "the Apocalypse is doctrinally the uniting link between the Synoptists and the Fourth Gospel" (Westcott). Great as are the differences between the Revelation and the Gospel, the leading ideas of both are the same. The one gives us in a magnificent vision, the other in a great historic drama, the supreme conflict between good and evil and its issue. In both Jesus Christ is the

central figure, whose victory through defeat is the issue of the conflict. In both the Jewish dispensation is the preparation for the Gospel, and the warfare and triumph of the Christ is described in language saturated with the O. T. Some remarkable similarities of detail will be pointed out in the notes (see on i. 14; xi. 44; xix. 2, 5, 13, 17, 20, 37). The difference of date will go a long way towards explaining the difference of style.

(3 *a*) The question, 'How could S. John have studiously elevated himself in every way above the Apostle Peter?' reminds us of the famous question of Charles II. to the Royal Society. The answer to it is that S. John does nothing of the kind. S. Peter takes the lead in the Fourth Gospel as in the other three. His introduction to Christ and significant naming stand at the very opening of the Gospel (i. 41, 42); he answers in the name of the Twelve (vi. 68); he is prominent if not first at the feet-washing (xiii. 6); he directs S. John to find out who is the traitor (xiii. 24); he takes the lead in defending his Master at the betrayal (xviii. 10); the news of the Resurrection is brought to him first (xx. 2); his companion does not venture to enter the sepulchre until he has done so (xx. 6—8); he is mentioned first in the list of disciples given xxi. 2, and there takes the lead (xxi. 3); he continues to take the lead when Jesus appears to them (xxi. 7, 11); he receives the last great charge, with which the Gospel concludes (xxi. 15—22).

(*b*) To suppose that the phrase 'the disciple whom Jesus loved' implies self-glorification at the expense of others is altogether to misunderstand it. It is not impossible that the designation was given to him by others before he used it of himself. At any rate the affection of the Lord for him was so well known that such a title would be well suited for an oblique indication of the author's personality. Besides thus gently letting us behind the scenes the phrase serves two purposes: (1) it is a permanent expression of gratitude on the part of the Evangelist for the transcendent benefit bestowed upon him; (2) it is a modest explanation of the prominent part which he was called upon to play on certain occasions. Why was he singled out to be told who was the traitor (xiii. 23)? Why was the care of the Lord's mother entrusted to him (xix. 26)? Why was he allowed to recognise the Lord at the sea of Tiberias (xxi. 7) before any of the rest did so? The recipient of these honours has only one explanation to give: Jesus loved him.

(4) In the controversy as to the right time of keeping Easter S. Polycarp defended the Asiatic custom of keeping the Christian Passover at the same time as the Jewish Passover, viz. the evening of the 14th Nisan, "because he had always (so) observed it *with John the disciple of our Lord*, and the rest of the Apostles, with whom he associated" (Eus. *H. E.* v. xxiv. 16). On this ground he refused to yield to Anicetus, Bishop of Rome, though he did not require Anicetus to give way to him. But, as we shall see (Appendix A), the Fourth Gospel clearly represents the Crucifixion as taking place on the 14th Nisan, and the Last Supper as taking place the evening before. Therefore, either Polycarp falsely appeals to S. John's authority (which is most improbable), or the Fourth Gospel is not by S. John. But this objection confuses two things, the Christian Passover or Easter, and the Last Supper or institution of the Eucharist. The latter point was not in dispute at all. The question debated was whether the Christian Churches in fixing the time of Easter were to follow the Jewish Calendar exactly or a Christian modification of it. S. Polycarp claimed S. John as sanctioning the former plan, and nothing in the Fourth Gospel is inconsistent with such a view. Schürer, who denies the authenticity of the Gospel, has shewn that no argument against the authenticity can be drawn from the Paschal controversy.

CHAPTER III.

THE PLACE AND DATE.

Tradition is unanimous in giving Ephesus as the place where S. John resided during the latter part of his life, and where the

Fourth Gospel was written. There is no sufficient reason for doubting this strong testimony, which may be accepted as practically certain.

There is also strong evidence to shew that the Gospel was written at the request of the elders and disciples of the Christian Churches of Asia. We have this on the early and independent authority of the Muratorian Fragment (c. A.D. 170) and of Clement of Alexandria (c. A.D. 190); and this is confirmed by Jerome. No doubt S. John had often delivered the contents of his Gospel orally; and the elders wished before he died to preserve it in a permanent form. Moreover, difficulties had arisen in the Church which called for a recasting of Apostolic doctrine. The destruction of Jerusalem had given altogether a new turn to Christianity: it had severed the lingering and hampering connexion with Judaism; it had involved a readjustment of the interpretations of Christ's promises about His return. Again, the rise of a Christian philosophy, shading off by the strangest compromises and colouring into mere pagan speculation, called for a fresh statement, in terms adequate to the emergency, and by a voice sufficient in authority, of Christian truth. There is both external and internal evidence to shew that a crisis of this kind was the occasion of the Fourth Gospel.

The precise date cannot be determined with certainty. There are indications in the Gospel itself that it was written late in the author's life time. In his narrative he seems to be looking back after a long lapse of time (vii. 39, xxi. 19). And as we study it, we feel that it is the result of a larger experience of God's Providence and of a wider comprehension of the meaning of His Kingdom than was possible at the time when the other Evangelists, especially the first two of them, wrote their Gospels. All this induces us to place the date of the Fourth Gospel as late as possible; and tradition (as we have seen in Chap. 1) represents S. John as living to extreme old age. S. John would not begin to teach at Ephesus until some time after S. Paul left it, i.e. not much before A.D. 70. If Irenaeus is right in saying that S. Luke's Gospel was not written till after the death of S. Peter and S. Paul (*Haer.* III. i. 1), this would again place the writing of the Fourth Gospel considerably later than A.D. 70. It is not improbable that the first twenty chapters were written a considerable time before the Gospel was published, that the last chapter was added some years later, and then the whole given to the church (see introductory note to chap. xxi.). S. John may have lived almost if not quite to the end of the century; therefore from A.D. 80 to 95 would seem to be the period within which it is probable that the Gospel was published.

Those who deny that S. John is the author have tried almost every date from A.D. 110 to 165. Dividing this period into two, we have this dilemma:—If the Gospel was published between 110 and 140, why did not the *hundreds* of Christians, who had known S. John during his later years, denounce it as a forgery? If it was not published till between 140 and 165, how did it become universally accepted by 170?

CHAPTER IV.

THE OBJECT AND PLAN.

i. *The Object.*

These two subjects, the object and the plan, naturally go together, for the one to a large extent determines the other: the purpose with which the Evangelist wrote his Gospel greatly influences the form which it assumes. What that purpose was he tells us plainly himself: 'These have been written *that ye may believe that Jesus is the Christ, the Son of God, and that believing ye may have life in His name*' (xx. 31). His object is not to write the life of Christ; if it were, we might wonder that out of his immense stores of personal knowledge he has not given us a great deal more than he has done. Rather, out of these abundant stores he has made a careful and self-denying selection with a view to producing a particular effect upon his readers, and by means of that effect to open to them an inestimable benefit. In this way his object manifestly influences his plan. He might have given himself the delight of pouring forth streams of information, which he alone possessed, to a community ardently thirsting for it. But such prodigality would have obscured rather than strengthened his argument: he therefore rigidly limits himself in order to produce the desired effect.

The effect is twofold: (1) to create a belief that Jesus is the Christ; (2) to create a belief that Jesus is the Son of God. The first truth is primarily for the Jew; the second is primarily for the Gentile; then both are for all united. The first truth leads the Jew to become a Christian; the second raises the Gentile above the barriers of Jewish exclusiveness; the two together bring eternal life to both.

To the Jews the Evangelist would prove that Jesus, the Man who had been known to them personally or historically by that name, is the Christ, the Messiah for whom they had been looking, in whom all types and prophecies have been fulfilled, to whom therefore the fullest allegiance is due. To the Gentiles the Evangelist would prove that this same Jesus, of whom they also have heard, is the Son of God, the Only God, theirs as well as His, the Universal Father, their Father as well as His; whose Son's mission, therefore, must be coextensive with His Father's family and kingdom. Long before the promise was made to Abraham 'all things came into being through Him' (i. 3): if therefore the Jews had a claim on the Christ, the Gentiles had a still older claim on the Son of God.

These two great truths, that Jesus is the Christ, and that Jesus is the Son of God, being recognised and believed, the blessed result follows that believers have life in His name, i.e. in Him as revealed to them in the character which His name implies. There is neither Gentile nor Jew, circumcision nor uncircumcision, barbarian, Scythian, bond nor free; but Christ is all and in all; all are one in Christ Jesus (Col. iii. 11; Gal. iii. 28).

There is no need to look for any additional object over and above that which the Evangelist himself states; although this is frequently done. Thus from the time of Irenaeus (*Haer.*

III. xi.) it has been common to say that S. John wrote his Gospel against Cerinthus and other heretics. By clearly teaching the main truths of the Gospel S. John necessarily refutes errors; and it is possible that here and there some particular form of error was in his mind when he wrote: but the refutation of error is not his object in writing. If his Gospel is not a Life of Christ, still less is it a polemical treatise.

Again, from the time of Eusebius (*H. E.* III. xxiv. 11) and earlier it has been maintained that S. John wrote to supplement the Synoptists, recording what had not been recorded by them. No doubt he does supplement them to a large extent, especially as regards the ministry in Judæa: but it does not follow from this that he wrote in order to supplement them. Where something not recorded by them would suit his purpose equally well he would naturally prefer it; but he has no hesitation in retelling what has already been told by one, two, or even all three of them, if he requires it for the object which he has in view (see introductory note to chap. vi.).

ii. *The Plan.*

In no Gospel is the plan so manifest as in the Fourth. Perhaps we may say of the others that they scarcely have a plan. We may divide and subdivide them for our own convenience; but there is no clear evidence that the three Evangelists had any definite scheme before them in putting together the fragments of Gospel history which they have preserved for us. It is quite otherwise with the Fourth Evangelist. The different scenes from the life of Jesus Christ which he puts before us, are not only carefully selected but carefully arranged, leading up step by step to the conclusion expressed in the confession of S. Thomas, 'My Lord and my God.' But if there is a development of faith and love on the one side in those who accept and follow Jesus, so also there is a development of unbelief and hatred on the other in those who reject and persecute Him. 'The Word became flesh;' but, in as much as He was not generally recognised and welcomed, His presence in the world necessarily involved a separation and a conflict; a separation

INTRODUCTION. 37

of light from darkness, truth from falsehood, good from evil, life from death, and a conflict between the two. It is the critical episodes in that conflict round the person of the Incarnate Word that the Evangelist places before us one by one. These various episodes taken one by one go far to shew,—taken all together and combined with the issue of the conflict irrefragably prove,—'that Jesus is the Christ, the Son of God.'

The main outlines of the plan are these :—

I. THE PROLOGUE OR INTRODUCTION (i. 1—18).
   1. The Word in His own Nature (i. 1—5).
   2. His revelation to men and rejection by them (i. 6—13).
   3. His revelation of the Father (i. 14—18).

II. FIRST MAIN DIVISION. CHRIST'S MINISTRY, OR HIS REVELATION OF HIMSELF TO THE WORLD (i. 19—xii. 50).
  a. **The Testimony** (i. 19—51)
   1. of John the Baptist (i. 19—37),
   2. of the disciples (i. 38—51),
   3. of the first sign (ii. 1—11).
  b. **The Work** (ii. 13—xi. 57)
   1. among Jews (ii. 13—iii. 36),
   2. among Samaritans (iv. 1—42),
   3. among Galileans (iv. 43—54),

(*The work has become a Conflict*). 4. among mixed multitudes (v.—xi.).
  c. **The Judgment** (xii.)
   1. of men (1—36),
   2. of the Evangelist (37—43),
   3. of Christ (44—50).
  Close of Christ's public ministry.

III. SECOND MAIN DIVISION. THE ISSUES OF CHRIST'S MINISTRY, OR HIS REVELATION OF HIMSELF TO HIS DISCIPLES (xiii.—xx.).
  d. **The inner Glorification of Christ in His last Discourses** (xiii.—xvii.).
   1. His love in humiliation (xiii. 1—30).
   2. His love in keeping His own (xiii. 31 —xv. 27).

3. The promise of the Comforter and of His return (xvi.).
4. The prayer of the High-Priest (xvii.).

e. **The outer Glorification of Christ in His Passion** (xviii., xix.).
1. The betrayal (xviii. 1—11).
2. The ecclesiastical and civil trials (xviii. 12—xix. 16).
3. The crucifixion and burial (xix. 17—42).

f. **The Resurrection** (xx.).
1. The manifestation to Mary Magdalene (1—18).
2. The manifestation to the ten (19—23).
3. The manifestation to S. Thomas with the ten (24—29).
4. The conclusion (30, 31).

IV. THE EPILOGUE OR APPENDIX (xxi.).

CHAPTER V.

THE CHARACTERISTICS OF THE GOSPEL.

Here again, only a few leading points can be noticed : the subject is capable of almost indefinite expansion.

1. From the time of Clement of Alexandria (c. A.D. 190) this Gospel has been distinguished as a 'SPIRITUAL GOSPEL' (Eus. *H. E.* VI. xiv. 7). The Synoptists give us mainly the external acts of Jesus Christ: S. John lays before us glimpses of the inner life and spirit of the Son of God. Their narrative is chiefly composed of His manifold and ceaseless dealings with men: in S. John we have rather His tranquil and unbroken union with His Father. The heavenly element which forms the background of the first three Gospels is the atmosphere of the Fourth.

It is quite in harmony with this characteristic of the Gospel that it should contain such a much larger proportion of Christ's words than we find in the others: discourses here form the principal part, especially in the latter half of the Gospel. Not even in the Sermon on the Mount do we learn so much of 'the spirit of Christ' as in the discourses recorded by S. John. And what is true of the central figure is true also of the numerous characters which give such life and definiteness to S. John's narrative: they also make themselves known to us by what they say rather than by what they do. And this suggests to us a second characteristic.

2. No Gospel is so rich in TYPICAL but thoroughly REAL AND LIFELIKE GROUPS AND INDIVIDUALS as the Fourth. They are sketched, or rather by their words are made to sketch themselves, with a vividness and precision which, as already observed, is almost proof that the Evangelist was an eyewitness of what he records.

Among the groups we have *the disciples* strangely misunderstanding Christ (iv. 33, xi. 12) yet firmly believing on Him (xvi. 30); *His brethren*, dictating a policy to Him and not believing on Him (vii. 3—5); *John's disciples*, with their jealousy for the honour of their master (iii. 26); *the Samaritans*, proud to believe from their own experience rather than on the testimony of a woman (iv. 42); *the multitude*, sometimes thinking Jesus possessed, sometimes thinking Him the Christ (vii. 20, 26, 41); *the Jews*, claiming to be Abraham's seed and seeking to kill the Messiah (viii. 33, 37, 40); *the Pharisees*, haughtily asking, 'Hath any one of the rulers or of the Pharisees believed on Him?' (vii. 48) and 'are we also blind?' (ix. 40); *the chief priests*, professing to fear that Christ's success will be fatal to the national existence (xi. 48), and declaring to Pilate that they have no king but Caesar (xix. 15). In the sketching of these groups nothing is more conclusive evidence of the Evangelist being contemporary with his narrative than the way in which the conflict and fluctuations between belief and unbelief among the multitude and 'the Jews' is indicated.

The types of individual character are still more varied, and as in the case of the groups they exemplify both sides in the great conflict, as well as those who wavered between the two.

On the one hand we have the Mother of the Lord (ii. 3—5, xix. 25—27), the beloved disciple and his master the Baptist (i. 6—37, iii. 23—36), S. Andrew and Mary of Bethany, all unfailing in their allegiance ; S. Peter falling and rising again to deeper love (xviii. 27, xxi. 17); S. Philip rising from eager to firm faith (xiv. 8), S. Thomas from desponding and despairing love (xi. 16, xx. 25) to faith, hope, and love (xx. 28). There is the sober but uninformed faith of Martha (xi. 21, 24, 27), the passionate affection of Mary Magdalene (xx. 1—18). Among conversions we have the instantaneous but deliberate conviction of Nathanael (i. 49), the gradual but courageous progress in belief of the schismatical Samaritan woman (see on iv. 19) and of the uninstructed man born blind (see on xi. 21), and in contrast with both the timid, hesitating confessions of Nicodemus, the learned Rabbi (iii. 1, vii. 50, xix. 39). On the other side we have the cowardly wavering of Pilate (xviii. 38, 39, xix. 1—4, 8, 12, 16), the unscrupulous resoluteness of Caiaphas (xi. 49, 50), and the blank treachery of Judas (xiii. 27, xviii. 2—5). Among the minor characters there is the 'ruler of the feast' (ii. 9, 10), the 'nobleman' (iv. 49), the man healed at Bethesda (v. 7, 11, 14, 15).

If these groups and individuals are creations of the imagination, it is no exaggeration to say that the author of the Fourth Gospel is a genius superior to Shakspere.

3. From typical characters we pass on to typical or symbolical events. SYMBOLISM is a third characteristic of this Gospel. Not merely does it contain the three great allegories of the Sheep-fold, the Good Shepherd, and the Vine, from which Christian art has drawn its symbolism from the very earliest times ; but the whole Gospel from end to end is penetrated with the spirit of symbolical representation. In nothing is this more apparent than in the eight miracles which the Evangelist has selected for the illustration of his Divine Epic. His own word for them leads us to expect this : to him they are not so much miracles as 'signs.' The first two are introductory, and seem to be pointed out as such by S. John (ii. 11, iv. 54). The turning of the water into wine exhibits the Messiah's sovereign

power over inanimate matter, the healing of the official's son His power over the noblest of living bodies. Moreover they teach two great lessons which lie at the very root of Christianity; (1) that Christ's Presence hallows the commonest events and turns the meanest elements into the richest; (2) that the way to win blessings is to trust the Bestower of them. The third sign, healing the paralytic, shews the Messiah as the great Restorer, repairing the physical as well as the spiritual ravages of sin (v. 14). In the feeding of the 5000 the Christ appears as the Support of life, in the walking on the sea as the Guardian and Guide of His followers. The giving of sight to the man born blind and the raising of Lazarus shew that He is the Source of Light and of Life to men. The last sign, wrought by the Risen Christ, sums up and concludes the whole series (xxi. 1—12). Fallen man, restored, fed, guided, enlightened, delivered from the terrors of death, passes to the everlasting shore of peace, where the Lord is waiting to receive him.

In Nicodemus coming by night, in Judas going out into the night, in the dividing of Christ's garments and the blood and water from His side, &c. &c. we seem to have instances of the same love of symbolism. These historical details are singled out for notice *because* of the lesson which lies behind them. And if we ask for the source of this mode of teaching, there cannot be a doubt about the answer: it is the form in which almost all the lessons of the Old Testament are conveyed. This leads us to another characteristic.

4. Though written in Greek, S. John's Gospel is in thought and tone, and sometimes in the form of expression also, thoroughly HEBREW, AND BASED ON THE HEBREW SCRIPTURES. Much has been already said on this point in Chapter II. ii. (2), in shewing that the Evangelist must have been a Jew. The Gospel sets forth two facts in tragic contrast: (1) that the Jewish Scriptures in endless ways, by commands, types, and prophecies, pointed and led up to the Christ; (2) that precisely the people who possessed these Scriptures, and studied them most diligently, failed to recognise the Christ or refused to believe in Him. In this aspect the Gospel is a long comment

on the mournful text, 'Ye search the Scriptures; because in them ye think ye have eternal life: and they are they which testify of Me. And ye will not come to Me, that ye may have life' (v. 39, 40). To shew, therefore, the way out of this tragical contradiction between a superstitious reverence for the letter of the law and a scornful rejection of its true meaning, S. John writes his Gospel. He points out to his fellow-countrymen that they are right in taking the Scriptures for their guide, ruinously wrong in the use they make of them: Abraham, Moses and the Prophets, rightly understood, will lead them to adore Him whom they have crucified. This he does, not merely in *general statements* (i. 45, iv. 22, v. 39, 46), but in detail, both by *allusions;* e.g. to Jacob (i. 47, 51) and to the rock in the wilderness (vii. 37), and by *direct references;* e.g. to Abraham (vii. 56), to the brazen serpent (iii. 14), to the Bridegroom (iii. 29), to the manna (vi. 49), to the paschal lamb (xix. 36), to the Psalms (ii. 17, x. 34, xiii. 18, xix. 24, 37), to the Prophets generally (vi. 45, [vii. 38]), to Isaiah (xii. 38, 40), to Zechariah (xii. 15), to Micah (vii. 42).

All these passages (and more might easily be added) tend to shew that the Fourth Gospel is saturated with the thoughts, imagery, and language of the O. T. "Without the basis of the Old Testament, without the fullest acceptance of the unchanging divinity of the Old Testament, the Gospel of S. John is an insoluble riddle" (Westcott, *Introduction*, p. lxix.).

5. Yet another characteristic of this Gospel has been mentioned by anticipation in discussing the plan of it (chap. IV. ii); —its SYSTEMATIC ARRANGEMENT. It is the only Gospel which clearly has a plan. What has been given above as an outline of the plan (IV. ii.), and also the arrangement of the miracles in section 3 of this chapter, illustrate this feature of the Gospel. Further examples in detail will be pointed out in the subdivisions of the Gospel given in the notes.

6. The last characteristic which our space will allow us to notice is its STYLE. The style of the Gospel and of the First Epistle of S. John is unique. But it is a thing to be felt rather than to be defined. The most illiterate reader is conscious of it; the ablest critic cannot analyse it satisfactorily. A few

main features, however, may be pointed out; the rest being left to the student's own powers of observation.

Ever since Dionysius of Alexandria (c. A.D. 250) wrote his masterly criticism of the differences between the Fourth Gospel and the Apocalypse (Eus. *H. E.* VII. xxv.), it has been not uncommon to say that the Gospel is written in very pure Greek, free from all barbarous, irregular, or uncouth expressions. This is true in a sense; but it is somewhat misleading. The Greek of the Fourth Gospel is pure, as that of a Greek Primer is pure, because of its extreme simplicity. And it is faultless for the same reason; blemishes being avoided because idioms and intricate constructions are avoided. Elegant, idiomatic, classical Greek it is not.

(*a*) This, therefore, is one element in the style,—*extreme simplicity*. The clauses and sentences are connected together by simple conjunctions co-ordinately; they are not made to depend one upon another; 'In Him was life, *and the life* was the light of men;' not '*which* was the light, &c.' Even where there is strong contrast indicated a simple 'and' is preferred to 'nevertheless' or 'notwithstanding;' 'He came unto His own home, *and* His own people received Him not.' In passages of great solemnity the sentences are placed side by side without even a conjunction; 'Jesus answered...Pilate answered...Jesus answered' (xviii. 34—36). The words of others are given in direct not in oblique oration. The first chapter (19—51), and indeed the first half of the Gospel, abounds in illustrations.

(*b*) This simple co-ordination of sentences and avoidance of relatives and dependent clauses involves a good deal of repetition; and even when repetition is not necessary we find it employed for the sake of close connexion and emphasis. This *constant repetition* is very impressive. A good example of it is where the predicate (or part of the predicate) of one sentence becomes the subject (or part of the subject) of the next; or where the subject is repeated; 'I am *the good Shepherd; the good Shepherd* giveth His life for the sheep;' 'The light shineth in *the darkness;* and *the darkness* comprehended it not;' 'In the beginning was *the Word*, and *the Word* was with God, and *the Word* was God. Sometimes instead of repeating the subject S. John introduces an apparently superfluous demonstrative pronoun; 'He that seeketh the glory of Him that sent Him, *this one* is true' (vii. 18); 'He that made me whole, *that man* said unto me' (v. 11). The personal pronouns are frequently inserted for emphasis and repeated for the same reason. This is specially true of ' I ' in the discourses of Christ.

(*c*) Although S. John connects his sentences so simply, and sometimes merely places them side by side without conjunctions, yet he very frequently *points out a sequence in fact or in thought*. His two most characteristic particles are 'therefore' (οὖν) and 'in order that' (ἵνα). 'Therefore' occurs almost exclusively in narrative, and points out that one fact is a consequence of another, sometimes in cases where this would not have been obvious; 'He came *therefore* again into Cana of Galilee' (iv. 46), because of the welcome He had received there before; 'They sought *therefore* to take Him' (vii. 30), because of His claim to be sent from God.—While the frequent use of 'therefore' points to the conviction that nothing happens without a cause, the frequent use of 'in order that' points to the belief that nothing happens without a purpose. S. John uses 'in order that' not only where some other construction would have been suitable, but also where another construction would seem to be much more suitable; 'I am not worthy *in order that* I may unloose' (i. 27), 'My meat is *in order that* I may do the will' (iv. 34); 'This is the work of God, *in order that* ye may believe' (vi. 29); 'Who sinned, this man or his parents, *in order that* he should be born blind?' (ix. 2); 'It is expedient for you, *in order that* I go away' (xvi. 7). S. John is specially fond of this construction to point out the working of the Divine purpose, as in some of the instances just given (comp. v. 23, vi. 40, 50, x. 10, xi. 42, xiv. 16, &c. &c.) and in particular of the fulfilment of prophecy (xviii. 9, xix. 24, 28, 36). In this connexion an elliptical expression 'but in order that' (=but *this was done* in order that) is not uncommon; 'Neither this man sinned, nor his parents, *but in order that*, &c.' (ix. 3; comp. xi. 52, xiv. 31, xv. 25, xviii. 28).

(*d*) S. John, full of the spirit of Hebrew poetry, frequently employs that *parallelism* which to a large extent is the very form of Hebrew poetry: 'A servant is not greater than his lord; neither one that is sent greater than he that sent him' (xiii. 16); 'Peace I leave with you, My peace I give unto you... Let not your heart be troubled, neither let it be fearful' (xiv. 27). Sometimes the parallelism is antithetic, and the second clause denies the opposite of the first; 'He confessed, and denied not' (i. 20); 'I give unto them eternal life, and they shall never perish' (x. 28).

(*e*) Another peculiarity, also of Hebrew origin, is *minuteness of detail*. Instead of one word summing up the whole action, S. John uses two or three stating the details of the action; 'They *asked* him and *said* to him' (i. 25); 'John *bare witness, saying*' (i. 32); 'Jesus *cried aloud* in the Temple *teaching* and *saying*' (vii. 28). The frequent phrase 'answered and said,' illustrates both this particularity and also the preference for co-ordinate sentences (*a*). 'Answered and said' occurs thirty-four times in S. John, and only two or three times in the Synoptists, who commonly write 'having answered said,' or 'answered saying.'

(*f*) In conclusion we may notice a few of S. John's favourite words and phrases; 'Abide' especially in the phrases expressing abiding in one another; 'believe on' a person; 'true' as opposed to lying, and 'true' as opposed to spurious, 'truly,' and 'truth;' 'witness' and 'bear witness;' 'the darkness,' of moral darkness; 'the light,' of spiritual light; 'life;' 'love;' eternal life;' 'in frankness' or 'openly;' 'keep My word;' 'manifest;' 'the Jews,' of the opponents of Christ; 'the world,' of those alienated from Christ. The following words and phrases are used by S. John only; 'the Paraclete' or 'the Advocate,' of the Holy Spirit; 'the Word,' of the Son; 'only-begotten,' of the Son; 'come out from God,' of the Son; 'lay down My life,' of Jesus Christ; 'Verily, verily;' 'the ruler of this world,' of Satan; 'the last day.'

These characteristics combined form a book which stands alone in Christian literature, as its author stands alone among

Christian teachers; the work of one who for threescore years and ten laboured as an Apostle. Called to follow the Baptist when only a lad, and by him soon transferred to the Christ, he may be said to have been the first who from his youth up was a Christian. Who, therefore, could so fitly grasp and state in their true proportions and with fitting impressiveness the great verities of the Christian faith? He had had no deep-seated prejudices to uproot, like his friend S. Peter and others who were called late in life. He had had no sudden wrench to make from the past, like S. Paul. He had not had the trying excitement of wandering abroad over the face of the earth, like most of the Twelve. He had remained at his post at Ephesus, directing, teaching, meditating; until at last when the fruit was ripe it was given to the Church in the fulness of beauty which it is still our privilege to possess and learn to love.

CHAPTER VI.

ITS RELATION TO THE SYNOPTIC GOSPELS.

The Fourth Gospel presupposes the other three; the Evangelist assumes that the contents of his predecessors' Gospels are known to his readers. The details of Christ's birth are summed up in 'the Word became flesh.' His subjection to His parents is implied by contrast in His reply to His mother at Cana. The Baptism is involved in the Baptist's declaration, 'I have seen (the Spirit descending and abiding on Him) and have borne witness' (i. 34). The Ascension is promised through Mary Magdalene to the Apostles (xx. 17), but left unrecorded. Christian Baptism is assumed in the discourse with Nicodemus, and the Eucharist in that on the Bread of Life; but the reference in each case is left to speak for itself to Christians familiar with both those rites. S. John passes over their institution in silence.

The differences between the Fourth Gospel and the three first are real and very marked: but it is easy to exaggerate them. They are conveniently grouped under two heads; (1) differences as to the scene and extent of Christ's ministry; (2) differences as to the view given of His Person.

(1) With regard to the first, it is urged that the Synoptists represent our Lord's ministry as lasting for one year only, including only one Passover and one visit to Jerusalem, with which the ministry closes. S. John, however, describes the ministry as extending over three or possibly more years, including at least three Passovers and several visits to Jerusalem.

In considering this difficulty, if it be one, we must remember two things : (*a*) that all four Gospels are very incomplete and contain only a series of fragments; (*b*) that the date and duration of Christ's ministry remain and are likely to remain uncertain. (*a*) In the gaps in the Synoptic narrative there is plenty of room for all that is peculiar to S. John. In the spaces deliberately left by S. John between his carefully arranged scenes there is plenty of room for all that is peculiar to the Synoptists. When all have been pieced together there still remain large interstices which it would require at least four more Gospels to fill (xxi. 25). Therefore it can be no serious difficulty that so much of the Fourth Gospel has nothing parallel to it in the other three. (*b*) The additional fact of the uncertainty as to the date and duration of the Lord's public ministry is a further explanation of the apparent difference in the amount of time covered by the Synoptic narrative and that covered by the narrative of S. John. There is no contradiction between the two. The Synoptists nowhere say that the ministry lasted for only one year, although some commentators from very early times have proposed to understand 'the acceptable year of the Lord' (Luke iv. 19) literally. The three Passovers of S. John (ii. 13, vi. 4, xi. 55 ; v. 1 being omitted as very doubtful), compel us to give at least a little over two years to Christ's ministry. But S. John also nowhere implies that he has mentioned all the Passovers within the period ; and the startling statement of Irenaeus (*Haer.* II. xxii. 5) must be borne in mind, that our Lord fulfilled the office of a Teacher until He was over forty years old, "even as the Gospel and all the elders bear witness, who consorted with John the disciple of the Lord in Asia, (stating) that John had handed this down to them." Irenaeus makes the ministry begin when Christ was nearly thirty years of age (Luke iii. 23); so that he gives it a duration of more than ten years on what seems to be very high authority. All that can be affirmed with certainty is that the ministry cannot have begun earlier than A.D. 28 (the earlier alternative for the fifteenth year of Tiberius; Luke iii. 1), and cannot have ended later than A.D. 37, when Pilate was recalled by Tiberius shortly before his death. Indeed as Tiberius died in March, and Pilate found him already dead when he reached Rome, the recall probably took place in A.D. 36; and the Passover of A.D. 36 is the latest date possible for the Crucifixion. Chronology is not what the Evangelists aimed at giving us; and the fact that S. John spreads his narrative over a longer period than the Synoptists will cause a difficulty to those only who have mistaken the purpose of the Gospels.

(2) As to the second great difference between S. John and the Synoptists, it is said that, while they represent Jesus as a great Teacher and Reformer, with the powers and authority of a Prophet, who exasperates His countrymen by denouncing their immoral traditions, S. John gives us instead a mysterious Personage, invested with Divine attributes, who infuriates the hierarchy by claiming to be one with the Supreme God. It is urged, moreover, that there is a corresponding difference in the teaching attributed to Jesus in each case. The discourses in the Synoptic Gospels are simple, direct, and easily intelligible, inculcating for the most part high moral principles, which are enforced and illustrated by numerous parables and proverbs. Whereas the discourses in the Fourth Gospel are many and intricate, inculcating for the most part deep mystical truths, which are enforced by a ceaseless reiteration tending to obscure the exact line of the argument, and illustrated by not a single parable properly so called.

These important differences may be to a very great extent explained by two considerations: (*a*) the peculiarities of S. John's own temperament; (*b*) the circumstances under which he wrote. (*a*) The main features of S. John's character, so far as we can gather them from history and tradition, have been stated above (chapter I. ii.), and we cannot doubt that they have affected not only his choice of the incidents and discourses selected for narration, but also his mode of narrating them. No doubt in both he was under the guidance of the Holy Spirit (xiv. 26): but we have every reason for supposing that such guidance would work with, rather than against, the mental endowments of the person guided. To what extent the substance and form of his Gospel has been influenced by the intensity of his own nature we cannot tell : but the intensity is there, both in thought and language, both in its devotion and in its sternness; and the difference from the Synoptists shews that *some* influence has been at work. (*b*) The circumstances under which S. John wrote will carry us still further. They are very different from those under which the first Gospels were written. Christianity had grown from infancy to manhood and believed itself to be near the great consummation of the Lord's return. It was 'the last time.' Antichrist, who, as Jesus had foretold, was to precede His return, was already present in manifold shapes in the world (1 John ii. 18). In the bold speculations which had mingled themselves with Christianity, the Divine Government of the Father and the Incarnation of the Son were being explained away or denied (1 John ii. 22, iv. 3). The opposition, shewn from the first by 'the Jews' to the disciples of the Teacher whom they had crucified, had settled down into a relentless hostility. And while the gulf between Christianity and Judaism had thus widened, that between the Church and the world had also become more evident. The more the Christian realised the meaning of being 'born of God,' the more manifest became the truth, that 'the whole world lieth in wickedness' (1 John v. 18, 19). A Gospel that was to meet the needs of a society so changed both in its internal and external relations must obviously be very different from those which had suited its infancy. And a reverent mind will here trace the Providence of God, in that an Apostle, and he the Apostle S. John, was preserved for this crisis. It is scarcely too much to say that, had a Gospel, claiming to have been written by him near the close of the first century, greatly resembled the other three in matter and form, we should have had reasonable grounds for doubting its authenticity. (The special difficulty with regard to the discourses as reported by the Synoptists and by S. John is discussed in the introductory note to chap. iii.)

It must be remarked on the other side that, along with these important differences as regards the things narrated and the mode of narrating them, there are *coincidences* less conspicuous, but not less real or important.

Among the most remarkable of these are the characters of the Lord, of S. Peter, of Mary and Martha, and of Judas. The similarity in most cases is too subtle for the picture in the Fourth Gospel to have been drawn from that in the Synoptic account. It is very much easier to believe that the two pictures agree because both are taken from life.

The invariable use by the Synoptists of the expression 'Son of Man' is rigidly observed by S. John. It is always used by Christ of Himself; never by, or of, any one else. See notes on i. 51; and also on ii. 19 and xviii. 11 for two other striking coincidences.

The student will find tabulated lists of minor coincidences in Dr Westcott's *Introduction*, pp. lxxxii., lxxxiii. He sums up thus: "The general conclusion stands firm. The Synoptists offer not only historical but also spiritual points of connexion between the teaching which they record and the teaching in the Fourth Gospel; and S. John himself in the Apocalypse completes the passage from the one to the other."

CHAPTER VII.

ITS RELATION TO THE FIRST EPISTLE.

The chronological relation of the Gospel to the First Epistle of S. John cannot be determined with certainty. The Epistle presupposes the Gospel in some shape or other: but as the Gospel was given orally for many years before it was written, it is possible that the Epistle may have been written first. Probably they were written within a few years of one another, whichever was written first of the two.

In comparing the Fourth Gospel with the Synoptists we found great and obvious differences, accompanied by real but less obvious correspondences. Here the opposite is rather the case. The coincidences both in thought and expression between the Gospel and the First Epistle of S. John are many and conspicuous; but closer inspection shews some important differences.

The object of the Gospel, as we have seen, is to create a conviction 'that Jesus is the Christ, the Son of God.' The object of the Epistle is rather to insist that the Son of God is Jesus. The Gospel starts from the historical human Teacher and proves that He is Divine; the Epistle starts rather from the Son of God and contends that He has come in the flesh. Again, the Gospel is not polemical: the truth is stated rather than error attacked. In the Epistle definite errors are attacked.

The lesson of both is one and the same; faith in Jesus Christ leading to fellowship with Him, and through fellowship with Him to fellowship with the Father and with one another: or, to sum up all in one word, Love.

CHAPTER VIII.

THE TEXT OF THE GOSPEL.

The authorities are abundant and various. It will suffice to mention twelve of the most important; six Greek MSS. and six Ancient Versions.

Greek Manuscripts.

CODEX SINAITICUS (ℵ). 4th century. Discovered by Tischendorf in 1859 at the monastery of S. Catherine on Mount Sinai, and now at St Petersburg. The whole Gospel.

INTRODUCTION.

CODEX ALEXANDRINUS (A). 5th century. Brought by Cyril Lucar, Patriarch of Constantinople, from Alexandria, and afterwards presented by him to Charles I. in 1628. In the British Museum. The whole Gospel, excepting vi. 50—viii. 52.

CODEX VATICANUS (B). 4th century, but perhaps later than the Sinaiticus. In the Vatican Library. The whole Gospel.

CODEX EPHRAEMI (C). 5th century. A palimpsest: the original writing has been partially rubbed out and the works of Ephraem the Syrian have been written over it. In the National Library at Paris. Eight fragments; i. 1—41; iii. 33—v. 16; vi. 38—vii. 3; viii. 34—ix. 11; xi. 8—46; xiii. 8—xiv. 7; xvi. 21—xviii. 36; xx. 26—xxi. 25.

CODEX BEZAE (D). 6th or 7th century. Given by Beza to the University Library at Cambridge in 1581. Remarkable for its interpolations and various readings. The whole Gospel, excepting i. 16—iii. 26: but xviii. 13—xx. 13 is by a later hand, possibly from the original MS.

CODEX REGIUS PARISIENSIS (L). 8th or 9th century. Nearly related to the Vaticanus. At Tours. The whole Gospel, excepting xxi. 15—xxi. 25.

Ancient Versions.

OLD SYRIAC (Curetonian). 2nd century. Four fragments; i.—42; iii. 5—vii. 35; vii. 37—viii. 53, *omitting* vii. 53—viii. 11; xiv. 11—29.

VULGATE SYRIAC (Peschito). 3rd century. The whole Gospel.

HARCLEAN SYRIAC (a revision of the Philoxenian Syriac; 5th or 6th century). 7th century. The whole Gospel.

OLD LATIN (Vetus Latina). 2nd century. The whole Gospel in several distinct forms.

VULGATE LATIN (mainly a revision of the Old Latin by Jerome, A.D. 383—5). 4th century. The whole Gospel.

MEMPHITIC (Coptic, in the dialect of Lower Egypt). 3rd century. The whole Gospel.

CHAPTER IX.

THE LITERATURE OF THE GOSPEL.

It would be impossible to give even a sketch of this within a small compass, so numerous are the works on S. John and his writings. All that will be attempted here will be to give more advanced students some information as to where they may look for greater help than can be given in a handbook for the use of schools.

Of the earliest known commentary, that of Heracleon (c. A.D. 150), only quotations preserved by Origen remain. Of Origen's own commentary (c. A.D. 225—235) only portions remain. Of the Greek commentators of the fourth century, Theodorus of Heraclea and Didymus of Alexandria, very little has come down to us. But we have S. Chrysostom's 88 *Homilies* on the Gospel, which have been translated in the Oxford 'Library of the Fathers.' S. Augustine's 124 *Lectures* (*Tractatus*) on S. John may be read in the 'Library of the Fathers,' or in the new translation by Gibb, published by T. & T. Clark, Edinburgh. But no translation can fairly represent the epigrammatic fulness of the original. The *Commentary* of Cyril of Alexandria has been translated by P. E. Pusey, Oxford, 1875. With Cyril the line of great patristic interpreters of S. John ends.

The *Catena Aurea* of Thomas Aquinas (c. A.D. 1250) was published in an English form at Oxford, 1841—45. It consists of a 'chain' of comments selected from Greek and Latin authors. Unfortunately Thomas Aquinas was the victim of previous forgers, and a considerable number of the quotations from early authorities are taken from spurious works.

Of modern commentaries those of Cornelius à Lapide (Van der Steen) and Maldonatus in the sixteenth century and of Lampe in the eighteenth must be mentioned. The last has been a treasury of information for many more recent writers.

The following foreign commentaries have all been published in an English form by T. & T. Clark, Edinburgh; Bengel,

Godet, Luthardt, Meyer, Olshausen, Tholuck. Of these the works of Godet and Meyer may be specially commended. The high authority of Dr Westcott pronounces the commentary of Godet, "except on questions of textual criticism," to be "unsurpassed"—we may add, except by Dr Westcott's own.

Among original English commentaries those of Alford, Dunwell, McClellan, Watkins, and Wordsworth are or are becoming well known to all students. But immensely superior to all preceding works is the one noticed above, that by Dr Westcott in Vol. II. of the *Speaker's Commentary on N. T.* Murray, 1880.

Other works which give very valuable assistance are Ellicott's *Historical Lectures on the Life of our Lord*, Liddon's *Bampton Lectures*, 1866, Sanday's *Authorship and Historical Character of the Fourth Gospel*, and *The Gospels in the Second Century*, and Westcott's *Introduction to the Study of the Gospels*.

The present writer is bound to express his obligations, in some cases very great, to the works mentioned above of Alford, Dunwell, Ellicott, Liddon, McClellan, Sanday, Meyer, Watkins, and Westcott, as well as to many others. The debt to Canon Westcott would probably have been still greater if the notes to the first fifteen chapters had not been written before the writer of them had seen Vol. II. of the *Speaker's Commentary:* but they have been revised with its help. It was originally intended that Mr Sanday should undertake the present commentary, but press of other work induced him to ask leave to withdraw after having written notes on the greater part of the first chapter. His successor has had the advantage of these notes and has made large use of them, and throughout has aimed at in some measure remedying the loss caused by Mr Sanday's retirement by frequently quoting from his work on the Fourth Gospel. These quotations are marked simply 'S.' with a reference to the page.

ANALYSIS OF THE GOSPEL IN DETAIL.

I. 1—18. THE PROLOGUE.
  1. The Word in His own nature (1—5).
  2. His revelation to men and rejection by them (6—13).
  3. His revelation of the Father (14—18).

I. 19—XII. 50. THE MINISTRY.
  a. I. 19—II. 11. **The Testimony.**
    1. The Testimony of the Baptist (i. 19—37)
        to the deputation from Jerusalem (19—28),
        to the people (29—34),
        to Andrew and John (35—37).
    2. The Testimony of Disciples (i. 38—51).
    3. The Testimony of the First Sign (ii. 1—11).
  b. II. 13—XI. 57. **The Work.**
    1. The Work among Jews (ii. 13—iii. 36).
        First cleansing of the Temple (13—22).
        Belief without devotion (23—25).
        The discourse with Nicodemus (iii. 1—21).
        The baptism and final testimony of John (22—36).
    2. The Work among Samaritans (iv. 1—42).
    3. The Work among Galileans (iv. 43—54).
    4. The Work and conflict among mixed multitudes (v.—xi.).
      (a) CHRIST THE SOURCE OF LIFE (v.).
          The sign at the pool of Bethsaida (1—9).
          The sequel of the sign (10—16).
          The discourse on the Son as the Source of Life (17—47).

  (β) Christ the Support of Life (vi.).
    The sign on the land; feeding the 5000 (1—15).
    The sign on the lake; walking on the water (16—21).
    The sequel of the two signs (22—25).
    The discourse on the Son as the Support of Life (26—59).
    Opposite results of the discourse (60—71).

  (γ) Christ the Source of Truth and Light (vii. viii.).
    The controversy with His brethren (vii. 1—9).
    The discourse at the F. of Tabernacles (10—39).
    Opposite results of the discourse (40—52).
    [*The woman taken in adultery* (vii. 53—viii. 11)].
    Christ's true witness to Himself and against the Jews (viii. 12—59).

  Christ the Source of Truth and Life Illustrated by a Sign (ix.).
    The prelude to the sign (1—5).
    The sign (6—12).
    Opposite results of the sign (13—41).

  (δ) Christ is Love (x.).
    Allegory of the Door of the Fold (1—9).
    Allegory of the Good Shepherd (11—18).
    Opposite results of the teaching (19—21).
    The discourse at the F. of the Dedication (22—38).
    Opposite results of the discourse (39—42).

  Christ is Love Illustrated by a Sign (xi.)
    The prelude to the sign (1—33).
    The sign (33—44).
    Opposite results of the sign (45—57).

c. XII. **The Judgment.**
 1. The Judgment of men (1—36).
    The devotion of Mary (1—8).
    The hostility of the priests (9—11).
    The enthusiasm of the people (12—18).
    The discomfiture of the Pharisees (19).
    The desire of the Gentiles (20—33).
    The perplexity of the multitude (34—36).

    2. The Judgment of the Evangelist (37—43).
    3. The Judgment of Christ (44—50).

XIII.—XX. THE ISSUES OF THE MINISTRY.

  d. XIII.—XVII. **The inner Glorification of Christ in His last Discourses.**
    1. His love in Humiliation (xiii. 1—30).
    2. His Love in keeping His own (xiii. 31—xv. 27).
        Their union with Him illustrated by the allegory of the Vine (xv. 1—11).
        Their union with one another (12—17).
        The hatred of the world to both Him and them (18—25).
    3. The Promise of the Paraclete and of Christ's Return (xvi.).
        The World and the Paraclete (xvi. 1—11).
        The disciples and the Paraclete (12—15).
        The sorrow turned into joy (16—24).
        Summary and conclusion (25—33).
    4. The Prayer of the Great High Priest (xvii.).
        The prayer for Himself (xvii. 1—5),
            for the Disciples (6—19),
            for the whole Church (20—26).

  e. XVIII. XIX. **The outer Glorification of Christ in His Passion.**
    1. The Betrayal (xviii. 1—11).
    2. The Jewish or Ecclesiastical Trial (12—27).
    3. The Roman or Civil Trial (xviii. 28—xix. 16).
    4. The Death and Burial (xix. 17—42).
        The crucifixion and the title on the cross (17—22).
        The four enemies and the four friends (23—27).
        The two words, 'I thirst,' 'It is finished' (28—30).
        The hostile and the friendly petitions (31—42).

  f. XX. **The Resurrection and threefold Manifestation of Christ.**
    1. The first Evidence of the Resurrection (1—10).
    2. The Manifestation to Mary Magdalene (11—18).
    3. The Manifestation to the Ten and others (19—23).
    4. The Manifestation to S. Thomas and others (24—29).
    5. The Conclusion and Purpose of the Gospel (30, 31).

XXI. THE EPILOGUE OR APPENDIX.
   1. The Manifestation to the Seven and the Miraculous Draught of Fishes (1—14).
   2. The Commission to S. Peter and Prediction as to his Death (15—19).
   3. The misunderstood Saying as to the Evangelist (20—23).
   4. Concluding Notes (24, 25).

THE GOSPEL ACCORDING TO
S. JOHN.

CHAP. I. 1—18. *The Prologue or Introduction.*

THE GOSPEL ACCORDING TO ST JOHN] This title exists in very different forms, both ancient and modern, and is not original. As we might expect, the oldest authorities are the simplest, and the heading gradually increases in fulness; thus, 1. *According to John*, or *Of John;* 2. *Gospel according to John;* 3. *The Gospel according to John;* 4. *The holy Gospel,* &c. So also with the English Versions, from Wiclif's simple *Joon*, or *The Gospel of Joon*, to *The Holy Gospel of Jesus Christ according to John* of the Geneva Bible.

CHAP. I. 1—18. THE PROLOGUE OR INTRODUCTION.

That the first eighteen verses are introductory is universally admitted: commentators are not so unanimous as to the main divisions of this introduction. A division into three nearly equal parts has much to commend it:

1. *The Word in His own Nature* (1—5).
2. *His Revelation to men and rejection by them* (6—13).
3. *His Revelation of the Father* (14—18).

Some throw the second and third part into one, thus:

2. *The historical manifestation of the Word* (6—18).

Others again divide into two parts thus:

1. *The Word in His absolute eternal Being* (v. 1).
2. *The Word in relation to Creation* (2—18).

And there are other schemes besides these. In any scheme the student can scarcely fail to feel that the first verse is unique. Throughout the prologue the three great characteristics of this Gospel, simplicity, subtlety, and sublimity, are specially conspicuous; and the majesty of the first verse surpasses all. The Gospel of the Son of Thunder opens with a peal.

1—5. *The Word in His own Nature.*

1 IN the beginning was the Word, and the Word was with
2 God, and the Word was God. The same was in the

1—5. THE WORD IN HIS OWN NATURE.

1. *In the beginning*] The meaning must depend on the context.
In Gen. i. 1 it is an act done 'in the beginning;' here it is a Being
existing 'in the beginning,' and therefore prior to all beginning. That
was the first moment of time; this is eternity, transcending time. Thus
we have an intimation that the later dispensation is the confirmation
and infinite extension of the first. 'In the beginning' here equals
'before the world was,' xvii. 5. Compare xvii. 24; Eph. i. 4; and
contrast 'the beginning of the gospel of Jesus Christ,' Mark i. 1, which
is the historical beginning of the public ministry of the Messiah (John
vi. 64): 'the beginning' here is prior to all history. To interpret
'Beginning' of God as the Origin of all things is not correct, as the context shews.

was] Not 'came into existence,' but was already in existence before
the creation of the world. The generation of the Word or Son of God is
thus thrown back into eternity. Thus S. Paul calls Him (Col. i.
15) 'the firstborn of every creature,' or (more accurately translated)
'begotten before all creation,' like 'begotten before all worlds' in
the Nicene creed. Comp. Heb. i. 8, vii. 3; Rev. i. 8. On these
passages is based the doctrine of the Eternal Generation of the Son:
see *Articles of Religion*, I. and II. The Arians maintained that there
was a period when the Son was not: S. John says distinctly that
the Son or Word was existing *before time began*, i.e. from all eternity.

the Word] As early as the second century *Sermo* and *Verbum* were
rival translations of the Greek term *Logos* = Word. Tertullian (fl. A.D.
195—210) gives us both, but seems himself to prefer *Ratio*. *Sermo* first
became unusual, and finally was disallowed in the Latin Church. The
Latin versions all adopted *Verbum*, and from it comes our translation,
'the Word.'

None of these translations are at all adequate: but neither Latin nor
any modern language supplies anything really satisfactory. *Verbum*
and 'the Word' do not give the whole of even *one* of the two sides of
Logos: the other side, which Tertullian tried to express by *Ratio*, is not
touched at all; for ὁ λόγος means not only 'the spoken word,' but 'the
thought' expressed by the spoken word; it is *the spoken word as expressive of thought*. It is not found in the N.T. in the sense of ' reason.'

The expression *Logos* is a remarkable one; all the more so, because
S. John assumes that his readers will at once understand it. This
shews that his Gospel was written in the first instance for his own
disciples, who would be familiar with his teaching and phraseology.

Whence did S. John derive the expression, *Logos*? It has its origin
in the Targums, or paraphrases of the Hebrew Scriptures, in use in
Palestine, rather than in the mixture of Jewish and Greek philosophy
prevalent at Alexandria and Ephesus, as is very commonly asserted.

(1) In the *Old Testament* we find the Word or Wisdom of God personified, generally as an instrument for executing the Divine Will. We have a faint trace of it in the 'God said' of Gen. i. 3, 6, 9, 11, 14, &c. The personification of the Word of God begins to appear in the Psalms, xxxiii. 6, cvii. 20, cxix. 89, cxlvii. 15. In Prov. viii. and ix. the Wisdom of God is personified in very striking terms. This Wisdom is manifested in the *power* and *mighty* works of God; that God is *love* is a revelation yet to come. (2) In the *Apocrypha* the personification is more complete than in O.T. In Ecclesiasticus (c. B.C. 150—100) i. 1—20, xxiv. 1—22, and in the Book of Wisdom (c. B.C. 100) vi. 22 to ix. 18 we have Wisdom strongly personified. In Wisd. xviii. 15 the 'Almighty Word' of God appears as an agent of vengeance. (3) In the *Targums*, or Aramaic paraphrases of O.T., the development is carried still further. These, though not yet written down, were in common use among the Jews in our Lord's time; and they were strongly influenced by the growing tendency to separate the Godhead from immediate contact with the material world. Where Scripture speaks of a direct communication from God to man, the Targums substituted the *Memra*, or 'Word of God.' Thus in Gen. iii. 8, 9, instead of 'they heard the voice of the Lord God,' the Targums have 'they heard the voice of the *Word* of the Lord God;' and instead of 'God called unto Adam,' they put 'the *Word* of the Lord called unto Adam,' and so on. 'The Word of the Lord' is said to occur 150 times in a single Targum of the Pentateuch. In the *theosophy of the Alexandrine Jews*, which was a compound of theology with philosophy and mysticism, we seem to come nearer to a strictly personal view of the Divine Word or Wisdom, but really move further away from it. Philo, the leading representative of this religious speculation (fl. A.D. 40—50), admitted into his philosophy very various, and not always harmonious elements. Consequently his conception of the *Logos* is not fixed or clear. On the whole his *Logos* means some intermediate agency, by means of which God created material things and communicated with them. But whether this *Logos* is one Being or more, whether it is personal or not, we cannot be sure; and perhaps Philo himself was undecided. Certainly his *Logos* is very different from that of S. John; for it is scarcely a Person, and it is not the Messiah. And when we note that of the two meanings of Λόγος, Philo dwells most on the side which is less prominent, while the Targums insist on that which is more prominent in the teaching of S. John, we cannot doubt the source of his language. The Logos of Philo is preeminently the Divine *Reason*. The Memra of the Targums is rather the Divine *Word*; i.e. the Will of God manifested in personal action; and this rather than a philosophical abstraction of the Divine Intelligence is the starting point of S. John's expression.

To sum up:—the personification of the Divine Word in O.T. is poetical, in Philo metaphysical, in S. John historical. The Apocrypha and Targums help to fill the chasm between O.T. and Philo; history itself fills the far greater chasm which separates all from S. John. Between Jewish poetry and Alexandrine speculation on the one hand,

3 beginning with God. All *things* were made by him; and
4 without him was not any *thing* made that was made. In

and the Fourth Gospel on the other, lies the historical fact of the Incarnation of the *Logos*, the life of Jesus Christ.

The Logos of S. John, therefore, is not a mere attribute of God, but the Son of God, existing from all eternity, and manifested in space and time in the Person of Jesus Christ. In the Logos had been hidden from eternity all that God had to say to man; for the Logos was the living expression of the nature, purposes, and Will of God. (Comp. the impersonal designation of Christ in 1 John i. 1.) Human thought had been searching in vain for some means of connecting the finite with the Infinite, of making God intelligible to man and leading man up to God. S. John knew that he possessed the key to this enigma. He therefore took the phrase which human reason had lighted on in its gropings, stripped it of its misleading associations, fixed it by identifying it with the Christ, and filled it with that fulness of meaning which he himself had derived from Christ's own teaching.

with God] i.e. with the Father. 'With'=*apud*, or the French *chez:* it expresses the distinct Personality of the Logos. We might render 'face to face with God,' or 'at home with God.' So, 'His sisters, are they not all *with* us?' Matt. xiii. 56; comp. Mark vi. 3, ix. 19, xiv. 49; 1 Cor. xvi. 7; Gal. i. 18; 1 Thess. iii. 4; Philem. 13; 1 John i. 2.

the Word was God] i.e. the Word partook of the Divine *Nature*, not was identical with the Divine *Person*. The verse may be thus paraphrased, 'the Logos existed from all eternity, distinct from the Father, and equal to the Father.' Comp. 'neither confounding the Persons nor dividing the Substance.'

2. *The same*] More literally, **He** or **This** (Word), with emphasis (comp. vii. 18). This verse takes up the first two clauses and combines them. Such recapitulations are characteristic of S. John.

3. *by him*] Rather, **through** *Him*. The universe was created *by* the Father *through the agency* of the Son. Comp. 1 Cor. viii. 6; Col. i. 16 (where see Lightfoot's note); Rom. xi. 36; Heb. xi. 10. That no inferiority is necessarily implied by 'through,' as if the Son were a mere instrument, is shewn by 1 Cor. i. 9, where the same construction is used of the Father, '*through* Whom ye were called, &c.' Note the climax in what follows; the sphere contracts as the blessing enlarges: existence for everything; life for the vegetable and animal world; light for men.

without him, &c.] Better, **apart** *from Him*, &c. Comp. xv. 5. Antithetic parallelism; emphatic repetition by contradicting the opposite: frequent in Hebrew: one of the many instances of the Hebrew cast of S. John's style. Comp. *v.* 20, x. 28; 1 John i. 5, ii. 4, 27, 28; Ps. lxxxix. 30, 31, 48, &c., &c.

not anything] *No, not one;* **not even one**: stronger than 'nothing.' Every single thing, however great, however small, throughout all the realms of space, came into being through Him. No event takes place *without* Him,—apart from His presence and power. Matt. x. 29; Luke xii. 6.

him was life; and the life was the light of men. And the 5
light shineth in darkness; and the darkness comprehended
it not.

that was made] Better, *that* **hath been** *made*. The aorist refers to the fact of creation; the perfect to the permanent result of that fact. Contrast 'was made' and 'hath been made' here with 'was' in *vv.* 1 and 2. 'Was made' denotes the springing into life of what was once non-existent; 'was' denotes the perpetual pre-existence of the Word.
Some both ancient and modern writers would give the last part of *v.* 3 to *v.* 4, thus: *That which hath been made in Him was life;* i.e. those who were born again by union with Him felt His influence as life within them. It is very difficult to decide between the two punctuations. Tatian (*Orat. ad Graecos,* XIX.) has 'All things [were] by Him and without Him hath been made not even one thing.' See on *v.* 5.
4. *In him was life*] He was the well-spring from which every form of life—physical, intellectual, moral, spiritual, eternal—flows. See on v. 26.
Observe how frequently S. John's thoughts overlap and run into one another. Creation leads on to life, and life leads on to light. Without life creation would be unintelligible; without light all but the lowest forms of life would be impossible.
the light] Not 'light,' but '**the** Light,' the one true Light; absolute Truth both intellectual and moral, free from all ignorance and all stain. The Source of life is the Source of light.
the light of men] Man shares life with all organic creatures; light, or Revelation, is for him alone. The communication of Divine truth before the Fall is specially meant.
5. *shineth*] Note the present tense; the only one in the section. It brings us down to the Apostle's own day: now, as of old, the Light shines—in reason, in creation, in conscience,—and shines in vain. Note also the progress: in *vv.* 1 and 2 we have the period before Creation; in *v.* 3, the Creation; *v.* 4, man before the Fall; *v.* 5, man after the Fall.
in darkness] Better, *in* **the** *darkness*. The Fall is presupposed.
and the darkness] Mark the strong connexion between the two halves of *v.* 5 as also between *v.* 4 and *v.* 5, resulting in both cases from a portion of the predicate of one clause becoming the subject of the next clause. Such strong connexions are frequent in St John. Sometimes the whole of the predicate is taken; sometimes the subject or a portion of the subject is repeated.—By 'the darkness' is meant all that the Divine Revelation does not reach, whether by God's decree or their own stubbornness, ignorant Gentile or unbelieving Jew. 'Darkness' in a metaphorical sense for spiritual and moral darkness is peculiar to S. John, viii. 12, xii. 35, 46; 1 John i. 5, ii. 8, 9, 11.
comprehended it not] Or, **apprehended** *it not:* very appropriate of that which requires mental and moral effort. Comp. Eph. iii. 18. The darkness remained apart, unyielding, and unpenetrated. The words 'the darkness apprehendeth not the light' are given by Tatian as a

6—13. *The Word revealed to Men and rejected by them.*

6 There was a man sent from God, whose name *was* John. 7 The same came for a witness, to bear witness of the Light, 8 that all *men* through him might believe. He was not *that* 9 Light, but *was sent* to bear witness of *that* Light. That

quotation (*Orat. ad Graecos*, XIII.). He flourished A.D. 150—170: so this is early testimony to the existence of the Gospel. This and the reference to v. 3 (see note) are quite beyond reasonable dispute.

We have here an instance of what has been called the "tragic tone" in S. John. He frequently states a gracious fact, and in immediate connexion with it the very opposite of what might have been expected to result from it. The Light shines in Darkness, and (instead of yielding and dispersing) the darkness shut it out. Comp. vv. 10 and 11, (ii. 24,) iii. 11, 19, 32, v. 39, 40, vi. 36, 43, viii. 45, &c. The word rendered 'comprehended' may also mean '*overcame*;' and this makes good sense. Comp. xii. 35.

6—13. THE WORD REVEALED TO MEN AND REJECTED BY THEM.

6. *There was a man*] Rather, *There* **arose** *a man*, in contrast to the 'was' in v. 1. The word *was* from all eternity; John *arose*, came into existence, in time. Comp. x. 19. Note once more the noble simplicity of language.

sent from God] i.e. a Prophet. Comp. 'I will *send* my messenger,' Mal. iii. 1; 'I will *send* you Elijah the Prophet,' iv. 5. From the Greek for 'send' (*apostello*) comes our word 'Apostle.'

whose name was John] In the Fourth Gospel John is mentioned 20 times, and is never once distinguished as 'the Baptist.' The other three Evangelists carefully distinguish the Baptist from the son of Zebedee: to the writer of the Fourth Gospel there is only one John. This in itself is strong incidental evidence that he himself is the other John. See on xi. 16.

7. *for a witness*] Better, **for witness**, i.e. to bear witness, not to be a witness: what follows shews the meaning. The word 'witness' and 'to bear witness' are very frequent in S. John's writings, and this frequency should be marked by retaining the same translation throughout: testimony to the truth is one of his favourite thoughts.

through him] i.e. through the Baptist, the Herald of the Truth. Comp. v. 33; Acts x. 37, xiii. 24.

8. *not that Light*] Better, **not the** *Light*. The Baptist was not the Light, but 'the lamp that is lighted and shineth' (see on v. 35). He was *lumen illuminatum*, not *lumen illuminans*. At the close of the first century it was still necessary for S. John to insist on this. At Ephesus, where this Gospel was written, S. Paul in his third missionary journey had found disciples still resting in 'John's baptism,' Acts xix. 1—6. 'By lamp-light we may advance to the day' (Augustine).

but was sent to] 'was sent' is not in the Greek. 'But (in order) that'

was the true Light, which lighteth every man *that* cometh
into the world. He was in the world, and the world was 10
made by him, and the world knew him not. He came unto 11

is an elliptical phrase occurring several times in this Gospel. It calls
attention to the Divine purpose. Comp. ix. 3, xiii. 18, xiv. 31, xv. 25.

9. *That was*, &c.] This verse is ambiguous in the Greek. Most
of the Ancient Versions, Fathers, and Reformers agree with our translators. Many modern commentators translate—**the true Light, which
lighteth every man, was coming into the world**: but 'was' and 'coming' are almost too far apart in the Greek for this. There is yet a
third way;—**there was the true Light, which lighteth every man by
coming into the world.** 'Was' is emphatic: 'there *was* the true Light,'
even while the Baptist was preparing the way for Him. The Baptist
came once for all; the Light was ever coming.

The word for 'true' (*alēthinos*) is remarkable: it means true as opposed to 'spurious,' not true as opposed to 'lying.' It is in fact the
old English 'very,' e.g. 'very God of very God.' Christ then is the
true, the genuine, the perfect Light, just as He is 'the perfect Bread'
(vi. 32) and 'the perfect Vine' (xv. 1): not that He is the only Light,
and Bread, and Vine, but that He is in reality what all others are in
figure and imperfectly. All words about *truth* are very characteristic
of S. John.

every man] not 'all men:' the Light illumines each one singly, not all
collectively. God deals with men separately as individuals, not in
masses. But though every man is illumined, not every man is the
better for it: that depends upon himself.

that cometh into the world] A Jewish phrase for being born, frequent in S. John (ix. 39, xi. 27, xvi. 28); see on xviii. 37. 'The world'
is another of the expressions characteristic of S. John: it occurs nearly
80 times in the Gospel and 22 in the First Epistle. This verse, Hippolytus tells us (*Refut.* VII. x.), was used by Basilides in defending his
doctrine, and as he began to teach about A.D. 125, this is very early
evidence of the use of the Gospel.

10. *and the world*] Note three points; (1) the close connexion
obtained by repetition, as in *vv.* 4 and 5; (2) the tragic tone, as in *v.* 5;
(3) the climax. 'He was in the world' (therefore the world should have
known Him); 'and the world was His own creature' (therefore still
more it should have known Him); 'and (yet) the world knew Him
not.' 'And' = 'and yet' is very frequent in S. John; but it is best not
to put in the 'yet;' the simple 'and' is more forcible. Comp. *vv.* 5
and 11.

Note that 'the world' has not the same meaning in *vv.* 9 and 10.
Throughout N.T. it is most important to distinguish the various meanings of 'the world.' It means (1) 'the universe;' Rom. i. 20: (2) 'the
earth;' *v.* 9; Matt. iv. 8: (3) 'the inhabitants of the earth;' *v.* 29, iv.
42: (4) 'those outside the Church,' alienated from God; xii. 31, xiv. 17,
and frequently. In this verse the meaning slips from (2) to (4).

12 his own, and his own received him not. But as many as
received him, to them gave he power to become the sons of
13 God, *even* to them that believe on his name: which were

knew him not] Did not *acquire* knowledge of its Creator; did not recognise and acknowledge Him. Comp. Acts xix. 15.

11. *unto his own*] In the Greek the first 'own' is neuter, the second is masculine, and this difference should be preserved: *He came unto His own* **inheritance**; *and His own* **people** *received Him not* (see on vi. 37). In the parable of the Wicked Husbandmen (Matt. xxi. 33—41) the vineyard is 'His own inheritance,' the husbandmen are 'His own people,' the Jews. Or, for 'His own *inheritance*' we might say 'His own *home*,' as in xix. 27, where the Greek is the same. The tragic tone is very strong here as in *vv.* 5 and 10.

received] A stronger word than 'knew.' The exact meaning of the Greek word is 'to accept what is *offered.*' Mankind in general did not recognise the Messiah; the Jews, to whom He was specially sent, did not *welcome* Him. See on xix. 16.

Once more there is a climax;—'He was' (*v.* 9); 'He was in the world' (*v.* 10); 'He came unto His own inheritance' (*v.* 11).

12. *received*] Not the same Greek word as before: this denotes the spontaneous acceptance of the Messiah by *individuals*, whether Jews or Gentiles. He was not specially offered to any individuals as He was to the Jewish nation.

power] i.e. right, liberty, **authority.** We are born with a *capacity* for becoming sons of God; that we have as men. He gives us a *right* to become such; that we receive as Christians. Comp. v. 27, x. 18.

to become] Christ *is* from all eternity the Son of God; men are empowered to *become* sons of God. Comp. Matt. v. 45.

the sons of God] Omit 'the:' **children** *of God*. Both S. John and S. Paul insist on the fundamental fact that the relation of believers to God is a *filial* one. S. John gives us this fact on the human side; man 'must be born again' (iii. 3). S. Paul gives us the Divine side; God by 'adoption' makes us sons (Rom. viii. 16, 17, 21, 23; Gal. iv. 5).

even to them that believe] Explains who are the sons of God. The test of a child of God is no longer descent from Abraham, but belief in God's Son.

on his name] The construction 'to believe *on*' is characteristic of S. John: it occurs about 35 times in the Gospel and 3 times in the First Epistle; elsewhere in N.T. about 10 times. It expresses the very strongest belief; motion to and repose on the object of belief. 'His Name' is a frequent phrase in Jewish literature, both O. and N.T. It is not a mere periphrasis. Names were so often significant, given sometimes by God Himself, that a man's name told not merely *who* he was, but *what* he was: it was an index of character. So 'the Name of the Lord' is not a mere periphrasis for 'the Lord;' it suggests His attributes and His relations to us as Lord. Perhaps the name of *Logos* is specially meant here; and the meaning would then be to give one's entire ad-

born, not of blood, nor of the will of the flesh, nor of the will of man, but of God.

14—18. *The Incarnate Word's revelation of the Father.*

And the Word was made flesh, and dwelt among us, 14

hesion to Him as the Incarnate Son, the expression of the Will and Nature of God. Comp. iii. 18, xx. 31.

13. S. John denies thrice most emphatically that human generation has anything to do with Divine regeneration. Man cannot become a child of God in right of human parentage: descent from Abraham confers no such 'power.' A bitter word to Jewish exclusiveness.

were born] Literally, **were begotten.** Comp. 1 John v. 1, 4, 18.

not of blood] The blood was regarded as the seat of physical life. Gen. ix. 4; Lev. xvii. 11, 14, &c.

nor of the will of the flesh] Better, **nor yet from will of flesh**, i.e. from any fleshly impulse. A second denial of any physical process.

nor of the will of man] Better, **nor yet from will of man**, i.e. from the volition of any earthly father: it is the Heavenly Father who wills it. A third denial of any physical process.

There is an interesting false reading here. Tertullian (c. A.D. 200) had '*was* born' for '*were* born,' making it refer to Christ; and he accused the Valentinians of corrupting the text in reading '*were* born,' which is undoubtedly right. This shews that as early as A.D. 200 there were corruptions in the text, the origin of which was already lost. Such things take some time to grow: by comparing them and tracing their roots and branches we arrive at a sure conclusion that this Gospel cannot have been written later than A.D. 85—100. See on *v.* 18 and ix. 35.

14—18. THE INCARNATE WORD'S REVELATION OF THE FATHER.

14. *And the Word was made flesh*] Or, **became** *flesh*. This is the gulf which separates S. John from Philo. Philo would have assented to what precedes; from this he would have shrunk. From *v.* 9 to 13 we have the *subjective* side; the inward result of the Word's coming to those who receive Him. Here we have the *objective;* the coming of the Word as a historical fact. The Logos, existing from all eternity with the Father (*vv.* 1 and 2), not only manifested His power in Creation (*v.* 3) and in influence on the minds of men (*vv.* 9, 12, 13), but manifested Himself in the form of a man of flesh. The important point is that the Word became terrestrial and material: and thus the inferior part of man is mentioned, the flesh, to mark His humiliation. He took the whole of man's nature, including its frailty. "The majestic fulness of this brief sentence," *the Word became flesh*, which affirms once for all the union of the Infinite and the finite, "is absolutely unique." The Word *became* flesh; did not merely *assume* a body: and the Incarnate Word is one, not two personalities. Thus various heresies, Gnostic and Eutychian, are refuted by anticipation.

(and we beheld his glory, the glory as of the only begotten
15 of the Father,) full of grace and truth. John bare witness of
him, and cried, saying, This was he of whom I spake, He

dwelt among us] Literally, **tabernacled** *among us*, dwelt as in a tent.
The Tabernacle had been the seat of the Divine Presence in the wilderness: when God became incarnate in order to dwell among the Chosen People, 'to tabernacle' was a natural word to use. The word forms a link between this Gospel and the Apocalypse: it occurs here, four times in the Apocalypse, and nowhere else. Our translators render it simply 'dwell,' which is inadequate. Rev. vii. 15, xii. 12, xiii. 6, xxi. 3
among us] In the midst of those of us who witnessed His life.
we beheld] Or, **contemplated**. Comp. 1 John i. 1. No need to make a parenthesis.
his glory] The Shechinah. Comp. ii. 11, xi. 40, xii. 41, xvii. 5, 24; 2 Cor. iii. 7—18; Rev. xxi. 11. There is probably a special reference to the Transfiguration (Luke ix. 32; 2 Pet. i. 17); and possibly to the vision at the beginning of the Apocalypse. In any case it is the Evangelist's own experience that is indicated. Omit 'the' before the second 'glory.'
as of] i.e. exactly like. The glory is *altogether such as* that of an only-begotten son. Comp. Matt. vii. 29. He taught *exactly as* one having full authority. No article before 'only-begotten;' He was an only-begotten Son, whereas Moses and the Prophets were but servants.
only begotten] *Unigenitus.* The Greek word is used of the widow's son (Luke vii. 12), Jairus' daughter (viii. 42), the demoniac boy (ix. 38), Isaac (Heb. xi. 17). As applied to Christ it occurs only in S. John's writings; here, *v.* 18, iii. 16, 18; 1 John iv. 9. It marks off His unique Sonship from that of the 'sons of God' (*v.* 12).
of the Father] Literally, **from the presence of a father**; an only son sent on a mission from a father: comp. *v.* 6.
full] Looks forward to 'fulness' in *v.* 16.
grace] The original meaning of the Greek word is 'that which causes pleasure.' Hence (1) *comeliness, winsomeness:* 'the words of grace' in Luke iv. 22 are 'winning words.' (2) *Kindliness, goodwill:* Luke ii. 52; Acts ii. 47. (3) The *favour* of God towards sinners. This distinctly theological sense has for its central point the *freeness* of God's gifts: they are not earned, He gives them *spontaneously* through Christ. 'Grace' covers all these three meanings. The third at its fullest and deepest is the one here. It is as the *Life* that the Word is 'full of grace,' for it is 'by grace' that we come to eternal life. Eph. ii. 5.
truth] It is as the *Light* that the Word is 'full of truth.'
15. *bare witness*] Better, **bears witness**. At the end of a long life this testimony of the Baptist abides still fresh in the heart of the aged Apostle. Three times in 20 verses (15, 27, 30) he records the cry which was such an epoch in his own life. The testimony remains as a memory for him, a truth for all.
and cried] Better, *and* **cries**. The word indicates strong emotion, characteristic of a prophet. Comp. vii. 28, 37, xii. 44; Is. xl. 3.

that cometh after me is preferred before me: for he was
before me. And of his fulness have all we received, and 16
grace for grace. For the law was given by Moses, *but* grace 17

of whom I spake] As if his first utterance under the influence of the Spirit had been scarcely intelligible to himself.
He that cometh after, &c.] The exact meaning seems to be—'He who is coming after me (in His ministry as in His birth) has become superior to me, for He was in existence from all eternity before me.' Christ's pre-existence in eternity a great deal more than cancelled John's pre-existence in the world; and as soon as He appeared as a teacher He at once eclipsed His forerunner. But this is not quite certain. The words translated 'is preferred before me,' or 'is become superior to me,' literally mean 'has come to be before me;' and this may refer to *time* and not to *dignity*. But the perfect tense 'has come to be, has become' points to dignity rather than time. Moreover if 'has become before me' refers to time, this is almost tautology with 'for He was before me,' which must refer to time.
he was before me] The Greek is peculiar, being the superlative instead of the comparative; not simply '*prior* to me,' but '*first* of me.' Perhaps it means 'before me and first of all.'
16. The testimony of the Baptist to the incarnate Word is confirmed by the experience of all believers. The Evangelist is the speaker.
And] The true reading gives **Because**.
fulness] The Greek word, *pleroma*, is 'a recognised technical term in theology, denoting the totality of the Divine powers and attributes.' This fulness of the Divine attributes belonged to Christ (*v*. 14), and by Him was imparted to the Church, which is His Body (Eph. i. 23); and through the Church each individual believer in his degree receives a portion of it. See Lightfoot on *Colossians*, i. 19 and ii. 9. 'Of His fulness' means literally '**out of** His fulness,' as from an inexhaustible store.
all we] shews that the Evangelist and not the Baptist is speaking.
grace for grace] Literally, *grace* **in the place of** *grace*, one grace succeeding another, and as it were taking its place. There is no reference to the Christian dispensation displacing the Jewish. The Jewish dispensation would have been called 'the Law,' not 'grace;' see next verse, and comp. xvii. 22.
17. The mention of 'grace' reminds the Evangelist that this was the characteristic of the Gospel and marked its superiority to the Law; for the Law could only condemn transgressors, grace forgives them.
For] Better, **Because**.
by Moses] The preposition translated 'by' in *vv*. 3, 10, 17, and 'through' in *v*. 7, is one and the same in the Greek. The meaning in all five cases is 'by means of.' Moses did not give the Law any more than he gave the manna (vi. 32): he was only the mediate agent by whose hand it was given (Gal. iii. 19).

18 and truth came by Jesus Christ. No *man* hath seen God at any time; the only begotten Son, which is in the bosom of the Father, he hath declared *him*.

truth] Like grace, truth is opposed to the Law, not as truth to falsehood, but as perfection to imperfection.

came] Note the change from 'was given.' The grace and truth which came through Christ were His own; the Law given through Moses was not his own.

Jesus Christ] S. John no longer speaks of the Logos: the Logos has become incarnate (*v.* 14) and is spoken of henceforth by the names which He has borne in history.

18. The Evangelist solemnly sums up the purpose of the Incarnation of the Logos—to be a visible revelation of the invisible God. It was in this way that 'the truth came through Jesus Christ,' for the truth cannot be fully known, while God is not fully revealed.

No man] Not even Moses. Until we see 'face to face' (1 Cor. xiii. 12) our knowledge is only partial. Symbolical visions, such as Ex. xxiv. 10, xxxiii. 23; 1 Kings xix. 13; Is. vi. 1, do not transcend the limits of partial knowledge.

hath seen] With his bodily eyes.

at any time] Better, **ever yet**; 'no one hath ever yet seen God;' but some shall see Him hereafter.

the only begotten Son] The question of reading here is very interesting. Most MSS. and versions have 'the only-begotten Son' or 'only-begotten Son.' But the three oldest and best MSS. and two others of great value have 'only-begotten *God*.' The test of the value of a MS., or group of MSS., on any disputed point, is the extent to which it admits false readings on other points not disputed. Judged by this test the group of MSS. which read 'only-begotten God' is very strong; while the far larger group of MSS. which have 'Son' for 'God' is comparatively weak, for the same group of MSS. might be quoted in defence of a multitude of readings which no one would think of adopting. Again, the revised Syriac, which is among the minority of versions that support 'God,' is here of special weight, because it agrees with MSS. from which it usually differs. We conclude, therefore, that the very unusual expression 'only-begotten God' is the true reading, which has been changed to the usual 'only-begotten Son,' a change which in an old Greek MS. would involve the alteration of only a single letter. Both readings can be traced up to the second century, which again is evidence that the Gospel was written in the first century. Such differences take time to spread themselves widely. See on *v.* 13 and ix. 35.

in the bosom] Literally, **into** *the bosom*, which may mean that the return to glory after the Ascension is meant. Comp. Mark ii. 1, xiii. 16; Luke ix. 61. On the other hand the Greek for 'which is' points to a *timeless* relation.

hath declared] Better, **declared**, acted as His interpreter. The Greek word is used both in the LXX. and in classical authors of interpreting

19—37. *The Testimony of the Baptist.*

19—28. *His Testimony to the Deputation from Jerusalem.*

And this is the record of John, when the Jews sent 19

the Divine Will. On the emphatic use of 'He' here comp. v. 33 and see on x. 1. In the First Epistle this pronoun (*ekeinos*) is used specially for Christ; ii. 6, iii. 3, 5, 7, 16, iv. 17.

In this prologue we notice what may be called a *spiral movement*. An idea comes to the front, like the strand of a rope, retires again, and reappears later on for development and further definition. Meanwhile another idea, like another strand, comes before us, and retires to reappear in like manner. Thus the Word is presented to us in v. 1, is withdrawn, and again presented to us in v. 14. The Creation comes next in v. 3, disappears, and returns again in v. 10. Then 'the Light' is introduced in v. 5, withdrawn, and reproduced in vv. 10, 11. Next the rejection of the Word is put before us in v. 5, removed, and again put before us in vv. 10, 11. Lastly, the testimony of John is mentioned in vv. 6, 7, repeated in v. 15, taken up again in v. 19, and developed through the next two sections of the chapter.

We now enter upon the first main division of the Gospel, which extends to the end of chap. xii., the subject being CHRIST'S MINISTRY, or, HIS REVELATION OF HIMSELF TO THE WORLD, and that in three parts; THE TESTIMONY (i. 19—ii. 11), THE WORK (ii. 13—xi. 57), and THE JUDGMENT (xii.). These parts will be subdivided as we reach them. 19—37 *The Testimony of the Baptist* (1) to the deputation from Jerusalem, (2) to the people, (3) to S. Andrew and S. John: 38—51 *The Testimony of the Disciples:* ii. 1—11 *The Testimony of the First Sign.*

19—37. THE TESTIMONY OF THE BAPTIST.

19—28. HIS TESTIMONY TO THE DEPUTATION FROM JERUSALEM.

This section describes a crisis in the Baptist's ministry. He had already attracted the attention of the Sanhedrin. It was a time of excitement and expectation respecting the Messiah. John evidently spoke with an authority greater than other teachers, and his success was greater than theirs. The miracle attending his birth, connected with the public ministry of Zacharias in the Temple, was probably well known. He had proclaimed that a new dispensation was at hand (Matt. iii. 2), and this was believed to refer to the Messiah. But what was John's own position? Was he the Messiah? This uncertainty led the authorities at Jerusalem to send and question John himself as to his mission. No formal deputation from the Sanhedrin seems to have been sent. The Sadducee members, acquiescing in the Roman dominion, would not feel much interest. But to the Pharisee members, who represented the religious and national hopes of their countrymen, the question was vital; and they seem to have sent an informal though influential depu-

priests and Levites from Jerusalem to ask him, Who art
20 thou? And he confessed, and denied not; but confessed, I
21 am not the Christ. And they asked him, What then? Art

tation of ministers of religion (*v.* 19) from their own party (*v.* 24). S. John was probably among the Baptist's disciples at this time, and heard his master proclaim himself not the Messiah, but His Herald. It was a crisis for him as well as for his master, and as such he records it.

19. *the record*] Better, *the* **witness**; see on *v.* 7 and comp. iii. 11, v. 31.

the Jews] This term in S. John's Gospel commonly means *the opponents of Christ*, a meaning not found in the Synoptists, who seldom use the term. Matt. xxviii. 15; Mark vii. 3; Luke vi. 3, xxiii. 51, are the only instances excepting the title 'King of the Jews.' In them it is the sects and parties (Pharisees, Scribes, Herodians, &c.) that are the typical representatives of hostility to Christ. But S. John, writing later, with a fuller realisation of the national apostasy, and a fuller experience of Jewish malignity in opposing the Gospel, lets the shadow of this knowledge fall back upon his narrative, and 'the Jews' are to him not his fellow countrymen, but the persecutors and murderers of the Messiah. 'The name of a race has become the name of a sect.' He uses the term about 70 times, almost always with this shade of meaning.

priests] The Baptist himself was of priestly family (Luke i. 5); hence priests were suitable emissaries. The combination 'priests and Levites' occurs nowhere else in N. T. Together they represent the hierarchy.

Levites] Levites were commissioned to *teach* (2 Chron. xxxv. 3; Neh. viii. 7—9) as well as serve in the Temple; and it is as teachers, similar to the Scribes, that they are sent to the Baptist. The mention of Levites as part of the deputation is the mark of an eyewitness. Excepting in the parable of the Good Samaritan (Luke x. 32), Levites are not mentioned by the Synoptists, nor elsewhere in N.T., excepting Acts iv. 36. Had the Evangelist been constructing a story out of borrowed materials, we should probably have had Scribes or Elders instead of Levites. These indications of eyewitness are among the strong proofs of the authenticity of this Gospel.

Who art thou?] with a strong emphasis on the 'thou.'

20. *confessed, and denied not*] Antithetic parallelism, as in *v.* 3.

but confessed] Rather, **and he** *confessed*, to introduce *what* he confessed.

I am not the Christ] 'I' is emphatic, implying that some one else not far distant is the Christ. Throughout the section (20—34) John contrasts himself with the Christ by an emphasis on 'I.'

the Christ] It is to be regretted that our translators have so often omitted the definite article before 'Christ,' although it is inserted in the Greek. In the Gospel *narratives* the article should always be preserved in English as here. Comp. Matt. xvi. 16, xxvi. 63; Mark viii. 29; and contrast Matt. xxiv. 5; Luke xxiii. 35, 39, &c. To us 'Christ' is a

thou Elias? And he saith, I am not. Art thou *that* prophet? And he answered, No. Then said they unto 22 him, Who art thou? that we may give an answer to them that sent us. What sayest thou of thyself? He said, I am 23 the voice of one crying in the wilderness, Make straight the way of the Lord, as said the prophet Esaias. And they which were sent were of the Pharisees. 24

proper name, but to the Evangelists it is a title, '*the* Christ,' the Messiah so long expected. See Lightfoot, *On Revision*, p. 100.

21. *What then?*] ' *What then* are we to think?' or, ' *What then* art thou?'

Art thou Elias?] The Scribes taught that Elijah would come again before the coming of the Messiah (Matt. xvii. 10), and this belief is repeatedly alluded to in the Talmud. Comp. Mal. iv. 5.

I am not] A forger would scarcely have ventured on this in the face of Matt. xi. 14, where Christ says that John *is* Elijah. But Christ is there speaking figuratively (comp. Luke i. 17); John is here speaking literally. He says he is not Elijah returned to the earth again.

that prophet] Rather, **the** *Prophet*, the well-known Prophet of Deut. xviii. 15, who some thought would be a second Moses, others a second Elijah, others the Messiah. From vii. 40, 41 we see that some distinguished 'the Prophet' from the Messiah; and from Matt. xvi. 14 it appears that Jeremiah or other prophets were expected to return. Comp. 2 Esdras ii. 18; 1 Macc. xiv. 41. This verse alone is almost enough to prove that the writer is a Jew. Who but a Jew would know of these expectations? Or if a Gentile chanced to know them, would he not explain them to his readers? In *v.* 25, vi. 14, 48, 69 our translators have repeated the error of translating the definite article by 'that' instead of 'the.'

No] The Baptist knows that 'the Prophet' is the Messiah. His replies grow more and more abrupt; 'I am not the Christ,' 'I am not,' 'No.'

22. *Who art thou?*] They continue asking as to his person; he replies as to his office. In the presence of the Messiah the personality of His Forerunner is lost.

23. *I am the voice*, &c.] Or, *I am* a *voice*. The Synoptists use these words of the Baptist as fulfilling prophecy. From this verse it would seem as if they were first so used by himself. The quotation is almost exact from the LXX. John was a Voice making known the Word, meaningless without the Word. There is an almost certain reference to this passage (19—23) in Justin Martyr, *Trypho*, LXXXVIII., which is evidence that this Gospel was known before A.D. 150.

24. *And they which*, &c.] Perhaps the better reading is, *and* **there had been sent some of the Pharisees.** S. John mentions neither Sadducees nor Herodians; only the Pharisees, the sect most opposed to Christ, is remembered by the Evangelist who had gone furthest from Judaism.

25 And they asked him, and said unto him, Why baptizest thou then, if thou be not *that* Christ, nor Elias, neither 26 *that* prophet? John answered them, saying, I baptize with water: but there standeth one among you, whom ye know 27 not; he it is, who coming after me is preferred before me, 28 whose shoe's latchet I am not worthy to unloose. These *things* were done in Bethabara beyond Jordan, where John was baptizing.

29—34. *The Testimony of the Baptist to the people.*

29   The next day John seeth Jesus coming unto him, and

25. *Why baptizest thou then?*] 'What right have you to treat Jews as if they were proselytes and make them submit to a rite which implies that they are impure?' Had they forgotten Zech. xiii. 1; Ezek. xxxvi. 25?
be not that Christ, &c.] Better, **art** *not* **the** *Christ, nor* **yet Elijah,** *nor* **yet the** *Prophet.* See on *v.* 21.
26. 'You ask for my credentials; and all the while He Who is far more than credentials to me is among you. I am not a prophet to foretell His coming, but a herald to proclaim that He has come.'
27. *He it is*] These words and 'is preferred before me' are wanting in authority: the sentence should run, **He that cometh after me, whose shoe's latchet,** &c., **is standing in the midst of you, and ye know Him not.** 'Ye' is emphatic; 'Whom *ye* who question me know not, but Whom I, the questioned, know.'
28. *Bethabara*] The true reading is **Bethany**, which was changed to *Bethabara* owing to the powerful influence of Origen, who could find no Bethany beyond Jordan known in his day. But in 200 years the very name of an obscure place might easily perish. Origen found 'Bethany' in almost all the MSS. The site of Bethabara or Bethany is lost now, but it must have been near Galilee: comp. *v.* 29 with *v.* 43, and see on the 'four days,' xi. 17. It is possible to reconcile the two readings. Bethabara has been identified with 'Abârah, one of the main Jordan fords about 14 miles south of the sea of Galilee: and 'Bethania beyond Jordan' has been identified with Bashan; Bethania or Batanea being the Aramaic form of the Hebrew Bashan, meaning ' soft level ground.' Thus Bethabara is the village or ford; Bethania, the district on the east side of the ford. See Conder, *Handbook of the Bible,* pp. 315, 320. But see Appendix D.

29—34. THE TESTIMONY OF THE BAPTIST TO THE PEOPLE.

29. *The next day*] These words prevent us from inserting the Temptation between *vv.* 28 and 29. The fact of the Baptist knowing who Jesus is shews that the Baptism, and therefore the Temptation, must have preceded the deputation from Jerusalem. The Evangelist

saith, Behold the Lamb of God, which taketh away the sin of the world. This is he of whom I said, After me 30 cometh a man which is preferred before me: for he was before me. And I knew him not: but that he should be 31 made manifest to Israel, therefore am I come baptizing with water. And John bare record, saying, I saw the 32 Spirit descending from heaven like a dove, and it abode

assumes that his readers are well acquainted with the history of the Baptism and Temptation.

the Lamb of God] Evidently some Lamb well known to John's hearers is meant, viz. the Lamb of Is. liii. (comp. Acts viii. 32); but there may be an indirect allusion to the Paschal Lamb. With 'Behold' comp. xix. 5, 14: with 'of God' comp. Gen. xxii. 8.

which taketh away, &c.] These words seem to make the reference to Is. liii., esp. *vv.* 4, 5, 10, clear. The marginal reading, *beareth*, is not right here (1 John iii. 5).

the sin] Regarding it as one great burden or plague.

of the world] Isaiah (liii. 8) seems to see no further than the redemption of the Jews: 'for the transgression *of my people* was he stricken.' The Baptist knows that the Messiah comes to save the whole human race, even those hostile to Him.

30. *of whom*] The best text gives, **in behalf** *of whom*.

31. *And I knew him not*] Or, *I also knew Him not;* I, like you, did not at first know Him to be the Messiah. There is no contradiction between this and Matt. iii. 14. (1) 'I knew Him not' need not mean 'I had no knowledge of Him whatever.' (2) John's professing that he needed to be baptized by Jesus does not prove that he had already recognised Jesus as the Messiah, but only as superior to himself.

that he should be made manifest] This was the Baptist's second duty. He had (1) to prepare for the Messiah by preaching repentance; (2) to point out the Messiah. The word for 'manifest' is one of S. John's favourite words (*phaneroun*); ii. 11, iii. 21, vii. 4, ix. 3, xvii. 6, xxi. 1, 14; 1 John i. 2, ii. 19, 28, iii. 2, 5, 8, 9; Rev. iii. 18, xv. 4.

therefore am I come] Better, **for this cause** (xii. 18, 27) **came I** (comp. v. 16, 18, vii. 22, viii. 47).

baptizing with water] In humble contrast to Him Who baptizeth with the Holy Ghost' (*v.* 33). '*With* water' is literally '**in** *water*' here and *v.* 26.

32. *bare record*] Better, *bare* **witness**; comp. *vv.* 7, 8, 15, 19, 34.

I saw] Better, *I* **have beheld**, or *contemplated* (1 John iv. 12, 14), the perfect of the verb used in *vv.* 14 and 38.

like a dove] This was perhaps visible to Christ and the Baptist alone. A real appearance is the natural meaning here and is insisted on by S. Luke (iii. 22). And if we admit the 'bodily shape' at all, there can be no sound reason for rejecting the dove. The marvel is that the Holy Spirit should be visible in any way (comp. 'the tongues of fire,' Acts ii. 3), not that He should assume the form of a dove in particular. Of

33 upon him. And I knew him not: but he that sent me to baptize with water, the same said unto me, Upon whom thou shalt see the Spirit descending, and remaining on him, 34 the same is he which baptizeth with the Holy Ghost. And I saw, and bare record that this is the Son of God.

course this visible descent of the Spirit made no change in the nature of Christ. It served two purposes, (1) to make the Messiah known to the Baptist, and through him to the world; (2) to mark the official commencement of the ministry of the Messiah, like the anointing of a king. The whole incident is very parallel to the Transfiguration. In both Christ is miraculously glorified previous to setting out to suffer; in both a voice from heaven bears witness to Him; at both 'the goodly fellowship of the Prophets' is nobly represented.

33. *And I knew him not*] Or, as before, *I also knew Him not*. The Baptist again protests, that but for a special revelation he was as ignorant as others that Jesus was the Messiah.

he that sent me] The special mission of a Prophet. Comp. v. 6.

the same said unto me] Better, **he** *said unto me*: see on x. 1. *When* this revelation was made we are not told.

and remaining on him] Better, *and* **abiding** *on Him*. It is the same word as is used in v. 32, and one of which S. John is very fond; but our translators have obscured this fact by capriciously varying the translation, sometimes in the same verse (v. 39, iv. 40; 1 John ii. 24, iii. 24). Thus, though most often rendered 'abide,' it is also rendered 'remain' (ix. 41, xv. 11, 16), 'dwell' (i. 39, vi. 56, xiv. 10, 17), 'continue' (ii. 12, viii. 31), 'tarry' (iv. 40, xxi. 22, 23), 'endure' (vi. 27), 'be present' (xiv. 25). In 1 John ii. 24 it is translated in *three* different ways. See on xv. 9.

which baptizeth with the Holy Ghost] See on xiv. 26. This phrase, introduced without explanation or comment, assumes that the readers of this Gospel are well aware of this office of the Messiah, i. e. are well-instructed Christians. The word *baptizeth* is appropriate, (1) to mark the analogy and contrast between the office of the Baptist and that of the Messiah; (2) because the gift of the Spirit is constantly represented as an *out-pouring*. 'With,' as in vv. 26 and 31, is literally '**in**.'

34. *And I saw, and bare record*] Better, *And I* **have seen** *and* **have borne witness**. 'I have seen' is in joyous contrast to 'I knew Him not,' vv. 31, 33. 'Have borne witness' is the same verb as in vv. 7, 8 and 32: hence 'witness' is preferable to 'record' both here and in v. 32.

the Son of God] The Messiah. This declaration of the Baptist agrees with and confirms the account of the voice from heaven (Matt. iii. 17).

These verses, 32—34, prove that S. John does not, as Philo does, identify the Logos with the Spirit.

35—37. *The Testimony of the Baptist to Andrew and John.*

Again the next day *after* John stood, and two of his 35 disciples; and looking upon Jesus as he walked, he saith, 36 Behold the Lamb of God. And the two disciples heard 37 him speak, and they followed Jesus.

38—51. *The Testimony of Disciples.*

Then Jesus turned, and saw them following, and saith 38

35—37. THE TESTIMONY OF THE BAPTIST TO ANDREW AND JOHN.

35. *Again*] Referring to *v.* 29: it should come second; *The next day* **again** *John* **was standing.**
The difference between this narrative and that of the Synoptists (Matt. iv. 18; Mark i. 16; Luke v. 2) is satisfactorily explained by supposing this to refer to an earlier and less formal call of these first four disciples, John and Andrew, Peter and James. Their call to be Apostles was a very gradual one. Two of them, and perhaps all four, began by being disciples of the Baptist, who directs them to the Lamb of God (*v.* 36), Who invites them to His abode (*v.* 39): they then witness His miracles (ii. 2, &c.); are next called to be 'fishers of men' (Matt. iv. 19); and are finally enrolled with the rest of the Twelve as Apostles (Mark iii. 13). See note on Mark i. 20.

Two of his disciples] One of these we are told was S. Andrew (*v.* 40); the other was no doubt S. John himself. The account is that of an eyewitness; and his habitual reserve with regard to himself fully accounts for his silence, if the other disciple *was* himself. If it was some one else, it is difficult to see why S. John pointedly omits to mention his name.

There was strong antecedent probability that the first followers of Christ would be disciples of the Baptist. The fact of their being so is one reason of the high honour in which the Baptist has been held from the earliest times by the Church.

36. *looking upon*] **having looked on** with a fixed penetrating gaze. Comp. *v.* 42; Mark x. 21, 27; Luke xx. 17, xxii. 61.

Behold the Lamb of God] This seems to shew that these disciples were present the previous day (*v.* 29): hence there was no need to say more than this. This appears to have been the last meeting between the Baptist and Christ.

37. *heard him speak*] Although the declaration had not been addressed to them in particular.

they followed Jesus] The first beginning of the Christian Church. But we are not to understand that they have already determined to become His disciples.

38—51. THE TESTIMONY OF DISCIPLES.

38. *saw them*] Same verb as in *vv.* 14 and 32. The context shews that He saw into their hearts as well. For 'Then' read **But.**

unto them, What seek ye? They said unto him, Rabbi,
(which is to say, being interpreted, Master,) where dwellest
39 thou? He saith unto them, Come and see. They came
and saw where he dwelt, and abode with him that day:
40 for it was about the tenth hour. One of the two which
heard John speak, and followed him, was Andrew, Simon
41 Peter's brother. He first findeth his own brother Simon,

What seek ye?] i.e. in Me. He does not ask '*Whom* seek ye?' It was evident that they sought Him.
Rabbi] A comparatively modern word when S. John wrote, and therefore all the more requiring explanation to Gentile readers. S. John often interprets between Hebrew and Greek; thrice in this section. (Comp. vv. 41, 42.)
where dwellest thou?] Better, *where* abidest *Thou?* (See on v. 33.) They have more to ask than can be answered on the spot. Perhaps they think Him a travelling Rabbi staying with friends close by; and they intend to visit Him at some future time. He bids them come at once: *now* is the day of salvation.
39. *Come and see*] The more probable reading gives, *Come and ye* shall *see*.
they came] Insert, therefore.
that day] That memorable day.
it was about the tenth hour] S. John remembers the very hour of this crisis in his life: all the details of the narrative are very lifelike.
It is sometimes contended that S. John reckons the hours of the day according to the modern method, from midnight to midnight, and not according to the *Jewish* method, from sunset to sunset, as everywhere else in N.T. and in Josephus. It is antecedently improbable that S. John should in this point vary from the rest of N.T. writers; and we ought to require strong evidence before accepting this theory, which has been adopted mainly in order to escape from the difficulty of xix. 14, where see notes. Setting aside xix. 14 as the cause of the question, we have four passages in which S. John mentions the hour of the day, this, iv. 6, 52 and xi. 9. None of them are decisive: but in no single case is the balance of probability strongly in favour of the modern method. See notes in each place. Here either 10 A.M. or 4 P.M. would suit the context: and while the antecedent probability that S. John reckons time like the rest of the Evangelists will incline us to 4 P.M., the fact that a good deal still remains to be done on this day makes 10 A.M. rather more suitable. Origen knows nothing of S. John's using the modern method of reckoning.
40. *Andrew, Simon Peter's brother*] Before the end of the first century, therefore, it was natural to describe Andrew by his relationship to his far better known brother. In Church History S. Peter is everything and S. Andrew nothing: but would there have been an Apostle Peter but for Andrew. In the lists of the Apostles S. Andrew is always in

and saith unto him, We have found the Messias, which is, being interpreted, the Christ. And he brought him to Jesus. 42 And when Jesus beheld him, he said, Thou art Simon the son of Jona: thou shalt be called Cephas, which is by interpretation, A stone.

the first group of four, but he is outside the chosen three, in spite of this early call.

41. *He first findeth*, &c.] The meaning of 'first' becomes almost certain when we remember S. John's characteristic reserve about himself. Both disciples hurry to tell their own brothers the good tidings, that the Messiah has been found: S. Andrew finds *his* brother *first*, and afterwards S. John finds *his;* but we are left to infer the latter point.

S. Andrew thrice brings others to Christ; Peter, the lad with the loaves (vi. 8), and certain Greeks (xii. 22); and excepting Mark xiii. 3 we know scarcely anything else about him. Thus it would seem as if in these three incidents S. John had given us the key to his character. And here we have another characteristic of this Gospel—the lifelike way in which the less prominent figures are sketched. Besides Andrew we have Philip, i. 44, vi. 5, xii. 21, xiv. 8; Thomas, xi. 16, xiv. 5; xx. 24—29; Nathanael, i. 45—52; Nicodemus, iii. 1—12, vii. 50—52, xix. 39; Martha and Mary, xi., xii. 1—3.

We have found] This does not prove that S. John is still with him, only that they were together when their common desire and expectation were fulfilled.

Messias] The Hebrew form of this name is used by S. John only, here and iv. 25. Elsewhere the LXX. translation, 'the Christ,' is used. Here 'the' before 'Christ' should be omitted.

42. *beheld*] Same word as in *v.* 36, implying a fixed earnest look; what follows shews that Christ's gaze penetrated to his heart and read his character.

Simon the son of Jona] The true reading here and xxi. 15, 16, 17 is *Simon the son of* **John**. There is a tradition that his mother's name was Johanna. The Greek form *Iônâ* may represent two distinct Hebrew names, Jonah and Johanan = John. There is no need to make Christ's knowledge of his name and parentage miraculous; Andrew in bringing Simon would naturally mention them.

A stone] The margin and text should change places, *Peter*, being in the text and 'a stone' in the margin, like 'the Anointed' in *v.* 41. This new name is given with reference to the new relation into which the person named enters; comp. the cases of Abraham, Sarah, Israel. It points to the future office of Simon rather than to his present character. The form Cephas occurs nowhere else in the Gospels or Acts: but comp. 1 Cor. i. 12, iii. 22, ix. 5; xv. 5, Gal. i. 18, ii. 9, 11, 14.

There is no discrepancy between this and Matt. xvi. 18. Here Christ gives the name Peter; there he reminds S. Peter of it. It is quite clear from this that S. Peter was not first called among the Apostles, a point on which the Synoptists leave us in doubt.

43 The day following Jesus would go forth into Galilee, and
44 findeth Philip, and saith unto him, Follow me. Now Philip
45 was of Bethsaida, the city of Andrew and Peter. Philip
findeth Nathanael, and saith unto him, We have found him,
of whom Moses in the law, and the prophets, did write,
46 Jesus of Nazareth, the son of Joseph. And Nathanael

43. *The day following*] Better, as in vv. 29, 35, *The* **next** *day:* the Greek is the same in all three verses. We thus have four days accurately marked, (1) v. 19; (2) v. 29; (3) v. 35; (4) v. 44. A writer of fiction would not have cared for such minute details; they might entangle him in discrepancies. They are thoroughly natural as coming from an eyewitness. See on ii. 1.

Follow me] In the Gospels these words seem always to be the call to become a disciple. Matt. viii. 22, ix. 9, xix. 21; Mark ii. 14, x. 21; Luke v. 27, ix. 59; John xxi. 19. With two exceptions they are always addressed to those who afterwards became Apostles.

44. *Philip was of Bethsaida*] In the Synoptists Philip is a mere name in the lists of the Apostles: our knowledge of him comes from S. John. See above on v. 42 and on xiv. 8. The local knowledge displayed in this verse is very real. S. John would possess it; a writer in the second century would not, and would not care to invent. This is Bethsaida of Galilee on the western shore, not Bethsaida Julias. See note on Matt. iv. 13.

45. *Nathanael*]='Gift of God.' The name occurs Num. i. 8; 1 Chron. ii. 14; 1 Esdras i. 9, ix. 22. Nathanael is commonly identified with Bartholomew; (1) Bartholomew is only a patronymic and the bearer would be likely to have another name (comp. Barjona of Simon, Barnabas of Joses); (2) S. John never mentions Bartholomew, the Synoptists never mention Nathanael; (3) the Synoptists in their lists place Bartholomew next to Philip, as James next his probable caller John, and Peter (in Matt. and Luke) next his caller Andrew; (4) all the other disciples mentioned in this chapter become Apostles, and none are so highly commended as Nathanael; (5) All Nathanael's companions named in xxi. 2 were Apostles (see note there). But all these reasons do not make the identification more than probable. The framers of our Liturgy do not countenance the identification: this passage appears neither as the Gospel nor as a Lesson for S. Bartholomew's Day.

We have found him, of whom, &c.] "A most correct representation of the current phraseology, both in regard to the divisions of the O.T., and the application of the Messianic idea." S. p. 35.

Moses] viz. in Deut. xviii. 15 and in all the Messianic types, promises to Adam, Abraham, &c.

Jesus of Nazareth, the son of Joseph] The words are Philip's, and express the common belief about Jesus. It was natural to say He was 'of' or 'from Nazareth,' as His home had been there; still more natural to call him 'the son of Joseph.' The conclusion that the Evangelist is ignorant of the birth at Bethlehem, or of the miraculous nature of that

said unto him, Can there any good *thing* come out of Nazareth? Philip saith unto him, Come and see. Jesus 47 saw Nathanael coming to him, and saith of him, Behold an Israelite indeed, in whom is no guile. Nathanael saith 48 unto him, Whence knowest thou me? Jesus answered and said unto him, Before that Philip called thee, when thou wast under the fig tree, I saw thee. Nathanael answered 49

birth, cannot be drawn from this passage. Rather, we may conclude that he is a scrupulously honest historian, who records exactly what was said, without making additions of his own.

46. *Can there any good thing*, &c.] All Galileans were despised for their want of culture, their rude dialect, and contact with Gentiles. They were to the Jews what Bœotians were to the Athenians. But here it is a Galilean who reproaches Nazareth in particular. Apart from the Gospels we know nothing to the discredit of Nazareth; neither in O.T. nor in Josephus is it mentioned; but what we are told of the people by the Evangelists is mostly bad. Christ left them and preferred to dwell at Capernaum (Matt. iv. 13); He could do very little among them, 'because of their unbelief' (xiii. 58), which was such as to make Him marvel (Mark vi. 6); and once they tried to kill Him (Luke iv. 29). S. Augustine would omit the question. Nathanael 'who knew the Scriptures excellently well. when he heard the name Nazareth, was filled with hope, and said, From Nazareth something good can come.' But this is not probable. Possibly he meant no more than 'Can any good thing come out of despised Galilee?' Nazareth being in Galilee.

Come and see] The best cure for ill-founded prejudice. Philip shews the depth of his own conviction in suggesting this test, which seems to have been in harmony with the practical bent of his own mind. See on xii. 21 and xiv. 8.

47. *saw Nathanael coming*] This contradicts the theory that Christ overheard Nathanael's question. S. John represents Christ's knowledge of Nathanael as miraculous; as in *v.* 42 He appears as the searcher of hearts.

an Israelite indeed] In character as well as by birth: what follows shews what is meant. The 'guile' may refer to the 'subtilty' of Jacob (Gen. xxvii. 35) before he became Israel: 'Behold a son of Israel, who is in no way a son of Jacob.' The 'supplanter' is gone; the 'prince' remains. His guilelessness appears in his making no mock repudiation of the character attributed to him (*v.* 48). He is free from 'the pride that apes humility.'

48. *under the fig tree*] This probably means 'at home,' in the retirement of his own garden (1 Kings iv. 25; Mic. iv. 4; Zec. iii. 10); the Greek implies *motion to* under. Nathanael had perhaps been praying or meditating there; he seems to see that Christ knew what his thoughts had been there. It was under a fig tree that S. Augustine heard the famous '*Tolle, lege.*'

and saith unto him, Rabbi, thou art the Son of God; thou
50 art the King of Israel. Jesus answered and said unto him,
Because I said unto thee, I saw thee under the fig tree,
believest thou? thou shalt see greater *things* than these.
51 And he saith unto him, Verily, verily, I say unto you,
Hereafter ye shall see heaven open, and the angels of God
ascending and descending upon the Son of man.

49. *thou art the Son of God*] We know from other passages that this was one of the recognised titles of the Messiah; xi. 27; Matt. xxvi. 63; Mark iii. 11, v. 7; Luke iv. 41. 'Son of David' was more common.

the King of Israel] Omit 'the.' This phrase "is especially important, because it breathes those politico-theocratic hopes, which since the taking of Jerusalem, Christians at least, if not Jews, must have entirely laid aside." S. How could a Christian of the second century have thrown himself back to this?

50. *believest thou?*] Or possibly, *thou believest*. Comp. xvi. 31, xx. 29. The interrogative form is here best: He who marvelled at the unbelief of the people of Nazareth here expresses joyous surprise at the ready belief of the guileless Israelite of Cana.

51. *Verily, verily*] The double 'verily' occurs 25 times in this Gospel, and nowhere else, always in the mouth of Christ. It introduces a truth of special solemnity and importance. The single 'verily' occurs about 30 times in Matt., 14 in Mark, and 7 in Luke. The word represents the Hebrew 'Amen,' which in the LXX. never means 'verily.' In the Gospels it has no other meaning. The 'Amen' at the end of sentences (Matt. vi. 13, xxviii. 20; Mark xvi. 20; Luke xxiv. 53; John xxi. 25) is in every case of doubtful authority.

unto you] Plural; all present are addressed, Andrew, John, Peter (James), and Philip, as well as Nathanael.

Hereafter] Better, **from henceforth**; from this point onwards Christ's Messianic work of linking earth to heaven, and re-establishing free intercourse between man and God, goes on. But the word is wanting in the best MSS.

heaven open] Better, **the** *heaven* **opened**; made open and remaining so.

the angels of God] Like v. 47, an apparent reference to the life of Jacob, perhaps suggested by the scene, which may have been near to Bethel. This does not refer to the angels which appeared after the Temptation, at the Agony, and at the Ascension: rather to the perpetual intercourse between God and the Messiah during His ministry.

the Son of man] This phrase in all four Gospels is invariably used by Christ Himself of Himself as the Messiah, upwards of 80 times in all. None of the Evangelists direct our attention to this strict limitation in the use of the expression: their agreement on this striking point is evidently undesigned, and therefore a strong mark of their veracity. See notes on Matt. viii. 20; Mark ii. 10. In O. T. the phrase 'Son of

vv. 1—4.] S. JOHN, II. 83

CHAP. II. 1—11. *The Testimony of the First Sign.*

And the third day there was a marriage in Cana of Gali- 2
lee; and the mother of Jesus was there: and both Jesus 2
was called, and his disciples, to the marriage. And when 3
they wanted wine, the mother of Jesus saith unto him, They
have no wine. Jesus saith unto her, Woman, what have I 4

Man' has three distinct uses; (1) in the Psalms, for the ideal man; viii.
4—8, lxxx. 17, cxliv. 3, cxlvi. 3: (2) in Ezekiel, as the name by which the
Prophet is addressed by God; ii. 1, 3, 6, 8, iii. 1, 3, 4, &c., &c., more
than 80 times in all; probably to remind Ezekiel, that in spite of the
favour shewn to him, and the wrath denounced against the children of
Israel, he, no less than they, had a mortal's frailty: (3) in the 'night
visions' of Dan. vii. 13, 14, where 'One like a son of man came with
the clouds of heaven, and came to the Ancient of Days...and there was
given Him dominion, and glory, and a kingdom, that all people,
nations, and languages should serve Him, &c.' That 'Son of man
henceforth became one of the titles of the looked-for Messiah' may be
doubted. Rather, the title was a *new* one assumed by Christ, and as
yet only dimly understood (comp. Matt. xvi. 13).

This first chapter alone is enough to shew that the Gospel is the work
of a Jew of Palestine, well acquainted with the Messianic hopes, and
traditions, and phraseology current in Palestine at the time of Christ's
ministry, and able to give a lifelike picture of the Baptist and of Christ's
first disciples.

CHAP. II. **1—11.** THE TESTIMONY OF THE FIRST SIGN.

1. *the third day*] From the calling of Philip (i. 43), the last date
given, making a week in all; the first week, perhaps in contrast to the
last week (xii. 1).

Cana of Galilee] To distinguish it from Cana of Asher (Josh. xix.
28). This Cana is not mentioned in O. T.; it was the home of
Nathanael (xxi. 2), and is now generally identified with Kânet el-Jelîl,
about six miles N. of Nazareth.

was there] Staying as a friend or relation of the family; she speaks
to the servants as if she were quite at home in the house (v. 5). Joseph
has disappeared: the inference (not quite certain) is that in the interval
between Luke ii. 51 and this marriage—about 17 years—he had died.

2. *and his disciples*] Now five or six in number, Andrew, John,
Peter, Philip, Nathanael, and probably James. For 'both Jesus' read
'Jesus **also.**'

3. *when they wanted wine*] Better, *when* **the wine failed.** Perhaps
the arrival of these six or seven guests caused the want; certainly it
would make it more apparent. To Eastern hospitality such a mishap
on such an occasion would seem a most disgraceful calamity.

They have no wine] Much comment has here obscured a simple text.
The family in which she was a guest was in a serious difficulty. Per-

5 to do with thee? mine hour is not yet come. His mother saith unto the servants, Whatsoever he saith unto you, do *it*.
6 And there were set there six waterpots of stone, after the manner of the purifying of the Jews, containing two or three

haps she felt herself partly responsible for the arrangements: certainly she would wish to help. What more natural than that she should turn to her Son and tell Him the difficulty? Probably she did not expect a miracle, still less wish Him to break up the party, or begin a discourse to distract attention from the want. The meaning simply is—'They have no wine; what is to be done?'

4. *Woman, what have I to do with thee?*] S. John alone of all the Evangelists never gives the Virgin's name. Here, as so often, he assumes that his readers know the main points in the Gospel narrative: or it may be part of the reserve which he exhibits with regard to all that nearly concerns himself. Christ's Mother had become his mother (xix. 26, 27). He nowhere mentions his brother James.

Treatises have been written to shew that these words do not contain a rebuke; for if Christ here rebukes His Mother, it cannot be maintained that she is immaculate. 'Woman' of course implies no rebuke; the Greek might more fairly be rendered 'Lady' (comp. xix. 26). At the same time it marks a difference between the Divine Son and the earthly parent: He does not say, 'Mother.' But 'what have I to do with thee?' *does* imply rebuke, as is evident from the other passages where the phrase occurs, Judg. xi. 12; 1 Kings xvii. 18; 2 Kings iii. 13; Matt. viii. 29; Mark i. 24; Luke viii. 28. Only in one passage does the meaning seem to vary: in 2 Chron. xxxv. 21 the question seems to mean 'why need we quarrel?' rather than 'what have we in common?' But such a meaning, if possible there, would be quite inappropriate here. The further question has been asked,—what was she rebuked *for?* Chrysostom thinks for vanity; she wished to glorify herself through her Son. More probably for interference: He will help, but in His own way, and in His own time. Comp. Luke ii. 51.

mine hour] The meaning of 'My hour' and 'His hour' in this Gospel depends in each case on the context. There cannot here be any reference to His death; rather it means His hour for 'manifesting forth His glory' (*v.* 11) as the Messiah by working miracles. The exact moment was still in the future. Comp. vii. 8, where He for the moment refuses what He soon after does; and xii. 23, xvii. 1, which confirm the meaning here given to 'hour.'

5. Between the lines of His refusal her faith reads a better answer to her appeal.

6. *six waterpots of stone*] As an eyewitness S. John remembers their number, material, and size. The surroundings of the first miracle would not easily be forgotten. It is idle to seek for any special meaning in the number six. Vessels of stone were preferred as being less liable to impurity.

purifying] Comp. Matt. xv. 2; Mark vii. 3 (see note); Luke xi. 39.

firkins apiece. Jesus saith unto them, Fill the waterpots 7
with water. And they filled them up to the brim. And he 8
saith unto them, Draw out now, and bear unto the governor
of the feast. And they bare *it*. When the ruler of the 9
feast had tasted the water *that was* made wine, and knew
not whence it was: (but the servants which drew the water
knew;) the governor of the feast called the bridegroom, and 10
saith unto him, Every man at the beginning doth set forth
good wine; and when *men* have well drunk, then that which

two or three firkins] 'Firkin' is an almost exact equivalent of the Greek *metrētes*, which was about nine gallons. The six pitchers, therefore, holding from 18 to 27 gallons each, would together hold 106 to 162 gallons.

7. *Fill the waterpots*] It is difficult to see the meaning of this command, if (as some contend) only the water which was drawn out was turned into wine. The pitchers had been partially emptied by the ceremonial ablutions of the company, i.e. pouring water over their hands. Note that in His miracles Christ does not *create*; He increases the quantity, or changes the quality of things already existing.

to the brim] His Mother's words (*v.* 5) have done their work. Our attention seems here to be called to the great quantity of water changed into wine.

9. *ruler of the feast*] Perhaps *manager of the feast* would be better. It is doubtful whether the head-waiter, who managed the feast and tasted the meat and drink, is meant, or the *rex convivii, arbiter bibendi*, the guest elected by the other guests to preside. The bad taste of his remark inclines one to the former alternative: Ecclus. xxxii. 1, 2 is in favour of the second. In any case the translation should be uniform in these two verses, not sometimes 'governor,' sometimes 'ruler.' It is the same Greek word in all three cases, a word occurring nowhere else in N.T. The words also for 'water-pot' or 'pitcher' and for 'draw out' are peculiar to this Gospel; but they occur again iv. 7, 15, 28.

the water that was made wine] Or, *the water now become wine*. The Greek seems to imply that all the water had become wine; there is nothing to mark a distinction between what was now wine and what still remained water. It is idle to ask at what precise moment the water became wine: nor is much gained by representing the miracle as a series of natural processes (rain passing through the vine into the grapes, being pressed out and fermented, &c.) compressed into an instant. Such compression is neither more nor less intelligible than simple transition from water to wine. Moreover there was no vine.

which drew] Better, **who had drawn**.
called] Rather, **calleth**.

10. *when men have well drunk*] Our translators have timidly shrunk from giving the full coarseness of the man's joke: it should be

is worse: *but* thou hast kept the good wine until now.
11 *This beginning of miracles did Jesus in Cana of Galilee, and manifested forth his glory; and his disciples believed on him.*

when they have become drunken, when they are *drunk.* In Matt. xxiv. 49; Acts ii. 15; 1 Cor. xi. 21; 1 Thess. v. 7; Rev. xvii. 2, 6, we have the same word rightly translated. Tyndall and Cranmer were more courageous here; they have 'be dronke;' and the Vulgate has *inebriati fuerint.* The error comes from the Geneva Bible. Of course he does not mean that the guests around him are intoxicated: it is a jocular statement of his own experience at feasts. Omit 'then.'

thou hast kept the good wine until now] This was true in a sense of which he never dreamed. The True Bridegroom was there, and had indeed kept the best dispensation until the last.

11. *This beginning,* &c.] Better, **this, as a beginning of His signs,** *did Jesus in Cana;* i.e. it is the first miracle of all, not merely the first at Cana. Thus S. John agrees with the Synoptists in representing the Messianic career as beginning in Galilee. This verse is conclusive against the miracles of Christ's childhood recorded in the Aprocryphal Gospels. See on iv. 48. Our translators often in this Gospel, though very rarely in the other three, turn 'signs' into 'miracles.'

manifested] The same Greek word occurs in connexion with His *last* miracle, xxi. 1, 14, and the same English word should be used in all the passages. Comp. vii. 4 and see on i. 31.

his glory] This is the final cause of Christ's 'signs,' His own and His Father's glory (xi. 4), and these two are one.

and his disciples believed on him] What a strange remark for a writer in the second century to make! His disciples believed on Him? Of course they did. Assume that a disciple himself is the writer, and all is explained: he well remembers how his own imperfect faith was confirmed by the miracle. A forger would rather have given us the effect on the guests. Three times in this chapter does S. John give us the disciples' point of view, here, *v.* 17 and *v.* 22; very natural in a disciple, not natural in a later writer. See on xi. 15 and xxi. 12.

Two objections have been made to this miracle (1) on rationalistic, (2) on 'Temperance' grounds. (1) It is said that it is a wasteful miracle, a parade of power, unworthy of a Divine Agent: a tenth of the quantity of wine would have been ample. But the surplus was not wasted any more than the twelve baskets of fragments (vi. 13); it would be a valuable present to a bridal pair. (2) It is urged that Christ would not have supplied the means for gross excess; and to avoid this supposed difficulty it is suggested that the wine made was not intoxicating, i.e. was not wine at all. But in all His dealings with men God allows the possibility of a temptation to excess. All His gifts may be thus abused. The 5000 might have been gluttonous over the loaves and fishes.

After this he went down to Capernaum, he, and his 12 mother, and his brethren, and his disciples: and they continued there not many days.

Christ's honouring a marriage-feast with His first miracle gives His sanction (1) to marriage, (2) to times of festivity.

Four hundred years had elapsed since the Jews had seen a miracle. The era of Daniel was the last age of Jewish miracles. Since the three children walked in the burning fiery furnace, and Daniel had remained unhurt in the lions' den, and had read the hand-writing on the wall, no miracle is recorded in the history of the Jews until Jesus made this beginning of His 'signs' at Cana of Galilee. No wonder therefore, that the almost simultaneous appearance of a Prophet like John and a worker of miracles like Jesus attracted the attention of all classes.

12. "Now follows a section of which we can only say with M. Renan, that it constitutes a decisive triumph for our Gospel. ...If it is at all an artificial composition, with a dogmatic object, why should the author carry his readers thus to Capernaum—for nothing?" S. p. 52. If S. John wrote it, all is simple and natural. He records this visit to Capernaum because it actually took place, and because he well remembers those ' not many days.'

went down] Capernaum (the modern Tell-Hûm) being on the shore of the lake. It was situated in one of the most busy and populous districts of Palestine, and was therefore a good centre.

his mother, and his brethren] Natural ties still hold Him; in the next verse they disappear. On the vexed question of the 'brethren of the Lord' see the *Introduction* to the *Epistle of S. James*. It is impossible to determine with certainty whether they are (1) the children of Joseph and Mary, born after the birth of Jesus; (2) the children of Joseph by a former marriage, whether levirate or not; or (3) adopted children. There is nothing in Scripture to warn us against (1), the most natural view antecedently; but it has against it the general consensus of the Fathers, and the prevailing tradition of the perpetual virginity of S. Mary. Jerome's theory, that they were our Lord's cousins, sons of Alphaeus, is the one most commonly adopted, but vii. 5 (see note there) is fatal to it, and it labours under other difficulties as well. (2) is on the whole the most probable.

continued there] Better, **abode** *there*. See on i. 33.

not many days] Because the Passover was at hand, and He must be about His Father's business.

II. 13—XI. 57. THE WORK.

We here enter on the second portion of the first main division of the Gospel, thus subdivided:—THE WORK (1) among *Jews*, (2) among *Samaritans*, (3) among *Galileans*, (4) among *mixed multitudes*.

II. 13—XI. 57. The Work.

II. 13—III. 36. The Work among Jews.

13 And the Jews' passover was at hand, and Jesus went up to Jerusalem,

14—22. The First Cleansing of the Temple.

14 And found in the temple those that sold oxen and sheep 15 and doves, and the changers of money sitting: and when he had made a scourge of small cords, he drove *them* all out of the temple, and the sheep and the oxen; and poured out 16 the changers' money, and overthrew the tables; and said

II. 13—III. 36. THE WORK AMONG JEWS.

13. *And the Jews' passover*] Or, *the passover* **of the Jews.** An indication that this Gospel was written outside Palestine: one writing in the country would hardly have added 'of the Jews.' It is perhaps also an indication that this Gospel was written after a Passover *of the Christians* had come into recognition. Passovers were active times in Christ's ministry; and this is the first of them. It was possibly the nearness of the Passover which caused this traffic in the Temple Court. It existed for the convenience of strangers. Certainly the nearness of the Feast would add significance to Christ's action. While the Jews were purifying themselves for the Passover He purified the Temple. S. John groups his narrative round the Jewish festivals: we have (1) Passover; (2) Purim (?), v. 1; (3) Passover, vi. 4; (4) Tabernacles, vii. 2; (5) Dedication, x. 22; (6) Passover, xi. 55.

14—22. THE FIRST CLEANSING OF THE TEMPLE.

14. *in the temple*] i.e. within the sacred enclosure, in the Court of the Gentiles. The traffic would be very great at the approach of the Passover. The account is very graphic, as of an eyewitness. Note especially 'the changers of money *sitting:*' the sellers of cattle, &c., would stand.

changers of money] Not the same Greek word as in *v.* 15. There the word points to the commission paid on exchanges; here the word indicates a change from large to small coins.

15. *when he had made a scourge*] Peculiar to this account; not in the similar narrative of the Synoptists.

and the sheep, &c.] Rather, **both** *the sheep and the oxen*. 'All' does not refer to the sellers and exchangers, but anticipates the sheep and the oxen. The men probably fled at once. The order is natural; first the driving out of the cattle, then the pouring out of the money and overturning the tables. The word for 'money' literally means 'something cut up small,' hence 'change.' The common exchange would be foreign money for Jewish, payments to the Temple being necessarily made in Jewish coin.

unto them that sold doves, Take these *things* hence; make not my Father's house a house of merchandise. And his 17 disciples remembered that it was written, The zeal of thine house hath eaten me up.

Then answered the Jews and said unto him, What sign 18 shewest thou unto us, seeing that thou doest these *things?*

16. *said unto them that sold doves*] The doves could not be driven out. He calls to the owners to take the cages away. Comp. Luke ii. 24.

my Father's house] A distinct claim to Messiahship: it reminds us of 'about My Father's business' (which may also mean 'in My Father's house') spoken in the same place some 17 years before, Luke ii. 49. Possibly some who heard the Child's claim heard the Man's claim also.

an house of merchandise] Two years later things seem to have grown worse instead of better; the Temple has then become 'a den of robbers' or 'a bandits' cave.' See notes on Matt. xxi. 13 and Mark xi. 17.

17. *remembered*] Then and there. Who could know this but a disciple? Who would think of inventing it? See above on *v.* 11.

was written] Better, **is** *written;* in the Greek it is the perf. part. pass. with the auxiliary, which S. John almost always uses in quotations, while the Synoptists commonly use the perf. pass. Comp. vi. 31, 45, x. 34, xii. 14 (xix. 19).

hath eaten me up] Rather, **will devour**, or **consume me**, i.e. wear me out. Ps. lxix. 9, a psalm referred to again xv. 25 and xix. 28.

It is difficult to believe that this cleansing of the Temple is identical with the one placed by the Synoptists at the *last* Passover in Christ's ministry; difficult also to see what is gained by the identification. If they are the same event, either S. John or the Synoptists have made a gross blunder in chronology. Could S. John, who was with our Lord at both Passovers, make such a mistake? Could S. Matthew, who was with Him at the last Passover, transfer to it an event which took place at the first Passover, a year before his conversion? When we consider the immense differences which distinguish the last Passover from the first in Christ's ministry, it seems incredible that anyone who had contemporary evidence could through any lapse of memory transfer a very remarkable incident indeed from one to the other. On the other hand the difficulty of believing that the Temple was twice cleansed is very slight. Was Christ's preaching so universally successful that one cleansing would be certain to suffice? And if two years later He found that the evil had returned, would He not be certain to drive it out once more? Differences in the details of the narratives corroborate this view.

18. *the Jews*] See on i. 19.

What sign shewest thou] We have a similar question Matt. xxi. 23, but the widely different answer shews that the occasion is not the same. Such demands would be made often.

19 Jesus answered and said unto them, Destroy this temple, 20 and in three days I will raise it up. Then said the Jews, Forty and six years was this temple in building, and wilt 21 thou rear it up in three days? But he spake of the temple

19. *Destroy this temple*] It is S. Matthew (xxvi. 61) and S. Mark (xiv. 58, see notes) who tell us that this saying was twisted into a charge against Christ, but they do not record the saying. S. John, who does record the saying, does not mention the charge. Such coincidence can scarcely be designed, and is therefore evidence of the truth of both statements. See on xviii. 11. The word used in these three verses for 'temple' means the central sacred building (*naos*), whereas that used in *v.* 14 means the whole sacred enclosure (*hieron*). The latter is never used figuratively.

raise it up] In the charge His accusers turn this into *build*, a word not appropriate to raising a dead body. There is no contradiction between Christ's declaration and the ordinary N. T. theology, that the Son was raised by the Father. The expression is figurative throughout; and 'I and My Father are one.' Comp. x. 18. This throwing out seeds of thought for the future, which could not bear fruit at the time, is one of the characteristics of Christ's teaching.

20. *Forty and six years*, &c.] This was the third Temple. Solomon's Temple was destroyed by Nebuchadnezzar. Zerubbabel's was rebuilt by Herod the Great. The Greek implies that the building began 46 years ago, but not that it is now completed. "The building of the Temple, we are told by Josephus (*Ant.* xv. ii. 1), was begun in the 18th year of Herod the Great, 734—735 A.U.C. Reckoning 46 years from this point, we are brought to 781 or 782 A.U.C.=28 or 29 A.D. Comparing this with the data given in Luke iii. 1, the question arises, whether we are to reckon the 15th year of Tiberius from his joint reign with Augustus, which began A.D. 12; or from his sole reign after the death of Augustus, A.D. 14. This would give us A.D. 27 or 29 for the first public appearance of the Baptist, and at the earliest A.D. 28 or 30 for the Passover mentioned in this chapter." S. p. 65. So that there seems to be exact agreement between this date and that of S. Luke, if we count S. Luke's 15 years from the *joint* reign of Tiberius. It is incredible that this coincidence can have been planned; it involves an intricate calculation, and even with the aid of Josephus absolute certainty cannot be obtained. "By what conceivable process could a Greek in the second century have come to hit upon this roundabout expedient for giving a fictitious date to his invention?" S. p. 67.

rear it up] Better, **raise** *it up;* the same verb as in *v.* 19. For other instances of gross misunderstanding of Christ's words comp. iii. 4, 9, iv. 11, 15, 33, vi. 34, 52, vii. 35, viii. 22, 33, 52, xi. 12, xiv. 5.

21. *spake*] Or, **was speaking**. Setting aside inspiration, S. John's explanation must be admitted as the true one. What better interpreter of the mind of Jesus can be found than 'the disciple whom Jesus loved?' And he gives the explanation not as his only, but

of his body. When therefore he was risen from the dead, 22 his disciples remembered that he had said this unto them; and they believed the scripture, and the word which Jesus had said.

23—25. Belief without Devotion.

Now when he was in Jerusalem at the passover, in the 23 feast *day*, many believed in his name, when they saw the miracles which he did. But Jesus did not commit himself 24 unto them, because he knew all *men*, and needed not that 25 any should testify of man: for he knew what was in man.

as that of the disciples generally. Moreover it explains the 'three days,' which interpretations about destroying the old Temple religion and raising up a new spiritual theocracy do not.

22. *was risen*] Better, *was* **raised.** Comp. xxi. 14; Acts iii. 15, iv. 10, v. 30.

his disciples remembered] They recollected it when the event that explained it took place; meanwhile what had not been understood had been forgotten. Would anyone but a disciple give us these details about the disciples' thoughts? See on *v.* 11.

the scripture] O.T. prophecy, viz., Ps. xvi. 10; see on x. 35.

had said] Better, **spake**, on the present occasion.

23—25. BELIEF WITHOUT DEVOTION.

23. *in Jerusalem at*, &c.] More accurately, *in Jerusalem, at the Passover*, **during** *the Feast*. Note the exactness of detail.

when they saw the miracles] None of these have been recorded. Comp. iv. 45, xx. 30. Faith growing out of such soil would be likely to cease when the miracles ceased. 'When they saw' should perhaps be '*whilst* they saw,' as if implying 'and no longer.' For 'miracles' read **signs**, as in *v.* 11.

24. *did not commit*] The same verb as 'many *believed*' in *v.* 23. 'Many *trusted* in His name; but Jesus did not *trust* Himself unto them.' The antithesis is probably intentional.

25. *And needed not*] Better, *and* **because He had no need.**

for he knew] Better, *for He* **of Himself** *knew*. We have instances of this supernatural knowledge in the cases of Peter, i. 42; Nathanael, i. 47, 48; Nicodemus, iii. 3; the woman at the well, iv. 29; the disciples, vi. 61, 64; Lazarus, xi. 4, 15; Judas, xiii. 11; Peter, xxi. 17.

CHAP. III. 1—21. THE DISCOURSE WITH NICODEMUS.

This is the first of the eleven discourses of our Lord which form the main portion, and are among the great characteristics, of this Gospel. They have been used as a powerful argument against its authenticity; (1) because they are unlike the discourses in the Synoptic Gospels, (2) because they are suspiciously like the First Epistle

CHAP. III. 1—21. *The discourse with Nicodemus.*

3 There was a man of the Pharisees, named Nicodemus, a

of S. John, which all admit was written by the author of the Fourth Gospel, (3) because this likeness to the First Epistle pervades not only the discourses of our Lord, but those of the Baptist also, as well as the writer's own reflections throughout the Gospel. The inference is that they are, as much as the speeches in Thucydides, if not as much as those in Livy, the ideal compositions of the writer himself.

On the question as a whole we may say at once with Matthew Arnold (*Literature and Dogma*, p. 170), "the doctrine and discourses of Jesus *cannot* in the main be the writer's, because in the main they are clearly out of his reach." 'Never man spake like this man' (vii. 46); not even S. John, and still less any one else, could invent such words.

But the objections urged above are serious and ought to be answered. (1) The discourses in S. John are unlike those in the Synoptists, but we must beware of exaggerating the unlikeness. They are longer, more reflective, less popular. But they are for the most part addressed to the educated and learned, to Elders, Pharisees, and Rabbis: even the discourse on the Bread of Life, which is spoken before a mixed multitude at Capernaum, is largely addressed to the educated portion of it (vi. 41, 52), the hierarchial party opposed to Him. The discourses in the first three Gospels are mostly spoken among the rude and simple-minded peasants of Galilee. Contrast the University Sermons with the Parish Sermons of an eminent modern preacher, and we should notice similar differences. This fact will account for a good deal. But (2) the discourses both in S. John and in the Synoptists are translations from an Aramaic dialect. Two translations may differ very widely, and yet both be faithful; they may each bear the impress of the translator's own style, and yet accurately represent the original. This will to a large extent answer objections (2) and (3). And we must remember that it is possible, and perhaps probable, that the peculiar tone of S. John, so unmistakeable, yet so difficult to analyse satisfactorily, may be a reproduction, more or less conscious, of that of his Divine Master.

But on the other hand we must remember that an eventful life of half a century separates the time when S. John heard these discourses from the time when he committed them to writing. Christ had promised (xiv. 26) that the Holy Spirit should 'bring all things to the remembrance' of the Apostles; but we have no right to assume that in so doing He would override the ordinary laws of psychology. Material stored up so long in the breast of the Apostle could not fail to be moulded by the working of his own mind. And therefore we may admit that in his report of the sayings of Christ and of the Baptist there is an element, impossible to separate now, which comes from himself. His report is sometimes a literal translation of the very words used, sometimes the substance of what was said put into

ruler of the Jews: the same came to Jesus by night, and ² said unto him, Rabbi, we know that thou art a teacher come from God: for no *man* can do these miracles that thou

his own words: but he gives us no means of distinguishing where the one shades off into the other.

Cardinal Newman has kindly allowed the following to be quoted from a private letter written by him, July 15th, 1878. "Every one writes in his own style. S. John gives our Lord's meaning in his own way. At that time the third person was not so commonly used in history as now. When a reporter gives one of Gladstone's speeches in the newspaper, if he uses the first person, I understand not only the matter, but the style, the words, to be Gladstone's: when the third, I consider the style, &c. to be the reporter's own. But in ancient times this distinction was not made. Thucydides uses the dramatic method, yet Spartan and Athenian speak in Thucydidean Greek. And so every clause of our Lord's speeches in S. John may be in S. John's Greek, yet every clause may contain the matter which our Lord spoke in Aramaic. Again, S. John might and did select or condense (as being inspired for that purpose) the matter of our Lord's discourses, as that with Nicodemus, and thereby the wording might be S. John's, though the matter might still be our Lord's."

1. *There was a man*] Better, **Now** *there was a man*. The conjunction shows the connexion with what precedes: Nicodemus was one of the 'many' who 'believed in His name,' when they beheld His signs (ii. 23).

Nicodemus] He is mentioned only by S. John. It is impossible to say whether he is identical with the Nicodemus of the Talmud, also called Bunai, who survived the destruction of Jerusalem. The name was common both among Greeks and Jews. Love of truth and fear of man, candour and hesitation, seem to be combined in his character. Comp. vii. 50, xix. 39. In xix. 39 his timidity is again noted and illustrated.

a ruler of the Jews] A member of the Sanhedrin, vii. 50. Comp. xii. 42; Luke xxiii. 13, xxiv. 20. His coming by night is to avoid the hostility of his colleagues: the Sanhedrin was opposed to Jesus. Whether or no S. John was present at the interview we cannot be certain: probably he was. Nicodemus would not fear the presence of the disciples.

2. *we know*] Others are disposed to believe as well as Nicodemus.

a teacher come from God] In the Greek the order is, *that Thou art come from God as teacher.* We are not sure that 'come from God' points to the Messiah, 'He that should come.' But if so, we see the timidity of Nicodemus; he begins with an admission of Christ's Messiahship, and ends with the weak word 'teacher;' the Messiah was never thought of as a mere teacher. But 'come from God' may only mean divinely *sent*, as a Prophet (i. 6), or even less.

these miracles] Better, *these* **signs**, as in ii. 11.

3 doest, except God be with him. Jesus answered and said unto him, Verily, verily, I say unto thee, Except a man be
4 born again, he cannot see the kingdom of God. Nicodemus saith unto him, How can a man be born when he is old? can he enter the second time into his mother's womb, and
5 be born? Jesus answered, Verily, verily, I say unto thee, Except a man be born of water and *of* the Spirit, he cannot

except God be with him] A similarly weak conclusion, shewing timidity: one expects 'unless he be a Prophet,' or 'the Messiah.'

3. *Jesus answered*] He answers his thoughts before they are expressed. See on ii. 25, and on i. 51.

born again] The word translated 'again' may mean either 'from the beginning,' or 'from above.' By itself it cannot exactly mean 'again.' S. John uses the same word *v.* 31; xix. 11, 23. In all three places, (see especially xix. 11), it means 'from above,' which is perhaps to be preferred here: 'from the beginning' would make no sense. To be 'born from above' recalls being 'born of God' in i. 13, (comp. 1 John iii. 9, iv. 7, v. 1, 4, 18). Of course being 'born from above' is necessarily being 'born again;' but 'again' comes not so much from the Greek word, as from the context. Comp. '*verily I say unto you*, except ye be converted *and become as little children*, ye shall not *enter into the kingdom of heaven.*' Matt. xviii. 3.

There is a probable reference to this passage (3—5) in Justin Martyr, *Apol.* I. lxi. If so, we have evidence that this Gospel was known before A.D. 150. See on i. 23 and ix. 1.

he cannot see] i.e. so as to partake of it. Comp. to 'see corruption,' Ps. xvi. 10; to 'see evil,' xc. 15; to 'see death,' John viii. 51; Luke ii. 26.

the kingdom of God] This phrase, so frequent in the Synoptists, occurs only here and *v.* 5 in S. John. We may conclude that it was the very phrase used.

4. *when he is old*] He purposely puts the most impossible case; the words do not imply that he was an old man himself. It is difficult to believe that Nicodemus really supposed Christ to be speaking of ordinary birth; the metaphor of 'new birth' for spiritual regeneration cannot have been unfamiliar to him. Either he purposely misunderstands, in order to reduce Christ's words to an absurdity; or, more probably, not knowing what to say, he asks what he knew to be a foolish question.

the second time] This expression has contributed to the word which probably means 'from above,' being translated 'again.' But 'to enter a second time into his mother's womb' is simply a periphrasis for 'to be born' in the case of an adult. The word which means 'from above' is not included in the periphrasis. It is precisely that which perplexes Nicodemus; so he leaves it out.

5. *of water and of the Spirit*] Christ leaves the foolish question of Nicodemus to answer itself: He goes on to explain what is the real

enter into the kingdom of God. That which is born of the 6
flesh is flesh; and that which is born of the Spirit is spirit.
Marvel not that I said unto thee, Ye must be born again. 7
The wind bloweth where it listeth, and thou hearest the 8

point, and what Nicodemus has not asked, the meaning of 'from above:'
'of water and (of the) Spirit.' The outward sign and inward grace of
Christian baptism are here clearly given, and an unbiassed mind can
scarcely avoid seeing this plain fact. This becomes still more clear
when we compare i. 26 and 33, where the Baptist declares 'I baptize
with water;' the Messiah 'baptizeth with the Holy Ghost.' The Fathers,
both Greek and Latin, thus interpret the passage with singular una-
nimity. Thus once more S. John assumes without stating the primary
elements of Christianity. Baptism is assumed here as well known to his
reader, as the Eucharist is assumed in chap. vi. To a well-instructed
Christian there was no need to explain what was meant by being born
of water and the Spirit. The words therefore had a threefold meaning,
past, present, and future. In the past they looked back to the time
when the Spirit moved upon the water causing the birth from above of
Order and Beauty out of Chaos. In the present they pointed to the
divinely ordained (i. 33) baptism of John: and through it in the future
to that higher rite, to which John himself bore testimony.

6. The meaning of 'birth from above' is still further explained by an
analogy. What a man inherits from his parents is a body with animal
life and passions; what he receives from above is a spiritual nature with
heavenly aspirations and capabilities. What is born of sinful, human
nature is sinful and human; what is born of the Holy Spirit is spiritual
and divine.

7. *Ye must*] The declaration is brought more closely home. In
vv. 3 and 5 Christ had made a very general statement, 'except a man.'
He now shews that none are exempt from it. 'Ye, the chosen people,
ye, the Pharisees, ye, the rulers, must all be born from above.'

8. *The wind bloweth*, &c.] This verse is sometimes taken very
differently: *the Spirit breatheth where He willeth, and thou hearest His
voice, but canst not tell whence He cometh and whither He goeth; so is
every one (born) who is born of the Spirit*. The advantages of this
rendering are (1) that it gives to *Pneuma* the meaning which it almost
invariably has in more than 350 passages in N.T. in which it occurs, of
which more than 20 are in this Gospel. Although *pneuma* may mean
'the breath of the wind,' yet its almost invariable use in N.T. is 'spirit'
or 'the Spirit,' while *anemos* is used for 'wind:' (2) that it gives a better
meaning to 'willeth,' a word more appropriate to a person than to anything inanimate: (3) that it gives to *phōnē* the meaning which it has in
14 other passages in this Gospel, viz., 'articulate *voice*,' and not 'inar-
ticulate *sound*.' On the other hand this rendering (1) gives to *pnei* the
meaning 'breathes,' a meaning quite unknown in N.T.: (2) uses the
expression 'the voice of the Spirit,' also unknown to Scripture: (3) requires the insertion of 'born' in the last clause, in order to make sense.

sound thereof, but canst not tell whence it cometh, and whither it goeth: so is every one that is born of the Spirit. 9 Nicodemus answered and said unto him, How can these 10 things be? Jesus answered and said unto him, Art thou 11 a master of Israel, and knowest not these *things*? Verily, verily, I say unto thee, We speak that we do know, and testify that we have seen; and ye receive not our witness.

For the usual rendering may be pleaded (1) that it gives to *pnei* the meaning which it has everywhere else in N.T., viz. in vi. 18 and five other passages. Although *pnei* may mean 'breathes,' yet its invariable use in N.T. is of the 'blowing' of the wind, while another word (xx. 22) is used for 'breathe:' (2) that it gives the most literal meaning to 'hearest:' (3) that the last clause makes excellent sense without any repetition of 'born.' The Aramaic word probably used by our Lord has both meanings, 'wind' and 'spirit,' so that it is not impossible that both meanings are meant to run concurrently through the passage. "It was late at night when our Lord had this interview with the Jewish teacher. At the pauses in the conversation, we may conjecture, they heard the wind without, as it moaned along the narrow streets of Jerusalem; and our Lord, as was His wont, took His creature into His service—the service of spiritual truth. The wind was a figure of the Spirit. Our Lord would have used the same word for both." (Liddon.) There is a clear reference to this passage in the Ignatian Epistles, *Philad.* VII. Thus we have evidence of the Gospel being known certainly as early as A.D. 150, and probably A.D. 115.

so is every one] i.e. such is the case of every one: he feels the spiritual influence, but finds it incomprehensible in its origin, which is from above, and in its end, which is eternal life.

born of the Spirit] The Sinaitic MS. and two ancient versions read, *born of water and of the Spirit*. The inserted words are a gloss.

9. *How can these things be?*] He is bewildered; there is no appearing not to understand, as in v. 4. 'Be,' **come to pass** (see on i. 6).

10. *Art thou a master of Israel*] Better, *art thou* **the teacher** *of Israel*, the well-known Rabbi, a representative of the supreme authority in the Church?

11. *We speak that we do know*] The plural is no *proof* that any of the disciples were present, though S. John at least may have been; nor does it *necessarily* include more than Christ Himself. The plurals may be rhetorical, giving the saying the tone of a proverb; but the next verse seems to shew that they do include others. Christ and his disciples tell of earthly things, Christ alone of heavenly.

testify] Or, **bear witness of** (see on i. 7).

we have seen] Of which we have immediate knowledge. Comp. i. 18; xiv. 7, 9.

and ye receive not] The tragic tone once more; see on i. 5. 'Ye teachers of Israel,' the very men who should receive it.

If I have told you earthly *things*, and ye believe not, how shall ye believe, if I tell you *of* heavenly *things?* And no man hath ascended up to heaven, but he that came down from heaven, *even* the Son of man which is in heaven. And as Moses lifted up the serpent in the wilderness, *even* so must the Son of man be lifted up: that whosoever believeth in him should not perish, but have eternal life. For God

12. *earthly things*] Things which take place on earth, even though originating in heaven, e.g. the 'new birth,' which though 'from above,' must take place in this world. See notes on 1 Cor. xv. 40 and James iii. 15.

heavenly things] The mysteries which are not of this world, the Divine counsels respecting man's salvation.

13. *no man hath ascended up to heaven*] No man has been in heaven, so as to see and know these heavenly things, excepting Christ.

came down from heaven] Literally, **out of** *heaven*; at the Incarnation. On 'the Son of Man' see on i. 51.

which is in heaven] These words are omitted in the best MSS. If they are retained, the meaning is 'Whose proper home is heaven.' Or the Greek participle may be the imperfect tense (comp. vi. 62, ix. 25, xvii. 5), *which was in heaven* before the Incarnation. It is doubtful whether in this verse we have any direct allusion to the Ascension, though this is sometimes assumed.

14. *the serpent*] We here have some evidence of the date of the Gospel. The Ophitic is the earliest Gnostic system of which we have full information. The serpent is the centre of the system, at once its good and evil principle. Had this form of Gnosticism been prevalent before this Gospel was written, this verse would scarcely have stood thus. An orthodox writer would have guarded his readers from error: an Ophitic writer would have made more of the serpent.

even so] Christ here testifies to the prophetic and typical character of the O. T.

must] It is so ordered in the counsels of God. Heb. ii. 9, 10.

be lifted up] On the cross: the lifting up does not refer to the exaltation of Christ to glory. The glory to which the cross led (*crux scala coeli*) is not included. Comp. viii. 28 and xii. 32; and for other symbolic language about His death comp. Matt. xii. 40.

15. *That*] The eternal life of believers is the purpose of the 'must' in *v.* 14. For 'should' read **may** both here and in *v.* 16.

not perish, but] These words are not genuine here, but have been taken from the next verse. When they are struck out it is better to take 'in Him' with 'have' than with 'believeth:' *that* **every one who believeth may have in Him** *eternal life.*

16—21. It is much disputed whether what follows is a continuation of Christ's discourse, or the comment of the Evangelist upon it. The fact that terms characteristic of S. John's theology are put into the mouth of Christ, e.g. 'only-begotten' and 'the Light,' cannot settle the

so loved the world, that he gave his only begotten Son, that whosoever believeth in him should not perish, but have 17 everlasting life. For God sent not his Son into the world to condemn the world; but that the world through him 18 might be saved. He that believeth on him is not condemned: but he that believeth not is condemned already, because he hath not believed in the name of the only

question: the substance may still be our Lord's, though the wording is S. John's. It seems unlikely that S. John would give us no indication of the change from Christ's words to his own, if the discourse with Nicodemus really came to a full stop in v. 15. See on vv. 31—36.

16. *For*] Explaining how God wills eternal life to every one that believeth.

loved the world] The whole human race: see on i. 10. This would be a revelation to the exclusive Pharisee, brought up to believe that God loved only the chosen people. The word for 'love,' *agapân*, is very frequent both in this Gospel and in the First Epistle, and may be considered characteristic of S. John.

that he gave his only begotten] This would be likely to remind Nicodemus of the offering of Isaac. Comp. 1 John iv. 9; Heb. xi. 17; Rom. viii. 32. See note on i. 14.

everlasting life] The Greek is the same as in the previous verse, and the translation should be the same, **eternal** *life*. 'Eternal life' is one of the phrases of which S. John is fond. It occurs 17 times in the Gospel (only eight in the Synoptics) and six times in the First Epistle. In neither Gospel nor Epistle is 'eternal' (*aiônios*) applied to anything but 'life.' On *aiônios*, which of itself does not necessarily mean 'everlasting' or 'unending,' see note on Matt. xxv. 46.

17. *the world*] Note the emphatic repetition: the whole human race is meant, as in v. 16, not the Gentiles in particular.

not...to condemn] This does not contradict ix. 39, 'For judgment am I come into this world.' Comp. Luke ix. 56. Since there are sinners in the world Christ's coming involves a separation of them from the good, a judgment, a sentence: but this is not the *purpose* of His coming; the purpose is salvation. 'Condemn' is too strong here for the Greek word, which is simply to **judge** between good and bad; but the word frequently acquires the notion of 'condemn' from the context (see on v. 29). Note the change of construction; not, 'to save the world,' but 'that the world might be saved through Him.' The world can reject Him if it pleases.

18. *is not condemned...is condemned already*] Better, *is not* **judged** ...**hath been judged** *already*. The change of tense from present to perfect must be preserved. Unbelievers have no need to be sentenced by the Messiah; their unbelief is of itself their sentence. The next verse explains how this is. 'Judge' and 'judgment' are among S. John's characteristic words.

begotten Son of God. And this is the condemnation, that 19 light is come into the world, and men loved darkness rather than light, because their deeds were evil. For every one 20 that doeth evil hateth the light, neither cometh to the light, lest his deeds should be reproved. But he that doeth 21 truth cometh to the light, that his deeds may be made manifest, that they are wrought in God.

19. *And this is the condemnation*] Rather, **But the judgment is this**; this is what it consists in: comp. xv. 12, xvii. 3.

and men loved darkness, &c.] The tragic tone came again (see on i. 5). Both words should have the article, *loved* **the** *darkness rather than* **the** *light*. An understatement; they hated the Light. There is probably no allusion to Nicodemus coming to Jesus by night. He chose the darkness, not because his deeds were evil, but because they were good. He wished to conceal, not an evil deed from good men, but a good deed from evil men.

deeds] Better, **works** here and *vv.* 20, 21.

20. *doeth evil*] The Greek word for 'doeth' is not the same as that in the next verse; but it is not quite certain that any distinction of meaning is intended, although v. 29 inclines one to think so. There the words are paired in precisely the same way as here. On the other hand in Rom. vii. 15—20 these same two words are interchanged indifferently, each being used both of doing good and of doing evil. In order to make a distinction *practiseth evil* has been suggested. But 'evil' also requires re-translation, for in the Greek it differs from 'evil' in *v.* 19. The meaning in this verse is rather 'frivolous, good-for-nothing, worthless.' *He that* **practiseth worthless things** (the aimless trifler), *hateth the light*, which would show him the true value of the inanities which fill up his existence.

lest his deeds should] Better, **in order that his works may not**.

reproved] The margin gives 'discovered.' In viii. 9 the same word is translated 'convict,' in viii. 46 'convince,' and in xvi. 8 'reprove' with 'convince' in the margin. Of all these 'convict' is perhaps the best; **in order that his works may not be convicted** of being worthless, proved to be what they really are. See note on Matt. xviii. 15.

21. *doeth truth*] Or, as in 1 John i. 6, *doeth* **the** *truth*, the opposite of 'doing' or 'making a lie,' Rev. xxi. 27, xxii. 15. It is moral rather than intellectual truth that is meant. To 'do the truth' is to do that which is true to the moral law (comp. viii. 32), that which has true moral worth, as opposed to 'practising worthless things.' In 1 Cor. xiii. 6 we have a similar antithesis: 'rejoicing with the *truth*' is opposed to 'rejoicing in *iniquity*.'

that his deeds may be made manifest] 'His' is emphatic, '*his* deeds' as opposed to those of him that doeth evil. 'Be made manifest' balances 'be reproved.' The one fears to be convicted; the other courts the light, not for self-glorification, but as loving that to which he feels his works are akin. See on i. 31.

22—36. *The Baptism and Final Testimony of John.*

22 After these *things* came Jesus and his disciples into the land of Judea; and there he tarried with them, and baptized. 23 And John also was baptizing in Aenon near to Salim,

wrought in God] Better, **have been** *wrought in God*. This is his reason for wishing them to be made manifest; it is a manifestation of something divine. The Greek for '*that* they are' may mean '*because* they are.'

These three verses (19—21) shew that *before* the Incarnation there were two classes of men in the world; a majority of evil-doers, whose antecedents led them to shun the Messiah; and a small minority of righteous, whose antecedents led them to welcome the Messiah. They had been given to Him by the Father (vi. 37, xvii. 6); they recognised His teaching as of God, because they desired to do God's will (vii. 17). Such would be Simeon, Anna (Luke ii. 25, 36), Nathanael, the disciples, &c.

We have no means of knowing how Nicodemus was affected by this interview, beyond the incidental notices of him vii. 50, 51, xix. 39, which being so incidental shew that he is no fiction.

22—36. THE BAPTISM AND FINAL TESTIMONY OF JOHN.

22, 23. We have here a mark of authenticity similar to ii. 12. These passages "it is impossible to regard as embodiments of dogma. It is equally impossible to regard them as fragments detached from the mass of tradition. The only conclusion remains, that they are *facts lodged in the memory of a living witness of the events described.*" S. p. 86. S. John records them, not for any theological purpose, but because he was there, and remembers what took place.

and baptized] Or, **was baptizing** during his stay there, through his disciples (iv. 2). Christ's baptism was not yet in the Name of the Trinity (vii. 39) as ordered to the Apostles (Matt. xxviii. 19). It was a continuation of John's baptism, accompanied by the operation of the Spirit (*v.* 5). We have abundant evidence that John baptized before Christ's public ministry commenced, and that the disciples baptized after His ministry closed. That the one baptism should be the offspring of the other is probable enough antecedently; "yet this is the one passage in which it is positively stated that our Lord authorised baptism during His lifetime." S. p. 85.

23. *John also was baptizing*] Not as a rival to the Messiah, but still in preparation for Him. Although John knew that the Messiah had come, yet He had not yet taken the public position which John had expected Him to take, and hence John was by no means led to suppose that his own office in preaching repentance was at an end. There is no improbability in Jesus and John baptizing side by side. But with this difference; Jesus seldom, if ever, administered His own baptism; John apparently always did administer his.

Aenon] The name means 'springs.' The identifications of both

vv. 24—27.]   S. JOHN, III.   101

because there was much water there: and they came, and were baptized. For John was not yet cast into prison. 24 Then there arose a question between *some* of John's disciples 25 and the Jews about purifying. And they came unto John, 26 and said unto him, Rabbi, *he* that was with thee beyond Jordan, to whom thou barest witness, behold, the same baptizeth, and all *men* come to him. John answered and 27 said, A man can receive nothing, except it be given him

Aenon and Salim remain uncertain. The most probable conjecture is the Wâdy Fâr'ah, running from Mount Ebal to Jordan, an open vale, full of springs. There is a Salim three miles south of the valley, and the name of Aenon survives in 'Ainûn, a village four miles north of the waters.

much water] For immersion; the Greek means literally **many waters**. The remark shews that these places were not on the Jordan. It would be gratuitous to say of the Jordan that 'there was much water there.'

24. This corrects the impression, naturally derived from the Synoptists, that Christ's public ministry did not commence till after the imprisonment of the Baptist. The whole of these first three chapters and part of the fourth must be placed before Matt. iv. 12, where there are great gaps in the history.

25. *Then there arose*] Better, *there arose* **therefore**; i.e. in consequence of John's baptizing at Aenon.

a question] Or, **questioning**.

between some of John's disciples and the Jews] Better, **on the part of *John's disciples* with a Jew**. 'A Jew' for 'Jews' is the reading of the best authorities. We do not know what the question was; probably the efficacy of John's baptism as compared with Christ's, or as compared with the ordinary ceremonial washings, for purifying from sin. There is no clue as to who this Jew was. His question makes the disciples of John go at once to their master for his opinion about Jesus and His success.

26. *to whom thou barest witness*] Rather, *to whom thou* **hast borne** *witness*. This was the monstrous thing in their eyes; that One who seemed to owe His position to the testimony of John should be competing with him and surpassing him.

behold, the same] Or perhaps, *behold,* **this fellow**, expressing astonishment and chagrin, and perhaps contempt.

all men] An exaggeration very natural in their excitement. The picture is very true to life. Comp. the excited statement of the Samaritan woman, iv. 29; and of the Pharisees, xii. 19; contrast v. 32 and see on vi. 15.

27. *A man can receive nothing,* &c.] Comp. xix. 11. The meaning of John's declaration is given in two ways: (1) 'Jesus could not have this great success, unless it were granted Him from Heaven. This

28 from heaven. Ye yourselves bear me witness, that I said, I 29 am not the Christ, but that I am sent before him. He that hath the bride is the bridegroom: but the friend of the bridegroom, which standeth and heareth him, rejoiceth greatly because of the bridegroom's voice: this my joy 30 therefore is fulfilled. He must increase, but I *must* decrease.

ought to satisfy you that He is sent by God;' (2) 'I cannot accept the position of supremacy, which you would thrust upon me; because I have not received it from Heaven.' The former is better, as being a more direct answer to 'all men come to Him.' But it is quite possible that both meanings are intended.

be given] More literally, **have been** *given*.

28. *Ye yourselves*] Though you are so indignant on my account.

bear me witness, that I said] They had appealed to his testimony (*v.* 26); he turns it against them.

before him] 'Before Him, of whom you complain, whom I proclaim to be the Christ.' In i. 26, 30, John spoke less clearly.

29. John explains by a figure his subordination to the Messiah.

He that hath the bride] Here only in this Gospel does this well-known symbol occur. It is frequent both in O. T. and N. T. Is. liv. 5; Hos. ii. 19, 20; Eph. v. 32; Rev. xix. 7; xxi. 2, 9. Comp. Song of Solomon, *passim;* Matt. ix. 15, xxv. 1. In O. T. it symbolizes the relationship between Jehovah and His chosen people, in N. T. that between Christ and His Church.

the friend of the bridegroom] The special friend, appointed to arrange the preliminaries of the wedding, to manage and preside at the marriage feast. Somewhat analogous to our 'best man,' but his duties were very much more considerable. A much closer analogy may be found among the lower orders in the Tyrol at the present day. Here the Messiah is the Bridegroom and the Church His Bride; John is His friend who has prepared the heart of the Bride and arranged the espousal. He rejoices to see the consummation of his labours.

heareth him] i.e. listens attentively to do his bidding.

because of the bridegroom's voice] Heard in the midst of the marriage-festivities.

is fulfilled] i.e. **has been** *fulfilled* and still remains complete. Comp. xv. 11, xvi. 24, xvii. 13; 1 John i. 4.

30. *must*] It is so ordained in the counsels of God. Comp. *vv.* 7, 14, ix. 4, x. 16, xx. 9. This joy of the friend of the Bridegroom, in full view of the inevitable wane of his own influence and dignity, is in marked contrast to the jealousy and vexation of his disciples.

31—36. A question is raised with regard to this section similar to that raised about *vv.* 16—21. Some regard what follows not as a continuation of the Baptist's speech, but as the Evangelist's comment upon it. But, as in the former case, seeing that the Evangelist gives us no intimation that he is taking the place of the speaker, and that

He that cometh from above is above all : he that is of the 31
earth is earthly, and speaketh of the earth : he that cometh
from heaven is above all. And what he hath seen and 32
heard, that he testifieth; and no *man* receiveth his testimony.

there is nothing in what follows to compel us to suppose that there is such a transition, it is best to regard the Baptist as still speaking. It is, however, quite possible that this latter part of the discourse is more strongly coloured with the Evangelist's own style and phraseology, while the substance still remains the Baptist's. Indeed a change of style may be noticed. The sentences become less abrupt and more connected; the stream of thought is continuous.

"The Baptist, with the growing inspiration of the prophet, unveils before his narrowing circle of disciples the full majesty of Jesus; and then, as with a swan-like song, completes his testimony before vanishing from history." Meyer, *in loco*.

There is no contradiction between this passage and Matt. xi. 2—6, whatever construction we put on the latter (see notes there). John was 'of the earth,' and therefore there is nothing improbable in his here impressing on his disciples the peril of not believing on the Messiah, and yet in prison feeling impatience, or despondency, or even doubt about the position and career of Jesus.

31. *that cometh from above*] i.e. Christ. Comp. *v.* 13, viii. 23, He 'is above all,' John included. No one, however exalted a Prophet, can rival Him.

is earthly] There is loss instead of gain in obliterating the emphatic repetition of the words 'of the earth' as they appear in the Greek. *He that is of the earth,* **of the earth** *he is, and of the earth he speaketh*. This was John's case: he spoke of 'earthly things' (see on *v.* 12), Divine Truth *as manifested in the world*, and as revealed to him. He could not, like Christ, speak from immediate knowledge of 'heavenly things.' Note that 'speaking of the *earth*' is a very different thing from 'speaking of the *world*' (1 John iv. 5). The one is to speak of God's work on earth; the other of what opposes, or at least is other than, God's work.

he that cometh from heaven] A repetition with further development, very characteristic of S. John's style.

32. *what he hath seen and heard*] In His pre-existence with God ; *v.* 11, i. 18. He has immediate knowledge of heavenly things.

that he testifieth] Better, *that he* **witnesseth** (see on i. 7). Precisely this is the substance of His witness.

and no man] The tragic tone again; see on i. 5, and comp. *v.* 11. 'No man' is an exaggeration resulting from deep feeling: comparatively speaking none, so few were those who accepted the Messiah. Comp. the similar exaggeration on the other side, *v.* 26, 'all men come to Him.' These extreme contradictory statements, placed in such close proximity, confirm our trust in the Evangelist as faithfully reporting what was actually said. He does not soften it down to make it look plausible.

33 He that hath received his testimony hath set to *his* seal that
34 God is true. For he whom God hath sent speaketh the
words of God: for God giveth not the Spirit by measure
35 *unto him*. The Father loveth the Son, and hath given all
36 *things* into his hand. He that believeth on the Son hath
everlasting life: and he that believeth not the Son shall
not see life; but the wrath of God abideth on him.

receiveth his testimony] Better, *receiveth His* **witness**. The Baptist takes up Christ's words in *v.* 11.
33. The Baptist shews at once that 'no man' is hyperbolical; there are some who received the testimony.
hath received...hath set to his seal] Better, **received...set** *his seal.*
his testimony] **his witness.** 'His' is emphatic, balancing 'God.' 'He that received *Christ's* witness, set his seal that *God* is true.' To believe the Messiah is to believe God, for the Messiah is God's interpreter, i. 18. The metaphor is from sealing a document to express one's trust in it and adherence to it. Comp. vi. 27; 1 Cor. ix. 2. On 'true' see note on i. 9; 'true' here is opposed to 'lying' not to 'spurious.'
34. *whom God hath sent*] Better, *whom God* **sent**, viz. Christ 'who cometh from above,' *v.* 31.
God giveth not the Spirit by measure unto him] 'God' is of doubtful authority; 'unto Him' is not in the Greek. We must translate **He** *giveth not the Spirit by measure;* or, **the Spirit** *giveth not by measure.* The former is better, and 'He' probably means God; so that the only question is whether 'unto Him' is rightly supplied or not. In translation it is best to omit the words, although there is a direct reference to Jesus. 'Not by measure giveth He the Spirit,' least of all to Jesus, 'for it pleased (the Father) that in Him the whole plenitude (of Divinity) should have its permanent abode,' Col. i. 19. Some take 'He' as meaning Christ, who gives the Spirit fully to His disciples.
35. *loveth the Son*] Comp. v. 20. This is the reason for His giving all things into His hand. Christ is thus made 'Head over all things' (Eph. i. 22), and 'Lord of all' (Acts x. 36).
36. *hath everlasting life*] Or, **eternal** *life* (see on *v.* 16). Note the tense; 'hath' not 'shall have.' Believers are already in possession of eternal life. Christians often think of eternal life as something yet to be won. It has been already given to them; the question is whether they will lose it again or not. The struggle is not to gain but to retain. Comp. xvii. 3.
he that believeth not] This may also mean *he that* **obeyeth** *not*, and this is better, for it is not the same word as 'he that believeth' with the negative added. The same correction seems to be needed, Acts xiv. 2, xix. 9; Rom. xi. 30 (see margin). Comp. Heb. iv. 6, 11; 1 Pet. iv. 17.
shall not see] Not only has not beheld, but has no prospect of beholding.

CHAP. IV. 1—42. *The Work among Samaritans.*

When therefore the Lord knew how the Pharisees had heard that Jesus made and baptized moe disciples than John, (though Jesus himself baptized not, but his disciples,) he left Judea, and departed again into Galilee. And he must needs go through Samaria. Then cometh he to a 4 2 3 4

the wrath of God] This phrase occurs nowhere else in the Gospels. It is the necessary complement of the love of God. If there is love for those who believe, there must be wrath for those who refuse to believe. Comp. Matt. iii. 7; Luke iii. 7; Rom. i. 18, ix. 22, xii. 19.

abideth] Not 'shall come to him:' this is his portion already. He is under a ban until he believes, and he refuses to believe: therefore the ban remains. He, like the believer, not only *will* have but *has* his portion; it rests with him also, whether the portion continues his. He has to struggle, not to avert a sentence, but to be freed from it.

CHAP. IV. 1—42. THE WORK AMONG SAMARITANS.

1. *When therefore the Lord knew*] The 'therefore' refers us back to iii. 26. Of the many who came to Christ some told the Pharisees of His doings, just as others told John.

the Pharisees] See on i. 24.

made and baptized] Literally, **is making and baptizing**, the very words of the report are given. This is important as shewing the meaning of the next verse, which is a correction not of the Evangelist's own statement but of the report. In the Authorised Version S. John seems to be correcting himself: he is really correcting the report carried to the Pharisees.

than John] They did not object so much to John's making disciples. He disclaimed being the Messiah, and he took his stand on the Law. Moreover, he 'did no miracle.' They could understand his position much better than that of Jesus, and feared it less. See on vi. 15.

2. *Jesus himself baptized not*] Because baptizing is the work of a minister, not of the Lord. Christ baptizes with the Holy Spirit (i. 33).

3. *He left Judæa*] The stronghold of the Pharisees and of the party opposed to Christ. We are to infer, therefore, that this report made them commence operations against Him.

departed again into Galilee] 'Again' is somewhat wanting in authority. It points to the period from i. 43 to ii. 12. Christ had come up from Capernaum to Jerusalem for the Passover (ii. 13): He now returns to Galilee. It is sometimes assumed that this visit to Galilee marks the beginning of the Galilean ministry recorded by the Synoptists (comp. Matt. iv. 12). This may be correct, but it is not quite certain. See note on Mark i. 14, 15.

4. *he must needs go through Samaria*] There was no other way,

city of Samaria, which is called Sychar, near to the parcel

unless he crossed the Jordan and went round by Perea, as Jews sometimes did to avoid annoyance from the Samaritans (on the Samaritans, see note on Matt. x. 5). As Christ was on his way *from* Jerusalem, and escaping from the ruling party there, He had less reason to fear molestation. Comp. Luke ix. 53.

5—42. Doubt has been thrown on this narrative in three different ways. (1) On *a priori* grounds. How could the Samaritans, who rejected the prophetical books, and were such bitter enemies of the Jews, be expecting a Messiah? The narrative is based on a fundamental mistake. But it is notorious that the Samaritans did look for a Messiah, and are looking for one to the present day. Though they rejected the Prophets, they accepted the Pentateuch, with all its Messianic prophecies. (2) On account of *Acts viii.* 5. How could Philip go and convert the Samaritans, if Christ had already done so? But is it to be supposed that *in two days* Christ perfected Christianity in Samaria (even allowing, what is not certain, that Christ and Philip went to the same town), so as to leave nothing for a preacher to do afterwards? Many acknowledged Jesus as the Messiah who afterwards, on finding Him to be very different from the Messiah they expected, fell away. This would be likely enough at Samaria. The seed had fallen on rocky ground. (3) On the supposition that the narrative is an *allegory*, of which the whole point lies in the words 'thou hast had five husbands, and he whom thou now hast is not thy husband.' The five husbands are the five religions from Babylon, Cuthah, Ava, Hamath, and Sepharvaim, brought to Samaria by the colonists from Assyria (2 Kings xvii. 24); and the sixth is the adulterated worship of Jehovah. If our interpreting Scripture depends upon our guessing such riddles as this, we may well despair of the task. But the allegory is a pure fiction. 1. When S. John gives us an allegory, he leaves no doubt that it is an allegory There is not the faintest hint here. 2. It would be extraordinary that in a narrative of 38 verses the whole allegory should be contained in less than one verse, the rest being mere setting. This is like a frame a yard wide round a miniature. 3. There is a singular impropriety in making the five heathen religions 'husbands,' while the worship of Jehovah is represented by a paramour.

The narrative is true to what we know of Jews and Samaritans at this time. The topography is well preserved. 'The gradual development of the woman's belief is psychologically true.' These and other points to be noticed as they occur may convince us that this narrative cannot be a fiction. Far the easiest supposition is that it is a faithful record of actual facts.

5. *Then cometh he*] Better, *He cometh* **therefore**; because that was His route.

a city of Samaria] City is used loosely, and must not be supposed to imply anything large. Capernaum, which Josephus calls a village, the Evangelists call a city. 'Town' would be better as a translation. Samaria is the insignificant province of Samaria into which

of ground that Jacob gave to his son Joseph. Now Jacob's 6
well was there. Jesus therefore, being weared with *his*
journey, sat thus on the well: *and* it was about the sixth
hour. There cometh a woman of Samaria to draw water: 7
Jesus saith unto her, Give me to drink. (For his disciples 8

the old kingdom of Jeroboam had dwindled. Omit 'which is' before
'called.'
called Sychar] 'Called' may be another indication that this Gospel
was written outside Palestine or it may mean that Sychar was a nickname ('liar' or 'drunkard'). In the one case Sychar is a different place
from Sychem or Shechem, though close to it, viz. the modern Askar:
in the other it is another name for Sychem, the Neapolis of S. John's
day, and the modern Naplûs. The former view is preferable, though
certainty is impossible. Would S. John have written 'Neapolis' if
Sychem were meant? He writes Tiberias (vi. 1, 23, xxi. 1): but
Tiberias was probably a new town as well as a new name, whereas
Neapolis was a new name for an old town; so the analogy is not perfect.
Eusebius and Jerome distinguish Sychar from Sychem. Naplûs has
many wells close at hand.
that Jacob gave to his son Joseph] Gen. xxxiii. 19, xlviii. 22; Josh.
xxiv. 32. Abraham bought the ground, Jacob gave it to Joseph, and
Joseph was buried there.
6. *Jacob's well*] Or, **spring** (*v.* 11). It still exists, but without
spring-water; one of the few sites about which there is no dispute, in
the entrance to the valley between Ebal and Gerizim.
sat thus on the well] Or, **was sitting** *thus* (just as He was) **by** *the*
spring. All these details mark the report as of one who had full
information.
about the sixth hour] See on i. 39. This case again is not decisive
as to S. John's mode of reckoning the hours. On the one hand, noon
was an unusual hour for drawing water. On the other, a woman whose
life was under a cloud (*v.* 18) might select an unusual hour; and at
6 P.M. numbers would probably have been coming to draw, and the
conversation would have been disturbed. Again, after 6 P.M. there
would be rather short time for all that follows. These two instances
(i. 39 and this) lend no strong support to the antecedently improbable
theory that S. John's method of counting the hours is different from the
Synoptists.
7. *a woman of Samaria*] i.e. of the province; not of the *city* of
Samaria, at that time called Sebaste, in honour of Augustus, who had
given it to Herod the Great. Herod's name for it survives in the modern
Sebustieh. A woman of the city of Samaria would not have come all
that distance to fetch water. In legends this woman is called Photina.
Give me to drink] Quite literal, as the next verse shews. He asked
her for refreshment *because* His disciples had gone away. 'Give me the
spiritual refreshment of thy conversion' is a meaning read into the words
and not found in them.

9 were gone away unto the city to buy meat.) Then saith the woman of Samaria unto him, How *is it that* thou, being a Jew, askest drink of me, which am a woman of Samaria?
10 For the Jews have no dealings with the Samaritans. Jesus answered and said unto her, If thou knewest the gift of God, and who it is that saith to thee, Give me to drink; thou wouldest have asked of him, and he would have given
11 thee living water. The woman saith unto him, Sir, thou hast nothing to draw with, and the well is deep: from

8. *to buy meat*] i.e. food, not necessarily flesh. The meat-offering was fine flour and oil without any flesh. Lev. ii. 1. The Greek word here means 'nourishment.'

9. *woman of Samaria*] In both places in this verse we should rather have **Samaritan woman**: the Greek is not the same as in *v.* 7. The adjective lays stress on the national and religious characteristics. For 'then' read **therefore**, as in *v.* 5.

How is it] Feminine pertness. She is half-amused and half-triumphant.

being a Jew] She knew Him to be such by His dress and by His language.

for the Jews, &c.] Omit the articles; *for Jews have no dealings with Samaritans.* This is a remark, not of the woman, but of S. John, to explain the woman's question. As He was on his way from Jerusalem she probably thought He was a Judaean. The Galileans seem to have been less strict; and hence His disciples went to buy food of Samaritans. Some important authorities omit the remark.

10. *the gift of God*] What He is ready to give thee, what is now held out to thee, thy salvation. For 'knewest' read **hadst known**. Comp. xi. 21, 32, xiv. 28, where we have the same construction; and contrast v. 46 and viii. 19, where the A. V. makes the converse mistake of translating imperfects as if they were aorists.

thou wouldest have asked of him] instead of His asking of thee: 'thou' is emphatic. 'Spiritually our positions are reversed. It is thou who art weary, and foot-sore, and parched, close to the well, yet unable to drink; it is I who can give thee the water from the well, and quench thy thirst for ever.' There is a scarcely doubtful reference to this passage in the Ignatian Epistles, *Romans,* VII. See on vi. 33, to which there is a clear reference in this same chapter. The passage with these references to the Fourth Gospel is found in the Syriac as well as in the shorter Greek versions of Ignatius; so that we have almost certain evidence of this Gospel being known as early as A.D. 115. See on iii. 3.

11. *Sir*] A decided change from the pert 'How is it?' in *v.* 9. His words and manner already begin to impress her.

the well is deep] Not the same word for '*well*' as in *v.* 6. There the *spring* in the well is the chief feature: here it is rather the *deep hole*

whence then hast thou *that* living water? Art thou greater 12
than our father Jacob, which gave us the well, and drank
thereof himself, and his children, and his cattle? Jesus 13
answered and said unto her, Whosoever drinketh of this
water shall thirst again: but whosoever drinketh of the 14

in which the spring was. Earlier travellers have called it over a 100
feet deep: at the present time it is about 75 feet deep.
that living water] Better, **the** *living water*, of which Thou speakest.
She thinks He means spring-water as distinct from cistern-water.
Comp. Jer. ii. 13, where the two are strongly contrasted. In Gen. xxvi.
19, as the margin shews, 'springing water' is literally 'living water,'
viva aqua. What did Christ mean by the 'living water?' Among the
various answers we may at once set aside any reference to baptism.
Faith, God's grace and truth, Christ Himself, are other answers. The
difference between them is at bottom not so great as appears on the
surface. Christ here uses the figure of water, as elsewhere of bread
(vi.) and light (viii. 12), the three most necessary things for life. But
He does not here *identify* Himself with the living water, as He does
with the Bread, and the Light: therefore it seems better to understand
the living water as the 'grace and truth' of which He is full (i. 14).
Comp. Ecclus. xv. 3; Baruch iii. 12.

12. *Art thou greater*] 'Thou' is very emphatic; *Surely Thou art
not greater*. Comp. viii. 53. The loquacity of the woman as contrasted with the sententiousness of Nicodemus is very natural, while on
the other hand she shews a similar perverseness in misunderstanding
spiritual metaphors.

our father Jacob] The Samaritans claimed to be descended from
Joseph; with how much justice is a question very much debated.
Some maintain that they were of purely heathen origin, although they
were driven by calamity to unite the worship of Jehovah with their own
idolatries: and this view seems to be in strict accordance with 2 Kings
xvii. 23—41. Renegade Jews took refuge among them from time to
time; but such immigrants would not affect the texture of the nation
more than the French refugees among ourselves. Others hold that the
Samaritans were from the first a mongrel nation, a mixture of heathen
colonists with Jewish inhabitants, left behind by Shalmaneser. But
there is nothing to shew that he did leave any behind (2 Kings
xviii. 11); Josephus says (*Ant.* IX. xiv. 1) that 'he transplanted *all* the
people.' When the Samaritans asked Alexander the Great to excuse
them from tribute in the Sabbatical year, because as true sons of
Joseph they did not till their land in the seventh year, he pronounced
their claim an imposture, and destroyed Samaria. Our Lord calls a
Samaritan a 'stranger' (Luke xvii. 18), literally 'one of a different
race.'

which gave us the well] This has no foundation in Scripture, but no
doubt was a Samaritan tradition. She means, the well was good enough
for him, and is good enough for us; hast Thou a better?

water that I shall give him shall never thirst; but the water that I shall give him shall be in him a well of water spring-
15 ing up into everlasting life. The woman saith unto him, Sir, give me this water, that I thirst not, neither come
16 hither to draw. Jesus saith unto her, Go, call thy husband,
17 and come hither. The woman answered and said, I have no husband. Jesus said unto her, Thou hast well said, I
18 have no husband: for thou hast had five husbands; and he whom thou now hast is not thy husband: *in* that saidst
19 thou truly. The woman saith unto him, Sir, I perceive that
20 thou art a prophet. Our fathers worshipped in this moun-

13, 14. Christ leaves her question unanswered, like that of Nicodemus (iii. 4, 5), and passes on to develop the metaphor rather than explain it, contrasting the literal with the figurative sense. Comp. iii. 6.

14. *shall never thirst*] Literally, **will certainly not thirst for ever**, for the craving is satisfied as soon as ever it recurs. See on viii. 51.

springing up into everlasting life] Not that eternal life is some *future* result to be realised hereafter; it is the *immediate* result. The soul in which the living water flows has eternal life. See on *v.* 36 and iii. 16.

15. She still does not understand, but does not wilfully misunderstand. This wonderful water will at any rate be worth having, and she asks quite sincerely (not ironically) for it. Had she been a Jew, she could scarcely have thus misunderstood, this metaphor of 'water' and 'living water' is so frequent in the Prophets. Comp. Isa. xii. 3, xliv. 3; Jer. ii. 13; Zech. xiii. 1, xiv. 8. But the Samaritans rejected all but the Pentateuch.

to draw] Same word as in ii. 8, 9; peculiar to this Gospel.

16. *Go, call thy husband*] Not that the man was wanted, either as a concession to Jewish propriety, which forbad a Rabbi to talk with a woman alone, or for any other reason. By a seemingly casual request Christ lays hold of her inner life, convinces her of sin, and leads her to repentance, without which her request, 'Give me this water,' could not be granted. The husband who was no husband was the plague-spot where her healing must begin.

17. *hast well said*] i.e. **saidst** *rightly*. Comp. viii. 48; Matt. xv. 7; Luke xx. 39. There is perhaps a touch of irony in the 'well.'

18. *five husbands*] To be understood quite literally. They were either dead or divorced, and she was now living with a man without being married to him.

in that saidst thou truly] Better, **this** (one thing) *thou* **hast said** *truly*. Christ exposes the falsehood which lurks in the literal truth of her statement.

19. *a prophet*] One divinely inspired with supernatural knowledge, 1 Sam. ix. 9. Note the gradual change in her attitude of mind towards

tain; and ye say, that in Jerusalem is the place where *men ought to worship*. Jesus saith unto her, Woman, believe 21 me, the hour cometh, when ye shall neither in this moun-

Him. First, off-hand pertness (*v.* 9); then, respect to His gravity of manner and serious words (*v.* 11); next, a misunderstanding belief in what He says (*v.* 15); and now, reverence for Him as a 'man of God.' Comp. the parallel development of faith in the man born blind (see on ix. 11) and in Martha (see on xi. 21).

20. Convinced that He can read her life she shrinks from inspection and hastily turns the conversation from herself. In seeking a new subject she naturally catches at one of absorbing interest to every Samaritan. Mount Gerizim shorn of its temple suggests the great national religious question ever in dispute between them and the Jews. Here was One who could give an authoritative answer about it; she will ask Him. To urge that such a woman would care nothing about the matter is unsound reasoning. Are irreligious people never keen about religious questions now-a-days? Does an immoral life destroy all interest in Romanism, Ritualism, and the like?

in this mountain] Gerizim; her not naming it is very lifelike. The Samaritans contended that here Abraham offered up Isaac, and afterwards met Melchisedek. The former is more credible than the latter. A certain Manasseh, a man of priestly family, married the daughter of Sanballat the Horonite (Neh. xiii. 28), and was thereupon expelled from Jerusalem. He fled to Samaria and helped Sanballat to set up a rival worship on Gerizim. It is uncertain whether the temple on Gerizim was built then (about B.C. 410) or a century later; but it was destroyed by John Hyrcanus B.C. 130, after it had stood 200 years or more. Yet the Samaritans in no way receded from their claims, but continue their worship on Gerizim to the present day.

ye say] Unconsciously she admits that One, whom she has just confessed to be a Prophet, is against her in the controversy. Comp. Deut. xii. 13.

21—24. "We shall surely be justified in attributing the wonderful words of verses 21, 23, 24, to One greater even than S. John. They seem to breathe the spirit of other worlds than ours—'of worlds whose course is equable and pure;' where media and vehicles of grace are unneeded, and the soul knows even as it is known. There is nothing so like them in their sublime infinitude of comprehension, and intense penetration to the deepest roots of things, as some of the sayings in the Sermon on the Mount (Matt. v. 45, vi. 6). It is words like these that strike home to the hearts of men, as in the most literal sense Divine." S. p. 95.

21. *believe me*] This formula occurs here only; the usual one is 'I say unto you.'

the hour cometh] No article in the Greek; *there cometh* an *hour*. Christ decides neither for nor against either place. The utter ruin on Gerizim and the glorious building at Jerusalem will soon be on an equality. Those who would worship the Father must rise above such

22 tain, nor *yet* at Jerusalem, worship the Father. Ye worship
ye know not what: we know what we worship: for salvation
23 is of the Jews. But the hour cometh, and now is, when the
true worshippers shall worship the Father in spirit and *in*

distinctions of place. A time is coming when all limitations of worship
will disappear.

22. *ye know not what*] Or, **that which ye know not.** The Samaritan
religion, even after being purified from the original mixture with idolatry
(2 Kings xvii. 33, 41), remained a mutilated religion; the obscurity of
the Pentateuch (and of that a garbled text) unenlightened by the clearer
revelations in the Prophets and other books of O.T. Such a religion
when contrasted with that of the Jews might well be called ignorance.

we know what we worship] Or, **we worship that which we know.**
The first person plural here is not similar to that in iii. 11 (see note there),
though some would take it so. Christ here speaks as a Jew, and in
such a passage there is nothing surprising in His so doing. As a rule
Christ gives no countenance to the view that He belongs to the Jewish
nation in any special way, though the Jewish nation specially belongs to
Him (i. 11): He is the Saviour of the world, not of the Jews only.
But here, where it is a question whether Jew or Samaritan has the
larger share of religious truth, He ranks Himself both by birth and
by religion among the Jews. 'We,' therefore, means 'we Jews.'

salvation is of the Jews] Literally, **the** *salvation*, the expected salvation, *is of the Jews;* i.e. *proceeds from* them (not *belongs to* them), in
virtue of the promises to Abraham (Gen. xii. 3, xviii. 18, xxii. 18) and
Isaac (xxvi. 4). This verse is absolutely fatal to the theory that this
Gospel is the work of a Gnostic Greek in the second century (see on
xix. 35). That salvation proceeded from the Jews contradicts the fundamental principle of Gnosticism, that salvation was to be sought in the
higher knowledge of which Gnostics had the key. Hence those who
uphold such a theory of authorship assume, in defiance of all evidence,
that this verse is a later interpolation. The verse is found in all MSS.
and versions.

23. *the hour cometh*] As before, *there cometh* **an** *hour*. What
follows, *and it is now here*, could not be added in *v.* 21. The local
worship on Gerizim and Zion must still continue for a while; but there
are already a few who are rising above these externals to the spirit of
true worship, in which the opposition between Jew and Samaritan
disappears.

the true worshippers] The same word for 'true' as in i. 9 (see note
there); 'true' as opposed to what is 'spurious' and 'unreal.' Worship
to be genuine, real, and perfect must be offered in spirit and truth.

in spirit] This is opposed to all that is carnal, material, and of the
earth earthy;—'this mountain,' the Temple, limitations of time and
place. Not that such limitations are wrong; but they are not of the
essence of religion, and become wrong when they are mistaken for the
essence of religion.

truth: for the Father seeketh such to worship him. God *is* 24
a Spirit: and they that worship him must worship *him* in
spirit and *in* truth. The woman saith unto him, I know 25
that Messias cometh, which is called Christ: when he is
come, he will tell us all *things*. Jesus saith unto her, I that 26
speak unto thee am *he*.

in truth] (Omit 'in') i.e. in harmony with the Nature and Will of God. In the sphere of intellect, this means recognition of His Presence and Omniscience; in the sphere of action, conformity with His absolute Holiness. 'Worship in spirit and truth,' therefore, implies prostration of the inmost soul before the Divine Perfection, submission of every thought and feeling to the Divine Will.

for the Father seeketh, &c.] Better, **for such the Father also seeketh for His worshippers.** 'Such' is very emphatic; 'this is the character which He also desires in His worshippers.' The 'also' must not be lost. That worship should be 'in spirit and truth' is required by the fitness of things: moreover God Himself desires to have it so, and works for this end. Note how three times in succession Christ speaks of God as *the Father* (*vv.* 21, 23): perhaps it was quite a new aspect of Him to the woman.

24. God is spirit, and must be approached in that part of us which is spirit, in the true temple of God, 'which temple ye are.' Even to the chosen three Christ imparts no truths more profound than these. He admits this poor schismatic to the very fountain-head of religion.

25. *Messias*] See note on i. 41. There is nothing at all improbable in her knowing the Jewish name and using it to a Jew. The word being so rare in N.T. we are perhaps to understand that it was the very word used; but it may be S. John's equivalent for what she said. Comp. *v.* 29. Throughout this discourse it is impossible to say how much of it is a translation of the very words used, how much merely the substance of what was said. S. John would obtain his information from Christ, and possibly from the woman also during their two days' stay. The idea that S. John was left behind by the disciples, and *heard* the conversation, is against the whole tenour of the narrative and is contradicted by *vv.* 8 and 27.

which is called Christ] Probably a parenthetic explanation of the Evangelist's (but contrast i. 41), not the woman's. The Samaritan name for the expected Saviour was 'the Returning One,' or (according to a less probable derivation) 'the Converter.' 'The Returner' points to the belief that Moses was to appear again.

when he is come] Or, *when He comes*. 'He' is in emphatic contrast to other teachers.

all things] In a vague colloquial sense.

26. *am he*] This is correct, although 'He' is not expressed in the Greek. It is the ordinary Greek affirmative (comp. Luke xxii. 70); there is no reference to the Divine name 'I AM,' Ex. iii. 14; Deut. xxxii. 39. This open declaration of His Messiahship is startling wher

27 And upon this came his disciples, and marvelled that he talked with *the* woman: yet no *man* said, What seekest
28 thou? or, Why talkest thou with her? The woman then left her waterpot, and went her way into the city, and saith
29 to the men, Come, see a man, which told me all *things* that
30 ever I did: is not this the Christ? Then they went out of the city, and came unto him.
31 In the mean while *his* disciples prayed him, saying,

we remember Matt. xvi. 20, xvii. 9; Mark viii. 30. But one great reason for reserve on this subject, lest the people should 'take him by force to make him a king' (vi. 15), is entirely wanting here. There was no fear of the Samaritans making political capital out of Him. Moreover it was one thing for Christ to avow Himself when He saw that hearts were ready for the announcement; quite another for disciples and others to make Him known promiscuously.

27. *talked with the woman*] Rather, **was talking** *with a woman*, contrary to the precepts of the Rabbis. 'Let no one talk with a woman in the street, no not with his own wife.' The woman's being a Samaritan would increase their astonishment.

What seekest thou?] Probably both questions are addressed (hypothetically) to Christ; not one to the woman, and the other to Him.

28. *The woman then*] Better, *The woman* **therefore**; because of the interruption.

left her waterpot] Same word for 'waterpot' as in the miracle at Cana, and used nowhere else. Her leaving it shews that her errand is forgotten, or neglected as of no moment compared with what now lies before her. This graphic touch comes from one who was there, and saw, and remembered.

29. *all things that ever I did*] How natural is this exaggeration! In her excitement she states not what He had really told her, but what she is convinced He could have told her. Comp. 'all men' in iii. 26, and 'no man' in iii. 32. This strong language is in all three cases thoroughly in keeping with the circumstances.

is not this the Christ?] Rather, *Is this*, **can this be**, *the Christ?* A similar error occurs xviii. 17, 25. Although she believes it she thinks it almost too good to be true. Moreover she does not wish to seem too positive and dogmatic to those who do not yet know the evidence. The form of question is similar to that in *v.* 33: both are put in a form that anticipates a negative answer; *num* not *nonne*.

30. *went out......and came*] Literally, *went out......and* **were coming**. The change of tense from aorist to imperfect gives vividness. We are to see them coming along across the fields as we listen to the conversation that follows, 31—38.

31. *In the mean while*] Between the departure of the women and the arrival of her fellow-townsmen.

Master, eat. But he said unto them, I have meat to eat ³² that ye know not of. Therefore said the disciples one to ³³ another, Hath any *man* brought him *ought* to eat? Jesus ³⁴ saith unto them, My meat is to do the will of him that sent me, and to finish his work. Say not ye, There are ³⁵ yet four months, and *then* cometh harvest? behold, I say unto you, Lift up your eyes, and look on the fields; for they are white already to harvest. And he that reapeth ³⁶

Master, eat] Better, **Rabbi**, *eat*. Here and in ix. 2 and xi. 8 our translators have rather regrettably turned 'Rabbi' into 'Master,' (comp. Matt. xxvi. 25, 49; Mark ix. 5; xi. 21, xiv. 45); while 'Rabbi' is retained i. 38, 49, iii. 2, 26, vi. 25 (comp. Matt. xxiii. 7, 8). Apparently their principle was that wherever a disciple addresses Christ, 'Rabbi' is to be translated 'Master;' in other cases 'Rabbi' is to be retained; thus obscuring the view which the disciples took of their own relation to Jesus. He was their Rabbi.

32. *I have meat*, &c.] The pronouns 'I' and 'ye' are emphatically opposed. His joy at the woman's conversion prompts Him to refuse food: not of course that His human frame could do without it, but that in His delight He feels for the moment no want of food.

33. *Hath any man brought him*] The emphasis is on 'brought.' 'Surely no one hath *brought* Him any thing to eat.' Another instance of dulness as to spiritual meaning. In ii. 20 it was the Jews; in iii. 4 Nicodemus; in *v.* 11 the Samaritan woman; and now the disciples. Comp. xi. 12, xiv. 5. These candid reports of what tells against the disciples add to the trust which we place in the narratives of the Evangelists.

34. *My meat is to do the will*, &c.] Literally, *My food is* that I may do *the will of Him that sent Me and thus finish His work*. It is Christ's aim and purpose that is His food. Comp. v. 36, viii. 56. These words recall the reply to the tempter 'man doth not live by bread alone,' and the reply to His parents 'Wist ye not that I must be about my Father's business.' Luke iv. 4, ii. 49.

35. *Say not ye*] The pronoun is again emphatic.

There are yet four months, &c.] This cannot be a proverb. No such proverb is known; and a proverb on the subject would have to be differently shaped; e.g. 'From seedtime to harvest is four months,' or something of the kind. So that we may regard this saying as a mark of time. Harvest began in the middle of Nisan or April. Four months from that would place this event in the middle of December: or, if (as some suppose) this was a year in which an extra month was inserted, in the middle of January.

are white already to harvest] In the green blades just shewing through the soil the faith of the sower sees the white ears that will soon be there. So also in the flocking of these ignorant Samaritans to Him for instruction Christ sees the abundant harvest of souls that is

8—2

receiveth wages, and gathereth fruit unto life eternal: that both he that soweth and he that reapeth may rejoice together. And herein is *that* saying true, One soweth, and another reapeth. I sent you to reap *that* whereon ye bestowed no labour: other *men* laboured, and ye are entered into their labours. And many of the Samaritans of that

to follow. 'Already' is the last word in the Greek sentence; and from very ancient times there has been a doubt whether it belongs to this sentence or the next. Some of the best MSS. give 'already' to the next sentence; 'already he that reapeth receiveth wages.' But MS. authority in punctuation is not of much weight. The received punctuation is perhaps better; 'already' at the end of *v.* 35 being in emphatic contrast to 'yet' at the beginning of it.

36. *unto life eternal*] Another small change without reason (comp. xii. 25, xvii. 3). Our translators vary between 'eternal life,' 'life eternal,' 'everlasting life,' and 'life everlasting' (xii. 50). The Greek is in all cases the same, and should in all cases be translated 'eternal life.' See on iii. 16. Here '*into* eternal life' would perhaps be better: 'eternal life' is represented as the granary into which the fruit is gathered, not the future result of the gathering. See on *v.* 14. Comp. for similar imagery, 'The harvest truly is plenteous, but the labourers are few, &c.' Matt. ix. 37, 38.

that both] i.e. *In order that both:* shewing that this was God's purpose and intention.

he that soweth] Christ, not the Prophets. The Gospel is not the fruit of which the O.T. is the seed; rather the Gospel is the seed for which the O.T. prepared the ground.

he that reapeth] Christ's ministers.

37. *And herein is that saying true*] Rather, For *herein is the saying* (*proved*) *true*, i.e. is shewn to be the genuine proverb capable of realisation, not a mere empty phrase. 'True' is opposed to 'unreal' not to 'lying.' See on *v.* 23, i. 9 and vii. 28. 'Herein' refers to what precedes: comp. xv. 8 and 'by this' which represents the same Greek in xvi. 30.

38. *I sent you*, &c.] The pronouns are again emphatically opposed, as in *v.* 32.

other men] Christ, the Sower; but put in the plural to balance 'ye' in the next clause. In *v.* 37 both are put in the *singular* for the sake of harmony; 'One soweth' (Christ), 'another reapeth' (the disciples). All the verbs in this verse are perfects excepting 'sent;' *have not laboured, have laboured, have entered.*

39. *many of the Samaritans*] Strong proof of the truth of *v.* 35. These Samaritans outstrip the Jews, and even the Apostles, in their readiness to believe. The Jews rejected the testimony of their own Scriptures, of the Baptist, of Christ's miracles and teaching. The Samaritans accept the testimony of the woman, who had suddenly become an Apostle to her countrymen.

city believed on him for the saying of the woman, which testified, He told me all that ever I did. So when the 40 Samaritans were come unto him, they besought him that *he* would tarry with them: and he abode there two days. And many moe believed because of his own word; and 41 said unto the woman, *Now* we believe, not because of thy 42 saying: for we have heard *him* ourselves, and know that this is indeed the Christ, the Saviour of the world.

43—54. *The Work among Galileans.*

Now after two days he departed thence, and went into 43 Galilee. For Jesus himself testified, that a prophet hath no 44

40. *besought him*] Or, **kept beseeching** *Him*. How different from His own people at Nazareth; Matt. xiii. 58; Luke iv. 29. Comp. the thankful Samaritan leper, Luke xvii. 16, 17.

tarry with them] Better, **abide** *with them*. See on i. 33. They perhaps mean, take up His abode permanently with them, or at any rate for some time.

42. *thy saying*] Not the same word as in *v.* 39, the Greek for which is the same as that translated 'word' in *v.* 41. *Vv.* 39 and 41 should be alike, viz. 'word,' meaning 'statement' in *v.* 39 and 'teaching' in *v.* 41. Here we should have 'speech' or 'talk.' In classical Greek *lalia* has a slightly uncomplimentary turn, 'gossip, chatter.' But this shade of meaning is lost in later Greek, though there is *perhaps* a slight trace of it here; 'not because of *thy* talk;' but this being doubtful, 'speech' will be the safer translation. The whole should run, **no longer is it because of thy speech that we believe.** In viii. 43 *lalia* is used by Christ of His own words; see note there.

we have heard him ourselves] Better, *we have heard* **for** *ourselves.* There is no 'Him' in the Greek. 'The Christ' is also to be omitted. It is wanting in the best MSS.

the Saviour of the world] It is not improbable that such ready hearers would arrive at this great truth before the end of those two days. It is therefore unnecessary to suppose that S. John is here unconsciously giving one of his own expressions (1 John iv. 14) for theirs.

43—54. THE WORK AMONG GALILEANS.

43. *after two days*] Literally, *after* **the** *two days* mentioned in *v.* 40.

and went] These words are wanting in the best MSS.

44. *For Jesus himself testified*] This is a well-known difficulty. As in xx. 17, we have a reason assigned which seems to be the very opposite of what we should expect. This witness of Jesus would account for His *not* going into Galilee: how does it account for His going thither? It seems best to fall back on the old explanation of

45 honour in his own country. Then when he was come into Galilee, the Galileans received him, having seen all *the things* that he did at Jerusalem at the feast: for they also 46 went unto the feast. So Jesus came again into Cana of Galilee, where he made the water wine. And there was a certain nobleman, whose son was sick at Capernaum. 47 When he heard that Jesus was come out of Judea into Galilee, he went unto him, and besought him that he would come down, and heal his son: for he was at the point of 48 death. Then said Jesus unto him, Except ye see signs and 49 wonders, ye will not believe. The nobleman saith unto

Origen, that by 'his own country' is meant Judaea, 'the home of the Prophets.' Moreover, Judaea fits in with the circumstances. He had not only met with little honour in Judaea; He had been forced to retreat from it. No Apostle had been found there. The appeal to Judaea had in the main been a failure.

45. *all the things that he did*] Of these we have a passing notice ii. 23. 'The Feast' means the Passover, but there is no need to name it, because it has already been named, ii. 23.

46. *where he made the water wine*] and therefore would be likely to find a favourable hearing. For 'So Jesus came' read **He** *came* **therefore**. See on vi. 14.

nobleman] Literally, *king's man*, i.e. **officer in the service of the king**, Herod Antipas; but whether in a civil or military office, there is nothing to shew. 'Nobleman' is, therefore, not at all accurate: the word has nothing to do with birth. It has been conjectured that this official was Chuza (Luke viii. 3), or Manaen (Acts xiii. 1).

47. *that he would come down*] Literally, **in order that he might** *come down*; comp. v. 34, v. 7, 36, vi. 29, 50.

at Capernaum] 20 miles or more from Cana.

48. *signs and wonders*] Christ's miracles are never mere 'wonders' to excite astonishment; they are 'signs' of heavenly truths as well, and this is their primary characteristic. Where these two words are joined together 'signs' always precedes, excepting four passages in the Acts, where we have 'wonders and signs.' This is the only passage in which S. John uses 'wonders' at all. In ii. 11 the word translated 'miracles' is the same as the one here translated 'signs.' See below, v. 54.

ye will not believe] In marked contrast to the ready belief of the Samaritans. The form of negation in the Greek is of the strong kind; *ye will in no wise believe*. See note on 1 Cor. i. 22. Faith based on miracles is of a low type comparatively, but Christ does not reject it. Comp. x. 38, xiv. 11, xx. 29. This man's faith is strengthened by being put to test. The words are evidently addressed to him and those about him, and they imply that those addressed are Jews.

him, Sir, come down ere my child die. Jesus saith unto 50 him, Go *thy way;* thy son liveth. And the man believed the word that Jesus had spoken unto him, and he went *his way.* And as he was now going down, his servants met 51 him, and told *him,* saying, Thy son liveth. Then inquired 52 he of them the hour when he began to amend. And they said unto him, Yesterday at the seventh hour the fever left him. So the father knew that *it was* at the same hour, in 53 the which Jesus said unto him, Thy son liveth: and himself believed, and his whole house. This *is* again the second 54

49. *ere my child die*] This shews both the man's faith and its weakness. He believes that Christ's presence can save the child; he does not believe that He can save him without being present.

50. *the man believed*] The father's faith is healed at the same time as the son's body.

had spoken] Better, **spake**; aorist, not pluperfect.

52. *began to amend*] Or, **was somewhat better**; a colloquial expression. The father fancies that the cure will be gradual. The fever will depart at Christ's word, but will depart in the ordinary way. He has not yet fully realised Christ's power. The reply of the servants shews that the cure was instantaneous.

Yesterday at the seventh hour] Once more we have to discuss S. John's method of counting the hours of the day. (See on i. 39 and iv. 6.) Obviously the father set out as soon after Jesus said 'thy son liveth' as possible; he had 20 or 25 miles to go to reach home, and he would not be likely to loiter on the way. 7 A.M. is incredible; he would have been home long before nightfall, and the servants met him some distance from home. 7 P.M. is improbable; the servants would meet him before midnight. Thus the modern method of reckoning from midnight to midnight does not suit. Adopting the Jewish method from sunset to sunset, the seventh hour is 1 P.M. He would scarcely start at once in the mid-day heat; nor would the servants. Supposing they met him after sunset, they might speak of 1 P.M. as 'yesterday.' (But see on xx. 19, where S. John speaks of the late hours of the evening as belonging to the day *before* sunset.) Still, 7 P.M. is not impossible, and this third instance must be regarded as not decisive. But the balance here seems to incline to what is antecedently more probable, that S. John reckons the hours, like the rest of the Evangelists, according to the Jewish method.

53. *himself believed*] This is the last stage in the growth of the man's faith, a growth which S. John sketches for us here as in the case of the Samaritan woman. In both cases the spiritual development is thoroughly natural, as also is the incidental way in which S. John places it before us.

and his whole house] The first converted family.

54. *This is again the second,* &c.] Rather, *This again as a second* miracle *that* Jesus did, when he was come out of Judea into Galilee.

miracle (or *sign*) *did Jesus, after He had come out of Judaea into Galilee.* Both first and second had similar results: the first confirmed the faith of the disciples, the second that of this official.

The question whether this foregoing narrative is a discordant account of the healing of the centurion's servant (Matt. viii. 5; Luke vii. 2) has been discussed from very early times, for Origen and Chrysostom contend against it. Irenaeus seems to be in favour of the identification, but we cannot be sure that he is. He says, 'He healed the son of the centurion though absent with a word, saying, Go, thy son liveth.' Irenaeus may have supposed that this official was a centurion, or 'centurion' may be a slip. Eight very marked points of difference between the two narratives have been noted. Together they amount to something like proof that the two narratives cannot refer to one and the same fact, unless we are to attribute an astonishing amount of carelessness or misinformation either to the Synoptists or to S. John.

(1) Here a 'king's man' pleads for his son; there a centurion for his servant.

(2) Here he pleads in person; there the Jewish elders plead for him.

(3) Here the father is probably a Jew; there the centurion is certainly a Gentile.

(4) Here the healing words are spoken at Cana; there at Capernaum.

(5) Here the malady is fever; there paralysis.

(6) Here the father wishes Jesus to come; there the centurion begs him not to come.

(7) Here Christ does not go; there apparently he does.

(8) Here the father has weak faith and is blamed (*v.* 48); there the centurion has strong faith and is commended.

And what difficulty is there in supposing two somewhat similar miracles? Christ's miracles were 'signs;' they were vehicles for conveying the spiritual truths which Christ came to teach. If, as is almost certain, He often repeated the same instructive sayings, may He not sometimes have repeated the same instructive acts? Here, therefore, as in the case of the cleansing of the Temple (ii. 13—17), it seems wisest to believe that S. John and the Synoptists record different events.

CHAPS. V.—XI. THE WORK AMONG MIXED MULTITUDES, CHIEFLY JEWS.

The Work now becomes a CONFLICT between Christ and "the Jews;" for as Christ reveals Himself more fully, the opposition between Him and the ruling party becomes more intense; and the fuller revelation which excites the hatred of His opponents serves also to sift the disciples; some turn back, others are strengthened in their faith by what they see and hear. The Evangelist from time to time points out the

CHAPS. V.—XI. *The Work among mixed multitudes, chiefly Jews.*

CHAP. V. *Christ the Source of Life.*

1—9. *The Sign at the Pool of Bethesda.*

After this there was a feast of the Jews; and Jesus went 5

opposite results of Christ's work: comp. vi. 60—71, vii. 40—52, ix. 13—41, x. 19, 21, 39—42, xi. 45—57.

Thus far we have had the announcement of the Gospel to the world, and the reception it is destined to meet with, set forth in four typical instances; *Nathanael*, the guileless Israelite, truly religious according to the light allowed him; *Nicodemus*, the learned ecclesiastic, skilled in the Scriptures, but ignorant of the first elements of religion; the *Samaritan woman*, immoral in life and schismatical in religion, but simple in heart and readily convinced; and the *royal official*, weak in faith, but progressing gradually to a full conviction. But as yet there is little evidence of hostility to Christ, although the Evangelist prepares us for it (i. 11, ii. 18—20, iii. 18, 19, 26, iv. 44). Henceforth, however, hostility to Him is manifested in every chapter of this division. Two elements are placed in the sharpest contrast throughout; the Messiah's clearer manifestation of His Person and Work, and the growing animosity of 'the Jews' in consequence of it. Two miracles form the introduction to two great discourses: two miracles illustrate two discourses. The healing at Bethesda and the feeding of the 5000 lead to discourses in which Christ is set forth as *the Source and the Support of Life* (v., vi.). Then He is set forth as *the Source of Truth and Light;* and this is illustrated by His giving physical and spiritual sight to the blind (vii.—ix.). Finally He is set forth as *Love* under the figure of the Good Shepherd giving His life for the sheep; and this is illustrated by the raising of Lazarus, a work of love which costs Him His life (x., xi.). Thus, of four typical miracles, two form the introduction and two form the sequel to great discourses. The prevailing idea throughout is truth and love provoking contradiction and enmity.

CHAP. V. CHRIST THE SOURCE OF LIFE.

In chaps. v. and vi. the word 'life' occurs 18 times; in the rest of the Gospel 18 times.

This chapter falls into two main divisions; (1) *The Sign at the Pool of Bethesda and its Sequel* (1—16); (2) *The Discourse on the Son as the Source of Life* (17—47).

1—9. THE SIGN AT THE POOL OF BETHESDA.

1. *After this*] Better, *After* **these things**, a more indefinite sequence.

a feast of the Jews] This is the reading of highest authority, although some important MSS. read '*the* feast of the Jews,' probably because from very early times this feast was believed to be the Passover.

² up to Jerusalem. Now there is at Jerusalem by the sheep *market* a pool, which is called in the Hebrew tongue Be-
³ thesda, having five porches. In these lay a great multitude

If '*a* feast' is the true reading, this alone is almost conclusive against its being the Passover; S. John would not call the Passover 'a feast of the Jews.' Moreover in all other cases where he mentions Passovers he lets us know that they are Passovers and not simply feasts, ii. 13, vi. 4, xi. 55, &c. He gives us three Passovers; to make this a fourth would be to put an extra year into our Lord's ministry for which scarcely any events can be found, and of which there is no trace elsewhere. Almost every other feast, and even the Day of Atonement, have been suggested; but the only one which fits in satisfactorily is Purim. We saw from iv. 35 that the two days in Samaria were either in December or January. The next certain date is vi. 4, the eve of the Passover, i.e. April. Purim, which was celebrated in March (14th and 15th Adar), falls just in the right place in the interval. This feast commemorated the deliverance of the Jews from Haman, and took its name from the *lots* which he caused to be cast (Esther iii. 7, ix. 24, 26, 28). It was a boisterous feast, and some have thought it unlikely that Christ would have anything to do with it. But we are not told that He went to Jerusalem *in order to keep the feast*; Purim might be kept anywhere. More probably He went because the multitudes at the feast would afford great opportunities for teaching. Moreover, it does not follow that because some made this feast a scene of unseemly jollity, therefore Christ would discountenance the feast itself.

2. *there is at Jerusalem*] This is no evidence whatever that the Gospel was written before the destruction of Jerusalem. The pool would still exist, even if the building was destroyed; and such a building, as being of the nature of a hospital, would be likely to be spared. Even if all were destroyed the present tense would be natural here. See on xi. 18.

by the sheep market] There is no 'market' in the Greek, and no reason for supposing that it ought to be supplied. The margin is probably right: *sheep*-gate. We know from Neh. iii. 1, 32, xii. 39 that there was a sheep-gate; so called probably from sheep for sacrifice being sold there. It was near the Temple. The adjective for 'sheep-' occurs nowhere else in N.T. but here, and nowhere in O.T. but in the passages in Nehemiah. But so little is known of this gate, and the ellipsis of 'gate' is so unparalleled that we cannot regard this explanation as certain. Another translation is possible, with a change of case in the word for pool; *Now there is in Jerusalem, by the sheep-pool, a place called in the Hebrew tongue Bethesda.*

in the Hebrew tongue] 'Hebrew' means Aramaic, the language spoken at the time, not the old Hebrew of the Scriptures. See on xx. 16.

Bethesda] 'House of mercy,' or possibly 'House of the Portico,' or again 'of the Olive.' The name Bethesda does not occur elsewhere.

of impotent *folk*, of blind, halt, withered, waiting for the moving of the water. For an angel went down at a *certain* 4 season into the pool, and troubled the water: whosoever then first after the troubling of the water stepped in, was made whole of whatsoever disease he had. And a certain 5 man was there, which had an infirmity thirty *and* eight years. When Jesus saw him lie, and knew that he had 6 been now a long time *in that case*, he saith unto him, Wilt thou be made whole? The impotent *man* answered him, 7

The traditional identification with *Birket Israel* is not commonly advocated now. The 'Fountain of the Virgin' is an attractive identification, as the water is intermittent to this day. This fountain is connected with the pool of Siloam, and some think that Siloam is Bethesda. That S. John speaks of Bethesda here and Siloam in ix. 7, is not conclusive against this: for Bethesda might be the name of the building and Siloam of the pool; and the Greek for 'called' here is strictly 'called *in addition*' or '*sur*named,' as if the place had some other name.

five porches] Or, *colonnades*. These would be to shelter the sick. The place seems to have been a kind of charitable institution.

3. *lay a great multitude*] Better, **were lying a multitude**.

blind, halt, withered] These are the special kinds of 'impotent folk.'

waiting for the moving of the water] These words and the whole of *v.* 4 are almost certainly an interpolation, though a very ancient one. They are omitted by the best MSS. Other important MSS. omit *v.* 4 or mark it as suspicious. Moreover, those MSS. which contain the passage vary very much. The passage is one more likely to be inserted without authority than to be omitted if genuine; and very probably it represents the popular belief with regard to the intermittent bubbling of the healing water, first added as a gloss, and then inserted into the text. The water was probably mineral in its elements, and the people may or may not have been right in supposing that it was most efficacious when the spring was most violent.

5. *which had an infirmity*, &c.] Literally, *who had passed thirty-eight years in his infirmity*. Not that he was 38 years old; evidently he was more; but he had had this malady 38 years.

6. *knew*] Or, **perceived**, perhaps supernaturally (see on xvi. 19), but He might learn it from the bystanders: the fact was very likely notorious.

Wilt thou?] Or, more strongly, **Dost thou will?** Note that the man does not ask first. Here and in the case of the man born blind (ix.), as also of Malchus' ear (Luke xxii. 51), Christ heals without being asked to do so. Excepting the healing of the royal official's son all Christ's miracles in the Fourth Gospel are spontaneous. On no other occasion does Christ ask a question without being addressed first: why does He now ask a question of which the answer was so obvious?

Sir, I have no man, when the water is troubled, to put me into the pool: but while I am coming, another steppeth 8 down before me. Jesus saith unto him, Rise, take up 9 thy bed, and walk. And immediately the man was made whole, and took up his bed, and walked: and on the same day was the sabbath.

10—16. *The Sequel of the Sign.*

10 The Jews therefore said unto him that was cured, It is the sabbath day: it is not lawful for thee to carry *thy* 11 bed. He answered them, He that made me whole, the

Probably in order to rouse the sick man out of his lethargy and despondency. It was the first step towards the man's having sufficient faith: he must be inspired with some expectation of being cured. The question has nothing to do with religious scruples; 'Art thou willing to be made whole, although it is the Sabbath?'

7. *I have no man*] He is not only sick but friendless.

is troubled] No doubt this took place at irregular intervals, else there would be no need to wait and watch for it.

to put me into the pool] Literally, **in order to** (iv. 47) **throw** *me into the pool;* perhaps implying that the gush of water did not last long and there was no time to be lost in quiet carrying. But in this late Greek *ballein* (=throw) has become weakened in meaning. Comp. xiii. 2, xx. 25.

while I am coming] Unaided, and therefore slowly.

another steppeth down] This seems to shew that the place where the bubbling appeared was not large. He does not say 'others step down before me:' one is hindrance enough.

8. *Rise, take up thy bed*] As in the case of the paralytic (Mark ii. 9), Christ makes no enquiry as to the man's faith. Christ knew that he had faith; and the man's attempting to rise and carry his bed after 38 years of impotency was an open confession of faith. His bed would probably be only a mat or rug, still common in the East.

It is scarcely necessary to discuss whether this miracle can be identical with the healing of the paralytic let down through the roof (Matt. ix.; Mark ii.; Luke v.). Time, place, details and context are all different, especially the important point that this miracle was wrought on the Sabbath.

10—16. THE SEQUEL OF THE SIGN.

10. *The Jews*] The hostile party, as usual: probably members of the Sanhedrin (see on i. 19). They ignore the cure and notice only what can be attacked. They had the letter of the law very strongly on their side. Comp. Exod. xxiii. 12, xxxi. 14, xxxv. 2, 3; Num. xv. 32; Neh. xiii. 15; and especially Jer. xvii. 21.

11. *He that made me whole*] The man's defiance of them in the

same said unto me, Take up thy bed, and walk. Then 12
asked they him, What man is that which said unto thee,
Take up thy bed, and walk? And he that was healed 13
wist not who it was: for Jesus had conveyed himself away,
a multitude being in *that* place. Afterward Jesus findeth 14
him in the temple, and said unto him, Behold, thou art
made whole: sin no more, lest a worse *thing* come unto

first flush of his recovered health is very natural. He means, 'if He
could cure me of a sickness of 38 years He had authority to tell me to
take up my bed.' They will not mention the cure; he flings it in their
face. There is a higher law than that of the Sabbath, and higher
authority than theirs. Comp. the conduct of the blind man, chap. ix.

the same said unto me] Better, '**He** *said to me*,' 'He' being emphatic: see on x. 1.

12. *What man is that which*] Better, **Who is the man that**, 'man' being contemptuous, almost = 'fellow.' Once more they ignore the miracle, and attack the command. They ask not, 'Who cured thee, and therefore must have Divine authority?' but, 'Who told thee to break the Sabbath, and therefore could not have it?' Christ's command was perhaps aimed at these erroneous views about the Sabbath.

13. *had conveyed himself away*] Better, **withdrew**. Originally the word signified 'to stoop out of the way of,' 'to bend down as if to avoid a blow.' Here only in N.T. The word might also mean, '*swam out of*,' which would be a graphic expression for making one's way through a crowd.

a multitude being in that place] This is ambiguous. It may explain either *why* Jesus withdrew, viz. to avoid the crowd, or *how* he withdrew, viz. by disappearing among the crowd. Both make good sense.

14. *Afterward*] Literally, *after* **these things**, as in *v.* 1. Probably the same day; we may suppose that one of his first acts after his cure would be to offer his thanks in the Temple. On *vv.* 13 and 14 Augustine writes, 'It is difficult in a crowd to see Christ; a certain solitude is necessary for our mind; it is by a certain solitude of contemplation that God is seen......He did not see Jesus in the crowd, he saw Him in the Temple. The Lord Jesus indeed saw him both in the crowd and in the Temple. The impotent man, however, does not know Jesus in the crowd; but he knows Him in the Temple.'

sin no more] Or perhaps, **continue no longer in sin.** Comp. [viii. 11,] xx. 17. The man's conscience would tell him what sin. Comp. [viii. 7]. What follows shews plainly not merely that physical suffering in the aggregate is the result of sin in the aggregate, but that this man's 38 years of sickness were the result of his own sin. This was known to Christ's heart-searching eye (ii. 24, 25), but it is a conclusion which we may not draw without the clearest evidence in any given case. Suffering serves other ends than being a punishment for sin: 'whom the Lord loveth He chasteneth;' and comp. ix. 3.

a worse thing] Not necessarily hell: even in this life there might be

15 thee. The man departed, and told the Jews that it was Jesus, which had made him whole.

16 And therefore did the Jews persecute Jesus, and sought to slay him, because he had done these *things* on the sabbath day.

17—47. *The Discourse on the Son as the Source of Life.*

17 But Jesus answered them, My Father worketh hitherto,

a worse thing than the sickness which had consumed more than half man's threescore and ten. So terrible are God's judgments; so awful is our responsibity. Comp. Matt. xii. 45; 2 Pet. ii. 20.

15. *told the Jews*] Not in malice against Jesus, nor in any hope of converting His opponents. Neither of these is probable, nor is there the least evidence of either. Rather, he continues his defiance of them (*v.* 11). He had given as his authority for breaking the Sabbath 'He that made me whole.' Having found out that it was the famous teacher from Galilee, he returns to give them this additional proof of authority.

16. *And therefore*] Better, *And on this account*, or, *and* for this cause (xii. 18, 27). It is not St John's favourite particle 'therefore,' but a preposition and pronoun. Comp. *v.* 18.

and sought to slay him] These words are not genuine here, but have been inserted from *v.* 18. The other two verbs are both in the imperfect tense expressing continued action; 'used to persecute, continued to persecute;' 'used to do, habitually did.' From which we may infer that some of the unrecorded miracles (ii. 23, iv. 45) were wrought on the Sabbath: unless the Evangelist is speaking from their point of view; 'because (as they said) He habitually did these things on the Sabbath.'

17—47. THE DISCOURSE ON THE SON AS THE SOURCE OF LIFE.

17. *answered them*] This was how He met their constant persecution. The discourse which follows (see introductory note to chap. iii.) may be thus analysed. (S. p. 106.) It has two main divisions—I. *The prerogatives of the Son of God* (17—30). II. *The unbelief of the Jews* (31—47). These two are subdivided as follows: I. 1. Defence of healing on the Sabbath based on the relation of the Son to the Father (17, 18). 2. Intimacy of the Son with the Father further enforced (19, 20). 3. This intimacy proved by the twofold power committed to the Son (*a*) of communicating spiritual life (21—27), (*b*) of raising the dead (28, 29). 4. The Son's qualification for these high powers is the perfect harmony of His Will with that of the Father (30). II. 1. The Son's claims rest not on His testimony alone, nor on that of John, but on that of the Father (31—35). 2. The Father's testimony is evident (*a*) in the works assigned to the Son (36), (*b*) in the revelation which the Jews reject (37—40). 3. Not that the Son needs honour from men, who are too worldly to receive Him (41—44). 4. Their appeal to Moses is vain; his writings condemn them.

17—30. *The Prerogatives and Powers of the Son of God.*
and I work. Therefore the Jews sought the more to kill him, because he not only had broken the sabbath, but said also that God was his Father, making himself equal with God. Then answered Jesus and said unto them, Verily, verily, I say unto you, The Son can do nothing of himself, but what he seeth the Father do: for

17—30. THE PREROGATIVES AND POWERS OF THE SON OF GOD.

17, 18. *Defence of healing on the Sabbath based on the relation of the Son to the Father.*

My Father worketh hitherto, &c.] Or, **My Father is working even until now; I am working also.** From the Creation up to this moment God has been ceaselessly working for man's salvation. From such activity there is no rest, no Sabbath: for mere cessation from activity is not of the essence of the Sabbath; and to cease to do good is not to keep the Sabbath but to sin. Sabbaths have never hindered the Father's work; they must not hinder the Son's. Elsewhere (Mark ii. 27) Christ says that the Sabbath is a blessing not a burden; it was made for man, not man for it. Here He takes far higher ground for Himself. He is equal to the Father, and does what the Father does. Mark ii. 28 helps to connect the two positions. If the Sabbath is subject to man, much more to the Son of Man, who is equal to the Father.

18. *Therefore*] Better, **For this cause.** See on *v.* 16, vi. 65, vii. 21, 22, viii. 47, ix. 23, x. 17, xii. 39, xiii. 11, xv. 19, xvi. 15.

the more] Shewing that the persecution spoken of in *v.* 16 included attempts to compass His death. Comp. Mark iii. 6. This 'seeking to kill' is the blood-red thread which runs through the whole of this section of the Gospel: comp. vii. 1, 19, 25, viii. 37, 40, 59, x. 31, xi. 53, xii. 10.

had broken] Literally, *was loosing* or *relaxing;* i.e. making less binding. As in *v.* 15, the A.V. puts pluperfect for imperfect.

making himself equal] They fully understand the force of the parallel statements, 'My Father is working; I am working also.' 'Behold,' says Augustine, 'the Jews understand what the Arians fail to understand.' If Arian or Unitarian views were right, would not Christ at once have explained that what they imputed to Him as blasphemy was not in His mind at all? But instead of explaining that He by no means claims equality with the Father, He goes on to reaffirm this equality from other points of view: see especially *v.* 23.

19, 20. *Intimacy of the Son with the Father further enforced.*

19. *can do nothing of himself*] It is impossible for Him to act with individual self-assertion independent of God, because He is the Son: Their Will and working are one. The Jews accuse Him of blasphemy; and blasphemy implies opposition to God: but He and the Father are most intimately united.

what *things* soever he doeth, these also doeth the Son
20 likewise. For the Father loveth the Son, and sheweth
him all *things* that himself doeth: and he will shew him
21 greater works than these, that ye may marvel. For as the
Father raiseth up the dead, and quickeneth *them;* even so
22 the Son quickeneth whom he will. For the Father judgeth

but what he seeth, &c.] Better, **unless He seeth the Father doing it.**
20. *For the Father loveth the Son*] Moral necessity for the Son's doing what the Father does. The Father's love for the Son compels Him to make known all His works to Him; the Son's relation to the Father compels Him to do what the Father does. The Son continues on earth what He had seen in heaven before the Incarnation.

he will shew him, &c.] Or, **Greater works than these will He shew Him.** 'The Father will give the Son an example of greater works than these healings, the Son will do the like, and ye unbelievers will be shamed into admiration.' He does not say that they will believe. 'Works' is a favourite term with S. John to express the details of Christ's work of redemption. Comp. *v.* 36, ix. 4, x. 25, 32, 37, xiv. 11, 12, xv. 24.

21—29. *The intimacy of the Son with the Father proved by the twofold power committed to the Son* (a) *of communicating spiritual life,* (b) *of causing the bodily resurrection of the dead.*

21—27. The Father imparts to the Son the power of raising the spiritually dead. It is very important to notice that 'raising the dead' in this section is *figurative;* raising from moral and spiritual death: whereas the resurrection (*vv.* 28, 29) is *literal;* the rising of dead bodies from the graves. It is impossible to take both sections in one and the same sense, either figurative or literal. The wording of *v.* 28 and still more of *v.* 29 is quite conclusive against spiritual resurrection being meant there: what in that case could 'the resurrection of damnation' mean? Verses 24 and 25 are equally conclusive against a bodily resurrection being meant here: what in that case can 'an hour is coming, *and now is*' mean?

21. *raiseth up the dead*] This is one of the 'greater works' which the Father sheweth the Son, and which the Son imitates, the raising up those who are spiritually dead. Not all of them: the Son imparts life only to 'whom He will:' and He wills not to impart it to those who will not believe. The 'whom He will' would be almost unintelligible if actual resurrection from the grave were intended.

22. *For the Father judgeth no man*] Rather, *For* **not even doth the Father** (to Whom judgment belongs) **judge any** *man.* The Son therefore has both powers, to make alive whom He will, and to judge: but the second is only the corollary of first. Those whom He does not will to make alive are by that very fact judged, separated off from the living, and left in the death which they have chosen. He does not make them dead, does not slay them. They are spiritually dead already, and will

no *man*, but hath committed all judgment unto the Son: that all *men* should honour the Son, even as they honour 23 the Father. He that honoureth not the Son honoureth not the Father which hath sent him. Verily, verily, I say unto 24 you, He that heareth my word, and believeth on him that sent me, hath everlasting life, and shall not come into condemnation; but is passed from death unto life. Verily, 25 verily, I say unto you, The hour is coming, and now is, when the dead shall hear the voice of the Son of God: and

not be made alive. Here, as in iii. 17, 18, the judgment is one of condemnation; but this comes from the context, not from the word.

hath committed] Or, **given**; there is no reason for varying the common rendering.

23. *honoureth not the Father*] Because he refuses to honour the Father's representative.

which hath sent] Better, *which* **sent**. See on xx. 21.

24. *He that heareth*] We see from this that 'whom He will' (*v.* 21) implies no arbitrary selection. It is each individual who decides for himself whether he will hear and believe.

believeth on him that sent me] Omit 'on;' there is no preposition in the Greek.

hath everlasting life] Or, *hath* **eternal** *life*: see on iii. 16. Note the tense; he hath it already, it is not a reward to be bestowed hereafter: see on iii. 36.

shall not come into condemnation] Better, **cometh not into judgment**.

is passed from death into life] Or, *is passed* **over out of** *death* **into** *life* (comp. xiii. 1; 1 John iii. 14). This is evidently equivalent to escaping judgment and attaining eternal life, clearly shewing that death is spiritual death, and the resurrection from it spiritual also. This cannot refer to the resurrection of the body.

25. Repetition of *v.* 24 in a more definite form, with a cheering addition: *v.* 24 says that whoever hears and believes God has eternal life; *v.* 25 states that already some are in this happy case.

The hour is coming] Better, **There cometh an hour**: comp. iv. 21, 23.

and now is] These words also exclude the meaning of a *bodily* resurrection; the hour for which had not yet arrived. The few cases in which Christ raised the dead cannot be meant; (1) the statement evidently has a much wider range; (2) the widow's son, Jairus' daughter, and Lazarus were not yet dead, so that even of them 'and *now is*' would not be true; (3) they died again after their return from death, and 'they that hear shall live' clearly refers to *eternal* life, as a comparison with *v.* 24 shews. If a *spiritual* resurrection be understood, 'and now is' is perfectly intelligible: Christ's ministry was already winning souls from spiritual death.

26 they that hear shall live. For as the Father hath life in himself; so hath he given to the Son to have life in himself; 27 and hath given him authority to execute judgment also, 28 because he is the Son of man. Marvel not at this: for the

> **26.** *so hath he given to the Son*] Better, *so* **gave He also** *to the Son*. Comp. 'the living Father hath sent Me, and I live by the Father' (vi. 57). The Father is the absolutely living One, the Fount of all Life. The Messiah, however, imparts life to all who believe; which He could not do unless He had in Himself a fountain of life; and this the Father *gave* Him when He sent Him into the world. The Eternal Generation of the Son from the Father is not here in question; it is the Father's communication of Divine attributes to the Incarnate Word that is meant.
>
> **27.** *Hath given him authority to execute judgment also*] Better, **gave** *Him authority to execute judgment*, when He sent Him into the world. 'Also' is not genuine. See on i. 12, and comp. x. 18.
>
> *because he is the Son of man*] Rather, *because He is* **a son of man**; i.e. not because He is the Messiah, but because He is a human being. In the Greek neither 'son' nor 'man' has the article. Where 'the Son of Man,' i.e. the Messiah, is meant, both words have the article: comp. i. 51, iii. 13, 14, vi. 27, 53, 62, viii. 28, &c. Because the Son emptied Himself of all His glory and became a man, therefore the Father endowed Him with these two powers; to have life in Himself, and to execute judgment.
>
> Before passing on to the last section of this half of the discourse we may remark that "the relation of the Son to the Father is seldom alluded to in the Synoptic Gospels. But a single verse in which it is, seems to contain the essence of the Johannean theology, Matt. xi. 27: 'All things are delivered unto Me of My Father; and no man knoweth the Son but the Father; neither knoweth any man the Father, save the Son, and he to whomsoever the Son will reveal Him.' This passage is one of the best authenticated in the Synoptic Gospels. It is found in exact parallelism both in S. Matthew and S. Luke...... And yet once grant the authenticity of this passage, and there is nothing in the Johannean Christology that it does not cover." S. p. 109. The theory, therefore, that this discourse is the composition of the Evangelist, who puts forward his own theology as the teaching of Christ, has no basis. If the passage in S. Matthew and S. Luke represents the teaching of Christ, what reason have we for doubting that this discourse does so? To invent the substance of it was beyond the reach even of S. John; how far the precise wording is his we cannot tell. This section of it (21—27) bears very strong impress of his style.
>
> **28, 29.** The intimacy between the Father and the Son further proved by the power committed to the Son of causing the bodily resurrection of the dead.
>
> **28.** *Marvel not*] Comp. iii. 7. Marvel not that the Son can grant spiritual life to them that believe, and separate from them those who will

hour is coming, in the which all that are in the graves shall hear his voice, and shall come forth; they that have done 29 good, unto the resurrection of life; and they that have done evil, unto the resurrection of damnation. I can of mine 30 own self do nothing: as I hear, I judge: and my judgment is just; because I seek not mine own will, but the will of the Father which hath sent me.

31—47. *The unbelief of the Jews.*

If I bear witness of myself, my witness is not true. 31

not believe. There cometh an hour when He shall cause a general resurrection of men's bodies, and a final separation of good from bad, a final judgment. He does not add 'and now is,' which is in favour of the resurrection being *literal*.

all that are in the graves] Not 'whom He will;' there are none whom He does not will to come forth from their **sepulchres** (see on xi. 7). All, whether believers or not, must rise. This shews that spiritual resurrection cannot be meant.

29. *done evil*] Or, **practised worthless things.** See on iii. 20.

unto the resurrection of damnation] Better, *unto the resurrection of* **judgment.** It is the same Greek word as is used in *vv.* 22, 27. These words are the strongest proof that spiritual resurrection cannot be meant. Spiritual resurrection must always be a resurrection of life, a passing from spiritual death to spiritual life. A passing from spiritual death to *judgment* is not spiritual resurrection. This passage, and Acts xxiv. 15, are the only *direct* assertions in N.T. of a bodily resurrection of the wicked. It is implied, Matt. x. 28; Rev. xx. 12, 13. A satisfactory translation for the Greek words meaning 'judge' and 'judgment' cannot be found: they combine the notions of 'separating' and 'judging,' and from the context often acquire the further notion of 'condemning.' See on iii. 17, 18.

30. *The Son's qualification for these high powers is the perfect harmony between His Will and that of the Father.*

I can of mine own self] Change to the first person. He identifies Himself with the Son. It is because He is the Son that He cannot act independently: it is impossible for Him to will to do anything but what the Father wills.

as I hear] From the Father: Christ's judgment is the declaration of that which the Father communicates to Him. And hence Christ's judgment must be just, for it is in accordance with the Divine Will; and this is the strongest possible guarantee of its justice. Comp. Matt. xxvi. 39.

31—47. THE UNBELIEF OF THE JEWS.

31—35. *These claims rest not on My testimony alone, nor on that of John, but on that of the Father.*

31. *my witness is not true*] Nothing is to be understood; the words

32 There is another that beareth witness of me; and I know that the witness which he witnesseth of me is
33 true. Ye sent unto John, and he bare witness unto the
34 truth. But I receive not testimony from man: but these
35 *things* I say, that ye might be saved. He was a burning and a shining light: and ye were willing for a season
36 to rejoice in his light. But I have greater witness than

are to be taken quite literally: 'If I bear any witness other than that which My Father bears, that witness of Mine is not true.' In viii. 14 we have an apparent contradiction to this, but it is only the other side of the same truth: 'My witness is true because it is really My Father's.'

32. *There is another*] Not the Baptist, as seems clear from *v.* 34; but the Father, comp. vii. 28, viii. 26. It has been already remarked how much there is in this Gospel about 'witness,' 'bearing witness,' and the like: see on i. 7.

33. *Ye sent unto John, and he bare witness*] Better, *Ye* **have sent** *unto John, and he* **hath borne** *witness*. 'What ye have heard from him is true; but I do not accept it, for I need not the testimony of man. I mention it for your sakes, not My own. If ye believe John ye will believe Me and be saved.' 'Ye' and 'I' in these two verses (33, 34) are in emphatic opposition.

35. *He was a burning and a shining light*] A grievous mistranslation, ignoring the Greek article twice over, and also the meaning of the words; and thus obscuring the marked difference between the Baptist and the Messiah: better, *he was* **the lamp which is kindled and (so) shineth**. Christ is the Light; John is only the lamp kindled at the Light, and shining only after being so kindled, having no light but what is derived. The word here, and Matt. vi. 22, translated 'light,' is translated 'candle' Matt. v. 15; Mark iv. 21; Luke viii. 16, xi. 33, 36, xv. 8; Rev. xviii. 23, xxii. 5. 'Lamp' would be best in all places. No O. T. prophecy speaks of the Baptist under this figure. David is so called 2 Sam. xxi. 17 (see margin), and Elijah (Ecclus. xlviii. 1). The imperfects in this verse seem to imply that John's career is closed; he is in prison, if not dead.

were willing for a season] Like children, they were glad to disport themselves in the blaze, instead of seriously considering its meaning. And even that only for a season: their pilgrimages to the banks of the Jordan had soon ended; when John began to preach repentance they left him, sated with the novelty and offended at his doctrine.—For another charge of frivolity and fickleness against them in reference to John comp. Matt. xi. 16—19.

36—40. *The Father's testimony is evident*, (a) *in the works assigned to Me*, (b) *in the revelation which ye do not receive*.

36. *I have greater witness than that of John*] Better, *I have* **the**

that of John: for the works which the Father hath given me to finish, the same works that I do, bear witness of me, that the Father hath sent me. And the Father 37 himself, which hath sent me, hath borne witness of me. Ye have neither heard his voice at any time, nor seen his shape. And ye have not his word abiding in you: for 38

witness which is greater than John; or, the witness which I have is greater than John, viz. the works which as the Messiah I have been commissioned to do. Among these works would be raising the spiritually dead to life, judging unbelievers, as well as miracles: certainly not miracles only; iv. 48, x. 38.

to finish] Literally, **in order that I may accomplish**; comp. xvii. 4. This was God's purpose. See on iv. 34, 47, ix. 3. S. John is very fond of the construction 'in order that,' especially of the Divine purpose.

37—40. The connexion of thought in the next few verses is very difficult to catch, and cannot be affirmed with certainty. This is often the case in S. John's writings. A number of simple sentences follow one another with an even flow; but it is by no means easy to see how each leads on to the next. Here there is a transition from the *indirect* testimony to the Messiahship of Jesus given by the *works* which He is commissioned to do (*v.* 36), to the *direct* testimony to the same given by the *words* of Scripture (37—40). The Jews were rejecting both.

which hath sent me, hath borne witness] There is a difference of tense in the Greek which should be retained: *the Father* **which sent** *Me* (once for all at the Incarnation) **He** *hath borne witness* (for a long time past, and is still doing so) *of Me*.

Ye have neither, &c.] These words are a *reproach;* therefore there can be no allusion (as suggested in the margin) to the Baptism or the Transfiguration. The Transfiguration had not yet taken place, and very few if any of Christ's hearers could have heard the voice from heaven at the Baptism. Moreover, if that particular utterance were meant, 'voice' in the Greek would have had the article. Nor can there be any reference to the theophanies, or symbolical visions of God, in O.T. It could be no matter of *reproach* to these Jews that they had never beheld a theophany. A paraphrase will shew the meaning; 'neither with the ear of the heart have ye ever heard Him, nor with the eye of the heart have ye ever seen Him, in the revelation of Himself given in the Scriptures; and so ye have not the testimony of His word present as an abiding power within you.' There should be no full stop at 'shape,' only a comma or semi-colon. Had they studied Scripture rightly they would have had a less narrow view of the Sabbath (*v.* 16), and would have recognised the Messiah.

38. *And ye have not his word*] 'And hence it is that ye have no inner appropriation of the word'—seeing that ye have never received it either by hearing or vision. 'His word' is not a fresh testimony different from the 'voice' and 'shape:' all refer to the same thing,— the testimony of Scripture to the Messiah.

³⁹ whom he hath sent, him ye believe not. Search the Scriptures; for in them ye think ye have eternal life: and they ⁴⁰ are they which testify of me. And ye will not come to me, ⁴¹ that ye might have life. I receive not honour from men.

for whom he hath sent] Better, **because** *whom He* **sent.** This is the proof of the previous negation: one who had the word abiding in his heart could not reject Him to whom that word bears witness. Comp. 1 John ii. 14, 24.

39. *Search the Scriptures*] It will never be settled beyond dispute whether the verb here is *imperative* or *indicative*. As far as the Greek shews it may be either, 'search,' or 'ye search,' and both make sense. The question is, which makes the best sense, and this the context must decide. The context seems to be strongly in favour of the indicative, **ye search** *the Scriptures*. All the verbs on either side are in the indicative; and more especially the one with which it is so closely connected, 'and ye will not come.' *Ye search the Scriptures, and* (instead of their leading you to Me) *ye are not willing to come to Me.* The tragic tone once more: see on i. 5. The reproach lies not in their searching, but in their searching to so little purpose. Jewish study of the Scriptures was too often learned trifling and worse; obscuring the text by frivolous interpretations, 'making it of none effect' by unholy traditions.

for in them ye think] 'Ye' is emphatic; **because** *ye are the people who think;* it is your own opinion. Not that they were wrong in thinking that eternal life was to be found in the Scriptures; their error was in thinking that they, who rejected the Messiah, had found it. Had they searched aright they would have found both the Messiah and eternal life.

they are they] See on x. 1.

40. *ye will not come to me*] Not the future of 'to come,' but the present of 'to will:' *ye* **are not willing to** *come to Me.* This is at the root of their failure to read Scripture aright, their hearts are estranged. They have no *will* to find the truth, and without that no intellectual searching will avail. Note that here again man's will is shewn to be free; the truth is not forced upon him; he can reject it if he likes. Comp. iii. 19.

that ye might have life] 'Ye fancy ye find life in your searching of the Scriptures, and ye refuse to come to Me in order to have it in reality.'

41—44. *Not that I seek glory from men; had I done so, you would have received Me. Your worldliness prevents you from receiving One whose motives are not worldly.*

41. *I receive not honour*] It is nothing to Me; I have no need of it, and refuse it: comp. *v*. 34. **Glory** would perhaps be better than 'honour' both here and in *v*. 44, and than 'praise' in ix. 24 and xii. 43; see notes there. Christ is anticipating an objection, and at the same

But I know you, that ye have not the love of God in you. 42
I am come in my Father's name, and ye receive me not: 43
if another shall come in his own name, him ye will receive.
How can ye believe, which receive honour one of another, 44
and seek not the honour that *cometh* from God only? Do 45
not think that I will accuse you to the Father: there is *one*

time shewing what is the real cause of their unbelief. 'Glory from men is not what I seek; think not the want of that is the cause of My complaint. The desire of glory from men is what blinds your eyes to the truth.'

42. *But I know you*] Once more Christ appears as the searcher of hearts; comp. i. 47, 50, ii. 24, 25, iv. 17, 18, 48, v. 14.

in you] Or, *in* **yourselves**, *in your hearts*. 'Thou shalt love the Lord thy God with all thy heart' (Deut. vii. 5) was written on their broad phylacteries (see note on Matt. xxiii. 5), but it had no place in their hearts and no influence on their lives. It is the want of *love*, the want of *will* (*v*. 40) that makes them reject and persecute the Messiah.

43. *and ye receive me not*] The tragic tone as in *vv*. 39, 40, 'I come with the highest credentials, as My Father's representative (comp. viii. 42), and ye reject Me.'

come in his own name] As a false Messiah or as Antichrist. Sixty-four pretended Messiahs have been counted. Comp. Matt. xxiv. 24.

44. *How can ye believe*] The emphasis is on 'ye.' How is it possible, for *you*, who care only for the glory that man bestows, to believe on One who rejects such glory. This is the climax of Christ's accusation. They have reduced themselves to such a condition that they *cannot* believe. They must change their whole view and manner of life before they can do so, comp. *v*. 47.

from God only] Rather, *from* **the only God**, from Him who alone is God; whereas by receiving glory from one another they were making gods of one another; so that it is they who really 'make themselves equal with God' (*v*. 18). The Greek is not similar to Matt. xvii. 8 or Luke v. 21, but to xvii. 3; 1 Tim. vi. 16. Comp. Rom. xvi. 27; 1 Tim. i. 17; Jude 25. Note the absence of the article before the first 'honour' and its presence before the second: they receive glory, such as it is, from one another, and are indifferent to *the* glory, which alone deserves the name.

The whole verse should run thus, *How can ye believe*, **seeing that ye receive glory** *one of another; and the* **glory** *which cometh from* **the only God** *ye seek not*.

45—47. *Do not appeal to Moses; his writings condemn you.*

Thus the whole basis of their confidence is cut away. Moses on whom they trust as a defender is their accuser.

45. *Do not think*] As you might be disposed to do after hearing these reproaches.

46 that accuseth you, *even* Moses, in whom ye trust. For had ye believed Moses, ye would have believed me: for he 47 wrote of me. But if ye believe not his writings, how shall ye believe my words?

that I will accuse you] If this refers to the day of judgment (and the future tense seems to point to that), there are two reasons why Christ will not act as accuser (1) because it would be needless; there is another accuser ready; (2) because He will be acting as Judge.

there is one] Your accuser exists already; he is there with his charge. Note the change from future to present: Christ *will* not be, because Moses *is*, their accuser.

in whom ye trust] Literally, **on** *whom ye* **have set your hope.**

46. *had ye believed Moses, ye would have believed me*] Better, **If** *ye believed Moses, ye* **would believe** *Me:* the verbs are imperfects, not aorists. See on viii. 19 (where we have a similar mistranslation), 42, ix. 41, xv. 19, xviii. 36. Contrast the construction in iv. 10, xi. 21, 32, xiv. 28. This proves that Moses is their accuser.

for he wrote of me] Christ here stamps with His authority the authority of the Pentateuch. He accepts, as referring to Himself, the Messianic types and prophecies which it contains. Comp. Luke xxiv. 27, 44.

47. *if ye believe not*] The emphatic words are 'his' and 'My.' Most readers erroneously emphasize 'writings' and 'words.' The comparison is between Moses and Christ. It was a simple matter of fact that Moses had written and Christ had not: the contrast between writings and words is no part of the argument. Comp. Luke xvi. 31; 'If they hear not Moses and the prophets, neither will they be persuaded though one rose from the dead.'

my words] Or, *My sayings*. It is not the plural of 'word' (λόγος) in *v.* 38, but another substantive (ῥήματα) used by S. John only in the plural. Comp. vi. 63, 68, viii. 47, xii. 47, xv. 7; where the separate sayings are meant; whereas in vi. 60, viii. 43, 51, xii. 48, xv. 3 it is rather the teaching as a whole that is meant.

CHAP. VI.

We see more and more as we go on, that this Gospel makes no attempt to be a complete or connected whole. There are large gaps in the chronology. The Evangelist gives us not a biography, but a series of typical scenes, very carefully selected, and painted with great accuracy and minuteness, but not closely connected. As to what guided him in his selection, we know no more than the general purpose stated xx. 31, and it is sufficient for us. Those words and works of Jesus, which seemed most calculated to convince men that He 'is the Christ, the Son of God,' were recorded by the beloved Apostle. And the fact that they had already been recorded by one or more of the first Evangelists did not deter him from insisting on them again; although he naturally more often chose what they had omitted. In this chapter we

Chap. VI. *Christ the Support of Life.*

1—15. *The Sign on the Land; Feeding the Five Thousand.*

After these *things* Jesus went over the sea of Galilee, 6 *which is* the *sea* of Tiberias. And a great multitude 2

have a notable instance of readiness to go over old ground in order to work out his own purpose. The miracle of feeding the Five Thousand is recorded by all four Evangelists, the only miracle that is so. Moreover, it is outside the Judaean ministry; so that for this reason also we might have expected S. John to omit it. But he needs it as a text for the great discourse on the Bread of Life; and this though spoken in Galilee was in a great measure addressed to Jews from Jerusalem ; so that both text and discourse fall naturally within the range of S. John's plan.

As in Chap. V. Christ is set forth as the *Source of Life*, so in this chapter He is set forth as the *Support of Life*.

Chap. VI. Christ the Support of Life.

This chapter, like the last, contains a discourse arising out of a miracle. It contains moreover an element wanting in the previous chapter,—the results of the discourse. Thus we obtain three divisions; 1. *The Sign on the Land, the Sign on the Lake, and the Sequel of the Signs* (1—25). 2. *The Discourse on the Son as the Support of Life* (26—59). 3. *The opposite Results* (60—71).

1—15. The Sign on the Land; Feeding the Five Thousand.

1. *After these things*] See on v. 1. How long after we cannot tell; but if the feast in v. 1 is rightly conjectured to be Purim, this would be about a month later in the same year, which is probably A.D. 29. But S. John is not careful to mark the precise interval between the various scenes which he gives us. Comp. the indefinite transitions from the First Passover to Nicodemus, ii. 23, iii. 1; from Nicodemus to the Baptist's discourse, iii. 22, 25; from that to the scene at Sychar iv. 1—4; &c., &c. The chronology is doubtless correct, but it is not clear: chronology is not what S. John cares to give us. The historical connexion with what precedes is not the same in the four accounts. Here it is in connexion with the miracles at Bethesda and probably after the death of the Baptist (see on v. 25): in S. Matthew it is in connexion with the death of the Baptist: in S. Mark and S. Luke it is after the death of the Baptist, but in connexion with the return of the Twelve. The notes on Matt. xiv. 13—21; Mark vi. 40—44, and Luke ix. 10—17 should be compared throughout.

went over the sea of Galilee] To the eastern or north-eastern shore. The scene shifts suddenly from Judaea (v. 18) to Galilee; but we are told nothing about the transit.

which is the sea of Tiberias] (Here, v. 23 and xxi. 1 only). Added to describe the sea more exactly, especially for the sake of foreign readers.

followed him, because they saw his miracles which he did
3 on them that were diseased. And Jesus went up into a
4 mountain, and there he sat with his disciples. And the
5 passover, a feast of the Jews, was nigh. When Jesus then

Another slight indication that this Gospel was written outside Palestine: inside Palestine such minute description would be less natural. Perhaps we are to understand that the *southern* half of the lake is specially intended; for here on the western shore Tiberias was situated. The name Tiberias is not found in the first three Gospels. The town was built during our Lord's life time by Herod Antipas, who called it Tiberias out of compliment to the reigning Emperor; one of many instances of the Herods paying court to Rome. Comp. Bethsaida Julias, where this miracle took place, called Julias by Herod Philip after the infamous daughter of Augustus. The new town would naturally be much better known and more likely to be mentioned when S. John wrote than when the earlier Evangelists wrote.

2. *a great multitude*] All the greater seeing that the Baptist was no longer a counter-attraction, and that the Twelve had returned from their mission, in which they had no doubt excited attention. This multitude went round by land while Christ crossed the water. All the verbs which follow are imperfects and express continued and habitual action; **were following** *Him, because they* **were beholding** *the* **signs** *which he* **was doing**, &c., i.e. after He landed He kept on working miracles of healing, and these continually attracted fresh crowds.

3. *into a mountain*] Rather, *into* the *mountain*, or, perhaps *the mountainous part* of the district. The definite article indicates familiarity with the locality. Comp. *v*. 15. We have no means of determining the precise eminence.

4. *And the passover*] Better, **Now** *the Passover*.

a feast of the Jews] Rather, **the** *feast of the Jews*. Possibly this near approach of the Passover is given merely as a date to mark the time. As already noticed (see on ii. 13), S. John groups his narrative round the Jewish festivals. But the statement may also be made as a further explanation of the multitude. Just before the Passover large bands of pilgrims on their way to Jerusalem would be passing along the east shore of the lake. But we find that the multitude in this case are quite ready (*v*. 24) to cross over to Capernaum, as if they had no intention of going to Jerusalem; so that this interpretation of the verse is uncertain. Still more doubtful is the theory that this verse gives a key of interpretation to the discourse which follows, the eating of Christ's flesh and blood being the antitype of the Passover. Of this there is no indication whatever. It is safest to regard the verse as a mere note to time. In any case the addition of 'the feast of the Jews' again indicates that the author is writing away from Palestine. From vii. 1 it would seem that Jesus did not go up to Jerusalem for this Passover

vv. 6—8.] S. JOHN, VI. 139

lift up *his* eyes, and saw a great company come unto him, he saith unto Philip, Whence shall we buy bread, that these may eat? And this he said to prove him: for he himself 6 knew what he would do. Philip answered him, Two 7 hundred pennyworth of bread is not sufficient for them, that every one of them may take a little. One of his 8

5. *When Jesus then*, &c.] Better, **Jesus therefore having lifted up His eyes and seen that a great multitude cometh.**
he saith unto Philip] Why Philip? Because he was nearest to Him; or because his forward spirit (xiv. 8) needed to be convinced of its own helplessness; or because, as living on the lake (i. 44) he would know the neighbourhood. Any or all of these suggestions may be correct. As Judas kept the bag it is not likely that Philip commonly provided food for the party. A more important question remains: "we notice that the impulse to the performance of the miracle comes in the Synoptists from the disciples; in S. John, solely from our Lord Himself." This is difference, but not contradiction: S. John's narrative does not preclude the possibility of the disciples having spontaneously applied to Christ for help either before or after this conversation with Philip. "For the rest the superiority in distinctness and precision is all on the side of S. John. He knows to whom the question was put; he knows exactly what Philip answered; and again the remark of Andrew, Simon Peter's brother......Some memories are essentially pictorial; and the Apostle's appears to have been one of these. It is wonderful with what precision every stroke is thrown in. Most minds would have become confused in reproducing events which had occurred so long ago; but there is no confusion here. The whole scene could be transferred to canvas without any difficulty." S. pp. 121—123.
Whence shall we buy] Or, *whence* **must** *we buy;* the deliberative subjunctive.
6. *to prove him*] This *need* not mean more than to try whether he could suggest any way out of the difficulty; but the more probable meaning is to test his faith, to try what impression Christ's words and works have made upon him.
he himself] without suggestions from others.
would do] Or, **was about to do.**
7. *Two hundred pennyworth*] *Two hundred shillingsworth* would more accurately represent the original. The *denarius* was the ordinary wage for a day's work (Matt. xx. 2; comp. Luke x. 35); in weight of silver it was less than a shilling; in purchasing power it was more. Two hundred *denarii* from the one point of view would be about £7, from the other, nearly double that. S. Philip does not solve the difficulty; he merely states it in a practical way; a much larger amount than they can command would still be insufficient. See notes on Mark viii. 4.
8. *One of his disciples*] Of course this does not imply that Philip

disciples, Andrew, Simon Peter's brother, saith unto him,
9 There is a lad here, which hath five barley loaves, and two
10 small fishes: but what are they among so many? And
Jesus said, Make the men sit down. Now there was much
grass in the place. So the men sat down, *in* number about
11 five thousand. And Jesus took the loaves; and when he
had given thanks, he distributed to the disciples, and the
disciples to them that were set down; and likewise of the

was *not* a disciple; the meaning rather is, that a disciple had been appealed to without results, and now a disciple makes a communication out of which good results flow. There seems to have been some connexion between S. Andrew and S. Philip (i. 44, xii. 22). In the lists of the Apostles in Mark iii. and Acts i. S. Philip's name immediately follows Andrew's. On S. Andrew see notes on i. 40, 41. The particulars about Philip and Andrew here are not found in the Synoptists' account.

9. *a lad*] And therefore able to carry very little. The word is a diminutive in the Greek, *a little lad;* it might also mean 'servant,' but this is less likely.

barley loaves] The ordinary coarse food of the lower orders; Judg. vii. 13. S. John alone mentions their being of barley, and that they belonged to the lad, who was probably selling them. With homely food from so scanty a store Christ will feed them all. These minute details are the touches of an eyewitness.

two small fishes] Better, **two fishes**, although the Greek (*opsaria*) is a diminutive. The word occurs in this Gospel only (*v.* 11, xxi. 9, 10, 13), and literally means a *little relish*, i.e. anything eaten with bread or other food: and as salt fish was most commonly used for this purpose, the word came gradually to mean 'fish' in particular. Philip had enlarged on the greatness of the difficulty; Andrew insists rather on the smallness of the resources for meeting it.

10. *much grass*] As we might expect early in April (*v.* 4). S. Mark (vi. 39, 40) mentions how they reclined in parterres, by hundreds and by fifties, *on the green grass*. This arrangement would make it easy to count them.

the men sat down] The women and children were probably apart by themselves. S. Matthew (xiv. 21) tells us that the 5000 included the men only. Among those going up to the Passover there would not be many women or children.

11. *when he had given thanks*] The usual grace before meat said by the head of the house or the host. 'He that enjoys aught without thanksgiving, is as though he robbed God.' Talmud. But it seems clear that this giving of thanks or blessing of the food (Luke ix. 16) was the *means* of the miracle, because (1) all four narratives notice it; (2) it is pointedly mentioned again *v.* 23; (3) it is also mentioned in both accounts of the feeding of the 4000 (Matt. xv. 36; Mark viii. 6).

to the disciples, and the disciples] These words are wanting in

fishes as much as they would. When they were filled, he said unto his disciples, Gather up the fragments that remain, that nothing be lost. Therefore they gathered *them* together, and filled twelve baskets with the fragments of the five barley loaves, which remained over and above unto them that had eaten. Then *those* men, when they had seen the miracle that Jesus did, said, This is of a truth *that* prophet that should come into the world.

authority; the best texts run, **He distributed to them that were lying down.** It is futile to ask whether the multiplication took place in Christ's hands only: the *manner* of the miracle eludes us, as in the turning of the water into wine. That was a change of quality, this of quantity. This is a literal fulfilment of Matt. vi. 33.

12. *Gather up the fragments*] S. John alone tells of this command, though the others tell us that the fragments were gathered up. It has been noticed as a strong mark of truth, most unlikely to have been invented by the writer of a fiction. We do not find the owner of Fortunatus' purse careful against extravagance. How improbable, from a human point of view, that one who could multiply food at will should give directions about saving fragments!

13. *baskets*] All four accounts have the same word for basket, *cophinus*, i.e. the wallet which every Jew carried when on a journey, to keep himself independent of Gentile food, which would be unclean. Comp. Juvenal III. 14. Each of the Twelve gathered into his own wallet, and filled it full. Moreover in referring to the miracle the word *cophinus* is used (Matt. xvi. 9). In the feeding of the 4000 (Matt. xv. 37; Mark viii. 8), and in referring to it (Matt. xvi. 10), a different word for basket, *spuris*, is used. Such accuracy is evidence of truth. See note on Mark viii. 8. S. Mark tells us that fragments of fish were gathered also. The remnants far exceed in quantity the original store.

The expedients to evade the obvious meaning of the narrative are worth mentioning, as shewing how some readers are willing to 'violate all the canons of historical evidence,' rather than admit the possibility of a miracle: (1) that food had been brought over and concealed in the boat; (2) that some among the multitude were abundantly supplied with food and were induced by Christ's example to share their supply with others; (3) that the whole is an allegorical illustration of Matt. vi. 33. How could either (1) or (2) excite even a suspicion that He was the Messiah, much less kindle such an enthusiasm as is recorded in *v.* 15? And if the whole is an illustration of Matt. vi. 33, what meaning in the allegory can be given to this popular enthusiasm? There are "rationalising expedients that are considerably more incredible than miracles." S. p. 126.

14. *Then those men*] Rather, **The** *men* **therefore.**
the miracle that Jesus did] Better, *the* **sign** *that* **He** *did.* The name Jesus has been inserted here, as elsewhere, because this once

15 When Jesus therefore perceived that they would come and take him by force, to make him a king, he departed again into a mountain himself alone.

was the beginning of a lesson read in church. The same thing has been done in our own Prayer Book in the Gospels for Quinquagesima and the 3rd Sunday in Lent: in the Gospel for S. John's Day the names of both Jesus and Peter have been inserted; and in those for the 5th S. in Lent and 2nd S. after Easter the words 'Jesus said' have been inserted. In all cases a desire for clearness has caused the insertion. Comp. viii. 21.

that prophet that should come] Literally, **the** *Prophet that* **cometh**: the Prophet of Deut. xviii. 15 (see on i. 21). But perhaps the Greek participle here only represents the Hebrew participle, which is properly present, but is often used where a future participle would be used in Latin or Greek. S. John alone tells us the effect of the miracle on those who witnessed it: comp. ii. 11, 23. These two verses (14, 15) supply "a decisive proof that the narrative in the fourth Gospel is not constructed out of that of the Synoptists, and we might almost add a decisive proof of the historical character of the Gospel itself... The Synoptists have nothing of this... Yet how exactly it corresponds with the current Messianic expectations! Our Lord had performed a miracle; and at once He is hailed as the Messiah. But it is as the Jewish, not the Christian Messiah. The multitude would take Him by force and make Him king. At last they have found the leader who will lead them victoriously against the Romans and 'restore the kingdom to Israel.' And just because He refused to do this we are told a few verses lower down that many of His disciples 'went back, and walked no more with Him,' and for the same cause, a year later, they crucified Him. It is this contrast between the popular Messianic belief and the sublimated form of it, as maintained and represented by Christ, that is the clue to all the fluctuations and oscillations to which the belief in Him was subject. This is why He was confessed one day and denied the next..... It is almost superfluous to point out how impossible it would have been for a writer wholly *ab extra* to throw himself into the midst of these hopes and feelings, and to reproduce them, not as if they were something new that he had learned, but as part of an atmosphere that he had himself once breathed. There is no stronger proof both of the genuineness and of the authenticity of the fourth Gospel than the way in which it reflects the current Messianic idea." S. pp. 123, 124.

15. *take him by force*] Carry Him up to Jerusalem and proclaim Him king at the Passover. This again is peculiar to S. John. In his Epic he points out how the enmity of Christ's foes increases; and nothing increased it so much as popular enthusiasm for Him: comp. iii. 26, iv. 1—3, vii. 40, 41, 46, viii. 30, ix. 30—38, x. 21, 42, xi. 45, 46, xii. 9—11.

again] He had come down to feed them.

16—21. *The Sign on the Lake; Walking on the Water.*

And when even was *now* come, his disciples went down 16 unto the sea, and entered into a ship, and went over the sea 17 towards Capernaum. And it was now dark, and Jesus was not come to them. And the sea arose by reason of a great 18 wind that blew. So when they had rowed about five and 19 twenty or thirty furlongs, they see Jesus walking on the sea, and drawing nigh unto the ship: and they were afraid. But 20 he saith unto them, It is I; be not afraid. Then they 21

into a mountain] Better, as in *v.* 3, *into* **the** *mountain*, or *the hill country*.
himself alone] S. Matthew and S. Mark tell us that the solitude He sought was for prayer. S. Luke (ix. 18) mentions both the solitary prayer and also a question which seems to refer to this burst of enthusiasm for Christ; 'Whom say the people that I am?' Thus the various accounts supplement one another.

16—21. THE SIGN ON THE LAKE; WALKING ON THE WATER.

16. *when even was now come*] S. Matthew (xiv. 15, 23) makes two evenings; this was in accordance with Jewish custom. It is the second evening that is here meant, from 6 p.m. to dark.
went down] From Matt. xiv. 22 and Mark vi. 45 we learn that Christ 'constrained' His disciples to embark: this points either to their general unwillingness to leave Him, or to their having shared the wish to make Him a king by force. S. Luke omits the whole incident.
17. *toward Capernaum*] S. Mark says 'unto Bethsaida' which was close to Capernaum. See notes and map at Matt. iv. 13 and Luke v. 1. For 'went over the sea' we should read **were coming** *over the sea*, i.e. were on their way home.
was not come] More accurately, *was not yet come*.
18. *the sea arose*] Literally, *was becoming thoroughly agitated*, so that their Master's following them in another boat seemed impossible. For the vivid description comp. Jonah i. 13.
19. *five and twenty or thirty furlongs*] This pretty closely corresponds with 'in the midst of the sea' (Matt. xiv. 24). The lake is nearly seven miles across in the widest part.
walking on the sea] There is no doubt that this means on the surface of the water, although an attempt has been made to shew that the Greek may mean 'on the sea-shore.' Even if it can, which is perhaps somewhat doubtful, the context shews plainly what is meant. How could they have been afraid at seeing Jesus walking on the shore? S. Mark tells us that it was about the fourth watch, i.e. between 3.0 and 6.0 a.m. S. Matthew alone gives S. Peter's walking on the sea.
20. *It is I*] Literally, *I am* (comp. xviii. 5).

willingly received him into the ship: and immediately the
ship was at the land whither they went.

22—25. *The Sequel of the two Signs.*

22 The day following, when the people which stood on the

> 21. *they willingly received him*] Rather, *they* **were willing to
> receive** *Him*. The mistranslation seems to have arisen from a wish to
> make this account agree with that of S. Matthew and S. Mark, who
> say that he entered the boat. It is probably due to Beza, who for the
> Vulgate's *voluerunt recipere* substitutes *volente animo receperunt*. S.
> John leaves us in doubt whether He entered the boat or not; he is not
> correcting the other two accounts: this would require 'but before He
> could enter it the boat was at the land.'
> *immediately*] We are probably to understand that this was miracu-
> lous; not a mere favourable breeze which brought them to land before
> they had recovered from their surprise: but the point is uncertain and
> unimportant.
> *whither they went*] Better, *whither they* **were going**, or intending
> to go. The imperfect tense helps to bring out the contrast between
> the difficulty of the first half of the voyage, when they were alone, and
> the ease of the last half, when He was with them. The word for
> 'going' implies departure, and looks back to the place left.
> The Walking on the Sea cannot be used as evidence that the writer
> held Docetic views about Christ, i.e. believed that His Body was a
> mere phantom. A Docetist would have made more of the incident,
> and would hardly have omitted the cry of the disciples 'It is a *spirit*'
> (Matt. xiv. 26; comp. Mark vi. 49). Docetism is absolutely excluded
> from this Gospel by i. 14, and by the general tone of it throughout.
> Comp. xix. 34, 35, xx. 20, 27.
>
> 22—25. THE SEQUEL OF THE TWO SIGNS.
>
> 22—24. We have here a complicated sentence very unusual in
> S. John (but comp. xiii. 1—4); it betrays "a certain literary awk-
> wardness, but great historical accuracy......The structure of the sen-
> tence is no argument against the truth of the statements which it con-
> tains. On the contrary, if these had been fictitious, we may be sure
> that they would have been much simpler. Indeed a forger would
> never have thought of relating how the crowd got across the sea at all.
> We see the natural partiality with which the Evangelist dwells upon
> scenes with which he is familiar. He had been a fisherman on the sea
> of Galilee himself. He knew the boats of Tiberias from those of
> Capernaum and the other cities, and had probably friends or relations
> in that very crowd." S. pp. 126, 127.
> 22. *the people*] An instance of the caprice of our translators in
> creating differences. The same Greek word is translated 'multitude'
> in *v.* 2, 'company' in *v.* 5, and 'people' here, *v.* 24, &c.; **multitude**
> would be best throughout.

other side of the sea saw that there was none other boat there, save that one whereinto his disciples were entered, and that Jesus went not with his disciples into the boat, but *that* his disciples were gone away alone; (howbeit there 23 came other boats from Tiberias nigh unto the place where they did eat bread, after that the Lord had given thanks:) when the people therefore saw that Jesus was not there, 24 neither his disciples, they also took shipping, and came to Capernaum, seeking for Jesus. And when they had found 25 him on the other side of the sea, they said unto him, Rabbi, when camest thou hither?

26—59. *The Discourse on the Son as the Support of Life.*

Jesus answered them and said, Verily, verily, I say 26

on the other side of the sea] On the eastern side where the miracle took place.
save that one whereinto his disciples were entered] The only words of this sentence that are of certain authority are **save one**; the rest is probably an explanatory note.
were gone away] Better, **went** *away*.
23. *Howbeit there came*] This awkward parenthesis explains how there came to be boats to transport the people to the western shore after they had given over seeking for Christ on the eastern.
after that the Lord had given thanks] Unless the giving thanks was the turning-point of the miracle it is difficult to see why it is mentioned again here: see on *v.* 11.
24. *they also took shipping*] More literally, *they* **themselves entered into the boats**, i.e. the boats that had come from Tiberias, driven in very possibly by the gale which had delayed the Apostles: 'also' is not genuine. Of course there is no reason to suppose that *all* who had been miraculously fed crossed over; but a sufficient number of them to be called a 'multitude.'
25. *on the other side of the sea*] This now means the western shore; in *v.* 22 it meant the eastern. From *v.* 59 we have the locality fixed very distinctly as the synagogue at Capernaum.
when camest thou] Including *how?* they suspect something miraculous. Christ does not gratify their curiosity: if the feeding of the 5000, which they had witnessed, taught them nothing, what good would it do them to hear of the crossing of the sea? 'Camest Thou hither' is literally 'hast Thou come to be here:' comp. i. 15.

26—59. THE DISCOURSE ON THE SON AS THE SUPPORT OF LIFE.

God's revealed word and created world are unhappily alike in this; that the most beautiful places in each are often the scene and subject of strife. This marvellous discourse is a well-known field of controversy, as to whether it does or does not refer to the Eucharist. That it has no reference whatever to the Eucharist seems incredible, when we remember (1) the startling words here used about eating the Flesh of the Son of Man and drinking His Blood; (2) that just a year from this time Christ instituted the Eucharist; (3) that the primitive Church is something like unanimous in interpreting this discourse as referring to the Eucharist. A few words are necessary on each of these points. (1) Probably nowhere in any literature, not even among the luxuriant imagery of the East, can we find an instance of a teacher speaking of the reception of his doctrine under so astounding a metaphor as eating his flesh and drinking his blood. Something more than this must at any rate be meant here. The metaphor 'eating a man's flesh' elsewhere means to injure or destroy him. Ps. xxvii. 2 (xiv. 4); James v. 3. (2) The founding of new religions, especially of those which have had any great hold on the minds of men, has ever been the result of much thought and deliberation. Let us leave out of the account the Divinity of Jesus Christ, and place Him for the moment on a level with other great teachers. Are we to suppose that just a year before the Eucharist was instituted, the Founder of this, the most distinctive element of Christian worship, had no thought of it in His mind? Surely for long beforehand that institution was in His thoughts; and if so, 'Except ye eat the Flesh of the Son of Man and drink His Blood, ye have no life in you' cannot but have some reference to 'Take eat, this is My Body,' 'Drink ye all of it, for this is My Blood.' The coincidence is too exact to be fortuitous, even if it were probable that a year before it was instituted the Eucharist was still unknown to the Founder of it. That the audience at Capernaum could not thus understand Christ's words is nothing to the point: He was speaking less to them than to Christians throughout all ages. How often did He utter words which even Apostles could not understand at the time. (3) The interpretations of the primitive Church are not infallible, even when they are almost unanimous: but they carry great weight. And in a case of this kind, where spiritual insight and Apostolic tradition are needed, rather than scholarship and critical power, patristic authority may be allowed the very greatest weight.

But while it is incredible that there is *no* reference to the Eucharist in this discourse, it is equally incredible that the reference is solely or primarily to the Eucharist. The wording of the larger portion of the discourse is against any such exclusive interpretation; not until *v.* 51 does the reference to the Eucharist become clear and direct. Rather the discourse refers to *all* the various channels of grace by means of which Christ imparts Himself to the believing soul: and who will dare to limit these in number or efficacy?

To quote the words of Dr Westcott, the discourse "cannot refer primarily to the Holy Communion; nor again can it be simply prophetic of that Sacrament. The teaching has a full and consistent meaning in connexion with the actual circumstances, and it treats essentially of spiritual realities with which no external act, as such, can be extensive. The well-known words of Augustine, *crede et man-*

unto you, Ye seek me, not because ye saw *the* miracles, but because ye did eat of the loaves, and were filled. Labour not for the meat which perisheth, but for *that* 27 meat which endureth unto everlasting life, which the Son of man shall give unto you: for him hath God the

ducasti, 'believe and thou *hast* eaten,' give the sum of the thoughts in a luminous and pregnant sentence.

"But, on the other hand, there can be no doubt that the truth which is presented in its absolute form in these discourses is presented in a specific act and in a concrete form in the Holy Communion; and yet further that the Holy Communion is the divinely appointed means whereby men may realise the truth. Nor can there be any difficulty to any one who acknowledges a divine fitness in the ordinances of the Church, an eternal correspondence in the parts of the one counsel of God, in believing that the Lord, while speaking intelligibly to those who heard Him at the time, gave by anticipation a commentary, so to speak, on the Sacrament which He afterwards instituted." *Speaker's Commentary*, II. p. 113.

The discourse may be thus divided; I. 26—34, Distinction between the material bread and the Spiritual Bread; II. 35—50 (with two digressions, 37—40; 43—46), Identification of the Spiritual Bread with Christ; III. 51—58, Further definition of the identification as consisting in the giving of His Body and outpouring of His Blood. S. p. 128. On the language and style see introductory note to chap. III.

26—34. *Distinction between the material bread and the Spiritual Bread.*

26. *not because ye saw the miracles*] Better, **not because ye saw signs.** There is no article in the Greek; and the strict meaning of 'signs' should be retained. They *had* seen the *miracle*, but it had *not* been a *sign* to them; it had excited in them nothing better than wonder and greediness. The plural does not necessarily refer to more than the one sign of the Feeding; the generic plural.

27. *Labour not for*, &c.] Better, **Work** *not for*, &c. The translation in the margin is preferable, to keep up the connexion with verses 28, 29, 30. The people keep harping on the word 'work.'

the meat which perisheth] Better (to avoid all ambiguity), *the* **food** *that perisheth:* 'meat' in the sense of 'flesh-meat' is not intended. Comp. (iv. 13) 'whosoever drinketh of this water shall thirst again.' The discourse with the Samaritan woman should be compared throughout: 'the food which abides' here corresponds with 'the living water' there; 'the food that perisheth' with the water of the well. 'Perisheth' not merely in its sustaining power, but in itself: it is digested and dispersed (Matt. xv. 17; 1 Cor. vi. 13).

endureth unto everlasting life] Better, **abideth** *unto* **eternal** *life:* see on i. 33 and iii. 16.

28 Father sealed. Then said they unto him, What shall we
29 do, that we might work the works of God? Jesus answered
and said unto them, This is the work of God, that ye
30 believe on *him* whom he hath sent. They said therefore
unto him, What sign shewest thou then, that we may see,
31 and believe thee? what dost thou work? Our fathers did
eat manna in the desert; as it is written, He gave them
32 bread from heaven to eat. Then Jesus said unto them,
Verily, verily, I say unto you, Moses gave you not *that*

for him hath God the Father sealed] Better (preserving the emphasis of the Greek order), *for Him* **the Father sealed, even God.** 'Sealed,' i.e. authenticated (iii. 33), as the true giver of this food (1) by direct testimony in the Scriptures, (2) by the same in the voice from Heaven at His Baptism, (3) by indirect testimony in His miracles and Messianic work.

28. *Then said they*] They said **therefore.**
What shall we do, that we might work] Better, *what* **must** *we do that we* **may** *work*. They see that His words have a moral meaning; they are to do works pleasing to God. But how to set about this?

29. *the work of God*] They probably were thinking of works of the law, tithes, sacrifices, &c. Christ tells them of one work, one moral act, from which all the rest derive their value,—belief in Him whom God has sent.

that ye believe] Literally, *that ye may believe*. S. John's favourite form of expression, indicating the Divine purpose. Comp. *v.* 50 and v. 36.

30. *What sign shewest thou then*] 'Thou' is emphatic: 'what dost Thou on Thy part?' They quite understand that in the words 'Him whom He hath sent' Jesus is claiming to be the Messiah; but they want a proof. Their enthusiasm had cooled, their curiosity had increased, during the night. After all, the feeding of the 5000 was less marvellous than the manna, and Moses was not the Messiah. Note that whereas He uses the strong form, 'believe *on* Him,' they use the weak one, 'believe Thee.' See last note on i. 12.

what dost thou work] They purposely choose the very word that He had used in *v.* 29. The emphasis is on 'what.'

31. *manna*] More exactly, **the** manna.
He gave them bread from heaven to eat] A rough quotation of 'had rained down manna upon them to eat' (Ps. lxxviii. 24). They artfully suppress the nominative (which in the Psalm is 'God'), and leave 'Moses' to be understood. Possibly Neh. ix. 15 is in their thoughts; if so, there is the same artfulness. On 'it is written' see on ii. 17. 'From heaven' is literally **out of** heaven.'

32. *Moses gave you not*] Christ shews them that He quite understands their insinuation: they are comparing Him unfavourably with

bread from heaven; but my Father giveth you the true bread from heaven. For the bread of God is he which 33 cometh down from heaven, and giveth life unto the world. Then said they unto him, Lord, evermore give us this 34 bread. And Jesus said unto them, I am the bread of life: 35

Moses. He denies both their points; (1) that Moses gave the manna; (2) that the manna was in the truest sense bread from heaven.
giveth you the true bread, &c.] Literally, *giveth you the bread out of heaven* (*which is*) *the true bread;* 'true' in the sense of 'real' and 'perfect' (see on i. 9); the manna was but the type, and therefore imperfect. Note the change of tense from 'gave' to 'giveth:' God is continually giving the true bread; it is not a thing granted at one time and then no more, like the manna.

33. *the bread of God is he which*] Better, *the bread of God is that which*. Christ has not yet identified Himself with the Bread; it is still impersonal, and hence the present participle in the Greek. Contrast v. 41. There is a clear reference to this passage in the Ignatian Epistles, *Romans* vii. The whole chapter is impregnated with the Fourth Gospel. See on iv. 10.
giveth life unto the world] Without this Bread mankind is spiritually dead; and this is the point of the argument (the introductory 'for' shews that the verse is argumentative); we have proof that it is the Father who gives the really heavenly Bread, *for* it is His Bread that quickens the whole human race.

34. *Then said they*] They said **therefore.**
Lord, evermore give us this bread] 'Lord' is too strong, and makes the request too much like the prayer of a humble believer. Our translators wisely vary the rendering of *Kyrie*, using sometimes 'Lord,' and sometimes 'Sir.' Here, as in the conversation with the Samaritan woman, 'Sir' would be better. Not that the request is ironical; it is not the mocking prayer of the sceptic. Rather it is the selfish petition of one whose beliefs and aspirations are low. As the Samaritan woman thought that the living water would at any rate be very useful (iv. 15), so these Jews think that the true bread is at least worth having. He fed them yesterday, and they are hungry again; He talks to them of food that endureth; it will be well to be evermore supplied with this food, which is perhaps another manna with greater sustaining powers. They do not disbelieve in His power, but in His mission.

35—50. *Identification of the Spiritual Bread with Christ.*

35. *I am the bread of life.* The pronoun is very emphatic: comp. iv. 26. As in v. 30, He passes from the third to the first person. 'Bread of life' means 'bread that giveth life.' Comp. 'the tree of life' (Gen. ii. 9, iii. 22, 24), 'the water of life' (Rev. xxi. 6, xxii. 1). In the remainder of the verse 'He that cometh to Me'='he that believeth on Me,' and 'shall never hunger'='shall never thirst;' i.e. the believer shall experience the continual satisfaction of his highest spiri-

he that cometh to me shall never hunger; and he that
36 believeth on me shall never thirst. But I said unto you,
37 That ye also have seen me, and believe not. All that the
Father giveth me shall come to me; and him that cometh
38 to me I will in no wise cast out. For I came down from
heaven, not to do mine own will, but the will of him that
39 sent me. And this is the Father's will which hath sent me,

tual needs. The superiority of Christ to the manna consists in this, that while it satisfied only bodily needs for a time, He satisfies spiritual needs for ever.

36. *I said unto you*] When? no such saying is recorded. Ewald thus finds some slight evidence for his theory that a whole sheet of this Gospel has been lost between chapters v. and vi. But the reference may easily be to one of the countless unrecorded sayings of Christ, or possibly to the general sense of v. 37—44. In the latter case 'you' must mean the Jewish nation, for those verses were addressed to Jews at Jerusalem. See on x. 26, where there is a somewhat similar case. That 'I said' means 'I would have you to know,' and has no reference to any previous utterance, does not seem very probable.

ye also have seen me] 'Also' belongs to 'have seen,' not to 'ye,' as most English readers would suppose: *ye have even seen me* (not merely heard of me), *and* (yet) *do not believe*. The tragic tone again. See on i. 5, 10, 11.

37—40. Digression on the blessedness of those who come to Christ as believers.

37. *All that the Father giveth...him that cometh*] There is a significant change of gender in the Greek which is obscured in the English version: 'all that' is neuter, **all that which**; what is given is treated as impersonal, mankind *en masse;* what comes, with free will, is masculine. Men are given to Christ without their wills being consulted; but each individual can, if he likes, refuse to come. There is no coercion. Comp. similar changes of gender in i. 11, xvii. 2.

shall come to me, and him that cometh...For I came down] The verb 'come' here represents three different Greek verbs, but there is no such great difference between them as to make it worth while to change so familiar a text; yet it would be more literal to translate *all that the Father giveth Me, to Me shall come, and him that approacheth Me I will in no wise cast out; for I have descended,* &c. The second '*Me*' is emphatic, the first and third are not.

38. *I came down*] Better, **I am come** *down* or *have descended*. Four times in this discourse Christ declares that He is come down from heaven; verses 38, 50, 51, 58. The drift of these three verses (38—40) is;—How could I cast them out, seeing that I am come to do my Father's will, and He wills that they should be received?

39. *this is the Father's will,* &c.] The true reading is; *this is* **the will of Him that sent Me.**

that of all which he hath given me I should lose nothing, but should raise it up *again* at the last day. And this is 40 the will of him that sent me, that every one which seeth the Son, and believeth on him, may have everlasting life: and I will raise him up *at* the last day.

The Jews then murmured at him, because he said, I am 41 the bread which came down from heaven. And they said, 42 Is not this Jesus, the son of Joseph, whose father and

that of all] Literally, *in order that of all:* see on *v.* 29.
all which he hath given me] 'All' is neuter as in *v.* 37, and is placed first for emphasis. In the Greek it is a *nominativus pendens*.
raise it up again at the last day] This gracious utterance is repeated as a kind of refrain, verses 40, 44, 54. 'Again' may be omitted. This is 'the resurrection of life' (v. 29), 'the first resurrection,' the resurrection of the just.
the last day] This phrase is peculiar to S. John, and occurs seven times in this Gospel. Elsewhere it is called 'the Day of the Lord,' 'the Great Day,' &c.
40. *And this is the will of him that sent me*] The true reading is: For *this is the will* of My Father. The opening words of verses 39 and 40, being very similar, have become confused in inferior MSS. The best MSS. have 'Father' in this verse, where 'the Son' is mentioned, not in *v.* 39, where He is not. Moreover this verse is explanatory of *v.* 40, and opens with 'for;' it shews who are meant by 'all which He hath given me,' viz. *every one that contemplateth the Son and believeth on Him.* 'Seeth' is not strong enough for the Greek word here used: the Jews had seen Jesus; they had not contemplated Him so as to believe. 'Contemplate' is frequent in S. John and the Acts, elsewhere not. Comp. xii. 45, xiv. 19, xvi. 10, 16, 19. 'That' again = *in order that.*
I will raise him up] The Greek construction is ambiguous; possibly 'raise' depends upon 'that' as in *v.* 39: *and that I should raise him up.* 'I' is here very emphatic; 'by My power as Messiah.'
41. *The Jews then murmured at him*] Better, *The Jews* **therefore muttered respecting** *Him,* talked in an under tone among themselves about Him: it does not necessarily mean that they found fault, though the context shews that they did (comp. *v.* 61, vii. 12). From the mention of the Jews we are to understand that there were some of the hostile party among the multitude, perhaps some members of the Sanhedrin; but not that the whole multitude were hostile, though carnally-minded and refusing to believe without a further sign. Comp. i. 19, ii. 18, v. 10, vii. 11, &c.
I am the bread which came down from heaven] They put together the statements in verses 33, 35, 38.
42. *Is not this*] Or, *Is not this* **fellow**; the expression is contemptuous.

mother we know? how *is it* then *that* he saith, I came
43 down from heaven? Jesus therefore answered and said unto
44 them, Murmur not among yourselves. No *man* can come
to me, except the Father which hath sent me draw him:
45 and I will raise him up *at* the last day. It is written in the
prophets, And they shall be all taught of God. Every
man therefore that hath heard, and hath learned of the
46 Father, cometh unto me. Not that any *man* hath seen the

whose father and mother we know] 'We know all about His parentage; there is nothing supernatural or mysterious about His origin.' Nothing can be inferred from this as to Joseph's being alive at this time: the probability is that he was not, as he nowhere appears in the Gospel narrative; but this cannot be proved.

how is it then, &c.] Better, *How* **doth He now say, I am come down**.

43—46. Digression on the difficulty of coming to Christ as a believer.

43. *Murmur not*] Christ does not answer their objection or explain. Even among the first Christians the fact of his miraculous conception seems to have been made known only gradually, so foul were the calumnies which the Jews had spread respecting His Mother. This certainly was not the place to proclaim it. He directs them to something of more vital importance than the way by which He came into the world, viz. the way by which they may come to Him.

44. *draw him*] It is the same word as is used xii. 32; 'will draw all men unto Me.' The word does not necessarily imply force, still less irresistible force, but merely *attraction* of some kind, some inducement to come. Comp. 'with loving-kindness have I *drawn* thee' (Jer. xxxi. 3), and Virgil's *trahit sua quemque voluptas*.

45. *in the prophets*] The direct reference is to Isa. liv. 13, but there are similar passages Jer. xxxi. 33, 34; Joel iii. 16, 17. The quotation explains what is meant by the Father's *drawing* men, viz., enlightening them. The 'therefore' in the second half of the verse is not genuine: 'therefore' is very common in the narrative portion of this Gospel, very rare in the discourses. On 'it is written' see on ii. 17. Here, as in xiii. 18 and xix. 37, the quotation agrees with the Hebrew against the LXX. This is evidence that the writer knew Hebrew and therefore was probably a Jew of Palestine.

Every man therefore that hath heard, &c.] And no others: only those who have been enlightened by the Father can come to the Son.

46. *Not that any man hath seen*] To be enlightened and taught by the Father it is not necessary to see Him. "That is a privilege reserved for a later stage in the spiritual life, and is only to be attained mediately through the Son (comp. i. 18)." S. p. 129.

Father, save he which is of God, he hath seen the Father. Verily, verily, I say unto you, He that believeth on me hath everlasting life. I am *that* bread of life. Your fathers did eat manna in the wilderness, and are dead. This is the bread which cometh down from heaven, that a man may eat thereof, and not die. I am the living bread which came down from heaven: if any *man* eat of this bread, he shall live for ever: and the bread that I will give is my flesh, 47 48 49 50 51

he which is of God] Or, *He which is* **from** *God*, with whom He was previous to the Incarnation; i. 1, 14, viii. 42, xvi. 27.

47—50. Christ returns from answering the Jews to the main subject.

47. *hath everlasting life*] *Hath* **eternal** *life* (iii. 16). Note the tense. Christ solemnly assures them (the double 'Verily') that the believer is already in possession of eternal life. See on iii. 36 and v. 24.

48. *that bread of life*] Better, **the** *Bread of life*. Comp. *v.* 32, i. 21, 25, vi. 14, where the same exaggerated translation of the Greek article occurs.

49. Christ answers them out of their own mouths. They had spoken of the manna as superior to the multiplied loaves and fishes; but the manna did not preserve men from death. The same word is used both in *v.* 49 and *v.* 50; therefore for 'are dead' it will be better to substitute **died.** Moreover, the point is, not that they are dead now, but that they perished then; the manna did not save them. They **ate the** *manna and* **died.**

50. *that a man may eat*] S. John's favourite form of expression again, indicating the Divine intention: comp. *v.* 29, vi. 34, viii. 56, &c. 'Of this purpose is the Bread which cometh down from heaven; in order that a man may eat thereof and so not die.' Comp. 1 John v. 3.

51—58. *Further definition of the identification of the Spiritual Bread with Christ as consisting in the giving of His Body and the outpouring of His Blood.*

In *vv.* 35—50 Christ in His *Person* is the Bread of Life: here He is the spiritual food of believers in the Redemptive *work* of His Death.

51. *the living bread*] Not merely the Bread of life (*v.* 48), the life-giving Bread, but the living Bread, having life in itself, which life is imparted to those who partake of the Bread.

which came down] At the Incarnation. Now that the Bread is identified with Christ, we have the past tense of what took place once for all. Previously (verses 33, 50) the present tense is used of what is continually going on. In one sense Christ is perpetually coming down from heaven, in the other He came but once: He is ever imparting Himself to man; He only once became man.

he shall live for ever] Just as 'living Bread' is a stronger expression than 'Bread of life,' so 'live for ever' is stronger than 'not die.'

and the bread that I will give] The precise wording of this sentence

52 which I will give for the life of the world. The Jews therefore strove amongst themselves, saying, How can this *man*
53 give us *his* flesh to eat? Then Jesus said unto them, Verily, verily, I say unto you, Except ye eat the flesh of the Son of man, and drink his blood, ye have no life in you.
54 Whoso eateth my flesh, and drinketh my blood, hath eternal

is somewhat uncertain, but the best reading seems to be: *and the Bread that I will give is* My Flesh for *the life of the world*. That in Christ's mind these words looked onwards to the Eucharist, and that in thus speaking to believers throughout all time He included a reference to the Eucharist has already been stated to be highly probable. (See above, Introduction to 26—58). But that the reference is not exclusively, nor even directly, to the Eucharist is shewn from the use of ' Flesh '(*sarx*) and not ' Body ' (*sôma*). In all places where the Eucharist is mentioned in N. T. we have 'Body,' not 'Flesh;' Matt. xxvi. 26; Mark xiv. 22; Luke xxii. 19; 1 Cor. xi. 24 ff. Moreover the words must have had some meaning for those who heard them at Capernaum. Evidently they have a wider range than any one Sacrament. Christ promises to give His Flesh (by His bloody death soon to come) for the benefit of the whole world. But this benefit can only be appropriated by the faith of each individual; and so that which when offered by Christ is His Flesh appears under the figure of bread when partaken of by the believer. The primary reference, therefore, is to Christ's propitiatory death; the secondary reference is to *all* those means by which the death of Christ is appropriated, especially the Eucharist. Not that Christ is here promising that ordinance, but uttering deep truths, which apply, and which He intended to apply, to that ordinance, now that it is instituted.

52. *strove among themselves*] Their excitement increases; they have got beyond muttering among themselves (*v.* 41).

give us his flesh to eat] 'To eat' is their own addition; they wish to bring out in full the strangeness of His declaration.

53. *Then said Jesus*] Better, Therefore *said Jesus:* see on *v.* 45.

and drink his blood] Christ not only accepts what they have added to His words, but still further startles them by telling them that they must drink His Blood; an amazing statement to a Jew, who was forbidden to taste even the blood of animals (Gen. ix. 4; Lev. xvii. 10—16). These words point still more distinctly to His propitiatory death; for 'the blood is the life' which He offered up for the sins of the world. The eating and drinking are not faith, but the appropriation of His death; faith leads us to eat and drink and is the means of appropriation. Taken separately, the Flesh represents sacrifice and sustenance, the Blood represents atonement and life.

no life in you] Literally, *no life in* yourselves: for the source of life is absent. The next four verses explain more fully how this is.

54. The gracious positive of the previous minatory negative. From the warning as to the disastrous consequences of not partaking He

life; and I will raise him up *at* the last day. For my flesh is meat indeed, and my blood is drink indeed. He that eateth my flesh, and drinketh my blood, dwelleth in me, and I in him. As the living Father hath sent me, and I live by the Father: so he that eateth me, even he shall live by me. This is *that* bread which came down from heaven: not as your fathers did eat manna, and are dead: he that eateth *of* this bread shall live for ever.

passes to a declaration of the blessed consequences of partaking, viz. eternal life, and that at once, with resurrection among the just hereafter.

55. *my flesh is meat indeed*, &c.] According to the best reading; *My Flesh is* **true food** *and My Blood is* **true** *drink;* i.e. this is no misleading metaphor, but an actual fact.

56. *dwelleth in me, and I in him*] Or, **abideth** *in Me and I in him.* This is one of S. John's very characteristic phrases to express the most intimate mutual fellowship and union. The word 'abide' is also characteristic, as we have seen. Comp. xiv. 10, 20, xv. 4, 5, xvii. 21; 1 John iii. 24, iv. 16. Christ is at once the centre and circumference of the life of the Christian; the source from which it springs, and the ocean into which it flows; its starting-point and its goal.

57. Not a mere repetition of the previous statement but an enlargement of it. The result of this close union is perfect life, proceeding as from the Father to the Son, so in like manner from the Son to all believers.

the living Father] The absolutely Living One, the Fount of all life, in whom is no element of death. The expression occurs nowhere else. Comp. Matt. xvi. 16; 2 Cor. vi. 16; Hebr. vii. 25. For 'hath sent' read **sent**.

By the Father] Better **because of** *the Father*, i.e. because the Father is the Living One. Similarly, 'by Me' should be **because of** *Me*, i.e. because he thus derives life from Me.

he that eateth me] Instead of the Flesh and Blood we have Christ Himself; the two modes of partaking are merged in one, the more appropriate of the two being retained.

even he] Or, **he also**.

58. *This is that bread*] Better, *this is* **the** *Bread:* see on *v.* 48. The verse is a general summing up of the whole, returning from the imagery of Flesh and Blood to the main expression of the discourse—the Bread that came down from heaven and its superiority to all earthly food.

not as your fathers did eat manna, and are dead] Better, *not as* **the fathers did eat and died** (see on *v.* 49): 'your' and 'manna' are wanting in the best MSS. It is not in that way that *the* Bread comes down from heaven, nor is it such food.

eateth of] Omit 'of,' as in *vv.* 54, 56: 'of' is rightly inserted in *vv.* 26, 50, 51.

59 These *things* said he in the synagogue, as he taught in Capernaum.

60—71. Opposite Results of the Discourse.

60 Many therefore of his disciples, when they had heard **61** *this*, said, This is a hard saying; who can hear it? When Jesus knew in himself that his disciples murmured at it, he **62** said unto them, Doth this offend you? *What* and if ye

59. *in the synagogue*] Or, *in synagogue*, as we say 'in church:' there is no article in the Greek. Comp. xviii. 20. The verse is a mere historical note, stating definitely what was stated vaguely in v. 22 as 'the other side of the sea.' 'These things' naturally refers to the whole discourse from v. 26; we have no sufficient evidence of a break between v. 40 and v. 41. On the other hand there is strong evidence that from v. 26 to v. 58 forms one connected discourse spoken at one time in the synagogue at Capernaum. The site of Capernaum is not undisputed (see on Matt. iv. 13); but assuming Tell Hûm to be correct, the ruins of the synagogue there are probably those of the very building in which these words were uttered. On one of the stones a pot of manna is sculptured.

60—71. OPPOSITE RESULTS OF THE DISCOURSE.

60. *Many therefore of his disciples*] Including many more than the Apostles.

This is a hard saying] Or, **Hard is this speech.** Not hard to understand, but hard to accept. The word for 'hard' means originally 'dry,' and so 'rough;' and then in a moral sense, 'rough, harsh, offensive.' Nabal the churl has this epithet, 1 Sam. xxv. 3; and the slothful servant in the parable of the Talents calls his master a '*hard* man,' Matt. xxv. 24. Here the meaning is: 'This is a repulsive speech; who can listen to it?' It was the notion of eating flesh and drinking blood that specially scandalized them. See on v. 47.

61. *knew in himself*] Again He appears as the reader of the heart. Comp. i. 42, 47, ii. 24, 25, iv. 18, v. 14, 42, vi. 26, &c. More literally the verse runs: *Now Jesus knowing in Himself that His disciples are muttering about it:* see on v. 41, vii. 12. They talked in a low tone so that He could not hear: but He knew without hearing.

62. *What and if*, &c.] Literally, **If therefore ye should behold the Son of man ascending** *where He was before?* The sentence breaks off (*aposiopesis*) leaving something to be understood: but what is to be understood? The answer to this depends on the meaning assigned to 'behold the Son of man ascending.' The most literal and obvious interpretation is of an actual beholding of the Ascension: and in that case we supply; 'Would ye still take offence then?' Against this interpretation it is urged (1) That S. John does not record the Ascension. But it is assumed, if not here and iii. 13, yet certainly xx. 17 as a

shall see the Son of man ascend up where he was before?
It is the spirit that quickeneth; the flesh profiteth nothing: 63
the words that I speak unto you, *they* are spirit, and *they*
are life. But there are some of you that believe not. For 64
Jesus knew from the beginning who they were that believed
not, and who should betray him. And he said, Therefore 65

fact; and in all three cases it is in the words of our Lord that the
reference occurs. S. John throughout assumes that the main events of
Christ's life and the fundamental elements of Christianity are well known
to his readers. (2) That none but the Twelve witnessed the Ascension,
while this is addressed to a multitude of doubting disciples. But some
of the Twelve were present: and Christ speaks hypothetically; '*if* ye
should behold,' not '*when* ye *shall* behold.' (3) That in this case we
should expect 'but' instead of 'therefore.' Possibly, but not necessarily. The alternative interpretation is to make the 'ascending' refer
to the whole drama which led to Christ's return to glory, especially the
Passion (comp. vii. 33, xiii. 3, xiv. 12, 28, xvi. 5, 28, xvii. 11, 13):
and in that case we supply; 'Will not the sight of a suffering Messiah
offend you still more?'

63. *that quickeneth*] Literally, *that maketh alive* or **giveth life.**
The latter would perhaps be better to bring out the connexion with
'they are life' at the end of the verse.

the flesh] Not, '*My* Flesh,' which would contradict *v.* 51. The
statement is a general one, but has reference to Himself. 'My Flesh'
in *v.* 51 means 'My death' to be *spiritually* appropriated by every
Christian, and best appropriated in the Eucharist. 'The flesh' here
means the flesh *without the Spirit*, that which can only be appropriated
physically, like the manna. Even Christ's flesh in this sense 'profiteth
nothing.' (Comp. iii. 6.) Probably there is a general reference to
their carnal ideas about the Messiah: it is "in our Lord's refusal to
assume the outward insignia of the Messianic dignity, and in His persistent spiritualisation of the Messianic idea" that we must seek "the
ultimate cause" of the defection of so many disciples. S. pp. 141,
142.

the words] Or, *the sayings:* see on v. 47.

that I speak] The true reading is; *that I* **have spoken**, in the discourse just concluded.

64. *some of you that believe not*] There were some of those who followed
Him and called themselves His disciples, who still did not believe on
Him. The better order is, there are **of you some.**

knew from the beginning] It is impossible to fix the exact limits of
this; the meaning of 'the beginning' must depend on the context (see
on i. 1). Here the most natural limit is 'knew from the beginning of
their discipleship,' when they first became His followers. Comp. ii.
24, 25.

who should betray him] Or, *who* **it was that should** *betray Him*.
To ask, 'Why then did Jesus choose Judas as an Apostle?' is to ask in

said I unto you, that no *man* can come unto me, except it were given unto him of my Father.
66 From that *time* many of his disciples went back, and
67 walked no more with him. Then said Jesus unto the
68 twelve, Will ye also go away? Then Simon Peter answered him, Lord, to whom shall we go? thou hast the words of
69 eternal life. And we believe and are sure that thou art

a special instance for an answer to the insoluble enigma 'Why does Omniscience allow wicked persons to be born? Why does Omnipotence allow evil to exist?' The tares once sown among the wheat, both must 'grow together till the harvest,' and share sunshine and rain alike.

65. *Therefore*] Better, **For this cause** (xii. 18, 27): see on v. 16, 18, vii. 22, viii. 47.

said I unto you] v. 44; comp. v. 37, and see notes on both.

were given unto him of my Father] **Have been** *given unto him of* the *Father*.

66. *From that time*] This may be the meaning, but more probably it means *in consequence of that*. **Hereupon** has somewhat of the ambiguity of the Greek, combining the notions of time and result. The Greek phrase occurs here and xix. 12 only in N. T.

67. *the twelve*] The first mention of them; S. John speaks of them familiarly as a well-known body, assuming that his readers are well acquainted with the expression (see on *v.* 62). This is a mark of truth: all the more so because the expression does not occur in the earlier chapters; for it is probable that down to the end of chap. iv. at any rate 'the Twelve' did not yet exist.

Pilate and Mary Magdalene are introduced in the same abrupt way (xviii. 29, xix. 25).

Will ye also go away?] Better, **Surely ye also do not wish to** *go away?* 'Will' is too weak; it is not the future tense, but a separate verb, 'to will.' There is a similar error vii. 17 and viii. 44. Christ knows not only the unbelief of the many, but the belief and loyalty of the few.

68. *Then Simon Peter*] Omit 'Then.' S. Peter, as leader, *primus inter pares*, answers here as elsewhere in the name of the Twelve (see note on Mark iii. 17), and answers with characteristic impetuosity. The firmness of His conviction shews the appropriateness of the name given to him i. 42. His answer contains three reasons in logical order why they cannot desert their Master: (1) there is no one else to whom they can go; the Baptist is dead. Even if there were (2) Jesus has all that they need; He has 'sayings of eternal life.' And if there be other teachers who have them also, yet (3) there is but one Messiah, and Jesus is He. See on *v.* 47.

69. *we believe*] Rather, *we* **have believed**: the perfect tense implies that the faith and knowledge which they possess have been theirs for some time past. 'Are sure' means literally '*have come to know.*'

that Christ, the Son of the living God. Jesus answered 70 them, Have not I chosen you twelve, and one of you is a devil? He spake of Judas Iscariot *the son* of Simon: for 71 he *it was that* should betray him, being one of the twelve.

thou art that Christ, &c.] These words seem to have been imported hither from S. Peter's Confession, Matt. xvi. 16. The true reading here is; *Thou art* **the Holy One of God**. This is altogether a different occasion from Matt. xvi. 16, and probably previous to it. The Confessions are worth comparing. 1. 'Thou art the Son of God' (Matt. xiv. 33); in this the other Apostles joined. 2. 'Thou art the Holy One of God' (John vi. 69). 3. 'Thou art the Christ, the Son of the living God' (Matt. xvi. 16). They increase in fulness, as we might expect.

70. *Have I not chosen you twelve*] Or, **Did not I choose you the Twelve** (comp. xiii. 18)? Here probably the question ends: *and one of you is a devil* is best punctuated without an interrogation; it is a single statement in tragic contrast to the preceding question. It would be closer to the Greek to omit the article before 'devil' and make it a kind of adjective; *and one of you is devil*, i.e. devilish in nature: but this is hardly English. The words contain a half-rebuke to S. Peter for his impetuous avowal of loyalty in the name of them *all*. The passage stands alone in the N.T. (comp. Matt. xvi. 23), but its very singularity is evidence of its truth. S. John is not likely to have forgotten what was said, or in translating to have made any serious change.

71. *Judas Iscariot, the son of Simon*] The better reading is; **Judas, the son of Simon Iscariot**. If, as seems probable, the name Iscariot means 'man of Kerioth,' a place in Judah, it would be natural enough for both father and son to have the name. Assuming this to be correct, Judas was the only Apostle who was not a Galilean.

that should betray] *That was to betray;* not the same phrase as in *v.* 64.

being one of the twelve] 'Being' is of doubtful genuineness. The tragic contrast is stronger without the participle: *for he was to betray Him, one of the Twelve.*

With regard to the difficulty of understanding Christ's words in this sixth chapter, Meyer's concluding remark is to be borne in mind. "The difficulty is partly exaggerated; and partly the fact is overlooked that in all references to His death and the purpose of it Jesus could rely upon the light which the *future* would throw on these utterances: and sowing, as He generally did, for the future in the bosom of the present, He was compelled to utter much that was mysterious, but which would supply material and support for the further development and purification of faith and knowledge. The wisdom thus displayed in His teaching has been justified by *History.*"

CHAP. VII.

"Chapter vii., like chapter vi., is very important for the estimate of the fourth Gospel. In it the scene of the Messianic crisis shifts from

CHAP. VII. *Christ the Source of Truth and Light.*

1—9. *The controversy with His brethren.*

7 After these *things* Jesus walked in Galilee: for he would not walk in Jewry, because the Jews sought to kill him. ² Now the Jews' feast of tabernacles was at hand. His ³

Galilee to Jerusalem; and, as we should naturally expect, the crisis itself becomes hotter. The divisions, the doubts, the hopes, the jealousies, and the casuistry of the Jews are vividly portrayed. We see the mass of the populace, especially those who had come up from Galilee, swaying to and fro, hardly knowing which way to turn, inclined to believe, but held back by the more sophisticated citizens of the metropolis. These meanwhile apply the fragments of Rabbinical learning at their command in order to test the claims of the new prophet. In the background looms the dark shadow of the hierarchy itself, entrenched behind its prejudices and refusing to hear the cause that it has already prejudged. A single timid voice is raised against this injustice, but is at once fiercely silenced." S. p. 144.

As in chapters v. and vi. Christ is set forth as the *Source and Support of Life*, so in chapters vii., viii., and ix. He is set forth as the *Source of Truth and Light*.

CHAP. VII. CHRIST THE SOURCE OF TRUTH AND LIGHT.

Chapter vii. has three main divisions: 1. *The controversy with His brethren* (1—9); 2. *His teaching at the Feast of Tabernacles* (10—39); 3. *The effect of His teaching;* division both in the multitude and in the Sanhedrin (40—52).

1—9. THE CONTROVERSY WITH HIS BRETHREN.

1 *After these things*] The interval is again vague (see introductory note to chap. vi.); but comparing vi. 4 with vii. 2 we see that it covers about five months, the interval between the Passover and the Feast of Tabernacles.

walked in Galilee] To this ministry in Galilee, of which S. John tells us nothing, most of the incidents narrated Matt. xiv. 34—xviii. 35 belong. The tenses here are all imperfects, implying continued action.

he would not walk in Jewry] From this we understand that He did not go up to Jerusalem for the Passover mentioned vi. 4. 'Jewry' is found here in all the English versions excepting Wiclif's; it was common in the earlier translations. But in the A.V. it has been retained (probably by an oversight) only here, Luke xxiii. 5, and Dan. v. 13: elsewhere **Judæa** has been substituted. In Dan. v. 13 the same word is translated both 'Jewry' and 'Judah!' Comp. the Prayer Book version of Ps. lxxvi. 1.

2. *the Jews' feast of tabernacles*] Again an indication that the Gospel was written outside Palestine: see on vi. 1, 4. An author writing in Palestine would be less likely to specify it as 'the feast

brethren therefore said unto him, Depart hence, and go into Judea, that thy disciples also may see the works that thou doest. For *there is* no *man that* doeth any *thing* in 4 secret, and he himself seeketh to be known openly. If thou do these *things*, shew thyself to the world. For 5

of the Jews.' Tabernacles was the most joyous of the Jewish festivals. It had two aspects; (1) a commemoration of their dwelling in tents in the wilderness, (2) a harvest-home. It was therefore a thanksgiving (1) for a permanent abode, (2) for the crops of the year. It began on the 15th of the 7th month, Tisri (about our September), and lasted seven days, during which all who were not exempted through illness or weakness were obliged to live in booths, which involved much both of the discomfort and also of the merriment of a picnic. The distinctions between rich and poor were to a large extent obliterated in the general encampment, and the Feast thus became a great levelling institution. On the eighth day the booths were broken up and the people returned home: but it had special sacrifices of its own and was often counted as part of the Feast itself. The Feast is mentioned here, partly as a date, partly to shew what after all induced Christ to go up to Jerusalem.

3. *His brethren*] See on ii. 12.

Depart hence] The bluntness of this suggestion, given almost as a command, shews that they presumed upon their near relationship. It would be more natural in the mouths of men *older* than Christ, and therefore is in favour of their being sons of Joseph by a former marriage rather than sons of Joseph and Mary (comp. Mark iii. 21, 31). They shared the ordinary beliefs of the Jews about the Messiah, and therefore did not believe in their Brother. But His miracles perplexed them, and they wished the point brought to a decisive issue. There is no treachery in their suggestion; its object is not to put Him in the power of His enemies.

thy disciples also] His brethren seem to imply that they themselves are not His disciples even nominally.

4. *there is no man that doeth*] More simply, **no man** *doeth*.

and he himself seeketh] i.e. no one does anything in secret and is thereby personally seeking to act with openness. To conceal His miracles is to deny His Messiahship; the Messiah must accept His position.

to be known openly] Literally, *to be in openness* or *frankness*. The word for 'frankness' occurs nine times in this Gospel and four times in the First Epistle; not in Matt. or Luke; only once in Mark.

If thou do these things] Feeding the 5000, and other miracles. If Thou doest such miracles at all, do them at Jerusalem at the Feast and convince the whole nation. It is assuming a false position to do such things and hide them in obscure parts of Galilee: it is claiming to be the Messiah and being afraid to shew one's credentials.

162 S. JOHN, VII. [vv. 6—8.

6 neither did his brethren believe in him. Then Jesus said unto them, My time is not yet come: but your time is
7 alway ready. The world cannot hate you; but me it hateth, because I testify of it, that the works thereof are
8 evil. Go ye up unto this feast: I go not up yet unto this

They knew probably that He had not gone up to Jerusalem for the Passover.

shew thyself] Better, **manifest** *Thyself.* See on i. 31, xxi. 1, and comp. ix. 3, xvii. 6.

 5. *For neither did his brethren believe in him*] Or, *For* **not even** *did His brethren* (as one would expect) *believe on Him*. It is marvellous that in the face of this verse any one should have maintained that three of His brethren (James, Simon, and Judas) were Apostles. This verse is also fatal to the common theory, that these 'brethren' are really our Lord's cousins, the sons of Alphæus. Certainly *one* of the sons of Alphæus (James) was an Apostle; probably a *second* was (Matthew, if Levi and Matthew are the same person, as is almost universally admitted); possibly a third was (Judas, if 'Judas of James' means 'Judas, *brother* of James,' as is commonly supposed). By this time the company of the Twelve was complete (vi. 67, 70, 71); so that we cannot suppose that some of the Twelve have still to be converted. If then one, two, or three sons of Alphæus were Apostles, how could it be true that the sons of Alphæus 'did not believe on Him?' 'His brethren' cannot be the sons of Alphæus. They seem to have been converted by the Resurrection. Immediately after the Ascension we find them with the Apostles and the holy women (Acts i. 14; comp. 1 Cor. ix. 5, Gal. i. 19).

6. *Then Jesus said*] Better, *Jesus* **therefore saith.**

My time is not yet come] i.e. My time for manifesting Myself to the world; with special reference to the Passion. It is inadequate to interpret it of the time for going up to the Feast. Moreover, what sense would there be in 'Your time *for going up to the Feast* is always ready?' Whereas 'You can always manifest yourselves' makes excellent sense. See last note on ii. 4.

7. *The world*] Unbelievers; the common meaning in S. John. In v. 4 'the world' means all mankind. See on i. 10.

cannot hate you] Because you and it are of one mind; because you are part of it: it cannot hate itself; see on xv. 19. Hence it is that they can always manifest themselves: they can always count upon favourable surroundings and a sympathetic audience.

me it hateth] Comp. iii. 20, vii. 34, 36, viii. 21, xii. 39.

8. *Go ye up unto this feast*] 'Ye' is emphatic; 'this' is wanting in authority; we should read, *go ye up unto* **the** *feast*.

I go not up yet] 'Yet,' though very ancient, is possibly no part of the original text: it may have been inserted to avoid the charge of the heathen critic Porphyry, that Jesus here shews fickleness or deceit, and therefore cannot be Divine. But the sense is the same, whether

feast; for my time is not yet full come. When he had said 9 these *words* unto them, he abode *still* in Galilee.

10—39. *The Discourse at the Feast of Tabernacles.*
But when his brethren were gone up, then went he also 10 up unto the feast, not openly, but as it were in secret. Then the Jews sought him at the feast, and said, Where is 11

'yet' is inserted or not. He means 'I am not going now; not going publicly in the general caravan of pilgrims; not going with you, who do not believe on Me.' He does not say 'I shall not go.' The next two verses shew exactly what is meant by the negative.

9. *he abode still in Galilee*] This in conjunction with *v.* 1 shews that S. John is quite aware that Galilee is the main scene of Christ's ministry, as the Synoptists represent. The gaps in his narrative leave ample room for the Galilean ministry.

This opening scene (1—9) "is described by M. Renan as a 'gem of history' (*un petit trésor historique*). He argues justly that an apologist, writing merely *ad probandum*, would not have given so much prominence to the unbelief which Jesus met with in His own family. He insists, too, on the individualising traits which the whole section bears. The brethren of Jesus are not 'types' but living men; their ill-natured and jealous irony is only too human." S. pp. 144, 145.

10—39. THE DISCOURSE AT THE FEAST OF TABERNACLES.

Of this section *vv.* 10—15 form a sort of introduction.

"An equal degree of authenticity belongs to the verses which follow, 10—15. The whispered enquiries and debatings among the people, the secret journey, the sudden appearance in the temple in the midst of the Feast, and in particular the question that alludes to the Rabbinical schools and the custom of professed teachers to frequent them, compose a varied, clear, and graphic picture that has every circumstance of probability in its favour." S. pp. 145, 146.

10. *unto the feast*] These words have become transposed; they belong to the first clause, not to the second; *Now when His brethren were* **gone up to the feast,** *then He also went up.* This being so, it becomes possible, if not probable, that Christ's declaration 'I go not up to this Feast' is true, even when made to mean 'I shall not go up at all.' All that is certain is that Christ appeared when the Feast was half over (*v.* 14).

not openly] Not in the general caravan, but either by a different route (e.g. through Samaria, as in iv. 4, instead of down the eastern bank of Jordan), or several days later. One suspects that traces of Docetism are difficult to find in this Gospel when it is maintained that this verse contains such.

11. *the Jews*] The hostile party, as usual: comp. *v.* 1. Both here and in *v.* 6 'then' should rather be **therefore**: comp. vi. 53, 67, 68.

12 he? And there was much murmuring among the people concerning him : *for* some said, He is a good *man:* others 13 said, Nay; but he deceiveth the people. Howbeit no *man* spake openly of him for fear of the Jews.

14 Now about the midst of the feast Jesus went up into the 15 temple, and taught. And the Jews marvelled, saying, How 16 knoweth this *man* letters, having never learned? Jesus

The force of the 'therefore' here is 'because they did not find Him in the caravan of pilgrims from Galilee.'

sought...and said] Both verbs are imperfects of continued action. They do not mention His name,—perhaps in contempt; 'Where is that man?' Comp. ix. 28.

12. *murmuring*] Talking in an under tone, not necessarily complaining: see on vi. 41, 61. Here some are for, and some against Him. 'Among the people' should rather be *among the* **multitudes**; the word is plural, and this is the only place in the Gospel where the plural is used: the singular (*He* **leadeth the multitude astray**) is common.

13. *no man*] Quite literally; no man dared speak openly either for or against Him, they were so afraid of the hierarchy. Experience had taught them that it was dangerous to take any line which the rulers had not formally sanctioned; and though the rulers were known to be against Christ, yet they had not committed themselves beyond recall, and might turn against either side. 'A true indication of an utterly jesuitical domination of the people.' Meyer.

for fear of the Jews] Literally, *for* **the** *fear of the Jews*, i.e. on account of the *prevalent* fear of the hierarchy and official representatives of the nation.

14. *about the midst of the feast*] Literally, *But now, when the feast was at the middle*, or *was half way past*; i.e. about the fourth day. But the expression is a vague one, so that we cannot be certain which day.

went up into the temple] Whether He had been in Jerusalem or not since the beginning of the Feast, is uncertain: see on *v.* 10. This is perhaps the first occasion of His publicly teaching in the Temple; when He cleansed it (ii. 13—17) He delivered no discourse.

15. *And the Jews marvelled*] According to the best MSS., *The Jews* **therefore** *marvelled*. 'Therefore' should also be inserted in *v.* 16; *Jesus* **therefore** *answered them.* S. John's extreme fondness for this particle in narrative is worth keeping in view.

How knoweth this man letters] Or, *this* **fellow**, as in vi. 42. Their question is so eminently characteristic, that it is very unlikely that a Greek writer of the second century would have been able to invent it for them; he would probably have made them too cautious to commit themselves to any expression of astonishment about Him. The substance of His doctrine excites no emotion in them, but they are astounded that He should possess learning without having got it according to ordinary routine. He had never attended the schools of the

answered them, and said, My doctrine is not mine, but his that sent me. If any *man* will do his will, he shall know 17 of the doctrine, whether it be of God, or *whether* I speak of myself. He that speaketh of himself seeketh his own 18 glory: but he that seeketh his glory that sent him, the same is true, and no unrighteousness is in him. Did not Moses 19

Rabbis, and yet His interpretations of Scripture shewed a large amount of biblical and other knowledge. That *does* excite them. In Acts xxvi. 24, 'much learning doth make thee mad,' the word there translated 'learning' is the same as the one here translated 'letters.'

16—36. The remark made on the Jews' question in *v.* 15 applies also to their questions and comments throughout this dialogue. They are too exactly in keeping with what we know of the Jews in our Lord's day to be the invention of a Greek more than a century later. They "are all exactly what we should expect from the popular mode of interpreting and applying the Messianic prophecies." S. p. 146.

16. *My doctrine is not mine*] 'The teaching which I give does not originate with Me; that is the reason why I have no need to learn in the schools. He Who sent Me communicates it to Me.'

17. *If any man will do his will*] As in vi. 67 and viii. 44, 'will' is too weak; it is not the simple future, but the verb 'to will:' *If any man* **willeth to do** *His will*. The mere mechanical performance of God's will is not enough; there must be an inclination towards Him, a wish to make our conduct agree with His will; and without this agreement Divine doctrine cannot be recognised as such. There must be a moral harmony between the teaching and the taught, and this harmony is in the first instance God's gift (vi. 44, 45), which each can accept or refuse at will. Comp. xiv. 21.

he shall know] Literally, *He shall come to know, recognise*. See on *v.* 26 and viii. 55.

whether it be of God, &c.] Literally, *whether it proceeds from God* (as its Fount), *or I speak from Myself*. Comp. v. 30, xv. 4.

18. Proof almost in the form of a syllogism that He does not speak of Himself. It applies to Christ alone. Human teachers who seek God's glory are not thereby secured from erroneous teaching. These verses (16—18) remind us, and might remind some of His hearers of an earlier discourse delivered in Jerusalem some seven months before: comp. v. 19, 30, 37, 44.

the same is true] and therefore does not speak of himself, for whoever speaks what comes from himself is not true.

no unrighteousness is in him] Or, **unrighteousness is not in him**. S. John does not say 'falsehood' as we might expect, but uses a wider word which points out the moral root of the falsehood. Comp. viii. 46. Throughout S. John's writings the connexion between truth and righteousness, falsehood and unrighteousness is often brought before us. Hence his peculiar phrases 'to *do* the truth' (1 John i. 6), 'to do a lie' (Rev. xxi. 27, xxii. 15).

give you the law, and *yet* none of you keepeth the law?
20 Why go ye about to kill me? The people answered and
said, Thou hast a devil: who goeth about to kill thee?
21 Jesus answered and said unto them, I have done one work,
22 and ye all marvel. Moses therefore gave unto you circumcision, not because it is of Moses, but of the fathers;

There is no need to suppose that anything is omitted between 18 and 19, though the transition is abrupt. Christ has answered them and now takes the offensive. He exposes the real meaning of their cavillings; they seek His life.

19. *Did not Moses give you the law?*] Here the question should probably end: *and none of you doeth the law* should be a simple statement in contrast to the question preceding. The argument is similar to v. 45; Moses in whom they trust condemns them. Moreover it is an *argumentum ad hominem*: 'ye are all breakers of the law, and yet would put Me to death as a breaker of it.'

20. *Thou hast a devil*] The multitude who have come up from the provinces know nothing of the designs of the hierarchy, although dwellers in Jerusalem (*v.* 25) are better informed. These provincials think He must be possessed to have such an idea. Comp. x. 20, and also Matt. xi. 18, where the same is quoted as said of the Baptist. In both cases extraordinary conduct is supposed to be evidence of insanity, and the insanity is attributed to demoniacal possession. In viii. 48 the same remark is made, but in a much more hostile spirit (see note there); and there Christ answers the charge. Here, where it is the mere ignorant rejoinder of a perplexed multitude, He takes no notice of the interruption.

21. *I have done*] Better, **I did.** Comp. *v.* 23.

one work] The healing of the impotent man at Bethesda: it excited the astonishment of all as being wrought on the Sabbath. Christ reminds them that on that occasion all, and not the rulers only, were offended.

Most modern editors add to this verse the words translated 'therefore' in *v.* 22 [it is not S. John's favourite particle (see on *v.* 15), but a preposition with a pronoun=*for this cause, on account of this*]; 'and ye all marvel on account of this.' But this is cumbrous, and unlike S. John, who *begins* sentences with this phrase (v. 16, 18, viii. 47, x. 17, xii. 39; mistranslated 'therefore' in all cases) rather than ends them with it. The old arrangement is best.

22. *Moses therefore gave*] Better, **For this cause** (xii. 18, 27) **Moses hath given.** Comp. viii. 47.

of Moses...of the fathers] 'Originating with Moses...originating with the fathers.' Circumcision originated with the Patriarchs, and was a more ancient institution than the Sabbath. When, therefore, the two ordinances clashed, the younger had to give place; it was more fit that the Sabbath should be broken, than that circumcision should be administered on the wrong day. If then the Sabbath

vv. 23—27.] S. JOHN, VII. 167

and ye on the sabbath day circumcise a man. If a man 23 on the sabbath day receive circumcision, that the law of Moses should not be broken; are ye angry at me, because I have made a man every whit whole on the sabbath day? Judge not according to the appearance, but judge righteous 24 judgment. Then said some of them of Jerusalem, Is not 25 this he, whom they seek to kill? But lo, he speaketh 26 boldly, and they say nothing unto him. Do the rulers know indeed that this is the very Christ? Howbeit we 27 know this *man* whence he is: but when Christ cometh, no

could give way to a mere ceremonial observance, how much more might it give way to a work of mercy? The law of charity is older and higher than any ceremonial law.
on the sabbath] Rather, *on a Sabbath;* so also in *v.* 23.
23. *that the law of Moses should not be broken*] i.e. the law about circumcision on the eighth day (Lev. xii. 3), which was a re-enactment of the patriarchal law (Gen. xvii. 12). Some adopt the inferior rendering in the margin; 'without breaking the law of Moses,' or 'without the law of Moses being broken;' in which case 'the law of Moses' means the law about the Sabbath.
are ye angry] The word occurs nowhere else in N.T. It signifies bitter and violent resentment.
because I have made] Better, *because* **I made.** Comp. *v.* 21.
24. *according to the appearance*] 'According to the appearance' Christ's act was a breach of the Sabbath. This is almost certainly the meaning, although the word translated 'appearance' may mean 'face,' and is rightly translated 'face' in xi. 44 (see note there). There is no reference here to Christ's having 'no form nor comeliness,' as if He meant 'Judge not by My mean appearance.'
25. *Then said some*] Or, **Some therefore** *said* (see on vi. 53, vii. 11, 15), i.e. in consequence of Christ's vindication of Himself. These inhabitants of the capital know better than the provincials, who speak in *v.* 20, what the intentions of the hierarchy really are.
26. *boldly*] Or, *with frankness*, or *openness;* the same word as in *v.* 4, where (as in xvi. 29) it has a preposition; here and *v.* 13 it is the simple dative.
Do the rulers know] The word here translated 'know' is not the one translated 'know' in *vv.* 28, 29. The latter is the most general word for 'know:' this means rather to 'acquire knowledge.' *Have the rulers come to know* (or *recognised*)? See on i. 10. In the next verse we have both words. Comp. viii. 55.
that this is the very Christ] 'Very' is wanting in authority: *that this* **man is the Christ** is the right reading. This suggestion, however, is only a momentary thought. They at once raise a difficulty which for them demolishes the suggestion.
27. *when Christ cometh*] Better, *when* **the** *Christ cometh:* see on i. 20.

28 *man* knoweth whence he is. Then cried Jesus in the temple as he taught, saying, Ye both know me, and ye know whence I am: and I am not come of myself, but he 29 that sent me is true, whom ye know not. But I know him:

no man knoweth whence he is] Literally, *no man comes to know* (see on v. 26 and viii. 55) *whence He is*. 'Whence' does not refer to the Messiah's *birthplace*, which was known (*vv*. 41, 42); nor to His *remote descent*, for He was to be the Son of David (*ibid.*); but to His parentage (vi. 42), immediate and actual. This text is the strongest, if not the only evidence that we have of the belief that the immediate parents of the Messiah would be unknown: but the precision and vivacity of this passage carries conviction with it, and shews how familiar the ideas current among the Jews at that time were to S. John. It never occurs to him to explain. The belief might easily grow out of Isa. liii. 8, 'Who shall declare His generation?' Justin Martyr tells us of a kindred belief, that the Messiahship of the Messiah would be unknown, even to Himself, until He was anointed by Elijah. (*Trypho*, pp. 226, 336.)

28. *Then cried Jesus*] Better, **Jesus therefore cried aloud**. The word translated 'cried' signifies a loud expression of strong emotion. He is moved by their gross misconception of Him, a fact which the weakening of 'therefore' into 'then' obscures. Comp. *v*. 37, i. 15, xii. 44.

in the temple] S. John well remembers that moving cry in the Temple; the scene is still before him and he puts it before us, although neither 'in the Temple' nor 'as He taught' is needed for the narrative (see *v*. 14).

Ye both know me, &c.] Various constructions have been put upon this: (1) that it is a question; (2) that it is ironical; (3) a mixture of the two; (4) a reproach, i.e. that they knew His Divine nature and maliciously concealed it. None of these are satisfactory. The words are best understood quite simply and literally. Christ admits the truth of what they say: they have an outward knowledge of Him and His origin (vi. 42); but He has an inner and higher origin, of which they know nothing. So that even their self-made test, for the sake of which they are willing to resist the evidence both of Scripture and of His works, is complied with; for they know not His real immediate origin.

and I am not come of myself] 'Of Myself' is emphatic; *and* (*yet*) *of Myself I am not come*. Comp. viii. 42. The 'and' introduces a contrast, as so often in S. John: 'ye know My person, and ye know My parentage; and yet of the chief thing of all, My Divine mission, ye know nothing. See on *v*. 30.

but he that sent me is true] The word for 'true' here is the same as occurs i. 9 in 'the *true* Light' (see note there): the meaning, therefore, is not 'truthful' but 'real, perfect;' *He that sendeth Me is a real sender*, One who in the highest and most perfect sense can give a mis-

for I am from him, and he hath sent me. Then they 30
sought to take him: but no *man* laid hands on him,
because his hour was not yet come. And many of the 31
people believed on him, and said, When Christ cometh, will
he do moe miracles than these which this *man* hath done?
The Pharisees heard that the people murmured such *things* 32
concerning him; and the Pharisees and the chief priests

sion. But perhaps here and in Rev. iii. 7 and xix. 11 the distinction
between the two words for 'true' is not very marked. Such refine-
ments (the words being alike except in termination) have a tendency to
become obscured.

29. *I know him*] 'I' in emphatic contrast to the preceding 'ye,'
which is also emphatic. 'I know Him, for I came forth from Him,
and it is He, and no other, that sent Me.' 'Sent' is aorist, not perfect.
Comp. the very remarkable passage Matt. xi. 27.

30. *Then they sought*] Better, **Therefore they kept seeking** (imperfect of continued action) in consequence of His publicly claiming
Divine origin and mission. 'They' means the rulers, the Sanhedrin;
not the people, who are mentioned in the next verse.

but no man laid hands] Rather, **and** *no man laid hands*, 'and'
introducing a contrast as in *v.* 28. See on xxi. 3. That 'and' in
S. John often = 'and yet,' as here, is most true; that 'and' ever = 'but'
is true neither of S. John nor of any other Greek writer.

because his hour] The hour appointed by God for His Passion (xiii.
1), this meaning being clearly marked by the context (see on *v.* 6 and
ii. 4). The immediate cause of their not seizing Him was that they
were as yet afraid to do so; but S. John passes through proximate
causes to the prime cause of all, the Will of God. When the hour
was come God no longer allowed their fear, which still existed (Matt.
xxvi. 5), to deter them.

31. *And many of the people*] Our version is somewhat perverse;
in *v.* 30 'and' is arbitrarily turned into 'but;' here 'but' is turned
into 'and.' **But** (on the other hand, i.e. in contrast to the rulers) **of
the multitude** *many believed on Him* (as the Messiah) *and* **kept saying**
(in answer to objectors), *When* **the** *Christ* (see on *v.* 27 and i. 20)
cometh, will He do more **signs** *than this man* **did**? They express not
their own doubts but those of objectors in saying '*when* the Christ
cometh:' *they* believe that He has come. Some of them perhaps had
witnessed the numerous Galilean miracles; they have at any rate
heard of them.

32. *heard that the people murmured such things*] Better, *heard* **the
multitude muttering these** *things* (see on *v.* 12): it was not reported
to them, they heard it themselves, and they went and reported it in the
Sanhedrin, which gives an order for His apprehension. Note that in
this the reckless hierarchy, who were mainly Sadducees, combine with
the Pharisees (comp. *v.* 45, xi. 47, 57, xviii. 3).

33 sent officers to take him. Then said Jesus unto them, Yet a little while am I with you, and *then* I go unto him that 34 sent me. Ye shall seek me, and shall not find *me:* and 35 where I am, *thither* ye cannot come. Then said the Jews among themselves, Whither will he go, that we shall not find him? will he go unto the dispersed among the Gentiles,

33. *Then said Jesus*] Better, as in *v.* 30 and often, **Therefore** *said Jesus*, i.e. in consequence of their sending to arrest Him: probably He recognised the officers waiting for an opportunity to take Him. According to the best MSS., 'Unto them' should be omitted: Christ's words are addressed to the officers and those who sent them.

It is very difficult to decide on the precise meaning of Christ's words. Perhaps the simplest interpretation is the best. 'I must remain on earth a little while longer, and during this time ye cannot kill Me: then ye will succeed, and I shall go to My Father. Thither ye will wish to come, but ye cannot; for ye know Him not (*v.* 28), and such as ye cannot enter there.' This is the first formal attempt upon His life. It reminds Him that His death is not far off, and that it will place a tremendous barrier between Him and those who compass it. It is the beginning of the end; an end that will bring a short-lived loss and eternal triumph to Him, a short-lived triumph and eternal loss to them.

unto him that sent me] One suspects that here S. John is translating Christ's words into plainer language than He actually used. Had He said thus clearly 'unto Him that sent Me,' a phrase which they elsewhere understand at once of God (see on *v.* 30), they could scarcely have asked the questions which follow in *v.* 35. Unless we are to suppose that they here *pretend* not to understand; which is unlikely, as they speak not to Him but 'among themselves.'

34. *Ye shall seek me*] From xiii. 33 it seems almost certain that these words are not to be understood of seeking His *life:* rather of seeking for *help* at His hands. Comp. viii. 21. It is best, however, not to limit their application to any particular occasion, such as the destruction of Jerusalem, the great hour of Jewish need.

where I am, thither ye cannot come] 'Thither' is not in the Greek and is perhaps better omitted, so as to bring out the emphatic opposition between 'I' and 'ye.'

35. *Then said the Jews*] The **Jews therefore** *said*, i.e. in consequence of what Christ had said, shewing that it is to the official representatives of the nation that His words are addressed.

Whither will he go, &c.] Better, **Where does this fellow intend to go, seeing** *that we shall not find Him?* **Does He intend to go unto the dispersion among** *the Gentiles*, &c.

the dispersed] Or, **the dispersion**, meaning those Jews who were dispersed among the heathen outside Palestine; the abstract for the concrete, like 'the circumcision' for the Jews generally. The word for 'dispersion' (*diaspora*), occurs James i. 1 and 1 Pet. i. 1 (see

and teach the Gentiles? What *manner of* saying is this 36
that he said, Ye shall seek me, and shall not find *me:* and
where I am, *thither* ye cannot come?

In the last day, *that* great *day* of the feast, Jesus stood 37
and cried, saying, If any *man* thirst, let him come unto me,

notes there), and nowhere else in N.T. There were three chief colonies of these 'dispersed' or 'scattered' Jews, in Babylonia, Egypt, and Syria, whence they spread over the whole world. 'Moses of old time hath in every city them that preach him,' Acts xv. 21. These opponents of Christ, therefore, suggest that He means to go to the Jews scattered among the Gentiles in order to reach the Gentiles and teach them—the very mode of proceeding afterwards adopted by the Apostles. But here it is spoken in sarcasm. Christ's utter disregard of Jewish exclusiveness and apparent non-observance of the ceremonial law gave a handle to the sneer; which would be pointless if the word translated 'Gentiles' (margin 'Greeks') were rendered 'Hellenists,' i.e. Grecised Jews. *Hellenes*, or 'Greeks,' in N.T. *always* means Gentiles or heathen. See on xii. 20.

36. *What manner of saying is this*] Or, **What is this saying?** 'this' being contemptuous, like 'this precious saying.' They know that their scornful suggestion is not true.

37. *In the last day, that great day*] **Now on** *the last day*, **the** *great day*. This was probably not the seventh day, but the eighth day, which according to Lev. xxiii. 36, 39; Num. xxix. 35; Neh. viii. 18, was reckoned along with the seven days of the feast proper. To speak of the seventh day as 'the great day of the feast' would not be very appropriate; whereas the eighth day on which the people returned home was, like the first day, kept as a Sabbath (Lev. xxiii. 39), and had special sacrifices (Num. xxix. 36—38). In keeping with the solemnity of the day Christ solemnly takes up His position and cries aloud with deep emotion (see on *v.* 28).

stood] Or, **was standing.**

If any man thirst] The conjectural reference to the custom of pouring water at the Feast of Tabernacles is probably correct. On all seven days water was brought from the pool of Siloam and poured into a silver basin on the western side of the altar of burnt offering, a ceremony not mentioned in O.T. Apparently this was *not* done on the *eighth* day. Accordingly Christ comes forward and fills the gap, directing them to a better water than that of Siloam. The fact that the water was poured and not drunk, does not seem to be a reason for denying the reference, especially when we remember how frequently Christ took an external fact as a text (comp. iv. 10, v. 17, 19, vi. 26, 27, (viii. 12?) ix. 39, xiii. 8, 10, 12—17; Mark x. 15, 16, 23, 24, &c.). The pouring of the water would be suggestive enough. In such cases there is no need for the analogy to be complete, and in the present case it would add point to the reference that it was not complete. Mere pouring of water could not quench even bodily thirst;

38 and drink. He that believeth on me, as the scripture hath 39 said, out of his belly shall flow rivers of living water. (But this spake he of the Spirit, which they that believe on him should receive: for the Holy Ghost was not yet *given;* because that Jesus was not yet glorified.)

40—52. *Opposite Results of the Discourse.*

40 Many of the people therefore, when they heard *this* saying,

Christ could satisfy spiritual thirst. 'Therefore with joy shall ye draw water out of the wells of salvation.' Isa. xii. 3.

38. *as the scripture hath said*] This phrase undoubtedly refers to the words that follow: but inasmuch as no such text is found in Scripture, some have tried to force the phrase into connexion with what precedes, as if the meaning were 'He that believeth on me in the way that Scripture prescribes.' Although the exact words are not found in Scripture there are various texts of similar import: Isa. xliv. 3, lviii. 11; Zech. xiii. 1, xiv. 8, &c. But none of them contain the very remarkable expression 'out of his belly.'

rivers of living water] In the Greek 'rivers' stands first with strong emphasis; *rivers out of his belly shall flow*, (rivers) *of living water*, in marked contrast to the *ewer* of water poured each day during the Feast. 'He that believeth on me' is of course a stage far in advance of 'if any one thirst.' A man may thirst for spiritual satisfaction, and yet not end in believing on Christ. But the believer cannot end in satisfying his own thirst; he at once becomes a fount whence others may derive refreshment. Whether he wills to be a teacher or no, the true Christian cannot fail to impart the spirit of Christianity to others.

39. *this spake he of the Spirit*] S. John's interpretation is to be accepted, whatever may be our theory of inspiration, (1) because no better interpreter of Christ's words ever lived, even among the Apostles; (2) because it is the result of his own inmost experience. The principle of Christian activity has ever been the Spirit. He moves the waters, and they overflowed at Pentecost. Till then 'the Spirit was not yet;' the dispensation of the Spirit had not come.

the Holy Ghost was not yet given] Both 'the Holy' and 'given' are of doubtful authority: 'given' is omitted by nearly all MSS. except the Vatican; it gives the right sense. Like 'Holy Spirit' in i. 33, 'Spirit' has no article and means a power of the Spirit.

because that Jesus was not yet glorified] Comp. xvi. 7; Ps. lxviii. 18. The Spirit, "though given in His fulness to Christ Himself (iii. 34), and operating through Him in His people (vi. 63), was not, until after Christ's return to glory, to be given to the faithful as the Paraclete and representative of Christ for the carrying on of His work." Meyer.

40—52. OPPOSITE RESULTS OF THE DISCOURSE.

40. *Many of the people*, &c.] According to the best authorities;

said, Of a truth this is the Prophet. Others said, This is the 41
Christ. But some said, Shall Christ come out of Galilee?
Hath not the scripture said, That Christ cometh of the seed 42
of David, and out of the town of Bethlehem, where David
was? So there was a division among the people because 43
of him. And some of them would have taken him; but no 44
man laid hands on him.
Then came the officers to the chief priests and Pharisees; 45

Of the multitude, therefore, some, when they heard these words,
were saying, or, began to say.
Of a truth this is the Prophet] The Prophet of Deut. xviii. 15,
whom some identified with the Messiah, others supposed would be the
fore-runner of the Messiah. Here he is plainly distinguished from the
Messiah. See on i. 21 and vi. 14.
41. *Others said...some said*] Both verbs, as in *v.* 40, are imperfects
of repeated action; *kept saying, used to say.*
Shall Christ come out of Galilee] We have here an instance how
little attention our translators paid to the Greek article: in the same
verse they translate the article in one place and ignore it in another.
In the next verse they ignore it again. In all three places it should
be '*the* Christ' (see on i. 20). **Why, doth the Christ** *come out of
Galilee?* It is quite inadmissible to infer, because S. John does not
correct this mistake of supposing that Jesus came from Galilee, that he
is either ignorant of the truth or indifferent to it. He knew that his
readers would be well aware of the facts. On the other hand, could
a Greek of the second century invent these discussions of the Jewish
multitude?
42. *of the seed of David*] Ps. cxxxii. 11; Jer. xxiii. 5; Isa. xi. 1, 10.
out of the town of Bethlehem] Literally, **from Bethlehem, the
village** *where David was.* Mic. v. 2; 1 Sam xvi.
43. *a division*] *Schisma*, whence our word 'schism.' It means a
serious and possibly violent division: ix. 16, x. 19; 1 Cor. i. 10,
xii. 25; comp. Acts xiv. 4, xxiii. 7. In N. T. it is never used in the
modern sense of a separation *from* the Church, but of parties *in* the
Church. In the Synoptists it is used only in its original sense of
physical severing; 'a worse *rent* is made;' Matt. ix. 16; Mark ii. 21.
among the people] **In the multitude.**
44. *some of them*] Some of the multitude, provoked by the controversy, would on their own responsibility have carried Him before the
Sanhedrin. These 'some' are not the officers mentioned in the next
verse.
45. *Then came the officers*] Better, **Therefore** *came the officers*,
i.e. because neither they nor any of the multitude had ventured to
arrest Him. Under the control of God's providence (*v*. 30), they had
been unable to find any good opportunity for taking Him, and had
been over-awed by the majesty of His words (*v*. 46).

and they said unto them, Why have ye not brought him?
46 The officers answered, Never man spake like this man.
47 Then answered them the Pharisees, Are ye also deceived?
48 Have any of the rulers or of the Pharisees believed on him?
49 But this people who knoweth not the law are cursed.
50 Nicodemus saith unto them, (he that came to *Jesus* by
51 night, being one of them,) Doth our law judge any man,

to the chief priests and Pharisees] See on *v.* 32. It would seem as if the Sanhedrin had continued sitting, waiting for the return of its officers; an extraordinary proceeding on so great a day (see on *v.* 37), shewing the intensity of their hostility. Their question is quite in harmony with this.

they said] The pronoun used (*ekeinoi*) indicates that they are regarded as alien or hostile to the narrator.

Why have ye not brought] Why **did** *ye not* **bring**?

46. *Never man spake like this man*] The reading is doubtful; some of the best MSS. have *Never man* **so spake**. Possibly Christ said a good deal more than is recorded by S. John.

47. *the Pharisees*] That portion of the Sanhedrin which was most jealous of orthodoxy, regarded both by themselves and others as models of correct belief: see next verse. For 'then' read **therefore**.

Are ye also deceived] Strong emphasis on 'ye;' *Surely ye also have not been* **led astray**, ye, the officers of the Sanhedrin! Comp. *v.* 12.

48. What right have you to judge for yourselves, contrary to the declared opinion of the Sanhedrin and of the orthodox party? What right have you to wear our livery and dispute our resolutions?

49. *this people*] Very contemptuous; *this* **multitude** *of yours* (comp. 35, 36), whose ignorant fancies you prefer to our deliberate decisions.

who knoweth not the law] The form of negative used implies censure; knoweth not when it ought to know. They ought to know that a sabbath-breaker cannot be the Messiah.

are cursed] A mere outburst of theological fury. A formal excommunication of the whole multitude by the Sanhedrin (comp. ix. 22) would be impossible. How could such a sentence be executed on the right individuals? It was reserved for a Christian hierarchy to invent the interdict. Excommunication *en masse* was unknown to the Jews.

50. *he that came to Jesus by night*] The better reading seems to be, *he that came* **to Him** **before**. See on iii. 1, 2. His 'being one of them' contradicts what is implied in *v.* 48, that no member of the Sanhedrin believed on Him.

51. *Doth our law*] 'Law' is emphatic. 'You condemn the multitude for not knowing the law; but are we not forgetting the law in condemning a man unheard?' These learned theologians and lawyers were forgetting such plain and simple texts as Deut. i. 16, 17, xvii. 8, xix. 15; involving the most elementary principles of justice.

before it hear him, and know what he doeth? They 52 answered and said unto him, Art thou also of Galilee? Search, and look: for out of Galilee ariseth no prophet.

any man, before it hear him] Literally, **the** *man* (prosecuted) except it first hear from himself.

52. *Art thou also of Galilee?*] 'Surely thou dost not sympathize with Him as being a fellow-countryman?' They share the popular belief that Jesus was by birth a Galilean (*v.* 41).

out of Galilee ariseth no prophet] Either their temper makes them forgetful, or in the heat of controversy they prefer a sweeping statement to a qualified one. Jonah of Gath-hepher (2 Kings xiv. 25) was certainly of Galilee; Nahum of Elkosh may have been, but the situation of Elkosh is uncertain; Hosea was of the northern kingdom, but whether of Galilee or not is unknown; Abelmeholah, whence Elisha came, was in the north part of the Jordan valley, possibly in Galilee. Anyhow, their statement is only a slight and very natural exaggeration (comp. iv. *v.* 29). Judging from the past, Galilee was not very likely to produce a Prophet, much less the Messiah.

Of the various questions which arise respecting the paragraph that follows (vii. 53—viii. 11) one at least may be answered with something like certainty,—that it is *no part of the Gospel of S. John.* (1) In both tone and style it is very unlike his writings. His favourite words and expressions are wanting; others that he rarely or never uses are found. (2) It breaks the course of the narrative, which runs smoothly enough if this paragraph be omitted; and hence a few of the MSS. which contain it place it at the end of the Gospel. (3) All the very serious amount of external evidence which tells against the passage being part of the Gospel narrative at all of course tells against its being by S. John, and in this respect is not counterbalanced by other considerations. So that the internal and external evidence when put together is overwhelmingly against the paragraph being part of the Fourth Gospel.

With regard to the question whether the section is *a genuine portion of the Gospel history*, the internal evidence is wholly in favour of its being so, while the balance of external testimony is decidedly on the same side. (1) The style is similar to the Synoptic Gospels, especially to S. Luke; and four inferior MSS. insert the passage at the end of Luke xxi., the place in the history into which it fits best. (2) It bears the impress of truth and is fully in harmony with Christ's conduct on other occasions; yet it is quite original and cannot be a divergent account of any other incident in the Gospels. (3) It is easy to see how prudential reasons may in some cases have caused its omission (the fear of giving, as S. Augustine says, *peccandi impunitatem mulieribus*); difficult to see what, excepting its truth, can have caused its insertion. (4) Though it is found in no Greek MS. earlier than the sixth century, nor in the earliest versions, nor is quoted as by S. John until late in the fourth century, yet Jerome says that in his time it was

53 And every man went unto his own house. Jesus went
8
2 unto the mount of Olives. And early in the morning he
came again into the temple, and all the people came unto

contained '*in many Greek and Latin MSS.*' (*Adv. Pelag.* II. 17), and these must have been as good as, or better than, the best MSS. which we now possess.

The question as to *who is the author*, cannot be answered. There is not sufficient material for a satisfactory conjecture, and mere guesswork is worthless. The extraordinary number of various readings (80 in 183 words) points to more than one source.

One more question remains. *How is it that nearly all the MSS. that do contain it* (several uncials, including the Cambridge MS., and more than 300 cursives) *agree in inserting it here?* This cannot be answered with certainty. *Similarity of matter* may have caused it to have been placed in the margin in one copy, and thence it may have passed, as other things have done, into the text of the Cambridge and other MSS. In chap. vii. we have an unsuccessful attempt to ruin Jesus: this paragraph contains the history of another attempt, equally unsuccessful. Or, the incident may have been inserted in the margin in illustration of viii. 15, and hence have got into the text.

---

53. That this verse, as well as viii. 1, 2, is omitted in most MSS. shews that prudential reasons cannot explain the omission of the paragraph in more than a limited number of cases. Some MSS. omit only viii. 3—11.

every man went unto his own house] To what meeting this refers we cannot tell: of course not to the meeting of the Sanhedrin just recorded by S. John. It is unfortunate that the verse should have been left as the end of this chapter instead of beginning the next.

CHAP. VIII.

1. *the mount of Olives*] S. John nowhere mentions the Mount of Olives (comp. xviii. 1), and when he mentions a new place he commonly adds an explanation: i. 44, iv. 5, v. 2, vi. 1, xix. 13, 17. The phrase for 'went unto' is not found in S. John. Both occur in all three Synoptists.

2. *And early in the morning*, &c.] Comp. Luke xxi. 37, 38; 'and in the day time He was teaching in the temple, and at night He went out and abode in the mount that is called the mount of Olives. And all the people came early in the morning to Him in the temple for to hear Him.' The phrase for 'all the people' used by S. Luke is the phrase which occurs here: S. John never uses it. S. John uses the word for 'people' only twice; it occurs more than thirty times in S. Luke, and more than twenty times in the Acts. The word for 'came early' is a verb derived from the word for 'early' which occurs here: S. John uses neither.

him; and he sat down, and taught them. And the scribes 3
and Pharisees brought unto him a woman taken in adultery;
and when they had set her in the midst, they say unto him, 4
Master, this woman was taken in adultery, in the very act.
Now Moses in the law commanded us, that such should be 5
stoned: but what sayest thou? This they said, tempting 6
him, that they might have to accuse him. But Jesus

sat down] To teach with authority. Comp. Matt. v. 1, xxiii. 2;
Mark ix. 35.

3. *the scribes and Pharisees*] This phrase is used thrice by S. Luke,
once each by S. Matthew and S. Mark. S. John nowhere mentions
the scribes: he speaks of the hierarchy as 'the chief priests' or 'rulers'
with or without 'the Pharisees,' or else simply as 'the Jews.' Here
we are probably not to understand an official deputation from the
Sanhedrin: there is nothing to shew that the woman had been taken
before the Sanhedrin before being brought to Christ.

brought unto him] Literally, **bring** *unto Him*. The bringing her
was a wanton outrage both on her and on all generous and modest
spectators. She might have been detained while the case was referred
to Christ. The statement 'in the very act' is another piece of brutal
indelicacy; and the Greek verb, **hath been** *taken*, adds to this.

5. *Moses in the law*] Of the two texts given in the margin of our
Bible, Lev. xx. 10 and Deut. xxii. 22, probably neither is correct. It
is often assumed that 'put to death' in Jewish Law means stoning:
such however is not Jewish tradition. The Rabbis taught that it meant
strangulation; i.e. the criminal was smothered in mud and then a cord
was twisted round his neck. But for the case of a betrothed woman
sinning in the city, stoning is specified as the punishment (Deut. xxii.
23, 24), and this is probably what is indicated here. Such cases would
be rare, and therefore all the better suited for a casuistical question.

but what sayest thou?] Better, **What therefore** *sayest Thou?* This is
the only place in the whole paragraph where S. John's favourite particle
'therefore' occurs; and that not in the narrative, where S. John makes
such frequent use of it, but in the dialogue, where he very rarely
employs it. Scarcely anywhere in this Gospel can a dozen verses of
narrative be found without a 'therefore;' but see ii. 1—17, and contrast
iv. 1—26, xx. 1—9.

6. *tempting him*] The Greek word for 'tempting' is frequent in the
Synoptists of trying to place Christ in a difficulty; never so used in
S. John, who, however, uses it once of Christ 'proving' Philip
(vi. 6).

that they might have to accuse him] This clause must be borne in
mind in determining what the difficulty was in which they wished to
place Him. It seems to exclude the supposition that they hoped to
undermine His popularity, in case He should decide for the extreme
rigour of the law; the people having become accustomed to a lax
morality (Matt. xii. 39; Mark viii. 38). Probably the case is somewhat

stooped down, and with *his* finger wrote on the ground, *as
7 though he heard them not.* So when they continued asking
him, he lift up *himself*, and said unto them, He that is
without sin among you, let him first cast a stone at her.

parallel to the question about tribute, and they hoped to bring Him into
collision either with the Law and Sanhedrin or with the Roman Government.
If He said she was *not* to be stoned, He contradicted Jewish
Law; if He said she *was* to be stoned, He ran counter to Roman Law,
for the Romans had deprived the Jews of the right to inflict capital
punishment (xviii. 31). The Sanhedrin might of course pronounce
sentence of death (Matt. xxvi. 66; Mark xiv. 64; comp. John xix. 7),
but it rested with the Roman governor whether he would allow the
sentence to be carried out or not (xix. 16): see on xviii. 31 and
xix. 6.

stooped down, and with his finger wrote on the ground] It is said that
this gesture was a recognised sign of unwillingness to attend to what was
being said; a call for a change of subject. McClellan quotes Plut. II.
532: 'Without uttering a syllable, by merely raising the eyebrows, or
stooping down, or *fixing the eyes upon the ground*, you may baffle unreasonable
importunities.' 'Wrote' should perhaps be *'kept writing'*
(comp. vii. 40, 41), or *'began to write*, made as though He would write'
(comp. Luke i. 59). Either rendering would agree with this interpretation,
which our translators have insisted on as certain by inserting the
gloss (not found in any earlier English Version), 'as though He heard
them not.' But it is just possible that by writing on the stone pavement
of the Temple He wished to remind them of the 'tables of stone,
written with the finger of God' (Ex. xxxi. 18; Deut. ix. 10). They
were hoping that He would explain away the seventh commandment,
in order that they themselves might break the sixth.

7. *they continued asking*] They will not take the hint, whatever
His gesture meant.

without sin] The Greek word occurs nowhere else in N.T., but it is
quite classical: it may mean either 'free from the possibility of sin,
impeccable;' or 'free from actual sin, *sinless:*' if the latter, it may mean
either 'free from sin in general, *guiltless;*' or 'free from a particular sin,
not guilty.' The context shews that the last is the meaning here, 'free
from the sin of impurity:' comp. '*sin* no more,' *v.* 11, and 'sinner,'
Luke vii. 37, 39. The practical maxim involved in Christ's words is
that of Matt. vii. 1—5; Rom. xiv. 4. As to its application to them
comp. Matt. xii. 39; Mark viii. 38. He is contending not against
punishment being inflicted by human law, but against men taking the
law into their own hands.

a stone] Rather, **the** *stone*, according to the Received Text and some
MSS.; i.e. the stone required for executing the sentence. Others take
it of the *first* stone, which the witnesses were to throw (Deut. xvii. 7).
But Christ does not say 'let him cast the *first stone*,' but 'let him be *first
of you* to cast the stone.'

And again he stooped down, and wrote on the ground. 8
And they which heard *it*, being convicted by *their own* 9
conscience, went out one by one, beginning at the eldest,
even unto the last: and Jesus was left alone, and the woman
standing in the midst. When Jesus had lift up *himself*, 10
and saw none but the woman, he said unto her, Woman,
where are those thine accusers? hath no *man* condemned
thee? She said, No *man*, Lord. And Jesus said unto her, 11
Neither do I condemn thee: go, and sin no more.

    8. *again he stooped down*] He again declines to have the office of judge thrust upon Him. The Reader of men's hearts knew how His challenge must work: no one would respond to it.
    and wrote on the ground] A Venetian MS. ascribed to the tenth century has the remarkable reading 'wrote on the ground the sins of each one of them.' The same strange idea appears in Jerome, shewing how soon men began to speculate as to *what* He wrote. Others suppose that He wrote His answer in *v.* 7. As has been shewn (*v.* 6), it is not certain that He wrote anything.
    9. *being convicted by their own conscience*] These words are probably a gloss added by some copyist, like 'as though He heard them not,' added by our translators (*v.* 6).
    beginning at the eldest] Literally, *beginning at the* **elders**: but it means the elders in years, not the Elders; so that our translators have done well to avoid a literal rendering which would have been misleading. Meyer suggests that the oldest would be shrewd enough to slip away at once without compromising themselves further; certainly they would have the largest experience of life and its temptations.
    was left alone] Not that there were no witnesses, but that they had withdrawn to a distance. The graphic precision of this verse indicates the account of an eyewitness.
    standing in the midst] Literally, **being** *in the midst*, where the brutality of her accusers had placed her (*v.* 3).
    10. *none but the woman*] The word for 'but' or 'except' occurs nowhere in S. John's writings excepting Rev. ii. 25; frequently in S. Luke, five times in S. Matthew, five times in S. Paul's Epistles, once in S. Mark, and nowhere else.
    hath no man condemned thee?] Literally, **Did no man condemn** *thee?* But here the English perfect may idiomatically represent the Greek aorist: see on *v.* 29. The word for 'condemn' is a compound not found anywhere in S. John's writings, but occurring nine times in the Synoptists. S. John uses the simple verb, which means 'judge,' but often acquires the notion of judging unfavourably from the context (see on iii. 17 and v. 29).
    11. *No man, Lord*] We must bear in mind that 'Lord' may be too strong a translation of the Greek word, which need not mean more than 'Sir' (see on vi. 34). But as we have no such ambiguous word in English, 'Lord' is best.

VIII. 12—IX. 41. *Christ the Source of Truth and Light* (*continued*).

12 Then spake Jesus again unto them, saying, I am the light of the world: he that followeth me shall not walk in

Neither do I condemn thee] He maintains in tenderness towards her the attitude which He had assumed in sternness towards her accusers: He declines the office of judge. He came not to condemn, but to seek and to save. And yet He did condemn, as S. Augustine remarks, not the woman, but the sin. With regard to the woman, though He does not condemn, yet He does not pardon: He does not say 'thy sins have been forgiven thee' (Matt. ix. 2; Luke vii. 48), or even 'go in peace' (Luke vii. 50, viii. 48). "We must not apply in all cases a sentence, which requires His Divine knowledge to make it a just one" (Alford). He knew whether she was penitent or not.

go, and sin no more] Or, *go and* **continue no longer in sin**. The contrast between the mere negative declaration and the very positive exhortation is striking. See on v. 14.

VIII. 12—IX. 41. CHRIST THE SOURCE OF TRUTH AND LIGHT (*continued*).

In viii. 12—46 the word 'true' occurs six times, the word 'truth' seven times.

12. *Then spake Jesus again unto them*] The paragraph vii. 53 —viii. 11 being omitted, these words must be connected with vii. 52. The officers have made their report to the Sanhedrin, leaving Jesus unmolested. After an interval He continues His discourse: *again,* **therefore,** *Jesus spake unto them,* i.e. because the attempt to interfere with Him had failed. How long the interval was we do not know, but probably the evening of the same day.

I am the light of the world] Once more we have a possible reference to the ceremonies of the Feast of Tabernacles, somewhat less probable than the other (see on vii. 37), but not improbable. Large candelabra were lighted in the Court of the Women on the evening of the first day of the Feast, and these flung their light over the whole city. Authorities differ as to whether this illumination was repeated, but all are agreed that it did not take place on the last evening. Here, therefore, there was once more a gap, which Christ Himself may have designed to fill; and while the multitude were missing the festal light of the great lamps, He declares, 'I am the Light of the world.' In the case of the water we know that it was poured on each of the seven days, and that Christ spoke the probable reference to it on the last day of the Feast. But in this case the illumination took place possibly on the first night *only*, and Christ certainly did not utter this possible reference to it until the last day of the Feast, or perhaps not until the Feast was all over. But the fact that the words were spoken in the Court of the Women (see on *v.* 20) makes the reference not improbable.

darkness, but shall have the light of life. The Pharisees 13
therefore said unto him, Thou bearest record of thyself;
thy record is not true. Jesus answered and said unto them, 14
Though I bear record of myself, *yet* my record is true: for
I know whence I came, and whither I go; but ye cannot
tell whence I come, and whither I go. Ye judge after the 15

he that followeth me] This expression also is in favour of the reference. The illumination in the Court of the Women commemorated the pillar of fire which led the Israelites through the wilderness, as the pouring of the water of Siloam commemorated the water flowing from the Rock. 'The Lord went before them by day in a pillar of a cloud *to lead them the way;* and by night in a pillar of fire, *to give them light*' (Exod. xiii. 21). So Christ here declares that those who *follow* Him *shall in no wise walk in darkness.* The negative is very strong. This use of 'darkness' for moral evil is peculiar to S. John: see on i. 5, where (as here) we have light and life (*v.* 4) closely connected, while darkness is opposed to both.

shall have the light of life] Not merely with him but in him, so that he also becomes a source of light. See on vii. 38, and comp. 'Ye are the light of the world,' Matt. v. 14.

13. *Thou bearest record*] Our translators have again been somewhat capricious. The words which in verses 13 and 14 they render 'record' and 'bear record,' they render in verses 17 and 18 'witness' and 'bear witness.' The latter rendering is to be preferred. The Pharisees attempt to cancel the effect of Christ's impressive declaration by urging against Him a formal objection, the validity of which He had been heard to admit (v. 31): *Thou bearest* **witness** *of Thyself; Thy* **witness** *is not true.*

14. *Though I bear record*] Better, **even if** *I bear* **witness.** God can testify respecting Himself, and there are truths to which He alone can testify. Yet He condescends to conform to the standard of human testimony, and adds to His witness the words and works of His incarnate Son; who in like manner can bear witness of Himself, being supported by the witness of the Father (*v.* 16).

and whither I go] i.e. by Death and Ascension.

but ye cannot tell] Better, *But ye* **know not.** They knew neither of these points respecting themselves; how should they know it respecting Him? Man knows not either the origin or the issue of his life. 'Ye' is emphatic.

whence I came, and whither I go] For 'and' read **or** with the best MSS. Note the change from 'came,' which refers to the Incarnation, His having once come from the Father, to 'come,' which refers to His perpetual presence with mankind. Note also the balanced parallelism of the verse and comp. *vv.* 35, 38, vii. 6.

15. *Ye judge after the flesh*] According to His outward form, the form of a servant: comp. vii. 24. From the context 'judge' here acquires an adverse sense, and virtually means 'condemn:' comp.

16 flesh; I judge no *man*. And yet if I judge, my judgment is true: for I am not alone, but I and the Father that sent
17 me. It is also written in your law, that the testimony of
18 two men is true. I am *one* that bear witness of myself,
19 and the Father that sent me beareth witness of me. Then said they unto him, Where is thy Father? Jesus answered, Ye neither know me, nor my Father: if ye had known me,

iii. 17, 18, vii. 51. Judging Him to be a mere man they had condemned His testimony respecting Himself as invalid. 'Ye' and 'I' are in emphatic opposition.

I judge no man] Neither 'after the flesh,' nor 'as ye do,' nor anything else is to be supplied. No such addition can be made in *v*. 16, and therefore cannot be made here. The words are best taken quite simply and literally. 'My mission is not to condemn, but to save and to bless.' Comp. xii. 47.

16. *And yet if I judge*] Or, **But even** *if I judge*, like 'even if I bear witness' (*v*. 14). 'I judge no man; not because I have no authority, but because judging is not what I came to do. Even if I do in exceptional cases judge, My judgment is a genuine and authoritative one (see on i. 9), not the mock sentence of an impostor. It is the sentence not of a mere man, nor even of one with a Divine commission yet acting independently; but of One sent by God acting in union with His Sender.' Comp. v. 30.

17. *It is also written in your law*] Literally, *But in the law also, your law, it is written*. 'Your' is very emphatic; 'the Law about which you profess to be so jealous.' Comp. 'Thou art called a Jew, and restest on the Law' (Rom. ii. 17).

the testimony of two men is true] Better, *the* **witness** *of two*, &c. Not so much a quotation as a reference to Deut. xix. 15, xvii. 6. Note that the Law speaks of 'two or three *witnesses:*' here we have 'two *men*.' The change is not accidental, but introduces an argument *à fortiori:* if the testimony of two *men* is true, how much more the testimony of two Divine Witnesses. Comp. 'If we receive the witness of men, the witness of God is greater; for this is the witness of God which He hath testified of His Son' (1 John v. 9).

18. *I am one that bear witness of myself*] Or, **It is I who bear witness of Myself** (in My words and works), **and there beareth witness of Me the Father, who sent Me** (in Scripture and the voice from Heaven).

19. *Then said they*] *They said* **therefore.**

Where is thy Father?] They do not ask 'who' but 'where;' they know well enough by this time the meaning of Christ's frequent reference to 'Him that sent me:' v. 23, 24, 30, 37, 38, vi. 38, 39, 40, 44, vii. 16, 18, 28, 33. They ask, therefore, in mockery, what Philip (xiv. 8) asks with earnest longing, '*Shew us the Father:* we see one of Thy two witnesses; shew us the other.'

if ye had known me, &c.] Better, *If ye* **knew Me, ye would know,**

ye should have known my Father also. These words spake 20
Jesus in the treasury, as he taught in the temple : and no
man laid hands on him ; for his hour was not yet come.
Then said Jesus again unto them, I go my way, and ye 21
shall seek me, and shall die in your sins : whither I go, ye
cannot come. Then said the Jews, Will he kill himself? 22

&c. (There is a similar error v. 46). It is in the Son that the Father reveals Himself. Comp. xiv. 9, xvi. 3 ; and for the construction comp. *v.* 42.

20. *in the treasury*] *At the treasury* is an admissible and in one respect safer translation. It is not certain that there was a separate building called the treasury; and if there was, it is not probable that Christ would be able to address the multitude there. But the thirteen brazen chests, into which people put their offerings for the temple and other charitable objects, stood in the Court of the Women (see on Mark xii. 41), and these chests seem to have been called 'the treasury.' The point seems to be that in so public and frequented a place as this did He say all this, and yet no man laid hands on Him (see on vii. 30). Moreover the Hall Gazith, where the Sanhedrin met, was close to the Court of the Women ; so that He was teaching close to His enemies' head quarters.

21. *Then said Jesus again unto them*] The name 'Jesus' should be omitted both here and in the preceding verse (see on vi. 14), and 'then' should be **therefore** (see on vi. 45, 53, 68, vii. 15, 30, 33, 35, 45). *He said, therefore, again to them.* The 'therefore' does not compel us to place what follows on the same day with what precedes; 'therefore' merely signifies that, as no one laid hands on Him, He was able to address them again. 'Again' shews that there is some interval, but whether of minutes, hours, or days, we have no means of determining. There is no distinct mark of time between vii. 37 (the close of the Feast of Tabernacles) and x. 22 (the Feast of the Dedication), an interval of two months. See introductory note to chap. vi.

I go my way] There is no 'my way' in the Greek; the word is the same as for 'I go' in *v.* 14 and vii. 33 ; but to avoid abruptness we may render, *I go away.* Possibly in all three passages there is a side reference to the Jews who were now leaving Jerusalem in great numbers, the Feast of Tabernacles being over.

shall seek me] See on vii. 33, 34. Here Christ is more explicit ; He does not say 'shall not find Me,' but 'shall die in your sin.' So far from finding Him and being delivered by Him, they will perish most miserably. *In your sin shall ye die.* 'Sin' is emphatic, and is singular, not plural, meaning 'state of sin.'

22. *Will he kill himself?*] They see that He speaks of a voluntary departure, and perhaps they suspect that He alludes to His death. So with sarcasm still more bitter than the sneer in vii. 35 they exclaim 'Surely He does not mean to commit suicide? We certainly shall not be able to follow Him if He takes refuge in that!'

23 because he saith, Whither I go, ye cannot come. And he said unto them, Ye are from beneath; I am from above: 24 ye are of this world; I am not of this world. I said therefore unto you, that ye shall die in your sins: for if ye 25 believe not that I am *he*, ye shall die in your sins. Then said they unto him, Who art thou? And Jesus saith unto them, Even the same that I said unto you *from* the begin-

23. *Ye are from beneath*] At first sight it might seem as if this meant 'ye are from hell.' Christ uses strong language later on (*v.* 44), and this interpretation would make good sense with what precedes. 'Ye suggest that I am going to hell by self-destruction: it is ye who come from thence.' But what follows forbids this. The two halves of the verse are manifestly equivalent, and 'ye are from beneath' = 'ye are of this world.' The pronouns throughout are emphatically opposed. The whole verse is a good instance of 'the spirit of parallelism, the informing power of Hebrew poetry,' which runs more or less through the whole Gospel. Comp. xiv. 27.

24. *ye shall die in your sins*] Here 'die' is emphatic, not 'sin' as in *v.* 21. Moreover the plural is here correct; it is no longer the state of sin generally, but the separate sins of each that are spoken of. Before it was 'in your *sin* shall ye die;' here it is 'ye shall *die* in your sins.'

for if ye believe not] This is the only way in which they can be delivered—faith in Him. Comp. i. 12, iii. 15—18, vi. 40.

that I am he] Better, *that* **I am**. It not merely means 'that I am the Messiah,' but is the great name, which every Jew at once understood, I AM. Comp. *vv.* 28, 58, xiii. 19, xviii. 5; Ex. iii. 14; Deut. xxxii. 39; Isa. xliii. 10.

25. *Then said they*] *They said* **therefore**.

Who art thou?] It is incredible that the Jews can have failed to understand. Christ had just declared that He was from above, and not of this world. Even if the words 'I am' were ambiguous in themselves, in this context they are plain enough. As in *v.* 19, they pretend not to understand, and contemptuously ask, *Thou, who art Thou?* The pronoun is scornfully emphatic. Comp. Acts xix. 15. Possibly both in *v.* 19 and here they wish to draw from Him something more definite, more capable of being stated in a formal charge against Him.

Even the same that I said unto you from the beginning] This is a passage of well-known difficulty, and the meaning will probably always remain uncertain. (1) It is doubtful whether it is a question or not. (2) Of the six or seven Greek words all excepting the word meaning 'unto you' can have more than one meaning. (3) There is a doubt whether we have six or seven Greek words. To discuss all the possible renderings would go beyond the scope of this volume. *What I from the beginning am also speaking to you of* is perhaps as likely as any translation to be right. And it matters little whether it be made interrogative or not. Either, 'Do you ask that of which I have been speaking to you

ning. I have many *things* to say and to judge of you: 26
but he that sent me is true; and I speak to the world those
things which I have heard of him. They understood not 27
that he spake to them of the Father. Then said Jesus unto 28
them, When ye have lift up the Son of man, then shall ye
know that I am *he*, and *that* I do nothing of myself; but
as my Father hath taught me, I speak these *things*. And 29

from the first?', in which case it is not unlike Christ's reply to Philip
(xiv. 9); or, 'I am that of which I have been speaking to you all
along.'

26. Here again we have a series of simple sentences, the precise
meaning of which and their connexion with one another cannot be determined with certainty. See on vii. 33. The following seems to be
the drift of the verse: 'I have very much to speak concerning you, very
much to blame. But I keep to My immediate task of speaking to the
world those truths which before the world was I heard from God that
cannot lie, Who sent Me:' i.e. Christ will not desist from teaching
Divine truth in order to blame the Jews. It is as the Truth and the
Light that He appears in these discourses.

which I have heard of him] Better, **what I heard from Him, these
things I speak unto the world**, i.e. precisely these and nothing else.
Comp. *v*. 39.

27. *They understood not that he spake*] Better, they **perceived** not
that He **was speaking**. This statement of the Evangelist has seemed
to some so unaccountable after *v*. 18, that they have attempted to make
his words mean something else. But the meaning of the words is quite
unambiguous, and is not incredible. We have seen that there is an
interval, possibly of days, between *v*. 20 and *v*. 21. The audience may
have changed very considerably; but if not, experience shews that the
ignorance and stupidity of unbelief are sometimes almost unbounded.
Still we may admit that the dulness exhibited here is extraordinary;
and it is precisely because it is so extraordinary that St John records
it.

28. *Then said Jesus unto them*] Better, as so often (see on *v*. 21),
Therefore *said Jesus*, i.e. in consequence of their gross want of perception. 'Unto them' is of doubtful authority.

When ye have lifted up] On the Cross: comp. iii. 14 and xii. 32.
The Crucifixion was the act of the Jews, as Peter tells them in Solomon's
Porch (Acts iii. 13—15).

then shall ye know] Better, *then shall ye* **perceive**. It is the same
verb as is used in *v*. 27, and evidently refers back to that (comp. *v*. 43).
Had they known the Messiah they would have known His Father also
(xiv. 9). But when by crucifying Him they have brought about His
glory, then and not till then will their eyes be opened. Then will facts
force upon them what no words could teach them. Comp. xii. 32.

that I am he] See on *v*. 24.

but as my Father hath taught me] Better, *but* **that** *as My Father*

he that sent me is with me: the Father hath not left me
30 alone; for I do always those *things* that please him. As
he spake these *words*, many believed on him.
31 Then said Jesus to those Jews which believed on him,

taught *Me*, i.e. before the Incarnation; aorist, not perfect, like 'heard'
in *v*. 26. The construction depending on 'then shall ye understand'
continues to the end of this verse, and possibly down to 'is with Me.'
   29. *the Father hath not left me alone*] Here again we have an
aorist, not a perfect; '**He left** *Me not alone*' ('the Father' being omitted
in the best MSS.). It will depend on the interpretation whether the
aorist or perfect is to be used in English. If it refers to God sending the
Messiah into the world, then we must keep the aorist; *He left*. But if
it refers to Christ's experience in each particular case, the perfect may
be substituted: *He hath left*. In some cases it is the idiom in English
to use the perfect where the aorist is used in Greek, and then to translate
the Greek aorist by the English aorist would be misleading. See on
xvi. 32.
   for I do always] Or, **because the things which are pleasing to Him
I always do.** 'I' and 'always' are emphatic; and 'always' literally
means 'on every occasion,' which is somewhat in favour of the second
interpretation in the preceding note. 'He hath never left me alone,
because in every case I do what pleaseth Him.' The emphasis on 'I'
is perhaps in mournful contrast to the Jews. In any case it is a distinct
claim to Divinity. What blasphemous effrontery would such a declaration be in the mouth of any but the Incarnate Deity. The theory that
Jesus was the noblest and holiest of teachers, but nothing more, shatters
against such words as these. What saint or prophet ever dared to say,
'The things which are pleasing to God I in every instance do?' Comp.
v. 46. And if it be said, that perhaps Jesus never uttered these words,
then it may also be said that perhaps He never uttered any of the words
attributed to Him. We have the same authority for what is accepted
as His as for what is rejected as not His. History becomes impossible
if we are to admit evidence that we like, and refuse evidence that we
dislike.
   30. *many believed on him*] Nothing exasperated His opponents so
much as His success; and therefore in leading us on to the final catastrophe, the Evangelist carefully notes the instances in which He won,
though often only for a time, adherents and believers. See on vi. 15.
Among these 'many' were some of the hierarchy (*v*. 51). Their faith,
poor as it proves, is better than that of the many in ii. 23; belief that
results from teaching is higher than that which results from miracles.
Jesus recognises both its worth and its weakness, and applies a test,
which might have raised it to something higher, but under which it
breaks down.
   31. *Then said Jesus to those Jews which believed on him*] Better,
Jesus said, **therefore**, *to the Jews who* **had believed Him.** There is a
change in the expression respecting their belief. In *v*. 30 S. John

If ye continue in my word, *then* are ye my disciples indeed; and ye shall know the truth, and the truth shall make you 32 free. They answered him, We be Abraham's seed, and 33 were never in bondage to any *man:* how sayest thou, Ye shall be made free? Jesus answered them, Verily, verily, 34 I say unto you, Whosoever committeth sin is the servant of

uses the strong phrase 'believed *on* Him;' here he uses the much weaker 'believed Him' (see on i. 12), as if to prepare us for the collapse of their faith.

If ye continue, &c.] Or, *If ye* **abide** *in My word* (see on i. 33), *ye* **are truly My disciples.** Both 'ye' and 'My' are emphatic: 'you on your part'—'the word that is Mine.' "The new converts, who come forward with a profession of faith, receive a word of encouragement as well as of warning. They were not to mistake a momentary impulse for a deliberate conviction." S. p. 155. 'If ye abide in My word, so that it becomes the permanent condition of your life, then are ye My disciples in truth, and not merely in appearance after being carried away for the moment.'

32. *the truth*] Both Divine doctrine (xvii. 17) and Christ Himself (xiv. 6) 'whose service is perfect freedom.' See on xviii. 37.

shall make you free] Free from the moral slavery of sin. Comp. the Stoics' dictum—'The wise man alone is free.'

33. *They answered him*] Or, **unto Him**, according to the best MSS. 'They' must mean 'the Jews who had believed Him' (*v.* 31): it is quite arbitrary to suppose any one else. The severe words which follow (*v.* 44) are addressed to them, for turning back, after their momentary belief, as well as to those who had never believed at all.

Abraham's seed] Comp. 'kings of peoples shall be of her' (Sarah), and 'thy seed shall possess the gate of his enemies' (Gen. xvii. 16, xxii. 17). On texts like these they build the proud belief that Jews **have never yet been** *in bondage to any man.* But passion once more blinds them to historical facts (see on vii. 52). The bondage in Egypt, the oppressions in the times of the Judges, the captivity in Babylon, and the Roman yoke, are all forgotten. Some, who think such forgetfulness incredible, interpret 'we have never been *lawfully* in bondage.' 'The Truth' would not free them from *enforced* slavery. It might free them from *voluntary* slavery, by teaching them that it was unlawful for them to be slaves. 'But we know that already.' This, however, is somewhat subtle, and the more literal interpretation is not incredible. The power which the human mind possesses of keeping inconvenient facts out of sight is very considerable. In either case we have another instance of gross inability to perceive the spiritual meaning of Christ's words. Comp. iii. 4, iv. 15, vi. 34.

34. *Whosoever committeth sin is the servant of sin*] Better, **Everyone who continues to commit sin is the bond-servant** *of sin.* 'Committeth sin' is too weak for the Greek: Christ does not say that a single act of sin enslaves. 'To *commit* (*poiein*) sin' is the opposite of

35 sin. And the servant abideth not in the house for ever:
36 *but* the son abideth ever. If the Son therefore shall make
37 you free, ye shall be free indeed. I know that ye are
Abraham's seed; but ye seek to kill me, because my word
38 hath no place in you. I speak *that* which I have seen with

'to *do* the Truth' (iii. 21). Again, 'servant,' though often a good translation where nothing degrading is implied, is not strong enough, where, as here, the degradation is the main point. Moreover, the connexion with *v.* 33 must be kept up. The words for 'bondage' and 'servant' are cognate; therefore either 'bondage' and 'bond-servant,' or 'slavery' and 'slave,' must be our renderings.

Some have thought that we have here an echo of Rom. vi. 16, which of course S. John may have seen. But why may not both passages be original? The idea that vice is slavery is common in all literature: frequent in the classics. 2 Pet. ii. 19 is probably an echo either of this passage or of Rom. vi. 16. Comp. Matt. vi. 24.

35. *And the servant*, &c.] The transition is somewhat abrupt, the mention of 'bond-servant' suggesting a fresh thought. **Now the bond-servant** (not the bond-servant *of sin*, but any slave) *abideth not in the house for ever:* **the son** (not the Son of God, but any son) *abideth* **for** *ever.* "The thought is throughout profound and instructive; and to a Jew, always ready to picture to himself the theocracy or the kingdom of heaven under the form of a household, it would be easily intelligible." S. p. 157.

36. *If the Son therefore*, &c.] As before, any son is meant. 'If the son emancipates you, your freedom is secured; for he is always on the spot to see that his emancipation is carried out.' The statement is general, but of course with special reference to the Son of God. If they will abide in His word (*v.* 31), He will abide in them (vi. 56), and will take care that the bondage from which His word has freed them is not thrust upon them again.

shall be free indeed] Not the same word as is translated 'indeed' in *v.* 31. 'Indeed' or 'in reality' may do here; 'in truth' or 'truly' in *v.* 31. Both words are opposed to mere appearance.

37. Christ's words seem gradually to take a wider range. They are no longer addressed merely to those who for a moment had believed on Him, but to His opponents generally, whose ranks these short-lived believers had joined.

Abraham's seed] He admits their claim in their own narrow sense. They are the natural descendants of Abraham: his children in any higher sense they are not (*v.* 39). Comp. 'neither, because they are the seed of Abraham, are they all children' (Rom. ix. 8).

hath no place in you] Rather, **maketh no advance in you.** His word had found place in them for a very short time; but it made no progress in their hearts: it did not abide in them and they did not abide in it (*v.* 31). They had stifled it and cast it out.

38. *I speak*, &c.] The text here is a little uncertain, but the fol-

my Father: and ye do *that* which ye have seen with your father. They answered and said unto him, Abraham is our 39 father. Jesus saith unto them, If ye were Abraham's children, ye would do the works of Abraham. But now 40 ye seek to kill me, a man that hath told you the truth, which I have heard of God: this did not Abraham. Ye 41 do the deeds of your father. Then said they to him, We

lowing seems to have most authority; *I speak* the things which *I have seen with* (*My*) *Father: ye* also, therefore, do the things which ye heard from (*your*) *father.* 'I speak those truths of which I have had direct knowledge from all eternity with the Father; you, therefore, following My relation to the Father, commit those sins which your father suggested to you.' Christ does not say who their father is; but he means that morally they are the children of the devil. The 'therefore' (rare in discourses) is severely ironical. The connexion of *v.* 38 with *v.* 37 is not quite obvious. Perhaps it is this:—My words make no progress in you, because they are so different in origin and nature from your acts, especially your attempt to kill Me. It is possible to take the latter half of the verse as an imperative; **and do ye therefore the things which ye heard from the Father.**

39. *Abraham is our father*] They see that He means some other father than Abraham; possibly they suspect His full meaning, soon to be expressed (*v.* 44).

If ye were Abraham's children] The true reading seems to be, *if ye* **are** *Abraham's children*, which has been altered to 'if ye *were*,' so as to run more smoothly with the second clause. But the reading of the second verb is also doubtful, and perhaps we should read, **do** (imper.) *the works of Abraham.*

40. 'On the contrary, ye seek to commit murder, and a murder of the most heinous kind. Ye would kill One who hath spoken unto you the truth, truth which He learnt from God.'

a man that hath told you] This pointed insertion of 'man' possibly looks forward to *v.* 44, where they are called the children of the great *man-slayer*, lusting like him for blood. The Lord nowhere else uses this term of Himself.

this did not Abraham] A *litotes* or understatement of the truth. Abraham's life was utterly unlike the whole tenour of theirs. What could there be in common between 'the Friend of God' (Jas. ii. 23) and the enemies of God's Son?

41. *Ye do the deeds of your father*] Better, *Ye* **are doing** *the* **works** *of your father.* The word here rendered 'deeds' is the same as that rendered 'works' in *v.* 39. 'Ye' is emphatic, in contrast to Abraham. This shews them plainly that spiritual parentage is what He means. In *v.* 39 they still cling to Abraham, although He has evidently assigned them some other father. Here they drop literal parentage and adopt His figurative language. 'You are speaking of spiritual parentage. Well, our spiritual Father is God.'

be not born of fornication; we have one Father, *even* God.
42 Jesus said unto them, If God were your Father, ye would love me: for I proceeded forth and came from God; 43 neither came I of myself, but he sent me. Why do ye not understand my speech? *even* because ye cannot hear my

We be not born of fornication] The meaning of this is very much disputed. The following are the chief explanations: (1) Thou hast denied that we are the children of Abraham, then we must be the children of some one sinning with Sarah: which is false.' But this would be adultery, not fornication. (2) 'We are the children of Sarah, not of Hagar.' But this was lawful concubinage, not fornication. (3) 'We are not a mongrel race, like the Samaritans; we are pure Jews.' This is far-fetched, and does not suit the context. (4) 'We **were** not born of fornication, *as Thou art*.' But His miraculous birth was not yet commonly known, and this foul Jewish lie, perpetuated from the second century onwards (Origen, *c. Celsum* I. xxxii.), was not yet in existence. (5) 'We **were** not born of spiritual fornication; our sonship has not been polluted with idolatry. If thou art speaking of spiritual parentage, 'we have one Father, even God.' This last seems the best. Idolatry is so constantly spoken of as whoredom and fornication throughout the whole of the O.T., that in a discussion about spiritual fatherhood this image would be perfectly natural in the mouth of a Jew. Exod. xxxiv. 15, 16; Lev. xvii. 7; Judg. ii. 17; 2 Kgs. ix. 22; Ps. lxxiii. 27; Isa. i. 21; Jer. iii. 1, 9; Ezek. xvi. 15; &c. &c. See esp. Hos. ii. 4. There is a proud emphasis on 'we;'—'*we* are not idolaters, like Thy friends the Gentiles' (comp. vii. 35).

we have one Father] Or, **one Father we have**, with emphasis on the 'one,' in contrast to the many gods of the heathen.

42. Moral proof that God is not their father; if they were God's children they would love His Son. Comp. xv. 23, and 'every one that loveth Him that begat loveth Him also that is begotten of Him' (1 John v. 1). For the construction comp. *v.* 19, v. 46, ix. 41, xv. 19, xiii. 36: in all these cases we have imperfects, not aorists. Contrast iv. 10, xi. 21, 32, xiv. 28.

I proceeded forth and came from God] Rather, *I* **came out** (see on xvi. 28) *from God and* **am here** from God among you. Surely then God's true children would recognise and love Me.

neither came I of myself] Rather, **For not even of Myself have I come**. The 'for' must on no account be omitted; it introduces a proof that He is come from God. 'For (not only have I not come from any other than God) I have not even come of My own self-determination.'

43. *my speech...my word*] 'Speech' is the outward *expression*, the *language* used; 'thy speech bewrayeth thee' (Matt. xxvi. 73; comp. Mark xiv. 70). Besides these two passages the word for 'speech' is used only iv. 42, where it is rendered 'saying,' and here. 'Word' is the *meaning* of the expression, the teaching conveyed in the language used. They perpetually misunderstand His language, because they cannot

word. Ye are of *your* father the devil, and the lusts of 44
your father ye will do. He was a murderer from the
beginning, and abode not in the truth, because there is no

appreciate His meaning. They are 'from beneath' (*v.* 23), and He is
speaking of 'things above' (Col. iii. 1); they are 'of this world,' and
He is telling of 'heavenly things' (iii. 12); they are 'natural,' and He is
teaching 'spiritual things' (1 Cor. ii. 14; see note there). They '*cannot*
hear;' it is a moral impossibility: they have their whole character
to change before they can understand spiritual truths.

44. *Ye are of your father the devil*] At last Christ says plainly, what
He has implied in *vv.* 38 and 41. 'Ye' is emphatic; 'ye, who boast
that ye have Abraham and God as your Father, ye are morally the
Devil's children.' Comp. 1 John iii. 8, 10, which is perhaps an echo of
Christ's words.

This passage seems to be conclusive as to the real personal existence
of the devil. It can scarcely be an economy, a concession to ordinary
modes of thought and language. Would Christ have resorted to a
popular delusion in a denunciation of such solemn and awful severity?
Comp. 'the children of the wicked one' (Matt. xiii. 38); 'ye make him
twofold more the child of hell than yourselves' (Matt. xxiii. 15). With
this denunciation generally compare those contained in Matt. xi. 20—24,
xxiii. 13—36. "It is likely that dialogues of this sort would be of not
infrequent occurrence, especially just at this time when the conflict is
reaching its climax. It is likely too that they would be of the nature of
dialogues broken by impatient interruptions on the part of the Jews,
and not always a continuous strain of denunciation as in Matt. xxiii."
S. p. 159.

A monstrous but grammatically possible translation of these words is
adopted by some who attribute a Gnostic origin to this Gospel;—'ye are
descended from the father of the devil.' This Gnostic demonology,
according to which the father of the devil is the God of the Jews, is
utterly unscriptural, and does not suit the context here.

and the lusts of your father ye will do] Rather, *ye* **will to do.** See
on vi. 67, vii. 17; and comp. *v.* 40. 'Ye love to gratify the lusts which
characterize him, especially the lust for blood. Being his children, ye
are like him in nature.'

He was a murderer from the beginning] The word for 'murderer'
etymologically means 'man-slayer,' and seems to connect this passage
with *v.* 40 (see note there). The devil was a murderer by causing the
Fall, and thus bringing death into the world. Comp. 'God created
man to be immortal, and made him to be an image of His own eternity.
Nevertheless, *through envy of the devil came death into the world*, and
they that do hold of his side shall find it (Wisd. ii. 23, 24): and 'Cain
was of that wicked one and slew his brother:' and 'whosoever hateth
his brother is a murderer' (1 John iii. 12, 15).

and abode not in the truth] Rather, *and* **standeth** *not in the truth*.
The verb is not S. John's favourite word 'abide' (see on i. 33), but

truth in him. When he speaketh a lie, he speaketh of his
45 own: for he is a liar, and the father of it. And because I
46 tell *you* the truth, ye believe me not. Which of you convinceth me of sin? And if I say the truth, why do ye not
47 believe me? He that is of God heareth God's words: ye
48 therefore hear *them* not, because ye are not of God. Then

(according to the common reading) the same that is used in i. 35, iii. 29,
vii. 37, &c. Though perfect in form it is present in meaning: therefore
not 'hath stood,' still less 'stood' or 'abode,' but **standeth**. The true
reading, however, is probably not *hestēken*, but *estēken*, the imperfect of
stēkein (i. 26; Rom. xiv. 4), a stronger form of the verb; **stood firm**.
Truth is a region from which the devil has long since departed.

he speaketh of his own] Literally, *he speaketh out of his own;* out of
his own resources, out of his own nature: the outcome is what might be
expected from him.

for he is a liar, and the father of it] Better, **because** *he is a liar and
the father* **thereof**, i.e. father of the liar, rather than father of the lie
(understood in liar). Here again a monstrous misinterpretation is grammatically possible;—'for he is a liar, and his father also.' It is not strange
that Gnostics of the second and third centuries should have tried to wring
a sanction for their fantastic systems out of the writings of S. John. It *is*
strange that any modern critics should have thought demonology so
extravagant compatible with the theology of the Fourth Gospel.

45. *And because I tell you*, &c.] Better, **But** *because I* **speak** *the
truth, ye do not believe me*. 'Ye will listen to the devil (*v.* 38); ye will
believe a lie: but the Messiah speaking the truth ye will not believe.'
The tragic tone once more: comp. i. 5, 10, 11, ii. 24, iii. 10, 19, &c.

46. *Which of you convinceth me of sin?*] Or, **convicteth** *Me of sin* (see
on iii. 20). Many rebuked Christ and laid sin to His charge: none brought
sin home to His conscience. There is the majesty of Divinity in the challenge. What mortal man would dare to make it? See on *v.* 29, and
comp. xiv. 30, and xv. 10; 1 John iii. 5; 1 Pet. i. 19, ii. 22. Note
the implied connexion between sin generally and falsehood, as between
righteousness and truth, vii. 18.

And if I say the truth] Better, **If I say truth**. No MSS. have the
article, and the best MSS. omit the conjunction. 'If I am free from
sin (and none of you can convict Me of sin), I am free from falsehood
and speak the truth. Why then do ye on your part refuse to believe
Me?' 'Ye' is emphatic.

47. Christ answers His own question and at the same time gives a
final disproof of their claim to call God their father (*v.* 41).

heareth God's words] Christ here assumes, what He elsewhere
maintains explicitly, that He speaks the words of God (*v.* 26, iii. 34,
vii. 16, xvii. 8).

ye therefore hear them not] Better, **for this cause** (xii. 18, 27) *ye hear
not*. It is not S. John's favourite particle 'therefore,' but, as in
v. 16, 18, vi. 65, vii. 22 (see notes there), a preposition and pronoun

answered the Jews, and said unto him, Say we not well
that thou art a Samaritan, and hast a devil? Jesus an- 49
swered, I have not a devil; but I honour my Father, and

with which he not unfrequently begins a sentence to prepare the
way for a 'because' afterwards. These characteristics of his language
should be preserved in English, and kept distinct, so far as is possible.
In the First Epistle he uses the very same test as Christ here applies
to the Jews; 'We are of God: he that knoweth God heareth us; he
that is not of God heareth not us. Hereby know we the spirit of truth
and the spirit of error' (iv. 6).

48. *Then answered the Jews*] The best MSS. omit the particle,
which if it were genuine should be rendered 'therefore,' not 'then:'
The Jews answered. This denial of their national prerogative of being
sons of God seems to them malicious frenzy. He must be an enemy of
the peculiar people and be possessed.

Say we not well] i.e. rightly: comp. iv. 17, xiii. 13, xviii. 23. 'We'
is emphatic; 'we at any rate are right.'

that thou art a Samaritan] " Nowhere else do we find the designation 'a Samaritan;' yet it might naturally—we might say inevitably—
be given to one who seemed to attack the exclusive privileges of the
Jewish people." S. pp. 159, 160. It is therefore a striking touch of
reality, and another instance of the Evangelist's complete familiarity
with the ideas and expressions current in Palestine at this time.
Possibly this term of reproach contains a sneer at His visit to Samaria
in chap. iv., and at His having chosen the unusual route through
Samaria, as He probably did (see on vii. 10), in coming up to the Feast
of Tabernacles. The parable of the Good Samaritan was probably not
yet spoken.

and hast a devil] It is unfortunate that we have not two words in our
Bible to distinguish *diabolos*, '*the* Devil' (v. 44, xiii. 2; Matt. iv. 1;
Luke viii. 12; &c., &c.), from *daimonion* or *daimôn*, '*a* devil,' or 'unclean spirit.' 'Fiend,' which Wiclif *sometimes* employs (Matt. xii.
24, 28; Mark i. 34, 39, &c.), might have been used, had Tyndale
and Cranmer adopted it: **demon** would have been better still. But
here Tyndale, Cranmer, and the Geneva Version make the confusion
complete by rendering 'and hast *the* devil,' a mistake which they
make also in vii. 20 and x. 20. The charge here is more bitter than
either vii. 20 or x. 20, where it simply means that His conduct is
so extraordinary that He must be demented. We have instances more
similar to this in the Synoptists; Matt. ix. 34, xii. 24; Mark iii. 22;
Luke xi. 15.

49. *I have not a devil*] He does not notice the charge of being a
Samaritan. For Him it contained nothing offensive, for He knew that
Samaritans might equal or excel Jews (iv. 39—42; Luke x. 33, xvii. 16)
in faith, benevolence, and gratitude. There is an emphasis on 'I,' but
the meaning of the emphasis is not '*I* have not a demon, *but ye have.*'
Rather it means '*I* have not a demon, but honour My Father; while
you on the contrary dishonour My Father through Me.'

50 ye do dishonour me. And I seek not mine own glory:
51 there is *one* that seeketh and judgeth. Verily, verily, I say
unto you, If a man keep my saying, he shall never see
52 death. Then said the Jews unto him, Now we know that
thou hast a devil. Abraham is dead, and the prophets;
and thou sayest, If a man keep my saying, he shall never
53 taste of death. Art thou greater than our father Abraham,

50. *And I seek not mine own glory*] Better, **But** *I seek not My glory*. 'It is not because I seek glory for Myself that I speak of your dishonouring Me: My Father seeks that for Me and pronounces judgment on you.' Comp. *v.* 54 and v. 41.

51. *If a man keep my saying*] Better, *if a man keep My* **word**. This is important, to shew the connexion with verses 31 and 43 and also with v. 24. In all these the same Greek word is used, *logos*. The phrase 'keep My word' is one of frequent occurrence in this Gospel: verses 52, 55, xiv. 23, xv. 20, xvii. 6: as also the kindred phrase 'keep My commandments:' xiv. 15, 21, xv. 10: comp. 1 John ii. 3, 4, 5, iii. 22, 24, v. 2, 3. 'Keeping' means not merely keeping in heart, but obeying and fulfilling. This is the way in which they may escape the judgment just spoken of. So that there is no need to suppose that while verses 49, 50 are addressed to His opponents, *v.* 51 is addressed after a pause to a more friendly section, a change of which there is no hint.

shall never see death] Literally, *shall certainly not behold death for ever*. But 'for ever' belongs, like the negative, to the verb, not to 'death.' It does not mean 'he shall see death, but the death shall not be eternal:' rather 'he shall certainly never see death,' i.e. he already has eternal life (v. 24) and shall never lose it. This is evident from iv. 14, which cannot mean 'shall thirst, but the thirst shall not be eternal,' and from xiii. 8, which cannot mean 'shalt wash my feet, but the washing shall not be eternal.' In all three cases the meaning is the same, 'shall certainly never.' Comp. x. 28, xi. 26.

52. *Now we know that thou hast a devil*] 'It was somewhat of a conjecture before, but now we recognise clear evidence of it.'

Abraham is dead] *Abraham* **died**. Again they shew a gross want of perception and 'do not understand His speech' (*v.* 43). They cannot discern a spiritual truth, but understand Him to be speaking of physical death. 'My saying' should be 'My word' as in *v.* 51.

he shall never taste of death] In their excitement they exaggerate His language. The metaphor 'taste of death' is not taken from a death-cup, but from the general idea of bitterness. It is frequent in the classics.

53. *Art thou greater*] Exactly parallel to iv. 12. 'Thou' is emphatic: 'Surely *Thou* art not greater than our father Abraham, who **died?**— And the prophets **died.**' An anacoluthon, like their exaggeration, very natural. Strictly the sentence should run, 'and than the prophets, who died?'

which is dead? and the prophets are dead: whom makest thou thyself? Jesus answered, If I honour myself, my 54 honour is nothing: it is my Father that honoureth me; of whom ye say, that he is your God: yet ye have not known 55 him; but I know him: and if I should say, I know him not, I shall be a liar like unto you: but I know him, and keep his saying. Your father Abraham rejoiced to see my 56 day: and he saw *it*, and was glad. Then said the Jews 57

54—56. Christ first answers the insinuation that He is vain-glorious, implied in the question 'whom makest Thou Thyself?' Then He shews that He really is greater than Abraham.

54. *If I honour myself*] Better, *If I shall have glorified Myself, My glory is nothing*. It is not the same word as is rendered 'honour' in *v.* 49, therefore another English word is desirable. **There** *is My Father who* **glorifieth** *Me*—in miracles and the Messianic work generally. Comp. *v.* 50.

55. *Yet ye have not known him; but I know him*] Once more we have two different Greek words for 'know' in close proximity, and the difference is obliterated in our version (comp. vii. 15, 17, 26, 27, xiii. 7, xiv. 7, and see on vii. 26). Here the meaning is, **And** *ye have not* **recognised** *Him; but I know Him*, the latter clause referring to His immediate essential knowledge of the Father.

a liar like unto you] Or, **like unto you, a liar.** Referring back to *v.* 44.

keep his saying] Or, *keep His* **word**, as in verses 51, 52. Christ's whole life was a continual practice of obedience: Heb. v. 8; Rom. v. 19; Phil. ii. 8.

56. *rejoiced to see my day*] Literally, **exulted** *that he might see My day*, the object of his joy being represented as the goal to which his heart is directed. This is a remarkable instance of S. John's preference for the construction expressing a purpose, where other constructions would seem more natural. Comp. iv. 34, 47, vi. 29, 50, ix. 2, 3, 22, xi. 50, xvi. 7. Abraham exulted in anticipation of the coming of the Messiah through implicit belief in the Divine promises.

and he saw it, and was glad] A very important passage with regard to the intermediate state, shewing that the soul does not, as some maintain, remain unconscious between death and the Day of Judgment. The Old Testament saints in Paradise were allowed to know that the Messiah had come. *How* this was revealed to them we are not told; but here is a plain statement of the fact. The word for 'was glad' expresses a calmer, less emotional joy than the word for 'rejoiced,' and therefore both are appropriate: 'exulted' while still on earth; 'was glad' in Hades. Thus the 'Communion of Saints' is assured, not merely in parables (Luke xvi. 27, 28), but in the plainer words of Scripture. Comp. Heb. xii. 1.

57. *Then said the Jews*] Better, **Therefore** *said the Jews*.

13—2

unto him, Thou art not yet fifty years old, and hast thou
58 seen Abraham? Jesus said unto them, Verily, verily, I say
59 unto you, Before Abraham was, I am. Then took they up
stones to cast at him: but Jesus hid himself, and went out
of the temple, going through the midst of them, and so
passed by.

Thou art not yet fifty years old] The reading, 'forty years,' which Chrysostom and a few authorities give, is no doubt incorrect. It has arisen from a wish to make the number less wide of the mark; for our Lord was probably not yet thirty-five, although Irenaeus preserves a tradition that He taught at a much later age. He says (II. xxii. 5), *a quadrigesimo autem et quinquagesimo anno declinat jam in aetatem seniorem, quam habens Dominus noster docebat, sicut evangelium et omnes seniores testantur qui in Asia apud Joannem discipulum Domini convenerunt.* By 'evangelium' he probably means this passage. But 'fifty years' is a round number, the Jewish traditional age of full manhood (Num. iv. 3, 39, viii. 24, 25). There is no reason to suppose that Jesus was nearly fifty, or looked nearly fifty. In comparing His age with the 2000 years since Abraham the Jews would not care to be precise so long as they were within the mark.

58. *Before Abraham was, I am*] Here our translators have lamentably gone back from earlier translations. Cranmer has, 'Ere Abraham *was born*, I am;' and the Rhemish, 'Before that Abraham *was made*, I am,' following the Vulgate, *Antequam Abraham fieret, Ego sum.* See notes on 'was' in i. 1, 6. 'I am' denotes absolute existence, and in this passage clearly involves the pre-existence and Divinity of Christ, as the Jews see. Comp. *vv.* 24, 28; Rev. i. 4, 8; and see on *v.* 24.

59. *Then took they up stones*] Or, **Therefore** *took they up stones*, i.e. in consequence of His last words. They see clearly what He means. He has taken to Himself the Divine Name and they prepare to stone Him for blasphemy. Material lying there for completing and repairing the Temple would supply them with missiles. Comp. x. 31, 33.

but Jesus hid himself] Probably we are not to understand a miraculous withdrawal as in Luke iv. 30, where the 'passing through the midst of them' seems to be miraculous. Here we need not suppose more than that He drew back into the crowd away from those who had taken up stones. The Providence which ordered that as yet the fears of the hierarchy should prevail over their hostility (vii. 30, viii. 20), ruled that the less hostile in this multitude should screen Him from the fury of the more fanatical. It is quite arbitrary to invert the clauses and render, 'Jesus went out of the Temple and hid Himself.'

going through the midst of them, and so passed by] These words are apparently an insertion, and probably an adaptation of Luke iv. 30. No English Version previous to the one of 1611 contains the passage.

As a comment on the whole discourse see 1 Pet. ii. 22, 23, remembering that S. Peter was very possibly present on the occasion.

CHAP. IX. *Christ the Source of Truth and Light illustrated by a Sign.*

1—5. *The Prelude to the Sign.*

9 And as *Jesus* passed by, he saw a man *which was* blind from *his* birth. And his disciples asked him, saying, 2 Master, who did sin, this *man*, or his parents, that he was

"The whole of the Jews' reasoning is strictly what we should expect from them. These constant appeals to their descent from Abraham, these repeated imputations of diabolic possession, this narrow intelligence bounded by the letter, this jealousy of anything that seemed in the slightest degree to trench on their own rigid monotheism—all these, down to the touch in ver. 57, in which the age they fix upon in round numbers is that assigned to completed manhood, give local truth and accuracy to the picture; which in any case, we may say confidently, must have been drawn by a Palestinian Jew, and was in all probability drawn by a Jew who had been himself an early disciple of Christ." S. p. 160.

CHAP. IX. CHRIST THE SOURCE OF TRUTH AND LIGHT ILLUSTRATED BY A SIGN.

Light is given to the eyes of the man born blind and the Truth is revealed to his soul.

1—5. THE PRELUDE TO THE SIGN.

1. *And as Jesus passed by*] Or, *And as He was passing by*. This was possibly on His way from the Temple (viii. 59), or it may refer to a later occasion near the Feast of the Dedication (x. 22). We know that this man begged for his living (*v.* 8), and that beggars frequented the gates of the Temple (Acts iii. 2), as they frequent the entrances of foreign churches now.

blind from his birth] The man would be repeatedly stating this fact to passers by. The Greek for 'from his birth' occurs nowhere else in N. T. Justin Martyr uses the phrase twice of those whom Christ healed; *Trypho* LXIX.; *Apol.* I. xxii. No source is so probable as this verse, for nowhere else is there an account of Christ's healing a congenital disease. See on i. 23 and iii. 3.

2. *Master*] Better, **Rabbi**: see on iv. 31.

who did sin, this man, or his parents, that he was born blind?] Literally, *that he* **should be** *born blind* (see note on viii. 56). This question has given rise to much discussion. It implies a belief that some one *must* have sinned, or there would have been no such suffering: who then was it that sinned? Possibly the question means no more than this; the persons most closely connected with the suffering being specially mentioned, without much thought as to possibilities or probabilities. But this is not quite satisfactory. The disciples name

3 born blind? Jesus answered, Neither hath this *man* sinned, nor his parents: but that the works of God should be made 4 manifest in him. I must work the works of him that sent

two very definite alternatives; we must not assume that one of them was meaningless. That the sins of the fathers are visited on the children is the teaching of the Second Commandment and of every one's experience. But how could a man be born blind for his own sin? Four answers have been suggested. (1) The predestinarian notion that the man was punished for sins which God knew he would commit in the course of his life. This is utterly unscriptural and scarcely fits the context.

(2) The doctrine of the transmigration of souls, which was held by some Jews: he might have sinned in another body. But it is doubtful whether this philosophic tenet would be familiar to the disciples.

(3) The doctrine of the pre-existence of the soul, which appears Wisdom viii. 20: the man's soul sinned before it was united to the body. This again can hardly have been familiar to illiterate men.

(4) The current Jewish interpretation of Gen. xxv. 22, Ps. li. 5, and similar passages; that it was possible for a babe yet unborn to have emotions (comp. Luke i. 41—44) and that these might be and often were sinful. On the whole, this seems to be the simplest and most natural interpretation, and *v.* 34 seems to confirm it.

3. Christ shews that there is a third alternative, which their question assumes that there is not. Moreover He by implication warns them against assuming a connexion between suffering and sin in individuals (see on v. 14). *Neither* did *this man* sin (not 'hath sinned'), *nor his parents.* The answer, like the question, points to a definite act of sin.

but that] i.e. he was born blind *in order that.* This elliptical use of 'but (in order) that' is common in S. John, and illustrates his fondness for the construction expressing a purpose: see on i. 8 and viii. 56.

the works of God] All those in which He manifests Himself, not miracles only. Comp. xi. 4. There is an undoubted reference to this passage (1—3) in the Clementine Homilies (XIX. 22), the date of which is about A.D. 150. Comp. x. 9, 27.

4. *I must work,* &c.] The reading here is somewhat doubtful, as to whether 'I' or 'we,' 'Me' or 'us' is right in each case. The best authorities give, We *must work the works of Him that sent Me,* and this, the more difficult reading, is probably correct. Some copyists altered 'we' into 'I' to make it agree with 'Me,' others altered 'Me' into 'us' to make it agree with 'we.'

'*We* must work:' Christ identifies Himself with His disciples in the work of converting the world. '*Him that sent Me:*' Christ does *not* identify His *mission* with that of the disciples. They were both sent, but not in the same sense. So also He says 'My Father' and 'your Father,' 'My God' and 'your God;' but not 'our Father,' or 'our God' (xx. 17).

me, while it is day: the night cometh, when no *man* can work. As long as I am in the world, I am the light of 5 the world.

6—12. *The Sign.*

When he had thus spoken, he spat on the ground, 6 and made clay of the spittle, and he anointed the eyes of the blind man with the clay, and said unto him, Go, 7 wash in the pool of Siloam, (which is by interpretation,

while it is day] Or, *so long as it is day*, i. e. so long as we have life. Day and night here mean, as so often in literature of all kinds, life and death. Other explanations, e. g. opportune and inopportune moments, the presence of Christ in the world and His withdrawal from it,—are less simple and less suitable to the context. *If* all that is recorded from vii. 37 takes place on one day, these words would probably be spoken in the evening, when the failing light would add force to the warning, **night** *cometh* (no article), *when no* one *can work.* 'No one;' not even Christ Himself as man upon earth: comp. xi. 7—10; Ps. civ. 23.

5. *As long as I am in the world*] Better, **Whensoever** *I am in the world;* it is not the same construction as 'so long as it is day.' The Light shines at various times and in various degrees, whether the world chooses to be illuminated or not. Comp. i. 5, viii. 12. Here there is special reference to His giving light both to the man's eyes and to his soul. The Pharisees prove the truth of the saying that 'the darkness comprehended it not.'

I am the light of the world] Or, *I am* **light** to *the world:* no article. Contrast viii. 12.

6—12. THE SIGN.

6. *anointed the eyes of the blind man with the clay*] 'Of the blind man' should probably be omitted, 'of it' inserted, and the rendering in the margin adopted: **spread the clay of it** (clay made with the spittle) **upon his eyes.** Regard for Christ's truthfulness compels us to regard the clay as the *means* of healing; not that He could not heal without it, but that He willed this to be the channel of His power. Elsewhere He uses spittle; to heal a blind man (Mark viii. 23); to heal a deaf and dumb man (Mark vii. 33). Spittle was believed to be a remedy for diseased eyes (comp. Vespasian's reputed miracle, Tac. *Hist.* IV. 81, and other instances); clay also, though less commonly. So that Christ selects an ordinary remedy and gives it success in a case confessedly beyond its supposed powers (*v.* 32). This helps us to conclude *why* He willed to use means, instead of healing without even a word; viz. to help the faith of the sufferer. It is easier to believe, when means can be perceived; it is still easier, when the means seem to be appropriate.

7. *wash in the pool*] Literally, *wash into the pool*, i. e. 'wash off

Sent.) He went his way therefore, and washed, and came seeing. ⁸ The neighbours therefore, and they which before had seen him that he was blind, said, Is not this he that sat and ⁹ begged? Some said, This is he: others *said*, He is like ¹⁰ him: *but* he said, I am *he*. Therefore said they unto him, ¹¹ How were thine eyes opened? He answered and said, A man *that is* called Jesus made clay, and anointed mine

the clay into the pool,' or, 'go to the pool and wash.' The washing was probably part of the means of healing (comp. Naaman) and was a strong test of the man's faith.

Siloam] Satisfactorily identified with *Birket Silwân* in the lower Tyropoean valley, S. E. of the hill of Zion. This is probably the Siloah of Neh. iii. 15 and the Shiloah of Isa. viii. 6. 'The tower in Siloam' (Luke xiii 4) was very possibly a building connected with the water; perhaps part of an aqueduct.

which is by interpretation] Literally, *which is* **interpreted**.

Sent] This is an admissible interpretation; but the original meaning is rather *Sending*, i. e. outlet of waters, 'the waters of Shiloah that go softly' (Isa. viii. 6). S. John sees in the word '*nomen et omen*' of the man's cure. Perhaps he sees also that this water from the rock is an image of Him who was *sent* from the Father.

and came seeing] 'Came,' not back to Christ, who had probably gone away meanwhile (*v.* 12), but to his own home, as would appear from what follows. Has any poet ever attempted to describe this man's emotions on first seeing the world in which he had lived so long?

"The scene in which the man returns seeing and is questioned by his neighbours, is vividly described. So too is the whole of that which follows, when the Pharisees come upon the stage. We may accept it with little short of absolute credence. If the opponents of miracles could produce a single Jewish document, in which any event, known not to have happened, was described with so much minuteness and verisimilitude, then it would be easier to agree with them." S. pp. 162, 163.

8. *had seen him that he was blind*] The true reading is, **saw** *him that he was* a **beggar**, or perhaps, **because** *he was a beggar*, i. e. he was often seen in public places.

he that sat and begged] Or, *he that sitteth and beggeth;* present participles with the article to express his general habit.

9. *Some said*] Or, **Others** *said*, making three groups of speakers in all.

He is like him] The better reading is, **No**, **but** *he is like him*. The opening of his eyes would greatly change his look and manner: this added to the extreme improbability of a cure made them doubt his identity.

11. *A man that is called Jesus*] This looks as if he had heard

eyes, and said unto me, Go to the pool of Siloam, and wash: and I went and washed, and I received sight. Then said they unto him, Where is he? He said, I know 12 not.

13—41. *Opposite Results of the Sign.*

They brought to the Pharisees him that aforetime was 13 blind. And it was the sabbath day when Jesus made the 14

little of the fame of Jesus. But the better reading gives, '**The** man that is called Jesus,' which points the other way.

made clay] He does not say how, for this he had not seen. The rest he tells in order. Omit the words 'the pool of.'

I received sight] The Greek may mean either 'I looked up,' as in Mark vi. 41, vii. 34, xvi. 4, &c.; or 'I recovered sight,' as Matt. xi. 5; Mark x. 51, 52, &c. 'I looked up' does not suit *vv.* 15 and 18, where the word occurs again: and though 'I recovered sight' is not strictly accurate of a man *born* blind, yet it is admissible, as sight is natural to man.

Note the gradual development of faith in the man's soul, and compare it with that of the Samaritan woman (see on iv. 19) and of Martha (see on xi. 21). Here he merely knows Jesus' name and the miracle; in *v.* 17 he thinks Him 'a Prophet;' in *v.* 33 He is 'of God;' in *v.* 39 He is 'the Son of God.' What writer of fiction in the second century could have executed such a study in psychology?

12. *Where is he?*] That strange (*ekeinos*) Rabbi who perplexes us so much.

I know not] This shews that he did not return to Jesus after he was healed (*v.* 7). 'He said' should be, *He* **saith.**

13—41. OPPOSITE RESULTS OF THE SIGN.

13. *They brought,* &c.] Better, *they* **bring** *him to the Pharisees,* **him** *that once was blind.* These friends and neighbours are perhaps well-meaning people, not intending to make mischief. But they are uncomfortable because work has been done on the Sabbath, and they think it best to refer the matter to the Pharisees, the great authorities in matters of legal observance and orthodoxy (comp. vii. 47, 48). This is not a meeting of the Sanhedrin. S. John's formula for the Sanhedrin is 'the chief priests and (the) Pharisees' (vii. 45, xi. 47, 57, xviii. 3), or 'the Pharisees and the chief priests' (vii. 32).

14. *it was the sabbath*] We cannot be sure whether this is the last day of the Feast of Tabernacles (vii. 37) or the next Sabbath. There were seven miracles of mercy wrought on the Sabbath: 1. Withered hand (Matt. xii. 9); 2. Demoniac at Capernaum (Mark i. 21); 3. Simon's wife's mother (Mark i. 29); 4. Woman bowed down eighteen years (Luke xiii. 14); 5. Dropsical man (Luke xiv. 1); 6. Paralytic at Bethesda (John v. 10); 7. Man born blind.

15 clay, and opened his eyes. Then again the Pharisees also asked him how he had received his sight. He said unto them, He put clay upon mine eyes, and I washed, and do 16 see. Therefore said some of the Pharisees, This man is not of God, because he keepeth not the sabbath day. Others said, How can a man *that is* a sinner do such mira- 17 cles? And there was a division among them. They say unto the blind man again, What sayest thou of him, that he hath opened thine eyes? He said, He is a prophet. 18 But the Jews did not believe concerning him, that he had been blind, and received his sight, until they called the 19 parents of him that had received his sight. And they asked

15. *Then again*] Better, *Again*, **therefore.** The man is becoming impatient of this cross-questioning: he answers much more briefly than at first (*v.* 11).

16. *This man is not of God*] Comp. 'He casteth out devils through the prince of the devils' (Matt. ix. 34); like this, an argument of the Pharisees. The fact of a miracle is not denied: but it cannot have been done with God's help; therefore it was done with the devil's help.

How can a man that is a sinner, &c.] The less bigoted, men like Nicodemus and Joseph of Arimathea, shew that the argument cuts both ways. They also start from the 'sign,' but arrive at an opposite conclusion. Comp. Nicodemus' question, vii. 51. Perhaps Christ's teaching about the Sabbath (v. 17—23) has had some effect.

there was a division] See on vii. 43.

17. There being a division among them they appeal to the man himself, each side wishing to gain him. 'They' includes both sides, the whole body of Pharisees present. Their question is not twofold, but single; not, 'What sayest thou of Him? that He hath opened thine eyes?' but *What sayest thou of Him*, **because He opened** *thine eyes?* 'Thou' is emphatic; '*thou* shouldest know something of Him.' They do not raise the question of fact; the miracle as yet is not in dispute. His answer shews that only one question is asked, and that it is not the question of fact.

He is a prophet] i.e. one sent by God to declare His will; a man with a special and Divine mission; not necessarily predicting the future. Comp. iv. 19, iii. 2.

18. *But the Jews did not believe*] Better, *the Jews*, **therefore**, *did not believe.* The man having pronounced for the moderates, the bigoted and hostile party begin to question the *fact* of the miracle. Note that here and in *v.* 22 S. John no longer speaks of the Pharisees, some of whom were not unfriendly to Christ, but 'the Jews,' His enemies, the official representatives of the nation that rejected the Messiah (see on i. 19).

19. Three questions in legal form. Is this your son? Was he born blind? How does he now see?

them, saying, Is this your son, who ye say was born blind? how then doth he now see? His parents answered them 20 and said, We know that this is our son, and that he was born blind: but by what means he now seeth, we know 21 not; or who hath opened his eyes, we know not: he is of age; ask him: he shall speak for himself. These *words* 22 spake his parents, because they feared the Jews: for the Jews had agreed already, that if any *man* did confess that he *was* Christ, he should be put out of the synagogue. Therefore said his parents, He is of age; ask him. Then 23 24

who ye say] Emphasis on 'ye,' implying 'we do not believe it;' literally, **of whom** *ye say* **that he was** *born blind*.

21. *by what means*] Better, **how**, as in *vv*. 10, 15, 19, 26. In their timidity they keep close to the precise questions asked.

who hath opened] Better, *who* **opened**. This is the dangerous point, and they become more eager and passionate. Hitherto there has been nothing emphatic in their reply; but now there is a marked stress on all the pronouns, the parents contrasting their ignorance with their son's responsibility. 'Who opened his eyes, *we* know not: ask *himself*; *he himself* is of full age; *he himself* will speak concerning himself.' See on *v*. 23.

22. *had agreed*] It does not appear when; but we are probably to understand an informal agreement among themselves rather than a decree of the Sanhedrin. A formal decree would be easily obtained afterwards. The word for 'agreed' is used of the agreement with Judas (Luke xxii. 5, where it is translated 'covenanted'), and of the agreement of the Jews to kill S. Paul (Acts xxiii. 20), and nowhere else. 'Assented' in Acts xxiv. 9 is a different compound of the same verb.

that if any man] Literally, *in order that if any man:* what they agreed upon is represented as the *purpose* of their agreement. See on *vv*. 2, 3, and viii. 56.

put out of the synagogue] i.e. excommunicated. The Jews had three kinds of anathema. (1) Excommunication for thirty days, during which the excommunicated might not come within four cubits of any one. (2) Absolute exclusion from all intercourse and worship for an indefinite period. (3) Absolute exclusion for ever; an irrevocable sentence. This third form was very rarely if ever used. It is doubtful whether the second was in use at this time for Jews; but it would be the ban under which all Samaritans were placed. This passage and 'separate' in Luke vi. 22 probably refer to the first and mildest kind of anathema. The principle of all anathema was found in the Divine sentence on Meroz (Judg. v. 23): Comp. Ezra x. 8. The word for 'out of the synagogue' is peculiar to S. John, occurring xii. 42, xvi. 2, and nowhere else.

23. *Therefore*] Better, **For this cause** (xii. 18, 27): comp. i. 31, v. 16, 18, vi. 65, viii. 47.

He is of age; ask him] Or, *He is of* **full** *age; ask him* **himself**. This

again called they the man that was blind, and said unto him, Give God the praise: we know that this man is a
25 sinner. He answered and said, Whether he be a sinner *or no*, I know not: one *thing* I know, that, whereas I was
26 blind, now I see. Then said they to him again, What did
27 he to thee? how opened he thine eyes? He answered them, I have told you already, and ye did not hear: wherefore
28 would you hear *it* again? will ye also be his disciples? Then

is the right order of the clauses here, and they have been altered in the Received Text of *v.* 21 to match this verse.

24. *Then again called they*] Literally, *They called*, **therefore, a second time.** They had cross-questioned the parents apart from the son, and now try to browbeat the son, before he finds out that his parents have not discredited his story.

Give God the praise] Better, **Give glory to God** (comp. v. 41 and viii. 54); it is the same word for 'glory' as in i. 14, ii. 11, vii. 18, viii. 50. Even thus the meaning remains obscure: but 'Give God the praise' is absolutely misleading. The meaning is not 'Give God the praise for the cure;' they were trying to deny that there had been any cure: but, 'Give glory to God *by speaking the truth.*' The words are an adjuration to confess. Comp. Josh. vii. 19; 1 Sam. vi. 5; Ezra x. 11; 1 Esdr. ix. 8; 2 Cor. xi. 31. Wiclif, with the Genevan and Rhemish Versions, is right here. Tyndale and Cranmer have misled our translators.

we know that, &c.] 'We' with emphasis; 'we, the people in authority, who have the right to pronounce decisively. So it is useless for you to maintain that He is a Prophet.'

25. *He answered*] Better, **Therefore** *he answered*. He will not commit himself, but keeps to the incontrovertible facts of the case.

whereas I was blind] Literally, *being a blind man*, but the Greek participle may be either present or imperfect; either 'being by nature a blind man' or 'being formerly blind.' In iii. 13 and xix. 38 we have the same participle, and a similar doubt as to whether it is present or imperfect: so also in *v.* 8.

26. Being baffled, they return to the details of the fact, either to try once more to shake the evidence, or for want of something better to say.

27. *I have told you*] Rather, *I told you*.

and ye did not hear] Or possibly, *and did ye not hear?* This avoids taking 'hear' in two different senses; (1) 'pay attention,' (2) 'hear.' The man loses all patience, and will not go through it again.

wherefore would ye hear] Or, *wherefore do ye wish to hear.*

will ye also, &c.] Or, **Surely ye also do not wish to become** *His disciples.* The form of the question is similar to that in vi. 67 and vii. 52 (comp. iv. 29, vii. 35). Moreover, it is not the future tense, but the verb 'to will' or 'wish' (comp. v. 40, vi. 67, vii. 17, viii. 44). Lastly, the difference between 'be' and 'become' is easily preserved here, and is worth preserving (comp. viii. 58). The meaning of 'also' has been

they reviled him, and said, Thou art his disciple; but we are Moses' disciples. We know that God spake unto Moses: 29 as for this *fellow*, we know not from whence he is. The 30 man answered and said unto them, Why herein is a marvellous *thing*, that ye know not from whence he is, and *yet* he hath opened mine eyes. Now we know that God heareth 31 not sinners: but if any *man* be a worshipper of God, and

misunderstood. It can scarcely mean 'as well as I:' the man has not advanced so far in faith as to count himself a disciple of Jesus; and if he had, he would not avow the fact to the Jews. 'Also' means 'as well as His well-known disciples.' That Christ had a band of followers was notorious.

28. *Then they reviled him*] Omit 'then.' The word for 'revile' occurs nowhere else in the Gospels. Comp. 1 Pet. ii. 23. Argument fails, so they resort to abuse.

Thou art his disciple] Better, *Thou art* that man's *disciple*. They use a pronoun which expresses that they have nothing to do with Him. Comp. v. 12 and vii. 11.

The pronouns are emphatic in both *v.* 28 and *v.* 29: '*Thou* art His disciple; but *we* are Moses' disciples. *We* know that *God* hath spoken to Moses; but as for *this* fellow, &c.'

29. *that God spake*] Literally, *that God* **hath spoken**, i.e. that Moses received a revelation *which still remains*. This is a frequent meaning of the perfect tense—to express the permanent result of a past action. Thus the frequent formula 'it is written' is strictly 'it has been written,' or 'it *stands* written:' i.e. it once was written, and the writing still remains. But this is perhaps one of those cases where the Greek perfect is best represented by the English aorist (see on viii. 29, 10 for the converse).

we know not from whence he is] We know not what commission He has received, nor who has sent Him. Comp. viii. 14 and contrast vii. 27. Once more He is compared with Moses, as in the synagogue at Capernaum (vi. 31, 32).

30. *a marvellous thing*] Some of the best MSS. read '**the** marvellous thing.' '*You*, the very people who ought to know such things (iii. 10), know not whether He is from God or not, and yet He opened my eyes.' 'You' is emphatic, and perhaps is a taunting rejoinder to their '*we* know that this man is a sinner' (*v.* 24) and '*we* know that God hath spoken to Moses' (*v.* 29). The man gains courage at their evident discomfiture.

31. *God heareth not sinners*] i.e. wilful, impenitent sinners. Of course it cannot mean 'God heareth no one who hath sinned,' which would imply that God never answers the prayers of men. But the man's dictum, reasonably understood, is the plain teaching of the O.T., whence he no doubt derived it. 'The Lord is far from the wicked; but He heareth the prayer of the righteous' (Prov. xv. 29). Comp. Ps. lxvi. 18, 19; Job. xxvii. 8, 9; Isa. i. 11—15.

32 doeth his will, him he heareth. Since the world began was
it not heard that any *man* opened the eyes of one that was
33 born blind. If this *man* were not of God, he could do
34 nothing. They answered and said unto him, Thou wast
altogether born in sins, and dost thou teach us? And they
35 cast him out. Jesus heard that they had cast him out; and
when he had found him, he said unto him, Dost thou
36 believe on the Son of God? He answered and said, Who is

a worshipper of God] Or, **God-fearing**, religious. The word occurs
nowhere else in N.T. The man supposes that miracles must be answers
to prayer. Only good men can gain such answers to prayer. Only a
very good man could gain such an unprecedented answer as this.
    32. *Since the world began*] There is no healing of the blind in
O. T.
    33. *of God*] Or, **from** *God:* comp. i. 6.
    he could do nothing] The context limits the meaning—nothing at all
like this, no miracle.
    34. *Thou wast altogether born in sins*] 'In sins (first for emphasis)
every part of thy nature (comp. xiii. 10) has been steeped from thy
birth; thou wast born a reprobate.' They hold the same belief as the
disciples, that sin before birth is possible, and maliciously exclude not
only the alternative stated by Christ (*v*. 3) but even the one stated by
the disciples (*v*. 2), that his parents might have sinned. Their passion
blinds them to their inconsistency. They had been contending that no
miracle had been wrought; now they throw his calamity in his face as
proof of his sin.
    Dost thou teach us?] 'Dost thou, the born reprobate, teach us, the
authorized teachers?'
    they cast him out] Or, *they* **put him forth**: see on x. 4. This pro-
bably does not mean excommunication. (1) The expression is too
vague. (2) There could not well have been time to get a sentence of
excommunication passed. (3) The man had not incurred the threat-
ened penalty; he had not 'confessed that He was Christ' (*v*. 22). Provoked by his impracticability and sturdy adherence to his own view they
ignominiously dismiss him—turn him out of doors, if (as the 'out' seems
to imply) they were meeting within walls.
    35. *Dost thou believe*] There is a stress on 'thou.' 'Dost *thou*,
though others deny and blaspheme, believe?'
    On the Son of God] Again there is much doubt about the reading.
The balance of MSS. authority (including both the Sinaitic and the
Vatican MSS.) is in favour of 'the Son of **man**,' which moreover is the
expression that our Lord commonly uses respecting Himself in all four
Gospels (see on i. 51). But the reading 'The Son of God' is very
strongly supported, and is at least as old as the second century; for Tertullian, who in his work *Against Praxeas* quotes largely from this
Gospel, in chap. xxii. quotes this question thus, *Tu credis in Filium*

he, Lord, that I might believe on him? And Jesus said 37 unto him, Thou hast both seen him, and it is he that talketh with thee. And he said, Lord, I believe. And he 38 worshipped him.

Dei? In x. 36 and xi. 4 there is no doubt about the reading, and there Christ calls himself 'the Son of God.' Moreover, this appellation seems to suit the context better, for the man had been contending that Jesus came 'from God' (*v.* 33), and the term 'Son of man' would scarcely have been intelligible to him. Lastly, a copyist, knowing that the 'Son of man' was Christ's usual mode of designating Himself, would be very likely to alter 'the Son of God' into 'the Son of man.' Neither title, however, is very frequent in St John's Gospel. For all these reasons, therefore, it is allowable to retain the common reading. But in any case we once more have evidence of the antiquity of this Gospel. If both these readings were established by the end of the second century, the original text must have been in existence long before. Corruptions take time to spring up and spread. See on i. 13, 18.

36. *Who is he, Lord*] We should perhaps insert 'and' or 'then' with some of the best MSS., **and** *Who is He?* or, *Who is He* **then?** This 'and' or 'then' has the effect of intensifying the question. Comp. '*and* who is my neighbour?' (Luke x. 29); 'Who *then* can be saved?' (xviii. 26); 'Who is he *then* that maketh me glad?' (2 Cor. ii. 2). 'Lord' should perhaps be 'Sir' as in iv. 11, 15, 19, 49; v. 7 (see on vi. 34): not until *v.* 38 does he reach the point at which he would call Jesus 'Lord.' But it is the same Greek word in both cases, though the amount of reverence with which he uses it increases, as in the parallel case of the woman at the well.

that I might believe] Literally, *in order that I* **may** *believe*. S. John's favourite construction again, as in *vv.* 2, 3, 22.

37. *Thou hast both seen him*] Better, *Thou hast even seen Him, and He that speaketh with thee* **is He.** The latter half of the sentence is similar to the declaration in iv. 26. "This spontaneous revelation to the outcast from the synagogue *finds its only parallel* in the similar revelation to the outcast from the nation." Westcott. Not even Apostles are told so speedily.

38. *Lord, I believe*] Or, **I believe, Lord**: the order is worth keeping. Comp. the centurion's confession (Matt. xxvii. 54). There is no need to suppose that in either case the man making the confession knew anything like the full meaning of belief in the Son of God: even Apostles were slow at learning that. The blind man had had his own uninformed idea of the Messiah, and he believed that the realisation of that idea stood before him. His faith was necessarily imperfect, a poor 'two mites;' but it was 'all that he had,' and he gave it readily, while the learned Rabbis of their abundance gave nothing. It is quite gratuitous to suppose that a special revelation was granted to him. There is no hint of this in the narrative, nor can one see why so great an exception to God's usual dealings with man should have been made.

he worshipped him] This shews that his idea of the Son of God in-

39 And Jesus said, For judgment I am come into this world, that they which see not might see; and that they which
40 see might be made blind. And *some* of the Pharisees which were with him heard these *words*, and said unto him,
41 Are we blind also? Jesus said unto them, If ye were blind,

cludes attributes of Divinity. The word for 'worship' occurs elsewhere in this Gospel only in iv. 20—24 and xii. 20, always of the worship of God.

39—41. "The concluding verses contain a saying which is thoroughly in the manner of the Synoptists (cf. Matt. xv. 14; xxiii. 16, 17, 24, 26). It also supplies a warranty for ascribing a typical significance to miracles.

That the Synoptists do not relate this miracle does not affect its historical character, as the whole of these events in Judaea are equally omitted by them....... The vague and shifting outlines of the Synoptic narrative allow ample room for all the insertions that are made in them with so much precision by S. John." S. pp. 165, 166.

39. *And Jesus said*] There is no need to make a break in the narrative and refer these words to a subsequent occasion. This is not natural. Rather it is the sight of the man prostrate at His feet, endowed now with sight both in body and soul, that moves Christ to say what follows. His words are addressed to the bystanders generally, among whom are some of the Pharisees.

For judgment I am come] Better, *For judgment I* **came**. The precise form of word for 'judgment' occurs nowhere else in this Gospel. It signifies not the *act* of judging (v. 22, 24, 27, 30) but its *result*, a 'sentence' or 'decision' (Matt. vii. 2, Mark xii. 40, Rom. ii. 2, 3, &c.), Christ came not to judge, but to save (iii. 17, viii. 15); but judgment was the inevitable result of His coming, for those who rejected Him passed sentence on themselves (iii. 19). See on i. 9 and xviii. 37. The pronoun is emphatic.

they which see not] They who are conscious of their own blindness, who know their deficiencies; like 'they that are sick' and 'sinners' in Matt. ix. 12, 13, and 'babes' in Matt. xi. 25. This man was aware of his spiritual blindness when he asked, 'Who is He then, that I may believe on Him!'

might see] Better, **may see**, may really see, may pass from the darkness of which they are conscious, to light and truth.

they which see] They who fancy they see, who pride themselves on their superior insight and knowledge, and wish to dictate to others; like 'they that be whole,' and 'righteous' in Matt. ix. 12, 13, and 'the wise and prudent' in Matt. xi. 25. These Pharisees shewed this proud self-confidence when they declared, '*we* know that this man is a sinner,' and asked 'Dost *thou* teach *us*?'

might be made blind] Or, **may become** *blind*, really blind (Isa. vi. 10), may pass from their fancied light into real darkness.

40. *And some of*] Better, **Those** *of*.

Are we blind also?] Or, **Surely we also are not blind?** See on

ye should have no sin: but now ye say, We see; therefore your sin remaineth.

v. 27. Of course they understand Him to be speaking figuratively. It is strange that any should have understood their question as referring to bodily sight. They mean that they, the most enlightened among the most enlightened nation, must be among 'those who see.'

41. *If ye were blind*] Christ returns to His own meaning of 'blind' or 'they which see not' in *v.* 39. 'If ye were conscious of your own spiritual darkness, if ye yearned and strove to reach the light, *ye* **would not have sin** (see on xv. 22); for either ye would find the light, or, if ye failed, the failure would not lie at your door.' For the construction comp. v. 46; viii. 19, 42; xv. 19; xviii. 36.

therefore your sin remaineth] Better, *your sin* **abideth** (see on i. 33): 'therefore' is an insertion, and must be omitted. 'Ye profess to see: your sin in this false profession and in your consequent rejection of Me abideth.' It was a hopeless case. They rejected Him because they did not know the truth about Him; and they would never learn the truth because they were fully persuaded that they were in possession of it. Those who confess their ignorance and contend against it, (1) cease to be responsible for it, (2) have a good prospect of being freed from it. Those who deny their ignorance and contend against instruction, (1) remain responsible for their ignorance, (2) have no prospect of ever being freed from it. Comp. iii. 36.

CHAP. X. CHRIST IS LOVE.

In chapters v. and vi. two miracles, the healing of the paralytic and the feeding of the five thousand, formed the introduction to two discourses in which Christ is set forth as the *Source and the Support of Life*. In chapters vii. and viii. we have a discourse in which He is set forth as the *Source of Truth and Light*, and this is illustrated (ix.) by His giving physical and spiritual sight to the man born blind. In chap. x. we again have a discourse in which Christ is set forth as *Love*, under the figure of the Good Shepherd giving His life for the sheep, and this is illustrated (xi.) by the raising of Lazarus, a work of Love which costs Him His life. As already stated, the prevailing idea throughout this section (v.—xi.) is truth and love provoking contradiction and enmity. The more clearly the Messiah manifests Himself, and the more often He convinces some of His hearers of His Messiahship (vii. 40, 41, 46, 50, viii. 30, ix. 30—38, x. 21, 42, xi. 45), the more intense becomes the hostility of 'the Jews' and the more determined their intention to kill Him.

1—18. "The form of the discourse in the first half of chap. x. is remarkable. It resembles the Synoptic parables, but not exactly. The parable is a short narrative, which is kept wholly separate from the ideal facts which it signifies. But this discourse is not a narrative; and the figure and its application run side by side, and are interwoven with one another all through. It is an extended metaphor rather than a

CHAP. X. *Christ is Love.*
1—10. *The Allegory of the Door of the Fold.*

10 Verily, verily, I say unto you, He that entereth not by the

parable. If we are to give it an accurate name we should be obliged to fall back upon the wider term 'allegory.'

This, and the parallel passage in chap. xv., are the only instances of allegory in the Gospels. They take in the Fourth Gospel the place which parables hold with the Synoptists. The Synoptists have no allegories distinct from parables. The fourth Evangelist has no parables as a special form of allegory. What are we to infer from this? The parables certainly are original and genuine. Does it follow that the allegories are not?

(1) We notice, first, that along with the change of *form* there is a certain change of *subject*. The parables generally turn round the ground conception of the kingdom of heaven. They......do not enlarge on the relation which its King bears to the separate members...... Though the royal dignity of the Son is incidentally put forward, there is nothing which expresses so closely and directly *the personal relation of the Messiah to the community of believers*, collectively and individually, as these two 'allegories' from S. John. Their form seems in an especial manner suited to their subject matter, which is a fixed, permanent and simple relation, not a history of successive states. The form of the allegories is at least appropriate.

(2) We notice next that even with the Synoptists the use of the parable is not rigid. All do not conform precisely to the same type. There are some, like the Pharisee and Publican, the Good Samaritan, &c., which give direct patterns for action, and are not therefore parables in the same sense in which the Barren Fig-tree, the Prodigal Son, &c. are parables...... If, then, the parable admits so much deviation on the one side, may it not also on the other?

(3) Lastly, we have to notice the parallels to this particular figure of the Good Shepherd that are found in the Synoptists. These are indeed abundant. The parable of the Lost Sheep (Luke xv. 4—7; Matt. xviii. 12, 13)...... 'I am not sent but unto the lost sheep of the house of Israel' (Matt. xv. 24)...... 'But when He saw the multitudes, He was moved with compassion on them, because they fainted, and were scattered abroad, as sheep having no Shepherd' (Matt. ix. 36), which when taken with Matt. xi. 28, 29 ('Come unto Me all ye that labour,' &c.), gives almost an exact parallel to the Johannean allegory." S. pp. 167—169.

1—10. THE ALLEGORY OF THE DOOR OF THE FOLD.

1. *Verily, verily*] This double affirmation, peculiar to this Gospel (see on i. 51), never occurs at the beginning of a discourse, but either in continuation, to introduce some deep truth, or in reply. This verse is no exception. There is no break between the chapters,

door into the sheepfold, but climbeth up some other way, the
same is a thief and a robber. But he that entereth in by 2
the door is the shepherd of the sheep. To him the porter 3

which should perhaps have been divided at ix. 34 or 38 rather than
here. The scene continues uninterrupted from ix. 35 to x. 21, where we
have a reference to the healing of the blind man. Moreover x. 6 seems
to point back to ix. 41; their not understanding the allegory was
evidence of self-complacent blindness. This chapter, therefore, although
it contains a fresh subject, is connected with the incidents in chap. ix.,
and grows out of them. The connexion seems to be that the Pharisees
by their conduct to the man had proved themselves bad shepherds; but
he has found the Good Shepherd: they had cast him out of doors; but
he has found the Door: they had put him forth to drive him away;
the Good Shepherd puts His sheep forth to lead them. We are not
told where these words are spoken; so that it is impossible to say
whether it is probable that a sheepfold with the shepherds and
their flocks was in sight. There is nothing improbable in the supposition.

He that entereth not by the door] The Oriental sheepfolds are commonly walled or palisaded, with one door or gate. Into one of these
enclosures several shepherds drive their flocks, leaving them in charge
of an under-shepherd or porter, who fastens the door securely inside,
and remains with the sheep all night. In the morning the shepherds
come to the door, the porter opens to them, and each calls away his own
sheep.

some other way] Literally, *from another quarter:* the word occurs
here only in N.T.

the same] Better, **he**; literally, *that one*. It is a pronoun of which
S. John is very fond in order to recall with emphasis some person or
thing previously mentioned. Comp. i. 18, 33, v. ii. 39, ix. 37, xii. 48,
xiv. 21, 26, xv. 26. In i. 33 ('the same said unto me'), v. 11, and xii.
48 it is inaccurately translated, as here, 'the same.'

a thief and robber] Everywhere in this Gospel (8, 10, xii. 6, xviii.
40), as also 2 Cor. xi. 26, these words are given correctly as renderings
of the Greek equivalents; but everywhere else in N.T. (Matt. xxi. 13,
xxvi. 55, xxvii. 38, &c., &c.) the word here translated 'robber' is less
well translated 'thief.' The 'robber' is a brigand, a more formidable
criminal than the 'thief;' the one uses violence, the other cunning.

2. *is the shepherd of the sheep*] Better, *is* **a** *shepherd of the sheep*.
There is more than one flock in the fold, and therefore more than one
shepherd to visit the fold. The Good Shepherd has not yet appeared
in the allegory. The allegory indeed is two-fold; in the first part
(1—5), which is repeated (7—9), Christ is the Door of the fold; in the
second part (11—18) He is the Shepherd; *v*. 10 forming a link between
the two parts.

3. *To him the porter openeth*] The 'porter' is the door-keeper or
gate-keeper, who fastens and opens the one door into the fold. In the
allegory the fold is the Church, the Door is Christ, the sheep are the

openeth; and the sheep hear his voice: and he calleth his
4 own sheep by name, and leadeth them out. And when he
putteth forth his own sheep, he goeth before them, and the
5 sheep follow him: for they know his voice. And a stranger
will they not follow, but will flee from him: for they know
6 not the voice of strangers. This parable spake Jesus unto

elect, the shepherds are God's ministers. What does the porter represent? Possibly nothing definite. Much harm is sometimes done by trying to make every detail of an allegory or parable significant. There must be back ground in every picture. But if it be insisted that the porter here is too prominent to be meaningless, it is perhaps best to understand the Holy Spirit as signified under this figure; He who grants opportunities of coming, or of bringing others, through Christ into the Kingdom of God. Comp. 1 Cor. xvi. 9; 2 Cor. ii. 12; Col. iv. 3; Acts xiv. 27; Rev. iii. 8: but in all these passages 'door' does not mean Christ, but *opportunity*. See on 1 Cor. xvi. 9.

the sheep hear his voice] All the sheep, whether belonging to His flock or not, know from His coming that they are about to be led out. *His own sheep* (first for emphasis) *he calleth by name* (Exod. xxxiii. 12, 17; Isa. xliii. 1), *and leadeth them out* to pasture. Even in this country shepherds and shepherds' dogs know each individual sheep; in the East the intimacy between shepherd and sheep is still closer. The naming of sheep is a very ancient practice: see Theocritus V. 102.

4. *when he putteth forth his own sheep*] Better, *when he* **hath put forth all** *his own*. Most of the best MSS. have 'all' for 'sheep;' 'there shall not an hoof be left behind' (Exod. x. 26). The word for 'put forth' is remarkable; it is the same as is used in ix. 34, 35 of the Pharisees 'casting out' the man born blind. This is perhaps not accidental: the false shepherds put forth sheep to rid themselves of trouble; the true shepherds put forth sheep to feed them. But even the true shepherds must sometimes use a certain amount of violence to their sheep to 'compel them to come' (Luke xiv. 23) to the pastures. But note that there are no 'goats' in the allegory: all the flock are faithful. It is the ideal Church composed entirely of the elect. The object of the allegory being to set forth the relations of Christ to His sheep, the possibility of bad sheep is not taken into account. That side of the picture is treated in the parables of the Lost Sheep, and of the Sheep and the Goats.

5. *And a stranger will they not follow*] Better, **But** *a stranger they will* **assuredly** *not follow*. The form of negative is very strong, as in iv. 14, 48, vi. 35, 37, viii. 12, 51, 52: see on viii. 51. By 'a stranger' is meant quite literally anyone whom they do not know, not necessarily a thief or robber.

6. *This parable*] Better, *This* **allegory**. The word which the Synoptists use for 'parable' (*parabolē*) is never used by S. John; and the word here used by S. John (*paroimia*) is never used by the Synoptists. This should be brought out in translation; both are rendered

them: but they understood not what *things* they were which he spake unto them.

Then said Jesus unto them again, Verily, verily, I say 7 unto you, I am the door of the sheep. All that ever came 8 before me are thieves and robbers: but the sheep did not

by our translators sometimes 'parable' and sometimes 'proverb.' *Paroimia* occurs again xvi. 25, 29 and 2 Pet. ii. 22, and nowhere else in N.T. Everywhere but here it is translated 'proverb.' *Paroimia* means something *beside the way;* hence, according to some, a trite '*way side* saying;' according to others, a figurative '*out-of-the-way* saying.' On *parabolē* see on Mark iv. 2.

understood not] Did not recognise the meaning.

7. *Then said Jesus unto them again*] Better, **Therefore** *said Jesus again.* They did not understand; *therefore* He went through the allegory *again* more explicitly, interpreting the main features. 'Unto them' is of doubtful authority.

Verily, verily] This is *the* important point, to recognise that the one door of the fold, through which the sheep and the shepherds enter, is Christ. *I* (with great emphasis) *am the Door.* Comp. 'I am the Way' (xiv. 6).

the door of the sheep] Better, 'the Door *to* the sheep' (*vv.* 1, 2), and also 'the Door *for* the sheep' (*v.* 9). Sheep and shepherds alike have one and the same door. The elect enter the Church through Christ; the ministers who would visit the flocks must receive their commission from Christ. Note that Christ does not say, 'the Door of the *fold,*' but 'the Door of the *sheep.*' The fold has no meaning apart from the sheep.

8. *All that ever came before me are thieves and robbers*] These words are difficult, and some copyists seem to have tried to avoid the difficulty by omitting either 'all' or 'before Me.' But the balance of authority leaves no doubt that both are genuine. Some commentators would translate 'instead of Me' for 'before Me.' But this meaning of the Greek preposition is not common, and perhaps occurs nowhere in N.T. Moreover 'instead of Me' ought to include the idea of 'for My advantage;' and that is impossible here. We must retain the natural and ordinary meaning of 'before Me:' and as 'before Me in *dignity*' would be obviously inappropriate, 'before Me in *time*' must be the meaning. But who are 'all that came before Me?' The patriarchs, prophets, Moses, the Baptist *cannot* be meant, either collectively or singly. 'Salvation is of the Jews' (iv. 22); 'they are they which testify of Me' (v. 39); 'if ye believed Moses, ye would believe Me' (v. 46); 'John bare witness unto the truth' (v. 33): texts like this are quite conclusive against any such Gnostic interpretation. Nor can false Messiahs be meant: it is doubtful whether any had arisen at this time. Rather it refers to the 'ravening wolves in sheep's clothing' who had been, and still were, the ruin of the nation, who 'devoured widow's houses,' who were 'full of ravening and wickedness,' who had 'taken away the key of knowledge,' and were in

9 hear them. I am the door: by me if any *man* enter in, he shall be saved, and shall go in and out, and find pasture. 10 The thief cometh not, but for to steal, and to kill, and to destroy: I am come that they might have life, and that they might have *it more* abundantly.

very truth 'thieves and robbers' (Matt. vii. 15, xxiii. 14; Luke xi. 39, 52). Some of them were now present, thirsting to add bloodshed to robbery, and this denunciation of them is no stronger than several passages in the Synoptists: e.g. Matt. xxiii. 33; Luke xi. 50, 51. The tense also is in favour of this interpretation; not *were*, but '*are* thieves and robbers.'

but the sheep did not hear them] For they spoke with no authority (Matt. vii. 29); there was no living voice in their teaching. They had their hearers, but these were not 'the sheep,' but blind adherents, led by the blind.

9. *by me*] Placed first for emphasis; 'through Me and in no other way.' The main point is iterated again and again, each time with great simplicity, and yet most emphatically. "The simplicity, the directness, the particularity, the emphasis of S. John's style give his writings a marvellous power, which is not perhaps felt at first. Yet his words seem to hang about the reader till he is forced to remember them. Each great truth sounds like the burden of a strain, ever falling upon the ear with a calm persistency which secures attention." Westcott, *Introduction to the Study of the Gospels*, p. 250.

he shall be saved] These words and 'shall find pasture' seem to shew that this verse does not refer to the shepherds only, but to the sheep also. Although 'find pasture' may refer to the shepherd's work for the flock, yet one is inclined to think that if the words do not refer to both, they refer to the sheep only.

With the verse as a whole should be compared 'the strait gate and narrow way which leadeth unto life' (Matt. vii. 14). In the *Clementine Homilies* (III. lii.) we have 'He, being a true prophet, said, I am the gate of life; he that entereth in through Me entereth into life.' See on ix. 3.

10. *and to kill*] To slaughter as if for sacrifice.

I am come] Better, **I came**. 'I' is emphatic, in marked contrast to the thief. This is the point of transition from the first part of the allegory to the second. The figure of the Door, as the one entrance to salvation, is dropped; and that of the Good Shepherd, as opposed to the thief, is taken up; but this intermediate clause will apply to either figure, inclining towards the second one. In order to make the strongest possible antithesis to the thief, Christ introduces, not a shepherd, but Himself, the Chief Shepherd. The thief *takes* life; the shepherds *protect* life; the Good Shepherd *gives* it.

that they might have] Rather, in both clauses, *that they* **may** *have*.

have it more abundantly] Omit 'more;' it is not in the Greek, and

11—18. *The Allegory of the Good Shepherd.*

I am the good shepherd: the good shepherd giveth his life 11 for the sheep. But *he that is* a hireling, and not the shepherd, 12 whose own the sheep are not, seeth the wolf coming, and leaveth the sheep, and fleeth: and the wolf catcheth them, and

somewhat spoils the sense. More abundantly than what? Translate, *that they* **may have abundance.**

11—18. THE ALLEGORY OF THE GOOD SHEPHERD.

11. *I am the Good Shepherd*] The word translated 'good' cannot be adequately translated: it means 'beautiful, noble, good,' as opposed to 'foul, mean, wicked.' It sums up the chief attributes of ideal perfection. Christ is the Perfect Shepherd, as opposed to His own imperfect ministers; He is the true Shepherd, as opposed to the false shepherds, who are hirelings or hypocrites; He is the Good Shepherd, who gives His life for the sheep, as opposed to the wicked thief who takes their lives to preserve his own. Thus in Christ is realised the ideal Shepherd of O.T. Ps. xxiii.; Isa. xl. 11; Jer. xxiii.; Ezek. xxxiv., xxxvii. 24; Zech. xi. 7. Perhaps no image has penetrated more deeply into the mind of Christendom: Christian prayers and hymns, Christian painting and statuary, and Christian literature are full of it, and have been from the earliest ages. And side by side with it is commonly found the other beautiful image of this Gospel, the Vine: the Good Shepherd and the True Vine are figures of which Christians have never wearied.

giveth his life] Better, **layeth down** *His life*. The phrase is a remarkable one and peculiar to S. John, whereas 'to *give* His life' occurs in the Synoptists (Matt. xx. 20; Mark x. 45). 'To *lay* down' perhaps includes the notion of 'to *pay* down,' a common meaning of the words in classical Greek; if so, it is exactly equivalent to the Synoptic phrase 'to give as a *ransom.*' It occurs again, *vv.* 15, 17, xiii. 37, 38, xv. 13; 1 John iii. 16. In this country the statement 'the good shepherd lays down his life for his sheep' seems extravagant when taken apart from the application to Christ. It is otherwise in the East, where dangers from wild beasts and armed bands of robbers are serious and constant. Comp. Gen. xiii. 5, xiv. 12, xxxi. 39, 40, xxxii. 7, 8, xxxvii. 33; Job i. 17; 1 Sam. xvii. 34, 35.

12. *an hireling*] The word occurs nowhere else in N. T. excepting of the 'hired servants' of Zebedee (Mark i. 20). The Good Shepherd was introduced in contrast to the thief. Now we have another contrast to the Good Shepherd given, the *hired* shepherd, a mercenary, who tends a flock not his own for his own interests. The application is obvious; viz., to those ministers who care chiefly for the emoluments and advantages of their position, and retire when the position becomes irksome or dangerous.

and not the shepherd] Better, *and not* **a** *shepherd*, as in *v.* 2
the wolf] Any power opposed to Christ. See on *v.* 28.

13 scattereth the sheep. The hireling fleeth, because he is a 14 hireling, and careth not for the sheep. I am the good shep- 15 herd, and know my *sheep*, and am known of mine. As the Father knoweth me, *even* so know I the Father: and I lay down 16 my life for the sheep. And other sheep I have, which are not of this fold: them also I must bring, and they shall hear my voice; and there shall be one fold, *and* one shepherd.

and scattereth the sheep] The best authorities omit 'the sheep;' but the words might easily be omitted as apparently awkward and superfluous after the preceding 'them.' But in any case the meaning is 'snatcheth certain sheep and scattereth the flock.'

13. *The hireling fleeth*] These words are of still more doubtful authority. Omitting both the doubtful portions the sentence will run (The hireling) *leaveth the sheep and fleeth; and the wolf snatcheth them and scattereth (them); because he is an hireling and careth not*, &c.

14—18. Further description of the True Shepherd. (1) His intimate knowledge of His sheep; (2) His readiness to die for them. This latter point recurs repeatedly as a sort of refrain, like 'I will raise him up at the last day,' in chap. vi.

14. *and know my sheep, and am known of mine*] Better, *and* I **know Mine, and Mine know Me.**

15. *As the Father knoweth me, even so*, &c.] This rendering entirely obscures the true meaning. There should be no full stop at the end of *v.* 14, and the sentence should run; **I know Mine, and Mine know Me, even as the Father knoweth Me and I know the Father.** So intimate is the relation between the Good Shepherd and His sheep that it may be compared to the relation between the Father and the Son. The same thought runs through the discourses in the latter half of the Gospel: xiv. 20, xv. 10, xvii. 8, 10, 18, 21.

16. *other sheep I have*] Not the Jews in heathen lands, but Gentiles, for even among them He had sheep. The Jews had asked in derision, 'Will He go and teach the Gentiles?' (vii. 35). He declares here that among the despised heathen He has sheep. He was going to lay down His life, 'not for that nation only' (xi. 52), but that He might 'draw *all* men unto Him' (xii. 32). Of that most heathen of heathen cities, Corinth, He declared to S. Paul in a vision, 'I have much people in this city' (Acts xviii. 10).

not of this fold] Emphasis on 'fold,' not on 'this;' the Gentiles were in no fold at all, but 'scattered abroad' (xi. 52).

them also I must bring] Better, *them also I must* **lead.** No need for them to be removed; Christ can lead them in their own lands. 'Neither in this mountain, nor yet at Jerusalem' (iv. 21) is the appointed place. Note the 'must;' it is the Messiah's bounden duty, decreed for Him by the Father: comp. iii. 14, ix. 4, xii. 34, xx. 9.

there shall be one fold, and one shepherd] Rather, **they** *shall* **become** *one* **flock**, *one shepherd*. The distinction between 'be' and 'become' is worth preserving (see on ix. 27, 39), and that between 'flock' and

vv. 17, 18.]   S. JOHN, X.   217

Therefore doth *my* Father love me, because I lay down my 17
life, that I might take it again.   No *man* taketh it from me, 18

'fold' still more so. 'There shall become one fold' would imply that at present there are more than one: but nothing is said of any other fold. In both these instances our translators have rejected their better predecessors: Tyndale and Coverdale have 'flock,' not 'fold;' the Geneva Version has 'be made,' not 'be.' One point in the Greek cannot be preserved in English. The words for 'flock' and 'shepherd' are cognate and very similar, *poimnē* and *poimēn:* 'one herd, one herdsman' would be the nearest approach we could make, and to change 'flock' for 'herd' would be more loss than gain. The change from 'flock' to 'fold' has been all loss, leading to calamitous misunderstanding.

"The universalism of v. 16, which is so often quoted against the Gospel, seems rather to be exactly of the kind of which we have abundant evidence in the Synoptists: e.g. in Matt. viii. 11, xiii. 24—30, xxviii. 19; Luke xiii. 29. A certain precedence is assigned to Israel, but the inclusion of the Gentiles is distinctly contemplated." And if S. Matthew could appreciate this side of his Master's teaching, how much more S. John, who had lived to see the success of missions to the heathen and the destruction of Jerusalem. "On the other hand, the nature of S. John's universalism must not be mistaken. It implies a privileged position on the part of the Jews." S. pp. 172, 173. Moreover, even O.T. prophets seem to have had a presentiment that other nations would share in the blessings of the Messiah. Mic. iv. 2; Isa. lii. 15.

17. *Therefore*] Better, **On this account,** or, **For this cause** (xii. 18, 27). See on vii. 22 and viii. 47, and comp. v. 16, 18, vi. 65. The Father's love for the incarnate Son is intensified by the self-sacrifice of the Son.

that I might take it again] Literally, **in order that I may** *take it again*. This clause is closely connected with the preceding one: 'that' depends upon 'because.' Only because Christ was to take His human life again was His death such as the Father could have approved. Had the Son returned to heaven at the Crucifixion leaving His humanity on the Cross, the salvation of mankind would not have been won, the sentence of death would not have been reversed, we should be 'yet in our sins' (1 Cor. xv. 17). Moreover, in that case He would have ceased to be the Good Shepherd: He would have become like the hireling, casting aside his duty before it was completed. The office of the True Shepherd is not finished until all mankind become His flock; and this work continues from the Resurrection to the Day of Judgment.

18. *No man taketh it from me*] Better, *No* **one** *taketh it from Me;* not even God. See on *v.* 28. Two points are insisted on; (1) that the Death is entirely voluntary; (2) that both Death and Resurrection are in accordance with a commission received from the Father. Comp. 'Father, into Thy hands I commend My spirit' (Luke xxiii. 46). The precise words used by the two Apostles of Christ's death bring this out very clearly; 'yielded up (literally 'let go') the ghost' (Matt. xxvii. 50); 'gave up the ghost' (John xix. 30; see note there). The word used by

but I lay it down of myself. I have power to lay it down, and I have power to take it again. This commandment have I received of my Father.

19—21. *Opposite Results of the Teaching.*

19 There was a division therefore again among the Jews for
20 these sayings. And many of them said, He hath a devil,
21 and is mad; why hear ye him? Others said, These are not the words of him that hath a devil. Can a devil open the eyes of the blind?

S. Mark and S. Luke ('breathed His last,' or 'expired') is less strong. Here there is an emphasis on the pronoun; 'but *I* lay it down of Myself.'

I have power] i.e. **right**, authority, liberty: same word as in i. 12, v. 27, xvii. 2, xix. 10. This authority is the commandment of the Father: and hence this passage in no way contradicts the usual N.T. doctrine that Christ was raised to life again by the Father. Acts ii. 24.

This commandment have I received] Better, *This commandment received I*, viz., at the Incarnation: the commandment to die and rise again. Comp. iv. 34, v. 30, vi. 38.

19—21. OPPOSITE RESULTS OF THE TEACHING.

19. *again*] As about the man born blind (ix. 6) among the Pharisees, and at the Feast of Tabernacles (vii. 43), among the multitude. 'Therefore' should be omitted here as wanting authority; and 'there arose' would be more accurate than 'there was' (see on i. 6); *there* **arose** *a division again*. See on vii. 43.

among the Jews] Some even among the hostile party are impressed, and doubt the correctness of their position: comp. xi. 45.

20. *He hath a devil*] See last note on viii. 48, and comp. vii. 20.

21. *of him that hath a devil*] Better, *of* **one possessed with a demon**: the expression differs from that in v. 20.

Can a devil] Or, *Surely a* **demon** *cannot*. See on ix. 40. It was too great and too beneficent a miracle for a demon. But here they stop short: they state what He *cannot* be; they do not see, or will not admit, what He *must* be.

22—38. THE DISCOURSE AT THE FEAST OF THE DEDICATION.

Again we seem to have a gap in the narrative. Between *vv.* 21—22 (but see below) there is an interval of about two months; for the Feast of Tabernacles would be about the middle of October, and that of the Dedication towards the end of December. In this interval some would place Luke x. 1—xiii. 21. If this be correct, we may connect the sending out of the Seventy both with the Feast of Tabernacles and also with John x. 16. Seventy was the traditional number of the nations of the

22—38. *The Discourse at the Feast of the Dedication.*

And it was at Jerusalem *the feast of* the dedication, and it was winter. And Jesus walked in the temple in Solo-

earth; and for the nations 70 bullocks were offered at the Feast of Tabernacles—13 on the first day, 12 on the second, 11 on the third, and so on. The Seventy were sent out to gather in the nations; for they were not forbidden, as the Twelve were, to go into the way of the Gentiles or to enter any city of the Samaritans (Matt. x. 5). The Twelve were primarily for the twelve tribes; the Seventy for the Gentiles. The words 'other sheep I have which are not of this fold; them also I must lead,' must have been spoken just before the mission of the Seventy.

Dr Westcott, on the strength of a strongly attested reading in *v.* 22, **Then** *there took place the Feast of the Dedication*, would connect chap. ix. and x. 1—21 with this later feast rather than with the Feast of Tabernacles. In this case the interval of two months must be placed between chaps. viii. and ix.

22. *And it was at Jerusalem the feast of the dedication*] More literally, **Now there took place** *at Jerusalem the Feast of the Dedication*. This feast might be celebrated anywhere, and the pointed insertion of 'at Jerusalem' seems to suggest that in the interval between *v.* 21 and *v.* 22 Christ had been away from the city. It was kept in honour of the purification and restoration of the Temple (B.C. 164) after its desecration by Antiochus Epiphanes; 1 Macc. i. 20—60, iv. 36—59 (note esp. *vv.* 36 and 59); 2 Macc. x. 1—8. Another name for it was 'the Lights,' or 'Feast of Lights,' from the illuminations with which it was celebrated. Christian dedication festivals are its lineal descendants.

"The feast was of comparatively recent institution....It is not a feast the name of which would be likely to occur to any but a Jew; still less the accurate note of place in *v.* 23 ('in the temple in Solomon's porch'). Both these verses proclaim the eye-witness. So does the admirable question in the verse following. Attracted by His teachings and His miracles, but repelled by His persistent refusal to assume the Messianic character as they understood it, the Jews ask Jesus directly, 'How long, &c.' It is such a question as at this period of the ministry was inevitable, and the language in which it is expressed exactly represents the real difficulties and hesitation that the Jews would feel." S. pp. 174, 175.

and it was winter] Omit 'and,' which is wanting in authority, and join 'it was winter' to the next verse. The words explain why Jesus was walking under cover.

23. *in Solomon's porch*] This was a cloister or colonnade in the Temple-Courts, apparently on the east side. Tradition said that it was a part of the original building which had survived the various destructions and rebuildings. No such cloister is mentioned in the account of Solomon's Temple, and perhaps the name was derived from the wall against which it was built. It is mentioned again Acts iii. 11 (where see note) and *v.* 12. Foundations still remaining probably belong to it.

24 mon's porch. Then came the Jews round about him, and said unto him, How long dost thou make us to doubt? 25 If thou be the Christ, tell us plainly. Jesus answered them, I told you, and ye believe not: the works that I do 26 in my Father's name, they bear witness of me. But ye believe not, because ye are not of my sheep, as I said

24. *Then came the Jews round about*, &c.] Better, **The Jews therefore compassed Him about** (Luke xxi. 20; Hebr. xi. 30; Rev. xx. 9) *and* **kept saying** *to Him*. They encircled Him in an urgent and obtrusive manner, indicating that they were determined to have an answer.

How long dost thou make us to doubt?] The margin is better with **hold us in suspense.** The literal meaning is *How long dost Thou excite our mind? If Thou art the Christ tell us with openness* (see on vii. 4). They put a point-blank question, as the Sanhedrin do at the Passion (Luke xxii. 67). Their motives for urging this were no doubt mixed, and the same motive was not predominant in each case. Some were hovering between faith and hostility and (forgetting viii. 13) fancied that an explicit declaration from Him might help them. Others asked mainly out of curiosity: He had interested them greatly, and they wanted His own account of Himself. The worst wished for a plain statement which might form material for an accusation: they wanted Him to commit Himself.

25. *I told you, and ye believed not*] The best authorities have, *and ye* **believe** *not:* their unbelief still continues. To some few, the woman at the well, the man born blind, and the Apostles, Jesus had explicitly declared Himself to be the Messiah; to all He had implicitly declared Himself by His works and teaching.

the works] in the widest sense, not miracles alone; His Messianic work generally. See on v. 36. The pronouns are emphatically opposed; 'the works which *I* do...*they*....But *ye* believe not.

26. *as I said unto you*] These words are omitted by some of the best authorities, including the Vatican and Sinaitic MSS. But they may possibly have been left out to avoid a difficulty. *If* they are genuine they are best joined, as in our version, with what *precedes*. Nowhere in the Gospels does Christ make such a quotation from a previous discourse as we should have if we read, 'As I said unto you, My sheep hear My voice, &c.' The arrangement 'Ye are not of My sheep, as I said unto you,' is better, and the reference is to the general sense of the allegory of the sheep-fold, especially *vv.* 14, 15. He and His sheep have most intimate knowledge of one another; therefore these Jews asking who He is prove that they are not His sheep. Comp. vi. 36, where there seems to be a similar reference to the general meaning of a previous discourse. It is strange that an objection should have been made to His referring to the allegory after a lapse of two months. There is nothing improbable in His doing so, especially if He had been absent from the city in the interval (see on *v.* 22). Might not a speaker

unto you. My sheep hear my voice, and I know them, 27 and they follow me: and I give unto them eternal life; and 28 they shall never perish, neither shall any *man* pluck them out of my hand. My Father, which gave *them* me, is greater 29 than all; and no *man* is able to pluck *them* out of my Father's hand. I and *my* Father are one. Then the Jews 30 31

at the present time refer to a speech made two months before, especially if he had not spoken in public since then?

27, 28. Note the simple but very impressive coupling of the clauses by a simple 'and' throughout and comp. *vv.* 3 and 12: note also the climax.

28. *I give unto them*] Not '*will* give.' Here as in iii. 15, v. 24 and often, the gift of eternal life is regarded as already possessed by the faithful. It is not a *promise*, the *fulfilment* of which depends upon man's conduct, but a *gift*, the *retention* of which depends upon ourselves.

they shall never perish] This is parallel to viii. 51 (see note there); *shall certainly not perish for ever*, being the literal meaning. But the negative belongs to the verb, not to 'for ever;' and the meaning is, not 'they may die, but shall not die *for ever*,' but 'they shall never die for all eternity.' Comp. xi. 26.

neither shall any man pluck them] Better, **and no one shall snatch them**. 'No *one*' rather than 'no *man*' (as in *v.* 18), for the powers of darkness are excluded as well as human seducers. 'Snatch' rather than 'pluck,' for in the Greek it is the same word as is used of the wolf in *v.* 12, and this should be preserved in translation.

This passage in no way asserts the indefectibility of the elect, and gives no countenance to ultra-predestinarian views. Christ's sheep cannot be taken from Him *against their will;* but their will is free, and they may choose to leave the flock.

out of my hand] "His hand protects, bears, cherishes, leads them." Meyer.

29. *which gave them*] Better, *which* **hath given** *them*. Comp. xvii. 6, 24. This enforces the previous assertion. 'To snatch them out of My hand, he must snatch them out of My Father's hand; and My Father is greater than all:' even than the Son (xiv. 28). But the reading is not certain. The most probable text gives, **that which the Father hath given Me** *is greater than all*. The unity of the Church is strength invincible.

out of my Father's hand] The better reading is, *out of* **the** *Father's hand*. 'Out of His hand' would have sufficed; but 'Father' is repeated for emphasis.

30. *I and my Father are one*] 'One' is neuter in the Greek; not one Person, but one Substance. There is no 'My' in the Greek; *I and* **the** *Father are one*. Christ has just implied that His hand and the Father's hand are one, which implies that He and the Father are one; and this He now asserts. They are one in power, in will, and in

32 took up stones again to stone him. Jesus answered them, Many good works have I shewed you from my Father; for 33 which of those works do ye stone me? The Jews answered him, saying, For a good work we stone thee not; but for blasphemy; and because that thou, being a man, makest 34 thyself God. Jesus answered them, Is it not written in 35 your law, I said, Ye are gods? If he called them gods,

action: this at the very least the words must mean; the Arian interpretation of mere moral agreement is inadequate. Whether or no Unity of Essence is actually stated here, it is certainly implied, as the Jews see. They would stone Him for making Himself God, which they would not have done had He not asserted or implied that He and the Father were one in Substance, not merely in will. And Christ does not correct them, as assuredly He would have done, had their animosity arisen out of a gross misapprehension of His words. Comp. Rev. xx. 6, xxii. 3.

31. *Then the Jews*] Better, **Therefore** *the Jews:* their picking up stones was a direct consequence of His words. But 'therefore' should perhaps be omitted. They prepare to act on Lev. xxiv. 16 (Comp. 1 Kin. xxi. 10). 'Again' refers us back to viii. 59. The word for 'took up' is not the same in each case; the word used here is stronger, implying more effort; 'lifted up, bore.' But 'again' shews that it refers to raising up from the ground rather than carrying from a distance.

32. *Many good works*] It is the same word as is used *v.* 14 of the *Good* Shepherd: many beautiful, noble, excellent works. Comp. ' He hath done all things *well*' (Mark vii. 37) and 'God saw that it was *good*' (Gen. i. 8, 10, 12, &c.). These excellent works proceed from the Father and are manifested by the Son.

for which of those] Literally, *for what kind of work among these;* i.e. 'what is the character of the work for which ye are in the act of stoning me?' It was precisely the character of the works which shewed that they were Divine, as some of them were disposed to think (*v.* 21, vii. 26). Comp. Matt. xxii. 36, where the literal meaning is, 'what *kind* of a commandment is great in the law?' and 1 Cor. xv. 35, 'with what *kind* of body do they come?' See on xii. 33, xviii. 32, xxi. 19.

33. *For a good work*] The preposition is changed in the Greek; **concerning** *a good work.* 'That is not the subject-matter of our charge?'

and because] 'And' is explanatory, shewing wherein the blasphemy consisted: it does not introduce a separate charge.

34—38. Christ answers the formal charge of blasphemy by a formal argument on the other side.

34. *in your law*] 'Law' is here used in its widest sense for the whole of the Old Testament; so also in xii. 34 and xv. 25; in all three places the passage referred to is in the Psalms. Comp. vii. 19, 1 Cor. xiv. 21. The force of the pronoun is, 'for which you profess to have such a regard:' comp. viii. 17. On the Greek for 'is it written' see on ii. 17.

I said, Ye are gods] The argument is both *à fortiori* and *ad hominem*.

unto whom the word of God came, and the scripture
cannot be broken; say ye *of him*, whom the Father hath 36
sanctified, and sent into the world, Thou blasphemest;
because I said, I am the Son of God? If I do not the works 37

In the Scriptures (Ps. lxxxii. 6) even unjust rulers are called 'gods' on
the principle of the theocracy, that rulers are the delegates and representatives of God (comp. Ex. xxii. 28). If this is admissible without
blasphemy, how much more may He call Himself 'Son of God.'

35. *If he called them gods*] More probably, *If* it *called them gods*,
viz. the Law. 'Them' is left unexplained; a Jewish audience would at
once know who were meant. But how incredible that any but a Jew
should think of such an argument, or put it in this brief way! These
last eight verses alone are sufficient to discredit the theory that this
Gospel is the work of Greek Gnostic in the second century.

the word of God] Practically the same as 'the Scripture;' i.e. the
word of God in these passages of Scripture. The Word in the theological sense for the Son is not meant : this term appears nowhere in the
narrative part of S. John's Gospel. But of course it was through the
Word, not yet incarnate, that God revealed His will to His people.

cannot be broken] Literally, 'cannot be undone' or 'unloosed.' The
same word is rendered 'unloose' (i. 27), 'destroy' (ii. 19), 'break' (v. 18
and vii. 23), 'loose' (xi. 44). i. 27 and xi. 44 are literal, of actual unbinding ; the others are figurative, of dissolution or unbinding as a form
of destruction. Here either metaphor, dissolution or unbinding, would
be appropriate; either, 'cannot be explained away, made to mean
nothing;' or, 'cannot be deprived of its binding authority.' The latter
seems better. The clause depends upon 'if,' and is not parenthetical ;
'if the Scripture cannot be broken.' As in ii. 22, xvii. 12, xx. 9, 'the
Scripture' (singular) probably means a definite passage. Comp. vii. 38,
42, xiii. 18, xvii. 12, xix. 24, 28, 36, 37. Scripture as a whole is called
'the Scriptures' (plural); v. 39.

36. *Say ye*] 'Ye' with great emphasis, 'Do *ye*, in opposition to
the Scripture, say?'

of him, whom the Father hath sanctified] Omit 'hath;' both verbs
are aorists. This also is emphatic, in opposition to 'them unto whom
the word of God came.' Men on whom God's word has conferred a
fragment of delegated authority may be called 'gods' (Elohim) without
scruple ; He, Whom the Father Himself sanctified and sent, may not be
called **Son of God** (no article before 'Son') without blasphemy! By
'sanctified' is meant something analogous to the consecration of Jeremiah before his birth for the work of a Prophet (Jer. i. 5). When the
Son was sent into the world He was consecrated for the work of the
Messiah, and endowed with the fulness of grace and truth (see on i. 14),
the fulness of power (iii. 35), the fulness of life (v. 26). In virtue of this
Divine sanctification He becomes 'the Holy One of God' (vi. 69 ; Luke
iv. 34). See on xvii. 17, 19, the only other passages in S. John's
writings where the word occurs.

38 of my Father, believe me not. But if I do, though ye believe not me, believe the works: that ye may know, and believe, that the Father *is* in me, and I in him.

39—42. *Opposite Results of the Discourse.*

39 Therefore they sought again to take him : but he escaped

37, 38. Having met their technical charge in a technical manner He now proceeds to justify the assertion of His unity with the Father by an appeal to His works.

37. *believe me not*] A literal command. If His works are not those which His Father works, they *ought* not (not merely have no *need*) to believe what He says. Comp. v. 24, 46; vi. 30; viii. 31, 45. His works are His Father's (ix. 3, xiv. 10).

38. *believe the works*] 'Blessed are they that have not seen and yet have believed' (xx. 29); but it is better to have the faith that comes with sight than none at all.

that ye may know, and believe] The better reading probably is, *that ye may* **come to know and continually know**; 'attain to knowledge and advance in knowledge in contrast to your state of suspense' (*v.* 24). In the Greek it is the aorist and present of the same verb 'to come to know, perceive, recognise:' the aorist denotes the single act, the present the permanent growth. The apparent awkwardness of having the same verb twice in the same clause has probably caused a large number of authorities to substitute another verb in the second case. But the change of tense is full of meaning, especially in reference to the Jews. Many of them attained to a momentary conviction that He was the Messiah (ii. 23, vi. 14, 15, vii. 41, viii. 30, x. 42, xi. 45); very few of them went beyond a transitory conviction (ii. 24, vi. 66, viii. 31).

the Father is in me, and I in him] For 'in Him' read with the best authorities **in the Father**. An instance of the solemnity and emphasis derived from repetition, so frequent in this Gospel.

39—42. OPPOSITE RESULTS OF THE DISCOURSE.

39. *Therefore they sought again*] 'Therefore' is of rather doubtful authenticity; some important witnesses omit 'again' also. 'Again' refers us back to vii. 30, 32, 44, and shews that 'to take Him' means, not, take Him and stone Him (*v.* 31), but, arrest Him for the Sanhedrin.

he escaped] Literally, **went forth**. There being nothing in the text to shew that His departure was miraculous, it is safest (as in viii. 59, where the same word is used for 'went forth') to suppose that there was no miracle. He withdrew through the less hostile among those who encircled Him, while the others were making up their minds how to apprehend Him. The majesty of innocence suffices to protect Him, His hour not having come.

out of their hand, and went away again beyond Jordan into 40
the place where John at first baptized; and there he abode.
And many resorted unto him, and said, John did no miracle: 41
but all *things* that John spake of this *man* were true. And 42
many believed on him there.

40—42. "The chapter ends with a note of place which is evidently and certainly historical. No forger would ever have thought of the periphrasis 'where John at first baptized'...'John did no miracle: but all things that John spake of this man were true.' It would be impossible to find a stronger incidental proof that the author of the Gospel had been originally a disciple of the Baptist, or at least his contemporary, and also that he is writing of things that he had heard and seen. A Gnostic, writing in Asia Minor, even though he had come into relation with disciples of John, would not have introduced the Baptist in this way. In circles that had been affected by the Baptist's teaching, and were hesitating whether they should attach themselves to Jesus, this is precisely the sort of comment that would be heard." S. p. 179.

40. *again beyond Jordan*] Referring back to i. 28. The hostility of the hierarchy being invincible and becoming more and more dangerous Jesus retires into Peraea for quiet and safety before His Passion. This interval was between three and four months, from the latter part of December to the middle of April. But some portion of this time was spent at Ephraim (xi. 54) after going to Bethany in Judaea to raise Lazarus. Nothing is told us as to how much time was given to Bethany or Bethabara in Peraea, how much to Ephraim.

at first] John afterwards baptized at Aenon near Salim (iii. 23).
baptized] **was baptizing.**

41. *many resorted unto him*] There is no reason why the usual translation 'came' should be changed to 'resorted.' The testimony of the Baptist, and perhaps the miraculous voice at Christ's Baptism, were still remembered there. Since then there had been the mission of the Seventy and Christ's own work in Galilee.

and said] Or, **kept saying** or *used to say:* it was a common remark.

John did no miracle] Or **sign.** This is indirect evidence of the genuineness of the miracles recorded of Christ. It is urged that if Jesus had wrought no miracles, they would very possibly have been attributed to Him after His death. Let us grant this; and at the same time it must be granted that the same holds good to a very great extent of the Baptist. The enthusiasm which he awakened, as a Prophet appearing after a weary interval of four centuries, was immense. Miracles would have been eagerly believed of him, the second Elijah, and would be likely enough to be attributed to him. But more than half a century after his death we have one of his own disciples *quite incidentally* telling us that 'John did *no* miracle'; and there is no rival tradition to the contrary. *All* traditions concur in attributing miracles to Jesus.

42. *many believed on him there*] 'There' is emphatic. '*There*,'

CHAP. XI. *Christ is Love illustrated by a Sign.*

in contrast to Jerusalem which had rejected Him, 'many believed on Him'. Note the full expression 'believed *on*' (see on i. 12) as distinct from merely believing His statements (*vv.* 37, 38).

CHAP. XI. CHRIST IS LOVE ILLUSTRATED BY A SIGN.

Christ's love for His friends brings about His own death. Expressions of affection and tenderness abound in the chapter; comp. *vv.* 3, 5, 11, 15, 35, 36.

We have now reached 'the culminating point of the miraculous activity of our Lord', and at the same time the 'crucial question' of this Gospel—the Raising of Lazarus. Various objections have been urged against it, and through it against the Fourth Gospel as a whole. The principal objections require notice. They are based (1) on the extraordinary character of the miracle itself; (2) on the silence of the Synoptists; (3) on the fact that in spite of what is narrated *vv.* 47—53, no mention is made of the miracle in the accusation and condemnation of Jesus.

(1) The extraordinary character of the miracle "has been exaggerated by looking at it in the light of modern ideas. To us the raising of the dead stands apart from other miracles in a class by itself as peculiarly unexampled and incredible. But it was not so regarded at the time when the Gospel was written...In the Synoptists the answer that Jesus gives to the disciples of John groups together every class of miracle, the raising of the dead amongst them, without distinction. Similar narratives in the Synoptists, in the Acts, and in the Old Testament, are given without any special relief or emphasis." S. p. 186.

And surely this ancient view is both more reverent and more philosophical than the modern one. Only from a purely human standpoint can one miracle be regarded as more wonderful, i.e. more difficult of performance, than another. To Omnipotence all miracles, as indeed all works, are equal: distinctions of difficult and easy as applied to the Almighty are meaningless.

(2) It is certainly surprising that the Synoptists do not mention this miracle, all the more so because S. John tells us that it was the proximate cause of Christ's arrest and condemnation. But this surprising circumstance has been exaggerated. It seems too much to say that "it must always remain a mystery why this miracle, transcending as it does all other miracles which the Lord wrought,...should have been passed over by the three earlier Evangelists". Two considerations go a long way towards explaining the mystery. (i) "We are accustomed to regard the Synoptic Gospels as three; but in the outline and by far the greater part of their narrative they are virtually one. The groundwork of them all is supplied by a single document, that document itself a compilation, and (as there is ample evidence to show) *a very fragmentary one.*" S. p. 185. That a fragmentary document or tradition should omit important facts is not surprising: that three writers, making use of this defective evidence, should not

1—33. *The Prelude to the Sign.*

Now a certain *man* was sick, *named* Lazarus, of Bethany, 11

even in this very important instance supply the deficiency, is not more than surprising. And the second consideration greatly diminishes our surprise. (ii) The Synoptists, until they reach the last Passover, omit almost all events in or about Jerusalem: the ministry in Galilee is their province. Therefore "we cannot be surprised that they should omit an event which is placed at Bethany." S. p. 186. The omission of this raising by the Synoptists is very little more strange than the omission of the other raisings by John. Each side keeps to its own scheme of narration.

To explain that the Synoptists were silent in order not to draw attention, and perhaps persecution (xii. 10, 11), on Lazarus and his sisters, whereas when S. John wrote they were dead (just as S. John alone records that it was S. Peter who cut off the High Priest's servant's ear), is not very satisfactory. There is no evidence that Lazarus and his sisters were living when the first Gospel was written, still less when S. Luke wrote. And if they were alive, were the chief priests alive, and their animosity still alive also? The explanation is less easy than the difficulty.

(3) This last objection really tells in favour of the narrative. The hierarchy would have stood self-condemned if they had made His raising the dead a formal charge against Christ. The disciples had fled, and could not urge the miracle in His favour; and Christ Himself would not break the majestic silence which He maintained before His accusers to mention such a detail.

There are those who assume that miracles are impossible, and that no amount of evidence can render a miracle credible. This miracle is therefore dismissed, and we are to believe either (1) Lazarus was only *apparently dead*, i.e. that Christ was an impostor and S. John a dupe or an accomplice; or that (2) the *parable* of Lazarus and Dives has been *transformed* into a miracle; or that (3) the narrative is a *myth*, or (4) an *allegory*. (1) and (2) only need to be stated: of (3) and (4) we may say with Meyer, "No narrative of the N.T. bears so completely the stamp of being the very opposite of a later invention....And what an incredible height of art in the allegorical construction of history must we ascribe to the composer!" Instead of an historical miracle we have a literary miracle of the second century. Contrast this chapter with the miracles of the Apocryphal Gospels, and it will seem impossible that both can have come from the same source. To tear out this or any other page from S. John, and retain the rest, is quite inadmissible. "The Gospel is like that sacred coat 'without seam woven from the top throughout:' it is either all real and true or all fictitious and illusory; and the latter alternative is, I cannot but think, more difficult to accept than the miracle." S. p. 188.

1—33. The Prelude to the Sign.

1. *Now a certain man was sick*] Note once more the touching

2 the town of Mary and her sister Martha. (It was *that* Mary
which anointed the Lord with ointment, and wiped his feet
3 with her hair, whose brother Lazarus was sick.) Therefore
his sisters sent unto him, saying, Lord, behold, he whom

simplicity of the narrative. 'Now' should perhaps be 'but,' though the
Greek particle may mean either. Here it introduces a contrast to what
precedes. Christ went into Peraea for retirement, but the sickness of
Lazarus interrupted it.

named Lazarus] The theory that this narrative is a parable transformed into a miracle possibly represents something like the reverse of
the fact. The parable of Dives and Lazarus was apparently spoken
about this time, i.e. between the Feast of Dedication and the last Passover, and it may possibly have been suggested by this miracle. In no
other parable does Christ introduce a proper name. Some would
identify Lazarus of Bethany with the rich young ruler (Matt. xix. 16;
Mark x. 17; Luke xviii. 18), and also with the young man clad in a
linen cloth who followed Jesus in the Garden after the disciples had fled
(Mark xiv. 51; see note there). The name Lazarus is an abbreviated
Greek form of Eleazar='God is my help.' It is commonly assumed
without much evidence that he was younger than his sisters: S. Luke's
silence about him (x. 38, 39) agrees well with this.

Bethany] A small village on the S. E. slope of the Mount of Olives,
about two miles from Jerusalem (see on Matt. xxi. 9).

the town of Mary] Better, *of the* **village** *of Mary*. The same word
is used of Bethlehem (vii. 42) and in conjunction with 'towns' or 'cities'
(Luke xiii. 22). It is an elastic word; but its general meaning is
'village' rather than anything larger. Mary is here mentioned first,
although apparently the younger sister (Luke x. 28), because the
incident mentioned in the next verse had made her better known. They
would seem to have been people of position from the village being
described as their abode (to distinguish it from the other Bethany in
Peraea, to which Christ had just gone). The guests at the funeral (*vv.*
31, 45), the feast, the family burying-place (*v.* 38), and Mary's costly
offering (xii. 2, 3), point in the same direction.

2. *It was that Mary which anointed*] This of course does not
necessarily imply that the anointing had already taken place, as those
who identify Mary with the 'sinner' of Luke vii. 37 would insist: it
merely implies that when S. John wrote, this fact was well known
about her, as Christ had promised should be the case (Matt. xxvi. 13).
S. John tells two facts omitted in the earlier Gospels; (1) that the village of Martha and Mary was Bethany, (2) that the anointing at
Bethany was Mary's act. The identification of Mary of Bethany with
the prostitute of Luke vii. is altogether at variance with what S. Luke
and S. John tell us of her character. Nor is there any sufficient reason
for identifying either of them with Mary Magdalene. Mary of Bethany,
Mary of Magdala, and the 'sinner' of Luke vii. are three distinct persons.

3. *Therefore his sisters sent*] This shews that *v.* 2 ought not to be

vv. 4—6.]   S. JOHN, XI.   229

thou lovest is sick. When Jesus heard *that*, he said, This 4 sickness is not unto death, but for the glory of God, that the Son of God might be glorified thereby. Now Jesus 5 loved Martha, and her sister, and Lazarus. When he had 6

made a parenthesis: 'therefore' refers to the previous statement. Because of the intimacy, which every one who knew of the anointing would understand, the sisters sent. Note that they are not further described; S. John has said enough to tell his readers who are meant: but would not a forger have introduced them with more description?

he whom thou lovest is sick] Exquisite in its tender simplicity. The message implies a belief that Christ could, and probably would, heal a dangerous sickness. See on *v.* 5.

4. *is not unto death*] i.e. is not to have death as its final result. Christ foresaw both the death and the resurrection, and (as so often) uttered words which His disciples did not understand at the time, but recognised in their proper meaning after what He indicated had taken place. Comp. ii. 22, xii. 16, xxi. 23.

might be glorified] In two ways; because the miracle (1) would lead many to believe that He was the Messiah; (2) would bring about His death. 'Being glorified' is a frequent expression in this Gospel for Christ's Death regarded as the mode of His return to glory (vii. 39, xii. 16, 23, xiii. 31, 32); and this glorification of the Son involves the glory of the Father (v. 23, x. 30, 38). Comp. ix. 3; in the Divine counsels the *purpose* of the man's blindness and of Lazarus' sickness is the glory of God.

We ought perhaps to connect the special meaning of 'glorified' with the first clause: 'This sickness is to have for its final issue, not the temporal death of an individual, but the eternal life of all mankind.'

It is worth noting that both the first and the last of the seven miracles of the ministry recorded by S. John are declared to be manifestations of glory (ii. 11, xi. 4, 40) and confirmations of faith (ii. 11, xi. 15).

thereby] Both in the English and in the Greek this is ambiguous: it may refer either to the sickness or the glory. The former is correct.

5. *Now Jesus loved Martha*] The English Version loses much here, and still more in xxi. 15—17, by using the same word 'love' to translate two different Greek words: nor can the loss be remedied satisfactorily. The word used in *v.* 3, *philein* (Lat. *amare*), denotes a passionate, emotional warmth, which loves and cares not to ask why; the affection of lovers, parents, and the like. The word used here *agapân*, (Lat. *diligere*), denotes a calm, discriminating attachment, which loves because of the excellence of the loved object; the affection of friends. *Philein* is the stronger, but less reasoning; *agapân* the more earnest, but less intense. The sisters naturally use the more emotional word, describing their own feeling towards their brother; the Evangelist equally naturally uses the loftier and less impulsive word. The fact that the sisters are here included is not the reason for the change of expression.

Martha, and her sister, and Lazarus] The names are probably in

heard therefore that he was sick, he abode two days *still
7 in the same place where he was*. Then after that saith he
8 to *his* disciples, Let us go into Judea again. *His* disciples
say unto him, Master, the Jews of late sought to stone thee;
9 and goest thou thither again? Jesus answered, Are there
not twelve hours in the day? If any *man* walk in the day, he
stumbleth not, because he seeth the light of this world.
10 But if a man walk in the night, he stumbleth, because there

order of age. This and *v.* 19 confirm what is almost certain from Luke
x. 38, that Martha is the elder sister.
  6. *When he had heard therefore*] Omit 'had.' The connexion is a
little difficult. 'Therefore' after the statement in *v.* 5 prepares us for
'He set out immediately,' but instead of that we have the reverse.
'Therefore,' however, really leads on to *v.* 7, and consequently there
should be only a semicolon at the end of *v.* 6. **When, therefore, He
heard that he is sick, then indeed** *He abode two days in the place
where He was; then after* **this** *He saith*, &c. The question *why*
Christ remained the two days is futile: such was the Divine Will with
regard to the mode of working this miracle and to His Messianic work
generally. His life was a perfect fulfilment of the Preacher's rule; 'To
everything there is a season, and a time to every purpose under heaven'
(Eccl. iii. 1; comp. *v.* 9, ii. 4). There was a Divine plan, in conformity
with which He worked.
  7. *Let us go into Judea again*] The again refers us back to x. 40.
His using the general term, Judæa, instead of Bethany leads to the
disciples' reply. Judaea was associated with hostility, Bethany with
love and friendship.
  8. *Master, the Jews of late sought to stone thee*] Better, **Rabbi** (see on
iv. 31) **just now** *the Jews* **were seeking** *to stone Thee* (x. 31) *and* **art
Thou going** *thither again?* 'Again' is emphatic.
  9. *Are there not twelve hours in the day*] As so often, Christ gives
no direct answer to the question asked, but a general principle, involving the answer to the question. Comp. ii. 6, 19, iii. 5, 10, iv. 13, 21,
vi. 32, 53, viii. 7, 25, 54, x. 25. The meaning seems to be, 'Are there
not twelve working-hours in which a man may labour without fear of
stumbling? I have not yet reached the end of My working-day, and so
can safely continue the work I came to do. The night cometh, when I
can no longer work; but it has not yet come.' Comp. ix. 4. Thus it
is practically equivalent to 'Mine hour is not yet come;' it is still safe
for Him to work: but the figure here adopted is of wider application,
and contains a moral for the disciples and all Christians as well as an
application to Christ. The expression throws no light on S. John's
method of reckoning time. See on xix. 14.
  the light of this world] The sun.
  10. *he stumbleth*] Christ's night came when His hour came (xvii. 1).
Then the powers of darkness prevailed (Luke xxii. 53) and His enemies

is no light in him. These *things* said he: and after that he 11
saith unto them, Our friend Lazarus sleepeth; but I go, that
I may awake him out of sleep. Then said his disciples, 12
Lord, if he sleep, he shall do well. Howbeit Jesus spake of 13

became a stumblingblock in His path, bringing His work to a close
(xix. 30). The word for 'stumble' means literally to 'knock the foot
against' something.
there is no light in him] Rather, **the light is not** *in him*. This shews
that the meaning has slid from the literal to the figurative. 'The light'
in *v.* 9 is the physical light in the heavens; here it is the spiritual light
in the heart.

11. *and after that*] *and after* **this**. These words indicate a pause
in the narrative.

Our friend Lazarus sleepeth] Better, **Lazarus our friend is fallen
asleep**, or, *is gone to rest*. Sleep as an image of death is common from
the dawn of literature; but the Gospel has raised the expression from a
figure to a fact. Comp. Matt. xxvii. 52; Acts vii. 50, xiii. 36; 1 Cor.
vii. 39, xi. 30, xv. 6, 18; 1 Thess. iv. 13; 2 Pet. iii. 4. The thoroughly
Christian term 'cemetery' (=sleeping-place) in the sense of a place of
repose for the dead comes from the same Greek root. The exact time
of Lazarus' death cannot be determined, for we do not know how long
Christ took in reaching Bethany. Christ calls him '*our* friend,' as
claiming the sympathy of the disciples, who had shewn unwillingness
to return to Judæa.

that I may awake him] This shews that no messenger has come to
announce the death. Christ sees the death as He foresees the resurrection: comp. *v.* 4.

12. *Then said his disciples*] Better, **Therefore** *said the disciples* **to
Him**. They catch at any chance of escape from the dreaded journey.

if he sleep, he shall do well] Better, *if he* **be fallen asleep**, *he shall* **be
saved**, will be cured. Probably they thought that Christ meant to go
and cure Lazarus (*v.* 37, comp. ix. 3); and here they infer from his
sleeping that he will recover without Christ's aid: consequently Christ
need not go. They are too full of anxiety to notice Christ's significant
words 'I go, that I may awake him,' whereas the rendering in our Bible
reads like an expostulation against waking him, as if it meant 'a sick
man should not be disturbed.' For other instances in which the disciples grossly misunderstand Christ, see iv. 33, xiv. 5, 8, 22; Matt. xvi. 7;
and comp. iii. 4, 9, iv. 11, 15, vi. 34, 52, vii. 35, viii. 22, 33, 52. This
candour in declaring their own failings adds to our confidence in the
veracity of the Evangelists. It is urged that the misunderstanding here
is too gross to be probable: but they had not unnaturally understood
Christ Himself to have declared that Lazarus would not die (*v.* 4); this
being so, they could not easily suppose that by sleep He meant death.
Moreover, when men's minds are on the stretch the strangest misapprehensions become possible.

13. *Howbeit Jesus spake*] Or, **Now** *Jesus* **had spoken**.

his death: but they thought that he had spoken of taking of
14 rest in sleep. Then said Jesus unto them plainly, Lazarus
15 is dead. And I am glad for your sakes that I was not
there, to the intent ye may believe; nevertheless let us go
16 unto him. Then said Thomas, which is called Didymus,

had spoken] spake.
taking of rest in sleep] The word here translated 'taking of rest'
corresponds to 'sleepeth' or 'is gone to rest' in *v*. 11, and 'to sleep' in
v. 12. The word translated 'awake him out of sleep' in *v*. 11 is a compound of the word here rendered, 'sleep.'
    14. *Then said Jesus*] 'Then' here, as in Rom. vi. 21, is made to
cover two Greek words, 'then' of time, and 'then' of consequence:
translate, *Then* **therefore** *said Jesus*.
    plainly] Without metaphor: see on vii. 4 and x. 24.
    15. *I am glad*] Christ rejoices, not at his friend's death, but at His
own absence from the scene, for the disciples' sake. Had He been
there, Lazarus would not have died, and the disciples would have lost
this great sign of His Messiahship.
    to the intent ye may believe] S. John's favourite construction, indicating the Divine purpose: see on ix. 2, 3. Would any forger have written
this? Would it not seem utterly improbable that at the close of His
ministry Christ should still be working in order that Apostles might believe? Yet S. John, who heard the words, records them, and he knew
from sad experience (Mark xiv. 50, xvi. 11; Luke xxiv. 11, 21) that this
work was not superfluous. Just before the trial of faith which His
Passion and Death would bring to them, His disciples had need of all the
help and strength that He could give. See on ii. 11.
    nevertheless let us go] He breaks off suddenly.
    16. *Then said*] **Therefore** *said*.
    Thomas, which is called Didymus] S. John thrice (xx. 24, xxi. 2)
reminds his readers that Thomas is the same as he whom Gentile
Christians called Didymus. Thomas is Hebrew, Didymus is Greek, for
a twin. In all probability he was a twin, *possibly* of S. Matthew, with
whom he is coupled in all three lists of the Apostles in the Gospels: in
the Acts he is coupled with S. Philip. That S. Thomas received his name
from Christ (as Simon was called Peter, and the sons of Zebedee Boanerges) in consequence of his character, is pure conjecture. But the
coincidence between the name and his twin-mindedness (James i. 8,
iv. 8) is remarkable. " In him the twins, unbelief and faith, were contending with one another for mastery, as Esau and Jacob in Rebecca's
womb" (Trench). It is from S. John that we know his character: in
the Synoptists and the Acts he is a mere name (see on i. 41). He seems
to have combined devotion to Christ with a tendency to see the dark
side of everything. S. John's care in distinguishing him by his Gentile
name adds point to the argument derived from his never distinguishing
John as the Baptist (see on i. 6).

unto *his* fellow-disciples, Let us also go, that we may die with him.

Then when Jesus came, he found that he had *lien* in the 17 grave four days already. Now Bethany was nigh unto 18

fellow-disciples] The word occurs here only. It has been remarked that S. Thomas would scarcely have taken the lead in this way had S. Peter been present, and that had S. Peter been there he would probably have appeared in the previous dialogue. If he was absent, we have an additional reason for the absence of this miracle from S. Mark's Gospel, the Gospel of S. Peter, and undoubtedly the representative of the oldest form of the Synoptic narrative.

die with him] Of course with Christ (*v.* 8). It is strange that any should understand it of Lazarus. They could not die with him, for he was dead already, and S. Thomas knew this (*v.* 14).

17. *Then when Jesus came*] Better, *When* **therefore** *Jesus came*, not to the house, nor to Bethany, but to the vicinity (*vv.* 20, 30). In *v.* 16 also 'then' should be *therefore*, S. John's favourite particle to express a sequence in fact.

he found] i.e. on enquiry. It would seem as if Christ's miraculous power of knowing without the ordinary means of information was not in constant activity, but like His other miraculous powers was employed only on fitting occasions. It was necessary to His work that He should know of Lazarus' death; it was not necessary that He should know how long he had been buried, nor where he had been buried (*v.* 34). Comp. i. 48, iv. 18. Similarly, Peter's prison-gate opens 'of its own accord;' Mary's house-door does not (Acts xii. 10—16).

in the grave] Or, *in the* **sepulchre.** Our translators use three different English words for the same Greek word; 'grave' in this chapter, v. 28; Matt. xxvii. 52, &c.; 'tomb' Matt. viii. 28; Mark v. 2, vi. 29, &c.; 'sepulchre' of Christ's resting-place. 'Sepulchre' would be best in all cases. Another Greek word for 'tomb' used by S. Matthew only is rendered 'tomb' xxiii. 29, and 'sepulchre' xxiii. 27, xxvii. 61, 64, 66, xxviii. 1.

four days] No doubt he had been buried the day he died, as is usual in hot climates where decomposition is rapid; moreover, he had died of a malignant disease, probably a fever. Jehu ordered Jezebel to be buried a few hours after death (2 Kings ix. 34); Ananias and Sapphira were buried at once (Acts v. 6, 10). If Christ started just after Lazarus died, as seems probable, the journey had occupied four days. This fits in well with the conclusion that Bethabara or Bethany was in the north of Palestine, possibly a little south of the Sea of Galilee; near Galilee it must have been (comp. i. 28, 29, 43). But on the other hand Lazarus may have died soon after Christ heard of his illness; in which case the journey occupied barely two days.

18. *Now Bethany was nigh unto Jerusalem*] The 'was' *need* not imply that when S. John wrote Bethany had been destroyed, but this is the more probable meaning; especially as no other Evangelist speaks of

19 Jerusalem, about fifteen furlongs off: and many of the Jews came to Martha and Mary, to comfort them concerning 20 their brother. Then Martha, as soon as she heard that Jesus was coming, went and met him: but Mary sat *still*

places in the past tense, and S. John does not always do so. The inference is that he wrote after the destruction of Jerusalem; and that what was destroyed in the siege he speaks of in the past tense; *e.g.* Bethany (here), the garden of Gethsemane (xviii. 1), Joseph's garden (xix. 41) what was not destroyed, in the present tense; *e.g.* Bethesda (*v.* 2, where see note).

about fifteen furlongs] Literally, *about fifteen stades*. A Greek stade is 18 yards less than an English furlong; but the translation is sufficiently accurate, like 'firkin' (ii. 6). This distance, therefore, was under two miles, and is mentioned to account for the many Jews who came to condole with the sisters.

19. *many of the Jews came to Martha and Mary*] Better, *many from among the Jews had come*, &c. The received text with some good authorities has 'had come to Martha and Mary and their friends,' but this is not the best-attested reading. 'The Jews' here, as usual, means Christ's opponents; they would come mostly, if not entirely, from Jerusalem.

to comfort them] It was part of the Jewish ceremonial of mourning that many (ten at least) should come and condole. Gen. xxvii. 35; comp. 2 Sam. xii. 17; Job ii. 11. It is said that the usual period of mourning was thirty days; three of weeping, seven of lamentation, twenty of sorrow. But the instances in Scripture vary: Jacob, seventy days with an additional seven (Gen. l. 3, 10); Aaron and Moses, thirty days (Numb. xx. 29; Deut. xxxiv. 8); Saul and Judith, seven days (1 Sam. xxviii. 13; Jud. xvi. 24; comp. Ecclus. xxii. 12; 2 Esdr. v. 20). Josephus tells us that Archelaus mourned for his father seven days, and the Jews for himself, thirty days (*B. J.* II. i. 1; III. ix. 5). The Mishna prescribes seven days for near relations.

20. *Then Martha*] Or, *Martha*, **therefore**. Information would be brought to her as the elder sister and (apparently) mistress of the house (Luke x. 38). She as usual takes the lead in entertaining, and Mary shrinks from it. "One most remarkable feature in the history is the coincidence between the characters of Mary and Martha as depicted here and in S. Luke." S. p. 185. It is incredible that this coincidence should be either fortuitous or designed. It is much easier to believe that both Gospels give us facts about real persons. Christ is unwilling to mingle at once in the crowd of mourners, and halts outside the village.

Jesus was coming] Rather, *Jesus* is *coming*, probably the very words of the message. Perhaps they were still on the look-out for His arrival, although they supposed that it was too late for His coming to avail anything.

Mary sat still in the house] Or, **was sitting** *in the house:* the atti-

in the house. Then said Martha unto Jesus, Lord, if thou 21
hadst been here, my brother had not died. But I know, 22
that even now, whatsoever thou wilt ask of God, God will
give *it* thee. Jesus saith unto her, Thy brother shall rise 23
again. Martha saith unto him, I know that he shall rise 24
again in the resurrection at the last day. Jesus said unto 25

tude of sorrow and meditation (Job ii. 13). She does not know of
Christ's approach (*vv*. 28, 29): Martha, in discharging the duties of
hospitality to fresh arrivals, would be more likely to hear of it.

21. *if thou hadst been here*] Not a reproach, however gentle (she
does not say 'hadst Thou *come*'), but an expression of deep regret. This
thought had naturally been often in the sisters' minds during the last four
days (comp. *v*. 32). They believe that Christ could and would have
healed Lazarus: their faith and hope are not yet equal to anticipating
His raising him from the dead. The gradual progress of Martha's faith
is very true to life, and reminds us of similar development in the woman
of Samaria (iv. 19) and the man born blind (ix. 11), though she starts
at a more advanced stage than they do. If all these three narratives
are late fictions, we have three masterpieces of psychological study, as
miraculous in the literature of the second century as would be a Gothic
cathedral in the architecture of that age. For the construction comp.
iv. 10, xiv. 28.

22. *But I know, that even now*] 'But' must be omitted on critical
grounds; and the text should run, **and now** (that he is dead) *I know
that*, &c. She believes that had Christ been there, He could have
healed Lazarus by His own power (comp. iv. 47), and that now His
prayer may prevail with God to raise him from the dead. She has yet
to learn that Christ's bodily presence is not necessary, and that He can
raise the dead by His own power. He gradually leads her faith onwards to higher truth.

whatsoever thou wilt ask] She uses a word more appropriate to *human*
prayer, 'to ask *for oneself*' (comp. xiv. 13, 14, xv. 7, 16, xvi. 23, 26),
not used by Christ of His own prayers or by the Evangelists of Christ's
prayers (contrast xiv. 16, xvi. 26, xvii. 9, 15, 20; Matt. xxvi. 36, 39,
42, 44; Luke xxii. 32). She thus incidentally shews her imperfect idea
of His relation to God.

23. *shall rise again*] He uses an ambiguous expression as an exercise of her faith. Some think that these words contain no allusion to
the immediate restoration of Lazarus, and that Martha (*v*. 24) understands them rightly. More probably Christ includes the immediate
restoration of Lazarus, but she does not venture to do so, and rejects the
allusion to the final Resurrection as poor consolation.

24. *I know that he shall rise again*] This conviction was probably
in advance of average Jewish belief on the subject. The O.T. declara-
tions as to a resurrection are so scanty and obscure, that the Sadducees
could deny the doctrine, and the Pharisees had to resort to oral tradition
to maintain it (see on Mark xii. 18; Acts xxiii. 8).

her, I am the resurrection, and the life: he that believeth in 26 me, though he were dead, yet shall he live: and whosoever liveth and believeth in me shall never die. Believest thou 27 this? She saith unto him, Yea, Lord: I believe that thou art the Christ, the Son of God, which should come into the 28 world. And when she had so said, she went her way, and called Mary her sister secretly, saying, The Master is come, 29 and calleth for thee. As soon as she heard *that*, she arose 30 quickly, and came unto him. Now Jesus was not yet come

the last day] See on vi. 39.
25. *I am the resurrection, and the life*] He draws her from her selfish grief to Himself. There is no need for Him to pray as man to God (*v.* 22); *He* (and none else) is the Resurrection and the Life. There is no need to look forward to the last day; He *is* (not 'will be') the Resurrection and the Life. Comp. xiv. 6; Col. iii. 4. In what follows, the first part shews how He is the Resurrection, the second how He is the Life. 'He that believeth in Me, **even if** he shall have died (physically), shall live (eternally). And **every one** that liveth (physically) and believeth in Me, shall never die (eternally).'
26. *shall never die*] See on viii. 51; the form of expression is the same; 'shall assuredly never die.'
Believest thou this?] A searching question, suddenly put. She answers with confidence, and gives the ground of her confidence.
27. *I believe*] Literally, **I have believed**, i.e. *I have convinced myself and do believe.*
that thou art the Christ] She cannot have known the full import of her confession. With the Apostles she shared her countrymen's imperfect views of the character and office of the Messiah. See on ix. 38.
which should come] Literally, **that cometh.** Comp. vi. 14; Matt. xi. 3; Luke vii. 19; Deut. xviii. 15. She believes that He has the powers mentioned in *vv.* 25, 26, because He is the Messiah. How these powers will affect her own case she does not know, but with a vague hope of comfort in store for them all she returns to the house. See on i. 9 and xviii. 37.
28. *secretly*] Because she knew that some of Christ's enemies were among the guests (*vv.* 19, 31). 'Secretly' belongs to 'saying,' not to 'called.'
The Master is come] Or, *The Teacher is come.* It is not the Hebrew word 'Rabbi' that is here used, as in i. 50, iii. 2, 26, iv. 31, vi. 25, ix. 2; but the Greek word given in i. 39 as the translation of 'Rabbi,' and in xx. 16 as the translation of 'Rabboni,' and used by Christ (iii. 10) of Nicodemus. Comp. xiii. 13, 14; Mark xiv. 14. Martha avoids using His name for fear of being overheard.
29. *she arose quickly*] As was natural in one so fond of sitting at Jesus' feet.

into the town, but was in *that* place where Martha met him. The Jews then which were with her in the house, and comforted her, when they saw Mary, that she rose up hastily and went out, followed her, saying, She goeth unto the grave to weep there. Then when Mary was come where Jesus was, and saw him, she fell down at his feet, saying unto him, Lord, if thou hadst been here, my brother had not died.

33—44. *The Sign.*

When Jesus therefore saw her weeping, and the Jews also weeping which came with her, he groaned in the spirit,

30. *into the town*] Or, *into the* **village**; see on *v.* 1. By remaining outside He would be able to say what He wished to say to the sisters without fear of interruption.
was in that place] was **still** in that place.
31. *followed her, saying*] For 'saying' read with the best authorities, **thinking**. Their following interferes with the privacy at which Martha had aimed.
to weep there] The word rendered 'weep' here and in *v.* 33, as distinct from the one used in *v.* 35, indicates a loud expression of grief; wailing and crying, not merely shedding of tears.
32. *Then when Mary*] *Mary* **therefore** *when.*
she fell down at his feet] Nothing of the kind is reported of Martha, *v.* 21. Here again the difference of character between the two sisters appears.
Lord, if thou hadst been here] The same words as those of Martha, *v.* 21. No doubt the sisters had expressed this thought to one another often in the last few days. Mary's emotion is too strong for her; she can say no more than this; contrast *v.* 22. The Jews coming up prevent further conversation. For the construction comp. iv. 10, xiv. 28.

33—44. THE SIGN.

33. *weeping...weeping*] The repetition is for emphasis, and to point a contrast which is the key to the passage.
he groaned in the spirit] Better, *He* **was angered** *in the spirit*. The word translated 'groaned' occurs five times in N.T.; here, *v.* 38; Matt. ix. 30; Mark i. 43, xiv. 5 (see notes in each place). In all cases, as in classical Greek and in the LXX., it expresses not sorrow but *indignation* or severity. It means (1) literally, of animals, 'to snort, growl;' then metaphorically (2) 'to be very angry or indignant;' (3) 'to command sternly, under threat of displeasure.' What was He angered at? Some translate '*at* His spirit,' and explain (*a*) that He was indignant at the human emotion which overcame Him: which is out of harmony with all that we know about the human nature of Christ. Others, retaining '*in* His spirit,' explain (β) that He was indignant 'at

34 and was troubled, and said, Where have ye laid him? They
35/36 say unto him, Lord, come and see. Jesus wept. Then
37 said the Jews, Behold, how he loved him. And some of
them said, Could not this *man*, which opened the eyes of

the unbelief of the Jews and perhaps of the sisters:' but of this there is
no hint in the context. Others again, (γ) that it was 'at the sight of
the momentary triumph of evil, as death,...which was here shewn under
circumstances of the deepest pathos;' but we nowhere else find the Lord
shewing anger at the physical consequences of sin. It seems better to
fall back on the contrast pointed out in the last note. He was indignant at seeing the hypocritical and sentimental lamentations of His
enemies the Jews mingling with the heartfelt lamentations of His loving
friend Mary (comp. xii. 10): hypocrisy ever roused His anger.

was troubled] The margin is better; *He* **troubled Himself,** i.e. agitated Himself, allowed His emotion to become evident by external
movement such as a shudder.

34. *Where have ye laid him?*] This question is against the supposition, based on *v.* 31, that the place where Jesus halted outside the village was close to the grave.

They say unto him] 'They' are the two sisters: on both sides "grief
speaks in the fewest possible words."

35. *Jesus wept*] Or, **shed tears.** The word occurs nowhere else
in N.T.; it expresses less loud lamentation than the word used in
vv. 31, 33. He sheds tears on His way to their brother's grave, not
because He is ignorant or doubtful of what is coming, but because He
cannot but sympathize with the intensity of His friends' grief. "The
intense humanity attributed to Jesus, His affection, His visible suffering, the effort with which He collects Himself, are all strong marks of
authenticity, and the more so because they might be thought to conflict with the doctrine of the prologue. But this is but one more
proof how little that doctrine has disturbed the Evangelist's true historic recollection." S. pp. 186, 7.

36. *Then said......loved him*] Here, as in *vv.* 12, 14, 16, 17, 20,
21, 31, 32, 41, 45, 47, 53, 56, 'then' should rather be **therefore,**
as rightly given in *vv.* 3, 33, 38, 54: it is S. John's favourite particle
in all these verses. Both the verbs here are imperfects; '*kept* saying,'
'*used* to love.' What follows shews that this remark was not made by
all the Jews. The word for 'love' is the more passionate word used
in *v.* 3 by the sisters, not the higher word used in *v.* 5 by the Evangelist.

37. *And some of them*] Better, **But** *some of them,* in contrast to
those who speak in *v.* 36, who are not unfriendly, while these sneer.
The drift of this remark is 'He weeps; but why did He not come in
time to save His friend? Because He knew that He could not. And
if He could not, did he really open the eyes of the blind?' They
use the death of Lazarus as an argument to throw fresh doubt on the
miracle which had so baffled them at Jerusalem. Their reference to

the blind, have caused that even this *man* should not have died? Jesus therefore again groaning in himself cometh to ₃₈ the grave. It was a cave, and a stone lay upon it. Jesus ₃₉ said, Take ye away the stone. Martha, the sister of him that was dead, saith unto him, Lord, by this time he stinketh: for he hath been *dead* four days. Jesus saith unto her, Said ₄₀ I not unto thee, that, if thou wouldest believe, thou shouldest see the glory of God? Then they took away the stone *from* ₄₁ *the place* where the dead was laid. And Jesus lift up *his*

the man born blind instead of to the widow's son, or Jairus' daughter, has been used as an objection to the truth of this narrative. It is really a strong confirmation of its truth. An inventor would almost certainly have preferred more obvious parallels. But these Jews of course did not believe in those raisings of the dead: they much more naturally refer to a reputed miracle within their own experience. Moreover they are not hinting at raising the dead, but urging that if Jesus could work miracles He ought to have prevented Lazarus from dying.

should not have died] Rather, *should not* **die**.

38. *groaning in himself*] See on *v.* 33. This shews that '*in* His spirit' not '*at* His spirit' is the right translation there. Their sneering scepticism rouses His indignation afresh.

to the grave] See on *v.* 17. Insert **now** before 'it was a cave.' The having a private burying-place indicates that the family was well off. The large attendance of mourners and the very precious ointment (xii. 3) point to the same fact.

upon it] The Greek may mean 'against it,' so that an excavation in the side of a rock or mound is not excluded. What is now shewn as the sepulchre of Lazarus is an excavation in the ground with steps down to it. The stone would keep out beasts of prey.

39. *the sister of him that was dead*] Not inserted gratuitously. It was because she was his sister that she could not bear to see him or allow him to be seen disfigured by corruption. The remark comes much more naturally from the practical Martha than from the reserved and retiring Mary. There is nothing to indicate that she was mistaken; though some would have it that the miracle had begun from Lazarus' death, and that the corpse had been preserved from decomposition.

he hath been dead four days] Literally, *he is of the fourth day.*

40. *Said I not*] Apparently a reference to *vv.* 25, 26, and to the reply to the messenger, *v.* 4: on both occasions more perhaps was said than is recorded. See notes on *v.* 4.

41. *from the place where the dead was laid*] These words are omitted by an overwhelming number of authorities. They are a needless explanation added by a later hand.

And Jesus lift] The verb is identical with that translated 'took

eyes, and said, Father, I thank thee that thou hast heard
42 me. And I knew that thou hearest me always: but
because of the people which stand by I said *it*, that they
43 may believe that thou hast sent me. And when he thus had
spoken, he cried with a loud voice, Lazarus, come forth.
44 And he that was dead came forth, bound hand and foot
with graveclothes: and his face was bound about with a
napkin. Jesus saith unto them, Loose him, and let *him* go.

away' in the preceding clause. Both should be translated alike; moreover, 'and' should be 'but.' *They* **lifted therefore** *the stone.* But *Jesus lifted* **His eyes upwards.**

Father, I thank thee] Jesus thanks the Father as a public acknowledgment that the Son can do 'nothing of Himself,' but that the power which He is about to exhibit is from the Father (v. 19—26).

that thou hast heard] Better, *that Thou* **didst hear.** The prayer to which this refers is not recorded.

42. *And I knew*] Better, **But** *I knew*, 'I' being very emphatic. This verse is added to prevent misunderstanding: no one must suppose from this act of thanksgiving that there are any prayers of the Son which the Father does not hear.

I said it] i.e. I said the words 'I thank Thee, &c.'

that thou hast sent me] Or, **didst send** *Me.* 'Thou' is emphatic; 'Thou and no one else.'

43. *cried*] The Greek word (rare in N.T. except in this Gospel) is nowhere else used of Christ. It is elsewhere used of the shout of a multitude; xii. 13, xviii. 40, xix. 6, (12), 15. Comp. Matt. xii. 19; Acts xxii. 23. This loud cry was perhaps the result of strong emotion, or in order that the whole multitude might hear. It is natural to regard it as the direct means of the miracle, awakening the dead: though some would have it that 'I thank Thee' implies that Lazarus is already alive and needs only to be called forth.

44. *came forth*] It is safest not to regard this as an additional miracle. The winding-sheet may have been loosely tied round him, or each limb may have been swathed separately: in Egyptian mummies sometimes every finger is kept distinct.

graveclothes] The Greek word occurs here only in N.T. Comp. Prov. vii. 16. It means the bandages which kept the sheet and the spices round the body. Nothing is said about the usual spices (xix. 40) here; and Martha's remark (*v.* 39) rather implies that there had been no embalming. If Lazarus died of a malignant disease he would be buried as quickly as possible.

face] The Greek word occurs in N.T. only here, vii. 24, and Rev. i. 16: one of the small indications of a common authorship (see on xv. 20 and xix. 37).

napkin] A Latin word is used meaning literally 'a sweat-cloth.' It occurs xx. 7; Luke xix. 20; Acts xix. 12. Here the cloth bound

45—57. Opposite Results of the Sign.

Then many of the Jews which came to Mary, and had 45 seen *the things* which Jesus did, believed on him. But some 46 of them went their ways to the Pharisees, and told them what *things* Jesus had done. Then gathered the chief priests and 47 the Pharisees a council, and said, What do we? for this man doeth many miracles. If we let him thus alone, all *men* will 48

under the chin to keep the lower jaw from falling is probably meant. These details shew the eyewitness.

let him go] The expression is identical with 'let these go their way' (xviii. 8); and perhaps 'let him go his way' would be better here. Lazarus is to be allowed to retire out of the way of harmful excitement and idle curiosity.

The reserve of the Gospel narrative here is evidence of its truth, and is in marked contrast to the myths about others who are said to have returned from the grave. Lazarus makes no revelations as to the unseen world. The traditions about him have no historic value: but one mentioned by Trench (*Miracles*, p. 425) is worth remembering. It is said that the first question which he asked Christ after being restored to life was whether he must die again; and being told that he must, he was never more seen to smile.

45—57. OPPOSITE RESULTS OF THE SIGN.

45. *Then many of the Jews*] The English Version is here misleading, owing to inaccuracy and bad punctuation. It should run thus:—*Many* **therefore** *of the Jews*, **even they that came** *to Mary and* **beheld that** *which* **He** *did* (see on vi. 14). The Jews who witnessed the miracle *all* believed: 'of the Jews' means of the Jews generally.

But some of them went] Some of the Jews generally, not of those who saw and believed, went and told the Pharisees; with what intention is not clear, but probably not out of malignity. Perhaps to convince the Pharisees, or to seek an authoritative solution of their own perplexity, or as feeling that the recognised leaders of the people ought to know the whole case. The bad *result* of their mission has made some too hastily conclude that their *intention* was bad, and that therefore they could not be included in those who believed.

47. *a council*] They summon a meeting of the Sanhedrin. Even the adversaries of Jesus are being converted, and something decisive must be done. The crisis unites religious opponents. The chief priests, who were mostly Sadducees, act in concert with the Pharisees; jealous ecclesiastics with religious fanatics (comp. vii. 32, 45, xviii. 3).

What do we?] Implying that something *must* be done.

this man] Contemptuous, as in ix. 16, 24; comp. vii. 49.

doeth many miracles] It is no longer possible to deny the fact of the **signs**. Instead of asking themselves what these 'signs' must mean,

believe on him: and the Romans shall come and take away
both our place and nation. And one of them, *named*
Caiaphas, being the high priest that *same* year, said unto

their only thought is how to prevent others from drawing the obvious
conclusion.

48. *the Romans will come*] They do not inquire whether He is or
is not the Messiah; they look solely to the consequences of admitting
that He is. " The Sanhedrin, especially the Pharisaic section of it, was
a national and patriotic body. It was the inheritor and guardian of the
Rabbinical theories as to the Messiah. There can have been no class in
the nation in which these were so inveterately ingrained, and therefore
none that was so little accessible to the teaching of Jesus. It was from
first to last unintelligible to them. It seemed to abandon all the national
hopes and privileges, and to make it a sin to defend them. If it were
successful, it seemed as if it must leave the field open to the Romans....
It is rarely in ancient literature that we find a highly complicated situation so well understood and described." S. pp. 188, 189. This last
remark is eminently true of the whole narrative portion of the Fourth
Gospel.

our place and nation] 'Our' is very emphatic; *both our place* and
our nation. 'Place' is perhaps best understood of Jerusalem, the seat of
the Sanhedrin, and the abode of the bulk of the hierarchy. Other interpretations are (1) the Temple, comp. 2 Mac. v. 19; (2) the whole land;
so that the expression means 'our land and people,' which is illogical:
the land may be taken from the people, or the people from the land, but
how can both be taken away? (3) 'position, *raison d'être*.' In any
case the sentiment is parallel to that of Demetrius, and his fellow-
craftsmen (Acts xix. 27). They profess to be very zealous for religion,
but cannot conceal their interested motives.

49. *Caiaphas*] This was a surname; 'who was *called* Caiaphas' Matt.
xxvi. 3 (where see note on the Sanhedrin). His original name was
Joseph. Caiaphas is either the Syriac form of Cephas, a 'rock,' or, according to another derivation, means 'depression.' The highpriesthood had long since ceased to descend from father to son. Pilate's pre-
decessor, Valerius Gratus, had deposed Annas and set up in succession
Ismael, Eleazar (son of Annas), Simon, and Joseph Caiaphas (son-in-law
of Annas); Caiaphas held the office from A.D. 18 to 36, when he was deposed by Vitellius. Annas in spite of his deposition was still regarded
as in some sense high-priest (xviii. 13; Luke iii. 2; Acts iv. 6), possibly
as president of the Sanhedrin (Acts v. 21, 27, vii. 1, ix. 1, 2, xxii. 5,
xxiii. 2, 4, xxiv. 1). Caiaphas is not president here, or he would not be
spoken of merely as ' one of them.'

that same year] This has been urged as an objection, as if the
Evangelist ignorantly supposed that the highpriesthood was an annual
office,—a mistake which would go far to prove that the Evangelist was
not a Jew, and therefore not S. John. But there is no 'same' in the
Greek (comp. i. 33, iv. 53, v. 9, 11), and 'that year' means 'that notable and fatal year.' The same expression recurs v. 51 and xviii. 13.

them, Ye know nothing at all, nor consider that it is 50 expedient for us, that one man should die for the people, and *that* the whole nation perish not. And this spake he 51 not of himself: but being high priest that year, he prophesied that Jesus should die for *that* nation; And not for *that* 52 nation only, but that also he should gather together in one the children of God that were scattered abroad. Then 53 from that day forth they took counsel together for to put

Even if there were not this obvious meaning for 'that year,' the frequent changes in the office at this period would fully explain the insertion without the notion of an *annual* change being implied. There had been some twenty or thirty high-priests in S. John's lifetime.

Ye know nothing at all] An inference from their asking 'What do we?' It was quite obvious what they must do. The 'ye' is contemptuously emphatic. The resolute but unscrupulous character of the man is evident.

50. *expedient for us*] For us members of the Sanhedrin. But the better reading gives, *for* **you** half-hearted Pharisees.

that one man] Literally, *in order that one man;* S. John's favourite particle pointing to the Divine purpose: comp. iv. 34, 36, vi. 29, 50, ix. 2, 3, 39, xii. 23, and especially xvi. 7.

the people] The Jews as a theocratic community (*laos*).

the whole nation] The Jews as one of the nations of the earth (*ethnos*). Comp. Luke vii. 5; Acts x. 22. The same word in the plural, 'the nations,' means the Gentiles.

51. *not of himself*] Like Saul, Caiaphas is a prophet in spite of himself.

being high priest] None but a Jew would be likely to know of the old Jewish belief that the high-priest by means of the Urim and Thummim was the mouth-piece of the Divine oracle. The Urim and Thummim had been lost, and the high-priest's office had been shorn of much of its glory, but the remembrance of his prophetical gift did not become quite extinct (Hos. iii. 4); and 'in that fatal year' S. John might well believe that the gift would be restored.

52. *not for that nation only*] S. John purposely uses the word which describes the Jews merely as one of the nations of the earth distinct from the Gentiles. Of course we are not to understand that Caiaphas had any thought of the gracious meaning contained in his infamous advice.

gather together in one] Comp. xvii. 21: for 'in one' read **into** *one*.

53. *Then from that day*] **Therefore** for 'then' is the more important here to bring out the meaning that it was in consequence of Caiaphas' suggestion that the Sanhedrin practically if not formally pronounced sentence of death. The question remained how to get the sentence executed.

54 him to death. Jesus therefore walked no more openly among the Jews; but went thence unto a country near to the wilderness, into a city called Ephraim, and there continued 55 with his disciples. And the Jews' passover was nigh at hand: and many went out of the country up to Jerusalem before 56 the passover, to purify themselves. Then sought they for Jesus, and spake among themselves, as they stood in the temple, What think ye, that he will not come to the feast? 57 Now both the chief priests and the Pharisees had given a commandment, that, if any *man* knew where he were, he should shew *it*, that they might take him.

54. *therefore*] The decree of the Sanhedrin for His apprehension had been published (*v.* 57); the sentence of death was probably a secret among themselves.

openly] Comp. vii. 10. He withdraws from all intercourse with His adversaries.

went thence unto a country] *Departed thence into* **the** *country*.

the wilderness] The desert of Judæa, which extended to the confines of Jericho, would naturally be meant by '*the* wilderness.'

Ephraim] This place cannot be identified with certainty. Eusebius makes it eight miles, Jerome twenty miles, N.E. of Jerusalem: both make it the same as Ephron. If the Ephraim of 2 Chron. xiii. 19 and Josephus (*B. J.* IV. ix. 9) be meant, the wilderness would be that of Bethaven.

55. *And the Jews' passover*] **Now the passover of the Jews.** See notes on ii. 13 and vi. 4.

to purify themselves] (Acts xxi. 24.) Again we have evidence that the Evangelist is a Jew. No purifications are ordered by the Law as a preparation for the Passover. But to be ceremonially unclean was to be excluded (xviii. 28); hence it was customary for those who were so to go up to Jerusalem in good time so as to be declared clean before the Feast began.

56. *sought...spake*] Both verbs are in the imperfect of what went on continually. There are two questions in their words; 'What think ye? that He certainly will not come to the Feast.'

57. *Now both the chief priests*, &c.] Omit 'both.' The word is wanting in authority, and even if it were genuine it would not mean 'both' but 'moreover.' The verse explains why the people doubted His coming to the feast. Note that once more the Sadducaean hierarchy takes the lead. Comp. *v.* 47; xii. 10, xviii. 3, 35, xix. 6, 15, 21. In the history of the Passion the Pharisees are mentioned only once (Matt. xxvii. 62), and then, as here, after the chief priests.

a commandment] The better reading is, **commands**, which has been made singular because only one command is mentioned. Comp. our phrase 'to give orders.'

that] Literally, *in order that* (see on *v.* 50).

CHAP. XII. *The Judgment.*
1—36. *The Judgment of Men.*
Then Jesus six days before the passover came to Bethany, 12

"We are not told how long our Lord stayed at Ephraim. If we are to put faith in the tradition in the Talmud, and in the inferences which Dr Caspari draws from it, an actual verdict of death was passed at the recent meeting of the Sanhedrin, and was only waiting for its execution until an opportunity offered, and the legal period for the production of witnesses in the defence had expired. This would make the interval between the retreat to Ephraim and the Passover coincide more or less nearly with the forty days allowed. The data, however, are not such as we can build on confidently." S. p. 191. So that once more we have an interval of uncertain amount. See the introductory note to chapter vi. and the note on vi. 1.

CHAP. XII. THE JUDGMENT.

We now enter upon the third section of the first main division of this Gospel. It may be useful to state the divisions once more. THE PROLOGUE, i. 1—18; THE MINISTRY, i. 19—xii. 50, thus divided— (1) THE TESTIMONY, i. 19—ii. 11; (2) THE WORK, ii. 13—xi. 57; (3) THE JUDGMENT, xii. This third section, which now lies before us, may be subdivided thus—(a) *the Judgment of men,* 1—36; (β) *the Judgment of the Evangelist,* 37—43; (γ) *the Judgment of Christ,* 44—50.

We must be content to leave the precise method of harmonizing this later portion of S. John's narrative with that of the Synoptists in uncertainty. "It is best to hold fast to the general scheme given by S. John, and to treat the Synoptic sections, especially those in S. Luke (ix. 51—xviii. 35), as fragments of a great picture which are more or less fortuitously thrown together, and are no longer capable of an exact reconstruction." S. p. 191.

1—36. THE JUDGMENT OF MEN.

Note the dramatic contrast between the different sections of this division; the devotion of Mary and the enmity of the hierarchy, Christ's triumph and the Pharisees' discomfiture, &c.

1. *Then Jesus*] The 'then' or **therefore** simply resumes the narrative from the point where it quitted Jesus, xi. 55. This is better than to make it depend on xi. 57, as if He went to Bethany to avoid His enemies. His hour is drawing near, and therefore He draws near to the appointed scene of His sufferings.

six days before the passover] The Passover began at sunset on Nisan 14: six days before this would bring us to Nisan 8. Assuming the year to be A. D. 30, Nisan 8 would be Friday, March 31. We may suppose, therefore, that Jesus and His disciples arrived at Bethany on the Friday evening a little after the Sabbath had commenced, having performed not more than 'a Sabbath-Day's journey' on the Sabbath, the bulk of the

where Lazarus was which had been dead, whom he raised from the dead.

2—8. *The Devotion of Mary.*

2 There they made him a supper; and Martha served: but Lazarus was one of them that sat at the table with
3 him. Then took Mary a pound of ointment of spikenard, very costly, and anointed the feet of Jesus, and wiped his

journey being over before the day of rest began. But it must be remembered that this chronology is tentative, not certain.

which had been dead] These words are omitted by a large number of the best authorities, which give *where Lazarus was, whom* **Jesus** *raised from the dead. They made Him* **therefore**, &c.

2—8. THE DEVOTION OF MARY.

2. *they made him a supper*] 'They' is indefinite: if we had only this account we should suppose that the supper was in the house of Martha, Mary, and Lazarus; but S. Mark (xiv. 3) and S. Matthew (xxvi. 6) tell us that it was in the house of Simon the leper, who had possibly been healed by Christ and probably was a friend or relation of Lazarus and his sisters. Martha's serving (comp. Luke x. 40) in his house is evidence of the latter point (see the notes on the accounts of S. Matthew and S. Mark).

Lazarus was one of them] This is probably introduced to prove the reality and completeness of his restoration to life: but it also confirms the Synoptic accounts by indicating that Lazarus was a guest rather than a host.

sat at the table] Literally, *reclined*, as was the custom.

3. *took Mary a pound*] S. John alone gives her name and the amount of ointment. The pound of 12 ounces is meant. So large a quantity of a substance so costly is evidence of her over-flowing love. Comp. xix. 39.

ointment of spikenard] The Greek expression is a rare one, and occurs elsewhere only Mark xiv. 3, which S. John very likely had seen: his account has all the independence of that of an eye-witness, but may have been influenced by the Synoptic narratives. The meaning of the Greek is not certain: it may mean (1) 'genuine nard,' and spikenard was often adulterated; or (2) 'drinkable, liquid nard,' and unguents were sometimes drunk; or (3) 'Pistic nard,' 'Pistic' being supposed to be a local adjective. But no place from which such an adjective could come appears to be known. Of the other two explanations the first is to be preferred.

very costly] Horace offers to give a cask of wine for a very small box of it; 'Nardi parvus onyx eliciet cadum.' *Odes* IV. xii. 17.

anointed the feet] The two Synoptists mention only the usual (Ps. xxiii. 5) anointing of the head; S. John records the less usual act, which again is evidence of Mary's devotion. The rest of this verse is peculiar to S. John, and shews that he was present.

feet with her hair: and the house was filled with the odour of the ointment. Then saith one of his disciples, Judas 4 Iscariot, Simon's *son*, which should betray him, Why was 5 not this ointment sold for three hundred pence, and given to the poor? This he said, not that he cared for the 6 poor; but because he was a thief, and had the bag, and bare what was put *therein*. Then said Jesus, Let her alone: 7 against the day of my burying hath she kept this. For 8

4. *Then saith*, &c.] Rather, **But** *Judas Iscariot*, &c. The best authorities omit 'Simon's son.'

one of his disciples, Judas Iscariot] S. Mark says quite indefinitely, 'some,' S. Matthew, 'his disciples.' Each probably states just what he knew; S. Mark that the remark was made; S. Matthew that it came from the group of disciples; S. John that Judas made it, and why he made it. S. John was perhaps anxious that the unworthy grumbling should be assigned to the right person.

which should betray] Comp. vi. 71.

5. *three hundred pence*] Here, as in vi. 7, the translation 'pence' is very inadequate and misleading; 'three hundred shillings' would be nearer the mark (see on vi. 7). S. Mark adds that some were very indignant at her.

to the poor] More accurately, *to* **poor people**; there is no article (comp. Luke xviii. 22).

6. *the bag*] Better, *the* **box**, the cash-box in which the funds of the small company were kept. The word means literally 'a case for mouthpieces' of musical instruments, and hence any portable chest. It occurs in the LXX. of 2 Chron. xxiv. 8, 11, but nowhere in N.T. excepting here and xiii. 29.

and bare] The Greek word may mean either 'used to carry' or 'used to carry away,' i.e. *steal:* comp. xx. 15. S. Augustine, commenting on 'portabat,' which he found in the Italic Version, and which survives in the Vulgate, says "portabat an exportabat? sed ministerio portabat, furto exportabat." We have the same play in 'lift,' e.g. 'shop-*lifting;*' and in the old use of 'convey:' 'To steal'..." *Convey* the wise it call." *Merry Wives of Windsor* I. 3. "O good! Convey?—*Conveyers* are you all." *Richard II.* IV. 1.

what was put therein] Literally, *the things that were being cast* into it from time to time; the gifts of friends and followers.

7. *hath she kept*] The large majority of authorities, including the best, read *that she may keep*, and the whole will run: *Let her alone* **that she may preserve it for the day of My burial.** The simplest interpretation of this is 'Let her preserve what remains of it; not, however, to be sold for the poor, but to be used for My burial, which is near at hand.' The text has probably been altered to bring it more into harmony with the Synoptists, with whom the present anointing appears as anointing for the burial by anticipation. The word for 'burial' or 'entombment' occurs only here and Mark xiv. 8.

the poor always ye have with you; but me ye have not always.

9—11. *The Hostility of the Priests.*

9 Much people of the Jews therefore knew that he was there: and they came not for Jesus' sake only, but that they might see Lazarus also, whom he had raised from the
10 dead. But the chief priests consulted that they might put
11 Lazarus also to death; because that by reason of him many of the Jews went away, and believed on Jesus.

8. *For the poor*, &c.] Comp. Deut. xv. 11. Every word of this verse occurs in the first two Gospels, though not quite in the same order. Here the emphasis is on 'the poor,' there on 'always.' The striking originality of the saying, and the large claim which it makes, are evidence of its origin from Him who spake as never man spake. Considering how Christ speaks of the poor elsewhere, these words may be regarded as quite beyond the reach of a writer of fiction.

9—11. THE HOSTILITY OF THE PRIESTS.

9. *Much people*] Large caravans would be coming up for the Passover, and the news would spread quickly through the shifting crowds, who were already on the alert (xi. 55) about Jesus, and were now anxious to see Lazarus. Note that it is a **'large multitude of the *Jews*'** who come; i.e. of Christ's usual opponents. This again (comp. xi. 45—47) excites the hierarchy to take decisive measures. See on v. 12.

10. *But the chief priests*] Nothing is here said about the Pharisees (comp. xi. 47, 57), who are, however, not necessarily excluded. Both would wish to put Lazarus out of the way for the reason given in v. 11: but the chief priests, who were mostly Sadducees, would have an additional reason, in that Lazarus was a living refutation of their doctrine that 'there is no resurrection' (Acts xxiii. 8). See on xi. 57.

put Lazarus also to death] Whatever may be true about xi. 53, we must not suppose that this verse implies a formal sentence of death: it does not even imply a meeting of the Sanhedrin.

These repeated references to the raising of Lazarus (xi. 45, 47, xii. 1, 9, 10, 17) greatly strengthen the historical evidence for the miracle. They are quite inconsistent with the theory either of a misunderstanding or of deliberate fraud.

11. *went away, and believed*] Better, **were going away and believing**. It is best to leave 'going away' quite indefinite: the notion of falling away from the hierarchy lies in the context but not in the word. The imperfects denote a continual process.

S. Augustine comments on the folly of the priests—as if Christ could not raise Lazarus a second time! But this ignores the 'also': the hierarchy meant to put *both* to death. Their folly consisted in failing to

12—18. *The Enthusiasm of the People.*

On the next day much people that were come to the feast, when they heard that Jesus was coming to Jerusalem, took branches of palm trees, and went forth to meet him, and cried, Hosanna: Blessed *is* the King of Israel that cometh in the name of the Lord. And Jesus, when he had found a young ass, sat thereon; as it is written, Fear not, 12 13 14 15

see, not that He could raise Lazarus again, but that He could raise Himself (ii. 19). Note that it is the unscrupulous hierarchy, who attempt this crime. Comp. xviii. 35, xix. 6, 15, 21.

12—18. THE ENTHUSIASM OF THE PEOPLE.

12. *On the next day*] From the date given *v.* 1, consequently Nisan 9, from Saturday evening to Sunday evening, if the chronology given on *v.* 1 is correct. S. John seems distinctly to assert that the Triumphal Entry followed the supper at Bethany: S. Matthew and S. Mark both place the supper after the entry, S. Matthew without any date and probably neglecting (as often) the chronological order, S. Mark also without date, yet *apparently* implying (xiv. 1) that the supper took place two days before the Passover. But the date in Mark xiv. 1 covers only two verses and must not be carried further in contradiction to S. John's precise and consistent arrangement. S. John omits all details respecting the procuring of the young ass.

much people] Not 'Jews', as in *v.* 9, but pilgrims without any bias against Christ. Here and in *v.* 9 the true reading perhaps is, *the common people.*

13. *branches of palm trees*] More literally, **the** *palm-branches of* **the** *palm-trees;* i.e. those which grew there, or which were commonly used at festivals. Comp. Simon's triumphal entry into Jerusalem (1 Macc. xiii. 51). The palm-tree was regarded by the ancients as characteristic of Palestine. 'Phœnicia' (Acts xi. 19, xv. 3) is probably derived from *phœnix* = 'palm.' The tree is now comparatively rare, except in the Philistine plain: at 'Jericho, the city of palm-trees' (Deut. xxxiv. 3; 2 Chron. xxxviii. 15) there is not one.

Hosanna] This is evidence that the writer of this Gospel knows Hebrew. In the LXX. at Ps. cxvii. 25 we have a translation of the Hebrew, 'save we pray,' not a transliteration as here. (Comp. 'Alleluia' in Rev. xix. 1, 6.) This Psalm is said by some to have been written for the Feast of Tabernacles after the return from captivity, by others for the founding or dedicating of the second Temple. In what follows the better reading is *Blessed* **is He that cometh in the name of the Lord even the king of Israel.** The cry of the multitude was of course not always the same, and the different Evangelists give us different forms of it.

14. *It is written*] See on ii. 17.

15. *Fear not,* &c. The quotation is freely made; 'fear not' is sub-

daughter of Sion: behold, thy King cometh, sitting
16 on an ass's colt. These *things* understood not his disciples at the first: but when Jesus was glorified, then remembered they that these *things* were written of him, and
17 *that* they had done these *things* unto him. The people therefore that was with him when he called Lazarus out of
18 *his* grave, and raised him from the dead, bare record. For this cause the people also met him, for that they heard that he had done this miracle.

19. *The Discomfiture of the Pharisees.*

19 The Pharisees therefore said among themselves, Perceive ye how ye prevail nothing? behold, the world is gone after him.

stituted fo; 'rejoice greatly,' and the whole is abbreviated, Zech. ix. 9. In adding 'thy' to 'king' and in writing 'an ass's colt' the Evangelist seems to be translating direct from the Hebrew. The best editions of the LXX. omit 'thy' and all have 'a young colt' for the words here rendered 'an ass's colt.' Comp. i. 29, vi. 45, xix. 37. If the writer of this Gospel knew the O.T. in the original Hebrew he almost certainly was a Jew.

16. *understood not*] A mark of candour (see on xi. 12); comp. ii. 22 (where see note) and xx. 9. Would a Christian of the second century have invented this dulness of apprehension in Apostles? After Pentecost, however, much that had passed unnoticed or had been obscure before was brought to their remembrance and made clear (xiv. 26). Note 'these things' thrice repeated; *vv.* 14, 15 shew that the placing Him on the young ass is primarily meant.

was glorified] Comp. vii. 39 and xi. 4, where see notes.

17. *when he called Lazarus*] See on *v.* 10. There is another reading, well supported, which gives '*that* He called Lazarus,' and the whole will then run;—*The* **multitude**, *therefore, which was with Him,* **kept bearing witness** (i. 7) *that He called Lazarus out of the sepulchre and raised him from the dead.* But 'when' is to be preferred; so that there are two multitudes, one coming with Jesus from Bethany and one (*vv.* 13, 18) meeting Him from Jerusalem. See on *v.* 41.

18. *this miracle*] 'This' is emphatic: other miracles had made comparatively little impression, but this **sign** had convinced even His adversaries.

19. THE DISCOMFITURE OF THE PHARISEES.

19. *Perceive ye*] Rather, **Behold** *ye*. The Greek may also mean 'Behold' (imperat.) or **ye behold**: the last is perhaps best; 'Ye see what a mistake we have made; we ought to have adopted the plan of Caiaphas long ago.'

the world] The exaggerated expression of their chagrin, which in

20—33. *The Desire of the Gentiles and the Voice from Heaven.*

And there were certain Greeks among them that came up 20 to worship at the feast: the same came therefore to Philip, 21 which was of Bethsaida of Galilee, and desired him, saying, Sir, we would see Jesus. Philip cometh and telleth An- 22

this Divine epic is brought into strong contrast with the triumph of Jesus. Comp. a similar exaggeration from a similar cause iii. 26; '*all* men come to Him.'
is gone after him] Literally, *is gone* **away** *after Him*. The Greek word is not the same but is similar in meaning to that used in v. 11. After this confession of helplessness the Pharisees appear no more alone; the reckless hierarchy help them on to the catastrophe.

20—33. THE DESIRE OF THE GENTILES AND THE VOICE FROM HEAVEN.

20. *Greeks*] The same word is translated 'Gentiles' vii. 35, where see note. Care must be taken to distinguish in the N.T. between *Hellenes* or 'Greeks,' i.e. born Gentiles, who may or may not have become either Jewish proselytes or Christian converts, and *Hellenistae* or 'Grecians,' as our Bible renders the word, i.e. Jews who spoke Greek and not Aramaic. Neither word occurs in the Synoptists. *Hellenes* are mentioned here, vii. 35, and frequently in the Acts and in S. Paul's Epistles. *Hellenistae* are mentioned only in the Acts, vi. 1 and ix. 29: in Acts xi. 20 the right reading is probably *Hellenes*.
that came up to worship] Better, *that* **were wont** *to go up to worship*. This shews that they were 'proselytes of the gate,' like the Ethiopian eunuch (Acts viii. 27): see on Matt. xxiii. 15. In this incident we have an indication of the salvation rejected by the Jews passing to the Gentiles: the scene of it was probably the Court of the Gentiles; it is peculiar to S. John.

21. *to Philip*] Their coming to S. Philip was the result either (1) of accident; or (2) of previous acquaintance, to which the mention of his home seems to point; or (3) of his Greek name, which might attract them. See on i. 45, vi. 5, xiv. 8.
Sir] Indicating respect for the disciple of such a Master: comp. iv. 11, 15, 19.
we would see Jesus] This desire to 'come and see' for themselves would at once win the sympathy of the practical Philip. See on i. 46 and xiv. 8.

22. *telleth Andrew*] Another Apostle with a Greek name. They were both of Bethsaida (i. 44), and possibly these Greeks may have come from the same district. S. Philip seems to shrink from the responsibility of introducing Gentiles to the Messiah, and applies in his difficulty to the Apostle who had already distinguished himself by bringing others to Christ (i. 41, vi. 8, 9).

23 drew: and again Andrew and Philip tell Jesus. And Jesus answered them, saying, The hour is come, that the Son of 24 man should be glorified. Verily, verily, I say unto you, Except a corn of wheat fall into the ground and die, it abideth alone: but if it die, it bringeth forth much fruit. 25 He that loveth his life shall lose it; and he that hateth his 26 life in this world shall keep it unto life eternal. If any *man*

and again] The true reading is **Andrew cometh, and Philip, and they** *tell Jesus*.

23. *And Jesus answered*] Better, **But** *Jesus* **answereth.** He anticipates the Apostles and addresses them before they introduce the Greeks. We are left in doubt as to the result of the Greeks' request. Nothing is said to them in particular, though they may have followed and heard this address to the Apostles, which gradually shades off into soliloquy.

These men from the West at the close of Christ's life set forth the same truth as the men from the East at the beginning of it—that the Gentiles are to be gathered in. The wise men came to His cradle, these to His cross, of which their coming reminds Him; for only by His death could 'the nations' be saved.

The hour is come] The verb first for emphasis in the Greek as in iv. 21, 23: 'it hath come—the fated hour.' Comp. xiii. 1.

that the Son of man] Literally, *in order that*, of the Divine purpose, as in xi. 50 and xiii. 1, where see notes. See also the last note on i. 51.

glorified] By His Passion and Death through which He must pass to return to glory. See on vii. 39 and xi. 4.

24. *Verily, verily*] Strange as it may seem to you that the Messiah should die, yet this is but the course of nature: a seed cannot be glorified unless it dies. A higher form of existence is obtained only through the extinction of the lower form that preceded it. See on i. 51.

25. *loveth his life...hateth his life...life eternal*] 'Life' is here used in two senses, and in the Greek two different words are used. In the first two cases 'life' means the life of the individual, in the last, life in the abstract. By sacrificing life in the one sense, we may win life in the other. See notes on Matt. x. 39, xvi. 25; Mark viii. 35; Luke ix. 24, xvii. 33. A comparison of the texts will shew that most of them refer to different occasions, so that this solemn warning must have been often on His lips. The present utterance is distinct from all the rest.

shall lose it] Better, **loseth** *it;* the Greek may mean **destroyeth** *it.*

hateth his life] i.e. is ready to act towards it as if he hated it, if need so require. Neither here nor in Luke xiv. 26 must 'hate' be watered down to mean 'be not too fond of;' it means that and a great deal more. The word rendered 'life' in 'loveth his life' and 'hateth his

serve me, let him follow me; and where I am, there shall also my servant be: if any *man* serve me, him will *my* Father honour. Now is my soul troubled; and what shall 27 I say? Father, save me from this hour: but for this cause

life' might also mean 'soul,' and some would translate it so: but would Christ have spoken of hating one's soul as the way to eternal life?
26. *let him follow me*] in My life of self-sacrifice: Christ Himself has set the example of hating one's life in this world. These words are perhaps addressed through the disciples to the Greeks listening close at hand. If they 'wish to see Jesus' and know Him they must count the cost first. 'Me' is emphatic in both clauses.
where I am] i.e. where I shall be then, in My kingdom. Comp. xiv. 3, xvii. 24. Some would include in the 'where' the *road* to the kingdom, viz. death. 'I' and 'My' are emphatic.
serve...honour] Here the verbs are emphatic (not 'Me'), and balance one another. This verse is closely parallel to *v.* 35: 'let him follow Me' corresponds to 'hateth his life in this world;' 'him will the Father honour,' to 'shall keep it unto life eternal.'
27. This is a verse of well-known difficulty, and the meaning cannot be determined with certainty, several meanings being admissible. The doubtful points are (1) the position of the interrogation, whether it should come after 'I say' or 'from this hour;' (2) the meaning of 'for this cause.'
Now is my soul troubled] The word rendered 'soul' is the same as that rendered 'life' in 'loveth his life' and 'hateth his life.' To bring out this and the sequence of thought, 'life' would perhaps be better here. 'He that would serve Me must follow Me and be ready to hate his life; for My life has long since been tossed and torn with emotion and sorrow.' 'Is troubled' = *has been and still is troubled;* a frequent meaning of the Greek perfect.
what shall I say?] Or, *what* must *I say?* This appears to be the best punctuation; and the question expresses the difficulty of framing a prayer under the conflicting influences of fear of death and willingness to glorify His Father by dying. The result is first a prayer under the influence of fear—'save Me from this hour' (comp. 'Let this cup pass from Me,' Matt. xxvi. 39), and then a prayer under the influence of ready obedience—'Glorify Thy Name' through My sufferings. But the Greek means 'save me *out of*' (*sôson ek*), i.e. 'bring Me safe out of;' rather than 'save Me *from*' (*sôson apo*), i.e. 'keep Me altogether away from,' as in 'deliver us *from* the evil' (Matt. vi. 13). S. John omits the Agony in the garden, which was in the Synoptists and was well known to every Christian; but he gives us here an insight into a less known truth, which is still often forgotten, that the agony was not confined to Gethsemane, but was part of Christ's whole life. Others place the question at 'from this hour,' and the drift of the whole will then be, 'How can I say, Father save Me from this hour? Nay, I came to suffer; therefore My prayer shall be, Father, glorify Thy Name.'

28 came I unto this hour. Father, glorify thy name. Then came there a voice from heaven, *saying*, I have both glori- **29** fied *it*, and will glorify *it* again. The people therefore, that stood *by*, and heard *it*, said that it thundered: others said, **30** An angel spake to him. Jesus answered and said, This **31** voice came not because of me, but for your sakes. Now is the judgment of this world: now shall the prince of this

for this cause] These words are taken in two opposite senses; (1) that I might be saved out of this hour; (2) that Thy Name might be glorified by My obedience. Both make good sense. If the latter be adopted it would be better to transpose the stops, placing a full stop after 'from this hour' and a colon after 'unto this hour.'

28. *Then came there*] Better, *There came* **therefore**, i.e. in answer to Christ's prayer. There can be no doubt what S. John *wishes* us to understand;—that a voice was heard speaking articulate words, that some could distinguish the words, others could not, while some mistook the sounds for thunder. To make the thunder the reality, and the voice and the words mere imagination, is to substitute an arbitrary explanation for the Evangelist's plain meaning. For similar voices comp. that heard by Elijah (1 Kings xix. 12, 13); by Nebuchadnezzar (Dan. iv. 31); at Christ's Baptism (Mark i. 11) and Transfiguration (Mark ix. 7); and at S. Paul's Conversion (Acts ix. 4. 7, xxii. 9), where it would seem that S. Paul alone could distinguish the words, while his companions merely heard a sound (see on Acts ix. 4). One of the conditions on which power to distinguish what is said depends is sympathy with the speaker.

have glorified it] in all God's works from the Creation onwards, especially in the life of Christ.

will glorify it] in the death of Christ and its results.

29. *The people...thundered...spake*] Better, *The* **multitude...had thundered...hath spoken**.

30. *Jesus answered*] He answered their discussions about the sound, and by calling it a voice He decides conclusively against those who supposed it to be thunder. But those who recognised that it was a voice were scarcely less seriously mistaken; *their* error consisted in not recognising that the voice had a meaning for *them*. **Not for My sake hath this voice come**, *but for your sakes*, i.e. that ye might believe. Comp. xi. 42.

31. *Now...now*] With prophetic certainty Christ speaks of the victory as already won.

the judgment of this world] The sentence passed on this world (see on iii. 17 and v. 29) for refusing to believe. The Cross is the condemnation of all who reject it.

the prince of this world] Literally, *the* **ruler** *of this world*. This is one of the apparently Gnostic phrases which may have contributed to render this Gospel suspicious in the eyes of the Alogi (see *Introduction*, Chap. II. i.): it occurs again xiv. 30, xvi. 11, and nowhere else. It

world be cast out. And I, if I be lifted up from the earth, 32 will draw all *men* unto me. This he said, signifying what 33 death he should die.

34—36. *The Perplexity of the Multitude.*

The people answered him, We have heard out of the 34 law that Christ abideth for ever: and how sayest thou,

was a Gnostic view that the creator and ruler of the material universe was an evil being. But in the Rabbinical writings 'prince of this world' was a common designation of Satan, as ruler of the Gentiles, in opposition to God, the Head of the Jewish theocracy. But just as the Messiah is the Saviour of the believing world, whether Jew or Gentile, so Satan is the ruler of the unbelieving world, whether Gentile or Jew.

shall...be cast out] By the gradual conversion of unbelievers. This is a process which will continue until the last day.

32. *And I*] 'I' is very emphatic in opposition to 'the ruler of this world.' The glorified Christ will rule men's hearts in place of the devil.

be lifted up] Raised up to heaven by means of the Cross: we need not, as in iii. 14 and viii. 28, confine the meaning to the Crucifixion, although the lifting up on the Cross may be specially indicated. The words 'from the earth' (literally, *out of the earth*) seem to point to the Ascension; yet the Cross itself, apparently so repulsive, has through Christ's Death become an attraction; and this *may* be the meaning here. For the hypothetical form '*if* I be lifted up,' comp. '*if* I go,' xiv. 3. In both cases Christ is concerned not with the *time* of the act, but with the *consequences* of it; hence He does not say 'when,' but 'if.'

will draw] There are two Greek words for 'draw' in the N.T., one of which necessarily implies *violence*, the other does not: it is the latter that is used here and in vi. 44; the former is used Acts xiv. 19 and xvii. 6. Man's will is free; he can refuse to be drawn: and there is no violence; the attraction is moral. We see from vi. 44 that before the 'lifting up' it is the Father who draws men to the Son.

all men] Not only the Jews represented by the Twelve, but the Gentiles represented by these Greeks.

unto me] Better, *unto* **Myself**, up from the earth.

33. *what death*] Literally, **by** *what* **manner of** *death:* comp. x. 32, xviii. 32, xxi. 9.

should die] The word translated 'should' is the same as that used of the traitor, *v.* 4 and vi. 71. It is used (1) of what is *about* to happen, (2) of what (seeing that it *has* happened) may be regarded as necessary and fore-ordained.

34—36. THE PERPLEXITY OF THE MULTITUDE.

34. *The people answered*] *The* **multitude therefore** *answered*.

out of the law] In its widest sense, including the Psalms and the Prophets. Comp. Ps. lxxxix. 29, 36, cx. 4; Is. ix. 7; Ezek. xxxvii.

The Son of man must be lift up? who is this Son of
35 man? Then Jesus said unto them, Yet a little while
is the light with you. Walk while ye have the light, lest
darkness come upon you: for he that walketh in darkness
36 knoweth not whither he goeth. While ye have light, believe
in the light, that ye may be the children of light. These

25, &c. The people rightly understand 'lifted up from the earth' to
mean removal from the earth by death; and they argue—'Scripture
says that the Christ (see on i. 20) will abide for ever. You claim to be
the Christ, and yet *you* say that you will be lifted up and therefore *not*
abide.'

who is this Son of man?] 'This' is contemptuous: 'a strange Messiah this, with no power to abide!' (on 'Son of Man' see i. 51).
"Here we have the secret, unexplained by the Synoptists, why even
when the scale is seeming to turn for a moment in favour of belief, it is
continually swayed down again by the discovery of some new particular
in which the current ideas respecting the Messiah are disappointed and
contradicted." S. p. 199. One moment the people are convinced by
a miracle that Jesus is the Messiah, the next that it is impossible to
reconcile His position with the received interpretations of Messianic
prophecy. It did not occur to them to doubt the interpretations.

35. *Then Jesus said*] Better, *Jesus* **therefore** *said:* instead of answering their contemptuous question He gives them a solemn warning.

while ye have] The better reading is, as *ye have:* 'walk in a manner
suitable to the fact of there being the Light among you: make use of
the Light and work.'

darkness] **that** *darkness* 'in which no man can work.'

come upon you] like a bird of prey. The same Greek verb is used
of the last day; 1 Thess. v. 4; and in the LXX. of sin overtaking the
sinner; Num. xxxii. 23.

for he that walketh in darkness] And *he that walketh in* **the** *darkness.*

whither he goeth] Or, *goeth away;* knows not to what end he is
departing: comp. 1 John ii. 11.

36. *While ye have*] Here again the better reading is **as** *ye have;*
and 'light' should be '**the** Light.' Note the emphatic repetition so
common in S. John.

that ye may be] Rather, *that ye may* **become**. Faith is only the
beginning; it does not at once make us children.

children of light] No article: but in all the four preceding cases
'light' has the article and means Christ, the Light, as in i. 5, 7, 8, 9.
The expression 'child of' or 'son of' is frequent in Hebrew poetry to
indicate very close connexion as between product and producer (see on
xvii. 12). Thus, 'son of peace,' Luke x. 6; 'children of this world,'
xvi. 8; 'sons of thunder,' Mark iii. 17. Such expressions are very
frequent in the most Hebraistic of the Gospels: comp. Matt. v. 9,
viii. 12, ix. 15, xiii. 38, xxiii. 15.

things spake Jesus, and departed, and did hide himself from them.

37—43. *The Judgment of the Evangelist.*

But though he had done so many miracles before them, 37 yet they believed not on him: that the saying of Esaias the 38 prophet might be fulfilled, which he spake, Lord, who hath believed our report? and to whom hath the arm of the Lord been revealed? Therefore they could not 39

and departed] Probably to Bethany, to spend the last few days before His hour came in retirement. Comp. Matt. xxi. 17; Mark xi. 11; Luke xxi. 37.
did hide himself] Rather, **was hidden**.

37—43. THE JUDGMENT OF THE EVANGELIST.

S. John here sums up the results of the ministry which has just come to a close. Their comparative poverty is such that he can explain it in no other way than as an illustration of that judicial blindness which had been foretold and denounced by Isaiah. The tragic tone returns again: see on i. 5.

37. *so many miracles*] The Jews admitted His miracles, vii. 31; xi. 47. They are assumed by S. John as notorious, although he himself records only seven of them. Comp. ii. 23, iv. 45, vii, 31, xi. 47.
before them] i.e. before their very eyes.

38. *That*] Or, *in order that*, indicating the Divine purpose. Comp. xiii. 18, xv. 25, xvii. 12, xviii. 9, 32, xix. 24, 36. It is the two specially Hebraistic Gospels that most frequently remind us that Christ's life was a fulfilment of Hebrew prophecy. Comp. Matt. i. 22, ii. 15, 17, iv. 14, viii. 17, xii. 17, xiii. 35, xxi. 4, xxvi. 54, 56, xxvii. 9. See on Matt. i. 22.
Lord, who hath believed] The quotation closely follows the LXX.
our report] Literally, *that which they hear from us;* comp. Rom. x. 16.
the arm of the Lord] His power. There seems to be no sufficient authority for interpreting this expression of the Messiah, although it is the power of God as manifested in the Messiah that is here specially meant. Comp. Luke i. 51; Acts xiii. 17.

39. *Therefore*] Or, **For this cause** (*vv.* 18, 27); see on vii. 21, 22. It refers to what precedes, and the 'because' which follows gives the reason more explicitly. This use is common in S. John: comp. v. 18, viii. 47, x. 17.
they could not] It had become morally impossible. Grace may be refused so persistently as to destroy the power of accepting it. 'I will not' leads to 'I cannot.' Pharaoh first hardened his heart and then God hardened it. Comp. Rom. ix. 6 to xi. 32.

40 believe, because that Esaias said again, He hath blinded their eyes, and hardened their heart; that they should not see with *their* eyes, nor understand with *their* heart, and be converted, and I should 41 heal them. These *things* said Esaias, when he saw his 42 glory, and spake of him. Nevertheless among the *chief* rulers also many believed on him; but because of the Pharisees they did not confess *him*, lest they should be put 43 out of the synagogue: for they loved the praise of men more than the praise of God.

40. *He hath blinded*] Not Christ, nor the devil, but God. The quotation is free, following neither the Hebrew nor the LXX. very closely.

I should heal] 'I'=Christ. God has hardened their hearts so that they could not be converted, and therefore Christ could not heal them. Comp. Matt. xiii. 14, 15, where Christ quotes this text to explain why He teaches in parables; and Acts xxviii. 26, where S. Paul quotes it to explain the rejection of his preaching by the Jews in Rome.

41. *when he saw*] The better reading is, **because** *he saw*. We had a similar double reading in *v.* 17, where 'when' is to be preferred. In the Greek the difference is only a single letter, ὅτε and ὅτι. Christ's glory was revealed to Isaiah in a vision, and therefore he spoke of it. The glory of the Son before the Incarnation, when He was 'in the form of God' (Phil. ii. 6), is to be understood.

42. *Nevertheless*] In spite of the judicial blindness with which God had visited them many **even of** the Sanhedrin believed. We know of Joseph of Arimathea and Nicodemus.

because of the Pharisees] The recognised champions of orthodoxy both in and outside the Sanhedrin. Comp. vii. 13, ix. 22.

did not confess] Imperfect tense; they were perpetually omitting to do so.

43. *the praise of men* &c.] Better, *the* **glory** (*that cometh*) **from** *men* **rather than the glory** (*that cometh*) **from** *God* (see on v. 41, 44). The word rendered 'praise' is the same as that rendered 'glory' in v. 41. Moreover 'more than' is not strong enough; it should be *rather than*. Joseph and Nicodemus confessed their belief after the crisis of the Crucifixion. Gamaliel did not even get so far as to believe on Him.

44—50. THE JUDGMENT OF CHRIST.

The Evangelist has just summed up the results of Christ's ministry (37—43). He now corroborates that estimate by quoting Christ Himself. But as *v.* 36 seems to give us the close of the ministry, we are probably to understand that what follows was uttered on some occasion or occasions previous to *v.* 36. Perhaps it is given us as an epitome of what Christ often taught.

44—50. *The Judgment of Christ.*

Jesus cried and said, He that believeth on me, believeth 44 not on me, but on him that sent me. And he that seeth me 45 seeth him that sent me. I am come a light into the world, 46 that whosoever believeth on me should not abide in darkness. And if any *man* hear my words, and believe not, I 47 judge him not: for I came not to judge the world, but to save the world. He that rejecteth me, and receiveth not 48 my words, hath *one* that judgeth him: the word that I have spoken, the same shall judge him in the last day. For I 49

44. *cried*] Comp. vii. 28, 37. The expression implies *public* teaching.
believeth not on me] His belief does not end there; it must include more. This saying does not occur in the previous discourses; but in v. 36 and viii. 19 we have a similar thought. Jesus came as His Father's ambassador, and an ambassador has no meaning apart from the sovereign who sends him. Not only is it impossible to accept the one without the other, but to accept the representative is to accept *not him in his own personality* but the prince whom he personates. These words are, therefore, to be taken quite literally.
45. *seeth*] Or, **beholdeth**, *contemplateth*. The same verb is used vi. 40, 62, vii. 3 and frequently in S. John.
46. *I am come*] Emphatic; 'I and none other.' Comp. *vv.* 35, 36, viii. 12, ix. 5.
abide in darkness] Till the Light comes, all are in darkness; the question remains whether they will remain so *after* the Light has come.
47. *hear my words*] 'Hear' is a neutral word, implying neither belief nor unbelief. Matt. vii. 24, 26; Mark iv. 15, 16. For 'words' read **sayings** (see on v. 47) both here and in *v.* 48.
and believe not] The true reading is *and* **keep them not**, i.e. fulfil them (comp. Luke xi. 28, xviii. 21). One important MS. omits the 'not,' perhaps to avoid a supposed inconsistency between *v.* 47 and *v.* 48.
48. *my words*] Better, *My* **sayings** (see on *v.* 47): 'word' in the next clause is right.
hath one that judgeth him] Hath his judge already, without My sentencing him. Comp. iii. 18, v. 45. The hearer may refuse the word, but he cannot refuse the responsibility of having heard it.
in the last day] Peculiar to this Gospel: comp. vi. 39, 40, 44, 54, xi. 24. This verse is conclusive as to the doctrine of the last judgment being contained in this Gospel.
49. *For*] Or, **Because**: it introduces the reason why one who rejects Christ's word will be judged by His word;—because that word is manifestly Divine and proceeds from the Father.

have not spoken of myself; but the Father which sent me, he gave me a commandment, what I should say, and what 50 I should speak. And I know that his commandment is life everlasting: whatsoever I speak therefore, even as the Father said unto me, so I speak.

xiii.—xvii. *The inner Glorification of Christ in His last Discourses.*

of myself] Literally, *out of Myself* (*ek*) without commission from the Father. Comp. *from Myself* (*apo*) v. 30, vii. 16, 28, viii. 28.

he gave me] **Himself** (and none other) **hath given** *Me*. See on x. 18.

say...speak] 'Say' probably refers to the doctrine, 'speak' to the form in which it is expressed. See on viii. 43.

50. *And I know*] The Son's testimony to the Father. 'The commission which He hath given Me is **eternal life.**' (See on iii. 16.) His commission is to save the world.

as the Father said] The same distinction as in the previous verse: the matter of the revelation comes from the Father, the external expression of it from the Son.

With this the first main division of the Gospel ends. CHRIST'S REVELATION OF HIMSELF TO THE WORLD IN HIS MINISTRY is concluded. The Evangelist has set before us the TESTIMONY to the Christ, the WORK of the Christ, and the JUDGMENT respecting the work, which has ended in a conflict, and the conflict has reached a climax. We have reached the beginning of the end.

CHAP. XIII.

We now enter upon the second main division of the Gospel. The Evangelist has given us thus far a narrative of CHRIST'S MINISTRY presented to us in a series of typical scenes (i. 18—xii. 50). He goes on to set forth the ISSUES OF CHRIST'S MINISTRY (xiii—xx). The last chapter (xxi.) forms the EPILOGUE, balancing the first eighteen verses (i. 1—18), which form the PROLOGUE.

The second main division of the Gospel, like the first, falls into three parts: 1. THE INNER GLORIFICATION OF CHRIST IN HIS LAST DISCOURSES (xiii.—xvii.); 2. THE OUTER GLORIFICATION OF CHRIST IN HIS PASSION (xviii, xix.); 3. THE VICTORY COMPLETED IN THE RESURRECTION (xx.). These parts will be subdivided as we reach them.

xiii.—xvii. THE INNER GLORIFICATION OF CHRIST IN HIS LAST DISCOURSES.

1. *His Love in Humiliation* (xiii. 1—30); 2. *His Love in keeping His own* (xiii. 30—xv. 27); 3. *the Promise of the Paraclete and of Christ's Return* (xvi.): 4. *Christ's Prayer for Himself, the Apostles, and all Believers* (xvii.).

Chap. XIII. 1—30. *Love in Humiliation.*

Now before the feast of the passover, when Jesus knew 13 that his hour was come that he should depart out of this world unto the Father, having loved his own which were in the world, he loved them unto the end. And supper being 2 ended, the devil having now put into the heart of Judas

Chap. XIII. 1—30. Love in Humiliation.

This section has two parts in strong and dramatic contrast; 1. the washing of the disciples' feet (1—20); 2. the self-excommunication of the traitor (21—30).

1. *Now before the feast of the passover*] These words give a date not to any one word in the verse, whether 'knew' or 'having loved' or 'loved,' but to the narrative which follows. Their most natural meaning is that some evening before the Passover Jesus was at supper with His disciples. This was probably Thursday evening, the beginning of Nisan 14: but the difficult question of the Day of the Crucifixion is too long for a note and is discussed in Appendix A.

when Jesus knew] Or, *Jesus knowing* (*v.* 3). The Greek may mean either 'although He knew' or 'because He knew.' The latter is better: it was precisely because He knew that He would soon return to glory that He gave this last token of self-humiliating love.

his hour was come] See on ii. 4, vii. 6, xi. 9. Till His hour had come His enemies could do nothing but plot (vii. 30, viii. 20).

that he should] Literally, *in order that He should*, of the Divine purpose. See on xii. 23.

depart out of] Or, **pass over** *out of*: it is the same verb and preposition as in v. 24; 'hath *passed over* out of death into life.'

his own] Those whom God had given Him, i. 11, 12, xvii. 11; Acts iv. 23, xxiv. 23.

unto the end] The end of His life is the common interpretation, which may be right. Comp. Matt. x. 22 and xxiv. 13, where the same Greek expression is translated as it is here; and 1 Thess. ii. 16, where it is translated 'to the uttermost.' In Luke xviii. 5 'continual coming' is literally 'coming to the end.' In all these passages the meaning may either be 'at the last, finally,' or, 'to the uttermost, utterly.' **To the uttermost** is perhaps to be preferred here. Comp. the LXX. of Amos ix. 8; Ps. xii. 1.

2. *supper being ended*] There are two readings here, but neither of them means 'being ended,' moreover the supper is not ended (*v.* 26). The common reading would mean 'supper having begun,' and the better reading, 'when supper was at hand,' or, 'when supper was beginning.' "It was the custom for slaves to wash the feet of the guests before sitting down to meat; and we are tempted to suppose that the symbolical act, which our Evangelist relates here, took the place of this custom." S. p. 214.

3 Iscariot, Simon's *son*, to betray him; Jesus knowing that the
Father had given all *things* into his hands, and that he was
4 come from God, and went to God; he riseth from supper,
and laid aside *his* garments; and took a towel, and girded
5 himself. After that, he poureth water into a bason, and

the devil......to betray him] The true reading gives us, *The devil having now put it into the heart*, **that Judas, Simon's son, Iscariot, should betray Him.** Whose heart? Only two answers are possible grammatically; (1) the heart of Judas, (2) the devil's own heart. The latter is incredible, if only for the reason that S. John himself has shewn that the devil had long been at work with Judas. The meaning is that of the received reading, but more awkwardly expressed. 'To betray' is literally S. John's favourite form 'in order that he should betray.' The traitor's name is given in full for greater solemnity, and in the true text comes last for emphasis. Note the position of Iscariot, confirming the view (see on vi. 71) that the word is a local epithet rather than a proper name.

3. *Jesus knowing*] The Greek is the same as of 'when Jesus knew' in *v.* 1, and may have either of the two meanings given there. Here also 'because He knew' is better.

given all things] Comp. Eph. i. 22; Phil. ii. 9—11.

and went to God] Better, *and* **is going** *to God*.

4. *He riseth from supper*, &c.] Or, *from* **the** *supper:* the article perhaps marks the supper as no ordinary one. "This is the realism of history indeed...... The carefulness with which here, as in the account of the cleansing of the temple, the successive stages in the action are described, proclaim the eye-witness." S. p. 216. One is unwilling to surrender the view that this symbolical act was intended among other purposes to be a tacit rebuke to the disciples for the 'strife among them, which of them should be accounted the greatest' (Luke xxii. 24); and certainly 'I am among you as he that serveth' (*v.* 27) seems to point directly to this act. This view seems all the more probable when we remember that a similar dispute was rebuked in a similar way, viz. by symbolical action (Luke ix. 46—48). The dispute may have arisen about their places at the table. That S. Luke places the strife *after* the supper is not fatal to this view ; *he gives no note of time*, and the strife is singularly out of place there, immediately after their Master's self-humiliation and in the midst of the last farewells. We may therefore believe, in spite of S. Luke's arrangement, that the strife preceded the supper. "One thing is clear, that S. John, if he had read S. Luke's Gospel at this point, has not copied or followed it. He proceeds with the same peculiar independence which we have noticed in him all through." S. p. 215.

his garments] Or, *His* **upper garments**, which would impede His movements.

5. *into a bason*] Better, *into* **the** *bason*, which stood there for such purposes, the large copper bason commonly found in oriental houses.

began to wash the disciples' feet, and to wipe *them* with the towel wherewith he was girded. Then cometh he to Simon 6 Peter: and *Peter* saith unto him, Lord, dost thou wash my feet? Jesus answered and said unto him, What I do thou 7 knowest not now; but thou shalt know hereafter. Peter 8 saith unto him, Thou shalt never wash my feet. Jesus answered him, If I wash thee not, thou hast no part with

began to wash] Began is not a mere amplification as in the other Gospels (Matt. xi. 7, xxvi. 22, 37, 74; Mark iv. 1, vi. 2, 7, 34, 55; Luke vii. 15, 24, 38, 49; &c. &c.), and in the Acts (i. 1, ii. 4, xviii, 26, &c.). The word occurs nowhere else in S. John, and here is no mere periphrasis for 'washed.' He began to wash, but was interrupted by the incident with S. Peter. With whom He began is not mentioned: from very early times some have conjectured Judas.

Contrast the mad insolence of Caligula—*quosdam summis honoribus functos...ad pedes stare succinctos linteo passus est.* Suet. *Calig.* xxvi. *Linteum* in a Greek form is the very word here used for towel.

6. *Then cometh he*] Better, *He cometh* **therefore**, i.e. in consequence of having begun to wash the feet of each in turn. The natural impression is that S. Peter's turn at any rate did not come first. But if it did, this is not much in favour of the primacy of S. Peter, which can be proved from other passages, still less of a supremacy, which cannot be proved at all.

dost thou wash my feet?] There is a strong emphasis on 'Thou.' Comp. 'Comest *Thou* to me?' (Matt. iii. 14.)

7. *What I do thou knowest not*] Here both pronouns are emphatic and are opposed. Peter's question implied that he knew, while Christ did not know, what He was doing: Christ tells him that the very reverse of this is the fact. On 'now' see note on xvi. 31.

hereafter] Literally, *after these things* (iii. 22, v. 1, 14, vi. 1, vii. 1, xix. 38). 'Hereafter' conveys a wrong impression, as if it referred to the remote future. Had this been intended the words used for 'now' and 'afterwards' in *v*. 36 would probably have been employed here. The reference probably is to the explanation of this symbolical action given in *vv.* 12—17. This seems clear from the opening words (*v.* 12), '*Know* ye what I have done to you?'—all the more so, because it is the same word for 'know' as here for 'thou shalt know' (*ginōskein*); whereas the Greek for 'thou knowest' in this verse is a different and more general word (*oidas*): 'what *I* am doing, *thou* knowest not just now, but thou shalt recognise presently.' See notes on vii. 26 and viii. 55.

8. *Thou shalt never wash my feet*] The negative is the strongest form possible; 'thou shalt certainly not wash my feet for ever.' See on viii. 51, and comp. Matt. xvi. 22.

no part with me] The Greek is the same as in Matt. xxiv. 51 and Luke xii. 46. The expression is of Hebrew origin; comp. Deut. x. 9, xii. 12, xiv. 27. To reject Christ's self-humiliating love, because it humiliates Him (a well-meaning but false principle), is to cut oneself off

9 me. Simon Peter saith unto him, Lord, not my feet only,
10 but also *my* hands and *my* head. Jesus saith to him, He
that is washed needeth not save to wash *his* feet, but is
11 clean every whit : and ye are clean, but not all. For he
knew who should betray him; therefore said he, Ye are not
all clean.
12 So after he had washed their feet, and had taken his
garments, and was set down again, he said unto them,

from Him. It requires much more humility to accept a benefit which
is a serious loss to the giver than one which costs him nothing. In
this also the surrender of self is necessary.

9. *not my feet only*] The impetuosity which is so marked a characteristic of S. Peter in the first three Gospels (comp. especially Luke v. 8 and Matt. xvi. 22), comes out very strongly in his three utterances here. It is incredible that this should be deliberate invention; and if not, the independent authority of this narrative is manifest.

10. *He that is washed*] Rather, *He that is* bathed (comp. Heb. x. 22 and 2 Pet. ii. 22). In the Greek we have quite a different word from the one rendered 'wash' elsewhere in these verses: the latter means to wash part of the body, this to bathe the whole person. A man who has bathed does not need to bathe again when he reaches home, but only to wash the dust off his feet : then he is wholly clean. So also in the spiritual life, a man whose moral nature has once been thoroughly purified need not think that this has been all undone if in the walk through life he contracts some stains: these must be washed away, and then he is once more wholly clean. Peter, conscious of his own imperfections, in Luke v. 8, and possibly here, rushes to the conclusion that he is utterly unclean. But his meaning here perhaps rather is; 'If having part in Thee depends on being washed by Thee, wash all Thou canst.' S. Peter excellently illustrates Christ's saying. His love for his Master proves that he had bathed; his boastfulness (*v.* 37), his attack on Malchus (xviii. 10), his denials (25, 27) his dissimulation at Antioch (Gal. ii.), all shew how often he had need to wash his feet.

but not all] This is the second indication of the presence of a traitor among them (comp. vi. 70). Apparently it did not attract much attention: each, conscious of his own faults, thought the remark only too true. The disclosure is made gradually but rapidly now (*vv.* 18, 21, 26).

11. *who should betray him*] Or, *him that was betraying Him*. The Greek construction is exactly equivalent to that of 'He that should come' (Matt. xi. 3; Luke vii. 19); in both cases it is the present participle with the definite article—'the betraying one,' 'the coming one.'

therefore] Or, **for this cause**: see on xii. 39.

12. *was set down*] The Greek verb occurs frequently in the Gospels (and nowhere else in N.T.) of reclining at meals. It always implies a *change* of position (see on *v.* 25, and comp. vi. 10, xxi. 20; Matt. xv. 35; Mark vi. 40; Luke xi. 37).

Know ye what I have done to you? Ye call me Master 13
and Lord: and ye say well; for *so* I am. If I then, *your* 14
Lord and Master, have washed your feet; ye also ought to
wash one another's feet. For I have given you an example, 15
that ye should do as I have done to you. Verily, verily, I 16
say unto you, The servant is not greater than his lord;
neither he that is sent greater than he that sent him. If ye 17
know these *things*, happy are ye if ye do them. I speak 18

Know ye] 'Do ye recognise the meaning of it?' (see on *v.* 7). The question directs their attention to the explanation to be given.

13. *Master and Lord*] Or, **The** *Master* (*Teacher*) **and the** *Lord*. These are the ordinary titles of respect paid to a Rabbi: 'Lord' is the correlative of 'servant,' so that 'Master' might be a synonym for that also; but the disciples would no doubt use the word with deeper meaning as their knowledge of their Master increased. In the next verse the order of the titles is reversed, to give emphasis to the one with this deeper meaning.

14. *your Lord and Master, have washed*] Rather, **the** *Lord and* **the** *Master,* **washed.** For the construction comp. xv. 20 and xviii. 23.

ye also ought to wash one another's feet] The custom of 'the feet-washing' on Maundy Thursday in literal fulfilment of this typical commandment is not older than the fourth century. The Lord High Almoner washed the feet of the recipients of the royal 'maundy' as late as 1731. James II. was the last English sovereign who went through the ceremony. In 1 Tim. v. 10 'washing the saints' feet' is perhaps given rather as a *type* of devoted charity than as a definite act to be required.

15. *as I have done to you*] Not, '*what* I have done to you,' but '**even as** I have done:' this is the spirit in which to act—self-sacrificing humility—whether or no it be exhibited precisely in this way. Mutual service, and especially mutual cleansing, is the obligation of Christ's disciples. Comp. James v. 16.

16. *The servant is not greater than his lord*] This saying occurs four times in the Gospels, each time in a different connexion: (1) to shew that the disciples must expect no better treatment than their Master (Matt. x. 24); (2) to impress the Apostles with their responsibilities as teachers, for their disciples will be as they are (Luke vi. 40); (3) here; (4) with the same purpose as in Matt. x. 24, but on another occasion (xv. 20). We infer that it was one of Christ's frequent sayings: it is introduced here with the double 'verily' as of special importance (i. 51).

he that is sent] An Apostle (*apostolos*).

17. *happy are ye if ye do them*] Better, **blessed** *are ye*, &c. It is the same Greek word as is used in xx. 29 and in the Beatitudes both in S. Matthew and in S. Luke. Comp. Luke xi. 28, xii. 43; Matt. vii 21; Rev. i. 3.

not of you all: I know whom I have chosen: but that the scripture may be fulfilled, He that eateth bread with me hath lift up his heel against me. Now I tell you before it come, that, when it is come to pass, ye may

18. *I speak not of you all*] There is one who knows these things, and does not do them, and is the very reverse of blessed.

I know whom I have chosen] The first 'I' is emphatic: '*I* know the character of the Twelve whom I chose; the treachery of one has been foretold; it is no surprise to Me.' Comp. vi. 70.

but that] This elliptical use of 'but that' (='but this was done in order that') is frequent in S. John: i. 8, ix. 3, xiv. 31, xv. 25; 1 John ii. 19. Here another way of filling up the ellipsis is possible; 'But I chose them in order that.'

may be fulfilled] See on xii. 38. The quotation is taken, but with freedom, from the Hebrew of Ps. xli. 9; for 'lifted up his heel' both the Hebrew and the LXX. have 'magnified his heel.' (See on vi. 45.) The metaphor here is of one raising his foot before kicking, but the blow is not yet given. This was the attitude of Judas at this moment. It has been remarked that Christ omits the words 'Mine own familiar friend whom I trusted:' He had not trusted Judas, and had not been deceived, as the Psalmist had been: 'He knew what was in man' (ii. 25).

He that eateth bread with me] Or, *He that eateth the bread with Me.* The more probable reading gives, **My bread** for 'the bread with Me.' The variations from the LXX. are remarkable. (1) The word for 'eat' is changed from the common verb (ἐσθίω) used in Ps. xli. 10 to the much less common verb (τρώγω) used of eating Christ's Flesh and the Bread from Heaven (vi. 54, 56, 57, 58, where see notes), and nowhere else in the N. T., excepting Matt. xxiv. 38. (2) 'Bread' or 'loaves' (ἄρτους) has been altered to '*the* bread' (τὸν ἄρτον). (3) 'My' has possibly been strengthened to 'with Me:' to eat bread with a man is more than to eat his bread, which a servant might do. These changes can scarcely be accidental, and seem to point to the fact that the treachery of Judas in violating the bond of hospitality, so universally held sacred in the East, was aggravated by his having partaken of the Eucharist. That Judas did partake of the Eucharist seems to follow from Luke xxii. 19—21, but the point is one about which there is much controversy.

S. John omits the institution of the Eucharist for the same reason that he omits so much,—because it was so well known to every instructed Christian; and for such he writes.

19. *Now*] Better, as the margin, **From henceforth** (comp. i. 51, xiv. 7; Rev. xiv. 13). Hitherto Christ had been reserved about the presence of a traitor; to point him out would have been to make him desperate and deprive him of a chance of recovery. But every good influence has failed, even the Eucharist and the washing of his feet; and *from this time onward* Christ tells the other Apostles.

before it come] Add **to pass**, as in the next clause. Comp. xiv. 29.

believe that I am *he*. Verily, verily, I say unto you, He 20 that receiveth whomsoever I send receiveth me; and he that receiveth me receiveth him that sent me.

21—30. *The self-excommunication of the traitor.*

When Jesus had thus said, he was troubled in spirit, and 21 testified, and said, Verily, verily, I say unto you, that one of you shall betray me. Then the disciples looked one on 22 another, doubting of whom he spake. Now there was 23 leaning on Jesus' bosom one of his disciples, whom Jesus

The success of such treachery might have shaken their faith had it taken them unawares: by foretelling it He turns it into an aid to faith.

may believe that I am he] See on viii. 24, 28, 58.

20. *He that receiveth*, &c.] The connexion of this saying, solemnly introduced with the double 'verily,' with what precedes is not easy to determine. The saying is one with which Christ had sent forth the Apostles in the first instance (Matt. x. 40). It is recalled at the moment when one of them is being denounced for treachery. It was natural that such an end to such a mission should send Christ's thoughts back to the beginning of it. Moreover He would warn them all from supposing that such a catastrophe either cancelled the mission or proved it to be worthless from the first. Of every one of them, even of Judas himself, the saying still held good, 'he that receiveth *whomsoever* I send, receiveth Me.' The unworthiness of the minister cannot annul the commission.

21—30. THE SELF-EXCOMMUNICATION OF THE TRAITOR.

21. *he was troubled in spirit*] Once more the reality of Christ's human nature is brought before us (comp. xi. 33, 35, 38, xii. 27); but quite incidentally and without special point. It is the artless story of one who tells what he saw because he saw it and remembers it. The life-like details which follow are almost irresistible evidences of truthfulness.

22. *looked one on another*] 'Began to enquire among themselves' (Luke xxii. 23). The other two Evangelists say that all began to say to Him 'Is it I?' They neither doubt the statement, nor ask 'Is it *he?*' Each thinks it is as credible of himself as of any of the others. Judas asks, either to dissemble, or to see whether he really was known (Matt. xxvi. 25).

23. *there was leaning on Jesus' bosom*] Better, *there was* **reclining on Jesus' lap**. It is important to mark the distinction between this and the words rendered 'lying on Jesus' breast' in *v.* 25. The Jews had adopted the Persian, Greek, and Roman custom of reclining at meals, and had long since exchanged the original practice of standing at the Passover first for sitting and then for reclining. They reclined on the left arm and ate with the right. This is the posture of the beloved

24 loved. Simon Peter therefore beckoned to him, that *he*
25 should ask who it should be of whom he spake. He then
lying on Jesus' breast saith unto him, Lord, who is it?
26 Jesus answered, He it is, to whom I shall give a sop, when
I have dipped *it*. And when he had dipped the sop, he

disciple indicated here, which continued throughout the meal: in *v.* 25
we have a momentary change of posture.

whom Jesus loved] This explains how S. John came to be nearest
(see Introduction II. iii. 3 *b*), and "out of the recollection of that sacred,
never-to-be-forgotten moment, there breaks from him for the *first* time
this nameless, yet so expressive designation of himself" (Meyer). Comp.
xix. 26, xxi. 7, 20; not xx. 2. S. John was on our Lord's right. Who
was next to Him on the left? Some think Judas, who must have
been very close for Christ to answer him without the others hearing.

24. *that he should ask...spake*] The better reading gives, **and saith
to him, say who it is of whom He speaketh.** S. Peter thinks that the
beloved disciple is sure to know. The received reading, besides being
wanting in authority, contains an optative mood, which S. John never
uses.

25. *lying on Jesus' breast*] Our version does well in using different
words from those used in *v.* 23, but the distinction used is inadequate.
Moreover the same preposition, 'on,' is used in both cases; in the Greek
the prepositions differ also. In *v.* 23 we have the permanent posture;
here a change, the same verb being used as in *v.* 12 (see note). The
meaning is **leaning back on to Jesus' breast.** Comp xxi. 20, where
our translators give a similarly inadequate rendering. "This is among
the most striking of those vivid descriptive traits which distinguish the
narrative of the Fourth Gospel generally, and which are especially remarkable in these last scenes of Jesus' life, where the beloved disciple
was himself an eye-witness and an actor. It is therefore to be regretted
that these fine touches of the picture should be blurred in our English
Bibles." Lightfoot, *On Revision*, p. 73.

Some good MSS. insert 'thus' before 'on to Jesus' breast' (comp. iv.
6).

26. *to whom I shall give a sop, when I have dipped it*] The text
here is uncertain, but there is no doubt as to the meaning. Perhaps the
better reading is, **for whom I shall dip the morsel and give it to him.**
Copyists have possibly tried to correct the awkwardness of 'for
whom' and 'to him.' In any case 'sop' or 'morsel' must have the
article. The Greek word is derived from 'rub' or 'break,' and means
'a piece broken off:' it is still the common word in Greece for 'bread.'
To give such a morsel at a meal was an ordinary mark of goodwill,
somewhat analogous to taking wine with a person in modern times.
Christ, therefore, as a forlorn hope, gives the traitor one more mark of
affection before dismissing him. It is the last such mark: 'Friend,
wherefore art thou come?' (Matt. xxvi. 50) should rather be 'Comrade,
(do that) for which thou art come,' and is a sorrowful rebuke rather than

gave *it* to Judas Iscariot, *the son* of Simon. And after the 27
sop Satan entered into him. Then said Jesus unto him,
That thou doest, do quickly. Now no *man* at the table 28
knew for what intent he spake this unto him. For some *of* 29
them thought, because Judas had the bag, that Jesus had
said unto him, Buy *those things* that we have need of against
the feast; or that he should give something to the poor.
He then having received the sop went immediately out: 30
and it was night.

an affectionate greeting. Whether the morsel was a piece of the un-
leavened bread dipped in the broth of bitter herbs depends upon whether
this supper is regarded as the Paschal meal or not.
   And when, &c.] The true reading is, **Therefore,** *when He had dipped
the* **morsel He taketh and giveth it.** The name of Judas is once more
given with solemn fulness as in vi. 71, *Judas the son of* **Simon Iscariot.**
Comp. *v.* 2.
   27. *Satan entered into him*] Literally, **at that moment** *Satan
entered into him.* At first Satan made suggestions to him (*v.* 2) and
Judas listened to them; now Satan takes full possession of him. Desire
had conceived and brought forth sin, and the sin full grown had en-
gendered death (James i. 15). Satan is mentioned here only in S.
John.
   Then said] Once more we must substitute **therefore** for 'then.'
Jesus knew that Satan had claimed his own, and *therefore* bad him do
his work.
   do quickly] Literally, *do more quickly;* carry it out at once, even
sooner than has been planned. Now that the winning back of Judas
has become hopeless, delay was worse than useless: it merely kept Him
from His hour of victory. Comp. Matt. xxiii. 32.
   28. *no man...knew*] Even S. John, who now knew that Judas was the
traitor, did not know that he would act at once, and that it was to this
Jesus alluded.
   29. *For some of them*] Shewing that they could not have understood.
   had the bag] See on xii. 6.
   against the feast] This agrees with *v.* 1, that this meal precedes the
Passover.
   to the poor] Comp. xii. 5; Neh. viii. 10, 12; Gal. ii. 10.
   30. *He then having received the sop*] Better, *He* **therefore** *having
received the* **morsel.** The pronoun here and in *v.* 27 (*ekeinos*) indicates
that Judas is an alien. Comp. vii. 11, ix. 12, 28. The last two verses
are a parenthetical remark of the Evangelist; he now returns to the
narrative, repeating with solemnity the incident which formed the last
crisis in the career of Judas.
   went immediately out] This is no evidence as to the meal not being
a Paschal one. The rule that 'none should go out at the door of his

XIII. 31—XV. 27. *Christ's Love in keeping His own.*

31, 32 Therefore, when he was gone out, Jesus said, Now is the Son of man glorified, and God is glorified in him. If God

house until the morning' (Exod. xii. 22) had, like standing at the Passover, long since been abrogated. "When Satan entered into him, he went out from the presence of Christ, as Cain went out from the presence of the Lord."

and it was night] The tragic brevity of this has often been remarked, and will never cease to lay hold of the imagination. It can scarcely be meant merely to tell us that at the time when Judas went out night had begun. In the Gospel in which the Messiah so often appears as the Light of the World (i. 4—9, iii. 19—21, viii. 12, ix. 5, xii. 35, 36, 46), and in which darkness almost invariably means moral darkness (i. 5, viii. 12, xii. 35, 46) a use peculiar to S. John (1 John i. 5, ii. 8, 9, 11),—we shall hardly be wrong in understanding also that Judas went forth from the Light of the World into the night in which a man cannot but stumble 'because there is no light in him' (xi. 10). Thus also Christ Himself said some two hours later, 'This is your hour, and the power of darkness' (Luke xxii. 53). For other remarks of telling brevity and abruptness comp. 'Jesus wept' (xi. 35); 'He saith to them, I am He' (xviii. 5); 'Now Barabbas was a robber' (xviii. 40).

These remarks shew the impropriety of joining this sentence to the next verse; 'and it was night, therefore, when he had gone out;' a combination which is clumsy in itself and quite spoils the effect.

XIII. 31—XV. 27. CHRIST'S LOVE IN KEEPING HIS OWN.

31—35. Jesus, freed from the oppressive presence of the traitor, bursts out into a declaration that the glorification of the Son of Man has begun. Judas is already beginning that series of events which will end in sending Him away from them to the Father; therefore they must continue on earth the kingdom which He has begun—the reign of Love.

This section forms the first portion of those parting words of heavenly meaning which were spoken to the faithful eleven in the last moments before His Passion. At first the discourse takes the form of dialogue, which lasts almost to the end of chap. xiv. Then they rise from the table, and the words of Christ become more sustained, while the disciples remain silent with the exception of xvi. 17, 18, 29, 30. Then follows Christ's prayer, after which they go forth to the garden of Gethsemane (xviii. 1).

31. *Therefore, when he was gone out*] Indicating that the presence of Judas had acted as a constraint, but also that he had gone of his own will: there was no casting out of the faithless disciple (ix. 34).

Now] With solemn exultation: the beginning of the end has come.

the Son of man] See on i. 51.

glorified] In finishing the work which the Father gave Him to do (xvii. 4); and thus God is glorified in Him.

be glorified in him, God shall also glorify him in himself, and shall straightway glorify him. Little children, yet a 33 little while I am with you. Ye shall seek me: and as I said unto the Jews, Whither I go, ye cannot come; so now I say to you. A new commandment I give unto you, That 34 ye love one another; as I have loved you, that ye also love

32. *If God be glorified in him*] These words are omitted in the best MSS., and though they might easily be left out accidentally owing to the repetition, yet they spoil the balance and rhythm of the clauses.

God shall also glorify him] Better, **And** *God shall glorify Him*. This refers to the heavenly glory which He had with the Father before the world was. Hence the future tense: the glory of completing the work of redemption has already begun; that of departing to the Father as the Son of Man and returning to the Father as the Son of God will straightway follow.

in himself] i.e. in God: as God is glorified in the Messianic work of the Son, so the Son shall be glorified in the eternal blessedness of the Father. Comp. xvii. 4, 5; Phil. ii. 9.—Between this verse and the next some would insert the institution of the Eucharist.

33. *Little children*] Nowhere else in the Gospels does Christ use this expression of tender affection (*teknia*), which springs from the thought of His orphaned disciples. S. John appears never to have forgotten it. It occurs frequently in his First Epistle (ii. 1, 12, 28, iii. 7, 18, iv. 4, v. 21), and perhaps nowhere else in the N.T. In Gal. iv. 19 the reading is doubtful. 'Children' in xxi. 5 is a different word (*paidia*).

a little while] See on vii. 33, 34, viii. 21.

Ye shall seek me] Christ does not add, as He did to the Jews, 'and shall not find Me,' still less, 'ye shall die in your sin.' Rather, 'ye shall seek Me: and though ye cannot come whither I go, yet ye shall find Me by continuing to be My disciples and loving one another.' The expression 'the Jews' is rare in Christ's discourses; comp. iv. 22, xviii. 20, 36.

34. *A new commandment*] The commandment to love was not new, for 'thou shalt love thy neighbour as thyself' (Lev. xix. 18) was part of the Mosaic Law. But the motive is new; to love our neighbour because Christ has loved us. We have only to read the 'most excellent way' of love set forth in 1 Cor. xiii., and compare it with the measured benevolence of the Pentateuch, to see how new the commandment had become by having this motive added. There are two words for 'new' in Greek; one looks forward, 'young,' as opposed to 'aged;' the other looks back, 'fresh,' as opposed to 'worn out.' It is the latter that is used here and in xix. 41. Both are used in Matt. ix. 17, but our version ignores the difference—'They put *new* wine into *fresh* wineskins.' The phrase 'to give a commandment' is peculiar to S. John; comp. xii. 49; 1 John iii. 23.

as I have loved you] These words are rightly placed in the second

35 one another. By this shall all *men* know that ye are my disciples, if ye have love one to another.

36 Simon Peter said unto him, Lord, whither goest thou? Jesus answered him, Whither I go, thou canst not follow 37 me now; but thou shalt follow me afterwards. Peter said unto him, Lord, why cannot I follow thee now? I will lay 38 down my life for thy sake. Jesus answered him, Wilt thou lay down thy life for my sake? Verily, verily, I say unto

half of the verse. They do not mean 'love one another *in the same way* as I have loved you;' but they give the reason for the fresh commandment—'**even as** I have loved you.' S. John states the same principle in the First Epistle (iv. 11) 'If God so loved us, we ought also to love one another.' Comp. xv. 13.

35. *By this shall all men know that ye are my disciples*] This is the true 'Note of the Church;' not miracles, not formularies, not numbers, but *love*. "The working of such love puts a brand upon us; for see, say the heathen, how they love another," Tertullian, *Apol.* xxxix. Comp. 1 John iii. 10, 14. 'My disciples' is literally, *disciples to Me*.

36. *Lord, whither goest thou?*] The affectionate Apostle is absorbed by the declaration 'Whither I go, ye cannot come,' and he lets all the rest pass. His Master is going away out of his reach; he must know the meaning of that.

thou shalt follow me afterwards] Alluding probably not merely to the Apostle's death, but also to the manner of it: comp. xxi. 18, 19. But his hour has not yet come; he has a great mission to fulfil first (Matt. xvi. 18). The beautiful story of the *Domine, quo vadis?* should be remembered in connexion with this verse. See Introduction to the Epistles of S. Peter, p. 56.

37. *I will lay down my life*] St Peter seems to see that Christ's going away means death. With his usual impulsiveness (see on *v.* 9) he declares that he is ready to follow at once even thither. He mistakes strong feeling for moral strength. On the phrase 'lay down my life' see last note on x. 11.

38. *I say unto thee*] In the parallel passage in S. Luke (xxii. 34) Christ for the first and only time addresses the Apostle by the name which He had given him,—'I tell thee, *Peter;*' as if He would remind him that the rock-like strength of character was not his own to boast of, but must be found in humble reliance on the Giver.

S. Luke agrees with S. John in placing the prediction of the triple denial in the supper-room: St Matt. (xxvi. 30—35) and S. Mark (xiv. 26—30) place it on the way from the room to Gethsemane. It is possible but not probable that the prediction was repeated; though some would even make three predictions recorded by (1) S. Luke, (2) S. John, (3) S. Matt. and S. Mark. See introductory note to Chapter xii. and Appendix B.

thee, *The* cock shall not crow, till thou hast denied me thrice.

CHAP. XIV. *Christ's love in keeping His own (continued).*

Let not your heart be troubled: ye believe in God, 14

thrice] All four accounts agree in this. S. Mark adds two details: (1) that the cock should crow *twice*, (2) that the prediction so far from checking S. Peter made him speak only the more vehemently, a particular which S. Peter's Gospel more naturally contains than the other three. S. Matthew and S. Mark both add that all the disciples joined in S. Peter's protestations.

It has been objected that fowls were not allowed in the Holy City. The statement is wanting in authority, and of course the Romans would pay no attention to any such rule, even if it existed among the Jews.

CHAP. XIV.

" We come now to the last great discourse (xiv.—xvii.), which constitutes a striking and peculiar element in the Fourth Gospel.........we cannot but recognise a change from the compact lucid addresses and exposition of the Synoptists......This appears not so much in single verses as when we look at the discourse as a whole. In all the Synoptic Gospels, imperfectly as they are put together, there is not a single discourse that could be called involved in structure, and yet I do not see how it is possible to refuse this epithet to the discourse before us as given by S. John. The different subjects are not kept apart, but are continually crossing and entangling one another. The later subjects are anticipated in the course of the earlier; the earlier return in the later." Comp. the *spiral movement* noticed in the Prologue, i. 18.

"For instance, the description of the functions of the Paraclete is broken up......into five fragments (xiv. 16, 17; 25, 26; xv. 26; xvi. 8— 15; 23—25)...... The relation of the Church and the world is intersected just in the same way (xiv. 22—24, xv. 18—25, xvi. 1—3), besides scattered references in single verses...... We may consider the discourse perhaps under these heads: (1) the departure and the return, (2) the Paraclete, (3) the vine and its branches, (4) the disciples and the world." S. pp. 221—232. On the discourses in this Gospel generally see the introductory note to chapter iii.

CHAP. XIV. CHRIST'S LOVE IN KEEPING HIS OWN (continued).

1. *Let not your heart be troubled*] There had been much to cause anxiety and alarm; the denouncing of the traitor, the declaration of Christ's approaching departure, the prediction of S. Peter's denial. The last as being nearest might seem to be specially indicated; but what follows shews that 'let not your heart be troubled' refers primarily to 'whither I go, ye cannot come' (xiii. 33).

ye believe in God, believe also] The Greek for 'ye believe' and 'believe' is the same, and there is nothing to indicate that one is indicative

2 believe also in me. In my Father's house are many mansions: if *it were* not *so*, I would have told you. I go to 3 prepare a place for you. And if I go and prepare a place for you, I will come again, and receive you unto myself; 4 that where I am, *there* ye may be also. And whither I go

and the other imperative. Both may be indicative; but probably both are imperative: *believe in God*, and believe *in Me;* or perhaps, *trust in God, and trust in Me*. It implies the belief which moves towards and reposes on its object (see last note on i. 12). In any case a genuine belief in God leads to a belief in His Son.

2. *In my Father's house*] Heaven. Comp. 'The Lord's throne is in heaven,' Ps. xi. 4; 'Our Father, Which art in heaven' (Matt. vi. 9), &c.

are many mansions] Nothing is said about mansions differing in dignity and beauty. There may be degrees of happiness hereafter, but such are neither expressed nor implied here. What *is* said is that there are '*many* mansions;' there is room enough for all. The word for 'mansions,' common in classical Greek, occurs in the N. T. only here and *v*. 23. It is a substantive from the verb of which S. John is so fond, 'to abide, dwell, remain' (see note on i. 33), which occurs *vv*. 10, 16, 17, 25, and twelve times in the next chapter. This substantive, therefore, means 'an abode, dwelling, place to remain in.' 'Mansion,' Scotch 'manse,' and French 'maison,' are all from the Latin form of the same root.

if it were not so, I would have told you] The Greek may have more than one meaning, but our version is best. Christ appeals to His fairness: would He have invited them to a place in which there was not room for all? Others connect this with the next verse; 'should I have said to you, I go to prepare a place for you?' or, 'I would have said to you, I go, &c.' The latter cannot be right. Christ had already said, and says again, that He is going to shew them the way and to prepare for them (xiii. 36, xiv. 3).

I go to prepare] We must insert 'for' on overwhelming authority; '*for I go to prepare.*' This proves that there will be room for all.

3. *And if I go*] The 'if' does not here imply doubt any more than 'when' would have done: but we have 'if' and not 'when' because it is the *result* of the departure and not the date of it that is emphasized (see on xii. 32).

I will come again, and receive] Literally, *I am coming again and I will receive* (see on i. 11 and xix. 16). There is no doubt about the meaning of the going away; but the coming again may have various meanings, and apparently not always the same one throughout this discourse; either the Resurrection, or the gift of the Paraclete, or the death of individuals, or the presence of Christ in his Church, or the Second Advent at the last day. The last seems to be the meaning here (comp. vi. 39, 40).

vv. 5—7.] S. JOHN, XIV. 275

ye know, and the way ye know. Thomas saith unto him, 5
Lord, we know not whither thou goest; and how can we
know the way? Jesus saith unto him, I am the way, the 6
truth, and the life: no *man* cometh unto the Father, but by
me. If ye had known me, ye should have known my 7

4. *whither I go ye know, and the way ye know*] The true text seems once more to have been altered to avoid awkwardness of expression (see on xiii. 26). Here we should read, *Whither* **I go, ye know the way.** This is half a rebuke, implying that they ought to know more than they did know: they had heard but had not heeded (x. 7, 9, xi. 25). Thus we say 'you know, you see,' meaning 'you might know, you might see, if you would but take the trouble.'

5. *Thomas*] Nothing is to be inferred from the omission of 'Didymus' here (comp. xi. 16, xx. 24, xxi. 2). For his character see on xi. 16. His question here has a melancholy tone combined with some dulness of apprehension. But there is honesty of purpose in it. He owns his ignorance and asks for explanation. This great home with many abodes, is it the royal city of the conquering Messiah, who is to restore the kingdom to Israel (see on Acts i. 6); and will not that be Jerusalem? How then can He go away?

and how can we know] The true reading is, **How know we.**

6. *I am the way*] The pronoun is emphatic; I and no other: *Ego sum Via, Veritas, Vita*. S. Thomas had wished rather to know about the goal; Christ shews that for him, and therefore for us, it is more important to know the way. Hence the order; although Christ is the Truth and the Life before He is the Way. The Word is the Truth and the Life from all eternity with the Father: He becomes the Way for us by taking our nature. He is the Way to the many abodes in His Father's home, the Way to the Father Himself; and that by His doctrine and example, by His Death and Resurrection. In harmony with this passage 'the Way' soon became a recognised name for Christianity; Acts ix. 2, xix. 9, 23, xxii. 4, xxiv. 22 (comp. xxiv. 14; 2 Pet. ii. 2). But this is obscured in our version by the common inaccuracy '*this* way' or '*that* way' for '*the* Way.' (See on i. 21, 25, vi. 48.)

the truth] Better, **and** *the Truth*, being from all eternity in the form of God, Who cannot lie (Phil. ii. 6; Heb. vi. 18), and being the representative on earth of a Sender Who is true (viii. 26). To know the Truth is also to know the Way to God, Who must be approached and worshipped in truth (iv. 23). Comp. Heb. xi. 6; 1 John v. 20.

and the life] Comp. xi. 25. He is the Life, being one with the living Father and being sent by Him (vi. 57, x. 30). See on i. 4, vi. 50, 51, and comp. 1 John v. 12; Gal. ii. 20. Here again to know the Life is to know the Way to God.

no man cometh unto the Father, but by me] Christ continues to insist that the Way is of the first importance to know. 'Through Him we have access unto the Father' (Eph. ii. 18). Comp. Hebr. x. 19—22; 1 Pet. iii. 18.

7. *If ye had known me*] In the better MSS. we have here again

18—2

Father also: and from henceforth ye know him, and have
8 seen him. Philip saith unto him, Lord, shew us the Father,
9 and it sufficeth us. Jesus saith unto him, Have I been so
long time with you, and *yet* hast thou not known me, Philip?

two different words for 'know' (see on vii. 26, viii. 55, xiii. 7), and the emphasis in the first clause is on 'known' in the second on 'Father.' Beware of the common mistake of putting an emphasis on 'Me.' The meaning is: 'If ye had *recognised* Me, ye would have known My *Father* also.' The veil of Jewish prejudice was still on their hearts, hiding from them the true meaning both of Messianic prophecy and of the Messiah's acts.

from henceforth] The same expression as is mistranslated 'now' in xiii. 19: it is to be understood literally, not proleptically.

ye know him] Or, *recognise Him*. From this time onwards, after the plain declaration of Himself in *v*. 6, they begin to recognise the Father in Him. Philip's request leads to a fuller statement of *v*. 6.

8. *Philip*] For the fourth and last time S. Philip appears in this Gospel (see notes on i. 44—49, vi. 5—7, xii. 22). Thrice he is mentioned in close connexion with S. Andrew, who may have brought about his being found by Christ; twice he follows in the footsteps of S. Andrew in bringing others to Christ, and on both occasions it is specially to *see* Him that they are brought; 'Come and *see*' (i. 45); 'We would *see* Jesus' (xii. 21). Like S. Thomas he has a fondness for the practical test of personal experience; he would see for himself, and have others also see for themselves. His way of stating the difficulty about the 5000 (vi. 7) is quite in harmony with this practical turn of mind. Like S. Thomas also he seems to have been somewhat slow of apprehension, and at the same time perfectly honest in expressing the cravings which he felt. No fear of exposing himself keeps either Apostle back.

Lord, shew us the Father] He is struck by Christ's last words, 'Ye have seen the Father,' and cannot find that they are true of himself. It is what he has been longing for in vain; it is the one thing wanting. He has heard the voice of the Father from Heaven, and it has awakened a hunger in his heart. Christ has been speaking of the Father's home with its many abodes to which He is going; and Philip longs to see for himself. And when Christ tells him that he *has* seen, he unreservedly opens his mind: 'Only make that saying good, and it is enough.' He sees nothing impossible in this. There were the theophanies, which had accompanied the giving of the Law by Moses. And a greater than Moses was here—"that Prophet whom Moses had foretold. He looked, like all the Jews of his time, to see the wonders of the old dispensation repeated. Hence his question." S. p. 225.

9. *so long time*] Philip had been called among the first (i. 43).

hast thou not known me] Or, *hast not recognised Me*, as in *v*. 7. The Gospels are full of evidence of how little the Apostles understood of the life which they were allowed to share: and the candour with which this is confessed confirms our trust in the narratives. Not until

he that hath seen me hath seen the Father; and how sayest thou *then*, Shew us the Father? Believest thou not that I am in the Father, and the Father in me? the words that I speak unto you, I speak not of myself: but the Father that dwelleth in me, he doeth the works. Believe me that I *am* in the Father, and the Father in me: or else believe me for the very works' sake. Verily, verily, I say unto you, He that believeth on me, the works that I do shall he do

Pentecost were their minds fully enlightened. Comp. x. 6, xii. 16; Matt. xv. 16, xvi. 8; Mark ix. 32; Luke ix. 45, xviii. 34, xxiv. 25; Acts i. 6; Hebr. v. 12. Christ's question is asked in sorrowful but affectionate surprise; hence the tender repetition of the name. Had S. Philip recognised Christ, he would have seen the revelation of God in Him, and would never have asked for a vision of God such as was granted to Moses. See notes on xii. 44, 45. There is no reference to the Transfiguration, of which S. Philip had not yet been told; Matt. xvii. 9.

and how sayest thou then] The 'and' is of doubtful authority; 'then' is an insertion of our translators.

10. *Believest thou not*] S. Philip's question seemed to imply that he did not believe this truth, although Christ had taught it publicly (x. 38). What follows is stated in an argumentative form. 'That the Father is in Me is proved by the fact that My words do not originate with Myself; and this is proved by the fact that My works do not originate with Myself, but are really His.' No proof is given of this last statement: Christ's works speak for themselves; they are manifestly Divine. It matters little whether we regard the argument as *à fortiori*, the works being stronger evidence than the words; or as inclusive, the works covering and containing the words. The latter seems to agree best with viii. 28. On the whole statement that Christ's words and works are not His own but the Father's, comp. v. 19, 30, viii. 26—29, xii. 44.

the Father that dwelleth in me, he doeth the works] The better reading gives us, *the Father* **abiding in Me doeth His works** (*in Me*). And thus the saying 'Ye have seen the Father' (*v.* 7) is justified: the Father is seen in the Son.

11. *Believe me*] The English obliterates the fact that Christ now turns from S. Philip and addresses all the eleven: 'believe' is plural not singular. 'You have been with Me long enough to believe what I say; but if not, at any rate believe what I do. My words need no credentials: but if credentials are demanded, there are My works.' He had said the same, somewhat more severely, to the Jews (x. 37, 38); and he repeats it much more severely in reference to the Jews (xv. 22, 24). Note the progress from 'believe Me' here to 'believe *on* Me' in the next verse; the one grows out of the other.

12. *Verily, verily*] See notes on i. 51.

the works that I do shall he do also] i.e. like Me, he shall do the

also; and greater *works* than these shall he do; because I
13 go unto my Father. And whatsoever ye shall ask in my
name, that will I do, that the Father may be glorified in the
14 Son. If ye shall ask any *thing* in my name, I will do *it*.
15
16 If ye love me, keep my commandments. And I will

works of the Father, the Father dwelling in Him through the Son
(*v*. 23).
and greater works than these] There is no reference to healing by
means of S. Peter's shadow (Acts v. 15) or of handkerchiefs that had
touched S. Paul (Acts xix. 12). Even from a human point of view no
miracle wrought by an Apostle is greater than the raising of Lazarus.
But from a spiritual point of view no such comparisons are admissible;
to Omnipotence all works are alike. These 'greater works' refer
rather to the results of Pentecost; the victory over Judaism and
Paganism, two powers which for the moment were victorious over
Christ (Luke xxii. 53). Christ's work was confined to Palestine and
had but small success; the Apostles went everywhere, and converted
thousands.
because I go unto my Father] For 'My' read 'the' with all the best
MSS. The reason is twofold: (1) He will have left the earth and be
unable to continue these works; therefore believers must continue them
for Him; (2) He will be in heaven ready to help both directly and by
intercession; therefore believers will be able to continue these works
and surpass them.
It is doubtful whether there should be a comma or a full stop at the
end of this verse. Perhaps our punctuation is better; but to make
the 'because' run on into the next verse makes little difference to the
sense.
13. *whatsoever ye shall ask in my name*] Comp. xv. 16, xvi. 23,
24, 26. Anything that can rightly be asked in His name will be
granted; there is no other limit. By 'in My name' is not of course
meant the mere using the formula 'through Jesus Christ.' Rather, it
means praying and working as Christ's representatives in the same
spirit in which Christ prayed and worked,—'Not My will, but Thine
be done.' Prayers for other ends than this are excluded; not that it is
said that they will not be granted, but there is no promise that they
will. Comp. 2 Cor. xii. 8, 9.
that the Father may be glorified] See notes on xi. 4, xii. 28, xiii. 31.
14. *I will do it*] 'I' is emphatic. In both verses the prayer is
regarded as addressed to the Father, but granted by the Son, who is
one with the Father. But the most ancient authorities here add 'Me;'
if ye shall ask Me anything. In xv. 16 and xvi. 23 with equal truth
the Father grants the prayer; but in xv. 16 the Greek may mean either
'He may give' or 'I may give.'
15. *If ye love me*] The connexion with what precedes is again not
quite clear. Some would see it in the condition 'in My name,' which
includes willing obedience to His commands. Perhaps it is rather to

pray the Father, and he shall give you another Comforter,

be referred to the opening and general drift of the chapter. 'Let not your heart be troubled at My going away. You will still be Mine, I shall still be yours, and we shall still be caring for one another. I go to prepare a place for you, you remain to continue and surpass My work on earth. And though you can no longer minister to Me in the flesh, you can prove your love for Me even more perfectly by keeping *My* commandments when I am gone.' 'My' is emphatic; not those of the Law but of the Gospel.

keep] The better reading is **ye will keep**. Only in these last discourses does Christ speak of His commandments: comp. *v.* 21, xiii. 34, xv. 10, 12. See on *v.* 27.

16. *And I will pray the Father*] 'I' is emphatic: 'you do your part on earth, and I will do mine in Heaven.' Our translators have once more rightly made a distinction but an inadequate one (see on xiii. 23, 25). The word for 'pray' here is different from that for 'ask' *vv.* 13, 14; but of the two the one rendered 'pray' (*erôtân*) is (so far as there is a distinction) the *less* suppliant. It is the word always used by S. John when Christ speaks of His prayers to the Father (xvi. 26, xvii. 9, 15, 20); never the word rendered 'ask' (*aitein*), which however Martha, less careful than the Evangelist, uses of Christ's prayers (xi. 22). But the distinction must not be pressed as if *aitein* were always used of inferiors (against which Deut. x. 12; Acts xvi. 29; 1 Pet. iii. 15 are conclusive), or *erôtân* always of equals (against which Mark vii. 26; Luke iv. 38, vii. 3; John iv. 40, 47; Acts iii. 3 are equally conclusive), although the tendency is in that direction. In 1 John v. 16 both words are used. In classical Greek *erôtân* is never 'to make a request,' but always (as in i. 19, 21, 25, ix. 2, 15, 19, 21, 23, &c.) 'to ask a question.' (See on xvi. 23.)

another Comforter] Better, *another* **Advocate**. The Greek word, *Paraclete* (Παράκλητος) is employed five times in the N.T.—four times in this Gospel by Christ of the Holy Spirit (xiv. 16, 26, xv. 26, xvi. 7), once in the First Epistle by S. John of Christ (ii. 1). Our translators render it 'Comforter' in the Gospel, and 'Advocate' in the Epistle. As to the meaning of the word, usage appears to be decisive. It commonly signifies 'one who is summoned to the side of another' to aid him in a court of justice, especially the 'counsel for the *defence*.' It is *passive*, not active; 'one who is summoned to plead a cause,' not 'one who exhorts, or encourages, or comforts.' A comparison of the simple word (κλητός = 'called;' Matt. xx. 16, xxii. 14; Rom. i. 1, 6, 7; 1 Cor. i. 1, 2, &c.) and the other compounds, of which only one occurs in the N.T. (ἀνέγκλητος = 'unaccused;' 1 Cor. i. 8; Col. i. 22, &c.), or a reference to the general rule about adjectives similarly formed from transitive verbs, will shew that 'Paraclete' must have a passive sense. The rendering 'Comforter' has arisen from giving the word an active sense, which it cannot have. Moreover, 'Advocate' is the sense which the context suggests, wherever the word is used in the Gospel: the idea of pleading, arguing, convincing, instructing, is prominent in every

17 that he may abide with you for ever; *Even* the Spirit of truth; whom the world cannot receive, because it seeth him not, neither knoweth him: but ye know him; for he 18 dwelleth with you, and shall be in you. I will not leave

instance. Here the Paraclete is the 'Spirit of *truth*,' whose reasonings fall dead on the ear of the world, and are taken in only by the faithful. In *v.* 26 He is to *teach* and *remind* them. In xv. 26 He is to *bear witness* to Christ. In xvi. 7—11 He is to *convince* or *convict* the world. In short, He is represented as the Advocate, the Counsel, who suggests true reasonings to our minds and true courses for our lives, convicts our adversary the world of wrong, and pleads our cause before God our Father. In the *Te Deum* the Holy Spirit is rightly called 'the Comforter,' but that is not the function which is set forth here. To substitute 'Advocate' will not only bring out the right meaning in the Gospel, but will bring the language of the Gospel into its true relation to the language of the Epistle. 'He will give you *another* Advocate' acquires fresh meaning when we remember that S. John calls Christ our 'Advocate:' the Advocacy of Christ and the Advocacy of the Spirit mutually illustrating one another. At the same time an important coincidence between the Gospel and Epistle is preserved, one of the many which help to prove that both are by one and the same author, and therefore that evidence of the genuineness of the Epistle is also evidence of the genuineness of the Gospel. See Lightfoot, *On Revision*, pp. 50—56, from which nearly the whole of this note is taken.

It is worth noting that although S. Paul does not use the word Paraclete, yet he has the doctrine: in Rom. viii. 27, 34 the same language, 'maketh intercession for,' is used both of the Spirit and of Christ.

that he may abide with you for ever] Their present Advocate has come to them and will leave them again; this 'other Advocate' will come and never leave them. And in Him, who is the Spirit of Christ (Rom. viii. 9), Christ will be with them also (Matt. xxviii. 20).

17. *the Spirit of truth*] This expression confirms the rendering 'Advocate.' Truth is much more closely connected with the idea of advocating a cause than with that of comforting. Comp. xv. 26, xvi. 13; 1 John v. 6. The Paraclete is the Spirit of Truth as being the Bearer of the Divine revelation, bringing truth home to the hearts of men. In 1 John iv. 6 it is opposed to the 'spirit of error.' Comp. 1 Cor. ii. 12.

the world] See notes on i. 9, 10.

it seeth him not] Because the Spirit and 'the things of the Spirit' must be 'spiritually discerned' (1 Cor. ii. 14). The world may have intelligence, scientific investigation, criticism, learning; but not by these means is the Spirit of Truth contemplated and recognised; rather by humility, self-investigation, faith, and love.

for he dwelleth] **Because *He* abideth**: it is the same Greek word as in the previous clause. Comp. *v.* 28.

and shall be in you] A reading of higher authority gives us, '*and* is

you comfortless: I will come to you. Yet a little while, 19
and the world seeth me no more; but ye see me: because
I live, ye shall live also. At that day ye shall know that I 20
am in my Father, and you in me, and I in you. He that 21
hath my commandments, and keepeth them, he it is that
loveth me: and he that loveth me shall be loved of my
Father, and I will love him, and will manifest myself to

in you.' All the verbs are in the present tense. The Spirit was in the Apostles already, though not in the fulness of Pentecost.

Note throughout these two verses (16, 17) the definite personality of the Spirit, distinct both from the Father Who gives Him and from the Son Who promises Him. Note also the three prepositions (in *vv.* 16, 17): the Advocate is *with* us for fellowship (*meta*); He abides *by our side* to defend us (*para*); He is *in* us as a source of power to each individually (*en*).

18. *comfortless*] Rather (with Wiclif) **fatherless**, as the word is translated James i. 27, the only other place in the N. T. where it occurs; or (with the margin) *orphans*, the very word used in the Greek. The inaccurate rendering 'comfortless' gives unreal support to the inaccurate rendering 'Comforter.' In the Greek there is no connexion between orphans and Paraclete. We must connect this rather with the tender address in xiii. 33; He will not leave His 'little children' fatherless.

I will come to you] Or, *I* **am coming** *to you*, in the Holy Spirit, whom I will send. The context seems to shew clearly that Christ's spiritual reunion with them through the Paraclete, and not His bodily reunion with them either through the Resurrection or through the final Return is intended.

19. *a little while*] Comp. xiii. 33, xvi. 16.
but ye see me] In the Paraclete, ever present with you.
because I live, ye shall live also] i.e. that higher and eternal life over which death has no power either in Christ or His followers. Christ has this life in Himself (v. 26); His followers derive it from Him (v. 21).

20. *At that day*] Comp. xvi. 23, 26. Pentecost, and thenceforth to the end of the world. They will *come to know*, for experience will teach them, that the presence of the Spirit is the presence of Christ, and through Him of the Father.

ye in me, and I in you] Comp. xv. 4, 5; xvii. 21, 23; 1 John iii. 24, iv. 13, 15, 16.

21. *hath my commandments, and keepeth them*] Bears them in his mind and observes them in his life.

he it is] With great emphasis; he and no one else.

will manifest myself to him] Once more willing obedience is set forth as the road to spiritual enlightenment (see on vii. 17). The word for 'manifest' is not S. John's favourite word (*phaneroun*) but one which he uses only in these two verses (*emphanizein*).

22 him. Judas saith unto him, not Iscariot, Lord, how is it that thou wilt manifest thyself unto us, and not unto the 23 world? Jesus answered and said unto him, If a man love me, he will keep my words: and my Father will love him, and we will come unto him, and make *our* abode with him.

22. *Judas*] Excluding the genealogies of Christ we have six persons of this name in the N. T.
1. This Judas, who was the *son* of a certain James (Luke vi. 16; Acts i. 13): he is commonly identified with Lebbaeus or Thaddaeus (see on Matt. x. 3). 2. Judas Iscariot. 3. The brother of Jesus Christ, and of James, Joses, and Simon (Matt. xiii. 55; Mark vi. 3). 4. Judas, surnamed Barsabas (Acts xv. 22, 27, 32). 5. Judas of Galilee (Acts v. 37). 6. Judas of Damascus (Acts ix. 11). Of these six the third is probably the author of the Epistle; so that this remark is the only thing recorded in the N. T. of Judas the Apostle as distinct from the other Apostles. Nor is anything really known of him from other sources.

how is it] Literally, **What hath come to pass**; 'what has happened to determine Thee?'

manifest thyself] The word 'manifest' rouses S. Judas just as the word 'see' roused S. Philip (*v.* 7). Both go wrong from the same cause, inability to see the spiritual meaning of Christ's words, but they go wrong in different ways. Philip wishes for a vision of the Father, a Theophany, a suitable inauguration of the Messiah's kingdom. Judas supposes with the rest of his countrymen that the manifestation of the Messiah means a bodily appearance in glory before the whole world, to judge the Gentiles and restore the kingdom to the Jews. Once more we have the Jewish point of view given with convincing precision. Comp. vii. 4.

23. *Jesus answered*] The answer is given, as so often in our Lord's replies, not directly, but by repeating and developing the statement which elicited the question. Comp. iii. 5—8, iv. 14, vi. 44—51, 53—58, &c. The condition of receiving the revelation is loving obedience; those who have it not cannot receive it. This shews that the revelation cannot be universal, cannot be shared by those who hate and disobey (xv. 18).

my words] Rather, *My* **word**; the Gospel in its entirety.

we will come] For the use of the plural comp. x. 30.

abode] See on *v.* 2. The thought of God dwelling among His people was familiar to every Jew (Ex. xxv. 8, xxix. 45; Zech. ii. 10; &c.). This is a thought far beyond that,—God dwelling in the heart of the individual; and later Jewish philosophy had attained to this also. But the united indwelling of the Father and the Son by means of the Spirit is purely Christian.

In these two verses (23, 24) the changes ' words '......'sayings'...... ' word' give a wrong impression: they should run—' word '....'words'

He that loveth Me not keepeth not My sayings: and the 24 word which you hear is not mine, but the Father's which sent Me.

These *things* have I spoken unto you, being *yet* present 25 with you. But the Comforter, *which is* the Holy Ghost, 26 whom the Father will send in My name, he shall teach you all *things*, and bring all *things* to your remembrance, whatsoever I have said unto you. Peace I leave with you, my 27

...'word.' In the Greek we have the same substantive, twice n the singular and once in the plural.

24. *is not mine*] To be understood literally: see on xii. 44.

25. *being yet present*] Better, **while abiding**; it is S. John's favourite verb (see on i. 33). With this verse the discourse takes a fresh start returning to the subject of the Paraclete. Perhaps there is a pause after *v.* 24.

26. *But the Comforter*] Better, *But the* **Advocate** (see on *v.* 16).

which is the Holy Ghost] **Even** *the Holy* **Spirit.** The epithet 'holy' is given to the Spirit thrice in this Gospel; i. 33, xx. 22, and here (in vii. 39 the 'holy' is very doubtful). It is not frequent in any Gospel but the third; five times in S. Matthew, four in S. Mark, twelve in S. Luke. S. Luke seems fond of the expression, which he uses about forty times in the Acts; and he rarely speaks of the Spirit without prefixing the 'holy.' Here only does S. John give the full phrase, both substantive and epithet having the article: in i. 33 and xx. 22 there is no article.

in my name] As My representative, taking My place and continuing My work (see on *v.* 13). 'He shall not speak of Himself......He shall receive of Mine and shew it unto you' (xvi. 13, 14). The mission of the Paraclete in reference to the glorified Redeemer, is analogous to the mission of the Messiah in reference to the Father.

shall teach you all things] i. e. 'guide you into all the truth' (xvi. 13). He shall teach them the Divine truth in its fulness; all those things which they 'cannot bear now,' and also 'things to come.'

bring all things to your remembrance] Not merely the words of Christ, a particular in which this Gospel is a striking fulfilment of this promise, but also the meaning of them, which the Apostles often failed to see at the time: comp. ii. 22, xii. 16; Luke ix. 45, xviii. 34, xxiv. 8. "It is on the fulfilment of this promise to the Apostles, that their sufficiency as Witnesses of all that the Lord did and taught, and consequently the *authenticity of the Gospel narrative*, is grounded" (Alford).

27. *Peace I leave with you*] "Finally the discourse returns to the point from which it started. Its object had been to reassure the sorrowful disciples against their Lord's departure, and with words of reassurance and consolation it concludes. These are thrown into the form of a leave-taking or farewell." S. p. 226. 'Peace I leave with you' is probably a solemn adaptation of the conventional form of taking leave

peace I give unto you: not as the world giveth, give I unto you. Let not your heart be troubled, neither let it be 28 afraid. Ye have heard how I said unto you, I go away, and come *again* unto you. If ye loved me, ye would rejoice, because I said, I go unto the Father: for my Father 29 is greater than I. And now I have told you before it come

in the East: comp. 'Go in peace,' Judg. xviii. 6; 1 Sam. i. 17, xx. 42, xxix. 7; 2 Kings v. 19; Mark v. 34, &c. See notes on James ii. 16 and 1 Pet. v. 14. The Apostle of the Gentiles perhaps purposely substitutes in his Epistles '*Grace* be with you all' for the traditional Jewish 'Peace.'

my peace I give unto you] 'My' is emphatic; this is no mere conventional wish. Comp. xvi. 33, xx. 19, 21, 26. The form of expression, *peace that is mine*, is common in this Gospel. Comp. *the joy that is mine* (iii. 29, xv. 11, xvii. 13); *the judgment that is mine* (v. 30, viii. 16); *the commandments that are mine* (xiv. 15); *the love that is mine* (xv. 10).

not as the world giveth] It seems best to understand 'as' literally of the world's *manner* of giving, not of its *gifts*, as if 'as' were equivalent to 'what.' The world gives from interested motives, because it has received or hopes to receive as much again (Luke vi. 33, 34); it gives to friends and withholds from enemies (Matt. v. 43); it gives what costs it nothing or what it cannot keep, as in the case of legacies; it pretends to give that which is not its own, especially when it says 'Peace, peace,' when there is no peace (Jer. vi. 14). The manner of Christ's giving is the very opposite of this. He gives what is His own, what He might have kept, what has cost Him a life of suffering and a cruel death to bestow, what is open to friend and foe alike, who have nothing of their own to give in return.

Let not your heart be troubled] See on v. 1. Was He not right in giving them this charge? If He sends them another Advocate, through whom both the Father and He will ever abide with them, if He leaves them His peace, what room is there left for trouble and fear?

The word for 'be afraid' is frequent in the LXX. but occurs nowhere else in the N. T. '*Be* **fearful**' is the literal meaning.

28. *Ye have heard*, &c.] Literally, *Ye* **heard that** *I said to you, I* **am going** *away and* **I am coming unto** *you:* comp. vv. 1, 2, 18.

because I said, I go, &c.] Omit 'I said,' which is wanting in all the best authorities: *If ye* **had** *loved Me, ye would* **have rejoiced that I am going** *unto the Father*. The construction is the same as in iv. 10, xi. 21, 32, xiv. 28. Their affection is not free from selfishness: they ought to rejoice at His gain rather than mourn over their own loss.

for my Father is greater than I] **Because the** *Father is greater than I*. Therefore Christ's going to Him is gain. This was a favourite text with the Arians, as implying the inferiority of the Son. There is a real sense in which even in the Godhead the Son is subordinate to the Father: this is involved in the Eternal Generation and in the Son's

to pass, that, when it is come to pass, ye might believe. Hereafter I will not talk much with you: for the prince of 30 this world cometh, and hath nothing in me. But that the 31 world may know that I love the Father; and as the Father gave me commandment, *even* so I do. Arise, let us go hence.

being the Agent by whom the Father works in the creation and preservation of all things. Again, there is the sense in which the ascended and glorified Christ is 'inferior to the Father as touching His manhood.' Lastly, there is the sense in which Jesus on earth was inferior to His Father in Heaven. Of the three this last meaning seems to suit the context best, as shewing most clearly how His going to the Father would be a gain, and that not only to Himself but to the Apostles; for at the right hand of the Father, who is greater than Himself, He will have more power to advance His kingdom. See notes on 1 Cor. xv. 27, 28; Mark xiii. 32, [xvi. 19].

29. *ye might believe*] Better, *ye* **may** *believe.* The brevity of the expression makes it ambiguous. It may mean either, 'ye may believe *that I am He*' (as in xiii. 19), in which case 'I have told you' probably refers to the sending of the Paraclete; or, 'ye may believe *Me*' (as in v. 11), in which case 'I have told you' probably refers to Christ's going to the Father. The former seems better.

30. *Hereafter I will not talk much*] Literally, *No longer shall I speak many things:* comp. xv. 15.

the prince of this world cometh] Better, *the* **ruler** *of* **the** *world* **is coming.** The powers of darkness are at work in Judas and his employers. See on xii. 31.

and hath nothing in me] Quite literal: there is nothing in Jesus over which Satan has control. 'Let no one think that My yielding to his attack implies that he has power over Me. The yielding is voluntary in loving obedience to the Father.' This declaration, **in me he hath nothing,** could only be true if Jesus were sinless. On the import of this confident appeal to His own sinlessness see notes on viii. 29, 46 and xv. 10.

31. *But that*] Once more we have an instance of S. John's elliptical use of these words (see on xiii. 18), ' But (this is done, i. e. Satan cometh) in order that, &c.' Some, however, would omit the full stop at 'I do' and make 'that' depend upon 'Arise:' 'But that the world may know that I love the Father, and that as the Father commanded Me so I do, arise, let us go hence.' There is a want of solemnity, if not a savour of 'theatrical effect,' in this arrangement. Moreover it is less in harmony with S. John's style, especially in these discourses. The more simple construction is the more probable.

let us go hence] 'Let us go and meet the power before which I am willing in accordance with God's will to fall.'

We are probably to understand that they rise from table and prepare to depart, but that the contents of the next three chapters are spoken

CHAP. XV. 1—11. *The Union of the Disciples with Christ. The Allegory of the Vine.*

15 I am the true vine, and my Father is the husbandman.
2 Every branch in me that beareth not fruit he taketh away:

before they leave the room (comp. xviii. 1). Others suppose that the room is left now and that the next two chapters are discourses on the way towards Gethsemane, chap. xvii. being spoken at some halting place, possibly the Temple. See introductory note to chap. xvii.

CHAP. XV.

The general subject still continues from xiii. 31—CHRIST'S LOVE IN KEEPING HIS OWN. This is still further set forth in this chapter in three main aspects: 1. *Their union with Him*, illustrated by the allegory of the Vine (1—11); 2. *Their union with one another in Him* (12—17); 3. *The hatred of the world to both Him and them* (18—25).

1—11. THE UNION OF THE DISCIPLES WITH CHRIST.
THE ALLEGORY OF THE VINE.

The allegory of the Vine is similar in kind to that of the Door and of the Good Shepherd in chap. x. (see introductory note there): this sets forth union from within, the other union from without.

1. *I am the true vine*] We have here the same word for 'true' as in i. 9, vi. 32; Rev. iii. 14. Christ is the true, the genuine, the ideal, the perfect Vine, as He is the perfect Light, the perfect Bread, and the perfect Witness (see on i. 9). "'The material creations of God are only inferior examples of that finer spiritual life and organism in which the creature is raised up to partake of the Divine nature" (Alford). Whether the allegory was suggested by anything external,—vineyards, or the vine of the Temple visible in the moonlight, a vine creeping in at the window, the 'fruit of the vine' (Matt. xxvi. 29) on the table which they had just left,—it is impossible to say. Of these the last is far the most probable, as referring to the Eucharist just instituted as a special means of union with Him and with one another. But the allegory may easily have been chosen for its own merits and its O. T. associations (Ps. lxxx. 8—19; Is. v. 1—7; Jer. ii. 21; &c.) without any suggestion from without. The vine was a national emblem under the Maccabees and appears on their coins.

the husbandman] The Owner of the soil Who tends His Vine Himself and establishes the relation between the Vine and the branches. There is therefore a good deal of difference between the form of this allegory and the parable of the Vineyard (Mark xii. 1) or that of the Fruitless Fig-tree (Luke xiii. 6). The word 'husbandman' occurs nowhere else in the Gospels except of the wicked husbandmen in the parable of the Vineyard.

2. *Every branch*] The word for 'branch' in these six verses occurs here only in N. T., and in classical Greek is specially used of the vine.

and every *branch* that beareth fruit, he purgeth it, that it may bring forth more fruit. Now ye are clean through the word which I have spoken unto you. Abide in me, and I in you. As the branch cannot bear fruit of itself, except it abide in the vine; no more can ye, except ye abide in me. I am the vine, ye *are* the branches: He that abideth in me, and I in him, the same bringeth forth much fruit: for

3

4

5

The word used in the other Gospels (Matt. xiii. 32, xxi. 8, xxiv. 32; Mark iv. 32, xiii. 28; Luke xiii. 9), and in Rom. xi. 16—21, is of the same origin (from 'to break') but of more general meaning,—the smaller branch of any tree. So that the very word used, independently of the context, fixes the meaning of the allegory. It is every *vine*-branch, i.e. every one who is by origin a *Christian*. If they continue such by origin only, and give forth no fruit, they are cut off. The allegory takes no account of the branches of other trees: neither Jews nor heathen are included. Christ would not have called them branches 'in Me.'

he taketh away] Literally, *He taketh* it *away;* in both clauses we have a *nominativus pendens*.

he purgeth it] Better, *He* **cleanseth** *it*, in order to bring out the connexion with 'ye are clean' (*v.* 3). The Greek words rendered 'purgeth' and 'clean' are from the same root. There is also a similarity of *sound* between the Greek words for 'taketh away' and 'cleanseth,' like 'bear and forbear' in English (*airei* and *kathairei*). This may be intentional, but it cannot be reproduced in translation. By cleansing is meant freeing from excrescences and useless shoots which are a drain on the branch for nothing. The eleven were now to be cleansed by suffering.

bring forth] Better, as before, **bear**.

3. *Now ye are clean*] **Already** *are ye clean*. 'Ye' is emphatic; many more will be made clean hereafter.

through the word] Better, **on account of** *the word*. This is a frequent error in our version, διά with the accusative being translated as if it had the genitive. Comp. Matt. xv. 3, 6, where '*by* your tradition' should be '*for the sake of* your tradition.' 'The word' (xvi. 23) here means the whole teaching of Christ, not any particular utterance; but there may be special reference to the present discourses, through which Peter, Thomas, Philip, and Judas Lebbaeus have been cleansed from self-confidence and ignorance.

4. *Abide in me, and I in you*] See on vi. 56. 'And I in you' may be taken either as a promise ('and then I will abide in you') or as the other side of the command ('take care that I abide in you'); the latter seems to be better.

except ye abide] There is this mysterious property in the branches of the spiritual Vine, that they can cut *themselves* off, as Judas had done. Nature does something, and grace does more; but grace may be rejected.

5. *ye are the branches*] This has been implied, but not stated yet.

6 without me ye can do nothing. If a man abide not in me, he is cast forth as a branch, and is withered; and *men* gather them, and cast *them* into the fire, and they are 7 burned. If ye abide in me, and my words abide in you, ye shall ask what ye will, and it shall be done unto you. 8 Herein is my Father glorified, that ye bear much fruit; so 9 shall ye be my disciples. As the Father hath loved me, so

for without me] Better, **because apart from** *Me*, or (as the margin) *severed from Me*. Comp. i. 3; Eph. ii. 12.
ye can do nothing] Christians cannot live as Christians apart from Christ. Nothing is said here about those who are not Christians, although there is a sense in which the words are true of them also.
6. *he is cast forth*] The verb is in a past tense; he is already cast forth by the very fact of not abiding in Christ. This consequence follows so inevitably that to state the one is to state the other. The same remark applies to 'is withered.' But the cast-out branch may be grafted in again (Rom. xi. 23) and the dead branch may be raised to life again (v. 21, 25). The rest of the picture looks forward to the day of judgment. 'Men gather' should be quite indefinitely, **they** *gather* (see on Luke xii. 20).
they are burned] Or, *they burn*.
7. *my words*] Better, *My* **sayings**: see on *v.* 3 and v. 47.
ye shall ask what ye will] The better reading gives, **ask whatsoever** *ye will*, in the imperative. The promise is similar to that in xiv. 13, 14 both in its comprehensiveness and in its limitation. One who abides in Christ and has His words abiding in him cannot ask amiss.
8. *Herein is my Father glorified*] As in *v.* 6, the verb is the aorist passive; not 'is being glorified' but 'is glorified,' i.e. whenever the occasion arises. The aorist is used of an act regarded in itself as accomplished at any conceivable moment: comp. xvii. 26. 'When ye pray and obtain your prayers through abiding in Me, My Father is glorified already.' It is best to understand 'herein' as referring to what precedes (comp. iv. 37 and xvi. 30), in order to give the proper meaning to 'that.'
that ye bear] Literally, *in order that ye may bear:* it is S. John's favourite particle once more, expressing the Divine purpose (comp. viii. 56, ix. 2, 3, xi. 15, 50, xii. 23, xiii. 1, 2, &c.). 'Herein' cannot refer to 'in order that' without awkwardness.
so shall ye be my disciples] Rather, **and may become** *My disciples*. The construction introduced by 'in order that' continues to the end of the verse; moreover the difference between 'to be' and 'to become' should be preserved (see on x. 19, i. 6). The sense of the whole will therefore be; 'In granting your prayers My Father is glorified, in order that ye may be fruitful and become My disciples.'
9. *As the Father*, &c.] The Greek construction is ambiguous. It would be quite possible to translate, **Even as** *the Father* **loved** *Me* **and**

have I loved you: continue ye in my love. If ye keep my 10 commandments, ye shall abide in my love; even as I have kept my Father's commandments, and abide in his love.

These *things* have I spoken unto you, that my joy might 11 remain in you, and *that* your joy might be full.

I loved *you*, **abide** *in My love*. But our version is better as keeping in due prominence the main statement, that the love of Christ for His disciples is analogous to that of the Father for the Son. In any case 'abide' is better than 'continue;' the same Greek word is used throughout these verses (4—16), a fact which our translators obscure by giving three English words, 'abide,' 'continue,' and 'remain,' and that in three consecutive verses (9—11). Throughout the Gospel 'abide' should be maintained as the rendering of S. John's favourite verb μένειν (see on i. 33). The whole should run, **Even as** *the Father* **loved** *Me*, **I also loved** *you* (comp. xvii. 18, xx. 21); **abide** *in My love*. The verbs are aorists, not perfects, and Christ's work is regarded as a completed whole, already perfect in itself. But perhaps this is just one of those cases where the English perfect may be allowed to translate the Greek aorist: see on viii. 29.

in my love] The Greek might mean 'the love of Me,' but 'My love' for you is more natural and suits the context better, which speaks of His love towards them as similar to the Father's towards Him. The other, however, need not be altogether excluded. See on xiv. 27.

10. *If ye keep*] See on xiv. 15, 21, 24. To keep His commandments not only proves our love for Him but secures His love for us.

I have kept my Father's commandments] This being in a subordinate sentence the tremendous import of it is liable to pass unnoticed. Looking back over a life of thirty years Jesus says, 'I have kept the Father's commandments.' Would the best man that ever lived, if only a man, dare to make such a statement? See on xiv. 30.

11. *These things have I spoken*] The verse forms a conclusion to the allegory of the Vine. Comp. *v.* 17, xvi. 25, 33.

might remain] Better, **may abide**: but the reading is doubtful, and perhaps ought to be simply 'may be;' *that My joy* (see on xiv. 27) **may be** *in you*. This does not mean 'that I may have pleasure in you;' but that the joy which Christ experienced through consciousness of His fellowship with the Father, and which supported Him in His sufferings, might be in His disciples and support them in theirs. Here first, on the eve of His sufferings, does Christ speak of His joy.

might be full] Or, **may be fulfilled**. This expression of joy being fulfilled is peculiar to S. John (comp. iii. 29, xvi. 24, xvii. 13; 1 John i. 4; 2 John 12). The active occurs Phil. ii. 2; 'make my joy full;' but nowhere else. Human happiness can reach no higher than to share that joy which Christ ever felt in being loved by His Father and doing His will.

12—17. *The Union of the Disciples with one another in Christ.*

¹² This is my commandment, That ye love one another, as I ¹³ have loved you. Greater love hath no *man* than this, that ¹⁴ a man lay down his life for his friends. Ye are my friends, ¹⁵ if ye do whatsoever I command you. Henceforth I call you

12—17. THE UNION OF THE DISCIPLES WITH ONE ANOTHER IN CHRIST.

12. *This is my commandment*] Literally, *This is the commandment that is Mine* (see on xiv. 27). In *v.* 10 He said that to keep His commandments was the way to abide in His love. He now reminds them what His commandment is (see on xiii. 34). It includes all others. A day or two before this Christ had been teaching that all the Law and the Prophets hang on the two great commands, 'love God with all thy heart' and 'love thy neighbour as thyself' (Matt. xxii. 37—40). S. John teaches us that the second really implies the first (1 John iv. 20).

That ye love one another] Literally, *in order that ye love one another*: this is the *purpose* of the commandment. See next verse and on *v.* 8, vi. 29, and xvii. 3.

as I have loved] **Even as I loved**; comp. *v.* 9. Christ looks back from a point still further.

13. *that a man lay down*] Literally, *in order that a man lay down*: the greatest love is that of which the *purpose* is dying for those loved. On 'lay down his life' see note on x. 11.

for his friends] Needless difficulty has been made about this, as if it were at variance with Romans v. 6—8. Christ here says that the greatest love that any one can shew towards his friends is to die for them. S. Paul says that such cases of self-sacrifice for good men occur; but they are very rare. Christ, however, surpassed them, for He died not only for His friends but for His enemies, not only for the good but for sinners. There is no contradiction. Nor is there any emphasis on 'friends;' as if to suffer for friends were higher than to suffer for strangers or enemies. The order of the Greek words throws the emphasis on 'life:' it is the unique character of the thing sacrificed that proves the love. Christ says 'for His friends' because He is addressing His friends.

14. *Ye are my friends*] 'Ye' is emphatic: 'and when I say "friends," I mean you.' This shews that 'friends' was used simply because He was speaking to the Apostles.

whatsoever I command you] Better, **the things which I am commanding** *you*.

15. *Henceforth I call you not servants*] Better, **No longer do I call you** *servants* (comp. xiv. 30 and see on viii. 34). He had implied that they were servants before (xii. 26, xiii. 13—16). Perhaps the gentler word 'servant' is better here, although 'bond-servant' would bring

not servants; for the servant knoweth not what his lord doeth: but I have called you friends; for all *things* that I have heard of my Father I have made known unto you. Ye have not chosen me, but I have chosen you, and or- 16 dained you, that you should go and bring forth fruit, and *that* your fruit should remain: that whatsoever ye shall ask of the Father in my name, he may give it you. These 17 *things* I command you, that ye love one another.

out the contrast more strongly. Where the Apostles and others use it of themselves the gentler rendering is certainly to be preferred (Rom. i. 1; Gal. i. 10; Jas. i. 1; 2 Pet. i. 1; &c. &c.).

what his lord doeth] To be taken literally. The slave or servant may see what his master **is doing**, but does not know the meaning or purpose of it. 'Doeth' need not be made equal to a future.

I have called you friends] Or, **you have I called** *friends;* 'you' is emphatic. He who wills to do His will as a servant, shall know of the doctrine as a friend (vii. 17).

I have made known unto you] As they were able to bear it (xvi. 12). After Pentecost they would be able to bear much more. Both verbs are aorists;—**I heard**—**I made known**: comp. *vv.* 9 and 12.

16. *Ye have not,* &c.] Better, *Ye* **chose** *Me not, but I* **chose** *you:* 'Ye' and 'I' are emphatic; there is no emphasis on 'Me.' The reference is to their election to be Apostles, as the very word used seems to imply (comp. vi. 70, xiii. 18; Acts i. 2); therefore the aorist as referring to a definite act in the past should be preserved in translation.

ordained you] Better, **appointed** *you* (as 2 Tim. i. 11 and Heb. i. 2), in order to avoid an unreal connexion with ordination in the ecclesiastical sense. The same word used in the same sense as here is rendered 'set' in Acts xiii. 47 and 1 Cor. xii. 28, 'ordained' 1 Tim. ii. 7, and 'made' Acts xx. 28.

go and bring forth fruit] 'Go' must not be insisted on too strongly as if it referred to the missionary journeys of the Apostles. On the other hand it is more than a mere auxiliary or expletive: it implies the active carrying out of the idea expressed by the verb with which it is coupled (comp. Luke x. 37; Mat. xiii. 44, xviii. 15, xix. 21), and perhaps also separation from their Master (Matt. xx. 4, 7). The missionary work of gathering in souls is not specially indicated here: the 'fruit' is rather the holiness of their own lives and good works of all kinds. 'Bring forth' should be **bear** as in *v.* 5.

should remain] Better, *should* **abide** (see on *v.* 9). Comp. iv. 36.

whatsoever ye shall ask] See on *v.* 7 and xiv. 13.

he may give it] The Greek may also mean '*I* may give it' (comp. xiv. 13), the first and third persons being alike in this tense; and several ancient commentators take it as the first.

17. *These things I command you,* &c.] More literally, *These things I am commanding you, in order that ye may love one another.* 'These things' does not refer to 'that ye love one another,' but to what has

18—25. *The Hatred of the World to both Him and them.*

18 If the world hate you, ye know that it hated me before *it*
19 *hated* you. If ye were of the world, the world would love his own: but because ye are not of the world, but I have chosen you out of the world, therefore the world hateth you.
20 Remember the word that I said unto you, The servant is not greater than his lord. If they have persecuted me, they will

already been said about being one with Him and with each other. Comp. *v.* 11, xiv. 25, xvi. 25, 33.

18—25. THE HATRED OF THE WORLD TO BOTH HIM AND THEM.

In strong contrast to the love and union between Christ and His disciples and among the disciples themselves is the hatred of the world to Him and them. He gives them these thoughts to console them in encountering this hatred of the world. (1) It hated Him first : in this trial also He has shewn them the way. (2) The hatred of the world proves that they are not of the world. (3) They are sharing their Master's lot, whether the world rejects or accepts their preaching. (4) They will suffer this hatred not only with Him, but for His sake. All this tends to shew that the very hatred of the world intensifies their union with Him.

18. *ye know that it hated me*] Better, **know** *that it* **hath** *hated me* (comp. *v.* 20). As in xiv. 1 the principal verb may be either indicative or imperative, and the imperative is preferable : the second verb is the perfect indicative, of that which has been and still is the case.

before it hated you] 'It hated' is an insertion by our translators, and 'before you' is literally 'first of you,' like 'before me' in i. 15 (see note there) and 30; excepting that here we have the adverb and there the adjective.

19. *the world would love his own*] In vii. 7 He told His brethren, who did not believe on Him, that the world could not hate them. This shews why : in their unbelief it still found something of its own (comp. 1 John iv. 5). 'His own,' or **its** *own*, is neuter singular not masculine plural. The selfishness of the world's love is thus indicated: it loves not so much them, as that in them which is to its own advantage ; and hence the lower word for 'love' is used (*philein*), not the higher one (*agapân*) as in *v.* 17. It is mere natural liking. Note the solemn repetition of 'world' in this verse. For the construction comp. v. 46, viii. 19, 42, ix. 41, xviii. 36 and contrast iv. 10, xi. 21, xiv. 28.

I have chosen] I chose : see on *v.* 16.

therefore the world hateth you] Or, **for this cause** (see on viii. 47 and xii. 39) &c. Comp. 1 John iii. 13.

20. *Remember*] See note on xiii. 16: of the passages noticed there Matt. x. 24 is similar in meaning to this. Christ may here be alluding to the occasion recorded in Matt. x. 24. On the blessedness of sharing the lot of Christ comp. 1 Pet. iv. 12, 13.

also persecute you; if they have kept my saying, they will keep yours also. But all these *things* will they do unto you 21 for my name's sake, because they know not him that sent me. If I had not come and spoken unto them, they had not 22 had sin: but now they have no cloke for their sin. He 23 that hateth me hateth my Father also. If I had not done 24 among them the works which none other *man* did, they had

if they have kept my saying, they will keep] Better, *If they* **kept** (comp. xiii. 14, xviii. 23) *My* **word**, *they will keep*. 'Keep' must not be exchanged for 'watch, lay wait for,' in a hostile sense; as if both halves of the verse were alike instead of being opposed. The phrase 'keep the word (or words)' of any one is frequent in this Gospel (viii. 51, 52, 55, xiv. 23, 24, xvii. 6); always in the sense of the parallel phrase 'keep my commandments' (xiv. 15, 21, xv. 10). Both phrases form a link not only between the Gospel and the First Epistle (ii. 3, 4, 5, iii. 22, 24, v. 2, 3), but also between these two and the Apocalypse (iii. 8, 10, xii. 17, xiv. 12, xxii. 7, 9). Comp. John ix. 16; Rev. i. 3, ii. 26, iii. 3. (See on xi. 44, xix. 37, xx. 16). All these passages shew that it is impossible to take 'keep' in a hostile sense. The phrase 'to keep the word' of any one occurs in S. John's writings only. 'To keep the commandments (or commandment)' occurs elsewhere only Matt. xix. 17 (comp. xxviii. 20) and 1 Tim. vi. 14. The meaning of the verse as a whole is that both in failure and in success they will share His lot. For the construction comp. xiii. 14, xviii. 23.

21. *for my name's sake*] This thought is to turn their suffering into joy. Comp. Acts v. 41, xxi. 13; 2 Cor. xii. 10; Gal. vi. 14; Phil. ii. 17, 18; 1 Pet. iv. 14.

they know not him that sent me] Comp. vii. 28, xvi. 3, xvii. 25. They not merely did not know that God had sent Jesus; they did not know God Himself, for their idea of Him was radically wrong.

22. *If I had not come and spoken unto them*] He had spoken as man had never spoken before (vii. 46), and His words sufficed to tell unprejudiced minds Who He was. Their hatred was a sin against light; if there had been no light, there would have been no sin. 'To have sin' is a phrase peculiar to S. John (*v.* 24, ix. 41, xix. 11; 1 John i. 8).

no cloke] Better (with the margin), *no* **excuse**: not only have they sin, but they have sin without excuse. The same word is rendered 'cloke,' 1 Thess. ii. 5. But the notion is not that of hiding, but of excusing what cannot be hid: 'colour' (Acts xxvii. 30) is a better rendering than 'cloke.' Comp. Ps. cxl. 4.

for their sin] Literally, *concerning their sin:* comp. xvi. 8.

23. *hateth my Father also*] Comp. v. 23, xiv. 9.

24. *the works*] If they did not see that His words were Divine they might at least have seen that His works were such. Comp. x. 38, xiv. 11, v. 36. Here again their sin was against light; for they admitted the works (xi. 47).

not had sin: but now have they both seen and hated both
25 me and my Father. But *this cometh to pass*, that the word
might be fulfilled that is written in their law, They hated
26 me without a cause. But when the Comforter is come,
whom I will send unto you from the Father, *even* the Spirit
of truth, which proceedeth from the Father, he shall testify

which none other man did] Comp. ix. 32.
seen...my Father] Comp. xiv. 9, 10.
25. *in their law*] 'Law' is used in the wide sense for the O. T. generally. Comp. x. 34, xii. 34, xv. 25; Rom. iii. 19.
without a cause] The passage may be from either Ps. lxix. 4 or xxxv. 19: there are similar passages cix. 3 and cxix. 161. 'Without a cause,' gratuitously; so that here again they are without excuse.
26. *the Comforter*] Better, *the* **Advocate** (see on xiv. 16).
whom I will send] 'I' is emphatic. Here it is the Son Who sends the Paraclete from the Father. In xiv. 16 the Father sends in answer to the Son's prayer. In xiv. 26 the Father sends in the Son's name. These are three ways of expressing that the mission of the Paraclete is the act both of the Father and of the Son, Who are one.
from the Father] See note on 'from God' i. 6: the preposition and case are here the same; παρά with the genitive.
the Spirit of truth] See on xiv. 17.
which proceedeth from the Father] It seems best to take this much discussed clause as simply yet another way of expressing the fact of the *mission* of the Paraclete. If the Paraclete is sent by the Son from the Father, and by the Father in the Son's name and at the Son's request, then the Paraclete 'proceedeth from the Father.' If this be correct, then this statement refers to the *office* and not to the *Person* of the Holy Spirit, and has no bearing either way on the great question between the Eastern and Western Churches, the *Filioque* added in the West to the Nicene Creed. The word used here for 'proceed' is the same as that used in the Creed of Nicea, and the Easterns quote these words of Christ Himself as being against not merely *the insertion of the clause* 'and the Son' into the Creed (which all admit to have been made irregularly), but against the *truth* of the statement that the Spirit, not only in His temporal mission, but in His Person, from all eternity proceeds from both the Father and the Son. On the whole question see Pearson *On the Creed*, Art. viii.; *Reunion Conference at Bonn*, 1875, pp. 9—85, Rivingtons; Pusey *On the Clause "and the Son,"* a Letter to Dr Liddon, Parker, 1876. The word rendered 'proceedeth' occurs in this Gospel only here and v. 29, but is frequent in the other Gospels and in Revelation (Matt. iii. 5, iv. 4, xv. 11, 18; Mark vii. 15, 18, 20, 21, 23; Luke iv. 22, 37; Rev. i. 16, iv. 5, &c.), and there seems to be nothing in the word itself to limit it to the Eternal Procession. On the other hand the preposition used here (*para* = 'from the side of') is strongly in favour of the reference being to the mission. Comp. xvi. 27, xvii. 8.

of me: and ye also shall bear witness, because ye have been 27 with Me from the beginning.

CHAP. XVI.

The Promise of the Paraclete and of Christ's Return.

1—11. *The World and the Paraclete.*

These *things* have I spoken unto you, that ye should not 16

he shall testify of me] Better, *He shall* **bear witness.** It is the same word as is used in the next verse and is one of the words characteristic of this Gospel (see on i. 7). 'He' is emphatic, in opposition to the world which hates and rejects Christ. Christ has the witness of the Spirit of truth, which has the authority of the Father: it is impossible to have higher testimony than this.

27. *And ye also shall bear witness*] Better, **Nay, ye also bear witness**: the verb is present, not future. It is also possible to take the verb as an imperative (comp. *v.* 18 and xiv. 1), but the conjunctions used are against this. The testimony of the disciples is partly one and the same with the testimony of the Spirit, partly not. It is partly the same, so far as it depends on the illumination of the Spirit, who was to bring all things to their remembrance and lead them into all truth. This would not be true in its fulness until Pentecost. It is partly not the same, so far as it depends upon the Apostles' own personal experience of Christ and His work. This is the case at once; the experience is already there; and hence the present tense. Comp. Acts v. 32, where the Apostles clearly set forth the twofold nature of their testimony, and Acts xv. 28, where there is a parallel distinction of the two factors.

have been with me] Literally, **are** *with Me;* i.e. have been and still are.

from the beginning] As usual the context decides the meaning of 'beginning' (see on i. 1). Here plainly the meaning is from the beginning of Christ's ministry. They could bear witness as to what they themselves had seen and heard. Comp. Acts i. 22; Luke i. 2.

CHAP. XVI.

We are still in the first part of the second main division of the Gospel, THE INNER GLORIFICATION OF CHRIST IN HIS LAST DISCOURSES (xiii.—xvii.). We now enter upon the third division of this first part (see introductory note to chap. xiii.).

THE PROMISE OF THE PARACLETE AND OF CHRIST'S RETURN.

As has been remarked already, the subjects are not kept distinct; they cross and interlace, like the strands in a rope. But the following divisions may conduce to clearness; 1. *The World and the Paraclete* (1—11); 2. *The Disciples and the Paraclete* (12—15); *The Sorrow of Christ's Departure turned into Joy by His Return* (16—24); 4. *Summary and Conclusion of the Discourses* (25—33).

2 be offended. They shall put you out of the synagogues: yea, the time cometh, that whosoever killeth you will think 3 that he doeth God service. And these *things* will they do unto you, because they have not known the Father, nor me. 4 But these *things* have I told you, that when the time shall come, ye may remember that I told you of them. And these *things* I said not unto you at the beginning, because

1—11. THE WORLD AND THE PARACLETE.

1. *These things*] These discourses generally, especially the last section about the world's hatred of Him and them (xv. 18—27).

should not be offended] Literally, *should not be made to stumble*: comp. vi. 61; 1 John ii. 10. The metaphor is frequent in S. Matt. and S. Mark, occurs thrice in S. Luke (vii. 23, xvii. 1, 2), and twice in S. John. The fanatical hatred of the Jews might make Jewish Apostles stumble at the truth.

2. *out of the synagogues*] Or, *out of the* **synagogue**, i. e. excommunicate you. Comp. ix. 22; xii. 42.

yea, the time cometh] Better, **nay, there cometh an hour**. Comp. *v*. 25. 'You might think excommunication an extreme measure; *but* (ἀλλά) they will go far greater lengths than this.'

that whosoever] Literally, **in order that every one who**. The Divine purpose is again clearly indicated (see on xii. 23). *Every one*, Jew and Gentile alike, will put down the Christians as blasphemers and atheists and the perpetrators of every crime. The history of religious persecution is the fulfilment of this prophecy.

doeth God service] Better, **offereth service to God**. The verb expresses the offering of *sacrifice* (comp. Heb. v. 1, viii. 3, ix. 7); the substantive expresses a *religious* service (Rom. ix. 4; Heb. ix. 1. 6).

3. *unto you*] These words are of doubtful authority.

they have not known] Better, *they* **did not recognise**. The verb implies that they had the opportunity of knowing; but they had failed to see that God is Love, and that Jesus came not to shut out, but to bring in, not to destroy, but to save. The very names 'Father' (here used with special point) and 'Jesus' might have taught them better things.

4. *But*] Making a fresh start; *But, to return* (to *v.* 1).

have I told] See on *v.* 6.

when the time] Rather, *when* **their hour**, according to the better reading; i. e. the hour appointed for these things (*v.* 2).

ye may......of them] Better, *ye may* **remember them, that I told you**. 'I' is emphatic, 'I Myself, the object of your faith.'

And these things......beginning] Better, **But** *these things I* **told you not from** *the beginning*. Not exactly the same phrase as in xv. 27 (ἀπ' ἀρχῆς), but ἐξ ἀρχῆς (here and vi. 64 only): the one expresses simple departure, the other consequence and continuity. There is no inconsistency between this statement and passages like Matt. x. 16—39, xxiv. 9; Luke vi. 22, &c. 'These things' will cover a great deal more than the

I was with you. But now I go my way to him that sent 5
me; and none of you asketh me, Whither goest thou?
But because I have said these *things* unto you, sorrow hath 6
filled your heart. Nevertheless I tell you the truth; It is 7
expedient for you that I go away: for if I go not away,
the Comforter will not come unto you; but if I depart,
I will send him unto you. And when he is come, he 8

prediction of persecutions, e. g. the *explanation* of the persecutions, the promise of the Paraclete, &c.

because I was with you] See notes on Matt. ix. 15.

5. *I go my way to*] Or, *I go* **away unto**; the notion is that of withdrawal (see on *v.* 7). Hitherto He has been with them to protect them and to be the main object of attack : soon *they* will have to bear the brunt without Him. This is all that they feel at present,—how His departure affects themselves, not how it affects Him. And yet this latter point is all important even as regards themselves, for He is going in order to send the Paraclete.

none of you asketh] As far as words go S. Peter had asked this very question (xiii. 36) and S. Thomas had suggested it (xiv. 5); but altogether in a different spirit from what is meant here. They were looking only at their own loss instead of at His gain.

6. *I have said*] Better, *I have* **spoken** as in *v.* 1. A similar correction is needed in *v.* 4 for ' have I told :' it is the same Greek word in all three cases, and means 'to speak,' not 'to say' or 'to tell.'

sorrow hath filled] So that there is no room for thoughts of My glory and your future consolation.

7. *I tell you the truth*] 'I' is again emphatic; 'I who know, and who have never misled you.' Comp. xiv. 2.

It is expedient] So Caiaphas had said (xi. 50) with more truth than he knew; so also the taunt at the crucifixion, 'Himself He cannot save.' 'That' here='in order that' (S. John's favourite particle, *ἵνα*). Comp. *v.* 2 and xii. 43.

I go away] There are three different Greek verbs in *vv.* 5, 7, and 10, and our translators have not been happy in distinguishing them. The verb in *vv.* 5 and 10 should be **I go away**: here for 'I go away' we should have **I depart**, and for 'I depart' we should have **I go My way**. In the first the primary idea is *withdrawal;* in the second, *separation ;* in the third, *going on to a goal.*

the Comforter] *The* **Advocate** (see on xiv. 16). The Spirit could not come until God and man had been made once more *at one.* In virtue of His glorified and ascended Manhood Christ sends the Paraclete. ' Humanity was to ascend to heaven before the Spirit could be sent to humanity on earth.'

8. The threefold office of the Advocate towards those who do not believe but may yet be won over. *And* **He when He is come will convict** *the* **world concerning** *sin, and* **concerning** *righteousness, and* **concerning** *judgment.*

will reprove the world of sin, and of righteousness, and of judgment: of sin, because they believe not on me; of righteousness, because I go to my Father, and ye see me

he will reprove] 'Convince' (as the margin) or **convict** is to be preferred (see on iii. 20). This rendering gives additional point to the rendering 'Advocate' for Paraclete. To convince and convict is a large part of the duty of an advocate. He must vindicate and prove the truth; and whoever, after such proof, rejects the truth, does so with responsibility in proportion to the interests involved. The word occurs once in S. Matthew (xviii. 15) and once in S. Luke (iii. 19); but is somewhat frequent in the Epistles. Comp. 1. Cor. xiv. 24; Titus i. 9, 13, ii. 15; James ii. 9; Jude 15, [22], &c.

The conviction wrought by the Advocate may bring either salvation or condemnation, but it must bring one of the two. It is given to men 'for their wealth;' but it may 'be unto them an occasion of falling,' if it is wantonly set aside.

9. *Of sin*] Or, **Concerning** *sin*. This naturally comes first: the work of the Spirit begins with convincing man that he is a fallen, sinful creature in rebellion against God.

because they believe not on me] This is the source of sin—unbelief; formerly, unbelief in God, now unbelief in His Ambassador. Not that the sin is limited to unbelief, but this is the beginning of it: 'Because' does not explain 'sin,' but 'will convict.' The Spirit, by bringing the fact of unbelief home to the hearts of men, shews what the nature of sin is.

10. *righteousness*] The word occurs here only in this Gospel; but comp. 1 John ii. 29, iii. 7, 10; Rev. xix. 11. Righteousness is the keeping of the law, and is the natural result of faith; so much so that faith is reckoned as if it were righteousness (Rom. iv. 3—9), so certain is this result regarded. Here 'righteousness' is used not in the lower sense of keeping prescribed ordinances (Matt. iii. 15), but in the highest and widest sense of keeping the law of God; internal as well as external obedience. The lower sense was almost the only sense both to Jew and Gentile (Matt. v. 20). The Spirit, having convinced man that sin is much more than a breaking of certain ordinances, viz. a rejection of God and His Christ, goes on to convince him that righteousness is much more than a keeping of certain ordinances.

I go to my Father] Better, *I go away* (see on *v.* 7) *to the Father;* 'My' is wanting in the best texts. Once more 'because' explains 'will convict,' not 'righteousness.' The life of Christ on earth as the pattern for all mankind being completed, and the reconciliation of man to God being completed also, the Spirit makes known to man the nature of that life, and thus shews what the nature of righteousness is. Sin being resistance to God's will, righteousness is perfect harmony with it.

ye see me no more] 'Contemplate' or **behold** would be better than 'see' (comp. *v.* 16, vi. 40, 62, vii. 3, xiv. 19, &c.). He shews His disciples that He has sympathy for them; in speaking of His return to glory He does not forget the sorrow which they feel and expect (erroneously, as Acts ii. 46 shews) always to feel.

no more; of judgment, because the prince of this world is 11
judged.

12—15. *The Disciples and the Paraclete.*

I have yet many *things* to say unto you, but ye cannot 12
bear *them* now. Howbeit when he, the Spirit of truth, is 13
come, he will guide you into all truth: for he shall not
speak of himself; but whatsoever he shall hear, *that* shall he

11. *Of judgment......judged*] Better, **Concerning** *judgment, because the* **ruler** *of this world* **hath been** *judged* (see on xii. 31 and xiv. 30). As the world has had its own false views about sin and righteousness, so also it has had its own false standards of judgment. The Advocate convicts the world of its error in this point also. The world might think that 'the power of darkness' conquered at Gethsemane and Calvary, but the Resurrection and Ascension proved that what looked like victory was most signal defeat: instead of conquering he was judged. This result is so certain that from the point of view of the Spirit's coming it is spoken of as already accomplished.

12—15. THE DISCIPLES AND THE PARACLETE.

The Paraclete not only convicts and convinces the world, He also enlightens the Apostles respecting Christ and thereby glorifies Him, for to make Christ known is to glorify Him. These verses are very important as shewing the authority of the Apostles' teaching: it is not their own, but the truth of Christ revealed by the Spirit.

12. *many things to say*] They are His friends (xv. 15), and there is nothing which He wishes to keep back from them; He would give them His entire confidence. But it would be useless to tell them what they cannot understand; cruel to impart knowledge which would only crush them. 'Now' is emphatic (see on *v.* 31): at Pentecost they will receive both understanding and strength. The word here used for 'bear' appears again in xix. 17 of Christ bearing the Cross.

13. *the Spirit of truth*] See on xiv. 17.

he will guide you] 'He and no other will be your guide.' Christ is the Way and the Truth. The Spirit leads men into the Way and thus to the Truth. But He does no more than guide: He does not compel, He does not carry. They may refuse to follow, and if they follow they must exert themselves. Contrast Matt. xv. 14; Luke vi. 39; Acts viii. 31.

into all truth] Better, *into all* **the** *truth*, i. e. the truth in its entirety: this is very clearly expressed in the Greek.

he shall not speak of himself] This does not mean 'shall not speak *about* Himself' but '*from* Himself.' The Spirit, like the Son, cannot speak what proceeds from Himself as distinct from what proceeds from the Father: He is the Source of Divine energy and truth. Comp. v. 19 and vii. 18. This expression 'from himself, from itself' (ἀπό) is peculiar to S. John: comp. xi. 51, xv. 4.

14 speak: and he will shew you *things* to come. He shall glorify me: for he shall receive of mine, and shall shew *it* 15 unto you. All *things* that the Father hath are mine: therefore said I, that he shall take of mine, and shall shew *it* unto you.

16—24. *The sorrow of Christ's departure turned into joy by His return.*

16 A little while, and ye shall not see me: and again, a little while, and ye shall see me, because I go to the Father.

he will shew you things to come] Better, *He* **shall declare to you the things that are coming**. The Greek verb means 'to announce, proclaim, declare' rather than 'shew.' Note the thrice repeated 'He shall declare to you.' The phrase 'the things that are coming' is identical in form with 'He that cometh' (Luke vii. 19): among these things we may place the constitution of the Church and the revelation respecting the Last Judgment and its results.

14. *He shall glorify me*] Both pronouns are emphatic; 'Me shall that Spirit of truth glorify.' Just as the Son glorifies the Father by revealing Him (i. 18; xvii. 4) both in word and work, so does the Spirit glorify the Son by revealing Him. In both cases to reveal is necessarily to glorify: the more the Truth is known, the more it is loved and adored.

for he shall receive......unto you] Better, **because** *He shall* **take** *of Mine and shall* **declare** *it to you*. The verb rendered 'receive' is the same as that rendered 'take' in *v.* 15, and 'take' is better, as implying that the recipient is not wholly passive (*lambanein*, not *dechesthai*). Comp. x. 17, xii. 48, xx. 22.

15. *All things*] Literally, *All things whatsoever:* comp. xvii. 10. *therefore said I*] **For this cause** (xii. 18, 27) *said I:* see on v. 16, 18. *shall take*] Better, **taketh**: the Spirit is already revealing the Truth which is both of the Father and of the Son.

16—24. THE SORROW OF CHRIST'S DEPARTURE TURNED INTO JOY BY HIS RETURN.

16. *ye shall not see me*] Better, *ye* **behold Me no more** (comp. *v.* 10): the verb for 'see' in the second half of the verse is a more general term. When His bodily presence was withdrawn their view of Him was enlarged; no longer known after the flesh, He is seen and known by faith.

ye shall see me] In the spiritual revelation of Christ by the Paraclete from Pentecost onwards: Matt. xxviii. 20.

because I go to the Father] These words have probably been inserted to suit the next verse; the best MSS. omit them.

Then said *some* of his disciples among themselves, What 17 is this that he saith unto us, A little while, and ye shall not see me: and again, a little while, and ye shall see me: and, Because I go to the Father? They said therefore, What is 18 this that he saith, A little while? we cannot tell what he saith. Now Jesus knew that they were desirous to ask him, 19 and said unto them, Do ye inquire among yourselves of that I said, A little while, and ye shall not see me: and again, a little while, and ye shall see me? Verily, verily, I say unto 20 you, That ye shall weep and lament, but the world shall rejoice: and ye shall be sorrowful, but your sorrow shall be

17. *Then......disciples*] Better, *Some of His disciples* **therefore said**.
among themselves] Better, as in iv. 33, **one to another**; so also in xix. 24. The Greek for 'among themselves' (xii. 19) is different.

ye shall not see] **Ye behold Me not.** As in the previous verse we have two different verbs for 'see.'

and, Because I go] They refer to what was said in *v.* 10. The Apostles are perplexed both about the apparent contradiction of not beholding and yet seeing and also the departure to the Father. 'Because' (ὅτι) should probably be 'that,' to introduce the saying 'I go to the Father.' As already indicated, the reason, '*because* I go, &c.' in *v.* 16 is not genuine.

18. *we cannot tell what he saith*] More literally, *we* **know not** *what He* **speaketh**.

19. *Now Jesus knew*] More literally, *Jesus recognised* or **perceived** (see on viii. 55). We have here an indication that His supernatural power of reading the thoughts did not supersede His natural powers of observation, and perhaps was not used when the latter were sufficient: comp. v. 6, vi. 15. A different verb is used for His supernatural knowledge (vi. 61, 64; xiii. 1, 3, 11, 18, xviii. 4, xix. 28). But this distinction between *ginôskein* and *eidenai* is not always observed: comp. ii. 24, 25, where *ginôskein* is used of supernatural knowledge. Omit 'now' at the beginning of the verse.

among yourselves] Or, **with one another.** This is a third expression, differing from 'among yourselves' (xii. 19) and from 'one to another (iv. 33). See on *v.* 17. The whole should run, **Concerning this do ye enquire with one another,** *that I said*.

ye shall not see me] As in *vv.* 16, 17, *ye* **behold** *Me not*.

20. *ye shall weep and lament*] In the Greek 'ye' comes last in emphatic contrast to the world. The verbs express the outward manifestation of grief. Comp. xx. 11; Luke xxiii. 27. The world rejoiced at being rid of One whose life was a reproach to it and whose teaching condemned it.

and ye shall be sorrowful] Here we have the feeling as distinct from the manifestation of grief. Omit 'and.'

21 turned into joy. A woman when she is in travail hath sorrow, because her hour is come: but as soon as she is delivered of the child, she remembereth no more the anguish, 22 for joy that a man is born into the world. And ye now therefore have sorrow: but I will see you again, and your heart shall rejoice, and your joy no *man* taketh from you. 23 And in that day ye shall ask me nothing. Verily, verily, I say unto you, Whatsoever ye shall ask the Father in 24 my name, he will give *it* you. Hitherto have ye asked

sorrow shall be turned into joy] Not merely sorrow shall be succeeded by joy, but shall **become** joy. The withdrawal of the bodily presence of Christ shall be first a sorrow and then a joy. We have the same Greek construction of the rejected stone becoming the head of the corner (Matt. xxi. 42; Acts iv. 11), of the mustard sprout becoming a tree (Luke xiii. 19), of the first man Adam becoming a living soul (1 Cor. xv. 45).

21. *A woman*] Or, **The** *woman*, like 'the servant' (xv. 15): in each case the article is generic, expressing the general law. The figure is frequent in O. T.; Isai. lxvi. 7; Hos. xiii. 13; Mic. iv. 9. See on Mark xiii. 8.

for joy] Better, *for* **the** *joy*, the joy peculiar to the case.

a man] A human being, one of the noblest of God's creatures.

22. *And ye now therefore*] Or, *Ye* also *therefore now*. As in the case of childbirth, the suffering of the disciples was the necessary condition of the joy. This suffering was to repeat itself in a new form in the work of converting souls (Gal. iv. 19).

I will see you] In *vv.* 16, 17, 19 we had 'ye shall see Me:' here we have the other side of the same truth; and the same verb for 'see' is used in all four cases. In Gal. iv. 9 we have both sides of the truth stated (see on 1 Cor. viii. 3).

no man taketh] Or, according to some good authorities, *no one* **shall** *take.* Their sorrow shall depart, their joy shall remain.

23. *in that day*] Not the forty days of His bodily presence between the Resurrection and the Ascension, but the many days of His spiritual presence from Pentecost onwards. Comp. *v.* 26 and xiv. 20.

ye shall ask me nothing] The Greek is as ambiguous as the English. It is the same verb (*erōtān*) as is used in *v.* 19, and may mean either, as there, 'ask no question,' or, 'make no petition' (see on xiv. 16). The former is better. When they are illuminated by the Spirit there will be no room for such questions as 'What is this little while? How can we know the way? Whither goest Thou? How is it that Thou wilt manifest Thyself unto us and not unto the world?' His going to the Father will gain for them (1) perfect knowledge.

Verily, verily] See on i. 51.

Whatsoever......give it you] The better reading gives, **If** *ye shall ask* **anything of the Father, He will give it you in My name.** The word

nothing in my name: ask, and ye shall receive, that your joy may be full.

25—33. *Summary and conclusion of these discourses.*

These *things* have I spoken unto you in proverbs: 25 but the time cometh, when I shall no more speak unto you in proverbs, but I shall shew you plainly of the Father. At that day ye shall ask in my name: and I say not 26

for 'ask' here and in the next verse is *aitein* not *erôtân*. Note that the answer as well as the prayer (xiv. 13, xv. 16) is in Christ's name, and all such prayers will be answered. His return to the Father will gain for them (2) perfect response to prayer.

24. *nothing in my name*] Because Jesus was not yet glorified, was not yet fully known to the Apostles.

ask] The full meaning of the Greek is *go on asking;* it is the present not aorist imperative. Comp. v. 14, [viii. 11,] xx. 17, and contrast Matt. vii. 7 with Mark vi. 22.

may be full] Or, *may be* **fulfilled**, so as to be complete and remain so. His return to the Father will gain for them (3) perfect joy. See on xv. 11 and comp. xvii. 13; 1 John i. 4; 2 John 12.

25—33. SUMMARY AND CONCLUSION OF THESE DISCOURSES.

25. *These things*] As in *v.* 1 there is some uncertainty as to how much is included. Some refer 'these things' to *v.* 19—24; others to xv. 1—xvi. 24. Perhaps even the latter is too narrow a limit. The words can apply to all Christ's teaching, of which there was much which the multitudes were not allowed (Matt. xiii. 11) and the Apostles were not able (ii. 22) to understand at the time.

in proverbs] Better, *in* **allegories** (see on x. 6).

but the time cometh] Better, **there cometh an hour** (iv. 21, 23, v. 25, xvi. 2, 32). Omit 'but' with the best authorities.

shew] Or, **declare**, as in *vv.* 13, 14, 15. The best MSS. give a different compound of the same verb as is used in *vv.* 13, 14, 15, but the difference cannot well be marked in English.

plainly] Frankly, without reserve (see on vii. 4 and comp. vii. 13, 26, x. 24, xi. 14, 54, xviii. 20).

26. *At that day*] As in *v.* 23 and xiv. 20 from Pentecost onwards.

ye shall ask in my name] With the perfect knowledge just promised they will discern what may be asked in His name (see on xiv. 13): '*cognitio parit orationem.*'

I say not unto you] This does not mean 'I need not say unto you; for of course I shall do so;' which does not harmonize with *v.* 27. The meaning rather is, that so long as through the power of the Advocate they have direct communion with the Father in Christ's name, there is no need to speak of Christ's intercession. But this communion may be interrupted by sin, and then Christ becomes their Advocate (1 John ii. 1; Rom. viii. 34).

27 unto you, that I will pray the Father for you: for the Father himself loveth you, because ye have loved me, and have 28 believed that I came out from God. I came forth from the Father, and am come into the world: again, I leave the world, and go to the Father.

29 His disciples said unto him, Lo, now speakest thou 30 plainly, and speakest no proverb. Now are we sure that

that I will pray] The pronoun is emphatic. On the word here rendered 'pray' (*erōtân*) see on xiv. 16.
for you] More literally, *concerning you*.
27. *himself*] Without My intercession.
loveth you] On the difference between the two Greek verbs for 'love' see on xi. 5. It is the more emotional word that is used here in both cases. At first sight it appears the less appropriate to express God's love for the disciples: but the point is that it is a *Father's* love, it flows spontaneously from a *natural relationship* as distinct from discriminating friendship.
because ye have loved me] Both pronouns are emphatic and are next one another in the Greek, pointing to the closeness of the relationship; *because ye Me have loved*. Note the 'because;' it is their love for Christ which wins the Father's love (xiv. 21, 23).
have loved......have believed] Both perfects signify what has been and still continues. No argument can be drawn from the order of the verbs as to love preceding faith: 'have loved' naturally comes first on account of 'loveth' immediately preceding. 'Love begets love' is true both between man and man and between God and man. 'Faith begets faith' cannot have any meaning between God and man.
from God] The better reading is, *from* **the Father** (see on i. 6, xv. 26). It was specially because they recognised Him as the Son sent from the Father, and not merely as a Prophet sent from God (i. 6), that they won the Father's love.
28. *I came forth from*] Our translators are again right in marking a difference but not quite right in their way of doing so (see on *v.* 7). The Greek rendered 'I came *forth* from' here differs in the preposition used (*ek*) from that rendered 'I came *out* from' in *v.* 27 (*para*). It would be better to transpose the translations. In *v.* 27 it is the temporal mission of Christ from the Father that is meant (comp. xvii. 8); in *v.* 28 the Eternal Generation of the Son is also included (comp. viii. 42). The verse would almost form a creed. The Son, of one Substance with the Father, was born into the world, suffered, and returned to the Father.
29. *said*] Rather, **say.**
plainly] Literally, *in plainness* or *openness*. As in vii. 4, the word here has a preposition (see on vii. 26).
30. *are we sure*] Better, **we know**; it is the same verb as 'thou knowest,' and the capricious change of rendering is regrettable. There is a similarly capricious change 2 Cor. xii. 2, 3. Christ had spoken in

thou knowest all *things*, and needest not that any *man* should ask thee: by this we believe that thou camest forth from God. Jesus answered them, Do ye now believe? 31 Behold, the hour cometh, yea, is now come, that ye shall be 32 scattered, every man to his own, and shall leave me alone: and *yet* I am not alone, because the Father is with me.

the future tense (*v.* 23); they emphatically speak in the present; '*now we know.*' They feel that His gracious promise is already being fulfilled.

thou knowest all things] He had shewn them that He had read their hearts (*v.* 19); like the Samaritan woman (iv. 29, 39) they conclude that He knows all.

by this] Or, **Herein** (see on iv. 37); literally '*in* this.' His all-embracing knowledge is that in which their faith has root.

we believe that] The Greek might mean, 'we believe, because, &c.' But the A. V. is more in accordance with the context and with S. John's usage.

forth from God] They refer to Christ's mission only (*v.* 27), not to the Eternal Generation of the Son (*v.* 28).

31. *Do ye now believe?*] The words are only half a question (comp. xx. 29). The belief of which they are conscious is no illusion, but it is not yet as perfect as they in their momentary enthusiasm suppose. 'Now' means 'at this stage of your course;' it is not the word used by the Apostles (*vv.* 29, 30), but another of which S. John makes much use. The one (*nûn*) regards the present moment only, 'now' absolutely; the other (*arti*) regards the present in relation to the past and future, 'at this crisis.' Comp. *v.* 12, xiii. 7, 19, 33, 37, &c.

32. *the hour cometh*] Better (as in *v.* 25), **there cometh an hour.**

yea, is now come] Omit 'now;' the expression is not the same as iv. 23.

that ye shall be scattered] Rather, *that ye may be scattered*. 'That'= '*in order that*,' expressing the Divine purpose (comp. *v.* 2). This part of the allegory of the sheep-fold is to be illustrated even in the shepherds themselves (x. 12).

to his own] 'To his own home,' as the margin has it here and the text of xix. 27; or more generally 'to his own property and pursuits,' his belongings and surroundings. Comp. i. 11. The Greek in all three passages is the same, 'his own' being neuter plural.

shall leave] Rather, *may leave*, depending upon 'in order that.'

and yet] The 'yet' is not expressed in the Greek, but implied, as often in S. John, in the collocation of the sentences. Comp. i. 10, 11, iii. 19, 32, vi. 70, vii. 4, 26, viii. 20, ix. 30. Our translators have as a rule wisely omitted the 'yet,' leaving S. John's simple constructions to tell their own meaning. Here the 'yet' is almost necessary.

the Father is with me] The Divine *background* (as it seems to us) of Christ's life was to Him a *Presence* of which He was always conscious (viii. 29), with the awful exception in Matt. xxvii. 46.

33 These *things* I have spoken unto you, that in me ye might have peace. In the world ye shall have tribulation: but be of good cheer; I have overcome the world.

33. *These things*] These farewell discourses.
might have peace] Better, **may** *have peace*. Christ's ministry ends, as His life began, with a message of peace (Luke ii. 14).
ye shall have] Rather, **ye have**; the tribulation has already begun.
I have overcome] The pronoun is very emphatic. At the very moment when He is face to face with treachery, and disgrace, and death, Christ triumphantly claims the victory. Comp. 1 John ii. 13, 14, v. 4. In His victory His followers conquer also.

CHAP. XVII. THE PRAYER OF THE GREAT HIGH PRIEST.

"The prayer which follows the last discourse as its fit crown and conclusion has been designated by an old tradition *the Prayer of the High Priest*, now about to take upon Him His office, and to offer atonement for the sins of the people." S. p. 235. It is unique in the Gospels. The other Evangelists, especially S. Luke, mention the fact of Christ praying (Matt. xiv. 23; Mark i. 35; Luke iii. 21, v. 16, vi. 12, ix. 18, &c.), and give some words of His prayer at Gethsemane; but here the substance of a long act of devotion is preserved. S. John never mentions the fact of Christ praying, but in xii. 27 he perhaps gives us a few words of prayer, and in xi. 41 a thanksgiving which implies previous prayer. There is an approach to the first portion of this prayer in the thanksgiving in Matt. xi. 25, 26.

This ORATIO SUMMI SACERDOTIS falls naturally into three portions; 1. *for Himself* (1—5); 2. *for the disciples* (6—19); 3. *for the whole Church* (20—26), the last two verses forming a summary, in which the relations of Christ to the Father and to His own, and of His own to both Father and Son are gathered up.

The prayer was spoken aloud (*v.* 1), and thus was not only a prayer, but a source of comfort to those who heard it (*v.* 13), and by its preservation a means of faith and life to all (xx. 31). No doubt it was spoken in Aramaic, and we have here also, as in the discourses, no means of determining how far the Greek version preserves the very words, how far only the substance of what was spoken. We must take it reverently as it has been given to us, and we shall find abundant reason for believing that on the one hand it quite transcends even the beloved disciple's powers of invention; on the other that there is nothing in it to make us doubt that this report of it is from his pen. "It is urged that the triumphant elevation of this prayer is inconsistent with the Synoptic account of the Agony. But the liability to fluctuations of feeling and emotion is inherent in humanity, and was assumed with His manhood by Him Who was perfect man." S. p. 238. "All human experience bears witness in common life to the naturalness of abrupt transitions from joy to sadness in the contemplation of a supreme trial. The absolute insight and foresight of Christ makes such an alternation even

CHAP. XVII. *The Prayer of the Great High Priest.*

1—5. *The Prayer for Himself.*

These *words* spake Jesus, and lift up his eyes to heaven, 17 and said, Father, the hour is come; glorify thy Son, that thy Son also may glorify thee: as thou hast given him power over 2

more intelligible. He could see, as man cannot do, both the completeness of His triumph and the suffering through which it was to be gained." W. p. 237. The three characteristics of the Gospel, simplicity, subtlety, and sublimity, reach a climax here. Bengel calls this chapter the simplest in language, the profoundest in meaning, in the whole Bible.

The *place* where these words were spoken is not stated. If the view taken above (xiv. 31) is correct, they were spoken in the upper room, after the company had risen from supper, in the pause before starting for the Mount of Olives (xviii. 1). Westcott thinks that "the upper chamber was certainly left after xiv. 31," and that as "it is inconceivable that chap. xvii. should have been spoken anywhere except under circumstances suited to its unapproachable solemnity," these would best be found in the Temple Courts. Here the great Golden Vine, to suggest the allegory of the Vine (xvi. 1—11), and "nowhere could the outlines of the future spiritual Church be more fitly drawn than in the sanctuary of the old Church." It is perhaps slightly against this attractive suggestion, that surroundings so rich in meaning would probably have been pointed out by a writer so full of feeling for dramatic contrasts and harmonies as the writer of this Divine Epic (comp. iii. 2, iv. 6, xiii. 30, xviii. 3, 5, 28, 40, xix. 23—27, 31—42).

1—5. THE PRAYER FOR HIMSELF.

The Son was sent to give to men eternal life, which consists in the knowledge of God. This work the Son has completed to the glory of the Father, and therefore prays to be glorified by the Father.

1. *These words*] More exactly, *these* things, as in xvi. 1, 4, 6, 25, 33.

lifted up his eyes] in calm confidence and in the assurance of victory (xvi. 33). The attitude is in marked contrast to His falling on His face in the garden (Matt. xxvi. 39). 'To heaven' does not prove that He was in the open air: comp. Acts. vii. 55; Luke xviii. 13.

Father] This is His claim to be heard. Comp. 'Abba, Father' in Mark xiv. 36, and see Lightfoot on Gal. iv. 6.

the hour] See on ii. 4 and xii. 27. S. John loves to mark each great crisis in Christ's life; this is the last.

glorify thy Son] By His return to glory (*v.* 5) through suffering and death. Comp. Phil. ii. 9—11.

that thy Son also may glorify] By making known the glory of God, through the Son. To make God known is to glorify Him. 'Also' must be omitted, and for '*Thy* Son' we ought perhaps to read '*the* Son.'

all flesh, that he should give eternal life to as many as thou
3 hast given him. And this is life eternal, that they might
know thee the only true God, and Jesus Christ, whom thou
4 hast sent. I have glorified thee on the earth: I have finished

2. *As thou hast given him power*] Better, **Even as** *Thou* **gavest**
Him **authority**. The authority was given once for all, and is the
reason for the petition in v. 1. Comp. v. 27.

all flesh] A Hebraism not used elsewhere in this Gospel. Comp.
Matt. xxiv. 22; Luke iii. 6; Acts ii. 17; Rom. iii. 20, &c. Fallen man,
man in his frailty, is specially meant; but the Second Adam has dominion also over 'all sheep and oxen, yea, and the beasts of the field,
the fowl of the air, and the fish of the sea.' Ps. viii. 7, 8. In the following texts 'all flesh' includes the brute creation; Gen. vi. 19, vii. 15,
16, 21, viii. 17, ix. 11, 15, 16, 17; Ps. cxxxvi. 25; Jer. xxxii. 27, xlv. 5.
Once more, therefore, Jewish enclusiveness is condemned. The Messiah is King of 'all flesh,' not of the Jews only.

that he should give, &c.] Literally, **in order that all that Thou hast
given Him, He should give to them eternal life**. 'All that' is neuter
singular; 'to them' is masculine plural. Believers are given to Christ
as a united whole; they earn eternal life as individuals. Comp. i. 11,
vi. 37.

3. *And this is life eternal*] More exactly, **But the life eternal is
this**. '*The* life eternal' means that which has just been mentioned;
and 'is this' means 'this is what it consists in:' comp. iii. 19, xv. 12.

that they might know] Literally, **in order that they may recognise**;
comp. vi. 29, xv. 12; 1 John iii. 11, 23, v. 3; 2 John 6. The eternal
life is spoken of as already present (see on iii. 36, v. 24, vi. 47, 54);
hence 'may,' not 'might.' Moreover it is the *appropriation* of the
knowledge that is specially emphasized; hence 'recognise' rather than
simply 'know.' Comp. Wisdom xv. 3.

thee the only true God] i.e. 'Thee as the only true God.' For
'true' see note on i. 9 and comp. iv. 23, vi. 32, xv. 1: 'the only true
God' is directed against the many false, spurious gods of the heathen.
This portion of the truth was what *the Gentiles* so signally failed to
recognise.

Jesus Christ, whom thou hast sent] Better, **Him whom Thou didst
send—Jesus Christ**; or, *Jesus* as *Christ*. This portion of the truth
the Jews failed to recognise. But the words are not without difficulty,
even when we insert the 'as;' and the run of the Greek words is
rather against the insertion of 'as.' If 'Christ' were a predicate and
not part of the proper name we should expect 'Jesus, whom Thou didst
send, as Christ.' Probably in this verse we have the *substance* and not
the exact words of Christ's utterance. That He should use the name
'Jesus' here is perhaps improbable; that He should anticipate the use
of 'Jesus Christ' as a proper name is very improbable; and the expression 'the true God' is not used elsewhere by Christ and is used by S.
John (1 John v. 20). We conclude, therefore, that the *wording* here is
the Evangelist's, perhaps abbreviated from the actual words.

the work which thou gavest me to do. And now, O Father, 5 glorify thou me with thine own self with the glory which I had with thee before the world was.

6—19. *The Prayer for His Disciples.*

I have manifested thy name unto the men which thou 6 gavest me out of the world: thine they were, and thou gavest them me; and they have kept thy word. Now they have 7

4. *I have glorified*] Better, **I glorified.** In confident anticipation Christ looks backs from the point when all shall be accomplished, and speaks of the whole work of redemption as one act. Our translators have been very capricious throughout this chapter, rendering aorists as perfects and perfects as aorists. Comp. *vv.* 6, 8, 18, 21, 22, 23, 25, 26.

I have finished] According to the right reading, **having** *finished* or **perfected.** This is the way in which God is glorified, the completion of the work of revelation.

gavest me] Better, **hast given** *Me.* Christ did not choose for Himself.

to do] Literally, *in order that I may do it:* this was God's *purpose* in giving it. It is S. John's favourite particle; comp. v. 36 and see on *v.* 3.

5. *And now*] When the ministry is completed.

glorify thou me] The pronouns are placed side by side for emphasis, as in *v.* 4, where the Greek runs, 'I Thee glorified.' The two verses are parallels; 'I Thee glorified on earth; glorify Me Thou in heaven.'

with thine own self] In fellowship with Thee. The following great truths are contained in these two verses; (1) that the Son is in Person distinct from the Father; (2) that the Son, existing in glory with the Father from all eternity, working in obedience to the Father on earth, existing in glory with the Father now, is in Person one and the same.

I had] Imperfect tense, implying continual possession.

6—19. THE PRAYER FOR HIS DISCIPLES.

6—8. The basis of the intercession;—they have received the revelation given to them. The intercession itself begins *v.* 9.

6. *I have manifested*] Better, **I manifested:** see on *v.* 4 and i. 31.

which thou gavest] Better, *whom Thou* **hast given**: in the next clause 'gavest' is right. Sometimes the Father is said to 'give' or 'draw' men to Christ (*v.* 24, vi. 37, 44, 65, x. 29, xviii. 9); sometimes Christ is said to 'choose' them (vi. 70, xv. 16): but it is always in their power to refuse; there is no compulsion (i. 11, 12, iii. 18, 19, xii. 47, 48).

kept thy word] S. John's favourite phrase (see on viii. 51): the notion is that of intent watching. Christ's revelation of Himself and of

known that all *things* whatsoever thou hast given me are of
8 thee. For I have given unto them the words which thou
gavest me; and they have received *them*, and have known
surely that I came out from thee, and they have believed
9 that thou didst send me. I pray for them: I pray not for
the world, but for *them* which thou hast given me; for they
10 are thine. And all mine are thine, and thine are mine; and
11 I am glorified in them. And *now* I am no more in the

the Father is the Father's word (vii. 16, xii. 49); His doctrine as a whole.

7. *they have known*] Rather, *they* **know**: literally, 'they have recognised, come to know.' Comp. v. 42, vi. 69, viii. 52, 55, xiv. 9.

whatsoever thou hast given] Both His doctrine and His mission, as the next verse explains. The whole of Christ's work of redemption in word and act was in its origin and still is (present tense) of God.

8. *the words*] Or, *the* **sayings** (see on v. 47). This is not the plural of 'word' (*logos*) in *v.* 6; but the other noun (*rhemata*), the singular of which is not used by S. John. It means the separate utterances as distinct from the doctrine as a whole.

they have received...have known...have believed] Better, *they* **received ...recognised...believed.** See on *v.* 4.

came out from] Better, *came* **forth** *from* (see on xvi. 28). They recognised that His mission was Divine: they believed that He was sent as the Messiah. They had *proof* of the first point; the second was a matter of faith.

9—19. The intercession for the disciples based on their need.

9. *I pray for them*, &c.] Literally, *I am praying concerning them; concerning the world I am not praying, but concerning them whom*, &c. 'I,' 'them,' and 'the world' are emphatic. 'For them who have believed I in turn am praying; for the world I am not praying.' On the word here used for 'pray' see on xiv. 16. Of course this verse does not mean that Christ never prays for unbelievers; *v.* 23 and Luke xxiii. 34 prove the contrary; but it is for the chosen few, in return for their allegiance, that He is praying now.

they are thine] Although they have been given to the Son.

10. *all mine are thine*] Better, *all things that are Mine are Thine*. The statement does not refer to persons only, but continues and amplifies the reason with which *v.* 9 concludes; 'Because they are Thine, and all My things are Thine.' There should be no full stop at the end of *v.* 9.

thine are mine] Or, **the things that are Thine are Mine.** The statement is made conversely to insist on the perfect union between the Father and the Son.

I am glorified] Better, **I have been** *glorified;* have been and still am.

in them] As the vine is glorified in its branches and fruit. They are the vehicles and monuments of the glory. Comp. 1 Thess. ii. 20.

world, but these are in the world, and I come to thee. Holy Father, keep through thine own name those whom thou hast given me, that they may be one, as we *are*. While I was 12 with them in the world, I kept them in thy name: *those* that thou gavest me I have kept, and none of them is lost, but the son of perdition; that the scripture might be fulfilled.

11—16. In *vv*. 6—8 the disciples' acceptance of Christ is given as the basis of intercession for them: here another reason is added,—their need of help during Christ's absence. This plea is first stated in all simplicity, and then repeated at intervals in the petition.

11. *but these*] Rather, **and** *these*. The coupling of the sentences is solemnly simple; 'And now...and these...and I.'

Holy Father] The expression occurs nowhere else; but comp. Rev. vi. 10; 1 John ii. 20; and 'Righteous Father,' *v*. 25. The epithet agrees with the prayer that God would preserve the disciples from the unholiness of the world (*v*. 15) in the holiness which Christ had revealed to them and prays the Father to give them (*v*. 17).

keep...given] The true reading gives us, *keep* **them in Thy name which Thou hast given Me.** In any case the Greek here rendered '*through* Thy name,' and in *v*. 12 '*in* Thy name,' is the same, and should be translated in the same manner in both verses. Comp. Rev. ii. 17; xix. 12, xxii. 4. God has given His name to Christ to reveal to the disciples; and Christ prays that they may be kept true to that revelation. On the meaning of 'name' see on i. 12.

may be one] They had just received a new bond of union. For long there had been oneness of belief. Now they had been made one by union with Jesus; they were one bread and one body, for they had all partaken of the one Bread (1 Cor. x. 17).

as we are] Or, **even as** *we are* (comp. *v*. 2): in perfect spiritual union conforming to the essential union between the Father and the Son.

12. *in the world*] These words are omitted by the best authorities.

I kept] Literally, *I was keeping:* Christ's continual watching over His disciples is expressed. 'I' is emphatic, implying 'now that I am leaving them, do Thou keep them.'

I have kept] Rather, **I guarded**: both verb and tense are changed. This expresses the protection which is the result of the watching. Moreover the reading must be changed as in *v*. 11; *I kept them* **in Thy name which Thou hast given Me; and I guarded them.**

none of them is lost] Better, **not one of them perished.**

the son of perdition] The phrase is used twice only in N. T.; here of Judas, in 2 Thess. ii. 3 of the 'man of sin.' Comp. 'children of light,' 'children of darkness.' Such expressions are common in Hebrew (see on xii. 36). 'Children of perdition' occurs Is. lvii. 4, 'people of perdition' Ecclus. xvi. 9, and 'son of death' 2 Sam. xii. 5. We cannot here preserve the full force of the original, in which 'perish' and 'perdition' are represented by cognate words; 'none perished but the son of perishing.'

13 And now come I to thee; and these *things* I speak in the world, that they might have my joy fulfilled in themselves. 14 I have given them thy word; and the world hath hated them, because they are not of the world, even as I am not of the 15 world. I pray not that thou shouldest take them out of the world, but that thou shouldest keep them from the evil. 16 They are not of the world, even as I am not of the world. 17 Sanctify them through thy truth: thy word is truth. As thou 18

that the scripture] Ps. xli. 9: see on x. 35 and xiii. 18 and comp. xii. 38.

13. *And now come I*] Better, **But** *now I come.* The conjunction introduces a contrast. Hitherto Christ has been with them watching over them; 'but now' it is so no longer.

that they might] Better, *that they* **may.** Christ is praying aloud in order that His words may comfort them when they remember that He Himself consigned them to His Father's keeping. Comp. xi. 42.

my joy] Literally, *the joy that is Mine:* see on xiv. 27 and xv. 11.

14. *I have given*] 'I' in emphatic opposition to the world.

thy word] The revelation of God as a whole (see on *v.* 16 and v. 47).

hath hated] Rather, **hated**; the aorist expresses the single act of hate in contrast to the perfect, 'I have given' a gift which they continue to possess. These are the two results of discipleship; on the one side, Christ's protection (*v.* 12) and the gift of God's word; on the other, the hatred of the world.

15. *I pray not*] See on xiv. 16. The nature of the protection is made clear to the listening disciples; not exemption from attack and temptation, but freedom from the permanent influence of the enemy.

from the evil] Rather, *from the* **evil one**; comp. 1 John ii. 13, iii. 12, and especially v. 18. 'From'='out of:' just as Christ is that *in* which His disciples live and move, so the evil one, 'the ruler of this world' (xii. 31, xvi. 11), is that *out of* which He prays that they may be kept. Thus "the relation of man to good and evil is a *personal* relation:" comp. 1 John iv. 4.

16. *They are not...world*] What was stated in *v.* 14 as the reason for the world's hatred is repeated here as the introduction to a new and more definite petition; not merely protection, but sanctification. There is a slight change from the order of the words in *v.* 14; 'Of the world they are not, even as I am not of the world.' In both verses 'I' is **emphatic.**

17. *Sanctify*] Or, **consecrate.** The word expresses God's destination of them for their work and His endowment of them with the powers necessary for their work. The word is used of God's consecration of Jeremiah, Moses, and the chosen people (Jer. i. 5; Ecclus. xlix. 7, xlv. 4; 2 Mac. i. 25). This prayer has been called "the Prayer of Consecration."

through thy truth] Rather, **in the** *truth.* 'Thy' is a gloss, rightly explaining the text, but wanting in all the best MSS. The Truth is the

hast sent me into the world, even *so* have I also sent them into the world. And for their sakes I sanctify myself, that 19 they also might be sanctified through the truth.

20—26. *The Prayer for the whole Church.*

Neither pray I for these alone, but for them also which 20 shall believe on me through their word; that they all may be 21

whole Christian revelation, the new environment in which believers are placed, and which helps to work their sanctification; just as a sickly wild plant is strengthened and changed by transplanting it to a garden.

thy word] Literally, *the word that is Thine*, a mode of expression which gives prominence to the adjective. Comp. 'My doctrine is not Mine, but His that sent Me,' vii. 16. The Greek for 'word' is *logos*, God's revelation as a whole, not any single utterance or collection of utterances. See on v. 47.

18. *As thou hast sent*] Better, **Even as Thou didst send.** Comp. x. 36.

even so have I also sent] Better, **I also did send.** Comp. xx. 21, xv. 9. The Apostles had already received their commission (Matt. x. 5—15; Mark vi. 7; Luke ix. 2—5), which is about to be renewed.

19. *sanctify*] Or, **consecrate**, as in *v.* 17. Christ does for Himself that which He prays the Father to do for His disciples. In x. 36 He speaks of Himself as consecrated by the Father; set apart for a sacred purpose. But only thus far is the consecration of Christ and of His disciples the same. In them it also implied redemption and cleansing from sin; and in this sense the word is frequently connected with 'purify' (2 Cor. vii. 1; Eph. v. 26; 2 Tim. ii. 21; Heb. ix. 13). The radical meaning of the word is not separation, as is sometimes stated, but holiness, which involves separation, viz. the being set apart *for God*.

might be sanctified through the truth] Rather, **may be *sanctified* or consecrated in truth**. 'In truth'=in reality and not merely in name or appearance; the expression is quite distinct from 'in *the* truth' in *v.* 17. As a Priest consecrated by the Father (x. 36) He consecrates Himself as a Sacrifice (Eph. v. 2), and thereby obtains a real internal consecration for them through the Paraclete (xvi. 7).

20—26. THE PRAYER FOR THE WHOLE CHURCH.

20. *Neither pray I for these alone*] More accurately, **But *not concerning these only do I pray*** (see on xiv. 16). The limitation stated in *v.* 9 is at an end: through the Church He prays for the world (*v.* 21).

which shall believe] The true reading gives, **who believe**. The future body of believers is regarded by anticipation as already in existence: the Apostles are a guarantee and earnest of the Church that is to be.

on me through their word] Perhaps *through their word on Me* would be better. The order of the Greek insists on the fact that those who believe believe through the Apostles' word.

21. *That they all may be one*] This is the purpose rather than the

one; as thou, Father, *art* in me, and I in thee, that they also may be one in us: that the world may believe that thou hast
22 sent me. And the glory which thou gavest me I have given
23 them; that they may be one, even as we are one: I in them, and thou in me, that they may be made perfect in one; and that the world may know that thou hast sent me, and hast

purport of the prayer: Christ prays for blessings for His Church with this end in view,—that all may be one.

as] Or, **even as.** The unity of believers is like the unity of the Father with the Son (x. 30), not a merely moral unity of disposition and purpose, but a vital unity, in which the members share the life of one and the same organism (see on Rom. xii. 4, 5). A mere agreement in opinion and aim would not convince the world. See on *v.* 11. Omit 'art,' which is an insertion of our translators.

may be one in us] The balance of authority is against 'one,' which may be an explanatory gloss. In vi. 56 and xv. 4, 5 Christ's followers are said to abide in Him: this is to abide in His Father also.

hast sent] Better, *didst send* (comp. *v.* 18). The eternal unity of believers with one another will produce such external results ('see how these Christians love one another'), that the world will be induced to believe. Christian unity and love (Matt. vii. 12; Luke vi. 31; 1 Cor. xiii.) is a moral miracle, a conquest of the resisting will of man, and therefore more convincing than a physical miracle, which is a conquest of unresisting nature. Hence the divisions and animosities of Christians are a perpetual stumbling-block to the world.

22. Having prayed for them with a view to their unity, He states what He Himself has done for them with the same end in view.

gavest] Better, **hast given** (see on *v.* 4). The meaning of this gift of 'glory' seems evident from *v.* 24; the glory of the ascended and glorified Christ in which believers are 'joint-heirs' with Him (see on Rom. viii. 17). Looking forward with confidence to the issue of the conflict, Christ speaks of this glory as already given back to him (*v.* 5) and shared with His followers. Comp. xvi. 33.

23. *I in them, and thou in me*] And therefore, 'Thou in them and they in Thee.'

made perfect in one] Literally, *perfected into one;* i.e. completed and made one. In the unity the completeness consists. The expression 'into one' occurs elsewhere only xi. 52 (comp. 1 John v. 8). For 'perfected' comp. 1 John ii. 5; iv. 12, 17, 18.

may know] Or, **come to know, recognise** (*v.* 3) gradually and in time. This is the second effect of the unity of Christians, more perfect than the first. The first (*v.* 21) was that the world is induced to *believe* that God sent Christ; the second is that the world comes to *know* that God sent Christ, and moreover that He loved the world even as He loved Christ. 'Hast sent' and 'hast loved' in both places are literally **didst send** and **didst love**; but in the case of the second of the two verbs the English perfect is perhaps the best representative of the

loved them, as thou hast loved me. Father, I will that 24
they also, whom thou hast given me, be with me where
I am; that they may behold my glory, which thou hast
given me: for thou lovedst me before the foundation of
the world.

25, 26. *Summary.*

O righteous Father, the world hath not known thee: but 25

Greek aorist. The second 'Thou' in the verse and the last 'Me' are emphatic.

24. *Father*] Comp. *vv.* 1, 5, 11, xi. 41, xii. 27. The relationship is the ground of the appeal; He knows that His 'will' is one with His Father's.

I will] Comp. xxi. 22; Matt. viii. 3, xxiii. 37, xxvi. 39; Luke xii. 49. He has already granted this by anticipation (*v.* 22); He wills that this anticipation may be realised.

they whom] Literally, **that which**; the faithful as a body. See on *v.* 2.

where I am] Comp. xiv. 3.

behold] In the sense of sharing and enjoying it; for the faithful 'shall also reign with Him.' 2 Tim. ii. 12. This glory they behold with unveiled face, on which it is reflected as on the face of Moses. See on 2 Cor. iii. 18 and comp. 1 John iii. 2.

my glory] Literally, *the glory which is Mine*, a stronger expression than that in *v.* 22: see on *v.* 27.

which thou hast given me] Not the glory of the Word, the Eternal Son, which was His in His equality with the Father, but the glory of Christ, the Incarnate Son, with which the risen and ascended Jesus was endowed. In sure confidence Christ speaks of this as already given, and wills that all believers may behold and share it. Thus two gifts of the Father to the Son meet and complete one another: those whom He has given behold the glory that He has given.

for] Better, **because.**

the foundation of the world] Our Lord thrice uses this expression, here, Luke xi. 50, and Matt. xxv. 34. Two of those who heard it reproduce it (1 Pet. i. 20; Rev. xiii. 8, xvii. 8): comp. Eph. i. 4; Heb. iv. 3, ix. 26, xi. 11.

25, 26. SUMMARY.

25. *righteous Father*] The epithet (comp. *v.* 11) harmonizes with the appeal to the *justice* of God which follows, which is based on a simple statement of the facts. The world knew not God; Christ knew Him; the disciples knew that Christ was sent by Him. 'Shall not the Judge of all the earth do right?'

hath not known] Better, **knew** *not*. So also 'have known' should in both cases be **knew**, and 'hast sent' should be **didst send.** The verbs are all aorists. The conjunction *kai* before 'the world' may be

I have known thee, and these have known that thou hast
26 sent me. And I have declared unto them thy name, and
will declare it: that the love where*with* thou hast loved
me may be in them, and I in them.

rendered 'indeed,' meaning 'it is true the world knew Thee not, but yet &c.' Translate; **the world indeed knew Thee not, but I knew Thee.**

26. *have declared...will declare*] Better, **made known...will make known.** The verb is cognate with that rendered 'know' in *v.* 25, and here as there the aorist is used, not the perfect. Christ knows the Father and makes known His name, i.e. His attributes and will (see on i. 12), to the disciples. This imparting of knowledge is already accomplished in part,—'I made known' (comp. xv. 15); but the knowledge and the love which imparts it being alike inexhaustible, there is room for perpetual instruction throughout all time, especially after the Paraclete has been given,—'I will make known' (comp. xiv. 26, xvi. 13).

wherewith thou hast loved me] In the Greek we have a double accusative, as in Eph. ii. 4. 'Hast loved' should be **didst love** (see on *v.* 4): but possibly this is a case where the English present might be admitted as the best equivalent of the Greek aorist (see on xv. 8).

may be in them] May rule in their hearts as a guiding principle, without which they cannot receive the knowledge here promised; for 'he that loveth not, knoweth not God' (1 John iv. 8).

I in them] These last words of Christ's Mediatorial Prayer sum up its purpose. They are the thread which runs through all these farewell discourses. He is going away, and yet abides with them. His bodily presence passes away, His spiritual presence remains for ever; not seen with the eye without, but felt as life and strength within. Having known Christ after the flesh, now they know Him so no more: they are in Christ, a new creation (2 Cor. v. 16, 17).

Chap. XVIII.

We enter now upon the second part of the second main division of the Gospel. The Evangelist having given us the INNER GLORIFICATION OF CHRIST IN HIS LAST DISCOURSES (xiii.—xvii.), now sets forth HIS OUTER GLORIFICATION IN HIS PASSION AND DEATH (xviii., xix.). This part, like the former (see introduction to chap. xiii.), may be divided into four. 1. *The Betrayal* (xviii. 1—11); 2. *The Jewish Trial* (12—27); 3. *The Roman Trial* (xviii. 28—xix. 16); 4. *The Death and Burial* (17—42).

"We return once more from discourse to narrative, which preponderates in the whole of the remaining portion of the Gospel. Accordingly as we have found hitherto that in the narrative portions the marks of an eye-witness at once begin to multiply, so here especially they occur in such large amount and in such rapid succession that it appears impossible to resist the conviction that from an eye-witness and no one else the account proceeds." S. p. 239.

Dr Westcott (*Speaker's Commentary*, N.T., Vol. II. p. 249) observes; "1. It is a superficial and inadequate treatment of his narrative to regard it as a historical supplement of the other narratives, or of the current oral narrative on which they are based......*The record is independent and complete in itself.* It is a whole, and like the rest of the Gospel an interpretation of the inner meaning of the history which it contains.

Thus in the history of the Passion three thoughts among others rise into clear prominence :

(1) *The voluntariness of Christ's sufferings;* xviii. 4, 8, 11, 36; xix. 28, 30.

(2) *The fulfilment of a divine plan in Christ's sufferings;* xviii. 4, 9, 11; xix. ii. 24, 28, 36, 37.

(3) *The majesty which shines through Christ's sufferings*; xviii. 6, 20—23 (comp. Luke xxii. 53), 37; xix. 11, 26, 27, 30.

The narrative in this sense becomes a commentary on earlier words which point to the end ; (1) x. 17, 18; (2) xiii. 1; (3) xiii. 31.

2. In several places the full meaning of S. John's narrative is first obtained by the help of words or incidents preserved by the synoptists. *His narrative assumes facts found in them:* e. g. xviii. 11, 33, 40, xix. 41.

3. The main incidents recorded by more than one of the other Evangelists which are *omitted by S. John* are : (by *all three*) the agony, traitor's kiss, mockery as prophet, council at daybreak, impressment of Simon, reproaches of the spectators, darkness, confession of the centurion; (by *S. Matthew and S. Mark*) the desertion by all, examination before the Sanhedrin at night, false witness, adjuration, great Confession, mockery after condemnation, cry from Ps. xxii, rending of the veil.

Other incidents omitted by S. John are recorded by single Evangelists : (*S. Matthew*) power over the hosts of heaven, Pilate's wife's message, Pilate's hand-washing, self-condemnation of the Jews, earthquake; (*S. Mark*) flight of the young man, Pilate's question as to the death of Christ; (*S. Luke*) examination before Herod, lamentation of the women, three 'words' from the Cross (xxiii. 34, 43, 46), repentance of one of the robbers.

4. The main incidents *peculiar to S. John* are : the words of power at the arrest, examination before Annas, first conference of the Jews with Pilate and Pilate's private examination, first mockery and *Ecce Homo*, Pilate's maintenance of his words, the last charge (xix. 25—27), the thirst, piercing of the side, ministry of Nicodemus.

5. In the narrative of incidents recorded elsewhere *S. John constantly adds details*, often minute and yet most significant : e. g. xviii. 1, 2, 10, 11, 12, 15, 16, 26, 28, xix. 14, 17, 41. See the notes.

6. In the midst of great differences of detail *the Synoptists and S. John offer many impressive resemblances* as to the spirit and character of the proceedings : e. g. (1) the activity of the 'High Priests' (i. e. the Sadducaean hierarchy) as distinguished from the Pharisees; (2) the course of the accusation—civil charge, religious charge, personal influence ; (3) the silence of the Lord in His public accusations, with the

1—11. The Betrayal.

18   When Jesus had spoken these *words*, he went forth with his disciples over the brook Cedron, where was a garden, 2 into the which he entered, and his disciples. And Judas also, which betrayed him, knew the place: for Jesus ofttimes

significant exception, Matt. xxvi. 64; (4) the tone of mockery; (5) the character of Pilate."

1—11. THE BETRAYAL.

1.   *he went forth*] From the upper room. The same word is used of leaving the room, Matt. xxvi. 30; Mark xiv. 26; Luke xxii. 39. Those who suppose that the room is left at xiv. 31 (perhaps for the Temple), interpret this of the departure from the city, which of course it may mean in any case.

the brook Cedron] Literally, **the ravine of the Kedron, or of the cedars,** according to the reading, the differences of which are here exceedingly interesting. *Of the cedars* (τῶν Κέδρων) is the reading of the great majority of the authorities; but *of the Kedron* (τοῦ κεδροῦ or τοῦ κεδρών) is well supported. *Of the cedars* is the reading of the LXX. in 1 K. xv. 13 and occurs as a various reading 2 S. xv. 23; 1 K. ii. 37; 2 K. xxiii. 6, 12. The inference is that both names were current, the Hebrew having given birth to a Greek name of different meaning but very similar sound. Kedron or Kidron = 'black,' and is commonly supposed to refer to the dark colour of the water or the gloom of the ravine. But it might possibly refer to the black green of cedar trees, and thus the two names would be united. This detail of their crossing the 'Wady' of the Kidron is given by S. John alone; but he gives no indication of a "reference to the history of the flight of David from Absalom and Ahitophel" (2 S. xv. 23). 'Brook' is misleading; the Greek word means 'winter-torrent,' but even in winter there is little water in the Kidron. Neither this word nor the name Kedron occurs elsewhere in N. T.

a garden] Or, **orchard**. S. Matthew and S. Mark give us the name of the enclosure or 'parcel of ground' (John iv. 5) rather than 'place,' of which this 'garden' formed the whole or part. Gethsemane = oil-press, and no doubt olives abounded there. The very ancient olive-trees still existing on the traditional site were probably put there by pilgrims who replanted the spot after its devastation at the siege of Jerusalem. S. John gives no hint of a comparison between the two gardens, Eden and Gethsemane, which commentators from Cyril to Isaac Williams have traced. See on Mark i. 13 for another comparison.

and his disciples] Literally, **Himself** *and His disciples*, Judas excepted.

2.   *which betrayed*] Better, **who was betraying**: he was at that moment at work. Comp. *v.* 5.

knew the place] Therefore Christ did not go thither to hide or escape,

resorted thither with his disciples. Judas then, having 3
received a band *of men*, and officers from the chief priests
and Pharisees, cometh thither with lanterns and torches and

as Celsus scoffingly asserted. Origen (*Cels.* II. 10) appeals to *vv.* 4 and
5 as proving that Jesus deliberately surrendered Himself.

ofttimes] Comp. viii. 1, and see on Luke xxi. 37, xxii. 39. The
owner must have known of these gatherings, and may himself have been
a disciple.

resorted thither] Literally, **assembled there**; as if these gatherings
were for teaching of a more private kind than was given to the
multitude.

3. *Judas then*] Better, *Judas* **therefore**; S. John's favourite particle, as in *vv.* 4, 6, 7, 10, 11, 12, 16, 17, 19, 24, 27, 28, 29, 31, 33, 37,
40. It was because Judas knew that Jesus often went thither that he
came thither to take Him. "Our English version gives little idea of the
exactness of the description which follows." S. p. 241.

a band of men] Rather, **the band of soldiers**. This is one part of
the company; Roman soldiers sent to prevent 'an uproar' among the
thousands of pilgrims assembled to keep the Passover (see on Matt.
xxvi. 5). The word for band, *speira*, seems elsewhere in N. T. to mean
'cohort,' the tenth of a legion (Matt. xxvii. 27; Mark xv. 16; Acts x. 1,
xxi. 31, xxvii. 1), and with this Polybius (XI. xxi. 1; [xxiii. 1]) agrees.
But Polybius sometimes (VI. xxiv. 5, XV. ix. 7, III. cxiii. 3) appears
to use *speira* for 'maniple,' the third part of a cohort and about 200
men. In any case only a portion of the cohort which formed the garri-
son of the fortress of Antonia can here be meant: but that the arrest of
Jesus was expected to produce a crisis is shewn by the presence of the
chief officer of the cohort (*v.* 12). The Jewish hierarchy had no doubt
communicated with Pilate, and his being ready to try the case at so early
an hour as 5 A. M. may be accounted for in this way.

officers from the chief priests and Pharisees] i. e. from the Sanhedrin.
These may have been either officers of justice appointed by the Sanhedrin, or a portion of the Levitical temple-police: that some of the latter
were present is clear from Luke xxii. 4, 52. This is a second part
of the company. S. Luke (xxii. 52) tells us that some of the chief priests
themselves were there also. Thus there were (1) Roman soldiers,
(2) Jewish officials, (3) chief priests.

with lanterns and torches] The ordinary equipment for night duty,
which the Paschal full-moon would not render useless. It was possible
that dark woods or buildings would have to be searched. The word for
'lantern,' *phanos*, occurs here only in N. T.; and here only is *lampas*
rendered 'torch;' elsewhere either 'light' (Acts xx. 8) or 'lamp' (Matt.
xxv. 1—8; Rev. iv. 5, viii. 10). 'Torch' would perhaps be best in all
cases, even in Matt. xxv. 1—8, leaving 'lamp' free as the translation of
luchnos (v. 35; Matt. v. 15, vi. 22; Mark iv. 21; Luke viii. 16, xi. 33,
34, 36, &c.) for which 'light' and 'candle' are either inadequate or
misleading. Torches were fed with oil carried in a vessel (Matt. xxv. 4)
for the purpose.

4 weapons. Jesus therefore, knowing all *things* that should come upon him, went forth, and said unto them, Whom 5 seek ye? They answered him, Jesus of Nazareth. Jesus saith unto them, I am *he*. And Judas also, which betrayed 6 him, stood with them. As soon then as he had said unto

4. *all things that should come*] Better, **all the things that were coming.**
went forth] From what? (1) from the shade into the light; (2) from the circle of disciples; (3) from the depth of the garden; (4) from the garden itself. It is impossible to say which of these suggestions is right; the last is not contradicted by *v.* 26. The kiss of Judas is by some placed here, by others after *v.* 8. While 'His hour was not yet come' (vii. 30, viii. 20), He had withdrawn from danger (viii. 59, xi. 54, xii. 36); now he goes forth to meet it. He who had avoided notoriety (v. 13) and royalty (vi. 15), goes forth to welcome death.
said] The better reading gives **saith.** His question perhaps had two objects; to withdraw attention from the disciples (*v.* 8), and to make His captors realise what they were doing.
5. *Jesus of Nazareth*] Or, *Jesus* **the Nazarene** (Matt. ii. 23), a rather more contemptuous expression than 'Jesus of Nazareth' (i. 46; Acts x. 38; comp. Matt. xxi. 11). 'The Nazarene' in a contemptuous sense occurs xix. 19; Matt. xxvi. 71; Mark xiv. 67. It is sometimes used in a neutral sense (Mark x. 47; Luke xviii. 37, xxiv. 19). Later on the contempt of Jews and heathen became the glory of Christians (Acts ii. 22, iii. 6, iv. 10, vi. 14).
I am he] The 'he' is not expressed in the Greek: and 'I am' to Jewish ears was the name of Jehovah. We have had the same expression several times in this Gospel (iv. 26), vi. 20, viii. 24, 28, 58, xiii. 13 (see notes in each place). Judas, if not the chief priests, must have noticed the significant words. There is nothing in the narrative to shew that either the whole company were miraculously blinded (Luke xxiv. 16), or that Judas in particular was blinded or paralysed. Even those who knew Him well might fail to recognise Him at once by night and with the traces of the Agony fresh upon Him.
which betrayed him, stood] Literally, **who was betraying Him** (*v.* 2), **was standing.** This tragic detail is impressed on S. John's memory. In this as in the lanterns and torches, which he alone mentions, we have the vividness of the eye-witness. S. Luke (xxii. 47) tells us that 'Judas, one of the twelve, went before them, and drew near unto Jesus to kiss Him.' Apparently, after having done this, he fell back and rejoined Christ's enemies, standing in the foreground.
6. *As soon then as he had said*] Better, **when therefore** (see on *v.* 3) **He said.** The Evangelist intimates that what followed was the immediate consequence of Christ's words.
went backward, and fell] Whether this was the natural effect of guilt meeting with absolute innocence, or a supernatural effect wrought

them, I am *he*, they went backward, and fell to the ground. Then asked he them again, Whom seek ye? And they said, 7 Jesus of Nazareth. Jesus answered, I have told you that I 8 am *he:* if therefore ye seek me, let these go their way: that 9 the saying might be fulfilled, which he spake, Of them which thou gavest me have I lost none. Then Simon Peter 10

by Christ's will, is a question which we have not the means of determining. Moreover, the distinction may be an unreal one. Is it not His will that guilt should quail before innocence? The result in this case proved both to the disciples and to His foes that His surrender was entirely voluntary (x. 18). Once before, the majesty of His words had overwhelmed those who had come to arrest Him (vii. 46); and it would have been so now, had not He willed to be taken. Comp. Matt. xxvi. 53, where the expression '*legions* of angels' may have reference to the fragment of a legion that had come to superintend His capture.

7. *Then asked he them again*] *Again* therefore (*v.* 3) *He asked them*. Their first onset had been baffled; He Himself therefore gives them another opening. They repeat the terms of their warrant; they have been sent to arrest Jesus the Nazarene.

8. *I have told*] Rather, **I told.**

let these] At first Jesus had gone forward (*v.* 4) from His company, as Judas from his. Judas had fallen back on his followers while the disciples followed up and gathered round Christ. Thus the two bands confronted one another.

9. *thou gavest me have I lost*] Better, *Thou* **hast given me I lost** (see on xvii. 4). The reference is to xvii. 12, and is a strong confirmation of the historical truth of chap. xvii. If the prayer were the composition of the Evangelist to set forth in an ideal form Christ's mental condition at the time, this reference to a definite portion of it would be most unnatural. The change from 'not one of them perished' to 'I lost of them not one' brings out more clearly the protective intervention of Christ.

It does not follow, because S. John gives this interpretation of Christ's words, that therefore they have no other. This was a first fulfilment, within an hour or two of their utterance, an earnest of a larger fulfilment in the future. The meaning here must not be limited to bodily preservation. Had they been captured, apostasy (at least for a time) might have been the result, as was actually the case with S. Peter.

10. *Then Simon Peter*] *Simon Peter* **therefore** (*v.* 3), because he 'saw what would follow' (Luke xxii. 49). All four Evangelists mention this act of violence; S. John alone gives the names. While S. Peter was alive it was only prudent not to mention his name; and probably S. John was the only one who knew (*v.* 15) the servant's name. S. Peter's impetuous boldness now illustrates his impetuous words xiii. 37 and Mark viii. 32.

having a sword drew it, and smote the high priest's servant, and cut off his right ear. The servant's name was Malchus. 11 Then said Jesus unto Peter, Put up thy sword into the sheath: the cup which my Father hath given me, shall I not drink it?

12—27. The Jewish or Ecclesiastical Trial.

12 Then the band and the captain and officers of the Jews 13 took Jesus, and bound him, and led him away to Annas

having a sword] Probably one of the two produced in misunderstanding of Christ's words at the end of the supper (Luke xxii. 38). To carry arms on a feast-day was forbidden; so that we have here some indication that the Last Supper was not the Passover.

the high priest's servant] No doubt he had been prominent in the attack on Jesus, and S. Peter had aimed at his head. S. Luke also mentions that it was the *right* ear that was cut, and he alone mentions the healing, under cover of which S. Peter probably escaped.

11. *Then said Jesus*] *Jesus* **therefore** (*v.* 3) *said.*

the cup] S. John alone gives these words. On the other hand, the Synoptists alone give Christ's prayer in the garden (Matt. xxvi. 39, &c.) to which they obviously refer. Thus the two accounts confirm one another. See on ii. 19. For the metaphor comp. Ps. lxxv. 8, lx. 3; Job xxi. 20; Jer. xxv. 15; Rev. xiv. 10, xvi. 19, &c. S. Matthew gives another reason for putting up the sword into its place; 'all they that take the sword shall perish with the sword' (xxvi. 52).

12—27. THE JEWISH OR ECCLESIASTICAL TRIAL.

12. *Then the band, and the captain*] **Therefore** (*v.* 3) *the band* &c., because of this violent attempt at resistance. The captain or *chiliarch* is the tribune or chief officer of the Roman cohort. The representations of the hierarchy to the Romans are confirmed by S. Peter's act: Jesus the Nazarene is a dangerous character who stirs up His followers to rebellion; He must be properly secured and bound. Perhaps also their falling to the ground on meeting Him impressed them with the necessity of using the utmost caution, as with a powerful magician. The whole force is required to secure Him.

13. *to Annas first*] Whether Annas was 'chief' of the priests (2 K. xxv. 18), or president, or vice-president, of the Sanhedrin, we have no information. Certainly he was one of the most influential members of the hierarchy, as is shewn by his securing the high-priesthood for no less than five of his sons as well as for his son-in-law Caiaphas, after he had been deposed himself. He held office A. D. 7—14, his son Eleazar A.D. 16, Joseph Caiaphas A.D. 18—36; after him four sons of Annas held the office, the last of whom, another Annas (A. D. 62), put to death S. James, the first bishop of Jerusalem. The high-priests at this time were often mere nominees of the civil

first; for he was father in law to Caiaphas, which was the high priest that *same* year. Now Caiaphas was he, which 14 gave counsel to the Jews, that it was expedient that one man should die for the people.

And Simon Peter followed Jesus, and *so did* another 15 disciple: that disciple was known unto the high priest, and went in with Jesus into the palace of the high priest. But 16

power, and were changed with a rapidity which must have scandalised serious Jews. There were probably five or six deposed high-priests in the Sanhedrin which tried our Lord (see on Luke iii. 2). Other forms of the name Annas are Ananias, Ananus, and Hanan.

for he was father-in-law] And therefore Caiaphas would be sure to respect the results of a preliminary examination conducted by him. Possibly the chief priests thought that Annas was a safer man than Caiaphas, and the father-in-law having taken the lead which they wanted the high-priest would be compelled to follow. This examination before Annas is given us by S. John only, who tacitly corrects the impression that the examination before Caiaphas was the only one.

that same year] Omit 'same' and see on xi. 49. Comp. xx. 19 and Mark iv. 35, where 'same' is improperly inserted, as here.

14. *Now Caiaphas was he*] See on xi. 50—52. The remark is made here to recall the prophecy now so near fulfilment, and perhaps to intimate that with Caiaphas and his father-in-law to direct the trial it could have but one issue.

15. *followed*] Or, **was following**; the descriptive imperfect.

another disciple] Some good authorities read '*the* other disciple,' but the balance is very decidedly in favour of '*another.*' There is no reason for doubting the almost universal opinion that this 'other' was S. John himself; an opinion which agrees with the Evangelist's habitual reserve about himself (i. 40, xiii. 23—25, xix. 26, xx. 2—8, xxi. 20—24); and also with the fact that S. John frequently accompanies S. Peter (Luke xxii. 8; Acts iii. 1, iv. 13, viii. 14). But it must be allowed that the opinion is short of certain; although the fact that S. John elsewhere designates himself as 'the disciple whom Jesus loved' is in no degree against the identification. Here the description, 'the disciple whom Jesus loved,' would explain nothing and would therefore be out of place (see Introduction, chap. II. iii. (3) *b*). S. Augustine, Calvin and others suppose some person otherwise unknown to be meant. Other conjectures are, S. James, the Evangelist's brother, and (strangely enough) Judas Iscariot.

was known] The nature of this 'acquaintance' (Luke ii. 44, xxiii. 49) is nowhere explained.

the high priest] Caiaphas is probably meant (*vv.* 13, 24); but as deposed high priests still kept the title sometimes (Luke iii. 2; Acts iv. 6), it is possible that Annas is intended.

the palace] Rather, *the* **court** or open space in the centre or in front of the house (Luke xxii. 55). The same word is used for the 'sheep-

Peter stood at the door without. Then went out *that* other disciple, which was known unto the high priest, and spake 17 unto her that kept the door, and brought in Peter. Then saith the damsel that kept the door unto Peter, Art not thou 18 also *one* of this man's disciples? He saith, I am not. And the servants and officers stood *there*, who had made a fire of coals; for it was cold: and they warmed themselves: and Peter stood with them, and warmed himself.

19 The high priest then asked Jesus of his disciples, and of

fold' (x. 1, 16). It is not improbable that Annas lived in a portion of the official residence of his son-in-law; but even if this was not the case, it is no violent supposition that Annas conducted a preliminary examination in the house of Caiaphas (see on *v.* 13).

16. *stood*] Or, **was standing**; the descriptive imperfect again. Comp. *vv.* 5, 15. The details here also indicate the report of an eye-witness. 'At the door *without*' seems to indicate that the 'court' was inside rather than in front of the building.

her that kept the door] Comp. Rhoda, Acts xii. 13.

17. *Then saith the damsel*] **The damsel therefore** (*v.* 3) *saith.*

Art not thou also] Rather, **Art thou also** (as well as thy companion) or, *surely thou art not:* S. Peter's denial is thus, as it were, put into his mouth. See on iv. 29 and comp. iv. 33, vi. 67, vii. 47, ix. 40. In all these passages the form of the question anticipates a *negative* answer.

one of this man's disciples] Or, *one of the disciples of this man.* 'This man' and the turn of the sentence are contemptuous. Comp. ix. 16, 24, xi. 47. S. John had hurried on to the room where Christ was being examined; as at the Cross (xix. 26) he kept close to his Master; and in neither case was mole ted. S. Peter, who 'followed afar off' (Luke xxii. 54) and that rather out of curiosity 'to see the end' (Matt. xxvi. 58) than out of love, encountered temptation and fell.

18. *And the servants,* &c.] Better, **Now** *the servants and* **the** *officers, having made...*were standing and warming *themselves.* The tribune (*v.* 12) having deposited his prisoner in safety, has withdrawn with his men. Only the Jewish officials remain, joined now by the household servants of the high priests.

a fire of coals] Charcoal in a brazier, 'to the light' of which (Luke xxii. 56) S. Peter turned. Comp. xxi. 9; Ecclus. xi. 32.

for it was cold] Cold nights are exceptional but not uncommon in Palestine in April. Jerusalem stands high.

and Peter, &c.] Rather, *And Peter also* **was with them, standing and warming** *himself,* pretending to be indifferent, but restlessly changing his posture. S. Luke says he '*sat* to the light.'

19. *The high priest then*] Rather, **therefore** (*v.* 3), connecting what follows with *vv.* 13, 14. Again we are in doubt as to who is meant by the high-priest (see on *v.* 15), but it will be safest to consider that Caiaphas is meant throughout. Neither hypothesis is free from difficulty.

his doctrine. Jesus answered him, I spake openly to the 20 world; I ever taught in the synagogue, and in the temple, whither the Jews always resort; and in secret have I said nothing. Why askest thou me? ask them which heard *me*, 21 what I have said unto them: behold, they know what I said. And when he had thus spoken, one of the officers which 22 stood by stroke Jesus with the palm of his hand, saying, Answerest thou the high priest so? Jesus answered him, 23 If I have spoken evil, bear witness of the evil: but if well,

If the high priest here is Caiaphas, the difficulty is to explain *v*. 24 (see note there). But we may suppose that while Annas is conducting the examination Caiaphas enters and takes part in it.

of his disciples, &c.] It was hoped that some evidence might be obtained which would be of service in the formal trial that was to follow.

20. *I spake*] The true reading gives, **I have spoken**. There is a strong emphasis on 'I.' Christ answers no questions about His disciples; He bears the brunt Himself alone. Moreover He seems to contrast the openness of His proceedings with the secrecy of His enemies.

openly] See on vii. 4, 26.

to the world] Not to a secret society. Comp. viii. 26.

in the synagogue] All the best MSS. omit the article; **in synagogue**, as we say 'in church.' See on vi. 59.

whither the Jews always resort] The better reading gives, **where all the Jews come together**. The word rendered 'resort' is not the same as that rendered 'resort' in *v*. 2. 'I always taught in public places, where all the Jews meet.' Nothing could be more open than His teaching. Comp. Matt. x. 27.

have I said] Rather, **I spake**, the aorist of the verb in the first clause, which is in the perfect. See next verse.

21. *which heard*] Better, **who have heard**; and 'I have said' should again be **I spake**.

they know] Or, **these** *know*, as if implying that they were present and ought to be examined. According to Jewish rule witnesses for the defence were heard first. 'These' cannot refer to S. Peter and S. John. S. Peter is still outside by the fire.

22. *struck Jesus with the palm of his hand*] Literally, *gave a blow*, and the word for 'blow' (elsewhere xix. 3, Mark xiv. 65 only) etymologically means a 'blow with a rod,' but is also used for a 'blow with the open hand.' The word used for 'smite' in *v*. 23 is slightly in favour of the former: but Matt. v. 39 and Acts xxiii. 2 are in favour of the latter.

23. *If I have spoken*] Rather (as at the end of *vv*. 20, 21), *If I* **spake** (comp. xiii. 14, xv. 20). This seems to shew that Christ does not refer, as our version would lead us to suppose, to His answer to the high-priest, but to the teaching about which He is being examined.

24 why smitest thou me? Now Annas had sent him bound unto Caiaphas the high priest.

25 And Simon Peter stood and warmed himself. They said therefore unto him, Art not thou also *one* of his **26** disciples? He denied *it*, and said, I am not. One of the servants of the high priest, being *his* kinsman whose ear

He here gives His own illustration of His own precept (Matt. v. 39); to exclude personal retaliation does not exclude calm protest and rebuke.

24. *Now Annas had sent him bound*] The received text, following important authorities, has no conjunction. The Sinaitic MS. and some minor authorities insert 'now' or 'but' (δέ). But an overwhelming amount of evidence, including the Vatican MS., gives S. John's favourite particle, **therefore** (οὖν). Moreover the verb is aorist, not pluperfect. **Annas therefore sent Him.** It is not necessary to enquire whether the aorist may not virtually be pluperfect in meaning. Even if 'now' were genuine and the remark were an after-thought which ought to have preceded v. 19, the aorist might still be rendered literally, as in Matt. xxvi. 48 ('*gave* them,' not '*had given* them a sign'). Comp. Matt. xiv. 3, 4.

But 'therefore' shews that the remark is not an after-thought. Because the results of the preliminary investigation before Annas were such (there was a *primâ facie* case, but nothing conclusive), 'Annas *therefore* sent Him' for *formal* trial to Caiaphas, who had apparently been present (see on v. 19) during the previous interrogation and had taken part in it.

bound] He had been bound by the Roman soldiers and Jewish officials when He was arrested (v. 12). This was to prevent escape or rescue. During the examination he would be set free as possibly innocent. After the examination He was bound again as presumably guilty, or as before to prevent escape.

25. *And Simon Peter stood and warmed himself*] Better, **Now** *Simon Peter* **was standing and warming** *himself* (v. 18).

They said therefore] The movement in taking Jesus from Annas to Caiaphas once more attracted attention to the stranger by the fire.

Art not thou also] Rather, **Art thou also** (see on v. 17). A look of sympathy and distress on S. Peter's face, as His Master appears bound as a criminal, and perhaps with the mark of the blow (v. 22) on His face, provokes the exclamation, *Surely thou also art not one of His disciples?*

26. *his kinsman*] *A kinsman of him.* How natural that an acquaintance of the high-priest (v. 15) and known to his portress (v. 16) should know this fact also as well as Malchus' name (v. 10). This confirms the ordinary view that the 'other disciple' (v. 15) is the Evangelist himself. This third accusation and denial was, as S. Luke tells us, about an hour after the second; so that our Lord must have 'turned and looked upon Peter' either from a room looking into the

Peter cut off, saith, Did not I see thee in the garden with him? Peter then denied again: and immediately *the* cock 27 crew.

court, or as He was being led to receive the formal sentence of the Sanhedrin after the trial before Caiaphas, not as He was being taken from Annas to Caiaphas.
Did not I see thee] 'I' is emphatic; 'with my own eyes.'
27. *Peter then denied again*] *Again* **therefore** (*v.* 3) *Peter denied;* because he had denied before. S. John, like S. Luke, omits the oaths and curses (Mark xiv. 71; Matt. xxvi. 73). We may believe that S. Peter himself through S. Mark was the first to include this aggravation of his guilt in the current tradition.
the cock crew] Rather, a *cock crew*. In none of the gospels is there the definite article which our translation inserts. This was the second crowing (Mark xiv. 72). A difficulty has been made here because the Talmud says that fowls, which scratch in dunghills, are unclean. But (1) the Talmud is inconsistent on this point with itself; (2) not all Jews would be so scrupulous as to keep no fowls in Jerusalem; (3) certainly the Romans would care nothing about such scruples.

Just as the Evangelist implies (*v.* 11), without mentioning, the Agony in the garden, so he implies (xxi. 15), without mentioning, the repentance of S. Peter. The question has been raised, why he narrates S. Peter's fall, which had been thrice told already. There is no need to seek far-fetched explanations, as that "there might be contained in it some great principle or prophetic history, and perhaps both : some great principle to be developed in the future history of the Church, or of S. Peter's Church." Rather, it is part of S. John's own experience which falls naturally into the scope and plan of his Gospel, setting forth on the one side the Divinity of Christ, on the other the glorification of His manhood through suffering. Christ's foreknowledge of the fall of His chief apostle (xiii. 38) illustrated both: it was evidence of His Divinity (comp. ii. 24, 25), and it intensified His suffering. S. John, therefore, gives both the prophecy and the fulfilment. It has been noticed that it is "S. Peter's friend S. John, who seems to mention most what may lessen the fault of his brother apostle;" that servants and officers were about him; that in the second case he was pressed by more than one; and that on the last occasion a kinsman of Malchus was among his accusers, which may greatly have increased Peter's terror. Moreover, this instance of human frailty in one so exalted (an instance which the life of the great Exemplar Himself *could* not afford), is given us with fourfold emphasis, that none may presume and none despair.

On the difficulties connected with the four accounts of S. Peter's denials see Appendix B.

28—XIX. 16. THE ROMAN OR CIVIL TRIAL.

As already stated, S. John omits both the examination before Caiaphas and the Sanhedrin at an irregular time and place, at midnight and at 'the Booths' (Matt. xxvi. 57—68: Mark xiv. 53—65), and also the

28—XIX. 16. *The Roman or Civil Trial.*

28 Then led they Jesus from Caiaphas unto the hall of judgment: and it was early; and they themselves went not

formal meeting of the Sanhedrin after daybreak in the proper place (Matt. xxvii. 1; Mark xv. 1; Luke xxii. 66—71), at which Jesus was sentenced to death. He proceeds to narrate what the Synoptists omit, the conference between Pilate and the Jews (*vv.* 28—32) and two private examinations of Jesus by Pilate (*vv.* 33—38 and xix. 8—11). Here also we seem to have the evidence of an eyewitness. We know that S. John followed his Lord into the high priest's palace (*v.* 15), and stood by the Cross (xix. 26); it is therefore probable enough that he followed Him into the Procurator's court.

28. *Then led they*] Better, **They led therefore** (*v.* 3). S. John assumes that his readers know the result of Jesus being taken to Caiaphas (*v.* 24): He had been condemned to death; and now His enemies (there is no need to name them) take Him to the Roman governor to get the sentence executed.

the hall of judgment] The margin is better, *Pilate's house*, i.e. *the palace*. In the original it is *praitorion*, the Greek form of *praetorium*. Our translators have varied their rendering of it capriciously: Matt. xxvii. 27, 'common hall,' with 'governor's house' in the margin; Mark xv. 16, 'Praetorium;' John xviii. 33 and xix. 9, 'judgment-hall.' Yet the meaning must be the same in all these passages. Comp. Acts xxiii. 35, 'judgment-hall;' Phil. i. 13, 'the palace.' The meaning of *praetorium* varies according to the context. The word is of military origin; (1) 'the general's tent' or 'head quarters.' Hence, in the provinces, (2) 'the governor's residence,' the meaning in Acts xxiii. 35: in a sort of metaphorical sense, (3) a 'mansion' or 'palace' (Juvenal I. 75): at Rome, (4) 'the praetorian guard,' the probable meaning in Phil. i. 13. Of these leading significations the second is probably right here and throughout the Gospels; *the official residence of the Procurator*. Where Pilate resided in Jerusalem is not quite certain. We know that 'Herod's Praetorium,' a magnificent building on the western hill of Jerusalem, was used by Roman governors somewhat later (Philo, *Leg. ad Gaium*, p. 1034). But it is perhaps more likely that Pilate occupied part of the fortress Antonia, on the supposed site of which a chamber with a column in it has recently been discovered, which it is thought may possibly be the scene of the scourging.

S. John's narrative alternates between the *outside* and *inside* of the Praetorium. *Outside;* 28—32; 38—40; xix. 4—7; 12—16. *Inside;* 33—37; xix. 1—3; 8—11.

28—32. *Outside the Praetorium;* the Jews claim the execution of the Sanhedrin's sentence of death, and Pilate refuses it.

early] The same word, *proï*, is rendered 'morning' Matt. xvi. 3; Mark i. 35, xi. 20, xiii. 35, xv. 1; the last passage being partly parallel to this. In Mark xiii. 35 the word stands for the fourth watch (see on Mark vi. 48), which lasted from 3.0 to 6.0 A. M. A Roman court might

into the judgment hall, lest they should be defiled; but that they might eat the passover. Pilate then went out unto 29

be held directly after sunrise; and as Pilate had probably been informed that an important case was to be brought before him, delay in which might cause serious disturbance, there is nothing improbable in his being ready to open his court between 4.0 and 5.0 A.M. The hierarchy were in a difficulty. Jesus could not safely be arrested by daylight, and the Sanhedrin could not legally pronounce sentence of death by night: hence they had had to wait till dawn to condemn Him. Now another regulation hampers them: a day must intervene between sentence and execution. This they shuffled out of by going at once to Pilate. Of course if he undertook the execution, he must fix the time; and their representations would secure his ordering immediate execution. Thus they shifted the breach of the law from themselves to him.

As in the life of our Lord as a whole, so also in this last week and last day of it, the exact sequence and time of the events cannot be ascertained with certainty. Chronology is not what the Evangelists aim at giving us. For a tentative arrangement of the chief events of the Passion see Appendix C.

they themselves] In contrast with their Victim, whom they sent in under a Roman guard.

lest they should] Better, **that they might not,** omitting 'that they' in the next clause.

be defiled] by entering a house not properly cleansed of leaven (Ex. xii. 15).

eat the passover] It is quite evident that S. John does not regard the Last Supper as a Paschal meal. Comp. xiii. 1, 29. It is equally evident that the synoptic narratives convey the impression that the Last Supper was the ordinary Jewish Passover (Matt. xxvi. 17, 18, 19; Mark xiv. 14, 16; Luke xxii. 7, 8, 11, 13, 15). Whatever be the right solution of the difficulty, the independence of the author of the Fourth Gospel is manifest. Would anyone counterfeiting an Apostle venture thus to contradict what seemed to have such strong Apostolic authority? Would he not expect that a glaring discrepancy on so important a point would prove fatal to his pretensions? Assume that S. John is simply recording his own vivid recollections, whether or no we suppose him to be correcting the impression produced by the Synoptists, and *this* difficulty at any rate is avoided. S. John's narrative is too precise and consistent to be explained away. On the difficulty as regards the Synoptists see Appendix A; also Excursus V at the end of Dr Farrar's *S. Luke*.

29. *Pilate then*] *Pilate* **therefore** (*v.* 3). Because they would not enter, he went out to them. The Evangelist assumes that his readers know who Pilate is, just as he assumes that they know the Twelve (vi. 67) and Mary Magdalene (xix. 25); all are introduced without explanation.

went out] The verb stands first in the Greek for emphasis. The best MS. add 'outside' to make it still more emphatic; *went out there-*

them, and said, What accusation bring you against this man?
30 They answered and said unto him, If he were not a
malefactor, we would not have delivered him up unto thee.
31 Then said Pilate unto them, Take ye him, and judge him
according to your law. The Jews therefore said unto him,
32 It is not lawful for us to put any *man* to death: that the

fore Pilate outside unto them; as if attention were specially called to this
Roman concession to Jewish religiousness.
What accusation] Not that he does not know, but in accordance with
strict procedure he demands a formal indictment?
30. *a malefactor*] Literally, 'doing evil' or **an evil-doer**; not the
same expression as Luke xxiii. 32. The Jews are taken aback at
Pilate's evident intention of trying the case himself. They had expected
him merely to carry out their sentence, and had not come provided with
any definite accusation. Blasphemy, for which they had condemned
Him (Matt. xxvi. 65, 66), might be no crime with Pilate (comp. Acts
xviii. 16). Hence the vagueness of their first charge. Later on (xix. 7)
they throw in the charge of blasphemy; but they rely mainly on three
distinct charges, which being political, Pilate must hear; (1) seditious
agitation, (2) forbidding to give tribute to Caesar, (3) assuming the title,
'King of the Jews' (Luke xxiii. 3).
31. *Then said Pilate*] *Pilate* **therefore** (*v.* 3) *said.* If they will
not make a specific charge, he will not deal with the case. Pilate, impressed probably by his wife's dream (Matt. xxvii. 19) tries in various
ways to avoid sentencing Jesus to death. (1) He would have the Jews
deal with the case themselves; (2) he sends Jesus to Herod; (3) he proposes to release Him in honour of the Feast; (4) he will scourge Him
and let Him go. Roman governors were not commonly so scrupulous,
and Pilate was not above the average: a vague superstitious dread was
perhaps his strongest motive. Thrice in the course of these attempts
does he pronounce Jesus innocent (*v.* 39, xix. 4, 6).
Take ye, &c.] Literally, *Take him* **yourselves,** *and according to your
law judge Him.* 'Yourselves' and 'your' are emphatic and slightly
contemptuous. The 'therefore' which follows is wanting in most of
the best MSS.
It is not lawful, &c.] These words are to be taken quite literally,
and without any addition, such as 'at the Passover' or 'by crucifixion,'
or 'for high treason.' The question whether the Sanhedrin had or had
not the right to inflict capital punishment at this time is a vexed one.
On the one hand we have (1) this verse; (2) the statement of the Talmud
that 40 years before the destruction of Jerusalem the Jews lost this
power; (3) the evidence of Josephus (*Ant.* XX. ix. 1; comp. XVIII. i. 1;
XVI. ii. 4, and VI.) that the high priest could not summon a judicial
court of the Sanhedrin without the Procurator's leave; (4) the analogy
of Roman law. To this it is replied (Döllinger, *First age of the Church,*
Appendix II.); (1) that the Jews quibbled in order to cause Jesus to be
crucified at the Feast instead of stoned after all the people had dispersed;

saying of Jesus might be fulfilled, which he spake, signifying what death he should die. Then Pilate entered into 33 the judgment hall again, and called Jesus, and said unto

and Pilate would not have insulted the Jews from the tribunal by telling them to put Jesus to death, if they had no power to do so; (2) that the Talmud is in error, for the Roman dominion began 60 years before the destruction of Jerusalem; (3) that Josephus (xx. ix. 1) shews that the Jews *had* this power: Ananus is accused to Albinus not for *putting people to death*, but for *holding a court* without leave: had the former been criminal it would have been mentioned; (4) that the analogy of Roman law proves nothing, for cities and countries subject to Rome often retained their autonomy: and there are the cases of Stephen, those for whose death S. Paul voted (Acts xxvi. 10), and the Apostles, whom the Sanhedrin wished to put to death (Acts v. 33); and Gamaliel in dissuading the council never hints that to inflict death will bring trouble upon themselves. To this it may be replied again; (1) that Pilate would have exposed a quibble had there been one, and his dignity as judge was evidently not above shewing ironical contempt for the plaintiffs; (2) that the Talmud may be wrong about the date and right about the fact; possibly it is right about both; (3) to mention the holding of a court by Ananus was enough to secure the interference of Albinus, and more may have been said than Josephus reports; (4) autonomy in the case of subject states was the exception; therefore the burden of proof rests with those who assert it of the Jews. Stephen's death (if judicial at all) and the other cases (comp. John v. 18, vii. 1, 25, viii. 37, 59; Acts xxi. 31) only prove that the Jews sometimes ventured on acts of violence of which the Romans took little notice. Besides we do not know that in all these cases the Sanhedrin proposed to do more than to *sentence* to death, trusting to the Romans to execute the sentence, as here. Pilate's whole action, and his express statement xix. 10, seem to imply that he alone has the power to inflict death.

32. *the saying*] Or *word*, xii. 32; Matt. xx. 19.

what death] Rather, **by what manner of** *death*, as in xii. 33 and xxi. 19. So in x. 32 the Greek means 'for what *kind* of a work,' not merely 'for which work.' Comp. Matt. xxi. 23; xxii. 36; Luke vi. 32, xxiv. 19. Had the Sanhedrin executed Him as a blasphemer or a false prophet, He would have been stoned. The Jews had other forms of capital punishment, but crucifixion was not among them.

33—37. *Inside the Praetorium;* Jesus is privately examined by Pilate and makes 'a good confession' (1 Tim. vi. 13).

33. *Then Pilate*] *Pilate* **therefore** (*v.* 3). Because of the importunity of the Jews Pilate is obliged to investigate further; and being only Procurator, although *cum potestate*, has no Quaestor, but conducts the examination himself.

called Jesus] Probably the Roman guards had already brought Him inside the Praetorium: Pilate now calls Him before the judgment-seat.

34 him, Art thou the King of the Jews? Jesus answered him, Sayest thou this *thing* of thyself, or did others tell *it* thee of
35 me? Pilate answered, Am I a Jew? Thine own nation and the chief priests have delivered thee unto me: what hast
36 thou done? Jesus answered, My kingdom is not of this world: if my kingdom were of this world, then would my servants fight, that I should not be delivered to the Jews:
37 but now is my kingdom not from hence. Pilate therefore

The conversation implies that Jesus had not heard the previous conversation with the Jews.

Art thou the King of the Jews?] In all four Gospels these are the first words of Pilate to Jesus, and in all four there is an emphasis on 'Thou.' The pitiable appearance of Jesus was in such contrast to the royal title that Pilate speaks with a tone of surprise (comp. iv. 12). The question may mean either 'Dost Thou claim to be King?' or, 'Art Thou the so-called King?' The royal title first appears in the mouth of the wise men, Matt. ii. 1, next in the mouth of Pilate.

34. *answered him*] Omit 'him:' the introductions to *vv.* 34, 35, 36 are alike in form and are solemn in their brevity. The Synoptists give merely a portion of the reply in *v.* 37.

tell it thee] 'It' is not in the original and need not be supplied. Jesus claims a right to know the author of the charge. Moreover the meaning of the title, and therefore the truth of it, would depend on the person who used it. In Pilate's sense He was not King; in another sense He was.

35. *Am I a Jew?*] 'Is it likely that I, a Roman governor, have any interest in these Jewish questions?'

have delivered thee unto me: what hast thou done?] Better, **delivered Thee unto me: what didst Thou do** to make Thine own people turn against Thee?

36. *My kingdom*] There is a strong emphasis on 'My' throughout the verse; 'the kingdom that is Mine, the servants that are Mine;' i.e. those that are truly such (see on xiv. 27). The word for 'servants' here is the same as is rendered 'officers' in *vv.* 3, 12, 18, 22, vii. 32, 45, 46 (comp. Matt. v. 25), and no doubt contains an allusion to the officials of the Jewish hierarchy. In Luke i. 2, the only other place in the Gospels where the word is used of Christians, it is rendered 'ministers,' as also in 1 Cor. iv. 1, the only place where the word occurs in the Epistles. Comp. Acts xiii. 5.

is not of this world] Has not its origin or root there so as to draw its power from thence. Comp. viii. 23, x. 19, xvii. 14, 16.

if my kingdom] In the original the order is impressively reversed; *if of this world were My kingdom.* For the construction comp. v. 46.

fight] Better, **be striving** (comp. Luke xiii. 24; 1 Cor. ix. 25). For the construction comp. v. 46, viii. 19, 42, ix. 41, xv. 19.

but now] The meaning of 'now' is clear from the context and also

said unto him, Art thou a king then? Jesus answered, Thou sayest that I am a king. To this end was I born, and for this cause came I into the world, that I should bear witness unto the truth. Every one that is of the truth heareth my

from viii. 40, ix. 41, xv. 22, 24, 'as it is,' 'as the case really stands.' It does not mean 'My kingdom is not of this world *now*, but shall be so hereafter;' as if Christ were promising a millenium.

37. *Art thou a king then*] The Greek for 'then' (*oukoun*) occurs here only in N. T. The 'Thou' is even more emphatic than in *v*. 33. The two together give a tone of scorn to the question, which is half an exclamation. 'So then, *Thou* art a king!' Comp. i. 21.

Thou sayest that, &c.] This may be rendered, *Thou sayest* (truly); *because*, &c. But the A. V. is better: Christ leaves the title and explains the nature of His kingdom—the realm of truth.

To this end...for this cause] The Greek for both is the same, and should be rendered in the same way in English; **to this end.** Both refer to what precedes; not one to what precedes and one to what follows. To be a king, He became incarnate; to be a king, He entered the world.

was I born...came I] Better, **have I been born...am I come.** Both verbs are perfects and express not merely a past event but one which continues in its effects; Christ has come and remains in the world. The pronoun is very emphatic; in this respect Christ stands alone among men. The verbs point to His previous existence with the Father, although Pilate would not see this. The expression 'come into the world' is frequent in S. John (i. 9, ix. 39, xi. 27, xvi. 28): as applied to Christ it includes the notion of His *mission* (iii. 17, x. 36, xii. 47, 49, xvii. 18).

that I should] This is the Divine purpose of His royal power.

bear witness unto the truth] Not merely 'witness the truth,' i.e. give a testimony that is true, but bear witness to the objective reality of the Truth: again, not merely 'bear witness *of*,' i.e. respecting the Truth (i. 7, 15, ii. 25, v. 31—39, viii. 13—18, &c.), but 'bear witness *to*,' i.e. in support and defence of the Truth (v. 33). Both these expressions, 'witness' and 'truth,' have been seen to be very frequent in S. John (see especially chaps. i. iii. v. viii. *passim*). We have them combined here, as in v. 33. This is the object of Christ's sovereignty,—to bear witness to the Truth. It is characteristic of the Gospel that it claims to be 'the Truth.' "This title of the Gospel is not found in the Synoptists, Acts, or Apocalypse; but it occurs in the Catholic Epistles (James i. 18; 1 Pet. i. 22; 2 Pet. ii. 2) and in S. Paul (2 Thess. ii. 12; 2 Cor. xiii. 8; Eph. i. 13, &c). It is specially characteristic of the Gospel and Epistles of S. John." Westcott, *Introduction to S. John*, p. xliv.

that is of the truth] That has his root in it, so as to draw the power of his life from it. Comp. *v*. 36, iii. 31, viii. 47, and especially 1 John ii. 21, iii. 19.

"It is of great interest to compare this confession before Pilate with the corresponding confession before the high priest (Matt. xxvi. 64).

38 voice. Pilate saith unto him, What is truth? And when he had said this, he went out again unto the Jews, and 39 saith unto them, I find in him no fault *at all*. But ye have a custom, that I should release unto you one at the

The one addressed to the Jews is in the language of prophecy, the other addressed to a Roman appeals to the universal testimony of conscience. The one speaks of a future manifestation of glory, the other of a present manifestation of truth......... It is obvious how completely they answer severally to the circumstances of the two occasions." Westcott, *in loco*.

38. *What is truth?*] Pilate does not ask about '*the* Truth,' but truth in any particular case. His question does not indicate any serious wish to know what truth really is, nor yet the despairing scepticism of a baffled thinker; nor, on the other hand, is it uttered in a light spirit of 'jesting' (as Bacon thought). Rather it is the half-pitying, half-impatient, question of a practical man of the world, whose experience of life has convinced him that truth is a dream of enthusiasts, and that a kingdom in which truth is to be supreme is as visionary as that of the Stoics. He has heard enough to convince him that the Accused is no dangerous incendiary, and he abruptly brings the investigation to a close with a question, which to his mind cuts at the root of the Prisoner's aspirations. Here probably we must insert the sending to Herod Antipas, who had come from Tiberias, as Pilate from Caesarea, on account of the Feast, the one to win popularity, the other to keep order (Luke xxiii. 6—12).

38—40. *Outside the Praetorium;* Pilate pronounces Him innocent and offers to release Him in honour of the feast: the Jews prefer Barabbas.

38. *unto the Jews*] Apparently this means the mob and not the hierarchy. Pilate hoped that only a minority were moving against Jesus; by an appeal to the majority he might be able to acquit Him without incurring odium By pronouncing Him legally innocent he would gain this majority; by proposing to release Him on account of the Feast rather than of His innocence he would avoid insulting the Sanhedrin, who had already pronounced Him guilty. From S. Mark (xv. 8, 11) it would appear that *some* of the multitude hoped to deliver Jesus on the plea of the Feast and took the initiative in reminding Pilate of the custom, but were controlled by the priests and made to clamour for Barabbas.

I find in him no fault at all] Rather, *I find no* **ground of accusation** *in him*. As in xix. 6, the pronoun is emphatic; 'I, the Roman judge, in contrast to you Jewish fanatics.' The word here and xix. 4, 6 rendered 'fault' (*aitia*) is rendered 'accusation' Matt. xxvii. 37 and Mark xv. 26, and 'cause' Acts xiii. 28, xxviii. 18. In all these passages it seems to mean 'legal ground for prosecution.'

39. *ye have a custom*] Nothing is known of this custom beyond what is told us in the Gospels. Prisoners were sometimes released at Rome at certain festivals, and it would be quite in harmony with the

passover: will ye therefore *that* I release unto you the King of the Jews? Then cried they all again, saying, Not this 40 *man*, but Barabbas. Now Barabbas was a robber.

conciliatory policy of Rome to honour native festivals in this way in the case of subject nations. In Luke xxiii. 17 the custom is said to be an obligation; 'of necessity he must;' but the verse is of very doubtful genuineness.

that I should] Literally, *in order that I should*. See on xv. 12.
the King of the Jews] Expressive of scornful contempt. Comp. xix. 15.

40. *Then cried they all again*] Better, **They cried out therefore** (*v.* 3) *again all of them*. S. John has not mentioned any previous shout of the multitude; he once more assumes that his readers know the chief facts. See on xix. 6.

Barabbas] Or, *Bar-Abbas*, son of Abba (father). The innocent Son of the Father is rejected for the blood-stained son of a father. In Matt. xxvii. 16 and 17 some inferior authorities read '*Jesus* Barabbas' as his name, and Pilate asks 'Which do ye wish that I release to you, Jesus Barabbas, or Jesus Who is called Christ?' The reading is remarkable, but it is supported by no good MS.

Now Barabbas was a robber] There is a tragic impressiveness in this brief remark. Comp. 'Jesus wept' (xi. 35), and 'And it was night' (xiii. 30). It is to be regretted that 'robber' has not always been given as the translation of the Greek word used here ($\lambda\eta\sigma\tau\dot\eta s$ not $\kappa\lambda\dot\epsilon\pi\tau\eta s$). Thus we should have 'den of *robbers*' or '*robbers*' cave' (Matt. xxi. 13); 'as against a *robber*' (Matt. xxvi. 55); 'two *robbers*' (Matt. xxvii. 38, 44). The 'robber' is the bandit or brigand, who is more dangerous to persons than to property, and sometimes combines something of chivalry with his violence. In the case of Barabbas we know from S. Mark and S. Luke that he had been guilty of insurrection and consequent bloodshed rather than of stealing; and this was very likely the case also with the two robbers crucified with Jesus. Thus by a strange irony of fate the hierarchy obtain the release of a man guilty of the very political crime with which they charged Christ,—sedition. The people no doubt had some sympathy with the insurrectionary movement of Barabbas, and on this the priests worked. Barabbas had done, just what Jesus had refused to do, take the lead against the Romans. "They laid information against Jesus before the Roman government as a dangerous character; their real complaint against Him was precisely this, that He was not dangerous. Pilate executed Him on the ground that His kingdom was of this world; the Jews procured His execution precisely because it was not." *Ecce Homo*, p. 27.

CHAP. XIX.

19 Then Pilate therefore took Jesus, and scourged *him*. And
2 the soldiers platted a crown of thorns, and put *it* on his head,
3 and they put on him a purple robe, and said, Hail, King of

CHAP. XIX.

1—3. *Inside the Praetorium;* the scourging and mockery by the soldiers.

1. *Then Pilate therefore*] Because the attempt to release Him in honour of the Feast had failed, Pilate now tries whether the severe and degrading punishment of scourging will not satisfy the Jews. In Pilate's hands the boasted justice of Roman Law ends in the policy "What evil did He do? I found no cause of death in Him: I will *therefore* chastise Him and let Him go" (Luke xxiii. 22). Scourging was part of Roman capital punishment, and had we only the first two Gospels we might suppose that the scourging was inflicted immediately before the crucifixion: but this is not stated, and S. John, combined with S. Luke, makes it clear that scourging was inflicted as a separate punishment in the hope that it would suffice. The supposition of a second scourging as part of the execution is unnecessary and improbable. Pilate, sick of the bloody work and angry at being forced to commit a judicial murder, would not have allowed it; and it may be doubted whether any human frame could have survived a Roman scourging twice in one day. One infliction was sometimes fatal; *ille flagellis ad mortem caesus*, Hor. *S.* I. ii. 41. Comp. '*horribile flagellum*' *S.* I. iii. 119.

2. *And the soldiers*] Herod and his troops (Luke xxiii. 11) had set an example which the Roman soldiers were ready enough to follow. Pilate countenances the brutality as aiding his own plan of satisfying Jewish hatred with something less than death. The soldiers had inflicted the scourging; for Pilate, being only Procurator, would have no lictors.

a crown of thorns] The context seems to shew that this was in mockery of a royal crown rather than of a victor's wreath. The plant is supposed to be the thorny *nâbk*, with flexible branches, and leaves like ivy, abundant in the Jordan valley and round about Jerusalem.

a purple robe] S. Mark has 'purple,' S. Matthew 'scarlet,' S. Luke is silent. 'Purple' with the ancients was a vague term for bright rich colour and would be used of crimson as well as of violet. The robe was a military *chlamys*, or *paludamentum*, perhaps one of Pilate's cast-off cloaks. The garment in which Herod had mocked Jesus was probably white. Comp. 1 Macc. viii. 14, x. 20, 62. The scourging and mockery were very possibly visible to the Jews outside.

3. *And said*] The best authorities add a graphic touch not given by the Synoptists; *and* **they kept coming unto Him and saying.** We see each soldier coming up in turn to offer his mock homage.

Hail, King of the Jews] Like the Procurator, they mock the Jews as well as their Victim.

the Jews: and they smote him with their hands. Pilate 4
therefore went forth again, and saith unto them, Behold, I
bring him forth to you, that ye may know that I find no
fault in him. Then came Jesus forth, wearing the crown of 5
thorns, and the purple robe. And *Pilate* saith unto them,
Behold the man. When the chief priests therefore and 6
officers saw him, they cried out, saying, Crucify *him*, crucify
him. Pilate saith unto them, Take ye him, and crucify

smote him with their hands] Literally, **gave Him blows**, but whether with a rod, as the root of the word implies, or with the hand, as is more probable, we are uncertain (see on xviii. 22). The old Latin version adds *in faciem.*

4—7. *Outside the Praetorium;* Pilate's appeal, 'Behold the *man;*' the Jews' rejoinder, 'He made Himself *Son of God.*'

4. *Pilate therefore*] The true text gives, **and** *Pilate.* What follows is a continuance rather than a consequence of what has preceded.

I find no fault in him] There is a slight change from xix. 38, the emphasis here being on 'crime' instead of on 'I'; **ground of accusation I find none in Him.**

5. *Then came Jesus*] Better, *Jesus* **therefore** *came.* The Evangelist repeats the details of *v.* 2; they are details of a picture deeply imprinted on his memory. Whether or no he went into the Praetorium, he no doubt witnessed the *Ecce Homo.*

wearing] Not simply 'having' or 'bearing' (*phorôn* not *pherôn*). The crown and robe are now His permanent dress.

Behold the man!] In pity rather than contempt. Pilate appeals to their humanity: surely the most bitter among them will now be satisfied, or at least the more compassionate will control the rest. No one can think that this Man is dangerous, or needs further punishment. When this appeal fails, Pilate's pity turns to bitterness (*v.* 14).

6. *and officers*] Better (as in xviii. 18), *and* **the** *officers.* The leaders take the initiative, to prevent any expression of compassion on the part of the crowd. The sight of 'the Man' maddens rather than softens them.

cried out] The verb (*kraugazo*) expresses a *loud* cry, and (excepting Matt. xii. 19; Acts xxii. 23) occurs only in this Gospel in N.T. Comp. xi. 43, xii. 13, xviii. 40, xix. 12, 15.

Crucify him] Omit the pronoun, which is not in the Greek. The simple imperative better expresses the cry which was to give the cue to the multitude. According to all four Evangelists the demand for *crucifixion* was not made at first, but after the offer to release Jesus in honour of the Feast.

Take ye him] Better, *Take Him* **yourselves**, as in xviii. 31. We may admit that it ought to have been beneath the dignity of a Roman judge to taunt the people with a suggestion which he knew that they dare not follow; but there is nothing so improbable in it as to compel

7 *him:* for I find no fault in him. The Jews answered him, We have a law, and by our law he ought to die, because he made himself the Son of God.

8 When Pilate therefore heard that saying, he was the 9 more afraid; and went again into the judgment hall, and saith unto Jesus, Whence art thou? But Jesus gave him no 10 answer. Then saith Pilate unto him, Speakest thou not unto me? knowest thou not that I have power to crucify 11 thee, and have power to release thee? Jesus answered, Thou

us to believe that the Jews *had* the power of inflicting capital punishment (see on xviii. 31). Pilate is goaded into an exhibition of feeling unworthy of his office.

for I find] As in xviii. 38, the 'I' is emphatic; 'for *I* do not find in Him a ground of accusation.'

7. *We have a law*] The Jews answer Pilate's taunt by a plea hitherto kept in the background. He may think lightly of the seditious conduct of Jesus, but as a Procurator he is bound by Roman precedent to pay respect to the law of subject nationalities. He has challenged them to take the law into their own hands; let him hear what their law is.

by our law] Rather, *according to* **the** *law;* 'of us' is not genuine. They refer to Lev. xxiv. 16.

the Son of God] Omit 'the.' Pilate had said, 'Behold the *Man!*' The Jews retort, 'He made Himself *Son of God.*' Comp. v. 18, x. 33. They answer his appeal to their compassion by an appeal to his fears.

8—11. *Inside the Praetorium;* Christ's origin is asked and not told; the origin of authority is told unasked.

8. *that saying*] Better, **this word** (*logos*), the charge of blasphemy.

he was the more afraid] The message from his wife and the awe which Christ's presence was probably inspiring had already in some degree affected him. This mysterious claim still further excites his fears. Was it the offspring of a divinity that he had so infamously handled? Comp. Matt. xxvii. 54.

9. *judgment-hall*] See on xviii. 28.

Whence art thou?] Pilate tries a vague question which might apply to Christ's dwelling-place, which he already knew (Luke xxiii. 6), hoping for an answer as to His *origin.* Would the prisoner assert his mysterious claim to him, or explain it?

no answer] Pilate could not have understood the answer; and what had it to do with the merits of the case? Comp. Matt. xxvii. 12—14 and Christ's own precept, Matt. vii. 6.

10. *Then saith,* &c.] Better, *Pilate* **therefore** *saith to Him, To* **me** *Speakest thou not?* Whatever He might do before His Jewish persecutors, it was folly to refuse an answer to the Roman governor.

power] Or, **authority.** See on i. 12 and comp. v. 27, x. 18, xvii. 2. In the best texts 'to release' is placed first, 'to crucify' second.

couldest have no power *at all* against me, except it were given thee from above: therefore he that delivered me unto thee hath the greater sin. *And* from thenceforth Pilate 12 sought to release him : but the Jews cried out, saying, If thou let this *man* go, thou art not Cesar's friend : whoso-

11. *Thou couldest*] Or, **wouldest.** This is Christ's last word to Pilate ; a defence of the supremacy of God, and a protest against the claim of any human potentate to be irresponsible.
from above] i.e. from God. This even Pilate could understand : had Jesus said 'from My Father' he would have remained uninstructed. The point is not, that Pilate is an instrument ordained for the carrying out of God's purposes (Acts ii. 23); he was such, but that is not the meaning here. Rather, that the possession and exercise of all authority is the gift of God; iii. 27; Rom. xiii. 1—7 (see notes there). To interpret 'from above' of the higher tribunal of the Sanhedrin is quite inadequate. Comp. iii. 3, 7, 31; James i. 17, iii. 15, 17, where the same adverb, *anōthen*, is used: see notes in each place.
therefore] Better, **for this cause** (xii. 18, 27); comp. i. 31, v. 16, 18, vii. 22, viii. 47.
he that delivered me unto thee] Caiaphas, the representative of the Sanhedrin and of the nation. The expression rendered 'he that delivered' is used in xiii. 11, xviii. 2, 5 of Judas. But the addition 'to thee' shews that Judas is not meant; Judas had not betrayed Jesus to Pilate but to the Sanhedrin. The same verb is used of the Sanhedrin delivering Him to Pilate, xviii. 35.
hath the greater sin] Because he had the opportunity of knowing Who Jesus was. Once more we have the expression, peculiar to S. John, 'to have sin' (ix. 41, xv. 22, 24; 1 John i. 8).
12—16. *Outside the Praetorium;* the power from above controlled from below pronounces public sentence against the Innocent.
12. *And from thenceforth*] Or (as in vi. 66), **Hereupon.** Result rather than time seems to be meant; but the Greek (here and vi. 66 only in N.T.) may mean either. Omit 'and.'
sought] Imperfect tense, of continued efforts. Indirect means, such as the release in honour of the Feast, the appeal to compassion, and taunts having proved unsuccessful, Pilate now makes more direct efforts to release Jesus. What these were the Evangelist does not tell us.
If thou let this man go] Better, *If thou* **release** *this man;* it is the same verb as in the first clause. The Jews once more shift their tactics and from the ecclesiastical charge (*v.* 7) go back to the political, which they now back up by an appeal to Pilate's own political interests. They know their man: it is not a love of justice, but personal feeling which moves him to seek to release Jesus; and they will overcome one personal feeling by another still stronger. Pilate's unexplained interest in Jesus and supercilious contempt for His accusers must give way before a fear for his own position and possibly even his life.
Cesar's friend] Whether or no there was any such title of honour

13 ever maketh himself a king speaketh against Cesar. When Pilate therefore heard that saying, he brought Jesus forth, and sat down in the judgment seat in a place *that is* called 14 the Pavement, but in the Hebrew, Gabbatha. And it was

as *amicus Cesaris*, like our 'Queen's Counsel,' there is no need to suppose that any formal official distinction is intended here. The words probably mean no more than 'loyal to Cesar.'
whosoever] Literally, **every one who**.
maketh himself] Comp. v. 7, x. 33. The phrase perhaps implies action as well as words.
speaketh against Caesar] *ipso facto* declares himself a rebel; and for a Roman governor to countenance and even protect such a person would be high treason (*majestas*). The Jews perhaps scarcely knew how powerful their weapon was. Pilate's patron Sejanus (executed A.D. 31) was losing his hold over Tiberius, even if he had not already fallen. Pilate had already thrice nearly driven the Jews to revolt, and his character therefore would not stand high with an Emperor who justly prided himself on the good government of the provinces. Above all, the terrible *Lex Majestatis* was by this time worked in such a way that prosecution under it was almost certain death.
13. *that saying*] The better reading gives, **these words**. Pilate's mind seems to be made up at once.
brought Jesus forth] Sentence must be pronounced in public. Thus we find that Pilate, in giving judgment about the standards, which had been brought into Jerusalem, has his tribunal in the great circus at Caesarea, and Florus erects his in front of the palace (Josephus, *B. J.* II. ix. 3, xiv. 8).
sat down] The Greek verb (*kathizo*) may be either transitive, as in 1 Cor. vi. 4; Eph. i. 20, or intransitive, as in Matt. xix. 28; xxv. 31. If it is transitive here, the meaning will be, 'placed him on a seat,' as an illustration of his mocking exclamation, 'Behold your King!'—i.e. 'There He sits enthroned!' But [viii. 2;] xii. 14; Rev. iii. 21, xx. 4, the only places where S. John uses the word, and Acts xii. 21, xxv. 6, 17, where we have the same phrase as here, are against the transitive meaning in this place.
in the judgment seat] In the true text there is no article, which may mean that it was not the usual *Bema* but a temporary one. Every where else in N. T. 'judgment seat' has the definite article.
Pavement] Literally, *stone-paved*. Josephus (*Ant.* v. v. 2) says that the Temple-mount, on part of which the fortress of Antonia stood, was covered with a tesselated pavement.
in the Hebrew, Gabbatha] Omit 'the,' as in v. 20, and see on xx. 16. It was, we may conclude "from its having a Hebrew name, a fixed spot, and not the portable mosaic work which Roman generals sometimes carried about with them." S. p. 250. The fact that there was a fixed pavement supports this view; but Gabbatha (= *Gab Baitha*) means 'the ridge of the House' i.e. 'the Temple-mound,' and refers to the shape of the ground (like a *back*), not to the pavement upon it.

the preparation of the passover, and about the sixth hour:

14. *the preparation*] i.e. the day before the Passover, the 'eve.' See Appendix A.

and about the sixth hour] The best MSS. have 'it was' for 'and;' **it was** *about the sixth hour*. In two abrupt sentences S. John calls special attention to the day and hour; *now it was the eve of the Passover: it was about the sixth hour*. It is difficult to believe that he can be utterly mistaken about both. The question of the day is discussed elsewhere (Appendix A); the question as to the hour remains.

We have seen already (i. 39, iv. 6, 52, xi. 9), that whatever view we may take of the *balance* of probability in each case, there is nothing thus far which is conclusively in favour of the antecedently improbable view, that S. John reckons the hours of the day as we do, from midnight to noon and noon to midnight.

The modern method is sometimes spoken of as the *Roman* method. This is misleading, as it seems to imply that the Romans counted their hours as we do. If this were so, it would not surprise us so much to find that S. John, living away from Palestine and in the capital of a Roman province, had adopted the Roman reckoning. *But the Romans and Greeks, as well as the Jews, counted their hours from sunrise.* Martial, who goes through the day hour by hour (IV. viii.), places the Roman method beyond a doubt. The difference between the Romans and the Jews was not as to the *mode of counting the hours*, but as to the *limits of each individual day*. The Jews placed the boundary at sunset, the Romans (as we do) at midnight. (Comp. Pliny *Nat. Hist.* II. lxxvii.) The 'this day' of Pilate's wife (Matt. xxvii. 19) proves nothing; it would fit either the Roman or the Jewish method; and some suppose her to have been a proselyte. In this particular S. John *does* seem to have adopted the Roman method; for (xx. 19) he speaks of the evening of Easter Day as 'the *same* day at evening' (comp. Luke xxiv. 29, 33). This must be admitted as against the explanation that 'yesterday' in iv. 54 was spoken before midnight and refers to the time before sunset: but the servants may have met their master after midnight.

But there is some evidence of a custom of reckoning the hours from midnight in Asia Minor. Polycarp was martyred 'at the eighth hour' (*Mart. Pol.* XXI.), Pionius at 'the tenth hour' (*Acta Mart.* p. 137); both at Smyrna. Such exhibitions commonly took place in the morning (Philo, II. 529); so that 8.0 and 10.0 A.M. are more probable than 2.0 and 4.0 P.M.

McClellan adds another argument. "The phraseology of our present passage is unique in the Gospels. The *hour* is mentioned *in conjunction with the day*. To cite the words of St Augustine, but with the correct rendering of *Paraskeuê*, 'S. John does not say, *It was about the sixth hour of the day*, nor merely, *It was about the sixth hour*, but *It was the* FRIDAY *of the Passover; it was about the* SIXTH *hour*.' Hence in the straightforward sense of the words, the sixth hour that he means is the *sixth hour of the Friday;* and so it is rendered in the Thebaic Version.

15 and he saith unto the Jews, Behold your King. But they cried out, Away with *him*, away with *him*, crucify him. Pilate saith unto them, Shall I crucify your King? The 16 chief priests answered, We have no king but Cesar. Then delivered he him therefore unto them to be crucified. And they took Jesus, and led *him* away.

But *Friday* in S. John is the name of the whole *Roman civil day*, and the *Roman civil days* are reckoned from *midnight.*" *New Test.* I. p. 742.
 This solution may therefore be adopted, not as certain, but as less unsatisfactory than the conjecture of a false reading either here or in Mark xv. 25, or the various forced interpretations which have been given of S. John's words. If, however, the mode of reckoning in both Gospels be the same, the preference in point of accuracy must be given to the Evangelist who stood by the cross.
 Behold your King.] Like the title on the cross and unlike the "*Ecce Homo,*" these words are spoken in bitter irony. This man in His mock insignia is a fit sovereign for the miserable Jews. Perhaps Pilate would also taunt them with their own glorification of Him on Palm Sunday.
 15. *But they*] The true text gives, **They therefore**, with the pronoun of opposition (*ekeinoi*) in harmony with their cry. They will have nothing to do with such a king.
 Shall I] Or, **must** *I*. There is a strong emphasis on 'King,' which stands first in the original. Pilate begins (xviii. 33) and ends with the same idea, the one dangerous item in the indictment, the claim of Jesus to be King of the Jews.
 The chief priests] This depth of degradation was reserved for them. "The official organs of the theocracy themselves proclaim that they have abandoned the faith by which the nation had lived." Sooner than acknowledge that Jesus is the Messiah they proclaim that a heathen Emperor is their King. And their baseness is at once followed by Pilate's: sooner than meet a dangerous charge he condemns the innocent to death.
 16. *Then delivered he*, &c.] Better, *Then* **therefore** *delivered he,* &c. In none of the Gospels does it appear that Pilate pronounced sentence *on* Jesus; he perhaps purposely avoided doing so. But in delivering Him over to the priests he does not allow them to act for themselves: 'he delivered Him to them that *He might be crucified*' by Roman soldiers; not that they might crucify Him themselves.
 And they took] The best authorities give, *They* **therefore** *took*. The word for 'took' should rather be rendered *received*, as in the only other places in which it occurs in this Gospel, i. 11, xiv. 3. It means to 'accept what is offered, receive from the hands of another.' A comparison of the three texts is instructive. The eternal Son is given by the Father, comes to his own inheritance, and His own people received Him not (i. 11). The Incarnate Son is given up by Pilate to His own people, and they received Him to crucify Him (xix. 16). The glorified

17—42. *The Death and Burial.*

17—22. *The Crucifixion and the Title on the Cross.*

And he bearing his cross went forth into a place called 17 *the place* of a skull, which is called in the Hebrew Golgotha: where they crucified him, and two other with him, on either 18

Son comes again to His own people, to receive them unto Himself (xiv. 3).

and led him away] These words are of very doubtful authority.

17—42. THE DEATH AND BURIAL.

For what is peculiar to S. John's narrative in this section see the introductory note to chap. xviii. Besides this, the title on the cross, the Jews' criticism of it, and the conduct of the four soldiers, are given with more exactness by S. John than by the Synoptists.

The section falls into four double parts of which the second and fourth contain a marked dramatic contrast, such as S. John loves to point out:—

(1) *The Crucifixion and the title on the cross* (17—22).
(2) *The four enemies and the four friends* (23—27).
(3) *The two words,* 'I thirst,' 'It is finished' (28—30).
(4) *The hostile and the friendly petitions* (31—42).

17—22. THE CRUCIFIXION AND THE TITLE ON THE CROSS.

17. *bearing his cross*] The better reading gives, *bearing* **the cross** for Himself. S. John omits the help which Simon the Cyrenian was soon compelled to render, as also (what seems to be implied by Mark xv. 22) that at last they were obliged to carry Jesus Himself. Comp. the Lesson for Good Friday morning, Gen. xxii., especially *v.* 6.

went forth] "The place of public execution appears to have been situated north of the city. It was outside the gate (Heb. xiii. 12) and yet 'nigh unto the city' (*v.* 20). In the Mishna it is placed outside the city by a reference to Lev. xxiv. 14. It is said to have been 'two men high' (Sanh. vi. 1). The Jews still point out the site at the cliff, north of the Damascus gate, where is a cave now called 'Jeremiah's Grotto.' This site has therefore some claim to be considered as that of the Crucifixion. It was within 200 yards of the wall of Agrippa, but was certainly outside the ancient city. It was also close to the gardens and the tombs of the old city, which stretch northwards from the cliff; and it was close to the main north road, in a conspicuous position, such as might naturally be selected for a place of public execution." Conder, *Handbook to the Bible*, pp. 356, 7.

of a skull] Probably on account of its shape. It would be contrary to Jewish law to leave skulls unburied; and if this were the meaning of the name we should expect 'of skulls' rather than 'of a skull.'

18. *two other*] Robbers or bandits (not 'thieves'), as S. Matthew

19 side one, and Jesus in the midst.   And Pilate wrote
a title, and put *it* on the cross. And the writing was,
JESUS OF NAZARETH THE KING OF THE JEWS.
20 This title then read many of the Jews: for the place where
Jesus was crucified was nigh to the city: and it was written in
21 Hebrew, *and* Greek, *and* Latin. Then said the chief priests
of the Jews to Pilate, Write not, The King of the Jews;

and S. Mark call them, probably guilty of the same crimes as Barabbas
(see on xviii. 40). Jesus is crucified with them as being condemned
under a similar charge of sedition and treason.

Jesus in the midst]   Here also we seem to have a tragic contrast
—the Christ between two criminals. It is the place of honour mockingly given to Him as King.

19.   *a title*]   Better, *a title* **also.**   It was common to put on the cross
the name and crime of the person executed, after making him carry it
round his neck to the place of execution. S. John alone tells us that
Pilate wrote the title himself. The meaning of the 'also' is not quite
clear; perhaps it looks back to *v.* 16. S. John uses the Latin term,
titulus, in a Greek form, *titlos*. S. Matthew has 'His indictment'
(xxvii. 37); S. Mark, 'the inscription of His indictment' (xv. 26);
S. Luke, 'an inscription' (xxiii. 38).

the writing was]   Literally, **there was written** (see on ii. 17).   The
other three give the inscription thus;—S. Matthew, 'This is Jesus the
King of the Jews;' S. Mark, 'The King of the Jews;' S. Luke, 'This
is the King of the Jews.'

20.   *nigh to the city*]   Pictures are often misleading in placing the city
a mile or two in the background of the Crucifixion. S. John's exact
topographical knowledge comes out again here.

in Hebrew, and Greek, and Latin]   The better texts give, *In Hebrew
and* **in Latin** *and* **in Greek.**   The national and the official languages
would naturally be placed before Greek,—and for different reasons
either Hebrew or Latin might be placed first. In Luke xxiii. 38 the
order is Greek, Latin, Hebrew; but the clause is of very doubtful
authority. In any case the three representative languages of the world
at that time, the languages of religion, of empire, and of intellect, were
employed. Thus did they 'tell it out among the heathen that the Lord
is king,' or (according to a remarkable reading of the LXX. in Ps. xcvi.
10) 'that the Lord reigned from the tree.' (See on xx. 16.)

21.   *Then said*]   Better, *said* **therefore.**   Now that they have wrung
what they wanted out of Pilate they see that in granting it he has insulted them publicly before the thousands present at the Passover, and
in a way not easy to resent.

the chief priests of the Jews]   The addition 'of the Jews' is remarkable,
and it occurs nowhere else in N.T. It probably refers to the title:
these 'chief priests *of the Jews*' objected to His being called 'the King
of the Jews.'

but that he said, I am King of the Jews. Pilate answered, 22 What I have written I have written.

23—27. *The four Enemies and the four Friends.*

Then the soldiers, when they had crucified Jesus, took his 23 garments, and made four parts, to every soldier a part; and *also his* coat: now the coat was without seam, woven from the top throughout. They said therefore among themselves, 24 Let us not rent it, but cast lots for it, whose it shall be: that the scripture might be fulfilled, which saith, They parted my raiment among them, and for my vesture

22. *Pilate answered*] His answer illustrates the mixture of obstinacy and relentlessness, which Philo says was characteristic of him. His own interests are not at stake, so he will have his way: where he had anything to fear or to gain he could be supple enough. A shrewd, practical man of the world, with all a Roman official's contemptuous impartiality and severity, and all the disbelief in truth and disinterestedness which the age had taught him, he seems to have been one of the many whose self-interest is stronger than their convictions, and who can walk uprightly when to do so is easy, but fail in the presence of danger and difficulty.

23—27. THE FOUR ENEMIES AND THE FOUR FRIENDS.

23. *Then the soldiers*] Better, *The soldiers* **therefore.** The 'therefore' looks back to *v.* 18.

his garments] The loose, outer garment, or toga, with the girdle and fastenings. This was large enough to be worth dividing, and in some cases was the only garment worn.

four parts] A mark of accurate knowledge; a quaternion of soldiers has charge of the prisoner, as in Acts xii. 4; but there the prisoner has to be guarded and kept alive, so four quaternions mount guard in turn, one for each watch. The clothes of executed criminals were the perquisite of the soldiers on duty.

his coat] Better, **the** *coat* or **shirt**: it fitted somewhat close to the body, reaching from the neck to the knees or ancles.

without seam] Josephus tells us that that of the high-priest was seamless, whereas in other cases this garment was commonly made of two pieces (*Ant.* III. vii. 4).

24. *that the scripture*] It was *in order that* the Divine purpose, already declared by the Psalmist, might be accomplished, that this twofold assignment of Christ's garments took place. S. John quotes the LXX. verbatim, although there the difference, which both he and the original Hebrew mark between the upper and under garment, is obliterated. It is from this passage that the reference to Ps. xxii. 18 has been inserted in Matt. xxvii. 35; none of the Synoptists refer to the Psalm.

my raiment] A capricious change of translation; the same word is rendered **garments** in *v.* 23.

they did cast lots. These *things* therefore the soldiers did.

25 Now there stood by the cross of Jesus his mother, and his mother's sister, Mary the *wife* of Cleophas, and Mary 26 Magdalene. When Jesus therefore saw *his* mother, and the disciple standing by, whom he loved, he saith unto his 27 mother, Woman, behold thy son. Then saith he to the

25. *Now there stood*] Or, **But** *there* **were standing.** By two small particles (*men* in *v.* 23 and *de* here), scarcely translatable in English, S. John indicates the contrast between the two groups. On the one hand, the four plundering soldiers with the centurion; on the other, the four ministering women with the beloved disciple.

his mother's sister, Mary] The Greek, like the English, leaves us in doubt whether we here have two women or one, whether altogether there are four women or three. The former is much the more probable alternative. (1) It avoids the very improbable supposition of two sisters having the same name. (2) S. John is fond of *parallel* expressions; 'His mother and His mother's sister, Mary of Clopas and Mary Magdalene' are two pairs set one against the other. (3) S. Mark (xv. 40) mentions Mary Magdalene, Mary the mother of James the Less, and Salome. Mary Magdalene is common to both narratives, 'Mary the mother of James the Less' is the same as 'Mary of Clopas:' the natural inference is that Salome is the same as 'His mother's sister.' If this is correct, (4) S. John's silence about the name of 'His mother's sister' is explained: she was his own mother, and he is habitually reserved about all closely connected with himself. We have seen already that he never mentions either his own name, or his brother's, or the Virgin's. (5) The very ancient Peshito or Syriac Version adopts this view by inserting 'and' before 'Mary the (wife) of Clopas.'

the wife of Cleophas] Rather, *the wife of* **Clopas.** The Greek is simply 'the of Clopas,' and 'the *daughter* of Clopas' may be right, or 'the *mother*,' or even 'the *sister:*' but 'wife' is more probably to be supplied. There is no reason for identifying Clopas here with Cleopas in Luke xxiv. 18: Clopas is Aramaic, Cleopas is Greek. The spelling Cleop*h*as is a mistake derived from Latin MSS. All Greek authorities have Cleopas. If 'wife' is rightly inserted, and she is the mother of James the Less, Clopas is the same as Alphaeus (Matt. x. 3; comp. xxvii. 56). It is said that Clopas and Alphaeus may be different forms of the same Aramaic name.

Mary Magdalene] Introduced, like the Twelve (vi. 67) and Pilate (xviii. 29) abruptly and without explanation, as being quite familiar to the readers of the Gospel. See on Matt. xxvii. 56 and Luke viii. 2.

26. *whom he loved*] See on xiii. 23. The expression here is not a mere periphrasis to avoid giving the name, still less a boastful insertion: it explains why Jesus committed the two to one another. (See Introduction, II. iii. 3 *b.*)

Woman] See on ii. 4.

disciple, Behold thy mother. And from that hour *that disciple took her unto his own home.*

28—30. *The two words from the Cross, 'I Thirst,' 'It is finished.'*

After this, Jesus knowing that all *things* were now accom- 28 plished, that the scripture might be fulfilled, saith, I thirst.

behold thy son.] If, as has just been maintained (2nd note on *v.* 25), S. John was the Virgin's nephew, and if, as is probable (see on ii. 12), Christ's 'brethren' were the sons of Joseph by a former marriage, the fact that Christ committed His mother to her nephew and His own beloved disciple rather than to her step-sons requires no explanation. Even if His 'brethren' were the sons of Joseph and Mary, their not believing on Him (vii. 5) would sufficiently account for their being set aside; and we have no evidence that they believed until after the Resurrection (Acts i. 14).

27. *from that hour*] Quite literally, as soon as all was over (*v.* 30); or he may have led her away at once and then have returned (*v.* 35).

unto his own home] Although the commendation was double, each being given to the other, yet (as was natural) S. John assumes the care of Mary rather than she of him. This shews the untenability of the view that not only S. John, but in him all the Apostles, were committed by Christ to the guardianship of Mary. We have had the Greek expression for 'his own (home)' twice already in this Gospel: see on i. 11 and xvi. 32. That S. John was known to the high-priest (xviii. 15) and that his family had hired servants (Mark i. 20) would seem to imply that he was a man of some position and substance.

28—30. THE TWO WORDS FROM THE CROSS, 'I THIRST,' 'IT IS FINISHED.'

28. *After this*] See on *v.* 38.
knowing] Comp. xiii. 1.
were now accomplished] Rather, **are already finished**. The very same word is used here as in *v.* 30, and this identity must be preserved in translation.

that the scripture, &c.] Many critics make this depend on 'are already finished,' in order to avoid the apparent contradiction between all things being already finished and something still remaining to be accomplished. But this construction is somewhat awkward. It is better to connect 'that......fulfilled' with 'saith,' especially when Ps. lxix. 21 speaks so plainly of the thirst. The apparent contradiction almost disappears when we remember that the thirst had been felt sometime before it was expressed. All things were finished, including the thirst; but Christ alone knew this. In order that the prophecy *might be* **accomplished,** it was necessary that He should make known His thirst. 'Brought to its due end' or 'made perfect' is the natural meaning of the very unusual expression translated 'fulfilled.'

29 Now there was set a vessel full of vinegar: and they filled a spunge with vinegar, and put *it* upon hyssop, and put *it* to 30 his mouth. When Jesus therefore had received the vinegar, he said, It is finished: and he bowed *his* head, and gave up the ghost.

29. *Now...vinegar*] Omit 'now.' S. John's precise knowledge appears once more: the other three do not mention the vessel, but he had stood close to it. The 'vinegar' was probably the sour wine or *posca* in a large jar 'set' by the soldiers for their own use while on guard. Criminals sometimes lived for many hours, even a day or two, on the cross.
and they filled, &c.] The true text gives, **having placed therefore a sponge full of the vinegar upon hyssop they** *put it to his mouth*. The difference between the two verbs rendered 'put' is very graphic; the one expresses the placing of the sponge round the stalk (comp. Matt. xxi. 33, xxvii. 28, 48), the other the offering (xvi. 2) and applying (Mark x. 13) it to his lips.
hyssop] The plant cannot be identified with certainty. The caper-plant, which is as likely as any, has stalks which run to two or three feet, and this would suffice. It is not probable that Christ's feet were on a level with the spectators' heads, as pictures represent: this would have involved needless trouble and expense. Moreover the mockery of the soldiers recorded by S. Luke (see on xxiii. 36) is more intelligible if we suppose that they could almost put a vessel to His lips. S. John alone mentions the hyssop; another mark of exact knowledge.
put it to his mouth] The actors and their motive are left doubtful. Probably soldiers, but possibly Jews, and probably in compassion rather than mockery; or perhaps in compassion under cover of mockery (comp. Mark xv. 36).
30. *received*] He had refused the stupefying draught (Matt. xxvii. 34; Mark xv. 23), which would have clouded his faculties: He accepts what will revive them for the effort of a willing surrender of His life.
It is finished] Just as the thirst was there before he expressed it, so the consciousness that His work was finished was there (*v.* 28) before He declared it. The Messiah's work of redemption was accomplished; His Father's commandment had been obeyed; types and prophecies had been fulfilled; His life had been lived, and His teaching completed; His last earthly tie had been severed (*vv.* 26, 27); and the end had come. The final 'wages of sin' alone remained to be paid.
he bowed his head] Another detail peculiar to the Evangelist who witnessed it.
gave up the ghost] The two apostles mark with special clearness that the Messiah's death was entirely voluntary. S. Matthew says, 'He *let go* His spirit' (xxvii. 50); S. John, 'He *gave up* His spirit.' None of the four says 'He died.' The other two have '*He breathed out;*' and S. Luke shews clearly that the surrender of life was a willing one by giving the words of surrender 'Father into Thy hands I commend my spirit.'—'No one taketh it from Me, but I lay it down of Myself'

31—42. *The petition of the Jews and the petition of Joseph.*

The Jews therefore, because it was the preparation, that 31 the bodies should not remain upon the cross on the sabbath day, (for that sabbath day was a high day,) besought Pilate that their legs might be broken, and *that* they might be

It was the one thing which Christ claimed to do 'of Himself' (x. 18). Contrast v. 30, vii. 28, viii. 28, 42.

On 'the seven words from the cross' see on Luke xxiii. 34; Mark xv. 34; Matt. xxvii. 46. Between the two words recorded in these verses (28—30) there is again a contrast. 'I thirst' is an expression of suffering; the only one during the Passion. 'It is finished' is a cry of triumph; and the 'therefore' in *v.* 30 shews how the expression of suffering led on to the cry of triumph. S. John omits the 'loud voice' which all the Synoptists give as immediately preceding Christ's death. It proved that His end was voluntary and not the necessary result of exhaustion.

31—42. THE PETITION OF THE JEWS AND THE PETITION OF JOSEPH.

31. As in xviii. 28, the Jews shew themselves to be among those 'who strain out a gnat and swallow a camel.' In the midst of deliberate judicial murder they are scrupulous about ceremonial observances.

The Jews therefore] The 'therefore,' as in *v.* 23, probably does not refer to what immediately precedes: it looks back to *vv.* 20, 21. The Jews still continue their relentless hostility. They do not know whether any one of the three sufferers is dead or not; their request shews that; so that 'therefore' cannot mean in consequence of Jesus' death. In order to save the Sabbath, and perhaps also to inflict still further suffering, they ask Pilate for this terrible addition to the punishment of crucifixion. Certainly the lesson 'I will have mercy and not sacrifice,' of which Christ had twice reminded them, and once in connexion with the Sabbath (Matt. xii. 7, ix. 13), had taken no hold on them.

the preparation] The *eve* of the Sabbath; and the Sabbath on this occasion coincided with the 15th Nisan, the first day of the Passover. This first day ranked as a Sabbath (Exod. xii. 16; Lev. xxiii. 7); so that the day was doubly holy.

that...high day] Literally, *the day of that Sabbath was* **great** (comp. vii. 37).

legs might be broken] The *crurifragium*, like crucifixion, was a punishment commonly reserved for slaves. The two were sometimes combined, as here. Lactantius (IV. xxvi.) says, 'His executioners did not think it necessary to break His bones, *as was their prevailing custom;*' which seems to imply that to Jewish crucifixions this horror was commonly added, perhaps to hasten death. For even without a Sabbath to make matters more urgent, corpses ought to be removed before night-fall (Deut. xxi. 23); whereas the Roman custom was to leave them to putrefy on the cross, like our obsolete custom of hanging in chains.

32 taken away. Then came the soldiers, and brake the legs of
the first, and of the other which was crucified with him.
33 But when they came to Jesus, and saw that he was dead
34 already, they brake not his legs: but one of the soldiers
with a spear pierced his side, and forthwith came there out
35 blood and water. And he that saw *it* bare record, and his

32. *Then came the soldiers*] *The soldiers* therefore *came*, in consequence of the fresh order from Pilate which the Jews would bring. Two probably went to each of the robbers.

34. *pierced*] To make quite sure that He was dead. The Greek word is not the same as that used in *v.* 37; this means either to 'prick' or to 'stab,' that to 'pierce deeply.'

blood and water] There has been very much discussion as to the *physical* cause of Christ's death; and those who investigate this try to frame an hypothesis which will at the same time account for the effusion of blood and water. Two or three such hypotheses have been put forward. But it may be doubted whether they are not altogether out of place. It has been seen (*v.* 30) how the Evangelists insist on the fact that the Lord's death was a voluntary surrender of life, not a result forced upon Him. Of course it may be that the voluntariness consisted in welcoming causes which must prove fatal. But it is more simple to believe that He delivered up His life before natural causes became fatal. 'No one,' neither Jew nor Roman, 'took it from Him' by any means whatever: 'He lays it down of Himself' (x. 18). And if we decline to investigate the physical cause of the Lord's death, we need not ask for a physical explanation of what is recorded here. S. John assures us that he saw it with his own eyes, and he records it that we 'may believe:' i.e. he regards it as a 'sign' that the corpse was no ordinary one, but a Body that even in death was Divine.

We can scarcely be wrong in supposing that the blood and water are symbolical. The order confirms this. Blood symbolizes the work of redemption which had just been completed by His death; and water symbolizes the 'birth from above,' with its cleansing from sin, which was the result of His death, and is the means by which we appropriate it. Thus the two great Sacraments are represented.

35. *And he......is true*] Rather, *He that* **hath seen hath borne witness** *and his* **witness** *is true* (comp. i. 19, 32, 34; viii. 13, 14; xii. 17). Besides the change from 'record' to **witness**, for the sake of marking by uniform translation S. John's fondness for this verb and substantive, the correction from 'saw' to **hath seen** must be noted. The use of the perfect rather than the aorist is evidence that the writer himself is the person who saw. If he were appealing to the witness of another person he would almost certainly have written, as the A. V., 'he that *saw*.' The inference that the author is the person who saw becomes still more clear if we omit the centre of the verse, which is somewhat parenthetical: '*He that hath seen hath borne witness, in order that ye all also may believe.*' The natural sense of this statement is that the narrator is

record is true : and he knoweth that he saith true, that ye might believe. For these *things* were done, that the scripture should be fulfilled, A bone of him shall not be broken. And again another scripture saith, They shall look on *him* whom they pierced.

36

37

appealing to his own experience. Thus the Apostolic authorship of the Gospel is again confirmed. (See Westcott, *Introduction*, p. xxvii.)

is true] Not simply truthful, but genuine, perfect : it fulfils the conditions of sufficient evidence. (See on i. 9 and comp. viii. 16, vii. 28.)

saith true] Better, *saith* **things that are true.** There is no tautology, as in the A. V. S. John first says that his evidence is adequate ; he then adds that the contents of it are true. Testimony may be sufficient (e. g. of a competent eyewitness) but false : or it may be insufficient (e. g. of half-witted child) but true. S. John declares that his testimony is both sufficient and true ; both *alēthinos* and *alēthēs*.

that ye might] Better, *that ye* also may ; ye as well as the witness who saw for himself.

Why does S. John attest thus earnestly the trustworthiness of his narrative at this particular point? Four reasons may be assigned. This incident proved (1) the reality of Christ's *humanity* against Docetic views; and these verses therefore are conclusive evidence against the theory that the Fourth Gospel is the work of a Docetic Gnostic (see on iv. 22) : (2) the reality of Christ's *Divinity*, against Ebionite views ; while His human form was no mere phantom, but flesh and blood, yet He was not therefore a mere man, but the Son of God : (3) the reality of Christ's *death*, and therefore of His *Resurrection*, against Jewish insinuations of trickery (comp. Matt. xxviii. 13—15) : (4) the clear and unexpected fulfilment of two Messianic prophecies.

36. *were done*] Better, **came to pass.** Note that S. John uses the aorist (ἐγένετο), where S. Matthew, writing nearer to the events, uses the perfect (γέγονεν). 'Hath come to pass' implies that the event is not very remote : Matt. i. 22, xxi. 4, xxvi. 56. The 'for' depends upon 'believe.' Belief has the support of Scripture ; for the two surprising events, Christ's escaping the *crurifragium* and yet having His side pierced, were evidently preordained in the Divine counsels.

shall not be broken] Exod. xii. 46. Thus he who at the opening of this Gospel was proclaimed as the Lamb of God (i. 29, 36), at the close of it is declared to be the true Paschal Lamb. Once more we have evidence that S. John's consistent and precise view is, that *the death of Christ coincided with the killing of the Paschal Lamb.* And this seems also to have been S. Paul's view (see on 1 Cor. v. 7).

37. *They shall look*] All present, especially the Jews. The whole world was represented there.

pierced] See on v. 34. The word here used occurs nowhere else in N. T. excepting Rev. i. 7, and forms a connexion worth noting between the Gospel and the Apocalypse (see on xi. 44, xv. 20, and xx. 16); all the more so because S. John here agrees with the present Masoretic

S. JOHN, XIX. [vv. 38, 39.

38 And after this Joseph of Arimathea, being a disciple of Jesus, but secretly for fear of the Jews, besought Pilate that he might take away the body of Jesus: and Pilate gave *him* leave. He came therefore, and took the body of Jesus. 39 And there came also Nicodemus, which at the first came to Jesus by night, and brought a mixture of myrrh and aloes,

---

Hebrew text and in every word differs from the Greek of the LXX. The Greek softens down 'pierced through' (which seemed a strange expression to use of men's treatment of Jehovah) into 'insulted.' See on vi. 45, xii. 13, 15, where there is further evidence of the Evangelist having independent knowledge of Hebrew, and therefore being a Jew of Palestine.

38. *And after this*] More literally, **But** *after* **these things**. The 'but' marks a contrast between the hostile petition of the Jews and the friendly petition of Joseph. 'These things' as distinct from 'this' will shew that no one event is singled out with which what follows is connected: the sequence is indefinite. Comp. iii. 22, vi. 14. 'After *this*' in *v.* 28 is right: there the sequence is direct and definite. Comp. ii. 12, xi. 7, 11.

Joseph of Arimathea] See notes on Matt. xxvii. 57; Mark xv. 43; Luke xxiii. 50. The Synoptists tell us that he was rich, a member of the Sanhedrin, a good and just man who had not consented to the Sanhedrin's counsel and crime, one who (like Simon and Anna) waited for the kingdom of God, and had become a disciple of Christ.

secretly for fear of the Jews] This forms a coincidence with S. Mark, who says of him (xv. 43) that *'having summoned courage* he went in unto Pilate,' implying that like Nicodemus he was naturally timid. Joseph probably went to Pilate as soon as he knew that Jesus was dead: the vague 'after these things' need not mean that he did not act till after the piercing of the side.

took the body] As the friends of the Baptist (Matt. xiv. 12) and of S. Stephen (Acts viii. 2) did in each case.

39. *Nicodemus*] Another coincidence. Nicodemus also was a member of the Sanhedrin (iii. 1), and his acquaintance with Joseph is thus explained. And it is S. Mark who tells us that Joseph was one of the Sanhedrin, S. John who brings him in contact with Nicodemus. It would seem as if Joseph's unusual courage had inspired Nicodemus also. We are not told whether or no Nicodemus had 'consented to the counsel and deed of them.'

at the first] Either the first time that he came to Jesus, in contrast to other occasions; or simply at the beginning of Christ's ministry. Comp. x. 40).

myrrh and aloes] Myrrh-resin and pounded aloe-wood, both aromatic substances: 'All thy garments are myrrh and aloes' (Ps. xlv. 8). Comp. Matt. ii. 11. Aloes are not mentioned elsewhere in N. T. For 'mixture' (*migma*) the two best MSS. read **roll** (*eligma*), and the purpose of

about an hundred pound *weight*. Then took they the body 40 of Jesus, and wound it in linen clothes with the spices, as the manner of the Jews is to bury. Now in the place 41 where he was crucified there was a garden; and in the garden a new sepulchre, wherein was never man yet laid. There laid they Jesus therefore because of the Jews' prepa- 42 ration *day;* for the sepulchre was nigh at hand.

this large quantity was probably to cover the Body entirely. Comp. 2 Chron. xvi. 14.

about an hundred pound] 1200 ounces. There is nothing incredible in the amount. It is a rich man's proof of devotion, and possibly of remorse for a timidity in the past which now seemed irremediable: his courage had come too late.

40. *Then took they*] *They took* **therefore.**

wound it, &c.] Or, **bound** *it in linen* **cloths.** The 'cloths' seem to refer to the bandages which kept the whole together rather than the large 'linen sheet' mentioned by the other Evangelists, which Joseph had bought on purpose (Mark xv. 46). The word here used for 'linen cloths' occurs also in Luke xxiv. 12: see note there.

the manner of the Jews] As distinct from the manner of the Egyptians, whose three methods of embalming are elaborately described by Herodotus (II. lxxxvi. ff.). The Egyptians in all cases removed part of the intestines and steeped the body in nitre.

to bury] The Greek verb is rare in Scripture; in N. T. only Matt. xxvi. 12. The cognate substantive occurs xii. 7; Mark xiv. 8. In Gen. l. 2 it is used by the LXX. for the embalming of Jacob.

41. *there was a garden*] Contrast xviii. 1. S. John alone tells of the garden, which probably belonged to Joseph, for S. Matthew tells us that the sepulchre was his.

a new sepulchre] S. Matthew also states that it was new, and S. Luke that no one had ever yet been laid in it. S. John states this fact in both ways with great emphasis. Not even in its contact with the grave did 'His flesh see corruption.'

S. John omits what all the others note, that the sepulchre was hewn in the rock.

42. *the Jews' preparation day*] Perhaps another slight indication that the Gospel was written outside Palestine. Or the addition 'of the Jews' may point to the time when there was already a Christian 'preparation-day.' See notes on 'the Passover *of the Jews*' (ii. 13; xi. 55).

It would seem as if the burial was hastily and temporarily performed. They probably intended after the Sabbath to make a more solemn and complete burial elsewhere.

was nigh at hand] Perhaps this fact suggested to Joseph the thought of going to Pilate. He had a sepulchre of his own close to Golgotha.

CHAP. XX.

We enter now upon the third and last part of the second main division of the Gospel. The Evangelist having set before us the INNER GLORIFICATION OF CHRIST IN HIS LAST DISCOURSES (xiii.—xvii.), and HIS OUTER GLORIFICATION IN HIS PASSION AND DEATH (xviii, xix.), now gives us his record of THE RESURRECTION AND THREEFOLD MANIFESTATION OF CHRIST (xx.).

The chapter falls naturally into five sections. 1. *The first Evidence of the Resurrection* (1—10). 2. *The Manifestation to Mary Magdalene* (11—18). 3. *The Manifestation to the Ten and others* (19—23). 4. *The Manifestation to S. Thomas and others* (24—29). 5. *The Conclusion and Purpose of the Gospel* (30, 31).

S. John's Gospel preserves its character to the end. Like the rest of his narrative, the account of the Resurrection is not intended as a complete record;—it is avowedly the very reverse of complete (*v.* 30);—but a series of typical scenes selected as embodiments of spiritual truth. Here also, as in the rest of the narrative, we have individual characters marked with singular distinctness. The traits which distinguish S. Peter, S. John, S. Thomas, and the Magdalene in this chapter are both clear in themselves and completely in harmony with what is told of the four elsewhere.

Of the incidents omitted by S. John a good many are given in the other Gospels or by S. Paul: (S. Matthew and S. Mark) the angel's message to the two Marys and Salome; (*S. Matthew and* [*S. Mark*]) the farewell charge and promise; (*S. Luke and* [*S. Mark*]) the manifestation to two disciples not Apostles; (*S. Matthew*) the earthquake, angel's descent to remove the stone, soldiers' terror and report to the priests, device of the Sanhedrin, manifestation on the mountain in Galilee (comp. 1 Cor. xv. 6); ([*S. Mark*]) the reproach for unbelief; (*S. Luke*) the manifestation to S. Peter (comp. 1 Cor. xv. 5), conversation on the road to Emmaus, proof that He is not a spirit (xxiv. 38, 39), manifestation before the Ascension (50, 51; comp. Acts i. 6—9); (*S. Paul*) manifestations to the *Twelve*, to S. James, and to S. Paul himself (1 Cor. xv. 6, 7, 8).

To these incidents S. John adds, besides the contents of chap. xxi, the gift of the power of absolution, and the manifestation on the second Lord's Day, when S. Thomas was present.

It may be freely admitted that the difficulty of harmonizing the different accounts of the Resurrection is very great. As so often in the Gospel narrative, we have not the knowledge required for piecing together the fragmentary accounts that have been granted to us. To this extent it may be allowed that the evidence for the Resurrection is not what we should antecedently have desired.

But it is no paradox to say that for this very reason, as well as for other reasons, the evidence is sufficient. Impostors would have made the evidence more harmonious. The difficulty arises from independent witnesses telling their own tale, not caring in their consciousness of its truth to make it clearly agree with what had been told elsewhere. The writer of the Fourth Gospel must have known of some, if not all,

1—10. *The first Evidence of the Resurrection.*

The first *day* of the week cometh Mary Magdalene early, 20 when it was yet dark, unto the sepulchre, and seeth the stone taken away from the sepulchre. Then she runneth, 2 and cometh to Simon Peter, and to the other disciple, whom Jesus loved, and saith unto them, They have taken away the

of the Synoptic accounts; but he writes freely and firmly from his own independent experience and information. All the Gospels agree in the following very important particulars;
1. The Resurrection itself is left undescribed.
2. The manifestations were granted to disciples only, but to disciples wholly unexpectant of a Resurrection.
3. They were received with doubt and hesitation at first.
4. Mere reports were rejected.
5. The manifestations were granted to all kinds of witnesses, both male and female, both individuals and companies.
6. The result was a conviction, which nothing ever shook, that 'the Lord had risen indeed' and been present with them.
All four accounts also agree in some of the details;
1. The evidence begins with the visit of women to the sepulchre in the early morning.
2. The first sign was the removal of the stone.
3. Angels were seen before the Lord was seen.
(See Westcott, *Speaker's Commentary*, II. pp. 287, 8.)

1—10. THE FIRST EVIDENCE OF THE RESURRECTION.

1. *The first day*] Better, **But on** *the first day;* literally, 'day one.' We have the same expression Luke xxiv. 1.

the stone taken away] All four Gospels note the displacement of the stone; S. Mark alone notes the placing of it and S. Matthew the sealing. The words 'taken away from' should rather be **lifted out of**: the Synoptists all speak of '*rolling* away' the stone.

2. *Then she runneth*] *She runneth* **therefore**, concluding that the body must be gone.

Simon Peter] His fall was probably known and his deep repentance also: he is still chief of the Apostles, and as such the one consulted first.

and to the other] The repetition of 'to' implies that the two Apostles were not lodging together, although *v.* 3 implies that they were close to one another.

whom Jesus loved] Perhaps the expression is meant to apply to Simon Peter also; 'the *other* disciple whom Jesus loved.' This becomes probable when we notice that the word for 'loved' is not that used of S. John in xix. 26, xxi. 7, 20 (*agapân*), but the more general word (*philein*). See on xi. 5.

They have taken] She does not attempt to determine who, whether friends or foes.

Lord out of the sepulchre, and we know not where they
have laid him. Peter therefore went forth, and *that* other
disciple, and came to the sepulchre. So they ran both
together: and the other disciple did outrun Peter, and came
first to the sepulchre. And he stooping down, and looking
in, saw the linen clothes lying; yet went he not in. Then
cometh Simon Peter following him, and went into the
sepulchre, and seeth the linen clothes lie, and the napkin,
that was about his head, not lying with the linen clothes,
but wrapped together in a place by itself. Then went in
also *that* other disciple, which came first to the sepulchre,
and he saw, and believed. For as yet they knew not the

we know not] This possibly implies that other women had been
with her, as stated by the Synoptists. If so, she may have outstripped
them in going to the garden.

3. *and that...sepulchre*] Better, **and the** *other disciple, and they* **were
coming towards** *the sepulchre*.

4. *So they ran*] More exactly, **But** *they* **began to run.**

did outrun] Literally, **ran on more quickly than,** as being much the
younger man. Would a writer of the second century have thought of
this in inventing a narrative?

5. *stooping down, and looking in*] In the Greek this is expressed in
a single word, which occurs again *v.* 11 and Luke xxiv. 12, in a literal
sense, of 'bending down to look carefully at;' and in a figurative sense in
1 Pet. i. 12 and James i. 25 (see notes in both places). In Ecclus. xiv.
23 it is used of the earnest searcher after wisdom, in xxi. 23 of the rude
prying of a fool.

saw] Better, **seeth,** at a glance (*blepei*).

6. *Then cometh,* &c.] Better, *Simon Peter* **therefore also** *cometh;*
because S. John has remained standing there in awe and meditation.
S. Peter with his natural impulsiveness goes in at once. Both Apostles
act characteristically.

seeth] Or, **beholdeth** (*theōrei*). He takes a complete survey, and
hence sees the 'napkin,' which S. John in his short look had not
observed.

7. *the napkin*] See on xi. 44: the same word is used here.

about his head] Literally, **upon** *His head:* there is no need to mention His name. The writer is absorbed in his subject.

in a place by itself] Literally, **apart into one place.**

8. *Then......that other*] Better, **Therefore** *went in also* **the** *other.*
He is encouraged by his older companion. Note how all the details
tell of the eye-witness: he remembers even that the napkin was folded.
Contrast the want of detail in Luke xxiv. 12.

and believed] More difficulty has perhaps been made about this than is
necessary. 'Believed what?' is asked. That Jesus was risen. The

scripture, that he must rise again from the dead. Then the 10 disciples went away again unto their own home.

11—18. *The Manifestation to Mary Magdalene.*

But Mary stood without at the sepulchre weeping: and 11 as she wept, she stooped down, and looked into the sepulchre, and seeth two angels in white sitting, the one 12 at the head, and the other at the feet, where the body of Jesus had lain. And they say unto her, Woman, why 13

whole context implies it; and comp. *v.* 25. The careful arrangement of the grave-cloths proved that the body had not been taken away in haste as by a foe: and friends would scarcely have removed them at all. It is thoroughly natural that S. John speaks only of himself, saying nothing of S. Peter. He is full of the impression which the empty and orderly tomb made upon his own mind. S. Luke (xxiv. 12) speaks only of S. Peter's wonder, neither affirming nor denying his belief.

9. *they knew not the scripture*] S. John's belief in the Resurrection was as yet based only on what he had seen in the sepulchre. He had nothing derived from prophecy to help him. The candour of the Evangelists is again shewn very strongly in the simple avowal that the love of Apostles failed to grasp and remember what the enmity of the priests understood and treasured up. Even with Christ to expound Scripture to them, the prophecies about His Passion and Resurrection had remained a sealed book to them (comp. Luke xxiv. 25—27).

he must] Comp. iii. 14, xii. 34; Matt. xvi. 21, xxvi. 54; Mark viii. 31; Luke ix. 22, xvii. 25, xxii. 37, xxiv. 7, 26, 44. The Divine determination meets us throughout Christ's life on earth, and is pointed out with increasing frequency towards the close of it. Comp. Eph. iii. 11.

10. *Then the disciples*] *The disciples* **therefore**; because nothing more could be done at the sepulchre.

11—18. THE MANIFESTATION TO MARY MAGDALENE.

11. *But Mary*] She had returned to the sepulchre after the hurrying Apostles. Mark xvi. 9 states definitely, what we gather from this section, that the risen Lord's first appearance was to Mary Magdalene: the details of the meeting are given by S. John alone.

stood] Or, **continued standing**, after the other two had gone.

stooped down, and looked] See on *v.* 5.

12. *seeth*] Or, **beholdeth**, as in *v.* 6, a long contemplative gaze.

two angels] This is the only place where angels appear in S. John's narrative. Comp. i. 51, xii. 29, [v. 4].

in white] In the Greek 'white' is plural, 'garments' being understood, as in Rev. iii. 4: in Rev. iii. 5, 18, iv. 4 'garments' is expressed. Omit 'the' before 'one' and for 'the other' read 'one;' *one at the head and one at the feet.*

13. *Woman*] See on ii. 4, xix. 26.

weepest thou? She saith unto them, Because they have taken away my Lord, and I know not where they have 14 laid him. And when she had thus said, she turned herself back, and saw Jesus standing, and knew not that it 15 was Jesus. Jesus saith unto her, Woman, why weepest thou? whom seekest thou? She, supposing him to be the gardener, saith unto him, Sir, if thou have borne him *hence*, tell me where thou hast laid him, and I will take him away. 16 Jesus saith unto her, Mary. She turned herself, and saith

my Lord, and I know not] In *v*. 2 it was '*the* Lord and *we* know not.' In speaking to Apostles she includes other believers; in speaking to strangers she represents the relationship and the loss as personal. These words express the burden of her thoughts since she first saw that the stone had been removed. We may reasonably suppose that the Evangelist obtained his information from Mary Magdalene herself. "The extreme simplicity of the narrative, it may be added, reflects something of the solemn majesty of the scene. The sentences follow without any connecting particles till *v*. 19. (Comp. c. xv.)" Westcott *in loco*.

14. *And when*] Omit 'and.' Perhaps she becomes in some way conscious of another Presence.

saw] Better, **beholdeth**, as in *vv*. 6, 12.

knew not] Christ's Risen Body is so changed as not to be recognised at once even by those who had known Him well. It has new powers and a new majesty. Comp. xxi. 4; Luke xxiv. 16, 37; Matt. xxviii. 17; [Mark xvi. 12].

15. *the gardener*] Because he was there at that early hour.

if thou have borne him hence] The omission of the name is very lifelike: she is so full of her loss that she assumes that others must know all about it. 'Thou' is emphatic; 'Thou and not, as I fear, some enemy.'

I will take him away] In her loving devotion she does not measure her strength. Note that throughout it is 'the Lord' (*v*. 2), 'my Lord' (*v*. 13), 'Him' thrice (*v*. 15), never 'His body' or 'the corpse.' His lifeless form is to her still Himself.

16. *Mary*] The term of general address, 'Woman,' awoke no echo in her heart; the sign of personal knowledge and sympathy comes home to her at once. Thus 'He calleth His own sheep *by name*' (x. 3).

saith unto him] We must add with the best authorities, **in Hebrew.** The insertion is of importance as indicating the language spoken between Christ and His disciples. S. John thinks it well to remind Greek readers that Greek was not the language used. Comp. Acts xxii. 2, xxvi. 14. The expression here used (*Hebraïsti*) occurs only in this Gospel (v. 2, xix. 13, 17, 20) and in Revelation (ix. 11, xvi. 16). See on xix. 37.

unto him, Rabboni; which is to say, Master. Jesus saith 17
unto her, Touch me not; for I am not yet ascended to my
Father: but go to my brethren, and say unto them, I ascend
unto my Father, and your Father; and *to* my God, and your
God. Mary Magdalene came and told the disciples that 18

Rabboni] More exactly, **Rabbuni**. This precise form occurs also in Mark x. 51, but has been obliterated in the A. V. It is said to be Galilean, and if so natural in a woman of Magdala. Would any but a Jew of Palestine have preserved this detail?

Master] Or, *Teacher*. Its literal meaning is 'my Master,' but the pronominal portion of the word had lost almost all meaning. S. John's translation shews that as yet her belief is very imperfect: she uses a mere human title.

17. *Touch me not, for*, &c.] This is a passage of well-known difficulty. At first sight the reason given for refraining from touching would seem to be more suitable to a permission to touch. It is perhaps needless to enquire whether the 'for' refers to the whole of what follows or only to the first sentence, 'I am not yet ascended to the Father?' In either case the meaning would be, that the Ascension has not yet taken place, although it soon will do so, whereas Mary's action assumes that it has taken place. If 'for' refers to the first clause only, then the emphasis is thrown on Mary's mistake; if 'for' refers to the whole of what is said, then the emphasis is thrown on the promise that what Mary craves shall be granted in a higher way to both her and others very soon. The translation 'touch Me not' is inadequate and gives a false impression. The verb (*haptesthai*) does not mean to 'touch' and 'handle' with a view to seeing whether His body was real; this Christ not only allowed but enjoined (*v.* 27; Luke xxiv. 39; comp. 1 John i. 1): rather it means to 'hold on to' and 'cling to.' Moreover it is the present (not aorist) imperative; and the full meaning will therefore be, '*Do not continue holding Me*,' or simply, **hold Me not**. The old and often interrupted earthly intercourse is over; the new and continuous intercourse with the Ascended Lord has not yet begun: but that Presence will be granted soon, and there will be no need of straining eyes and clinging hands to realize it. (For a large collection of various interpretations see Meyer.)

to my Father] The better reading gives, *to the Father;* with this 'My brethren' immediately following agrees better. The general relationship applying both to Him and them, is stated first, and then pointedly distinguished in its application to Him and to them.

I ascend] Or, **I am ascending**. The change has already begun.

my God] The risen and glorified Redeemer is still perfect man. Comp. Rev. iii. 12. Thus also S. Paul and S. Peter speak of 'the God and Father of our Lord Jesus Christ.' Comp. Eph. i. 3; 2 Cor. xi. 31; 1 Peter i. 3; and see on Rom. xv. 6; 2 Cor. i. 3, where the expression is blurred in the A. V.

18. *came and told*] Better, **cometh and telleth**; literally, *cometh telling* instead of the more usual 'having come telleth.'

she had seen the Lord, and *that* he had spoken these *things* unto her.

19—23. *The Manifestation to the Ten and others.*

19 Then the same day at evening, being the first *day* of the week, when the doors were shut where the disciples were

Thus as Mary's love seems to have been the first to manifest itself (*v.* 1), so the first Manifestation of the Risen Lord is granted to her. It confirms our trust in the Gospel narratives to find this stated. A writer of a fictitious account would almost certainly have represented the first appearance as being to the Virgin, or to S. Peter, the chief of the Apostles, or to S. John, the beloved disciple, or to the chosen three. But these are all passed over, and this honour is given to her, who had once been possessed by seven devils, to Mary of Magdala, 'for she loved much.' A late and worthless tradition does assign the first appearance to the Virgin; but so completely has Christ's earthly relationship to her been severed (xix. 26, 27), that henceforth she appears only among the other believers (Acts i. 14).

19—23. THE MANIFESTATION TO THE TEN AND OTHERS.

19. *Then the same day*, &c.] Rather, **When therefore it was evening on that day, the first** day of the week. Note the great precision of the expression. 'That day,' that memorable day, the 'day of days.'

    Oh! day of days! shall hearts set free
    No minstrel rapture find for thee?
    Thou art the Sun of other days,
    They shine by giving back thy rays.
        KEBLE, *Christian Year, Easter Day.*

Comp. i. 39, v. 9, xi. 49, xviii. 13, where 'that' has a similar meaning. Evidently the hour is late; the disciples have returned from Emmaus (Luke xxiv. 23), and it was evening when they left Emmaus. At least it must be long after sunset, when the second day of the week, according to the Jewish reckoning, would begin. And S. John speaks of it as still part of the first day. This is a point in favour of S. John's using the modern method in counting the hours: it has a special bearing on the explanation of 'the seventh hour' in iv. 52. See notes there and on xix. 14.

when the doors were shut] This is mentioned both here and *v.* 26 to shew that the appearance was miraculous. After the Resurrection Christ's human form, though still real and corporeal, is not subject to the ordinary conditions of material bodies. Before the Resurrection He was visible, unless He willed it otherwise; after the Resurrection it would seem that He was invisible, unless He willed it otherwise. Comp. Luke xxiv. 31.

where the disciples were] The best authorities all omit 'assembled.' S. Luke says more definitely, 'the eleven and they that were with them'

assembled for fear of the Jews, came Jesus and stood in the midst, and saith unto them, Peace *be* unto you. And when 20 he had so said, he shewed unto them *his* hands and his side. Then were the disciples glad, when they saw the Lord. Then said Jesus to them again, Peace *be* unto you: as *my* 21

(xxiv. 33); 'the eleven' meaning the Apostolic company, although one was absent. It was natural that the small community of believers should be gathered together, not merely for mutual protection and comfort, but to discuss the reported appearances to the women and to S. Peter.

for fear of the Jews] Literally, *because of* the (prevailing) *fear of the Jews* (comp. vii. 13). It was not certain that the Sanhedrin would rest content with having put Jesus to death; all the less so as rumours of His being alive again were spreading.

came Jesus] It is futile to discuss how; that the doors were miraculously opened, as in S. Peter's release from prison, is neither stated nor implied.

Peace be unto you] The ordinary greeting intensified. His last word to them in their sorrow before His Passion (xvi. 33), His first word to them in their terror (Luke xxiv. 37) at His return, is 'Peace.' Possibly the place was the same, the large upper room where they had last been all together.

20. *his hands and his side*] S. Luke (xxiv. 40), who does not mention the piercing of the side, says 'His hands and His feet,' and adds that He told them to 'handle' Him, the very word used in 1 John i. 1.

Then were the disciples] *The disciples* therefore *were*. Their sorrow is turned into joy (xvi. 20), joy which at first made them doubt its reality (Luke xxiv. 41).

when they saw the Lord] Till then they had seen a form, but like Mary of Magdala and the two at Emmaus, knew not whose it was.

21. *Then said Jesus*] *Jesus* therefore *said;* because now they were ready to receive it. Their alarm was dispelled and they knew that He was the Lord. He repeats His message of 'Peace.'

as my Father, &c.] Better, *As* the *Father hath sent Me.* Christ's mission is sometimes spoken of in the *aorist* tense, as having taken place at a definite point in history (iii. 17, 34, v. 38, vi. 29, 57, vii. 29, viii. 42, x. 36, xi. 42, xvii. 3, 8, 18, 21, 23, 25), in which case the fact of the Incarnation is the prominent idea. Sometimes, though much less often, it is spoken of, as here, in the *perfect* tense, as a fact which continues in its results (v. 36; 1 John iv. 9, 14), in which case the present and permanent effects of the mission are the prominent idea. Christ's mission is henceforth to be carried on by His disciples.

The Greek for 'send' is not the same in both clauses; in the first, 'hath sent,' it is *apostellein;* in the second, 'send,' it is *pempein.* The latter is the most general word for 'send,' implying no special relation between sender and sent; the former adds the notion of a delegated authority constituting the person sent the envoy or representative of the sender. Both verbs are used both of the mission of Christ and of the

22 Father hath sent me, even *so* send I you. And when he had said this, he breathed on *them*, and saith unto them, 23 Receive ye the Holy Ghost: whose soever sins ye remit,

mission of the disciples. *Apostellein* is used of the mission of Christ in all the passages quoted above: it is used of the mission of the disciples, iv. 38, xvii. 18. (Comp. i. 6, 19, 24, iii. 28, v. 33, vii. 32, xi. 3.) *Pempein* is used of Christ's mission only in the aorist participle (iv. 34, v. 23, 24, 30, 37, vi. 38, 39, 40, 44, vii. 16, 18, 28, 33, viii. 16, 18, 26, 29, ix. 4; and in all the passages in chaps. xii—xvi.); the aorist participle of *apostellein* is not used by S. John, although the Synoptists use it in this very sense (Matt. x. 40; Mark ix. 37; Luke ix. 48, x. 16). *Pempein* is used of disciples here and in xiii. 20 (of the Spirit, xiv. 26, xvi. 7). "The general result...seems to be, that in this charge the Lord presents His own Mission as the one abiding Mission of the Father; this He fulfils through His Church. His disciples receive no new commission, but carry out His." Westcott *in loco*.

send I you] Or, **am I sending** *you*; their mission has already begun (comp. v. 17, xvii. 9); and the first and main part of it was to be the proclamation of the truth just brought home to themselves—the Resurrection (Acts i. 22, ii. 24, iv. 2, 33, &c.).

22. *he breathed on them*] The very same Greek verb (here only in N.T.) is used by the LXX. in Gen. ii. 7 (Wisdom xv. 11) of breathing life into Adam. This Gospel of the new Creation looks back at its close, as at its beginning (i. 1), to the first Creation.

We are probably to regard the breath here not merely as the emblem of the Spirit (iii. 8), but as the *means* by which the Spirit was imparted to them. 'Receive ye,' combined with the action of breathing, implies this. This is all the more clear in the Greek, because *pneuma* means both 'breath' and 'spirit,' a point which cannot be preserved in English; but at least 'Spirit' is better than 'Ghost.' We have here, therefore, an anticipation and earnest of Pentecost; just as Christ's bodily return from the grave and temporary manifestation to them was an anticipation of His spiritual return and abiding Presence with them 'even unto the end of the world.'

Receive ye] Or, **take** *ye*, implying that the recipient may welcome or reject the gift: he is not a mere passive receptacle. It is the very word used for '*Take*' (Matt. xxvi. 26; Mark xiv. 22; Luke xxii. 17) in the account of the institution of the Eucharist; which somewhat confirms the view that here, as there, there is an outward sign and vehicle of an inward spiritual grace. The expression still more plainly implies that some gift was offered and bestowed then and there: it is an unnatural wresting of plain language to make 'Take ye' a mere promise. There was therefore a Paschal as distinct from a Pentecostal gift of the Holy Spirit, the one preparatory to the other. It should be noticed that 'Holy Ghost' is without the definite article in the Greek, and this seems to imply that the gift is not made in all its fulness. See on xiv. 26, where both substantive and adjective have the article.

23. *Whose soever sins*, &c.] This power accompanies the gift of the

they are remitted unto them; *and* whose soever *sins* ye retain, they are retained.

24—29. *The Manifestation to S. Thomas and others.*

But Thomas, one of the twelve, called Didymus, was not with them when Jesus came. The other disciples therefore 24 25

Spirit just conferred. It must be noticed (1) that it is given to the whole company present; not to the Apostles alone. Of the Apostles one was absent, and there were others who were not Apostles present: no hint is given that this power is confined to the Ten. The commission therefore *in the first instance* is to the Christian community as a whole, not to the Ministry alone.

It follows from this (2) that the power being conferred on the community and never revoked, the power continues so long as the community continues. While the Christian Church lasts it has the power of remitting and retaining along with the power of spiritual discernment which is part of the gift of the Spirit. That is, it has the power to declare the conditions on which forgiveness is granted and the fact that it has or has not been granted.

It should be noted (3) that the expression throughout is plural on both sides. As it is the community rather than individuals that is invested with the power, so it is classes of men rather than individuals on whom it is exercised. *God* deals with mankind not in the mass but with personal love and knowledge soul by soul. His *Church* in fulfilling its mission from Him, while keeping this ideal in view, is compelled for the most part to minister to men in groups and classes. The plural here seems to indicate not what must always or ought to be the case, but what generally is.

are remitted...are retained] Both verbs are perfects, though there is some doubt about the reading as regards the former. The force of the perfect is—'are *ipso facto* remitted'—'are *ipso facto* retained.' When the community under the guidance of the Spirit has spoken, the result is complete.

retain] i.e. 'hold fast,' so that they do not depart from the sinner. The word occurs here only in this Gospel. In Revelation it is used of 'holding fast doctrine,' &c. (ii. 14, 15, 25, iii. 11; comp. 2 Thess. ii. 15).

24—29. THE MANIFESTATION TO S. THOMAS AND OTHERS.
Peculiar to S. John.

24. *Thomas*] See on xi. 16.
the twelve] See on vi. 67.
was not with them] His melancholy temperament might dispose him to solitude and to put no trust in the rumours of Christ's Resurrection if they reached him on Easter Day. And afterwards his despondency is too great to be removed by the testimony even of eye-witnesses. The test which he selects has various points of contact with the surroundings.

said unto him, We have seen the Lord. But he said unto them, Except I shall see in his hands the print of the nails, and put my finger into the print of the nails, and thrust my ²⁶hand into his side, I will not believe. And after eight days again his disciples were within, and Thomas with them: *then* came Jesus, the doors being shut, and stood in the midst, ²⁷and said, Peace *be* unto you. Then saith he to Thomas, Reach hither thy finger, and behold my hands; and reach *hither* thy hand, and thrust *it* into my side: and be not ²⁸faithless, but believing. And Thomas answered and said

The wounds had been the cause of his despair; it is they that must reassure him. The print of them would prove beyond all doubt that it was indeed His Lord that had returned to him. Moreover, the Ten had no doubt told him of their own terror and hesitation, and how Jesus had invited them to 'handle Him and see' in order to convince themselves. This would suggest a similar mode of proof to S. Thomas.

25. *print...put...print...thrust*] The A.V. preserves the emphatic repetition of 'print' but obliterates the similar repetition of 'put.' The verb (*ballein*) rendered 'thrust' here and in v. 27 is the same as that rendered 'put.' Its literal meaning is 'throw' or 'cast;' but in late Greek its meaning becomes more vague and general; 'place, lay, put.' Comp. v. 7, xiii. 2, xviii. 11. Here **put** would be better in all three places.

I will not believe] Or, *I will* **in no wise** *believe;* the negative is in the strongest form. Comp. iv. 48, vi. 37, &c.

26. *after eight days*] Including both extremes, according to the Jewish method. This is therefore the Sunday following Easter Day. We are not to understand that the disciples had not met together during the interval, but that there is no appearance of Jesus to record. The first step is here taken towards establishing 'the Lord's Day' as the Christian weekly festival. The Passover is over, so that the meeting of the disciples has nothing to do with that.

again...within] Implying that the place is the same. No hint is given as to the time of day.

then came Jesus] Better, in the simplicity of the original, **Jesus cometh.**

27. *saith*, &c.] He at once shews to S. Thomas that He knows the test that he had demanded.

behold] Better, **see**; it is the same word as S. Thomas used in v. 25.

be not] Rather, **become** *not*. The demand for this proof did not make S. Thomas faithless, but it placed him in peril of becoming so. 'Faithless' and 'believing' are verbal as well as actual contradictories in the Greek. 'Faithless' and 'faithful,' 'unbelieving' and 'believing' would in this respect be better; but it is best to leave it as in the A.V.

28. *And Thomas answered*] Omit 'and.' This answer and Christ's

unto him, My Lord and my God. Jesus saith unto him, 29
Thomas, because thou hast seen me, thou hast believed:
blessed *are* they that have not seen, and *yet* have believed.

comment, 'because thou hast *seen*,' seem to shew that S. Thomas did not use the test which he had demanded. In accordance with his desponding temperament he had underrated the possibilities of being convinced.

My Lord and my God] Most unnatural is the Unitarian view, that these words are an expression of astonishment addressed *to God*. Against this are (1) the plain and conclusive 'said *unto Him;*' (2) the words 'my Lord,' which manifestly are addressed to Christ (comp. v. 13); (3) the fact that this confession of faith forms a climax and conclusion to the whole Gospel. The words are rightly considered as an impassioned declaration on the part of a devoted but (in the better sense of the term) sceptical Apostle of his conviction, not merely that his Risen Lord stood before him, but that this Lord was also his God. And it must be noted that Christ does not correct His Apostle for this avowal, any more than He corrected the Jews for supposing that He claimed to be 'equal with God' (v. 18, 19); on the contrary He accepts and approves this confession of belief in His Divinity.

29. *Thomas, because,* &c.] 'Thomas' must be omitted on overwhelming evidence, although the addition of the name seems natural here as in xiv. 9. 'Thou hast believed' is half exclamation, half question (comp. xvi. 31).

blessed are they that have not seen] Rather, *Blessed are they that* **saw not.** There must have been some disciples who believed in the Resurrection merely on the evidence of others. Jesus had not appeared to every one of His followers.

This last great declaration of blessedness is a Beatitude which is the special property of the countless number of believers who have never seen Christ in the flesh. Just as it is possible for every Christian to become equal in blessedness to Christ's Mother and brethren by obedience (Matt. xii. 49, 50), so it is possible for them to transcend the blessedness of Apostles by faith. All the Apostles, like S. Thomas, had seen before they believed: even S. John's faith did not shew itself until he had had evidence (*v.* 8). S. Thomas had the opportunity of believing without seeing, but rejected it. The same opportunity is granted to all believers now.

Thus this wonderful Gospel begins and ends with the same article of faith. 'The Word was God,'—'the Word became flesh,' is the Evangelist's solemn confession of a belief which had been proved and deepened by the experience of more than half a century. From this he starts, and patiently traces out for us the main points in the evidence out of which that belief had grown. This done, he shews us the power of the evidence over one needlessly wary of being influenced by insufficient testimony. The result is the instantaneous confession, at once the result of questioning and the victory over it, 'My Lord and my God.'

30, 31. *The Conclusion and Purpose of the Gospel.*

30 And many other signs truly did Jesus in the presence of
31 his disciples, which are not written in this book: but
these are written, that ye might believe that Jesus is the
Christ, the Son of God; and that believing ye might have
life through his name.

30, 31. THE CONCLUSION AND PURPOSE OF THE GOSPEL.

30. *And many other signs truly*] The Greek cannot be exactly rendered without awkwardness: **Therefore** (as might be expected from what *has* been written here) *many* **and** *other signs*. The context shews that 'signs' must not be limited to proofs of the Resurrection: S. John is glancing back over his whole work—'this book;' and the 'signs' here, as elsewhere in this Gospel, are miracles generally. Comp. especially xii. 37. The expression 'many and other' points the same way; many in number and different in kind from those related. The signs of the Resurrection from the nature of the case were all similar in kind.

31. *but these are written*] On the one hand there were many unrecorded; *but* on the other hand some have been recorded. Note in the Greek the *men* and the *de* and comp. xix. 23, 25. It was not S. John's purpose to write a complete 'Life of Christ;' it was not his purpose to write a 'Life' at all. Rather he would narrate just those facts respecting Jesus which would produce a saving faith in Him as the Messiah and the Son of God. S. John's work is 'a Gospel and not a biography.'

that ye might believe] *That ye* **may** *believe*.

that Jesus is the Christ, &c.] That those who read this record may be convinced of two things,—identical in the Divine counsels, identical in fact, but separate in the thoughts of men,—(1) *that Jesus*, the well-known Teacher and true man, *is the Christ*, the long looked for Messiah and Deliverer of Israel, the fulfiller of type and prophecy; (2) that He is also *the Son of God*, the Divine Word and true God. Were He not the latter He could not be the former, although men have failed to see this. Some had been looking for a mere Prophet and Wonder-worker, —a second Moses or a second Elijah; others had been looking for an earthly King and Conqueror,—a second David or a second Solomon. These views were all far short of the truth, and too often obscured and hindered the truth. Jesus, the Lord's Anointed, must be and is not only very man but very God. Comp. 1 John iv. 14, 15.

ye might have life] *Ye* **may** *have life.* The truth is worth having for its own sake: but in this case to possess the truth is to possess eternal life. Comp. 1 John v. 13. Note once more that eternal life is not a a prize to be won hereafter; in believing these great truths we have eternal life already (see on v. 24).

through his name] Rather, **in** *His name* (see on i. 12). Thus the conclusion of the Gospel is an echo of the beginning (i. 4, 12). Comp. Acts iv. 10; 1 Cor. vi. 11.

CHAP. XXI. *The Epilogue or Appendix.*

1—14. *The Manifestation to the Seven and the Miraculous Draught of Fishes.*

After these *things* Jesus shewed himself again to the 21

It is quite manifest that this was in the first instance intended as the end of the Gospel. The conflict between belief and unbelief recorded in it reach a climax in the confession of S. Thomas and the Beatitude which follows: the work appears to be complete; and the Evangelist abruptly but deliberately brings it to a close. What follows is an afterthought, added by S. John's own hand, as the style and language sufficiently indicate, but not part of the original plan. There is nothing to shew how long an interval elapsed before the addition was made, nor whether the Gospel was ever published without it. The absence of evidence as to this latter point favours the view that the Gospel was not given to the world until after the appendix was written.
Sixteen distinct marks tending to shew that chap. xxi. is by S. John are pointed out in the notes and counted up by figures in square brackets, thus [1]. Besides these points it should be noticed that S. John's characteristic 'therefore' occurs seven times (*vv.* 5, 6, 7, 9, 15, 21, 23) in twenty-three verses.

CHAP. XXI. THE EPILOGUE OR APPENDIX.

This Epilogue to a certain extent balances the Prologue, the main body of the Gospel in two great divisions lying in between them; but with this difference, that the Prologue is part of the original plan of the Gospel, whereas the Epilogue is not. It is evident that when the Evangelist wrote xx. 30, he had no intention of narrating any more 'signs.' The reason for adding this appendix can be conjectured with something like certainty: the Evangelist wished to give a full and exact account of Christ's words respecting himself, about which there had been serious misunderstanding. In order to make the meaning of Christ's saying as clear as possible, S. John narrates in detail the circumstances which led to its being spoken.
The whole of the chapter is peculiar to S. John's Gospel. It falls into four parts. 1. *The Manifestation to the Seven and the Miraculous Draught of Fishes* (1—14). 2. *The Commission to S. Peter and Prediction as to his Death* (15—19). 3. *The misunderstood Saying respecting the Evangelist* (20—23). 4. *Concluding Notes* (24, 25).

1—14. THE MANIFESTATION TO THE SEVEN AND THE MIRACULOUS DRAUGHT OF FISHES.

1. *After these things*] This vague expression (see on v. 1, vi. 1, xix. 38) suits an afterthought which has no direct connexion with what immediately precedes.
shewed himself] Better, **manifested** *Himself.* The rendering of this verb (*phaneroun*), which is one of S. John's favourite words [1], should

disciples at the sea of Tiberias; and on this wise shewed he
2 *himself*. There were together Simon Peter, and Thomas
called Didymus, and Nathanael of Cana in Galilee, and the
3 *sons* of Zebedee, and two other of his disciples. Simon Peter
saith unto them, I go a fishing. They say unto him, We
also go with thee. They went forth, and entered into a ship
4 immediately; and that night they caught nothing. But

be kept uniform, especially here, ii. 11, vii. 4, xvii. 6, where the active voice is used. Comp. i. 31, iii. 21, ix. 3, xxi. 14; 1 John i. 2, ii. 19, 28, iii. 2, 5, 8, iv. 9. In the other Gospels the word occurs only Mark iv. 22; [xvi. 12, 14], in all cases in the passive form.

again] This (as *v.* 14 shews) points back to the manifestation to S. Thomas and the rest (xx. 26).

sea of Tiberias] See on vi. 1. S. John alone uses this name [2]. The return of the disciples from Jerusalem to Galilee is commanded Matt. xxviii. 7; Mark xvi. 7. They returned to Jerusalem soon, and remained there from the Ascension to Pentecost (Acts i. 4). S. Matthew notices only the appearances in Galilee, S. Luke [and S. Mark] only those in Jerusalem. S. John gives some of both groups.

on this wise shewed he] Better, **He manifested on this wise**. This repetition is S. John's style [3].

2. *There were together*] Probably all seven belonged to the neighbourhood; we know this of four of them.

Thomas] See on xi. 16, xiv. 5, xx. 24. All particulars about him are given by S. John [4].

Nathanael] See on i. 45: the descriptive addition 'of Cana of Galilee' occurs here only. S. John alone mentions Nathanael [5].

the sons of Zebedee] If one of the sons of Zebedee were not the writer, they would have been placed first after S. Peter, instead of last of those named [6]. The omission of their names also is in harmony with S. John's reserve about all closely connected with himself [7].

two other] Some conjecture Andrew and Philip; but if so, why are the names not given? More probably these nameless disciples are not Apostles.

3. *Simon Peter*] As so often, he takes the lead. In the interval of waiting for definite instructions the disciples have returned to their usual employment. Once more we have precise and vivid details, as of an eye-witness.

We also go] Rather, *we also* **come**.

went forth] From the town or village, probably Capernaum or Bethsaida.

into a ship] Better, *into* **the** *ships*. 'Immediately' must be omitted on decisive evidence.

that night] Better, **in** *that night*. 'That' perhaps indicates that failure was exceptional; or it may mean 'that memorable night' (comp. xix. 31; xx. 19). Night was the best time for fishing (Luke v. 5).

they caught nothing] Failure at first is the common lot of Christ's

when the morning was now come, Jesus stood on the shore: but the disciples knew not that it was Jesus. Then Jesus 5 saith unto them, Children, have ye any meat? They answered him, No. And he said unto them, Cast the net on 6 the right side of the ship, and ye shall find. They cast therefore, and now they were not able to draw it for the multitude of fishes. Therefore that disciple whom Jesus 7 loved saith unto Peter, It is the Lord. Now when Simon Peter heard that it was the Lord, he girt *his* fisher's coat

fishers. His Presence again causing success after failure might bring home to them the lesson that apart from Him they could do nothing (xv. 5).

The word here used for 'catch' does not occur in the Synoptists, but besides *v.* 10 is found six times in this Gospel (vii. 30, 32, 44, viii. 20, x. 39, xi. 57), and once in Revelation (xix. 20) [8]. Elsewhere only Acts iii. 7, xii. 4; 2 Cor. xi. 32.

4. *morning was now come*] The better reading gives, **dawn *was now* breaking**.

stood on the shore] Literally, *stood* **on to** *the* **beach**, i.e. He came and stood on the beach.

but] Nevertheless, or howbeit (*mentoi*, a particle rare in N.T. outside this Gospel); implying that this was surprising. Comp. iv. 27, vii. 13, xii. 42, xx. 5.

knew not] See on xx. 14.

5. *Then Jesus*] *Jesus* **therefore**; because they did not recognise Him.

Children] Perhaps a mere term of friendly address (*paidia*); not the affectionate term used xiii. 33 (*teknia*). *Paidia* occurs 1 John ii. 14, 18; *teknia* occurs 1 John ii. 1, 12, 28, iii. 7, 18, iv. 4, v. 21.

meat] The Greek word (*prosphagion*) occurs here only. It appears to mean something eaten with bread, especially fish. Perhaps we should translate, *Have ye any* **fish**?

6. *They cast therefore*] Perhaps they thought the stranger saw fish on the right side. Fish are at times seen "in dense masses" in the lake.

7. *Therefore that disciple*] The characteristics of the two Apostles are again most delicately yet clearly given (comp. xx. 2—9). S. John is the first to apprehend; S. Peter the first to act [9].

Now when Simon Peter heard] *Simon Peter* **therefore having** *heard*.

fisher's coat] The Greek word (*ependutes*) occurs here only. It was his upper garment, which he gathered round him "with instinctive reverence for the presence of his Master" (Westcott). 'Naked' need not mean more than 'stripped' of the upper garment. "No one but an eye-witness would have thought of the touch in *v.* 7, which *exactly inverts* the natural action of one about to swim, and yet is quite accounted for by the circumstances." S. p. 267.

unto him, (for he was naked,) and did cast himself into the
8 sea. And the other disciples came in a little ship; (for
they were not far from land, but as it were two hundred
9 cubits,) dragging the net with fishes. As soon then as they
were come to land, they saw a fire of coals there, and fish
10 laid thereon, and bread. Jesus saith unto them, Bring of
11 the fish which ye have now caught. Simon Peter went up,

cast himself] with his habitual impulsiveness.
8. *in a little ship*] Rather, *in the boat*, whether 'the ship' of *v.* 3 or a smaller boat attached to it, we cannot determine.
two hundred cubits] About 100 yards.
9. *As soon as...they saw*] Better, **When therefore...*they see***.
a fire of coals] See on xviii. 18: the word occurs only there and here in N.T. [10]. 'There' is literally **laid**.
fish laid thereon, and bread] Or possibly, a *fish laid thereon and* a **loaf**. But the singulars may be collectives as in the A.V. The word for fish (*opsarion*) is similar in meaning, though not in derivation, to the one used in *v.* 5. (See on vi. 9.) In *v.* 11 yet another word is used (*ichthus*), which means 'fish' generally, whether for eating or not.
10. *fish*] The same word as in *v.* 9, but in the plural.
caught] See on *v.* 3.
11. *went up*] Better, with the best texts, *went up* **therefore**: the meaning probably is 'went on board' the vessel, now in shallow water. The details in this verse are strong evidence of the writer having been an eye-witness: he had helped to count these 'great fishes' and gives the number, not because there is anything mystical in it, but because he remembers it.

The points of contrast between this Draught of Fishes and the similar miracle at the beginning of Christ's ministry are so numerous and so striking, that it is difficult to resist the conclusion that the spiritual meaning, which from very early times has been deduced from them, is divinely intended. Symbolical interpretations of Scripture are of three kinds: (1) Fanciful and illegitimate. These are simply misleading: they force into plain statements meanings wholly unreal if not false; as when the 153 fishes are made to symbolize Gentiles, Jews, and the Trinity. (2) Fanciful but legitimate. These are harmless, and may be edifying: they use a plain statement to inculcate a spiritual lesson, although there is no evidence that such lesson is intended. (3) Legitimate and divinely intended. In these cases the spiritual meaning is either pointed out for us in Scripture (Luke v. 10), or is so strikingly in harmony with the narrative, that it seems reasonable to accept it as purposely included in it. Of course it requires both spiritual and intellectual power to determine in any given case to which class a particular interpretation belongs; but in the present instance we may safely assign the symbolism to the third class.

The main points are these. The two Miraculous Draughts represent the Church Militant and the Church Triumphant. The one gathers

and drew the net to land full of great fishes, an hundred and fifty *and* three : and for all there were so many, *yet* was not the net broken. Jesus saith unto them, Come *and* dine. 12 And none of the disciples durst ask him, Who art thou? knowing that it was the Lord. Jesus then cometh, and 13 taketh bread, and giveth them, and fish likewise. This *is* 14 now the third time *that* Jesus shewed himself to his disciples, after that he was risen from the dead.

15—19. *The Commission to S. Peter and Prediction as to his death.*

So when they had dined, Jesus saith to Simon Peter, 15

together an untold multitude of both good and bad in the troubled waters of this world. Its net is rent with schisms and its Ark seems like to sink. The other gathers a definite number of elect, and though they be many contains them all, taking them not on the stormy ocean but on the eternal shore of peace.

12. *Come and dine*] The meal indicated is not the principal meal of the day (*deipnon*) which was taken in the afternoon, but the morning meal (*ariston*) or **breakfast**. See on Luke xi. 37.

And none] Omit 'and.' There is a solemn simplicity in the narrative. The sentences from *v.* 10 to *v.* 14 have no connecting particles: comp. chap. xv. and xx. 13—19.

none durst ask...knowing] A mixture of perplexity, awe, and conviction. They are convinced that He is the Lord, yet feel that He is changed, and reverence restrains them from curious questions. Comp. Matt. ii. 8, x. 11. The writer knows the inmost feelings of Apostles (comp. ii. 11, 17, 22, iv. 27, 33, vi. 21, ix. 2, xx. 20) [11].

13. *Jesus then cometh*] Omit 'then.' They are afraid to approach, so He comes to them. 'Bread' and 'fish' are in the singular, as in *v.* 9, but with the definite article, which points back to *v.* 9; '*the* bread' and '*the* fish' which had been mentioned before. Of course this is not the fish that had just been caught, and nothing is told us as to how it was provided. The food is a gift from the Lord to His disciples.

14. *This is now the third time*] We have a similar construction 2 Pet. iii. 1. The two previous manifestations are probably those related xx. 19—23, 26—29: but we have not sufficient knowledge to arrange the different appearances in chronological order. See on Luke xxiv. 49.

shewed himself] **Manifested** *Himself:* see on *v.* 1.

15—19. THE COMMISSION TO S. PETER AND PREDICTION AS TO HIS DEATH.

15. *dined*] See on *v.* 12.

saith to Simon Peter, Simon, son of Jonas] For 'Jonas' read **John** here and in *vv.* 16, 17, as in i. 42. Note that the writer himself calls

Simon, *son* of Jonas, lovest thou me more than these? He saith unto him, Yea, Lord; thou knowest that I love thee.

him Simon Peter, but represents the Lord as calling him 'Simon son of John.' This is not only in harmony with the rest of this Gospel, but with the Gospels as a whole. Although Jesus gave Simon the name of Peter, yet, with one remarkable exception (see on Luke xxii. 34), He never addresses him as Peter, but always as Simon. Matt. xvi. 17, xvii. 25; Mark xiv. 37; Luke xxii. 31. The Synoptists generally call him Simon, sometimes adding his surname. S. John always gives both names, excepting in i. 41, where the surname just about to be given would be obviously out of place. Contrast in this chapter *vv.* 2, 3, 7, 11 with 16, 17. Should we find this minute difference observed, if the writer were any other than S. John? [12] This being the general usage of our Lord, there is no reason to suppose that His calling him Simon rather than Peter on this occasion is a reproach, as implying that by denying his Master he had forfeited the name of Peter. That S. John should add the surname with much greater frequency than the Synoptists is natural. At the time when S. John wrote the surname had become the more familiar of the two. S. Paul never calls him Simon, but uses the Aramaic form of the surname, Cephas.

lovest thou me] The word for 'love' here and in the question in *v.* 16 is *agapân* (see on xi. 5). S. Peter in all three answers uses *philein*, and our Lord uses *philein* in the third question (*v.* 17). The change is not accidental; and once more we have evidence of the accuracy of the writer: he preserves distinctions which were actually made. S. Peter's preference for *philein* is doubly intelligible: (1) it is the less exalted word; he is sure of the natural affection which it expresses; he will say nothing about the higher love implied in *agapân*; (2) it is the warmer word; there is a calm discrimination implied in *agapân* which to him seems cold. In the third question Christ takes him at his own standard; he adopts S. Peter's own word, and thus presses the question more home.

more than these] 'More than these, thy companions, love Me.' The A. V. is ambiguous, and so also is the Greek, but there cannot be much doubt as to the meaning: 'more than thou lovest these things' gives a very inadequate signification to the question. At this stage in S. Peter's career Christ would not be likely to ask him whether he preferred his boat and nets to Himself. S. Peter had professed to be ready to die for His Master (xiii. 37) and had declared that though *all* the rest might deny Him, *he* would never do so (Matt. xxvi. 33). Jesus recalls this boast by asking him whether he *now* professes to have more loyalty and devotion than the rest.

Yea, Lord; thou knowest] "We have once more an exquisite touch of psychology. It is Peter's modesty that speaks, and his sense of shame at his own short-comings...He has nothing to appeal to, and yet he is conscious that his affection is not unreal or insincere, and He trusts to Him who searches the hearts." S. pp. 268, 9. Not only does he change the word for 'love' from *agapân* to *philein*, but he says nothing about

He saith unto him, Feed my lambs. He saith to him again 16
the second time, Simon, *son* of Jonas, lovest thou me? He
saith unto him, Yea, Lord; thou knowest that I love thee.
He saith unto him, Feed my sheep. He saith unto him the 17
third time, Simon, *son* of Jonas, lovest thou me? Peter was
grieved because he said unto him the third time, Lovest thou
me? And he said unto him, Lord, thou knowest all *things;*

'more than these:' he will not venture any more to compare himself
with others. Moreover he makes no professions as to the future; experience has taught him that the present is all that he can be sure of.
The 'Thou' in 'Thou knowest' is emphatic. This time he will trust
the Lord's knowledge of him rather than his own estimate of himself.
Can all these delicate touches be artistic fictions?

Feed my lambs] Not only is he not degraded on account of his fall,
he receives a fresh charge and commission. The work of the fisher
gives place to that of the shepherd: the souls that have been brought
together and won need to be fed and tended. And this S. Peter must
do.

16. *lovest thou me?*] Jesus drops the 'more than these,' which the
humbled Apostle had shrunk from answering, but retains His own word
for 'love.' S. Peter answers exactly as before.

Feed my sheep] Better, **Tend**, or *shepherd*, *My sheep*. The word rendered 'feed' in *vv.* 15 and 17 (*boskein*) means 'supply with food.' Comp.
Matt. viii. 30, 33; Mark v. 11, 14; Luke viii. 32, 34; xv. 15 (the only
other passages where the word occurs in N. T.) of the feeding of the
herd of swine. The word used here (*poimainein*) means rather 'be
shepherd to.' It is used literally Luke xvii. 7; 1 Cor. ix. 7; and
figuratively Matt. ii. 6; Acts xx. 28; 1 Pet. v. 2. Comp. Jude 12;
Rev. ii. 27, vii. 17, xii. 5, xix. 15. Tending implies more of guidance
and government than feeding does. The lambs, which can go no distance, scarcely require guidance, their chief need is food. The sheep
require both.

17. *the third time*] He had denied thrice, and must thrice affirm
his love. This time Jesus makes a further concession: He not only
ceases to urge the 'more than these,' but He adopts S. Peter's own
word, *philein*. The Apostle had rejected Christ's standard and taken
one of his own, about which he could be more sure; and Christ now
questions the Apostle's own standard. This is why 'Peter was grieved'
so much; not merely at the threefold question recalling his threefold
denial, not merely at his devotion being questioned more than once,
but that the humble form of love which he had professed, and that without boastful comparison with others, and without rash promises about
the future, should seem to be doubted by his Lord.

thou knowest all things; thou knowest] Once more we have two words
for 'know' in the original and only one in the A. V. (Comp. vii. 27,
viii. 55, xiii. 7, xiv. 7.) The first 'knowest' (*oidas*) refers to Christ's
supernatural intuition, as in *vv.* 15, 16: the second 'knowest' (*ginōskeis*)

thou knowest that I love thee. Jesus saith unto him, Feed
18 my sheep. Verily, verily, I say unto thee, When thou wast
young, thou girdest thyself, and walkedst whither thou
wouldest: but when thou shalt be old, thou shalt stretch
forth thy hands, and another shall gird thee, and carry *thee*

to His experience and discernment; *Thou recognisest, perceivest*, **seest**, *that I love Thee*. See on ii. 24, 25.
Feed my sheep] It is doubtful whether we have or have not precisely the same word for 'sheep' here as in *v*. 16. The Greek word here according to the best authorities is undoubtedly a diminutive (*probatia*, not *probata*); in *v*. 16 the evidence is pretty evenly balanced between *probatia* and *probata* ('little sheep' and 'sheep'). One is tempted to adopt S. Ambrose's order in *vv*. 15, 16, 17—'lambs,' 'little sheep,' 'sheep' (*agnos, oviculas, oves*), which seems also to have been the reading of the old Syriac: but the balance of evidence is against it. But without counting the possible difference between 'little sheep' and 'sheep,' there are three important distinctions obliterated in the A. V., —the two words rendered 'love,' the two rendered 'feed,' and the two rendered 'know.'
  S. Peter seems to recall this charge in his First Epistle (v. 2, 3), a passage which in the plainest terms condemns the policy of those who on the strength of this charge have claimed to rule as his successors over the whole of Christ's flock.
  18, 19. This high charge will involve suffering and even death. In spite of his boastfulness and consequent fall the honour which he once too rashly claimed (xiii. 37) will after all be granted to him.
  18. *Verily, verily*] This peculiarity of S. John's Gospel (see on i. 55) is preserved in the appendix to it [13].
  wast young] Literally, *wast* **younger** than thou art now. He was now between youth and age.
  stretch forth thy hands] For help.
  shall gird thee] As a criminal.
  whither thou wouldest not] To death. This does not mean that at the last S. Peter will be unwilling to die for his Lord, but that death, and especially a criminal's death, is what men naturally shrink from.
  The common interpretation that 'stretch forth thy hands' refers to the attitude in crucifixion, and 'gird thee' to binding to the cross, is precarious, on account of the order of the clauses, the taking to execution being mentioned after the execution. But it is not impossible; for the order of this group of clauses may be determined by the previous group, and the order in the previous group is the natural one. The girding naturally precedes the walking in the first half; therefore 'gird' precedes 'carry' in the second half, and 'stretch forth thy hands' is connected with 'gird' rather than 'carry' and therefore is coupled with 'gird.' Or again 'carry thee &c.' may possibly refer to the setting up of the cross after the sufferer was bound to it; in this way all runs smoothly.

whither thou wouldest not. This spake he, signifying by 19
what death he should glorify God. And when he had
spoken this, he saith unto him, Follow me.

20—23. *The Misunderstood Saying respecting the Evangelist.*

Then Peter, turning about, seeth the disciple whom Jesus 20
loved following; which also leaned on his breast at supper,
and said, Lord, which is he that betrayeth thee? Peter 21
seeing him saith to Jesus, Lord, and what *shall* this *man*

19. *This spake he*] Now this He spake.
signifying by what death] *Signifying by* **what manner of** *death.*
This comment is quite in S. John's style (comp. xii. 33, xviii. 32) [14].
It will depend on the interpretation of *v.* 18 whether we understand
this to mean crucifixion or simply martyrdom. That S. Peter was
crucified at Rome rests on sufficient evidence, beginning with Tertullian
(*Scorp.* xv.), and that he requested to be crucified head downwards is
stated by Eusebius (*H. E.* III. i. 2) on the authority of Origen.

he should glorify] Literally, *he* **shall** *glorify.*

Follow me] Perhaps the literal meaning is not altogether to be excluded; and it appears from S. Peter's 'turning about' (*v.* 20), that *he*
understood the words literally and began to follow. But no doubt this
command here, as elsewhere in the Gospels, is to be understood figuratively, the precise shade of meaning being determined by the context.
Comp. i. 43; Matt. viii. 22, ix. 9, xix. 21. In the present case there is
probably a reference to xiii. 36, 37; and the 'following' includes following to a martyr's death, and possibly the precise death of crucifixion.

20—23. THE MISUNDERSTOOD SAYING RESPECTING THE EVANGELIST.

20. *Peter, turning about, seeth*] Omit 'then.' The graphic details
are those of an eyewitness.

leaned] Better, *leaned* **back.** The allusion is to the momentary
change of posture (xiii. 25) in order to ask who was the traitor, not to
the position which he occupied next our Lord throughout the meal (xiii.
23).

21. *Peter seeing him*] *Peter* **therefore** *seeing him.* Once more we
see the intimacy between these two Apostles. When S. Peter is told
to follow, S. John does so also unbidden; and S. Peter having received
his own commission asks about that of his friend. Comp. xviii. 15,
xx. 1 [15].

and what shall this man do?] Literally, **but** *this man, what?* Not
so much 'what shall he *do?*' as 'what about him?' What is the lot in
store for him. The question indicates the natural wish to know the
future of a friend, all the more natural after having been told something
about his own future. Hence the 'therefore' at the beginning of the
verse. As usual, S. Peter acts on the first impulse.

22 *do?* Jesus saith unto him, If I will that he tarry till I come,
23 what *is that* to thee? follow thou me. Then went this
saying abroad among the brethren, that that disciple should
not die: yet Jesus said not unto him, He shall not die;
but, If I will that he tarry till I come, what *is that* to thee?

22. *If I will*] Christ died and rose again that He might become the Lord and Master both of the dead and the living (Rom. xiv. 9). He speaks here in full consciousness of this sovereignty. For the use of 'I will' by Christ comp. xvii. 24; Matt. viii. 3 and parallels, xxvi. 39. While the 'I will' asserts the Divine authority, the 'if' keeps the decision secret.

that he tarry] Better, *that he* **abide**; it is S. John's favourite word which we have had so often (i. 32, 33, 39, 40, ii. 12, iii. 36, iv. 40, &c., and twelve times in chap. xv.) [16]. S. Peter's lot was to suffer, S. John's to wait. For 'abide' in the sense of remain in life comp. xii. 34; Phil. i. 25; 1 Cor. xv. 6.

till I come] Literally, *while I am coming*. The words express rather the *interval* of waiting than the *end* of it. Comp. ix. 4; Mark vi. 45. This at once seems to shew that it is unnecessary to enquire whether Pentecost, or the destruction of Jerusalem, or the apocalyptic visions recorded in the Revelation, or a natural death, or the Second Advent, is meant by Christ's 'coming' in this verse. He is not giving an answer but refusing one. The reply is purposely hypothetical and perhaps purposely indefinite. But inasmuch as the longer the interval covered by the words, the greater the indefiniteness, the Second Advent is to be preferred as an interpretation, if a distinct meaning is given to the 'coming.'

what is that to thee?] The words are evidently a rebuke. There is a sense in which 'Am I my brother's keeper?' is a safeguard against curiosity and presumption rather than a shirking of responsibility.

follow thou me] 'Thou' is emphatic, contrasting with the preceding 'he,' which is emphatic also.

23. *Then went this saying*] *This saying* **therefore** *went.*

abroad among] Literally, *forth unto:* comp. Matt. ix. 26; Mark i. 28; Rom. x. 18.

the brethren] This phrase, common in the Acts (ix. 30, xi. 1, 29, xv. 1, 3, 22, 23, &c.), is not used elsewhere in the Gospels for believers generally; but we see the way prepared for it in the Lord's words to the disciples (Matt. xxiii. 8), to S. Peter (Luke xxii. 32), and to Mary Magdalene (xx. 17).

should not die] Literally, *doth not die;* so also 'shall not die' in the next clause. The mistake points to a time when Christians generally expected that the Second Advent would take place in their own time; and the correction of the mistake points to a time when the Apostle was still living. If this chapter was added by another hand after the Apostle's death it would have been natural to mention his death, as the simplest and most complete answer to the misunderstanding. The cautious character of the answer given, merely pointing out the hypo-

24, 25. *Concluding Notes.*

This is the disciple which testifieth of these *things*, and wrote these *things:* and we know that his testimony is true.

thetical form of Christ's language, without pretending to explain it, shews that the question had not yet been solved in fact. Thus we are once more forced back within the limits of the first century for the date of this Gospel.

24, 25. CONCLUDING NOTES.

Again the question of authorship confronts us. Are these last two verses by the writer of the rest of the chapter? Are they both by the same hand? The *external* evidence, as in the case of the preceding verses, is in favour of their being both by the same hand, and that the writer of the first twenty-three verses, and therefore S. John. No MS. or version is extant without *v.* 24, and all except the Sinaitic, have *v.* 25 also; nor is there any evidence that a copy was ever in existence lacking either this last chapter or *v.* 24.

The *internal* evidence is the other way. The natural impression produced by *v.* 24 is that it is not the writer of the Gospel who here bears witness to his own work, but a plurality of persons who testify to the trustworthiness of the Evangelist's narrative. So that we possibly have in this verse a note added by the Ephesian elders before the publication of the Gospel. The change to the singular in *v.* 25 would seem to imply that *this* verse is an addition by a third hand of a remark which the writer may have heard from S. John.

But the internal evidence is not conclusive, and the impression naturally produced by the wording of the verses need not be the right one. The aged Apostle in bringing his work a second time (xx. 30, 31) to a conclusion may have included that inmost circle of disciples (to whom he had frequently *told* his narrative by word of mouth) among those who were able to guarantee his accuracy. With a glance of affectionate confidence round the group of devoted hearers, he adds their testimony to his own, and gives them a share in bearing witness to the truth of the Gospel.

24. *which testifieth*] Better, *which* **beareth witness.** Whether 'these things' refers to the whole Gospel, or only to the contents of chap. xxi. cannot be determined.

wrote] Note the change from present to aorist. The witness still continues at the present time; the writing took place once for all in the past.

we know] Because S. John uses the singular, 'he knoweth,' in xix. 35, it does not follow that he would not use the plural here. It would have been out of place in the middle of his narrative to add the testimony of the Ephesian elders to his own as to details which he saw with his own eyes at the foot of the cross. But it is not unnatural that at the close of his Gospel he should claim them as joint witnesses to the fidelity with which he has committed to writing this last instalment of

25 And there are also many other *things* which Jesus did, the which, if they should be written every one, I suppose that even the world itself could not contain the books that should be written. Amen.

evangelical and apostolic traditions. Comp. 1 John v. 18, 19, 20, 15, iii. 14, i. 1; 3 John 12.

25. *every one*] Literally, **one by one**.

I suppose] The Greek word (*oimai*) occurs nowhere else in N. T. excepting Phil. i. 17; James i. 7. The use of the first person singular is very unlike S. John.

If this verse is an addition by an unknown hand it appears to be almost contemporary. The wording seems to imply that it would still be possible to write a great deal: additional materials still abound.

could not contain] The bold hyperbole (which may be S. John's, though added by another hand) expresses the yearnings of Christendom throughout all ages. The attempts which century after century continue to be made to write the 'Life of Christ' seem to prove that even the fragments that have come down to us of that 'Life' have been found in their manysidedness and profundity to be practically inexhaustible. After all that the piety and learning of eighteen hundred years have accomplished, Christians remain still unsatisfied, still unconvinced that the most has been made of the very fragmentary account of scarcely a tenth portion of the Lord's life on earth. What would be needed to make even this tenth complete? What, therefore, to complete the whole?

Amen] The addition of a copyist.

APPENDICES.

A. THE DAY OF THE CRUCIFIXION.

It can scarcely be doubted that if we had only the Fourth Gospel no question would have arisen as to the date of the Last Supper and of the Crucifixion. S. John's statements are as usual so clear and precise, and at the same time so entirely consistent, that obscurity arises only when attempts are made to force his plain language into harmony with the statements of the Synoptists which appear to contradict his.

S. John's gives five distinct intimations of the date.

1. '*Now before* the Feast of the Passover' (xiii. 1); a phrase which gives a date to the feet-washing and farewell discourses at the Last Supper.

2. 'Buy those things that we have need of *for the Feast*' (xiii. 29); which again shews that the Last Supper was not the Passover.

3. 'They themselves went not into the palace, that they might not be defiled, but *might eat the Passover*' (xviii. 28); which proves that 'early' on the day of the crucifixion the Jews who delivered our Lord to Pilate had not yet eaten the Passover.

4. 'It was the *preparation of the Passover*; it was about the sixth hour. And he saith to the Jews, Behold your King' (xix. 14); which shews that the Jews had not postponed eating the Passover because of urgent business: the Passover had not yet begun.

5. 'The Jews therefore, because it was *the preparation*, that the bodies should not remain upon the cross on the Sabbath day, (for that Sabbath day was an *high day*) asked Pilate &c.' (xix. 31). Here 'the preparation' (*paraskeuē*) may mean either the preparation for the Sabbath, i.e. Friday, or the preparation for the Passover, i.e. Nisan 14. But the statement that the Sabbath was a 'high day' most naturally means that the Sabbath in that week coincided with the first day of the Feast: so that the day was 'the preparation' for both the Sabbath and the Feast.

From these passages it is evident that *S. John places the Crucifixion on the preparation or eve of the Passover*, i.e. on Nisan 14, on the afternoon of which the Paschal Lamb was slain; and that he makes the Passover begin at sunset that same day. Consequently our Lord was in the grave before the Passover began, and *the Last Supper cannot have been the Paschal meal*.

Moreover these statements fall in very well with the almost universal view that the Crucifixion took place on a Friday, on the evening of which the Passover as well as the Sabbath began.

It is from the Synoptists that we inevitably derive the impression that the Last Supper *was* the Paschal meal (Matt. xxvi. 2, 17, 18, 19; Mark xiv. 14—16; Luke xxii. 7, 11, 13, 15). Whatever method of explanation be adopted, it is the impression derived from the Synoptists that must be modified, not that derived from S. John. Their statements refer rather to the *nature* of the Last Supper, his cover the whole field from the Supper to the taking down from the cross, giving clear marks of *time* all along. No doubt they are correct in stating that the Last Supper had *in some sense* the character of a Paschal meal; but it is quite evident from S. John that the Last Supper was not the Passover in the ordinary Jewish sense. When the Sabbath gave place to the Lord's Day the day was deliberately changed in order to mark the change of associations: a similar change for similar reasons may have been adopted when the Eucharist supplanted the Passover. The fact that the whole Church for eight centuries always used *leavened* bread at the Eucharist, and that the Eastern Church continues to do so to this day, may point to a tradition that the meal at which the Eucharist was instituted was not the Paschal meal. Moreover Jews, to whom the Gospel was to be preached first, might have found a serious stumbling-block in the fact that He who was proclaimed as the Paschal Lamb partook of the Paschal Feast and was slain afterwards. Whereas S. John makes it clear to them, that on the very day and at the very hour when the Paschal lambs had to be slain, the True Lamb was sacrificed on the Cross. (See note on Matt. xxvi. 17 and Excursus V. in Dr Farrar's *S. Luke.*)

B. S. PETER'S DENIALS.

The difficulties which attend all attempts at forming a Harmony of the Gospels are commonly supposed to reach something like a climax here. Very few events are narrated at such length by all four Evangelists; and in no case is the narrative so carefully divided by them into distinct portions as in the case of S. Peter's threefold denial of his Master. Here therefore we have an exceptionally good opportunity of comparing the Evangelists with one another piece by piece; and the result is supposed to be damaging to them. A careful comparison of the four accounts will establish one fact beyond the reach of reasonable dispute;—that, whatever may be the relation between the narratives of S. Matthew and S. Mark, those of S. Luke and S. John are independent both of the first two Gospels and of one another. So that we have at least three independent accounts.

It would be an instructive exercise for the student to do for himself what Canon Westcott has done for him (Additional Note on John xviii: comp. Alford on Matt. xxvi. 69), and tabulate the four accounts, comparing not merely verse with verse but clause with clause.

His first impression of great discrepancy between the accounts will convince him of the independence of at least three of them. And a further consideration will probably lead him to see that this independence and consequent difference are the result of fearless truthfulness. Each Evangelist, conscious of his own fidelity, tells the story in his own way without caring to correct his account by that of others. In the midst of the differences of details there is quite enough substantial agreement to lead us to the conclusion that each narrative would be found to be accurate if we were acquainted with all the circumstances. All four Evangelists tell us that *three denials were predicted* (Matt. xxvi. 34; Mark xiv. 30; Luke xxii. 34; John xiii. 38) and all four *give three denials* (Matt. xxvi. 70, 72, 74; Mark xiv. 68, 70, 71; Luke xxii. 57, 58, 60; John xviii. 17, 25, 27).

The *apparent discrepancy with regard to the prediction* is that S. Luke and S. John place it during the Supper, S. Mark and S. Matthew during

APPENDICES.

the walk to Gethsemane. But the words of the first two Evangelists do not quite necessarily mean that the prediction was made precisely where they mention it. Yet, if the more natural conclusion be adopted that they do mean to place the prediction on the road to Gethsemane; then, either the prediction was repeated, or they have placed it out of the actual chronological sequence. As already remarked elsewhere, chronology is not what the Evangelists care to give us.

The *numerous differences of detail with regard to the three denials*, especially the second and third, will sink into very small proportions if we consider that the attack of the maid which provoked the first denial, about which the four accounts are very harmonious, led to a series of attacks gathered into two groups, with intervals during which S. Peter was left unmolested. Each Evangelist gives us salient points in these groups of attacks and denials. As to the particular words put into the mouth of S. Peter and his assailants, it is quite unnecessary to suppose that they are intended to give us more than *the substance* of what was said (see Introductory Note to chap. iii.). Let us remember S. Augustine's wise and moderate words respecting the differences of detail in the narratives of the storm on the lake. "There is no need to enquire which of these exclamations was really uttered. For whether they uttered some one of these three, or other words which none of the Evangelists have recorded, yet conveying the same sense, *what does it matter?*" *De Cons. Ev.* II. xxiv. 55.

C. ORDER OF THE CHIEF EVENTS OF THE PASSION.

This part of the Gospel narrative is like the main portion of it in this, that the exact sequence of events cannot in all cases be determined with certainty, and that the precise date of events can in no case be determined with certainty. But for the sake of clearness of view it is well to have a tentative scheme; bearing in mind that, like a plan drawn from description instead of from sight, while it helps us to understand and realise the description, it must be defective and may here and there be misleading.

Thursday after 6.0 P.M.		
(Nisan 14)		The Last Supper and Last Discourses.
	11 P.M.	The Agony.
Midnight		The Betrayal.
Friday	1 A.M.	Conveyance to the high-priest's house.
	2 A.M.	Examination before Annas.
	3 A.M.	Examination before Caiaphas at an informal meeting of the Sanhedrin.
	4.30 A.M.	Condemnation to death at a formal meeting of the Sanhedrin.
	5 A.M.	First Examination before Pilate.
	5.30 A.M.	Examination before Herod.
	6 A.M.	Second Examination before Pilate.
		The scourging and first mockery by Pilate's soldiers.
	6.30 A.M.	Pilate gives sentence of Crucifixion.
		Second mockery by Pilate's soldiers.
	9 A.M	The Crucifixion.
		First Word. '*Father, forgive them*, &c.'
		Second — '*Woman, behold thy son.*'
		'*Behold, thy mother.*'
		Third — '*To-day thou shalt be,* &c.'

Friday Noon to 3 P.M.	The Darkness.
	Fourth Word. '*My God, My God,* &c.'
	Fifth — '*I thirst.*'
	Sixth — '*It is finished.*'
3 P.M.	Seventh — '*Father, into Thy hands,* &c.'
	The Centurion's Confession.
	The Piercing of the side.
3 to 5 P.M.	Slaughter of the Paschal lambs.
5 P.M.	The Burial.
6 P.M.	The Sabbath begins.
(Nisan 15)	The Passover.
Saturday	The Great Day of the Feast.
	Jesus in the Grave.

D. ON SOME POINTS OF GEOGRAPHY.

It seems to be quite certain that the attractive reconciliation of the two readings, Βηθανίᾳ and Βηθαβαρᾷ, derived from Lieutenant Conder's conjectures, and suggested in the note on i. 28, must be abandoned. And, what is of much more serious moment, it is becoming clear that Lieutenant Conder's identifications, when they depend upon philological theories, must be received with the utmost caution. It is true that the Arabs call Batanaea, the Baravala of Josephus, Băthănia; changing the Aramaic 't', corresponding to the Hebrew 'sh' in Bashan, to 'th', by a well-known phonetic relation between these three dialects. But a Jewish writer would not adopt a pure Arabic form, which is therefore impossible in a Gospel written by a Jew. And even if this point could be conceded there would remain the further improbability that the Arabic 'ă' in *Băthănîya* should be represented by η in Βηθανία. Bethania is a compound of Bêth, and some place on the Jordan. It might possibly mean 'boat-house'; and this would coincide pretty closely with Bethabara, which means 'ford-house' or 'ferry-house'.

In any map of Jerusalem there must of necessity be either serious omissions, or insertions which are more or less conjectural. In the present map the traditional name of Zion has been retained for the Western Hill, and also the name of Hippicus for the great Herodian tower which still stands close to the Jaffa Gate. Recent measurements, however, have shewn that of the three Herodian towers, Hippicus, Phasael, and Mariamne, the existing tower, often called the Tower of David, may be Phasael rather than Hippicus. The name, Tower of David, is mediaeval, and is a perpetuation of the error of Josephus, who supposed that the fortress of David belonged to the Upper City, and that the Western Hill had always been part of Jerusalem.

Again, the position of the Acra is much disputed. In the map it is not intended to affirm the special conjecture of Warren and Conder, but merely to retain, until something better is fully established, their present view. There is, however, good reason for doubting its correctness. On this and other topographical questions see the very interesting article on Jerusalem in the *Encycl. Britan.* (xiii. p. 641) by Professor Robertson Smith, to whom the writer of this Appendix is much indebted.

INDICES.

I. GENERAL.

Abraham's seed, supposed privileges of, 67, 187, 189
adultery, the woman taken in, 176—180; the paragraph part of the Gospel narrative, but not of the Fourth Gospel, 175
Aenon, 100
Ahitophel, 318
allegories in S. John, 210, 286
Alogi, rejection of the Fourth Gospel by the, 20, 21
analysis of the Gospel, 55—58
Andrew, character of, 79, 140, 251
angels, 82
Annas, his office and influence, 322; examination of Jesus by him peculiar to S. John, 323
Apocalypse, relation of the Fourth Gospel to, 30
Apocryphal Gospels, miracles of the Child Jesus in, 86
Apostles' defects stated without reserve, 91, 114, 115, 250, 263, 276, 357
Apostolic Fathers, assumed silence of, as to the Fourth Gospel, 18, 19
appearances after the resurrection, 354, 367
Arianism condemned, 127, 222
Arimathea, Joseph of, coincidence between S. John and S. Mark as to his character and connexion with Nicodemus, 352
attempts to arrest Jesus, 169, 173, 241, 248, 319
ascension, implied but not narrated by S. John, 156, 359, 97
Augustine quoted, 125, 146
authenticity, of the Gospel, by whom disputed, 18, 21; external evidence for, 20, 21; internal evidence for, 22—30, 50; internal evidence against, 30—32, 47—49; of the Appendix, 367, 377
baptism, Christian, referred to in the discourse with Nicodemus, 25: of Jesus, 100, 105; of John, 100
Baptist, his connexion with the Evangelist, 12, 77; argument from the Evangelist's calling him simply 'John,' 29, 64; crisis in his ministry, 71; he is a voice crying in the wilderness, 73

Barabbas, 335
Barnabas, epistle of, its evidence to the Fourth Gospel, 19
Bartholomew, reasons for identifying with Nathanael, 80
barley loaves, 140
Basilides, 19, 65
baskets, different kinds of at the feeding of 5000 and the feeding of 4000, 141
Bethabra, false reading for Bethany, 74
Bethany, two places of this name, 74, 228, 233
Bethesda, 122
Bethsaida, two places of this name, 80, 138
betrayal, 318
blasphemy, the Lord accused of, 127, 196, 222
blind, man born, healed, 199; his progressive faith, 201; his confession of faith, 207
brethren of the Lord, various theories respecting, 87; cannot be the sons of Alphaeus, 162
bridegroom, figure of the Messiah, 102

Caesar, speak against, 340
Caesarea, Pilate's residence, 334
Caiaphas, his office, 242; his prophecy, 243
Calvary or Golgotha, 343
Cana, two places of this name, 83; nature of the miracle at Cana of Galilee, 85
Capernaum, the modern *Tell Hûm*, 87, 156; argument from the mention of a visit to, 87
capital punishment, whether allowed to the Jews by the Romans, 178, 330
centurion's servant different from the nobleman's son, 120
Cerinthus, the Fourth Gospel attributed to, 21
characteristics of the Fourth Gospel, 38 —46, 63, 64, 65, 155; of S. John, 16, 46
chief priests, mostly Sadducees, 169, 241; their baseness, 342
chronology of the Fourth Gospel indefinite, 47, 137, 160, 218
Church, first beginning of the, 77; powers granted to, 362

circumcision prior to the Sabbath, 166
cleansing of the Temple in S. John distinct from that in the Synoptists, 89
Clement of Alexandria, 20, 33
Clementine homilies, 198, 214
cloths, 353, 356
Clopas or Alphaeus, 346
codices, the principal, containing the Gospel, 51, 52
coincidences, between S. Paul and S. John, 66, 280; between the Synoptists and S. John, 50
commandment, Christ's new, 271, 290
cocks, not excluded from Jerusalem, 327
cross, size of the, 348; title on, 344
crown of thorns, 336
cup of suffering, coincidence respecting, 322

date of the Gospel, 33
darkness, in a metaphorical sense, peculiar to S. John, 63
David, Christ's descent from, 173
death, punishment of, whether allowed to the Jews, 178, 330
Dedication, Feast of, 219
denials, S. Peter's, 326; why narrated by S. John, 327; difficulties respecting, 380
destruction of Jerusalem, S. John wrote after the, 234
devil, personal existence of the, 191; influence on Judas, 262
devil, or demon, Christ accused of being possessed by a, 166, 193, 194, 218
disciples' imperfections, 86, 91, 114, 115, 156, 250, 357
discourses in the Fourth Gospel contrasted with those in the Synoptic Gospels, 48, 91
discourses of Christ, with Nicodemus, 91; on the Source of life, 126; on the Support of life, 146; at the Feast of Tabernacles, 163; at the Feast of the Dedication, 219; at the last Passover, 261—316
Divinity claimed by Jesus, 186, 192, 196, 222, 285, 289
Docetism excluded from the Fourth Gospel, 144, 351
door of the fold, allegory of, 210, 213.
dove visible at the baptism, 75

Ecce homo quoted, 335
Elijah, argument from the Baptist's denial that he is, 73
Ephesus, the abode of S. John, 14; the place where he wrote his Gospel, 32; the elders of, 32, 377
Ephraim, city called, 244
Epilogue, an afterthought, 367
Epistle, first of S. John; relation to the Gospel, 19, 50, 280

eternal life already possessed by believers, 104, 129, 153, 155, 308
Eucharist, implied in the discourse on the Bread of Life, 146; why omitted by S. John, 266; symbolized at the crucifixion, 350
Evangelists, concurrence of all four, 50, 137, 317, 355, 381
evenings, the two Jewish, 143
excommunication, Jewish, 174, 203, 206

faith, the text of a child of God, 66
false readings, 67, 74, 101, 159, 196, 335, 346
feast, the unnamed in v. 1, probably not a Passover, 122
feasts, Jewish, S. John groups his narrative round, 88
five thousand, feeding of the, 137
forger of a gospel confronted by insuperable difficulties, 23
fragments, argument from the command to gather up, 141
funeral customs among the Jews, 234, 353

Gabbatha, not a mosaic pavement but the temple-mound, 340
Galileans, characteristics of, 10; ill repute of, 81, 173, 175
Galilee, mixed population in, 11; prophets from, 175; ministry in, 160
gaps in S. John's narrative, 47, 136, 160, 218
garments, 262
Gentiles seek Christ, 251, 252
Gerizim, temple on, 111
Gethsemane, anticipation of the agony in, 253
Gnostic demonology, 191, 192
Gnostics, the witness of, to the Fourth Gospel, 22
Gnosticism, excluded from the Fourth Gospel, 22, 112, 223, 351
Golgotha, 343
Gospel, not a Life of Christ, 34
grace before meat, 140
grave, 233, 239
Greek names among the Apostles, 251
Greeks desiring to see Jesus, 251
guards at the Cross, 345

Hebrew, evidence that the author of the Fourth Gospel knew, 152, 249, 266, 352
Herod Antipas, 118
high-priest, supposed to have prophetical gifts, 243; doubt as to who is meant by the title, 323, 324
Holy Ghost, 283
hyssop, 348

Ignatian epistles, their evidence to the Fourth Gospel, 19, 108
interpolations, 123, 175, 196
Irenaeus, evidence to the Fourth Gospel, 20; to the duration of the Lord's ministry, 47, 196

INDEX I. 385

Jacob's well, 107, 109
James, brother of S. John, 9; not mentioned by the Evangelist, 79, 346
Jerome, on the brethren of the Lord, 87; on Sychar, 107; on the paragraph of the woman taken in adultery, 175; on the Lord's writing on the ground, 179
Jerusalem, destroyed before S. John wrote, 234; his minute knowledge of, 26
JESUS:
(i) *The Ministry.*
Baptist's testimony to Him, 74; disciples' testimony to Him, 77; turns water into wine at Cana, 83; pays a brief visit to Capernaum, 17; cleanses the Temple, 88; discourses with Nicodemus, 92; converts many Samaritans, 105; heals the royal official's son, 118; heals a paralytic at Bethesda, 121; reasons with the Jews about the Son as the Source of life, 126; feeds five thousand, 137; who would make Him a king, 142; walks on the water, 143; reasons with the Jews about the Son as the Support of life, 145; with the Twelve about desertion of Him, 158; with His brethren about manifesting Himself, 160; with the Jews at the Feast of Tabernacles, 163; is marked for arrest, 173; [rescues the woman taken in adultery, 176;] charges the Jews with seeking to kill Him, 188; claims to be God, 196; heals the man born blind, 197; delivers the allegories of the Fold and of the Good Shepherd, 210; reasons with the Jews at the Feast of the Dedication, 219; retires into Peraea, 225; raises Lazarus from the dead, 227; is marked for death by Caiaphas, 243; is anointed by Mary of Bethany, 246; enters Jerusalem in triumph, 249; is sought for by Gentile proselytes, 251; retires from public teaching, 257
(ii) *The Issues of the Ministry.*
washes His disciples' feet, 261; points out the traitor, 267; delivers His farewell discourses to the eleven, 270; foretells Peter's denials, 272; answers Thomas, 275; Philip, 276; Judas not Iscariot, 282; delivers the allegory of the Vine, 286; promises to send the Paraclete and to return, 295; prays for Himself, His disciples, and His Church, 307; is arrested in the garden, 318; examined before Annas, 322; denied by Peter, 326; examined by Pilate, 328; mocked, sentenced, and crucified, 336; dies and is buried, 347; manifests Himself after His resurrection to Mary Magdalene,
357; to the ten Apostles, 360; to Thomas, 363; to seven disciples at the sea of Tiberias, 367; gives Peter his last commission and foretells his death; rebukes his curiosity about the Evangelist, 375
Jewish elements in the Fourth Gospel, 25—27
Jews, hostility of, to Christianity, 49; S. John's view of them, 72
John, the son of Zebedee; his parentage, 9; nationality, 10; connexion with the Baptist, 12, 77; fiery zeal, 13, 15; gives a home to the Blessed Virgin, 14, 347; life at Ephesus, 14; traditions about him, 15, 16; chief characteristics, 16, 17; probably the unnamed disciple in i. 35, 77; and in xviii. 15, 323; mode of reckoning time, 78,107,119, 341
John, the Baptist; the Evangelist's manner of naming him, 29, 64; not the Light but the Lamp, 64, 132; his witness to the Messiah, 68, 74, 75, 77, 101; the friend of the Bridegroom, 102; his baptism, 100, 105
John, the father of Peter, 79, 371
Jordan, ford of, at Bethany, 74; the country beyond, 225
Joseph, husband of the Virgin, 83
Joseph of Arimathea; his character and connexion with Nicodemus, 352
Judas Iscariot; his name and character, 159; murmurs at Mary of Bethany, 247; receives the sop and is entered by Satan, 269; helps to arrest Jesus, 318
Judas, not Iscariot, 282
Judas of Galilee, rising of, 11
Justin Martyr's evidence to the Fourth Gospel, 19, 73, 94, 197

Keble quoted, 360
Kedron, the ravine of the, 318
kingdom, nature of Christ's, 332

Last Day, 151
Last Supper, not a Passover, 379
Lazarus, raising of, objections to the, 226; identifications of, 228
Levites, argument from the mention of, 72
Liddon quoted, 96
Life, 63, 275
Light, 63, 64, 180
Lightfoot quoted, 19, 69, 268, 280
Lord, 149, 179, 207
Love, the Fourth Gospel the Gospel of, 17, 51, 209, 261, 270, 271, 290

Magdalene; *see* Mary
Majestas, Pilate's fear of being accused of, 340
Malchus, 322
Manasseh, founder of the rival worship on Gerizim, 111
Marcion's rejection of the Fourth Gospel, 20

INDEX I.

marriage, Christ gives his sanction to, 87; symbolical of His relation to His Church, 102
Martha, probably older than Mary and Lazarus, 229, 234; coincidence between S. John and S. Luke respecting her, 234; her progressive faith, 235
Mary Magdalene, introduced as a person well known, 346; visits the sepulchre, 355; manifestation to her, 357; nature of the rebuke to her, 359
Mary, the wife of Clopas, probably identical with the mother of James the less, 346
Mary, sister of Lazarus, not identical with the prostitute of Luke vii., nor with Mary Magdalene, 228; coincidence between S. John and S. Luke respecting her, 234; her devotion, 246; argument from the praise bestowed on her, 248
Mary, the Blessed Virgin, rebuked by Christ at Cana, 84; her relationship to His brethren, 87; to S. John, 10, 346, 347; no special manifestation to her after the Resurrection, 360
Messiah, Jewish ideas respecting wellknown to the Evangelist, 73, 82, 83, 142; Samaritan, 106, 113
Meyer quoted, 103, 159, 268
ministry, duration of Christ's, 47, 48
miracles in the Fourth Gospel symbolical, 40; spontaneous, 123
mission of Jesus distinct from that of His disciples, 198, 361; of the Holy Spirit, 279, 283, 294
money, 88, 139
Moses, contrasted with Christ, 149, 205; testifies to Christ, 80, 136; and against the Jews, 136, 166; the giver, neither of the Law, 69; nor of the manna, 149
Mount Gerizim, temple upon, 111
Mount of Olives not mentioned by S. John, 176
multitude, fickleness of the, 91, 142, 158, 160, 186, 256
Nathanael, reasons for identifying with Bartholomew, 80; his character, 81

Nazarene, 320
Nazareth, evil report of, 81
Neapolis, or Sychem, 107
New Commandment, 271, 290
Newman, Cardinal, quoted, 93
Nicodemus, mentioned by S. John only, 93; his character, 93; coincidence between S. John and S. Mark in connexion with him, 252
nobleman's son distinct from the centurion's servant, 120

Olives, Mount of, see Mount
orally, the Fourth Gospel delivered at first, 33, 51

Papias, 19
parables not found in the Fourth Gospel, 210
Paraclete, threefold office of the, 297; mission of, see Mission
parallelism in the Fourth Gospel, 45, 62, 72, 184
paralytic at Bethesda, 123
Passion, prominent thoughts in S. John's narrative of the, 317; probable order of the events of the, 381
Passover, customs at the, 267, 268, 269, 322; the first, 88; the second, 138; the last, 245; the Last Supper not the Passover, 379
Paul, coincidences between S. John and S., 66, 280
Pentecost anticipated, 362
Peter, brought to Jesus by his brother Andrew, 79; named by Jesus, 79; his impetuosity, 264, 272, 321, 356, 370; his denials, 324, 326, 380; his repentance implied but not recorded by S. John, 327; his visit to the sepulchre, 356; commission to him and prediction of his death, 371
Pharisees, the only sect mentioned by S. John, 73
Philip, called by Jesus, 80; consulted by Jesus, 139; rebuked by Jesus, 276; his character, 276
Philo, contrasted with S. John, 61, 67
Pilate, introduced in the narrative as well known, 329; his residence, 328; tries to avoid putting Jesus to death, 330; his famous question, 334; his conflicting fears, 338, 340; his character, 345
Polycarp's evidence to the First Epistle, 19; fallacious argument from his controversy with Anicetus, 32
Practorium, 328
prayer of the Great High Priest, 336
priests, 72; mostly Sadducees, yet combine with the Pharisees, 169, 241, 319
procession of the Holy Spirit, 294
Procurator, Pilate as, conducts the examination, 331
prophecies fulfilled in Christ, 89, 249, 345, 351
punctuation, differences of, 65, 166, 230, 253, 270, 278
purification, ceremonial, 84, 244
Purim, Feast of, 122
purple robe, 336
purpose, constructions implying, frequent in S. John, 115, 118, 148, 153, 195, 232, 243, 296, 297
purpose of the Gospel, 34, 366

readings, differences of, 67, 70, 104, 141, 151, 154, 162, 163, 189, 199, 206, 212, 220, 266, 311, 318, 326
remission of sins by the Church, 363

INDEX I. 387

reserve, a characteristic of S. John, 77, 79, 84, 346
resurrection, spiritual, 129; of the wicked, 130; of Christ, 355; Jewish belief as to, 235
robber or bandit, 211, 335; S. John and the robber, 15

Sabbath, of later origin than Circumcision, 166; Christ's attitude towards, 127; miracles wrought on, 201
Sadducees, not mentioned by S. John, 73; combine with the Pharisees, 169, 241
Salome, mother of S. John, 9; probably sister of the Virgin, 346
Samaria, 106
Samaritan, Jesus taunted with being a, 193
Samaritans, relations of, to the Jews, 108, 112; origin, 109; readiness to believe in Jesus, 116, 117
Samaritan Messiah, 106, 113
Samaritan woman, historical character of the narrative of, 106; her progressive faith, 111; the revelation vouchsafed to her, 114
Samaritan religion, 111, 112
Sanhedrin, 169, 174, 178, 327; in a difficulty respecting the execution of Jesus, 329
Satan, personal existence of, 191; influence on Judas, 262
scourging, Pilate's object in inflicting, 336
Sebaste, or Samaria, 107
sepulchre, 233, 339
serpent, argument from the mention of, 97
signs, 86
Siloam, pouring of water from, 171; identified with *Birket Silwân*, 200
Simon, S. John's usage in employing this name for S. Peter, 372
Solomon's porch, 219
Son of Man, use of the phrase in the Gospels, 82: in O. T., 83; its application to the Messiah, 83
spiral movement in the Prologue, 71
style of S. John, 42—46, 63, 64, 133
superscription, 344
Supper, the Last, 261
Sychar, 107
symbolical interpretations of Scripture, 370
symbolism in the Fourth Gospel, 40, 41
synagogue at Capernaum, 156
Synoptic Gospels, relation of to the Fourth, 46—50, 77, 91

Tabernacles, Feast of, 161; ceremonies at, 171, 180
table, mode of reclining at, 267
Talmud quoted, 140; declares fowls unclean, 327; declares that the Jews had lost the power to inflict capital punishment, 330
Targums, 61
Tatian, 63, 64

Temple, traffic in the, 88; Christ's public teaching in, 164, [177,] 183, 196; Solomon's porch in, 219
Tertullian, defender of a false reading, 67; witness to an early various reading, 206; gives the true 'Note of the Church', 272
Thaddaeus, or Judas, 282
Theophilus of Antioch: his evidence to the Fourth Gospel, 20
Thomas, name and character of, 232, 275, 363; compared with Philip, 276; nature of his scepticism, 364, 365
thorns, crown of, 336
Tiberias, not mentioned by the Synoptists, 138; a centre of education, 11; sea of, 137, 368; the boats of known to S. John, 144
Tiberius, chronology of his reign in connexion with Christ's ministry, 48; Pilate's fear of him, 340
title on the Cross, 344
tombs, 233, 339
tragic brevity in S. John, 270
tragic tone in S. John, 64, 99, 103
transfiguration, not recorded by S. John, 21; not alluded to in v. 37, 133
transmigration of souls, 198
treasury, 183
Trench quoted, 232
Truth, Jesus is the, 275; the Gospel is the, 333
trials, ecclesiastical and civil, of Jesus, 322—342
triumphal entry, 249
Twelve, the, spoken of as well-known, 158
typical characters in the Fourth Gospel, 39, 121
typical miracles, 40, 370

Uncial manuscripts, table of, 51, 52

versions, table of principal, 52
vine, allegory of the, 286
vinegar, 348
voice of one crying, &c., 73
voice from heaven, 254

washing the disciples' feet, 263
water, the living, 109
water, Christ walking on the, 143
Way, Jesus is the, 275
Westcott quoted, 30, 42, 50, 146, 214, 307, 316, 317, 333, 362, 369
wilderness, 244
wine, water turned into, 85; objections to the miracle, 86
woman of Samaria; see Samaritan woman.
woman taken in adultery; see adultery.
women minister to Christ, 10; at the cross, 346; visit the sepulchre, 354
words from the cross, 382

Zebedee, 9

II. WORDS AND PHRASES EXPLAINED.

abide, 76
Advocate, 279
Aenon, 100
after these things, 121, 352, 367
all flesh, 308
allegory, 212
ask, 235, 279, 302
arm of the Lord, 257
bag or box, 247
band, 319
Barabbas, 335
basket, 141
bear, 247
beginning, 60
believe on, 66
Bethesda, 122
born again, 94
branch, 286
breathe, 96, 362
brethren, 376
Caesar's friend, 339
Caiaphas, 242
captain, 322
changers of money, 88
children of God, 66
children of light, 256
cloke, 293
Comforter, 279
comfortless, 281
convey oneself away, 125
convince, 99, 192, 298
crurifragium, 349
darkness, 63
demon, 193
Didymus, 232
dispersion, 170
division or schism, 173
do the truth, 99
door, 211
early, 328
eternal life, 98
fault, 334
feast of the Jews, 138, 160
feed, 373
firkin, 85
fish, 140
fisher's coat, 369
fornication, 190
friend of the Bridegroom, 102
fulness, 69

Gentiles, 171, 251
give His life, 215
give glory to God, 204
glory, 68
Golgotha, 343
Good Shepherd, 215
grace, 68
grave, 233
Greeks, 171, 251
groan, 237
hall of judgment, 328
hard, 156
Hebrew, 122
Hellenes, 251
Hosanna, 249
hour, 84, 252
Iscariot, 159
Jewry, 160
Jews, 72
judge, 98, 181
keep, 293, 309
Lamb of God, 75
lamp, 132
last day of the feast, 171
life, 63
light, 63, 64
living water, 109
Logos, 60
Lord, 149, 179, 207
love, 229, 372
manifest, 367
mansions, 274
master, 96, 236
Messias, 79
murderer, 191
name, 66
napkin, 240
Nathanael, 80
new, 271
nobleman, 118
now, 305
ointment of spikenard, 246
offended, 296
only-begotten, 68, 70, 98
only God, the, 135
ordain, 291
palace, 323
parable, 212
Paraclete, 279
Passover of the Jews, 88
pennyworth, 139, 247
power, 66, 218

pray, 279
preparation, 349, 353
prince of this world, 254
proceed, 294
prophet, a, 64, 93, 110, 202
prophet, the, 73, 142, 173
proverb, 303
purge, 287
put, 364
Rabbi, 78, 96, 115
Rabboni, 359
reprove, 99, 298
righteousness, 298
robber, 211, 335
ruler of the feast, 85
ruler of the Jews, 93, 258
ruler of this world, 254
sanctify, 312, 313
sayings, 136
schism, 173
scripture, 223
seal, 148
send, 361
sepulchre, 233
signs, 86
Siloam, 200
sir, 149, 179, 207
sleep, 231
Son of Man, 82
son of man, 130
son of perdition, 311
sop, 268
speech, 117, 190
spirit, 95
Sychar, 107
tabernacled, 68
temple, 90
tempt, 177
Thomas, 232
true, 65, 351
verily, verily, 82
voice, 95
way, 275
wash, 264
wind, 95
without sin, 178
word, 190, 194
Word, the, 60
word of God, 223
words, 136
works, 128
world, 65

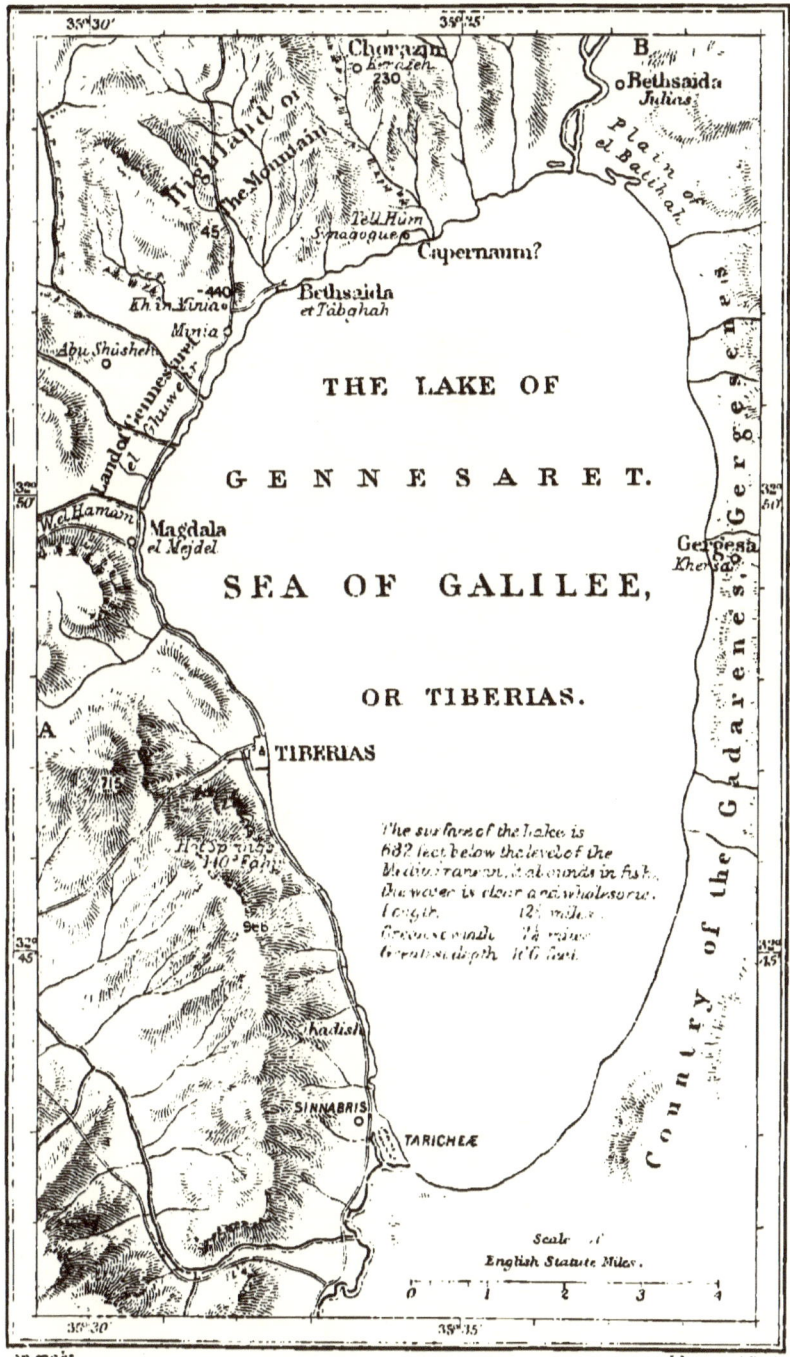

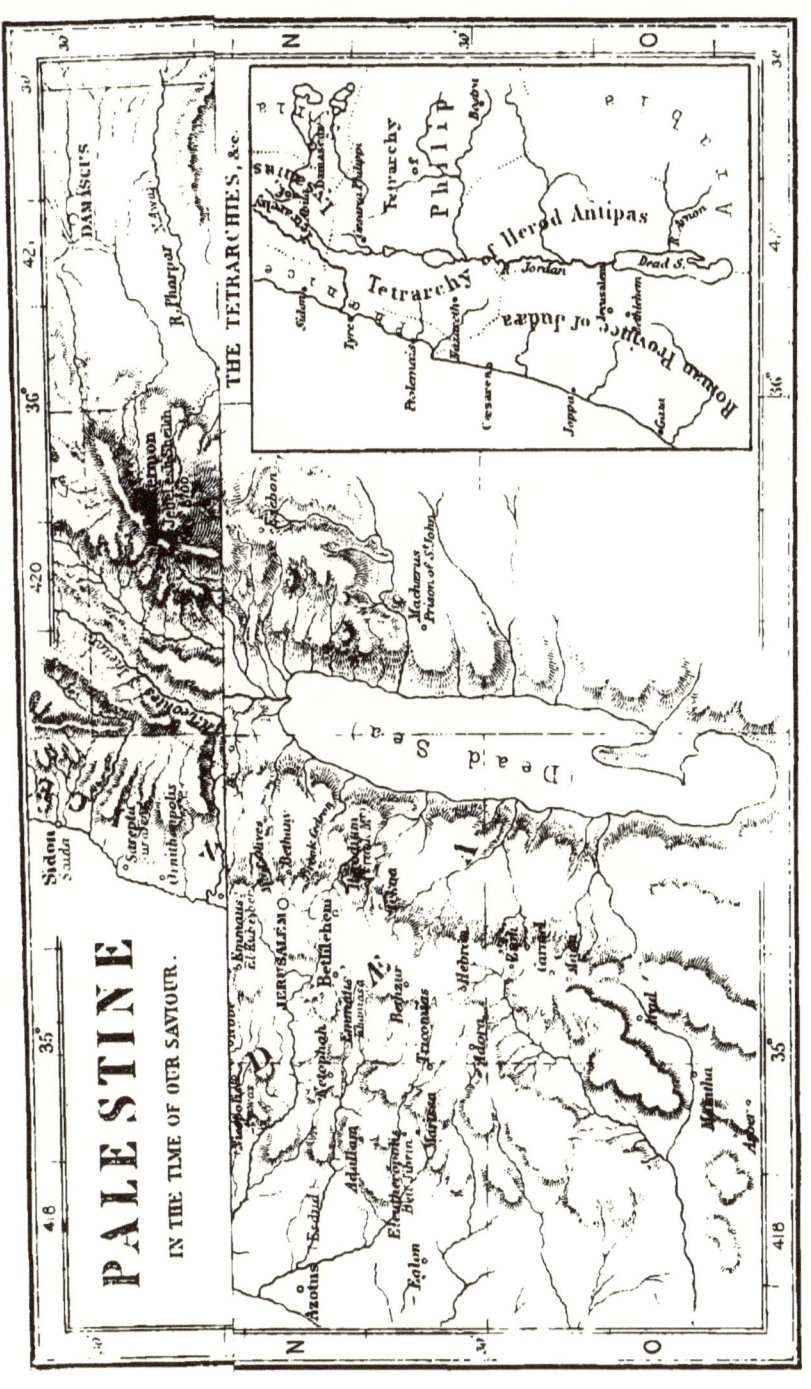

THE CAMBRIDGE BIBLE FOR SCHOOLS AND COLLEGES.
GENERAL EDITOR, J. J. S. PEROWNE,
BISHOP OF WORCESTER.

Opinions of the Press.

"*It is difficult to commend too highly this excellent series.*"—Guardian.

"*The modesty of the general title of this series has, we believe, led many to misunderstand its character and underrate its value. The books are well suited for study in the upper forms of our best schools, but not the less are they adapted to the wants of all Bible students who are not specialists. We doubt, indeed, whether any of the numerous popular commentaries recently issued in this country will be found more serviceable for general use.*"—Academy.

"*One of the most popular and useful literary enterprises of the nineteenth century.*"—Baptist Magazine.

"*Of great value. The whole series of comments for schools is highly esteemed by students capable of forming a judgment. The books are scholarly without being pretentious: and information is so given as to be easily understood.*"—Sword and Trowel.

"*The value of the work as an aid to Biblical study, not merely in schools but among people of all classes who are desirous to have intelligent knowledge of the Scriptures, cannot easily be over-estimated.*"—The Scotsman.

The Book of Judges. J. J. LIAS, M.A. "His introduction is clear and concise, full of the information which young students require, and indicating the lines on which the various problems suggested by the Book of Judges may be solved."—*Baptist Magazine.*

1 Samuel, by A. F. KIRKPATRICK. "Remembering the interest with which we read the *Books of the Kingdom* when they were appointed as a subject for school work in our boyhood, we have looked with some eagerness into Mr Kirkpatrick's volume, which contains the first instalment of them. We are struck with the great improvement in character, and variety in the materials, with which schools are now supplied. A clear map inserted in each volume, notes suiting the convenience of the scholar and the difficulty of the passage, and not merely dictated by the fancy of the commentator, were luxuries which a quarter of a century ago the Biblical student could not buy."—*Church Quarterly Review.*

"To the valuable series of Scriptural expositions and elementary commentaries which is being issued at the Cambridge University Press, under the title 'The Cambridge Bible for Schools,' has been added **The First Book of Samuel** by the Rev. A. F. KIRKPATRICK. Like other volumes of the series, it contains a carefully written historical and critical introduction, while the text is profusely illustrated and explained by notes."—*The Scotsman.*

II. Samuel. A. F. KIRKPATRICK, M.A. "Small as this work is in mere dimensions, it is every way the best on its subject and for its purpose that we know of. The opening sections at once prove the thorough competence of the writer for dealing with questions of criticism in an earnest, faithful and devout spirit; and the appendices discuss a few special difficulties with a full knowledge of the data, and a judicial reserve, which contrast most favourably with the superficial dogmatism which has too often made the exegesis of the Old Testament a field for the play of unlimited paradox and the ostentation of personal infallibility. The notes are always clear and suggestive; never trifling or irrelevant; and they everywhere demonstrate the great difference in value between the work of a commentator who is also a Hebraist, and that of one who has to depend for his Hebrew upon secondhand sources."—*Academy*.

"The Rev. A. F. KIRKPATRICK has now completed his commentary on the two books of Samuel. This second volume, like the first, is furnished with a scholarly and carefully prepared critical and historical introduction, and the notes supply everything necessary to enable the merely English scholar—so far as is possible for one ignorant of the original language—to gather up the precise meaning of the text. Even Hebrew scholars may consult this small volume with profit."—*Scotsman*.

I. Kings and Ephesians. "With great heartiness we commend these most valuable little commentaries. We had rather purchase these than nine out of ten of the big blown up expositions. Quality is far better than quantity, and we have it here."—*Sword and Trowel*.

I. Kings. "This is really admirably well done, and from first to last there is nothing but commendation to give to such honest work."—*Bookseller*.

II. Kings. "The Introduction is scholarly and wholly admirable, while the notes must be of incalculable value to students."—*Glasgow Herald*.

"It is equipped with a valuable introduction and commentary, and makes an admirable text book for Bible-classes."—*Scotsman*.

"It would be difficult to find a commentary better suited for general use."—*Academy*.

The Book of Job. "Able and scholarly as the Introduction is, it is far surpassed by the detailed exegesis of the book. In this Dr DAVIDSON's strength is at its greatest. His linguistic knowledge, his artistic habit, his scientific insight, and his literary power have full scope when he comes to exegesis....The book is worthy of the reputation of Dr Davidson; it represents the results of many years of labour, and it will greatly help to the right understanding of one of the greatest works in the literature of the world."—*The Spectator*.

"In the course of a long introduction, Dr DAVIDSON has presented us with a very able and very interesting criticism of this wonderful book. Its contents the nature of its composition, its idea and purpose, its integrity, and its age are all exhaustively treated of....We have not space to examine fully the text and notes before us, but we can, and do heartily, recommend the book, not only for the upper forms in schools, but to Bible students and teachers generally. As we wrote of a previous volume in the same series, this one leaves nothing to be desired. The notes are full and suggestive, without being too long, and, in itself, the introduction forms a valuable addition to modern Bible literature."—*The Educational Times.*

"Already we have frequently called attention to this exceedingly valuable work as its volumes have successively appeared. But we have never done so with greater pleasure, very seldom with so great pleasure, as we now refer to the last published volume, that on the **Book of Job**, by Dr DAVIDSON, of Edinburgh....We cordially commend the volume to all our readers. The least instructed will understand and enjoy it; and mature scholars will learn from it."—*Methodist Recorder.*

Job—Hosea. "It is difficult to commend too highly this excellent series, the volumes of which are now becoming numerous. The two books before us, small as they are in size, comprise almost everything that the young student can reasonably expect to find in the way of helps towards such general knowledge of their subjects as may be gained without an attempt to grapple with the Hebrew; and even the learned scholar can hardly read without interest and benefit the very able introductory matter which both these commentators have prefixed to their volumes. It is not too much to say that these works have brought within the reach of the ordinary reader resources which were until lately quite unknown for understanding some of the most difficult and obscure portions of Old Testament literature."—*Guardian.*

Ecclesiastes; or, the Preacher.—"Of the Notes, it is sufficient to say that they are in every respect worthy of Dr PLUMPTRE's high reputation as a scholar and a critic, being at once learned, sensible, and practical.... An appendix, in which it is clearly proved that the author of *Ecclesiastes* anticipated Shakspeare and Tennyson in some of their finest thoughts and reflections, will be read with interest by students both of Hebrew and of English literature. Commentaries are seldom attractive reading. This little volume is a notable exception."—*The Scotsman.*

"In short, this little book is of far greater value than most of the larger and more elaborate commentaries on this Scripture. Indispensable to the scholar, it will render real and large help to all who have to expound the dramatic utterances of **The Preacher** whether in the Church or in the School."—*The Expositor.*

"The '*ideal* biography' of the author is one of the most exquisite and fascinating pieces of writing we have met with, and, granting its starting-point, throws wonderful light on many problems connected with the book. The notes illustrating the text are full of delicate criticism, fine glowing insight, and apt historical allusion. An abler volume than Professor PLUMPTRE's we could not desire."—*Baptist Magazine.*

Jeremiah, by A. W. STREANE. "The arrangement of the book is well treated on pp. xxx., 396, and the question of Baruch's relations with its composition on pp. xxvii., xxxiv., 317. The illustrations from English literature, history, monuments, works on botany, topography, etc., are good and plentiful, as indeed they are in other volumes of this series."—*Church Quarterly Review,* April, 1881.

"Mr STREANE's **Jeremiah** consists of a series of admirable and well-nigh exhaustive notes on the text, with introduction and appendices, drawing the life, times, and character of the prophet, the style, contents, and arrangement of his prophecies, the traditions relating to Jeremiah,

4 CAMBRIDGE BIBLE FOR SCHOOLS & COLLEGES.

meant as a type of Christ (a most remarkable chapter), and other prophecies relating to Jeremiah."—*The English Churchman and Clerical Journal.*

Obadiah and Jonah. "This number of the admirable series of Scriptural expositions issued by the Syndics of the Cambridge University Press is well up to the mark. The numerous notes are excellent. No difficulty is shirked, and much light is thrown on the contents both of Obadiah and Jonah. Scholars and students of to-day are to be congratulated on having so large an amount of information on Biblical subjects, so clearly and ably put together, placed within their reach in such small bulk. To all Biblical students the series will be acceptable, and for the use of Sabbath-school teachers will prove invaluable."—*North British Daily Mail.*

"It is a very useful and sensible exposition of these two Minor Prophets, and deals very thoroughly and honestly with the immense difficulties of the later-named of the two, from the orthodox point of view."—*Expositor.*

"**Haggai and Zechariah.** This interesting little volume is of great value. It is one of the best books in that well-known series of scholarly and popular commentaries, 'the Cambridge Bible for Schools and Colleges' of which Dean Perowne is the General Editor. In the expositions of Archdeacon Perowne we are always sure to notice learning, ability, judgment and reverence .... The notes are terse and pointed, but full and reliable."—*Churchman.*

Malachi. "Archdeacon Perowne has already edited Jonah and Zechariah for this series. Malachi presents comparatively few difficulties and the Editor's treatment leaves nothing to be desired. His introduction is clear and scholarly and his commentary sufficient. We may instance the notes on ii. 15 and iv. 2 as examples of careful arrangement, clear exposition and graceful expression."—*Academy,* Aug. 2, 1890.

"**The Gospel according to St Matthew,** by the Rev. A. CARR. The introduction is able, scholarly, and eminently practical, as it bears on the authorship and contents of the Gospel, and the original form in which it is supposed to have been written. It is well illustrated by two excellent maps of the Holy Land and of the Sea of Galilee."—*English Churchman.*

"**St Matthew,** edited by A. CARR, M.A. **The Book of Joshua,** edited by G. F. MACLEAR, D.D. **The General Epistle of St James,** edited by E. H. PLUMPTRE, D.D. The introductions and notes are scholarly, and generally such as young readers need and can appreciate. The maps in both Joshua and Matthew are very good, and all matters of editing are faultless. Professor Plumptre's notes on 'The Epistle of St James' are models of terse, exact, and elegant renderings of the original, which is too often obscured in the authorised version."—*Nonconformist.*

"**St Mark,** with Notes by the Rev. G. F. MACLEAR, D.D. Into this small volume Dr Maclear, besides a clear and able Introduction to the Gospel, and the text of St Mark, has compressed many hundreds of valuable and helpful notes. In short, he has given us a capital manual of the kind required—containing all that is needed to illustrate the text, i.e. all that can be drawn from the history, geography,

OPINIONS OF THE PRESS.

customs, and manners of the time. But as a handbook, giving in a clear and succinct form the information which a lad requires in order to stand an examination in the Gospel, it is admirable......I can very heartily commend it, not only to the senior boys and girls in our High Schools, but also to Sunday-school teachers, who may get from it the very kind of knowledge they often find it hardest to get."—*Expositor*.

"With the help of a book like this, an intelligent teacher may make 'Divinity' as interesting a lesson as any in the school course. The notes are of a kind that will be, for the most part, intelligible to boys of the lower forms of our public schools; but they may be read with greater profit by the fifth and sixth, in conjunction with the original text."—*The Academy*.

"**St Luke.** Canon FARRAR has supplied students of the Gospel with an admirable manual in this volume. It has all that copious variety of illustration, ingenuity of suggestion, and general soundness of interpretation which readers are accustomed to expect from the learned and eloquent editor. Any one who has been accustomed to associate the idea of 'dryness' with a commentary, should go to Canon Farrar's **St Luke** for a more correct impression. He will find that a commentary may be made interesting in the highest degree, and that without losing anything of its solid value. . . . But, so to speak, it is *too good* for some of the readers for whom it is intended."—*The Spectator*.

"Canon FARRAR's contribution to The Cambridge School Bible is one of the most valuable yet made. His annotations on **The Gospel according to St Luke**, while they display a scholarship at least as sound, and an erudition at least as wide and varied as those of the editors of St Matthew and St Mark, are rendered telling and attractive by a more lively imagination, a keener intellectual and spiritual insight, a more incisive and picturesque style. His *St Luke* is worthy to be ranked with Professor Plumptre's *St James*, than which no higher commendation can well be given."—*The Expositor*.

"**St Luke.** Edited by Canon FARRAR, D.D. We have received with pleasure this edition of the Gospel by St Luke, by Canon Farrar. It is another instalment of the best school commentary of the Bible we possess. Of the expository part of the work we cannot speak too highly. It is admirable in every way, and contains just the sort of information needed for Students of the English text unable to make use of the original Greek for themselves."—*The Nonconformist and Independent*.

"As a handbook to the third gospel, this small work is invaluable. The author has compressed into little space a vast mass of scholarly information. . . The notes are pithy, vigorous, and suggestive, abounding in pertinent illustrations from general literature, and aiding the youngest reader to an intelligent appreciation of the text. A finer contribution to 'The Cambridge Bible for Schools' has not yet been made."—*Baptist Magazine*.

"We were quite prepared to find in Canon FARRAR'S **St Luke** a masterpiece of Biblical criticism and comment, and we are not disappointed by our examination of the volume before us. It reflects very faithfully the learning and critical insight of the Canon's greatest works, his 'Life of Christ' and his 'Life of St Paul', but differs widely from both in the terseness and condensation of its style. What Canon Farrar has evidently aimed at is to place before students as much information as possible within the limits of the smallest possible space, and in this aim he has hit the mark to perfection."—*The Examiner.*

The Gospel according to St John. "Of the notes we can say with confidence that they are useful, necessary, learned, and brief. To Divinity students, to teachers, and for private use, this compact Commentary will be found a valuable aid to the better understanding of the Sacred Text."—*School Guardian.*

"The new volume of the 'Cambridge Bible for Schools'—the **Gospel according to St John,** by the Rev. A. PLUMMER—shows as careful and thorough work as either of its predecessors. The introduction concisely yet fully describes the life of St John, the authenticity of the Gospel, its characteristics, its relation to the Synoptic Gospels, and to the Apostle's First Epistle, and the usual subjects referred to in an 'introduction'."—*The Christian Church.*

"The notes are extremely scholarly and valuable, and in most cases exhaustive, bringing to the elucidation of the text all that is best in commentaries, ancient and modern."—*The English Churchman and Clerical Journal.*

"(1) **The Acts of the Apostles.** By J. RAWSON LUMBY, D.D. (2) **The Second Epistle of the Corinthians,** edited by Professor LIAS. The introduction is pithy, and contains a mass of carefully-selected information on the authorship of the Acts, its designs, and its sources. ......The Second Epistle of the Corinthians is a manual beyond all praise, for the excellence of its pithy and pointed annotations, its analysis of the contents, and the fulness and value of its introduction."—*Examiner.*

"The concluding portion of the **Acts of the Apostles,** under the very competent editorship of Dr LUMBY, is a valuable addition to our school-books on that subject. Detailed criticism is impossible within the space at our command, but we may say that the ample notes touch with much exactness the very points on which most readers of the text desire information. Due reference is made, where necessary, to the Revised Version; the maps are excellent; and we do not know of any other volume where so much help is given to the complete understanding of one of the most important and, in many respects, difficult books of the New Testament."—*School Guardian.*

"The Rev. H. C. G. MOULE, M.A., has made a valuable addition to THE CAMBRIDGE BIBLE FOR SCHOOLS in his brief commentary on the **Epistle to the Romans.** The 'Notes' are very good, and lean, as the notes of a School Bible should, to the most commonly accepted and orthodox view of the inspired author's meaning; while the Introduction, and especially the Sketch of the Life of St Paul, is a model of condensation. It is as lively and pleasant to read as if two or three facts had not been crowded into well-nigh every sentence."—*Expositor.*

"**The Epistle to the Romans.** It is seldom we have met with a work so remarkable for the compression and condensation of all that is valuable in the smallest possible space as in the volume before us. Within its limited pages we have 'a sketch of the Life of St Paul,' we have further a critical account of the date of the Epistle to the Romans, of its language, and of its genuineness. The notes are numerous, full of matter, to the point, and leave no real difficulty or obscurity unexplained."—*The Examiner.*

"**The First Epistle to the Corinthians.** Edited by Professor LIAS. Every fresh instalment of this annotated edition of the Bible for Schools confirms the favourable opinion we formed of its value from the examination of its first number. The origin and plan of the Epistle are discussed with its character and genuineness."—*The Nonconformist.*

"**The Second Epistle to the Corinthians.** By Professor LIAS. **The General Epistles of St Peter and St Jude.** By E. H. PLUMPTRE, D.D. We welcome these additions to the valuable series of the Cambridge Bible. We have nothing to add to the commendation which we have from the first publication given to this edition of the Bible. It is enough to say that Professor Lias has completed his work on the two Epistles to the Corinthians in the same admirable manner as at first. Dr Plumptre has also completed the Catholic Epistles."—*Nonconformist.*

The Epistle to the Ephesians. By Rev. H. C. G. MOULE, M.A. "It seems to us the model of a School and College Commentary—comprehensive, but not cumbersome; scholarly, but not pedantic."—*Baptist Magazine.*

The Epistle to the Philippians. "There are few series more valued by theological students than 'The Cambridge Bible for Schools and Colleges,' and there will be no number of it more esteemed than that by Mr H. C. G. MOULE on the *Epistle to the Philippians.*"—*Record.*

"Another capital volume of 'The Cambridge Bible for Schools and Colleges.' The notes are a model of scholarly, lucid, and compact criticism."—*Baptist Magazine.*

Hebrews. "Like his (Canon Farrar's) commentary on Luke it possesses all the best characteristics of his writing. It is a work not only of an accomplished scholar, but of a skilled teacher."—*Baptist Magazine.*

"We heartily commend this volume of this excellent work."—*Sunday School Chronicle.*

"**The General Epistle of St James,** by Professor PLUMPTRE, D.D. Nevertheless it is, so far as I know, by far the best exposition of the Epistle of St James in the English language. Not Schoolboys or Students going in for an examination alone, but Ministers and Preachers of the Word, may get more real help from it than from the most costly and elaborate commentaries."—*Expositor.*

The Epistles of St John. By the Rev. A. PLUMMER, M.A., D.D. "This forms an admirable companion to the 'Commentary on the Gospel according to St John,' which was reviewed in *The Churchman* as soon as it appeared. Dr Plummer has some of the highest qualifications for such a task; and these two volumes, their size being considered, will bear comparison with the best Commentaries of the time."—*The Churchman.*

"Dr PLUMMER's edition of **the Epistles of St John** is worthy of its companions in the 'Cambridge Bible for Schools' Series. The subject, though not apparently extensive, is really one not easy to treat, and requiring to be treated at length, owing to the constant reference to obscure heresies in the Johannine writings. Dr Plummer has done his exegetical task well."—*The Saturday Review.*

THE CAMBRIDGE GREEK TESTAMENT
FOR SCHOOLS AND COLLEGES

with a Revised Text, based on the most recent critical authorities, and English Notes, prepared under the direction of the General Editor, THE BISHOP OF WORCESTER.

"*Has achieved an excellence which puts it above criticism.*"—Expositor.

St Matthew. "Copious illustrations, gathered from a great variety of sources, make his notes a very valuable aid to the student. They are indeed remarkably interesting, while all explanations on meanings, applications, and the like are distinguished by their lucidity and good sense."—*Pall Mall Gazette.*

St Mark. "The Cambridge Greek Testament of which Dr MACLEAR'S edition of the Gospel according to St Mark is a volume, certainly supplies a want. Without pretending to compete with the leading commentaries, or to embody very much original research, it forms a most satisfactory introduction to the study of the New Testament in the original....Dr Maclear's introduction contains all that is known of St Mark's life; an account of the circumstances in which the Gospel was composed, with an estimate of the influence of St Peter's teaching upon St Mark; an excellent sketch of the special characteristics of this Gospel; an analysis, and a chapter on the text of the New Testament generally."—*Saturday Review.*

St Luke. "Of this second series we have a new volume by Archdeacon FARRAR on *St Luke*, completing the four Gospels....It gives us in clear and beautiful language the best results of modern scholarship. We have a most attractive *Introduction*. Then follows a sort of composite Greek text, representing fairly and in very beautiful type the consensus of modern textual critics. At the beginning of the exposition of each chapter of the Gospel are a few short critical notes giving the manuscript evidence for such various readings as seem to deserve mention. The expository notes are short, but clear and helpful. For young students and those who are not disposed to buy or to study the much more costly work of Godet, this seems to us to be the best book on the Greek Text of the Third Gospel."—*Methodist Recorder.*

St John. "We take this opportunity of recommending to ministers on probation, the very excellent volume of the same series on this part of the New Testament. We hope that most or all of our young ministers will prefer to study the volume in the *Cambridge Greek Testament for Schools.*"—*Methodist Recorder.*

The Acts of the Apostles. "Professor LUMBY has performed his laborious task well, and supplied us with a commentary the fulness and freshness of which Bible students will not be slow to appreciate. The volume is enriched with the usual copious indexes and four coloured maps."—*Glasgow Herald.*

I. Corinthians. "Mr LIAS is no novice in New Testament exposition, and the present series of essays and notes is an able and helpful addition to the existing books."—*Guardian.*

The Epistles of St John. "In the very useful and well annotated series of the Cambridge Greek Testament the volume on the Epistles of St John must hold a high position...The notes are brief, well informed and intelligent."—*Scotsman.*

CAMBRIDGE: PRINTED BY C. J CLAY, M.A. AND SONS, AT THE UNIVERSITY PRESS.

CAMBRIDGE UNIVERSITY PRESS.

THE PITT PRESS SERIES.

₊ *Many of the books in this list can be had in two volumes, Text and Notes separately.*

I. GREEK.

Aristophanes. Aves—Plutus—Ranæ. By W. C. GREEN, M.A., late Assistant Master at Rugby School. 3s. 6d. each.
Aristotle. Outlines of the Philosophy of. By EDWIN WALLACE, M.A., LL.D. Third Edition, Enlarged. 4s. 6d.
Euripides. Heracleidae. By E. A. BECK, M.A. 3s. 6d.
——— **Hercules Furens.** By A. GRAY, M.A., and J. T. HUTCHINSON, M.A. New Edit. 2s.
——— **Hippolytus.** By W. S. HADLEY, M.A. 2s.
——— **Iphigeneia in Aulis.** By C. E. S. HEADLAM, B.A. 2s. 6d.
Herodotus, Book V. By E. S. SHUCKBURGH, M.A. 3s.
——— **Book VI.** By the same Editor. 4s.
——— **Books VIII., IX.** By the same Editor. 4s. each.
——— **Book VIII. Ch. 1—90. Book IX. Ch. 1—89.** By the same Editor. 3s. 6d. each.
Homer. Odyssey, Books IX., X. By G. M. EDWARDS, M.A. 2s. 6d. each. BOOK XXI. By the same Editor. 2s.
——— **Iliad. Book XXII.** By the same Editor. 2s.
——— **Book XXIII.** By the same Editor. [*Nearly ready.*]
Lucian. Somnium Charon Piscator et De Luctu. By W. E. HEITLAND, M.A., Fellow of St John's College, Cambridge. 3s. 6d.
——— **Menippus and Timon.** By E. C. MACKIE, M.A. [*Nearly ready.*]
Platonis Apologia Socratis. By J. ADAM, M.A. 3s. 6d.
——— **Crito.** By the same Editor. 2s. 6d.
——— **Euthyphro.** By the same Editor. 2s. 6d.
Plutarch. Lives of the Gracchi. By Rev. H. A. HOLDEN, M.A., LL.D. 6s.
——— **Life of Nicias.** By the same Editor. 5s.
——— **Life of Sulla.** By the same Editor. 6s.
——— **Life of Timoleon.** By the same Editor. 6s.
Sophocles. Oedipus Tyrannus. School Edition. By R. C. JEBB, Litt.D., LL.D. 4s. 6d.
Thucydides. Book VII. By Rev. H. A. HOLDEN, M.A., LL.D. [*Nearly ready.*]
Xenophon. Agesilaus. By H. HAILSTONE, M.A. 2s. 6d.
——— **Anabasis.** By A. PRETOR, M.A. Two vols. 7s. 6d.
——— **Books I. III. IV. and V.** By the same. 2s. each.
——— **Books II. VI. and VII.** By the same. 2s. 6d. each.
Xenophon. Cyropaedeia. Books I. II. By Rev. H. A. HOLDEN, M.A., LL.D. 2 vols. 6s.
——— ——— **Books III. IV. and V.** By the same Editor. 5s.
——— ——— **Books VI. VII. VIII.** By the same Editor. 5s.

London: Cambridge Warehouse, Ave Maria Lane.

50/12/90

II. LATIN.

Beda's Ecclesiastical History, Books III., IV. By J. E. B. MAYOR, M.A., and J. R. LUMBY, D.D. Revised Edition. 7s. 6d.

—— **Books I. II.** By the same Editors. [*In the Press.*

Caesar. De Bello Gallico, Comment. I. By A. G. PESKETT, M.A., Fellow of Magdalene College, Cambridge. 1s. 6d. COMMENT. II. III. 2s. COMMENT. I. II. III. 3s. COMMENT. IV. and V. 1s. 6d. COMMENT. VII. 2s. COMMENT VI. and COMMENT. VIII. 1s. 6d. each.

—— **De Bello Civili, Comment. I.** By the same Editor. 3s.

Cicero. De Amicitia.—De Senectute. By J. S. REID, Litt.D., Fellow of Gonville and Caius College. 3s. 6d. each.

—— **In Gaium Verrem Actio Prima.** By H. COWIE, M.A. 1s. 6d.

—— **In Q. Caecilium Divinatio et in C. Verrem Actio.** By W. E. HEITLAND, M.A., and H. COWIE, M.A. 3s.

—— **Philippica Secunda.** By A. G. PESKETT, M.A. 3s. 6d.

—— **Oratio pro Archia Poeta.** By J. S. REID, Litt.D. 2s.

—— **Pro L. Cornelio Balbo Oratio.** By the same. 1s. 6d.

—— **Oratio pro Tito Annio Milone.** By JOHN SMYTH PURTON, B.D. 2s. 6d.

—— **Oratio pro L. Murena.** By W. E. HEITLAND, M.A. 3s.

—— **Pro Cn. Plancio Oratio,** by H. A. HOLDEN, LL.D. 4s. 6d.

—— **Pro P. Cornelio Sulla.** By J. S. REID, Litt.D. 3s. 6d.

—— **Somnium Scipionis.** By W. D. PEARMAN, M.A. 2s.

Horace. Epistles, Book I. By E. S. SHUCKBURGH, M.A., late Fellow of Emmanuel College. 2s. 6d.

Livy. Book IV. By H. M. STEPHENSON, M.A. 2s. 6d.

—— **Book V.** By L. WHIBLEY, M.A. 2s. 6d.

—— **Books XXI., XXII.** By M. S. DIMSDALE, M.A., Fellow of King's College. 2s. 6d. each.

—— **Book XXVII.** By Rev. H. M. STEPHENSON, M.A. 2s. 6d.

Lucan. Pharsaliae Liber Primus. By W. E. HEITLAND, M.A., and C. E. HASKINS, M.A. 1s. 6d.

Lucretius, Book V. By J. D. DUFF, M.A. 2s.

Ovidii Nasonis Fastorum Liber VI. By A. SIDGWICK, M.A., Tutor of Corpus Christi College, Oxford. 1s. 6d.

Quintus Curtius. A Portion of the History (Alexander in India). By W. E. HEITLAND, M.A., and T. E. RAVEN, B.A. With Two Maps. 3s. 6d.

Vergili Maronis Aeneidos Libri I.—XII. By A. SIDGWICK, M.A. 1s. 6d. each.

—— **Bucolica.** By the same Editor. 1s. 6d.

—— **Georgicon Libri I. II.** By the same Editor. 2s.

—— —— **Libri III. IV.** By the same Editor. 2s.

—— **The Complete Works.** By the same Editor. Two vols. Vol. I. containing the Introduction and Text. 3s. 6d. Vol. II. The Notes. 4s. 6d.

London: Cambridge Warehouse, Ave Maria Lane.

III. FRENCH.

Corneille. La Suite du Menteur. A Comedy in Five Acts. By the late G. MASSON, B.A. 2s.

De Bonnechose. Lazare Hoche. By C. COLBECK, M.A. Revised Edition. Four Maps. 2s.

D'Harleville. Le Vieux Célibataire. By G. MASSON, B.A. 2s.

De Lamartine. Jeanne D'Arc. By Rev. A. C. CLAPIN, M.A. New edition revised, by A. R. ROPES, M.A. 1s. 6d.

De Vigny. La Canne de Jonc. By Rev. H. A. BULL, M.A., late Master at Wellington College. 2s.

Erckmann-Chatrian. La Guerre. By Rev. A. C. CLAPIN, M.A. 3s.

La Baronne de Staël-Holstein. Le Directoire. (Considérations sur la Révolution Française. Troisième et quatrième parties.) Revised and enlarged. By G. MASSON, B.A., and G. W. PROTHERO, M.A. 2s.

—— —— **Dix Années d'Exil. Livre II. Chapitres 1—8.** By the same Editors. New Edition, enlarged. 2s.

Lemercier. Fredegonde et Brunehaut. A Tragedy in Five Acts. By GUSTAVE MASSON, B.A. 2s.

Molière. Le Bourgeois Gentilhomme, Comédie-Ballet en Cinq Actes. (1670.) By Rev. A. C. CLAPIN, M.A. Revised Edition. 1s. 6d.

—— **L'École des Femmes.** By G. SAINTSBURY, M.A. 2s. 6d.

—— **Les Précieuses Ridicules.** By E. G. W. BRAUNHOLTZ, M.A., Ph.D. 2s.

—— —— **Abridged Edition.** 1s.

Piron. La Métromanie. A Comedy. By G. MASSON, B.A. 2s.

Racine. Les Plaideurs. By E. G. W. BRAUNHOLTZ, M.A. 2s.

—— —— **Abridged Edition.** 1s.

Sainte-Beuve. M. Daru (Causeries du Lundi, Vol. IX.) By G. MASSON, B.A. 2s.

Saintine. Picciola. By Rev. A. C. CLAPIN, M.A. 2s.

Scribe and Legouvé. Bataille de Dames. By Rev. H. A. BULL, M.A. 2s.

Scribe. Le Verre d'Eau. By C. COLBECK, M.A. 2s.

Sédaine. Le Philosophe sans le savoir. By Rev. H. A. BULL, M.A. 2s.

Thierry. Lettres sur l'histoire de France (XIII.—XXIV.). By G. MASSON, B.A., and G. W. PROTHERO, M.A. 2s. 6d.

—— **Récits des Temps Mérovingiens I.—III.** By GUSTAVE MASSON, B.A. Univ. Gallic., and A. R. ROPES, M.A. With Map. 3s.

Villemain. Lascaris ou Les Grecs du XVe Siècle, Nouvelle Historique. By G. MASSON, B.A. 2s.

Voltaire. Histoire du Siècle de Louis XIV. Chaps. I.— XIII. By G. MASSON, B.A., and G. W. PROTHERO, M.A. 2s. 6d. PART II. CHAPS. XIV.—XXIV. 2s. 6d. PART III. CHAPS. XXV. to end. 2s. 6d.

Xavier de Maistre. La Jeune Sibérienne. Le Lépreux de la Cité D'Aoste. By G. MASSON, B.A. 1s. 6d.

London: Cambridge Warehouse, Ave Maria Lane.

IV. GERMAN.

Ballads on German History. By W. WAGNER, Ph.D. 2s.

Benedix. Doctor Wespe. Lustspiel in fünf Aufzügen. By KARL HERMANN BREUL, M.A., Ph.D. 3s.

Freytag. Der Staat Friedrichs des Grossen. By WILHELM WAGNER, Ph.D. 2s.

German Dactylic Poetry. By WILHELM WAGNER, Ph.D. 3s.

Goethe's Knabenjahre. (1749—1759.) By W. WAGNER, Ph.D. New edition revised and enlarged, by J. W. CARTMELL, M.A. 2s.

—— **Hermann und Dorothea.** By WILHELM WAGNER, Ph.D. New edition revised, by J. W. CARTMELL, M.A. 3s. 6d.

Gutzkow. Zopf und Schwert. Lustspiel in fünf Aufzügen. By H. J. WOLSTENHOLME, B.A. (Lond.) 3s. 6d.

Hauff. Das Bild des Kaisers. By KARL HERMANN BREUL, M.A., Ph.D., University Lecturer in German. 3s.

—— **Das Wirthshaus im Spessart.** By A. SCHLOTTMANN, Ph.D. 3s. 6d.

—— **Die Karavane.** By A. SCHLOTTMANN, Ph.D. 3s. 6d.

Immermann. Der Oberhof. A Tale of Westphalian Life, by WILHELM WAGNER, Ph.D. 3s.

Kohlrausch. Das Jahr 1813. By WILHELM WAGNER, Ph.D. 2s.

Lessing and Gellert. Selected Fables. By KARL HERMANN BREUL, M.A., Ph.D. 3s.

Mendelssohn's Letters. Selections from. By J. SIME, M.A. 3s.

Raumer. Der erste Kreuzzug (1095—1099). By WILHELM WAGNER, Ph.D. 2s.

Riehl. Culturgeschichtliche Novellen. By H. J. WOLSTENHOLME, B.A. (Lond.). 3s. 6d.

Schiller. Wilhelm Tell. By KARL HERMANN BREUL, M.A., Ph.D. 2s. 6d.

—— —— **Abridged Edition.** 1s. 6d.

Uhland. Ernst, Herzog von Schwaben. By H. J. WOLSTENHOLME, B.A. 3s. 6d.

V. ENGLISH.

Ancient Philosophy from Thales to Cicero, A Sketch of. By JOSEPH B. MAYOR, M.A. 3s. 6d.

An Apologie for Poetrie by Sir PHILIP SIDNEY. By E. S. SHUCKBURGH, M.A. The Text is a revision of that of the first edition of 1595. 3s.

Bacon's History of the Reign of King Henry VII. By the Rev. Professor LUMBY, D.D. 3s.

Cowley's Essays. By the Rev. Professor LUMBY, D.D. 4s.

London: Cambridge Warehouse, Ave Maria Lane.

Milton's Comus and Arcades. By A. W. VERITY, M.A.,
sometime Scholar of Trinity College. 3s.
More's History of King Richard III. By J. RAWSON LUMBY,
D.D. 3s. 6d.
More's Utopia. By Rev. Prof. LUMBY, D.D. 3s. 6d.
The Two Noble Kinsmen. By the Rev. Professor SKEAT,
Litt.D. 3s. 6d.

VI. EDUCATIONAL SCIENCE.

Comenius, John Amos, Bishop of the Moravians. His Life
and Educational Works, by S. S. LAURIE, A.M., F.R.S.E. 3s. 6d.

Education, Three Lectures on the Practice of. I. On Marking, by H. W. EVE, M.A. II. On Stimulus, by A. SIDGWICK, M.A. III. On the Teaching of Latin Verse Composition, by E. A. ABBOTT, D.D. 2s.

Stimulus. A Lecture delivered for the Teachers' Training
Syndicate, May, 1882, by A. SIDGWICK, M.A. 1s.

Locke on Education. By the Rev. R. H. QUICK, M.A. 3s. 6d.

Milton's Tractate on Education. A facsimile reprint from
the Edition of 1673. By O. BROWNING, M.A. 2s.

Modern Languages, Lectures on the Teaching of. By C.
COLBECK, M.A. 2s.

Teacher, General Aims of the, and Form Management. Two
Lectures delivered in the University of Cambridge in the Lent Term, 1883, by F. W. FARRAR, D.D., and R. B. POOLE, B.D. 1s. 6d.

Teaching, Theory and Practice of. By the Rev. E. THRING,
M.A., late Head Master of Uppingham School. New Edition. 4s. 6d.

British India, a Short History of. By E. S. CARLOS, M.A.,
late Head Master of Exeter Grammar School. 1s.

Geography, Elementary Commercial. A Sketch of the Commodities and the Countries of the World. By H. R. MILL, D.Sc., F.R.S.E. 1s.

Geography, an Atlas of Commercial. (A Companion to the
above.) By J. G. BARTHOLOMEW, F.R.G.S. With an Introduction by HUGH ROBERT MILL, D.Sc. 3s.

VII. MATHEMATICS.

Euclid's Elements of Geometry. Books I. and II. By H. M.
TAYLOR, M.A., Fellow and late Tutor of Trinity College, Cambridge. 1s. 6d.

—— —— Books III. and IV. By the same Editor. 1s. 6d.

—— —— Books I.—IV., in one Volume. 3s.

Elementary Algebra (with Answers to the Examples). By
W. W. ROUSE BALL, M.A. 4s. 6d.

Elements of Statics. By S. L. LONEY, M.A. 5s.

Elements of Dynamics. By the same Editor. [*Nearly ready.*
Other Volumes are in preparation.

London: Cambridge Warehouse, Ave Maria Lane.

The Cambridge Bible for Schools and Colleges.

GENERAL EDITOR: J. J. S. PEROWNE, D.D.,
BISHOP OF WORCESTER.

"*It is difficult to commend too highly this excellent series.*—Guardian.

"*The modesty of the general title of this series has, we believe, led many to misunderstand its character and underrate its value. The books are well suited for study in the upper forms of our best schools, but not the less are they adapted to the wants of all Bible students who are not specialists. We doubt, indeed, whether any of the numerous popular commentaries recently issued in this country will be found more serviceable for general use.*"—Academy.

Now Ready. Cloth, Extra Fcap. 8vo. With Maps.

Book of Joshua. By Rev. G. F. MACLEAR, D.D. 2s. 6d.
Book of Judges. By Rev. J. J. LIAS, M.A. 3s. 6d.
First Book of Samuel. By Rev. Prof. KIRKPATRICK, B.D. 3s. 6d.
Second Book of Samuel. By the same Editor. 3s. 6d.
First Book of Kings. By Rev. Prof. LUMBY, D.D. 3s. 6d.
Second Book of Kings. By Rev. Prof. LUMBY, D.D. 3s. 6d.
Book of Job. By Rev. A. B. DAVIDSON, D.D. 5s.
Book of Ecclesiastes. By Very Rev. E. H. PLUMPTRE, D.D. 5s.
Book of Jeremiah. By Rev. A. W. STREANE, M.A. 4s. 6d.
Book of Hosea. By Rev. T. K. CHEYNE, M.A., D.D. 3s.
Books of Obadiah & Jonah. By Archdeacon PEROWNE. 2s. 6d.
Book of Micah. By Rev. T. K. CHEYNE, M.A., D.D. 1s. 6d.
Haggai, Zechariah & Malachi. By Arch. PEROWNE. 3s. 6d.
Book of Malachi. By Archdeacon PEROWNE. 1s.
Gospel according to St Matthew. By Rev. A. CARR, M.A. 2s. 6d.
Gospel according to St Mark. By Rev. G. F. MACLEAR, D.D. 2s. 6d.
Gospel according to St Luke. By Arch. FARRAR, D.D. 4s. 6d.
Gospel according to St John. By Rev. A. PLUMMER, D.D. 4s. 6d.
Acts of the Apostles. By Rev. Prof. LUMBY, D.D. 4s. 6d.
Epistle to the Romans. By Rev. H. C. G. MOULE, M.A. 3s. 6d.
First Corinthians. By Rev. J. J. LIAS, M.A. With Map. 2s.
Second Corinthians. By Rev. J. J. LIAS, M.A. With Map. 2s.
Epistle to the Galatians. By Rev. E. H. PEROWNE, D.D. 1s. 6d.

London: *Cambridge Warehouse, Ave Maria Lane.*

Epistle to the Ephesians. By Rev. H. C. G. MOULE, M.A. 2s. 6d.
Epistle to the Philippians. By the same Editor. 2s. 6d.
Epistles to the Thessalonians. By Rev. G. G. FINDLAY, M.A. 2s.
Epistle to the Hebrews. By Arch. FARRAR, D.D. 3s. 6d.
General Epistle of St James. By Very Rev. E. H. PLUMPTRE, D.D. 1s. 6d.
Epistles of St Peter and St Jude. By Very Rev. E. H. PLUMPTRE, D.D. 2s. 6d.
Epistles of St John. By Rev. A. PLUMMER, M.A., D.D. 3s. 6d.
Book of Revelation. By Rev. W. H. SIMCOX, M.A. 3s.

Preparing.

Book of Genesis. By the BISHOP OF WORCESTER.
Books of Exodus, Numbers and Deuteronomy. By Rev. C. D. GINSBURG, LL.D.
Books of Ezra and Nehemiah. By Rev. Prof. RYLE, M.A.
Book of Psalms. Part I. By Rev. Prof. KIRKPATRICK, B.D.
Book of Isaiah. By Prof. W. ROBERTSON SMITH, M.A.
Book of Ezekiel. By Rev. A. B. DAVIDSON, D.D.
Epistles to the Colossians and Philemon. By Rev. H. C. G. MOULE, M.A.
Epistles to Timothy & Titus. By Rev. A. E. HUMPHREYS, M.A.

The Smaller Cambridge Bible for Schools.

The Smaller Cambridge Bible for Schools *will form an entirely new series of commentaries on some selected books of the Bible. It is expected that they will be prepared for the most part by the Editors of the larger series (The Cambridge Bible for Schools and Colleges). The volumes will be issued at a low price, and will be suitable to the requirements of preparatory and elementary schools.*

Now ready.

First and Second Books of Samuel. By Rev. Prof. KIRKPATRICK, B.D. 1s. each.
First Book of Kings. By Rev. Prof. LUMBY, D.D. 1s.
Gospel according to St Matthew. By Rev. A. CARR, M.A. 1s.
Gospel according to St Mark. By Rev. G. F. MACLEAR, D.D. 1s.
Gospel according to St Luke. By Archdeacon FARRAR. 1s.
Acts of the Apostles. By Rev. Prof. LUMBY, D.D. 1s.

Nearly ready.

Second Book of Kings. By Rev. Prof. LUMBY, D.D.
Gospel according to St John. By Rev. A. PLUMMER, D.D.

London: Cambridge Warehouse, Ave Maria Lane.

The Cambridge Greek Testament for Schools and Colleges,

with a Revised Text, based on the most recent critical authorities, and English Notes, prepared under the direction of the

GENERAL EDITOR, J. J. S. PEROWNE, D.D.,
BISHOP OF WORCESTER.

Gospel according to St Matthew. By Rev. A. CARR, M.A.
With 4 Maps. 4s. 6d.

Gospel according to St Mark. By Rev. G. F. MACLEAR, D.D.
With 3 Maps. 4s. 6d.

Gospel according to St Luke. By Archdeacon FARRAR.
With 4 Maps. 6s.

Gospel according to St John. By Rev. A. PLUMMER, D.D.
With 4 Maps. 6s.

Acts of the Apostles. By Rev. Professor LUMBY, D.D.
With 4 Maps. 6s.

First Epistle to the Corinthians. By Rev. J. J. LIAS, M.A. 3s.

Second Epistle to the Corinthians. By Rev. J. J. LIAS, M.A.
[In the Press.

Epistle to the Hebrews. By Archdeacon FARRAR, D.D. 3s. 6d.

Epistle of St James. By Very Rev. E. H. PLUMPTRE, D.D.
[Preparing.

Epistles of St John. By Rev. A. PLUMMER, M.A., D.D. 4s.

London: C. J. CLAY AND SONS,
CAMBRIDGE WAREHOUSE, AVE MARIA LANE.
Glasgow: 263, ARGYLE STREET.
Cambridge: DEIGHTON, BELL AND CO.
Leipzig: F. A. BROCKHAUS.
New York: MACMILLAN AND CO.

www.ingramcontent.com/pod-product-compliance
Lightning Source LLC
Chambersburg PA
CBHW022121290426
44112CB00008B/763